The Strategic Managing of

The Strategic Managing of Human Resources

Second Edition

Edited by
John Leopold and Lynette Harris

FT Prentice Hall
FINANCIAL TIMES

An imprint of **Pearson Education**
Harlow, England • London • New York • Boston • San Francisco • Toronto • Sydney • Singapore • Hong Kong
Tokyo • Seoul • Taipei • New Delhi • Cape Town • Madrid • Mexico City • Amsterdam • Munich • Paris • Milan

Pearson Education Limited

Edinburgh Gate
Harlow
Essex CM20 2JE
England

and Associated Companies throughout the world

Visit us on the World Wide Web at:
www.pearsoned.co.uk

First published 2005
Second edition published 2009

ISBN: 978-0-273-71386-9

British Library Cataloguing-in-Publication Data
A catalogue record for this book is available from the British Library

Library of Congress Cataloging-in-Publication Data
The strategic managing of human resources / edited by John Leopold and Lynette Harris. — 2nd ed.
     p. cm.
  Includes bibliographical references and index.
  ISBN 978-0-273-71386-9 (pbk. : alk. paper) 1. Personnel management. 2. Strategic planning.
I. Leopold, John. II. Harris, Lynette.
  HF5549.S8865 2009
  658.3′01—dc22

2009000486

10 9 8 7 6 5 4 3 2 1
13 12 11 10 09

Typeset in 9.5/12pt stone serif by 35
Printed by Ashford Colour Press Ltd., Gosport

The publisher's policy is to use paper manufactured from sustainable forests.

Plan of the book

Part I Managing strategic human resourcing in a complex and uncertain organisational, social and economic context			
Chapter 1 Organisations, strategies and human resourcing	Chapter 2 Managing uncertainty or managing uncertainly?	Chapter 3 Employment law and human resourcing strategies	Chapter 4 Ethics and strategic human resourcing

Part II Human resourcing policies in practice					
Chapter 5 From equal opportunities to diversity management	Chapter 6 Assessment, selection and evaluation	Chapter 7 Performance management and performing management	Chapter 8 Reward strategies and paying for contribution	Chapter 9 Parting company: the strategic responsibility of exit management	Chapter 10 Human resourcing in international organisations

Part III Managing change and developing capability		
Chapter 11 Knowledge organisations, strategies and human resourcing	Chapter 12 Managing processes of human resource development	Chapter 13 Developing managers and managerial capacities

Part IV Managing employment and other human resourcing relationships		
Chapter 14 Strategic choice in patterns of employment relationships	Chapter 15 Employee participation, involvement and communications	Chapter 16 Managing consulting and consultancy relationships

Contents

PART I Managing strategic human resourcing in a complex and uncertain organisational, social and economic context

PART III Managing change and developing capability

PART IV Managing employment and other human resourcing relationships

Supporting resources

Visit **www.pearsoned.co.uk/leopold** to find valuable online resources

For instructors
- A comprehensive Instructor's manual that provides an introduction to the topics covered in each chapter and notes on the discussion questions, activities and case studies within the book
- A full set of PowerPoint slides to accompany the book

For more information please contact your local Pearson Education sales representative or visit **www.pearsoned.co.uk/leopold**

List of figures

List of tables

List of exhibits

List of case studies

List of activities

Contributing authors

Colin Bryson is Director of the Centre of Combined Studies at Newcastle University. He has a long-standing research interest in precarious employment, specifically the use of temporary and part-time employment in areas such as Higher Education in the UK. He has previously researched in industrial relations, HRM and the management of IT. Another current research interest is pedagogy in HE and particularly student engagement. His teaching focuses on student research projects and dissertations and developing graduate attributes in the undergraduate curriculum.

Dave Doughty is Director of International HR Developments in Nottingham Business School. Dave took an unusual route into academia, having started adult life with a career in professional football ahead. However, injuries curtailed this and after four years in Australia playing semi-professionally and working for the Australian Navy, academic studies were resumed. Over the latter part of his career Dave has been heavily involved in the international work of the Business School, including work in locations such as Azerbaijan, Poland, Bulgaria, India, Zimbabwe, France, the Netherlands, Greece, United Arab Emirates, Russia and Ukraine. Most of Dave's teaching is on a variety of postgraduate programmes and has involved considerable work with a range of major organisations such as BP. Research interests have been developed in the non-governmental organisation sector as well as cross-cultural management and the localisation of employment and development in multinational corporations.

Colin Fisher is Professor of Managerial Values and Ethics and author of *Resource Allocation in the Public Sector: Value of Priorities and Markets in the Management of the Public Services* (1998: Routledge). Colin has extensive experience teaching performance management, research methods and ethics to postgraduate students. In 2003 he published *Business Ethics and Values* with Alan Lovell and in 2004 a book on how to research and write a postgraduate dissertation in management. The third editions of both books will soon be published. He has recently completed a research report on metric manipulation in performance management.

Carley Foster is a Senior Lecturer in marketing and retail management at Nottingham Business School. Before joining NBS she worked for Boots the Chemists. She then went on to complete her PhD which explored diversity and equality issues in the retail industry and was an ESRC postdoctoral fellow. Besides diversity management, her other research interests include employer branding and the role of front-line staff in retail. She also recently led an ESF funded project which investigated the careers of female store staff in the retail industry.

Lynette Harris is Professor of Human Relations and Professional Practice in the Human Resource Management Division at Nottingham Business School. She is a researcher and consultant to organisations on contemporary issues in human resource management and the author of texts and articles in the academic and practitioner literature with a particular focus on human resourcing issues in public sector and smaller organisations. She is an independent arbitrator and mediator for ACAS and a Deputy Chair for the Central Arbitration Committee as well as undertaking a number of other roles in dispute resolution. Prior to joining the University, Lynette was a Personnel Director and has experience of working as a personnel specialist in both the public and private sector.

Luchien Karsten is Professor in the Foundations of Management, Faculty of Economics and Business, University of Groningen, the Netherlands and Visiting Professor at Newcastle University Business School. Having been trained as an economist and philosopher in Groningen and Paris, his research interests in time were developed through his doctoral thesis on the history of the international eight-hour day. Subsequent research has focused on the actual development of time–space orientation in organisations. Additionally, he is interested in management concepts that are used to describe and analyse flexibilisation in organisations. He is a Professor in the Energy Delta Institute, a joint venture between the Russian Gazprom and the Dutch Gasunie together with the University of Groningen, whose purpose is to strengthen managerial capabilities to coordinate the transition to deregulated energy markets. Furthermore he is involved in the coordination of cooperation with African countries (like Burkina Faso and Tanzania), Russia and Indonesia.

Susan Kirk is a Senior Lecturer and researcher, currently engaged in completing a PhD into international mobility of talented leaders. She lectures at postgraduate and post-experience levels both within the Business School and for corporate clients. Susan is a Chartered Fellow of the Chartered Institute of Personnel and Development and a Fellow of The Higher Education Academy. She is a regular reviewer for a number of major publishing houses. Susan has undertaken a variety of research and consultancy projects for SMEs and large organisations in both the public and private sectors and has published work derived from these studies.

John Leopold is Deputy Director of Newcastle University Business School and Professor of Human Resource Management. He is editor of *Personnel Review* and his research interests include HRM in greenfield sites in the UK and New Zealand and control over working time in the UK, France and the Netherlands. Previously employed at the Universities of Glasgow, Stirling and Nottingham Trent, his teaching interests include British and comparative industrial relations, employee involvement and consultation and human resource strategy. He is a Chartered Fellow of the CIPD and a member of the CIPD's Quality Assurance Panel.

Diannah Lowry is Principal Lecturer in Human Resource Management at Bristol Business School, University of the West of England. Her areas of interest in teaching and research include the ways in which mobile technologies re-shape the design and experience of work, ethics and HRM and organisational research methodology. Before joining Bristol Business School, Diannah was a Senior Research Fellow at the National Institute of Labour Studies at Flinders University in Australia, where she was also co-editor of the *Australian Bulletin of Labour*.

Edward Lugsden is a Lecturer in Human Resource Management at Newcastle University Business School; his main teaching interests are in human resource management and employee relations. He was previously employed as a Director of Human Resource Management in the NHS. His current research concerns the role of the HR function in developing and implementing strategy, the implications of changes to workforce composition, the application of lean production techniques to the NHS and changes in the nature of HRM in the public sector.

Jan Myers is an Assistant Professor in the School of Business Administration, Dalhousie University, Nova Scotia. She teaches across undergraduate and graduate business, commerce and management programmes on organisational behaviour and managing people. She is also part of a pan-Canadian research project on social economy organisations and her research interests focus on non-profit leadership and social entrepreneurship. In 2009, she will move to Cardiff School of Management, University of Wales Institute to undertake research into co-operatives, mutuals and social enterprises.

Sue Newell is the Cammarata Professor of Management, Bentley College, US and a part-time Professor of Information Management at Warwick University, UK. She has a BSc and PhD from Cardiff University, UK. Sue is currently the PhD Director at Bentley. Sue's research focuses on understanding the relationships between innovation, knowledge and organisational networking (ikon) – primarily from an organisational theory perspective. She was one of the founding members of ikon, a research centre based at Warwick University. She has been involved in many of the ikon projects and has recently completed a project titled 'The evolution of biomedical knowledge: interactive innovation in the UK and US'. She is also involved in research which focuses on exploring the implementation and use of packaged information systems, for example to support distributed project work or human resources. Her research emphasises a critical, practice-based understanding of the social aspects of innovation, change, knowledge management and inter-firm networked relations. Sue has published over 80 journal articles in the areas of organisation studies, management and information systems, as well as numerous books and book chapters.

Anne Sempik is Principal Lecturer in Human Resource Management. She joined Nottingham Business School in 1999. Her specialist areas include strategic human resourcing, succession planning and talent management, performance management and assessment and selection. Before joining NBS Anne spent 8 years as a research scientist in the pharmaceutical industry and 10 years as an HR practitioner working in the pharmaceutical and retail sectors. Anne is a Chartered Fellow of the CIPD and has served on the committee of the Derbyshire and Nottinghamshire Branch of the CIPD since 2004 as Policy Adviser and, from 2008, as Membership and CPD Adviser. Anne's current research interests include talent management, performance management and teaching and learning in the international arena. She also consults in the healthcare and pharmaceuticals sectors.

Pam Stevens is Senior Lecturer in Organisational Behaviour and Human Resource Management. She teaches across a range of HR subjects at postgraduate and post-experience level and until recently, was the Course Leader for the Business School's innovative MSc in Strategic HRM. Pam gained her undergraduate degree from McGill University in Montreal (her place of birth), and an MA in HRM from The University of Hull in 1995. She is a Chartered Fellow of the Chartered Institute of Personnel and Development. Her research interests are focused on the devolution of HR activities to line managers and the changing nature of the HR profession towards a more consultative model. Prior to her academic career, she was a Company Secretary for a plc in the IT industry for 11 years.

Jim Stewart is now Running Stream Professor of Human Resource Development at Leeds Business School having left Nottingham Business School to take up that post in March 2007. He is Director of the PhD Programme for the Faculty of Business and Law and Director of the DBA Programme. Jim is Reviews Editor of the *International Journal of Training and Development*, UK Editor of *Human Resource Development International* and Chair of the University Forum for HRD. He is author of *Employee Development Practice* (1999: FT Pitman) and joint editor of five books in the Routledge Studies in HRD series. His professional roles include being CIPD Chief Examiner for Learning and Development and he also chairs Quality Assurance Panel visits for the CIPD. While at Nottingham Business School Jim launched the highly successful NBS Doctorate in Business Administration and was for 10 years Joint Course Leader of that programme with Professor Colin Fisher. He teaches and supervises students on the Leeds Met PhD and DBA programmes as well as HRD-related topics on a number of undergraduate and postgraduate courses. An active researcher and writer, Jim is the author of numerous books, chapters, journal articles and research reports, including *Training in the Knowledge Economy*, published by the CIPD, which he co-authored with Professor Carole Tansley and *Talent: Strategy, management and measurement*, also published by the CIPD and co-authored with Professor Tansley and other colleagues.

Carole Tansley is Professor of HR Innovation in Nottingham Business School and Director of the International Centre of Talent Management and Development. Her areas of endeavour in teaching and research are talent management, human resource management and information systems, knowledge management and research methodology. Before joining NBS, Carole was an area manager for a search and selection consultancy, a senior human resourcing officer with Rolls Royce and Associates Ltd and an executive officer in the UK Civil Service. Carole's PhD was an ethnographic study entitled 'Identity, power and exchange in the development of human resource information systems' and she has since specialised on the development of the HR elements of Enterprise Resource Planning systems by HR specialists.

David Walsh is Principal Lecturer in Human Resource Management and Director of CIPD Programmes at Nottingham Trent University, which is a CIPD Centre of Research Excellence. His main teaching and research are currently in the area of multi-national human resource management, with particular interests in western companies operating in Azerbaijan, China, India and Russia. Hence, he undertakes reviews of texts in International HRM. He also teaches on the University's CIPD programmes and maintains his involvement in the study of employment relations and the sociology of the workplace. David's teaching of international HR at Master's level is both in and outside the UK and to students from a variety of countries. In addition, David has a particular interest in Malaysia and has been an external adviser to a leading UK university with degree programmes in that country.

Derek Watling is currently the Programme Leader for the Postgraduate Diploma in Human Resource Management and he is also the CIPD's Professional Assessment of Competence (PAC) Centre Manager at Nottingham Business School. From 2000 to 2006 he was a full-time member of the NBS Centre for Management Development (CMD) where he was responsible for the development, design and delivery of both Executive and Young Professional Development interventions. His specialist areas have focused on employee relations, employment law, strategic human resourcing and management development. Prior to embarking on a career in academia Derek spent eight years as an HR practitioner working variously for a public utility, a private steel manufacturer and in local government. His current research interests are in the areas of employee representation in non-unionised organisations and in graduate and management development.

Tony Watson is Professor of Organisational Behaviour in Nottingham University Business School. He teaches about and researches organisations, managerial work, strategy-making, entrepreneurship, HRM and industrial sociology. His books include

The Personnel Managers (1977), *In Search of Management* (1994/2001), and *Sociology, Work and Industry* (5th edition 2008). Current research focuses on the relationship between the emergent life strategies of managers, entrepreneurs and strategy-makers and emergent enterprises. A special interest is in ethnography and the concepts of narrative and identity as means of investigating, teaching and writing about the complexities, contradictions, pains and delights of organisational and business life.

Acknowledgements

We are particularly indebted to Wendy Patterson who nobly stepped in at short notice to take on the editing role for this revised text and whose experience, skills and phenomenal attention to detail helped us to meet the final deadline. We would also like to thank colleagues at Pearson who contributed to the project, and especially Amanda McPartlin our commissioning editor for her support and clear advice at all times.

Publisher's acknowledgements

The authors and the publishers would like to express their thanks to the following reviewers for their invaluable feedback throughout the development of this book:

Jocelyn Flemming – University of Gloucestershire
Dr Robert McMurray – The York Management School, University of York
Niels-Erik Wergin – University of Greenwich Business School
Dr Amanda Pyman – Kent Business School, University of Kent

We are grateful to the following for permission to reproduce copyright material:

Figures

Figure 4.2 adapted from Moral awareness in business organisations, *Human Relations*, 53 (7), p. 983 (Butterfield, K., Trevino, L. and Weaver, G. 2000), Copyright © 2000 by SAGE Publications Ltd. Reprinted by Permission of SAGE; Figure 7.2 from The differences between appraisal schemes: rhetoric and the design of schemes, *Personnel Review*, 24 (1), pp. 51–66 (Fisher, C.M. 1995), Copyright 1995 by Emerald Group Publishing Limited. Reproduced with permission of Emerald Group Publishing Limited in the format Textbook via Copyright Clearance Center; Figure 15.1 from Health and Safety Commission and Health and Safety Executive Collective Declaration on Worker Involvement, 2004, Reproduced under the terms of the Click-Use Licence; Figure 16.1 from Ethical consulting does not have to be an oxymoron, *Organizational Dynamics*, 28 (4), pp. 38–51 (Ozley *et al*., 2000), with permission from Elsevier.

Tables

Table 3.1 from Employment and the law: burden or benefit? Survey Report 2005, p. 9, http://www.cipd.co.uk/NR/rdonlyres/3359BAC2-5A40-43D0-B3A0-3A55C32EA477/0/emplawsr0605.pdf, Chartered Institute of Personnel and

Development/Lovells, with the permission of the publisher, the Chartered Institute of Personnel and Development, London (www.cipd.co.uk); Table 8.1 from *CIPD Reward Management Survey 2008* p. 12 (2008), CIPD, with the permission of the publisher, the Chartered Institute of Personnel and Development, London (www.cipd.co.uk); Table 13.2 adapted from *HRD in a Complex World*, Routledge (Lee, M. (ed.) 2003); Table 13.3 adapted from *Management Development: Strategies for Action*, 4th Edition, CIPD (Mumford, A. and Gold, J. 2004), with the permission of the publisher, the Chartered Institute of Personnel and Development, London (www.cipd.co.uk); Table 15.1 from *Managing Employee Involvement and Participation*, Sage (Hyman, J. and Mason, B. 1995), Reproduced by permission of SAGE Publications, London, Los Angeles, New Delhi and Singapore and reproduced by permission of Professor Jeff Hyman; Table 15.3 from The four faces of employee consultation, *Personnel Management*, May 1988 (Marchington, M.); Table 15.4 from Total quality management and employee involvement, *Human Resource Management Journal*, 2 (4), pp. 1–20 (Wilkinson, A., Marchington, M., Goodman, J. and Ackers, P. 1992), Copyright © 1992 Blackwell Publishing Ltd. Reproduced with permission of Blackwell Publishing Ltd.; Table 16.1 from Expertise and organizational boundaries: the varying roles of Australian management consultants, *Asia Pacific Business Review*, 9 (3), pp. 21–40 (Kitay, J. and Wright, C. 2003), reprinted by permission of the publisher (Taylor & Francis Ltd, http://www.informaworld.com); Table 16.2 from Alvesson, M. and Johansson, A. Professionalism and politics in management consultancy work, *Critical Consulting* (Clark, T. and Fincham, R. (eds.) 2002), Copyright © 2002 Blackwell Publishing Ltd. Reproduced with permission of Blackwell Publishing Ltd.

Text

Activity 2.2 adapted from *Excelleren = optimaliseren en innoveren*, Van Gorcum (Assen, van M., Berg, van den G., Wobben, J.J. 2008); Exhibit 3.1 from Editorial comment on a default retirement age, *Employers' Law*, June 2008, p. 3; Exhibit 3.3 from Avoiding tribunal trouble, *Employers' Law*, February 2008, pp. 12–13 (Cooper, N.); Exhibit 3.4 from Flexible working at ASDA, *Employers' Law*, August 2008, p. 19 (Fuller, G.); Exhibit 8.2 from Rewards and recognition at Denplan – Dental health insurer, *The Sunday Times*, 9 March 2008; Exhibit 15.1 from Consultation arrangements in a non-unionised organisation, http://www.ipa-involve.com/staging/40/45/?cmd=ViewCaseStudy&id=4237, Involvement and Participation Association; Exhibit 15.2 from Health and Safety Commission and Health and Safety Executive Collective Declaration on Worker Involvement, 2004, Reproduced under the terms of the Click-Use Licence.

The Financial Times

Exhibit 9.3 from Royal Mail managers threaten strike over job cuts postal services, *The Financial Times*, 16 March 2004; Exhibit 10.1 from A multinational cadre of managers is the key, *The Financial Times*, 8 October 1997 (Wagstyl, S.).

In some instances we have been unable to trace the owners of copyright material, and we would appreciate any information that would enable us to do so.

Foreword

Kevan Scholes

Co-author of *Exploring Corporate Strategy*, former Director of Sheffield Business School and Visiting Professor of Strategic Management, Sheffield Hallam University

One of the factors that characterises successful organisations is their ability to manage the relationship between overall 'business' strategy and strategies in different resource areas such as people, information, finance or technology. In many organisations this relationship is neglected and the worlds of 'strategy making' and resource management are entirely divorced. The consequences are clear: business strategies that sound impressive actually are not deliverable by the organisation. Also, those managing resource areas become immersed in day-to-day issues without any clear understanding as to how their decisions affect the overall success or failure of the organisation. Clearly the human resources of an organisation are a critically important resource area to which these general comments apply. The knowledge and experience of people can be the key factors enabling the success of strategies. But they can also hinder the successful adoption of new strategies too. So people-related issues need to be a central concern and responsibility of most managers in organisations and are not confined to a specialist human resource function. Indeed, although formal HR systems and structures may be vitally important in supporting successful strategies, it is quite possible that they may hinder strategy if they are not tailored to the types of strategies being pursued. Also, the relationship between people and successful strategies needs to go beyond the traditional agenda of the HR function and be concerned with behaviours as much as competences. The ability to change behaviours may be the key ingredient for success. Creating a climate where people strive to achieve success and the motivation of individuals are crucial roles of any manager and are a central part of their involvement in their organisation's strategy.

These opening remarks try to capture the way in which strategists view the relationship between overall business strategy and human resource strategies. It is especially pleasing for me to see that the spirit of these remarks is entirely captured by this book on *The Strategic Managing of Human Resources*. There are a number of aspects of the book that distinguish it from traditional HR books in ways that ensure that these strategic issues become the prominent concern of the reader. First, and somewhat unusual, is a clear starting point that human resources are not people. They are the knowledge, competences and behaviours that people bring to the work situation. This insight allows the issues of HR strategy to interface much more smoothly with other related themes such as knowledge management and strategic management approaches. Second is the clear acknowledgement that the responsibility for HR strategy must be shared between specialist HR professionals and line managers. They are both needed. Line managers are at the forefront of leading and motivating individuals but need to do so within a strategic framework. So this book is for line managers as much as HR specialists. But the strategic framework also needs to be practical and capable of operation on the ground. The book also addresses the rather obvious, but woefully neglected, point that HR strategies must go beyond the structures, policies and frameworks and be concerned with the *processes* through which human resources are managed and developed. It should be clear from the opening comments that it is this that will distinguish between the 'strategy dreamers' and those that can actually deliver successful strategies on the ground. So HR strategy must be about both *what* needs to be done and *how* it will be done. Again both line managers and HR specialists need to understand these issues. One of the things that frustrate strategists is the way in which many managers have a very parochial view about the boundaries of their work, responsibilities and influence. In particular, they seem content to do a good job managing their part of the organisation. This is clearly important but is usually not sufficient in terms of the strategic development of their area and the success of the organisation's overall strategies. For example, the strategic capability of the organisation may be crucially dependent on resources or activities that lie outside the organisation – perhaps in the supply or distribution chains. Any weaknesses there may create strategic problems, however well the in-house resource is being managed. In reverse, resource strengths outside the organisation may open up new strategic opportunities to which the organisation must respond. This has led many organisations to develop strategies for capitalising on external capabilities. At the extreme this has been through the outsourcing of whole areas of an organisation's activity. This has been a common solution with IT services. Less radical has been the development of relationships and alliances with other organisations – particularly where there are complementary competences or a need to create critical mass or share development costs. This has been common in many areas of technology development. One of the pleasing features of *The Strategic Managing of Human Resources* is that it avoids this parochial pitfall by discussing HR issues beyond just the 'strategies for employees' situation. From a strategist's point of view this is crucial.

Finally I welcome the way in which the choices of content and examples have helped to make this a practical as well as a theoretical book. This assists the reader in understanding how issues of sector or geographical location might influence the debate and priorities. The use of a wide range of examples from across Europe also makes the book useful to readers beyond the UK. Particularly helpful to readers is the Moddens case study that runs through the chapters providing useful connections.

Preface

John Leopold and Lynette Harris

The aims and objectives of this book

A basic assumption of the book is that it is most helpful to think about 'human resources' as the *capabilities and potential* that people bring to work organisations to enable organisations to fulfil tasks and to survive into the long term. This applies to all employing organisations – from manufacturing concerns to service providers, from small firms to giant corporations, from private enterprises to public bodies. It follows from this that managing organisations strategically needs to involve all managers in dealing with human resourcing matters in order to shape the human dimension of the organisation as a whole and taking the enterprise forward towards a healthy long-term future. It is nevertheless the case that there is a vital and distinctive role within this for HR specialists.

Organisational strategies are seen throughout the book as always 'emergent' and subject to *processes* of exchange in every aspect of their functioning – with human resourcing exchanges needing to take their place alongside issues of marketing, technology management, and the rest. All of these exchanges involve managers in processes of negotiation, argument, conflict and resolution. Within this, organisational managers need to make a series of strategic choices, at the heart of which is the choice to lean towards either a high commitment style of HR strategy or a low commitment strategic approach.

It is with this broad perspective on the strategic managing of human resources that a group of like-minded colleagues who at the time of the first edition were in the Department of Human Resource Management at Nottingham Business School have collaborated to write this book as a distinctive contribution to the literature on human resource management, for a number of reasons. It is distinctive, first, because it adopts a basic perspective which frames all the contributions that follow it. This perspective, with its emphasis on processes, rather than structures, and emergent patterns, rather than fixed systems, is firmly established and vividly illustrated in Chapter 1 and the approach it advocates is developed in various ways, and with reference to a number of specific aspects of human resourcing, in subsequent contributions. There is a clear emphasis on the processes that occur within organisations and between organisations and their human resourcing (and other) constituencies in a way that is better balanced with the structural arrangements that other texts tend to emphasise at the expense of attention to processes. Put simply, this means an emphasis on how things come about, not just an analysis of what patterns tend to exist within employing organisations.

Second, there is a recognition of the need for there to be a human resourcing involvement of line managers as well as HR managers and that the relationship between these two managerial interests will always involve tensions as well as a need to work together cooperatively. Third, there is also a recognition that although the employment relationship is central to human resourcing issues, human resources are increasingly obtained by work organisations through shorter-term market relationships with workers and suppliers of expert human resources. Finally, the influence of an increasingly regulated working environment on human resourcing processes, approaches to the employment relationship, and the need for specialist knowledge is recognised and examined.

Many of the chapters draw upon the research by members of the writing team, but all are designed to be authoritative overviews of the current situation in their field. The material in them, especially the activities and case studies, have been piloted, and subsequently refined, in our teaching on advanced undergraduate and specialised human resource management master's and professional programmes as well as with members of more general MBA and master's-type courses. In short, the book is the product of a team experienced in teaching the students it is aimed at, and the chapters are shaped by the pedagogic experience and research work of the authors.

The intended readership

The book will be of relevance and interest to managers studying on generalist management programmes such as the DMS and MBAs, to those on specialist HRM courses, such as students taking CIPD specialist electives en route to graduateship of the CIPD and to those students following dedicated master's programmes in human resource management. The book has also been written to support final-year undergraduates and people who have an interest in management but have not yet started in a managerial career. It is envisaged, therefore, that distinctive groups of students will benefit from reading significant sections of this book, but that the relevant chapters will depend on the specific course they follow, their personal interests and the guidance of tutors.

Using this book

The book is a postgraduate and advanced undergraduate textbook and each chapter contains a number of common features which will help readers to gain most benefit from them. Each chapter begins with a set of learning outcomes which readers should be able to achieve on completion of the chapter and its associated exercises. Throughout the chapters are activities that can be used in a number of ways depending on the learning context of the reader. At the end of each chapter is a major case study that attempts to draw on the key learning points in the chapter and offers the opportunity to examine and discuss a range of questions around each case. Activities and case studies can be used as either individual or group work exercises by course members as directed independent learning activities or as part of tutor-guided workshop discussions. Activities include full case studies, short organisational scenarios, direct investigatory exercises to develop research skills, preparation for debates and discussion, and self-directed exercises.

The case studies are ideal for use with a supporting lecture followed by workshop activity. All chapters conclude with a set of questions which can be used to develop further activities and discussion or as reflective exercises on what has been learned as well as providing possible topics where there is an assessment requirement. Finally, each chapter ends with suggestions for further reading.

In drawing up the exercises and case studies we have attempted to draw upon a range of organisational contexts, including profit-based firms, governmental institutions, small and medium-sized enterprises and large international multi-plant firms, to reflect the range of settings where the employment relationship is managed. Throughout the book we have tried to analyse the respective role and responsibilities of specialist and line managers in the selected areas of practice which we examine. Activities have been devised so that they can be engaged in as readily by people with limited direct experience of HR management and (especially strategic management) issues as they can by people with directly relevant organisational experience. This is to reflect the intended readership, potential specialists and managers who have to manage the employment relationship as part of their overall managerial role, and the way the relationship is practised. Connected to this is a further common feature, namely that managers have to make a whole series of informed judgements, and the book seeks to inform the choices, chances and circumstances that shape and influence these judgements. Each chapter also recognises that the HR specialist may have to operate as a consultant, either external or internal, to persuade line managers to pursue various policies and practices.

Web links

We have decided to produce a list of useful websites for the whole book rather than chapter by chapter to avoid unnecessary duplication as many of the sites are relevant to more than one chapter. We have indicated the likely usefulness of each site.

Advisory Conciliation and Arbitration Service (UK-based independent service offering advice on HR matters, especially employment law)
www.acas.org.uk

Age discrimination site (UK)
www.agepositive.gov.uk

Australian-based ethics network
www.ethics.org.au/

Australian Human Rights and Equal Opportunities
www.hreoc.gov.au/

Central Arbitration Committee (UK-based tribunal on statutory employment rights)
www.cac.gov.uk

Chartered Institute of Management
www.managers.org.uk

Chartered Institute of Personnel and Development (UK professional body for HR managers)
www.cipd.co.uk

Commission for the European Communities paper on modernizing labour law in the 21st century
http://ec.europa.eu/employment_social/labour_law/docs/2006/green_paper_en.pdf

Confederation of British Industry (UK central employers' organisation)
www.cbi.org.uk/home.html

Department for Business Enterprise and Regulation
www.berr.gov.uk

Department of Labor (USA government department)
www.dol.gov/

Department for Business Enterprise and Regulatory Reform (UK government department)
www.berr.gov.uk. This site asks for username and password

Equality and Human Rights Commission
http://www.equalityhumanrights.com

Europa – Gateway to the European Union (EU publications)
http://europa.eu/index_en.htm

European Centre for the Development of Vocational Training (CEDEFOP)
www.cedefop.eu.int

European Commission's report on Equality between Women and Men 2008
http://ec.europa.eu/employment_social/publications/2008/keaj08001_en.pdf

European Equal Opportunities
www.europa.eu.int/comm/equal

Dutch-based advisory body
www.agentschapszw.nl

Dutch-based advisory body
www.dagindeling.nl

Dutch HRM Network
http://hrm-network.nl

E.reward (an on line site to reward management)
www.e-reward.co.uk

European Industrial Relations Observatory Online (Useful for updates on
European employee relations)
www.eiro.eurofound.ie

European Experts in Human Resource Development / University Forum for
Human Resource Development – a research resource base of HRD in Europe
(EHRD)
www.ehrd-portal.org

European Business Ethic Network
www.eben-net.org

Government Equalities Office
www.equalities.gov.uk

Health and Safety Commission (UK-based body specialising in health and
safety at work)
http://hse.gov.uk

HRM The Journal (a web discussion area for HR academics, students and others)
http://hrmthejournal.ning.com/

HRLook (UK subscription-based HR information service)
www.hrlook.com

Institute for Employment Research (UK-based research organisation on
employment isues)
www.warwick.ac.uk/ier/

International Alliance for Human Resources Research
http://www.yorku.ca/hrresall

International Labour Office (Useful for updates on international HR)
www.ilo.org/public/english/index.htm

Learn Direct
www.learndirect.co.uk

Low Pay Commission (UK body focusing on low pay at work)
www.lowpay.gov.uk

Online update of new law
www.website-law.co.uk

Organisation for Economic Cooperation and Development (OECD)
www.oecd.org

Policy Studies Institute (UK-based research and policy body)
www.psi.org.uk/

Trades Union Congress (UK trade union congress)
www.tuc.org.uk

USA EEOC
www.eeoc.gov/

University Forum for Human Resource Development (UK network of university academics researching and teaching HRD)
www.ufhrd.co.uk

University for Industry
www.ufi.com/home/default.asp

Part I

Managing strategic human resourcing in a complex and uncertain organisational, social and economic context

Introduction to Part I

Human beings, since the beginning of time, have needed to develop social practices that utilise the talents and abilities of the people living in any community or work enterprise to ensure the completion of work tasks which need to be done to enable that community or enterprise to survive. However modern or fashionable 'Human Resource Management' might sound, it is important to recognise that it is an activity that deals with some very fundamental human social, economic and political problems. This is why Chapter 1 of *The Strategic Managing of Human Resources* opens with a case study of human work activity in prehistoric times. The intention behind looking at these ancient people is one of making us stop short and question the standard assumption that the managing of human resources is a distinctly modern activity. Whatever language might have been used, all human communities have needed to shape the way they used the human talents available to them to maintain and develop their economic and working activities. And this insight is one that has encouraged all the authors of *The Strategic Managing of Human Resources* to reject any notion of *people* themselves as 'human resources' and, instead, to identify human resources as the capabilities and the potential that people bring to work situations – capabilities that are strategically necessary for the continuation of the work enterprises in which those resources are deployed.

Having recognised that we are dealing with a rather fundamental aspect of work management when we look at human resourcing, and not just at a specialist and technical branch of contemporary managerial work, the issues raised by the activities of the ancient tribes people are shown throughout the book to be ones that arise, in a variety of different respects, in twenty-first century work organisations and societies. In the first chapter we see the dilemmas being faced by the owners and managers of a food manufacturing company, for example. This case study is taken up and extended at various points throughout the text. It establishes very clearly that we cannot understand *strategic* human resourcing – human resourcing work, that is, which both helps shape the work enterprise and contributes to its long-term survival – without paying close attention to the interests and priorities of the managers and business people who are in charge of such activities. Strategic human resourcing is something done by human beings, who are in no way free to manage in any way they like but who, at the same time, have certain key choices they can make about how to deal with human resourcing matters. We therefore see, in the chapters in the first part of the book, 'real' managers making choices of strategic direction – albeit choices constrained by the circumstances in which they operate. The theorising which is presented in these chapters is not there for any kind of ritualistic academic reason. It is included to help us all come to terms with just how this mix of choice, on the one hand,

and contextual or 'structural' constraints and opportunities, on the other hand, interrelate. And the analytical style, established in the first chapter and continued thereafter, is one which sees strategic directions as very much *emergent* matters, rather than as the outcomes of wholly rationally pre-planned decisions. Strategic directions involve managers sometimes leaning towards *high commitment* HR policies and practices and sometimes towards *low commitment* HR strategies. And whichever the managers in any particular organisation tend to lean towards, there is always interplay of managerial choice and preference, on the one hand, and contextual factors on the other.

Chapter 1, 'Organisations, strategies and human resourcing', establishes that the market-based and bureaucratised type of society and political economy within which strategic human resourcing occurs in the contemporary world is a funda-mental contextual factor to which all managerial choices inevitably relate. Thus, the economics and the politics of particular societies and the globalising pressures within which these operate are shown to be crucially relevant to managerial human resourcing activities – these activities being shaped by employment patterns emerging across the world and, at the same time, helping to shape them. And one of the reasons these human resourcing activities take the emergent strategic form that they do (as opposed to taking the form of big, pre-shaped, corporate plans) is that they have to cope with a context which is inherently *uncertain*. This notion of uncertainty is central to Chapter 2, 'Managing uncertainty or manag-ing uncertainly?'. The uncertainty of the world in which managerial choices are made is shown in this chapter to be the key to understanding the variety of flexible work practices and policies that play such an important part in the shaping of contemporary human resourcing strategies. Uncertainty has always been part of the human condition, even if the uncertainties facing human resource strategy-makers seem to be especially acute in a world of global change and intensifying competitive pressures. Human beings have, throughout history, created a variety of social institutions to help make manageable the potentially crippling uncer-tainties of human social life and, indeed, the potentially crippling conflicts of interest and value that arise as different individuals and groups pursue their various purposes.

Chapter 3, 'Employment law and human resourcing strategies', focuses on one particular institution that plays such a role in human society: the law. This chapter takes us back to ancient times again to point up the deep human significance of human legal arrangements generally. And it goes on to apply this insight to devel-opments in more recent times and to show how the regulative function of legal institutions both assists and constrains the effective managing of human resourc-ing issues. It is shown, too, to be a significant factor influencing the relationships between specialist human resource managers and other managers. Employment law is further shown to connect with matters of human rights. And this gives a connection to the concerns of Chapter 4, 'Ethics and strategic human resourcing'. It is shown here that ethical matters are at the heart of strategic human resourc-ing. They cannot be seen as an optional extra, or an indulgence of managers with particularly highly developed consciences. Applying several of the different criteria and 'ethical theories' discussed in this chapter, all of the people affected by an organisation's human resourcing strategies will make their own moral evaluations of the way they are treated. And they will be influenced in their actions and behaviour by the extent to which they perceive themselves to be treated ethically and fairly by that organisation and its managers. Those actions and behaviours inevitably make a significant difference to how well the organisation as a whole performs: how well, in effect, its strategic human resourcing work succeeds in taking the organisation forward into the future.

Organisations, strategies and human resourcing

Tony Watson

Learning outcomes

Having read this chapter and completed its associated activities, readers should be able to:

- Appreciate that issues of human resourcing, when taken back to basic principles, arise whenever human beings organise themselves, or are organised, to complete work tasks

- Understand why human resources are more usefully understood not as human beings themselves but as capacities that human beings bring to work situations, noting how such an insight relates to contemporary 'resource-based' thinking in strategic management generally

- Recognise that human resource issues in modern times can only be understood in the light of the nature of the societies and the economies in which they arise, as well as in the light of more general tendencies of human beings to resist being directed and to form coalitions of interest

- Analyse the strategies of organisations as patterns which *emerge* over time rather than as corporate plans

- Come to terms with the responsibility of organisational strategic human resourcing for shaping the human dimension of the organisation as a whole and for taking it forward into the future

- See why it can be argued that human resourcing is as much an influence on broad corporate strategy as something that follows from or serves it

- Understand why human resourcing work can be seen as 'essentially strategic' and why the responsibilities of HR specialists differ in certain respects from those of more functionally or departmentally focused managers

- Point to the fundamental strategic options that face HR strategy-makers – especially the choice between high commitment HR strategies and low commitment HR strategies

- Identify the variety of factors that influence the strategic direction followed in any particular organisation, noting the interplay of human choices and constraining and enabling circumstances in this

- Analyse the human resourcing practices of any organisation to assess the extent to which they are consistent with each other and are appropriate for the general environmental or business circumstances of the organisation

Human resourcing from the Stone Age to the twenty-first century

The nature of human resources

We tend to speak of human resource management as if it were something fairly new. It is spoken and written about as if it were the invention of late twentieth-century managers and of the academic experts who study such people. This is true. But it is only true in part. To appreciate this point we can helpfully imagine a prehistoric family group sitting around a fire talking about how they can make a better living in the small valley in which they have settled after giving up a nomadic way of life. Let us travel back in time and listen carefully to what is being said by the members of the Aynshent family.

Case Study 1.1a

Meet the Aynshents

One evening a conversation develops among the Aynshents, a prehistoric family group, with one of the women explaining that she had found a way of growing a much bigger crop of maize by preparing the ground more carefully. To increase this yield further, however, she needs more hands to work the land. Some babies were on the way in the little tribe, but they would not be able to work for some years. Perhaps the family should capture one or two of the travellers who passed this way now and again, and force them to work for the family. The speaker would be willing, she said, to organise and lead such an expedition. Or alternatively, one of the brothers who had recently proved to be a rather hopeless hunter could develop some farming skills and stop wasting his time pursuing animals that nearly always got away from him. Also, the eldest brother was hoping to get a strong young woman from across the other side of the valley to become his mate, and join the family group. If this happened, there would be another pair of hands available for work and there would be the potential for more babies to be born.

Further to this, an alliance with this woman's family would probably make available to the group some of the witch-doctoring expertise which was helping the people across the valley to get ahead of others in locating herds of prey. Further, it seemed that the young woman had a detailed knowledge of where to find wild crops of nuts and fruit that could be gathered. And an alliance with her family might also help the little tribe to fight off the intruders who had recently been appearing in the valley and who were competing for the scarce spring water supplies in the valley. The potential bride was already well known to her prospective mate's family and they both liked and trusted her, as she did them. The general view was that her joining the family would not only bring into it a further pair of hands together with valuable knowledge, skills and mothering 'potential' but that the general positive and cooperative atmosphere of the family group would be enhanced by her presence.

> ### Activity 1.1   HRM in prehistory and the present
>
> a) Thinking of the notion of *human resources* in a relatively common-sense way, identify any such resources that might be seen as arising in this conversation.
>
> b) If possible, identify any parallels that might be seen between what we think of as 'human resource management' in modern times and what is going on in this prehistoric scenario.

The first and most obvious 'human resource' that is mentioned in the conversation among the Aynshents is that of 'pairs of hands'. A member of the family has recognised the need for some fairly simple labour to be carried out – under her direct supervision, we might assume. Skill at hunting is a further resource that comes into the conversation, as are the notions of knowledge (of the location of wild crops), expertise (at witch doctoring) and organisational leadership (of a kidnapping expedition). In addition to the fairly obvious biological capacity of the women in the group to bear children and thus help reproduce the family, there are some more abstract human capacities alluded to. Among these is the capability of one of the brothers to make alliances with other groups in the valley and the capacity of his potential bride to bring into the group certain personal qualities that, it was felt, would enhance the cooperative spirit of the family. In the background here were even more abstract factors that have clear implications for how these 'resources' might be utilised: there is talk of the family and its prospective new member liking each other and, perhaps especially significant, *trusting* each other.

The Aynshents are a family, developing into a tribe, and are really quite different from a modern business or public corporation – settings where we would more likely expect to see human resourcing practices occurring. Yet the Aynshents can be seen as involved in a joint undertaking in which work tasks are undertaken both to ensure the survival of that enterprise and to enhance its economic performance to the benefit of certain of the people involved in it (note that there is the possibility of the family taking slaves; people who are not necessarily going to feel that they benefit from being brought into the tribe). Within this, we can see significant parallels between what was occurring around the campfire and what might occur in a modern work organisation. The conversation could be seen as involving analysis of managerial options with regard to human resources. Managerial decisions are being contemplated in the areas of recruitment (by slave-taking or marriage), retraining (the unsuccessful hunter to become a farmer), and strategic alliances (with the potential bride's family). As well as noting the opportunities open to the family, attention is given to the threat coming from competitors for water supplies. And, at the more general level, there is reflection in the group on what might be seen as the 'corporate culture' of the little tribe; the atmosphere of trust and cooperation that is felt to be conducive to the successful utilisation of the human resources that are the main topic of discussion.

Why has it been thought important to make this journey back in time and look at a pre-industrial case study in strategic human resourcing? One purpose was to make as forcefully as possible the point that 'strategic human resourcing' is not some new, or even recent, managerial or academic 'fad' or some novel and groundbreaking invention that is peculiar to modern circumstances. It is a profoundly commonsensical notion that would be sensibly taken up by people in charge of any human enterprise in which work tasks are undertaken and where there is a concern for that enterprise to continue into the future as a viable social and economic unit. The concept is as relevant to an ancient tribe, a commercial business, a football club, a government department or a university.

The application of an anthropological perspective to the topic of strategic human resourcing, rather than the more normal management studies or economics one, has purposes beyond this simple demystifying of human resourcing practices. It also helps us, by taking us back to basic principles, to conceptualise the issues with which we are concerned in a way that will most usefully inform our activities with regard to human resourcing matters – whether those activities are managerial ones concerned with enhancing practices or are research ones concerned with the advancing of knowledge. In other words, it can help us to *define our terms* in a way that will most successfully assist us in analysing and understanding the managerial processes with which we are concerned.

The key conceptual point that our Aynshents case helps us make is that it is better to focus on 'human resources' as human predispositions and capacities, such as skill, knowledge, commitment and a general predisposition of people to work cooperatively together, rather than to think of people themselves as 'resources'. To think of people as human resources, like the notion of 'managing people', can be seen as ethically suspect. To treat people as means to ends rather than as ends in themselves is to defy what Kant identified as an ethical categorical imperative, for instance. It is also unrealistic, given the human tendency, to which we will return shortly, to resent and resist attempts at control and manipulation by others (Watson, 2006). Human resources, in the context of modern work organisations, are thus most usefully seen as human capacities necessary for task performance and the continuation of the organisation into the future:

> *Human resources are the efforts, knowledge, capabilities and committed behaviours which people contribute to a work organisation as part of an employment exchange (or more temporary contractual arrangement) and which are managerially utilised to carry out work tasks and enable the organisation to continue in existence.*

Situating HRM in its historical and political-economic context

Work organisations, of the type we tend to take for granted, have developed only in the most recent period of human history. Like the family-based enterprise of the Aynshents, they use human resources to fulfil the purposes of their members (or, given the inequalities that have characterised human societies down the ages, to serve the purposes of *some* of their members). But they do this in a way which is characteristic of the *industrial capitalist* type of society and political economy which has emerged in the past few centuries. Modern work organisations make use of human resources in a context which is:

● *Market-based*. The relationship between the organisation and those supplying it with the human resources such as labour, skill and knowledge is fundamentally one of economic exchange. Resources are acquired in a context of labour markets with workers and organisational officials making bargains with workers who contract to work and behave in certain ways in exchange for various rewards or 'incentives'. On top of this basic economic exchange is a degree of *social exchange* whereby workers – to greatly varying levels across different circumstances – may seek such rewards as a sense of belonging, a feeling of security, or the opportunity to achieve status or power in return for giving to the organisation and its managerial officers a degree of loyalty or commitment.

● *Bureaucratised.* Modern work organisations are bureaucracies in the sense identified by Weber (1978). People are given a part to play in the division of labour of the organisation, not as in more 'traditional' times (as with the Aynshents) as a result of their birth or their possession of magical powers, but because they are deemed to be technically qualified for their posts. And work tasks are controlled and coordinated by office holders (typically these days called 'managers') whose authority derives from their expertise and who devise rules and procedures that are calculated to ensure that the most appropriate means are chosen to fulfil specific ends.

Human resources, in the modern industrial capitalist context, become qualities which are traded and bargained over in a very calculative manner. And given that organisations – especially business organisations – in the market context of the industrial capitalist economy compete with each other in order to survive, human resources become matters of considerable competitive significance. Kay (1993) locates them among an organisation's distinctive capabilities (the starting point, he argues, for the strategic analysis of any organisation) and Hamel and Prahalad (1994) identify the skills and knowledge of an organisation's staff as the *core competencies* that potentially give it advantages over other organisations. The contemporary emphasis on 'talent management' is a further development of this theme (Ashton and Morton, 2005; Tansley *et al.*, 2007).

This style of thinking of the strategic advantages of certain internal organisational qualities and capacities came increasingly to the fore as global competitive pressures grew in the latter decades of the twentieth century and has led to increasing use in the academic literature of what is called a *resource-based view (RBV) of the firm*. It was seen as necessary to balance attention to the external competitive strategies of firms with attention to the internal characteristics that made some outperform others. Barney (1991) emphasised the importance of firms exploiting their 'internal strengths' in human and non-human resources, ensuring that these resources stayed rare, unimitable and non-substitutable and would 'make a difference' in the sense of 'adding value' to business activities. In what we are identifying here as the 'human resourcing' area, Barney (1992) stressed that such a resource-based perspective can help us appreciate such socially complex resources as creativity, trust and a capacity to make both effective choices and changes in behaviour. Boxall (1996), who has concentrated on the application of resource-based thinking to human resource management, emphasises that an advantage in terms of the human capital (the skills, knowledge and capabilities) that reside in an organisation's staff only become effective once they are released, once there is what he calls a 'human process advantage'.

Strategic human resourcing is thus about much more than acquiring and retaining human capabilities but has to involve itself in such matters as trust-building and the seeking of what, in our definition earlier, were referred to as 'committed behaviours', forms of action where workers are choosing to act within a conception of what is appropriate for the wider organisation and not just for short-term or sectional gain. However, in spite of providing the above insights and in spite of its having become 'almost the assumed paradigm within strategic management research' (Allen and Wright, 2007: 90), there are difficulties with the RBV approach, as there are with its variants, such as the 'human capital' (Hitt *et al.*, 2001) and 'dynamic capabilities' (Teece *et al.*, 1997) approaches.

First, care has to be taken to recognise that work organisations are not free-standing entities competing with each other on a globally 'even playing field'. Different societies, with different cultures, educational and technological infra-structures, give a greater or a lesser degree of support in these broad resource areas to the organisations operating within them (Boxall and Purcell, 2002). And we can add to this the importance of class, gender and ethnic inequalities in any society as factors limiting or encouraging the development of high commitment and high trust relations as corporate human resources (Watson, 2004).

Second, we have to avoid the danger that RBV thinking leads us to talk too much about work organisations as if they were all capitalist firms engaged in the pursuit of 'competitive advantage' with other firms. It is undoubtedly the case that all work organisations in the industrial capitalist world have to cope with competitive pressures. Schools, hospitals, local authorities, police forces all have to compete with other organisations in the labour market for staff, for example. And they all, to some extent, compete with each other for state funding. But it is ludicrous to imply that when the managers of, say, a fire service, a university or a general medical practice concern themselves with developing their human resource capacity this is primarily to do with gaining competitive advantage over other fire-fighting provisions, higher education institutions or local health centres. This is something we will bear in mind when, later, we come to our own definition of 'strategy'.

The third issue which can be raised with regard to RBV thinking is that of whether it can help us very much in trying to understand better what *actually happens* when strategies are made in work organisations. There is, for example, very little information about *who* the practitioners are that actually shape human resourcing strategies or *how* those practitioners go about 'strategy-making'.

Valuable theoretical work is now emerging which sets a framework within which research might be done on what goes inside the strategy 'black box'. We thus have an emerging 'strategy as practice' perspective (Johnson *et al.*, 2003; Jarzabkowsky, 2005). This is 'essentially concerned with strategy as activity in organizations, typically the interaction of people . . . the practical performance of the people who engage in [these activities so that] two surprisingly neglected questions [can be answered]: what do the people engaged in strategizing actually do and how do they influence strategic outcomes?' (Johnson *et al.*, 2007). This interest is one taken up in the present chapter where we will see some particular practitioners of strategic HRM in action. We are partly applying a strategy-as-practice perspective here by looking at, in Jarzabkowsky's words, 'how practitioners act, what work they do, with whom they interact, and what practical reasoning they apply in their own localized experience of strategy' (2005: 9). However, the perspective adopted here, whilst incorporating the strategy-as-practice emphasis, is a wider one. Whereas 'strategy-as-practice' tends to characterise itself as a 'micro' and an activity-*based* (my emphasis) approach, the present one sets its relatively 'local' or microscopic concerns within a 'macro' structural and 'global' framework. It also relates its concerns to certain characteristics of the human species as whole – and specifically to the 'unmanageability' of human beings.

Human resources, people and work organisations

The impossibility of 'managing people'

In emphasising the importance to organisations of the human capabilities or resources that they draw upon as their managers strive either to compete with commercial rivals or to provide a public service that will be deemed worthy of continuing support by its users (and, critically, on their behalf, by the state), it is important not to separate people's work capacities from their humanity. Whether we are thinking ethically or expediently about people and work, it is necessary to recognise that the organisational worker – at whatever level they are engaged by the enterprise – is much more than a bundle of capabilities and that they have lives and priorities beyond their organisational involvement. People's identities and purposes are not influenced by their employment alone. And it is in the nature of the human beast, we might say, to assert a degree of independence in their relationships with other people, and with 'bosses' especially – although, strictly speaking, as Foucault (1980) points out, we read such ideas into our 'subjectivities' in the light of the discourses of our historical period (see Townley, 1994a on the particular relevance of this point to human resource management). This assertive aspect of human subjectivity tends to come into play regardless of how dependent people might be on these others and however much power or authority those others may possess. Thus, we might say, the managing of human resources is essentially problematic. Many managers would undoubtedly like to be able directly to 'manage people' and thus straightforwardly exploit the 'resources' which those people bring to the organisation. It would make life easier for managers if the workforce could be tended like a herd of cattle which, with careful husbandry, produces a regular supply of milk, butter and meat. The human animal, however, is fundamentally different from all others (Watson, 2001). 'Managing people' is an impossibility.

Human resources are essentially problematic because they are supplied by human beings. In spite of what is implied in many of the texts which regale management students with simplistic 'motivation theories' and personality inventories, people are not little biological machines having fixed personalities, given sets of 'needs' and a straightforward willingness to 'be managed' if their lower- and higher-level 'needs' are met, or their personality profiles matched to job demands (Watson, 2006). People are assertive, adaptable social beings with emergent identities who, with varying degrees of 'power', negotiate their roles and rewards with the employing organisation. When they go to work they are as much setting out to 'use' the organisation for their own ends as the organisation is concerned to 'use' them. People in modern societies, brought up to value notions of democracy and human rights, are especially likely to question the right of organisational officers to direct their activities, beyond certain tightly defined and agreed limits. But such characteristics have been part of the human experience since the species developed a brain large enough to use language and ask the question 'Why should I?'

Case Study 1.1b

An Aynshent dispute

The day after the conversation around the Aynshents' camp fire about changing how the family made its living, the sister who initiated the discussion approached the brother whose hunting skills had been questioned the night before. As soon as the man saw his sister approaching him, he turned his back on her. She immediately assumed that she had hurt his feelings with what she had said about his being better suited to farming than hunting. But once she eventually persuaded him to talk to her, she realised that it went deeper than this. In general he questioned the right of any family member to judge his abilities and, in particular, he claimed that her being his elder sister gave her no special position in the group. She responded to the effect that she was simply trying to find ways of making a better life for everyone in the tribe, by finding ways of ensuring that people's efforts were expended to best and most productive effect. The man listened carefully to this but then challenged his sister as to why he should be thought of primarily as a hunter who brought in meat or a farmer who grew crops. Why could he not simply be respected for himself? Well he was, she insisted. If that was so, he asked, could he not be allowed to spend his time doing what he loved best: studying the clouds and contemplating how the gods might be persuaded to look favourably on the tribe. This, his sister says, is impossible. Other family members simply would not accept that they should work to keep a man who was unwilling to work himself. At this, her brother stormed out of the cave, kicking up dust in his sister's face as he departed. He headed off to find other family members who he thought might agree with him that certain shifts in power in the group should be resisted.

Activity 1.2 — Handling human recalcitrance and resistance to management

1. Consider the extent to which the type of 'resistance to being managed' we see occurring here is a characteristic of an especially awkward character within the Aynshent family or is something that every human being has within them to some extent.

2. Think about any ways in which you have personally experienced this kind of human 'recalcitrance' in an organisational setting, either on your own behalf or in someone whose work patterns you were trying to influence.

3. Reflect on possible parallels between what the Aynshent sister is doing here and the work of a modern human resource manager and consider what, if you were her, you might do next.

In this second episode of the Ayshents' story, we see a fairly simple example of a human being refusing to separate their notions of self-identity and personal autonomy from their role as a 'supplier' of human resources. Reflection on personal experience is likely to indicate that this may be a bolder example of the normal human recalcitrance that we see every day. But it touches on something that is in every one of us. It would appear that even within slave systems, conscript armies or concentration camps, people fight to maintain a degree of human autonomy and self-respect, however great the power exerted over them.

There is little difficulty in seeing that the Aynshent sister is taking upon herself a role of changing how her family makes its living and is, in effect, utilising the human resources available to it. In doing this, she has quickly confronted the fact that the suppliers of human resources have feelings, feelings that can be hurt if they are slighted in some way. But the humanness of resource suppliers is more than just a matter of people having emotions. As we have already recognised, power of one human being over another is not automatically accepted. It has to be won – to be converted or, as Weber (1978) puts it, *legitimised* to make it into 'authority'. The Aynshent woman tries to do this in two ways. First, she justifies what she is doing by arguing that she is trying to benefit the tribe as a whole (making a better life for everyone in the tribe) and, later, she opposes his stated preferences by saying what would be acceptable to other family members. The first move is very similar to everyday modern managerial tactics where an HR manager might, for example, argue that they are redeploying a worker into a new job, not because the manager personally wants this, but 'for the sake of the business'. And the second move parallels classic HR managerial arguments about 'fairness' and 'comparable treatment' across the organisation when asking other organisational members, managers included, to 'stay in line' (Watson, 1977, 1986).

What might we envisage the Aynshent proto-HR manager doing next? It is unlikely that she has the authority simply to command her brother to retrain. One move she might make, however, would be to negotiate with him – and indeed with other family members – a role in which he combines some new farming responsibilities with certain priestly duties that allow him to draw out his currently hidden religious skills at the same time as taking his share of the basic labour of producing food. Even the modern HR manager, with the sort of formal authority that the Aynshent sister lacked and the ability to wield some of the power that every employer in market-based societies has over its employees, needs constantly to negotiate with other organisational members and to win people's consent to managerially initiated changes. Negotiation and bargaining are at the heart of all managerial work and strategic human resourcing.

Work organisations as negotiated orders

In the same way that organisational members are much more than bundles of human resources, organisations are much more than bunches of individuals. And they do not operate as simple people-processing machines. It may be helpful at times to analyse organisations as systems and procedures that transform inputs into outputs. But to understand the complexities of how organisations work in practice we need to see inside the 'black box' with which systems thinking presents us (Silverman, 1970; Watson, 2006). Every organisation has it own social order, with rules, values, official and unofficial interactions, formal and informal power structures and distinctive cultural patterns.

The human resourcing work that the Aynshent sister was undertaking was concerned with changing the social order of that human grouping. What she was doing clearly involved more than just dealing with individuals. Some cultural shift would need to be negotiated to accommodate the brother who was challenging her proposals. But also, there was the possibility that the brother was going to start a faction within the tribe, an interest group that might split the family and bring to the surface as yet latent conflicts of interest. The cooperative spirit that allowed the family to prosper and grow so far might be threatened. Part of the evolution of the human species as a whole has been the development of a capacity for cooperative effort. This has enabled achievements over the centuries that far exceed anything the Aynshents could have dreamt of. But equally important has been a tendency for people, both as individuals and group members, to assert their independence of others, to resist power and to pursue sectional interests.

All of these matters are key concerns of strategic human resourcing. And it is helpful to locate our understanding of human resource work within an understanding of work organisations as *negotiated orders*, recognising that the differences of interest and power arising in organisations both arise from and contribute to the class, power, gender and ethnic differences prevailing in society at large (Watson, 2008). To see work organisations as negotiated orders is to recognise that *they involve continually emergent patterns of activity and understanding that arise from the interplay of individual and group interests, ideas, initiatives and reactions – these interests and differences reflecting patterns of power and inequality applying in the society and economy of which the organisation is a part.*

Within any work organisation, ancient or modern, there will inevitably be different constituencies that have to be managerially bargained with, if the management is going to 'keep the organisational show on the road'. If managers are going to have any control whatsoever over the activities of the people working in the organisation they will need to win their consent and reward their compliance. And the interests of each group of office or factory workers need to be balanced with every other group, the aspirations of each departmental head have to be matched with the aspirations of every other, the demands of each professional faction set against the demands of every other, and so on. All of this has to be handled in a way equivalent to the bargaining and trading that has to occur on the organisation's behalf with customer, supplier and various other external constituencies to bring in the non-human resources of raw materials and revenue that are necessary to enable the enterprise to continue in existence. And to say this takes us towards a particular conception of strategic management: a 'processual' view that recognises the centrality of exchange relationships between organisations and various constituencies both inside and outside them.

Managing organisations strategically

Strategies as patterns that emerge over time

The normal way we tend to talk of strategies is as plans and, in the organisational context, we tend to talk of them as the plans the people in charge of organisations make to fulfil whatever goals they have set for that enterprise. It is increasingly being accepted that we can more usefully understand strategies as the outcomes of ongoing organisational processes involving a range of contributors rather than as pre-decided plans produced by specialist 'strategy-makers'. When doing strategic analysis – trying to understand how organisations are, or might be, shaped and directed over time – it is more helpful to utilise a concept of strategies as *realised patterns* rather than to treat strategies as managerial *plans*. A 'processual' view of strategy sees it as *the pattern emerging over time in an organisation as actions (of both a planned and unplanned nature) are carried out to enable the organisation as a whole to carry on into the future*.

It follows from this view that strategic choices or managerial decisions are those that have:

● a *corporate* dimension: relate to the whole organisation as opposed simply to a part of it;

● a *long-term* implication: whether this be a matter of just surviving in the sense of staying viable or a matter of aiming to operate at a higher level of performance (Boxall and Purcell, 2002).

Important studies by Quinn (1980) and Mintzberg (1994) adopted this perspective and established that strategy-making, when seen in practice, involves a great deal more than simply developing and implementing plans. The strategy of an organisation is thus best understood *not as the plan which an organisation follows* but as a *pattern which unfolds over time* in which formal planning can be found to occur to a greater or lesser extent. Quinn's (1980) research shows that organisations whose strategy-formation efforts are relatively successful in terms of conventional business criteria follow processes of *logical incrementalism*. This is 'a process of the gradual evolution of strategy driven by conscious managerial thought', as opposed to one involving operating with systematic preshaped strategic plans. At the centre of the 'process realm' is a 'network of information' which extends the perspective of operating managers and helps reduce their uncertainty about the future, as well as stimulating long-term 'special studies' (Quinn, 1980: 38–9). Mintzberg's 'McGill studies', which tracked the strategies of several organisations, similarly and 'in general' 'found strategy making to be a complex, interactive, and evolutionary process, best described as one of adaptive learning' (Mintzberg, 1994: 110). Strategy again *emerges* from complex processes rather than grand plans.

In the human resourcing area there is little evidence that very deliberate processes of carefully sequenced strategic analysis, planning and implementation are followed in practice. As Whipp put it, 'the application of over-rational, linear programmes of HRM as a means of securing competitive success is shown to be at odds with experience both in the UK and elsewhere' (1992: 33). More processual frameworks like those adopted in research by Hendry and Pettigrew (1992) and Pettigrew and Whipp (1991) show that integrating human resourcing with broader strategies is a 'highly complex and iterative process, much dependent on the interplay and resources of different stakeholders' (Legge, 1995: 135). There is rarely an 'easily isolated logic to strategic change' and, instead, the process is one which takes its motive force from an amalgam of economic, personal and political imperatives' (Whipp, 1992: 33). Bamberger and Meshoulam, in contrasting the processual or what they call 'incremental' approach to strategy with the more traditional 'rational planning' one, stress the value of the incremental perspective in recognising that 'the strategy formulation process is characterised by a high degree of informality, intra- and interorganisational politics, fragmentation, and, to a certain extent, even chance' (2000: 21).

Strategy-making in practice

All kinds of conflict and difference within the managerial political arena arise and lead to shifting priorities and varying practices. We can see this very clearly in the case of Moddens Foods where, at present, a single clear strategic direction for the firm and its human resourcing is not discernible.

Case Study 1.2a

Strategic debate at Moddens Foods

Moddens was for many years a small family firm that made sausages and supplied poultry to the gentry in a rural part of the country. These days it is a much larger business selling a range of food products across Europe and North America. Sam Modden is the company chairman and the only member of the family actively involved with the business. He is finding himself increasingly influenced by his daughter, Eva, who has nothing to do with the business and devotes all her time to her activities as an environmentalist and an 'anti-globalisation' activist. Her father, while disapproving of this, has come to take seriously some of her objections to the way the company is growing, in large part as a result of its applying industrial and chemical-based production methods to food products and the increasing use of cheap overseas labour at the cost of employment in the home country.

Tension has been growing for some time between Sam and the managing director, Juan Poort, who is keen to pursue a strategy of routinising production methods. This involves using whatever genetic manipulation of crops can offer to maximise the yield from harvests, for instance, and treating meat products in a way as close as possible to industrial raw materials. Connected with this is his determination to reduce labour costs to a minimum by hiring and firing workers across the globe in a way he deems to be most convenient and cost-effective. Poort is supported in all of this by Frank Angle, the operations director. Angle was brought up in the home town of the company and was once close to the Modden family. He has been increasingly loosening his local ties and seems to enjoy travelling the world and looking for supply and production opportunities in the Far East – especially in Thailand, where he has recently married a local woman. Hal Selz, the marketing director, not only personally dislikes Frank Angle but his religious principles, he says, lead him to sympathise with Sam Modden. He shares Sam's unhappiness about the company's shift to higher volume, lower quality output. They are both also very concerned about the increasingly ruthless human resourcing strategy which is associated with this.

The finance director, Ivan Kelp, has a degree of sympathy with these reservations about strategic trends but is also aware that the increasing profit levels which are being achieved are likely to be helpful in fighting off the takeover bid that he believes is likely to be made in the near future by a very large foreign-based international food company that, as yet, does not have a foothold in the country. Jean Frear, the human resources director, has a personal but very private preference for the company staying true to its high quality, broad range and 'premium product' roots. Her taste for gourmet food attracted her to the job at Moddens in the first place. But she tries hard to stay relatively neutral in the arguments and to mediate between the two factions on the board. She feels that she has a 'professional responsibility' to avoid dissension growing to an extent that will harm the business. She is also conscious that, as she put it to her colleagues in a recent board meeting, they cannot 'have it both ways' strategically: being both a 'mass producer of cheap chicken nuggets' and a 'purveyor of fine quality game and sausages to the discriminating classes'. She explained that two or three of their best chefs and food scientists were talking of leaving the company, a loss that would threaten several new products that were currently being developed. In Frank Angle's view, however, such people are 'more trouble than they are worth'. He prefers to employ, at the centre, 'a small number of straightforward chemists and food engineers' who would push forward the 'rationalisation and technological control' of every aspect of the business and forget trying to appeal either to 'ethically over-sensitive' customers or to the 'small clientele of food faddists'.

These differences are currently coming to a head over issues in the original headquarters and manufacturing centre in the town where the business began. Poort and Angle want to close the three chicken production centres in the town and replace them with plants in Thailand and, as production increases, China. They also want to close down the experimental organic food farm, which has been producing foods for Moddens' range of organic foods which Hal has been struggling to establish with two of the country's major supermarkets. They object, additionally, to Sam's belief in regularly producing new products to new recipes, especially when these are produced as a 'seasonal line' and are meant to stay on the market for only a short time. Moddens' share of the relatively small organic market has been growing only slowly and Poort would like to abandon it. This is in spite of the fact that Sam has been giving the organic and 'new seasonal foods' parts of the business his close and personal attention over recent months. Like Jean Frear he is aware that some of the very able and highly skilled agricultural experts, chefs and food scientists that Moddens employ are becoming anxious and are beginning to look for employment with rival companies. He is also concerned that the company is employing fewer and fewer of the local people whose families provided the labour and expertise that helped the business to grow over the years. But Frank Angle makes Sam and Jean exceedingly uncomfortable by pointing out to them that many of the workers employed locally are foreign workers, many of them refugees who are bussed in to the factories, often from miles away, to work long and often unsocial shifts for pay little above the national minimum wage. So why not, asks Poort, pay the even lower Thai national wage?

These events illustrate the point very well that if we want to understand how long-term changes to 'whole organisations' come about (i.e. strategy-making occurs), we need to look at the managerial politics of the organisation, at the various values and interests of the people responsible for shaping the organisation, instead of looking for wholly 'rational' plans made in the face of unambiguous market and other contextual information. This is by no means to argue that strategies result simply from personal arguments and political debates among decision-makers. Nor is it to argue that there is no degree of planning involved in what occurs. And it is certainly not to argue that issues in the organisation's business environment are not highly relevant to either strategic debates or strategic directions that are subsequently followed. Instead, it is to suggest that we look at all of these factors working out together. Let us consider some of these in the Moddens case.

Activity 1.3	'Human' and contextual factors in strategy-making

1. Identify the part played in this process of strategy-making by the personal interests, values and ideas of these people who are, in effect, Moddens' strategy-makers.
2. Identify the part played in this process of strategy-making by business, market and other contextual factors.

There appear to be two main factions developing among the key managerial decision-makers in Moddens, with the HR director, while favouring one of these, nevertheless trying to adopt a relatively neutral and mediating role and the finance director being equivocal. Sam Modden has perhaps the strongest personal feelings about developments, with his background as the remaining member of the founding family on the board. He clearly has strong feelings about the locality in which the firm developed and a conscience about employees and a degree of commitment to the local population. He is also influenced in his disquiet about the 'industrialising' tendencies in agriculture and food production by his daughter, who is a very committed critic of world trends of which Moddens, presumably to her distress, is becoming a part. Sam, we can assume, has also developed a commitment to the organic product line in which he has taken a strong personal interest. Juan Poort, the managing director, appears to have a simpler view of the business, unencumbered by sentiments about family or locality. Poort seems to find it easy to view workers as means of production rather than as people to whom an employer might have a longer-term commitment. Convenience and cost-effectiveness are his priority in the human resourcing field. Frank Angle seems to think similarly and appears to have some personal contempt for ethical ideas (at least for 'ethically over-sensitive customers') and for gourmet-oriented customers ('food faddists'). In speaking in this way, of course, he may well be attempting to upset or challenge Sam Modden or Jean Frear who, he is probably aware, is possibly one of these 'faddists'. Although we can infer that he once shared some of Sam's affection for the locality in which he built his career, we learn that he now likes to travel the world and it is not unreasonable to guess that some of his interest in moving production to the Far East is connected to his marriage to a Thai woman.

Jean Frear operates with certain ideas of 'professional' commitment and this, she clearly hopes, will keep her to some extent above these interpersonal wrangles as she tries to mediate between the factions. Nevertheless, it is apparent that her sentiments are with Modden. She and Sam, we hear, are made very uncomfortable by Angle's reminding them that some rather exploitative-sounding employment practices are occurring in the home town – let alone abroad. Whether or not she is likely, in the longer run, to bring Ivan Kelp into this middle ground is unclear. It looks like he is experiencing a tension between his value-based reservations about these trends and his awareness that the same trends might be helpful to him in his job, in so far as the rising profit figures help him fight off a possible takeover bid. Hal Selz, on the other hand, is in a less complicated position. From what we know, he has religious-based value objections to the 'ruthlessness' of human resourcing trends. And we might expect his personal dislike of Frank Angle to encourage him to support the Sam Modden position in questioning these trends.

All of these differences at the interpersonal value and personal-interest level can only be understood if we see them taking place in the light of a range of factors in Moddens Foods' business situation. A variety of relatively specific contextual factors arise within the more general political-economic context of Moddens' location within a capitalist culture and structure in which there are markets not just for products but for labour and for companies themselves:

- 'Globalising' trends and the opportunity to obtain supplies and labour from across the world, at a lower cost than in the company's home country; the availability of cheaper 'refugee' labour in the home country; the existence of growing overseas markets; the threat of takeover facing Moddens, one which relates to the apparent interest of a large international company in acquiring a business in Moddens' home country.

- Technological factors, with the increasing possibility of applying industrial and chemical methods to food processing.

- Legal factors, with the different minimum wages laws in different countries.

- Market factors and, especially, the existence of an apparently large market for 'industrialised foods' like chicken nuggets as well as the existence of a smaller, but higher price oriented, market for organic and other 'premium' and short-season food products.

In so far as we can see Moddens as a 'whole organisation', it is clearly one that, to survive into the long term, has to exchange resources or 'trade' with both *external* constituencies such as customers, suppliers and share owners and *internal* constituencies such as various employee constituencies and different significant managerial individuals and factions. Exactly how these exchange relations are to be shaped in the future is clearly the key strategic issue facing those in charge of the business. Are the main customers to be those wanting cheap homogenised foods or the more gourmet-inclined or environmentally sensitive consumers? Are the main employment exchanges to be with a relatively committed and tradi-tionally skilled local workforce or with workers recruited on a hire-and-fire basis wherever in the world they are cheapest and most convenient to employ? And, at the technical–professional level, is the employment exchange to be with what we have seen characterised by Frear as a group of 'highly skilled agricultural experts, chefs and food scientists' or with a group of what Angle calls 'straightforward chemists and food engineers'? As we will shortly see, the current position in which both of these strategic styles are being followed at the same time is increasingly being recognised by the directors as untenable.

The type of employment exchanges that Moddens makes with the various worker constituencies (these, of course, including the senior managerial workers whom we have met) are going to be central to the human resourcing strategy of Moddens Foods and to the type of company it becomes in the future.

Managing HR strategically

The nature of human resource strategies

In the light of our analysis so far we can conceptualise the human resourcing element of an organisation's overall strategy in terms of the 'general direction' that it follows in dealing with the human resources it needs to acquire through exchange relationships with the various human constituencies that can supply them. To follow a clear and consistent direction strategic human resourcing must involve the establishing of clear principles about 'how people are to be treated' and the shaping of practices that implement these values and principles.

We can thus most usefully define an organisation's human resourcing strategy as *the general direction followed by an organisation in how it secures, develops, retains and, from time to time, dispenses with the human resources it requires to carry out work tasks in a way that ensure that it continues successfully into the long term.* And, thus, 'strategic human resourcing' is to be understood as *the establishing of principles and the shaping of practices whereby the human resources which an organisation, seen as a corporate whole, requires to carry out work tasks that enable it to continue successfully into the long term.*

It would appear that, at Moddens, there is no clear 'general direction' being followed and there is inconsistency in the basic principles and values behind the shaping of human resourcing practices.

Activity 1.4   **Direction and consistency in emergent HR strategies**

1. Consider the extent to which an emergent human resourcing strategy (or 'general direction') can be seen in the account of managerial deliberations in Moddens Foods.

2. Assess the view stated by Jean Frear, the HR director, that there is an inconsistency in the current strategic approach ('having it both ways' as she puts it) and consider the implications of such an analysis for human resourcing in the future.

One of the reasons why we can so clearly see in the Moddens Foods case the role of organisational politics within strategy-making processes is that a strategic crisis has arisen. In the past there was a fairly clear strategic HR direction, one that might be seen as relatively paternalist, with employer and employee having some sense of long-term commitment to each other. This was associated with a broader business direction in which relatively high quality and expensive products were supplied, with highly skilled and innovative technicians being employed to bring about innovations to cope with developments in the tastes of more 'discriminating' customers. However, other markets were also developed in which a much more 'hire and fire' HR strategy appears to have developed alongside the older traditional Moddens' approach. And it is interesting that it is the HR director who points to a problem in these two business directions being followed at the same time. Jean says that the company cannot 'have it both ways': at the same time producing 'cheap chicken nuggets' and 'fine quality game and sausages'. In raising this, she is raising marketing problems and noting the challenge of the 'good name' of Moddens as a supplier of 'superior' foods being damaged through an association with a product of a very different nature. But there are significant human resourcing issues in her mind too. She explains this to her colleagues.

Case Study 1.2b

Strategic incoherence in Moddens' HR strategy

'As HR director I don't just think about staffing issues, you know. I've seen a couple of articles in the food press questioning how far the company can be trusted by the people who pay the high prices for our premium sausages and game pies when it is simultaneously operating in the same market as producers of junk foods who use all sorts of mechanically recovered bits and pieces, force a high water content into the meat and have no reservations about the indiscriminate use of antibiotics. So I don't see how we can stay in both markets – and here I know Hal feels the same as me. But my main input here has to be on the HR front. This damaging of our reputation is, as I have told you already, causing some of our top food and cookery experts to think of leaving us. These are the people we depend on for the innovations that we need to make to ensure our long-term future. And, let me tell you, I have already found that recruitment problems are occurring in these areas. The potential graduate recruits I have been talking to are pretty environmentally aware these days. I can see real recruitment problems for technical posts. Where does that leave us when looking to the future?'

'I have to admit that the increasing bussing-in of cheap foreign labour is also giving me headaches. It's not just that I am uneasy about some of the bullying and racism I have uncovered among supervisors that this has given rise to. I am also finding it difficult to pursue consistent pay, equal opportunity, promotion and disciplinary practices across a workforce that, in part, is local, long-serving and has fairly high expectations of us in welfare terms and is, in another part, untrusting and afraid, speaks a dozen different languages and may be sent back to their country of origin not long after I've got them trained and beginning to feel part of the company. It used to be a key part of the relationship of Moddens with all our employees that everyone was treated fairly. Nowadays nobody really knows where they stand and whether or not they might be replaced tomorrow by somebody on a lower wage who is willing to do whatever they are told.'

Human resourcing as essentially strategic

We noted earlier that to think about an organisation strategically is to think about the *whole organisation* and about the organisation's *long-term* future. Jean Frear, in her above statement, is looking at Moddens in both of these respects. Her responsibility for the HR strategy of the organisation leads her to look at the extent to which the organisation is 'holding together' as a human enterprise. She clearly worries about disintegration in this respect, with the danger, in effect, of a divided workforce leading to a divided organisation – one in which people will neither trust each other nor trust the company. And all of this is looked at with respect to the longer-term future of the organisation. She is particularly concerned about the innovative skills that she believes the organisation will require for the long term. These, she believes, are skills that will both be lost and prove irreplaceable if the emerging new strategic direction is followed.

These issues, raised by the HR director, might well be shared by other directors or senior managers. But, given the tendency for many managers to have specific functional or departmental concerns and objectives, there is an especially heavy strategic responsibility on the HR specialist to look at the human dimension of the organisation in a broader and more corporate sense. We could say that strategic HR management is *essentially strategic* (Watson and Watson, 1999). There are two reasons for this:

1. Whereas functional/operational/line managers have to focus on local or departmental performance, HR management must consider the whole organisation.
2. Whereas functional/operational/line managers have to focus on immediate or short-term performance, HR management has to look at the long term.

Strategic human resourcing, regardless of who takes formal responsibility for it, must be corporate and long term, for example:

- to avoid internal conflicts – and comparability claims – over perceived unfairness;
- to develop skills for the future as well as the present;
- to keep the organisation as an employer 'in line' with the law and public perceptions.

In the final analysis, a work organisation – be it a business, a public service or an administrative organisation – is a human enterprise. It fulfils tasks or achieves levels of performance greater than those that would be possible if people were to work on their own or in small groups. Using a mixture of power, negotiation, control and the seeking of consent, the management of an organisation has to pull that enterprise together and direct it in various ways. A human resourcing strategy is at the heart of this: without it there could not be an organisation.

HR strategy as mistress and servant of corporate strategy

It is possible to argue that human resources are not simply the *means* that an organisation uses to achieve organisational ends but are to some extent *ends* that the organisation exists in part to fulfil. The resource-based view of organisations (above, p. 10) discussed earlier takes us some way towards such a position: the organisation is a bundle of resources and organisational activities are undertaken to make use of those resources – the distinctive competences and capacities residing in the people who make up the organisation. Sam Modden suggests a view along these lines, recognising in the process that some of his fellow directors think quite differently.

Case Study 1.2c

Corporate and HR strategy in Moddens Foods

'I recognise that as chairman of a company that my family built up, I have a special loyalty to people who have given quite a lot of their lives to the business. Saying this sounds old fashioned but, as I said to Jean Frear when we recruited her as HR director, we have in this company a lot of skills and knowledge of farming, cooking and food processing and we have a lot of people who are willing and keen to make the firm ever more prosperous. I think we do such people an honour to exploit those capabilities and commitments. When I said this first to Jean she laughed and, quite rightly, pointed out that such a view was also 'good for business' and my own good standard of living. She is right, of course. But I see consideration of what makes up the business – in people terms – as something of a starting point when we are discussing the way the business should go. People like Ivan and Frank, however, start off from business opportunities and then simply treat human resources as means to those ends, similar to the way they think about the tractors and lorries that we buy. I see perfectly well that such an approach often makes business sense: that HR policies and practices are adopted to serve business strategies. I just think that we should recognise the possibility can also exist of things working the other way round. To put it another way: the human resources you start off with constitute, in themselves, an important business opportunity. I think you miss that point if you automatically talk of HR always being the servant and never the mistress of corporate strategy.'

It is clear that debating which comes first, the corporate/business strategy or the HR strategy, is rather like the old question about whether the chicken or the egg came first. However, the arguments of Sam Modden, and some of the assumptions of the resource-based view of organisations, provide an important corrective to certain common, influential and taken-for-granted ways of speaking about HR resourcing: one in which human resourcing considerations are made only *after* an organisation's management has decided its basic corporate and business strategies. It is perhaps not surprising that many tough-minded and 'macho' business leaders choose to speak in this way but it is more surprising that influential writers should support such a simplistic view. Lengnick-Hall and Lengnick-Hall (1988) made a similar observation. In arguing for a 'reciprocal interdependence' between corporate and HR strategies, they criticised standard thinking for 'matching people to strategy' rather than matching 'strategy to people' (Lengnick-Hall and Lengnick-Hall, 1988: 456) and Beaumont called for a 'close two-way relationship between business strategy' and 'HRM planning' (1993: 4). Yet, some years on from this, we see Ulrich (1997), to take one influential writer, pointing to the purpose of strategic human resource management as one of identifying what human capabilities are required to implement a 'business strategy' in order then to act to acquire those capabilities. And Schuler *et al.* (2001), in their systematic overview of 'HRM and its link with strategic management', clearly make HR strategy derivative of broader strategies. First, they suggest, strategists 'establish vision, mission values and general strategy'. They then 'identify strategic business issues and strategic business objectives'. Only then do they turn to HR issues, when they 'interpret' the 'HR meaning' of these issues and objectives (Schuler *et al.*, 2001: 16). One cannot help wondering if there is not a value assumption of 'business before everything' operating here and in the range of other textbooks that make HR part of the 'implementation' of strategy as opposed to a consideration that it can be part of the making of the corporate strategy in the first place.

To help with all the issues that we have been looking at so far we can move towards a general model for thinking about and analysing human resourcing choices and patterns. We need to recognise the existence both of the scope for managerial choice and the limitations on that scope that arise from the various circumstances of the organisations within which those managers are working.

Choices and circumstances in the shaping of HR strategies

'HRM best practices' vs. 'HR practices appropriate to organisational circumstances'

A significant trend in modern HR thinking has been to claim that in modern highly and globally competitive times there is really only one successful way for an organisation to deal with human resourcing issues. This is to adopt *high involvement* (sometimes called 'high performance' or 'high commitment') practices regardless of the organisation's circumstances. According to Wood and de Menezes (2008), work enrichment and flexible work practices are 'potential high involvement practices, as well as skill-acquisition (such as training and briefing methods, or training specifically geared to facilitating high involvement such as training in interpersonal skills or in teamwork) and motivational practices (including job security guarantees, internal career ladders, minimal status differentials, variable pay schemes, and skill-based pay)' (2008: 641). These 'best practices', along with others (Table 1.1), are sometimes characterised as 'HRM' practices and are contrasted with older 'personnel management' practices (Storey, 1992; Legge, 1995).

Table 1.1 HRM best practices

- Human resourcing issues are the concern of all managers.
- Human resourcing considerations are part of all strategic-level deliberations.
- A strong culture, with high levels of worker involvement and consultation, encourages high employee commitment to the organisation and its continuous improvement.
- High trust relations and teamworking practices make close supervision and strict hierarchies unnecessary.
- Employees undertake continually to develop their skills to achieve both personal 'growth' and task flexibility.

Considerable empirical research has been gathered to support the claim that such policies and 'best practices' pay off (Huselid, 1995; Becker and Gerhart, 1996; Ichniowski *et al.*, 1997; Macduffie, 1995; Guest, 1997; Patterson *et al.*, 1997; Pfeffer 1998). At a common-sense level, there is plausibility in this. If we recognise the existence of a general 'norm of reciprocity' in human societies (whereby if people treat us well, we tend to treat them well in return), it seems reasonable to expect that employers who act with respect and trust towards employees might expect their employees to return such trust and respect and to perform more effectively than if they were treated with limited trust or respect (Fox, 1974). However, as well as a range of logical and other problems (Boxall and Purcell, 2003; Marchington and Grugulis, 2000; Legge, 2001; Purcell and Hutchinson, 2007; Purcell and Kinnie, 2007) that arise with regard to the studies claiming to demonstrate the universal relevance of HR 'best practices', we have to ask why a vast number of employing organisations across the industrial capitalist world – often unresearched and certainly uncelebrated – have chosen not to adopt these practices and yet are not going out of business. We might well ask the question that if, for example, managers find they can somewhere in the world profitably recruit workers on hire-and-fire sweatshop conditions, low pay, insecure contracts to, say, kill and gut chickens, why should they move to high commitment relationships, with team-working and high levels of consultation? It is not unreasonable to expect that different types of HR strategy might work in different employment or business circumstances.

An alternative tradition to the 'best practice' or 'one best way approach' in writing about human resourcing has been the 'contingency thinking' tradition which has argued that different types of HR strategy and practice *fit* or *match* different organisational circumstances or contingencies. Some classic studies in the HRM literature have followed such a line, for example:

- Schuler and Jackson (1987) argued that different types of HR strategy are required for organisations that follow what Porter (1980, 1985) identifies as the three key strategic options for a business: innovation, quality enhancement or cost reduction. To take the example of just one facet of human resourcing, it would be appropriate within a cost reduction business strategy to reduce training and development activities to a minimum while, within an innovation strategy, the development of a broad range of skills among employees would require more sophisticated and extensive provision of employee development training.

- Kochan and Barocci (1985) suggested that different types of HR strategy are relevant to different stages in an organisation's life cycle. In the employee development area, again, a different set of practices would be needed when an organisation had achieved 'maturity' from when it was in a 'start-up' or 'growth' stage.

- Delery and Doty (1996) made use of Miles and Snow's (1978) notion of organisations having different *strategic configurations* and, to take an employee development example again, argue that organisations with a 'defender–internal employment system' configuration would be wise to develop people to climb well-defined career ladders while organisations adopting a 'prospector–market employment system' would be better adopting employee development practices that give personal responsibility to employees for their learning and development.

As with the universal 'best practice' view, there is plausibility in 'best fit' thinking. A hire-and-fire and low-job-discretion type of human resourcing strategy, for example, might work successfully in an organisation utilising simple technologies to provide goods for a stable and long-term market. But such a strategy would be likely to create considerable difficulties for the managers of an advanced technology enterprise operating in a rapidly changing market context. However, we must avoid letting the rather physical metaphor of 'fit' encourage us to think that managers can carefully 'blueprint' their human resourcing strategies to support a larger blueprint devised by corporate planners. Strategies are outcomes of human interpretations, conflicts, confusions, guesses and rationalisations rather than clear pictures unambiguously traced out on a corporate engineer's drawing board.

It is sensible to recognise that different human resourcing practices may indeed be appropriate to the different circumstances identified by 'best fit' thinkers and we can add that they are likely to fit better with other contingencies such as organisational size (Pugh and Hickson, 1976), technology (Woodward, 1994; Perrow, 1986) or market context (Burns and Stalker, 1994). But it is vital to recognise that these contingencies do not *determine* organisational shapes or human resourcing practices. Human resource strategies are the outcomes of *strategic choices* by managers (Child, 1972, 1997). To varying degrees, managers will take into account contingencies such as size, technology and organisational environment when making choices. To this extent 'contingencies' do influence organisational patterns. But it is an influence which is always *mediated* by managerial interpretation and political manoeuvring. Contingencies are, in Weick's (1979) terms, always *enacted* by human actors. The circumstances that Moddens Foods finds itself in are by no means unambiguous: the markets available to the company are not simply 'there', waiting to be met by the business. They are in part what, in the light of the interpretations made by Moddens' managers of the business opportunities and the relative success of the different management factions, the managers will help bring into being, by the nature of the products they offer and the way they advertise and generally market their wares. Human values about human resourcing issues held by members of the rival factions will also be *inputs* into these decision-making processes.

Choices and contingencies in HR strategy-making

The basic choice to be made about human resourcing strategy can most usefully be understood as one between a *low commitment* and a *high commitment* set of policies and practices (Table 1.2).

Table 1.2 High commitment and low commitment HR strategies

High commitment HR strategies	Low commitment HR strategies
Follow the 'best practice' HR model with the employer seeking a close relationship with workers who become psychologically or emotionally involved with the enterprise. Opportunities for personal and career development are built into people's employment, which is expected to continue over a longer-term period, potentially covering a variety of different tasks.	Follow 'hire and fire' principles with labour being acquired at the point when it is immediately needed. Workers are allocated to tasks for which they need very little training, with their employment being terminated when those tasks no longer need to be completed. The organisation–worker relationship is an 'arm's-length' and calculatingly instrumental one.

A choice to lean towards one rather than the other of these two basic strategic directions is clearly going to involve consideration of human values and ethical preferences by managers making the choice. But it is equally clear that strategy-makers are not free simply to choose which direction to follow regardless of all the contingent factors that we have identified above. What is it that, in the final analysis, within all the contingencies that come into play, encourages managers to move in one HR strategic direction rather than the other? To answer this we can say that, all things being equal, a low commitment type of human resourcing strategy is more appropriate to a situation where employees are not a major source of strategic uncertainty for the employing organisation. If an organisation has a simple technology and a relatively straightforward business environment that allows it to employ easily obtainable and replaceable employees, for example, it is not likely to require a highly participative set of working practices. But if strategic managers judge that the future of their organisation would be at risk without meeting the much higher demands that are likely to follow from employing a highly skilled or educated workforce to operate a complex technology or deal with an especially tricky business environment, it is much more likely to consider a high commitment employment strategy. Such a workforce would not be easy either to obtain or replace and 'best practice' HR arrangements are needed to encourage these people both to stay with the organisation and creatively and flexibly apply themselves to undertaking complex tasks.

Figure 1.1 suggests how managerial choices, together with political–economic, cultural and organisational contingency factors, come together within an arena of managerial politics and strategic debate to shape the human resourcing strategy of an organisation. Managerial strategy-makers, within all the politics of the

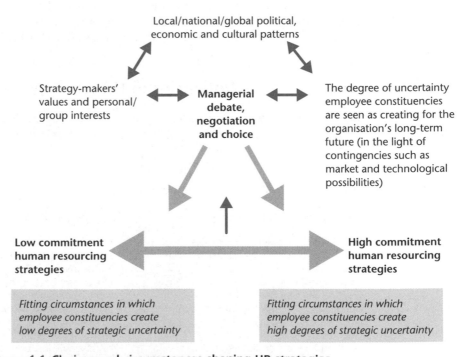

Figure 1.1 Choices and circumstances shaping HR strategies

organisational boardroom and their various personal priorities and values, debate and choose the basic direction to be followed in the light of their interpretation or 'reading' of the circumstances facing the organisation. In practice, all the factors identified in Figure 1.1 mutually influence each other and changes in any one area may instigate shifts in another. The double arrows used in the figure are intended to indicate this. And the upward-pointing arrow at the centre of the diagram is there to make a very important point. It takes up the point made earlier that the existing HR situation of an organisation can itself be seen as an 'input' to strategic decision-making. The strategic debate we have been following in Moddens Foods, for example, has arisen in part because of issues arising in the ways Moddens is currently treating the people it employs.

Activity 1.5	Uncertainty, employee constituencies and HR strategy-making

Assuming that the debate among the directors of Moddens Foods is taking them towards a choice *for the future* of either a low commitment HR strategy (associated with prioritising high-volume, low-cost food products) or a high commitment strategy (together with a prioritising of high-quality, 'premium' and short-season food products), consider the extent to which considerations of the *uncertainties* that employee constituencies create for managers have played in the debate so far – and might play as the directors continue their debate about how they are to go forward into the future.

The Juan Poort and Frank Angle faction within the Moddens' board appears to favour both a broadly predictable business strategy with relatively low uncertainty levels and an employment strategy to go with this. Angle comments that he prefers to employ a 'small number of straightforward chemists' rather than the currently favoured agriculturalists, chefs and food scientists. These are people who, he says, are 'more trouble than they are worth'. He appears to assume that the type of 'straightforward' technical experts he wants to employ would not cause uncertainty of the type currently being created by the people who, the board is told, are currently threatening to leave. And the 'rationalisation and technological control' over production that his type of technician would help bring about relates to the broad business strategy that he and Juan Poort favour – one in which the high-volume, low-price chicken nugget type of product predominates. The implication of this is that the older HR business strategy favoured by Sam Modden and his supporters of producing high-quality, lower-volume food products requires a type of labour that is less directly controllable and predictable (and is therefore a source of greater uncertainty) than the foreign and migrant labour and the less skilled technical labour that is increasingly being used.

Choices for the future of Moddens will inevitably take into account the extent to which human resources are going to be:

- a relatively predictable, certain and easily manageable aspect of organisational management – if they go for the 'chicken nuggets' option, for which a low commitment HR strategy will tend to be appropriate;

- a less malleable, uncertain and more challenging aspect of organisational management – if they go for the 'premium sausages and game pies' strategy option business (with its emphasis on innovation, novelty and high quality) for which a high commitment HR strategy will tend to be appropriate.

Case Study 1.2d

The Moddens sort themselves out

After a number of stormy boardroom meetings and a series of less formal discussions between the various individuals with an interest in the future of Moddens Foods, a settlement was made. This involved splitting the organisation into two divisions. Sam Modden and Juan Poort would stay in their positions as Group Executive Chairman and Group Managing Director, supported by Ivan Kelp who would take charge of finances for the whole group. But the Modden name would only be used on products made by the Gourmet Division, which would be headed by Hal Selz. The Volume Division, to be managed by Frank Angle, would re-brand its products and move into new and separate premises of its own. Jean Frear opted to work only for the Gourmet Division. She nominated one of her staff to take charge of HR issues for the Volume Division. Angle insisted that this would not be a senior management role and that he would be called their 'HR officer'. 'We don't need a big-time HR director like Gourmet will', he said, 'HR will be nice and straightforward for us.'

Successful human resourcing strategies, it can be argued, need to fulfil criteria of both *vertical integration*, whereby there is a 'fit' between HR strategies, broader organisational strategies and organisational contexts, and *horizontal integration*, where there is a 'fit' between 'different HR policies and practices, and the degree to which they support or contradict one another' (Marchington and Wilkinson, 2002a: 9). Moddens Foods had got into a state where neither of these criteria was being fulfilled. But by turning itself, in effect, into two separate organisations it was moving towards achieving both – with vertical and horizontal integration being achieved in different ways in each of the two divisions.

High commitment and low commitment HR strategies in practice

We have, in this chapter, focused on human resourcing strategies as 'broad directions' which are followed by organisations in the way they acquire and deal with the human resources they need to go forward successfully into the future. But implicit in this analysis has been a recognition that a significant range of different managerial practices are associated with each of the two broad strategic directions that we have considered. We can now end the chapter by identifying some of the more specific practices or 'strategic components' that tend to be associated with, or 'fit with', the two basic approaches to the strategic management of human resources that strategists can be seen to choose between (Table 1.3).

Table 1.3 Components of high commitment and low commitment HR strategies

	Components of a low commitment HR strategy (where human resources tend to create low levels of uncertainty for managers)	Components of a high commitment HR strategy (where human resources potentially create high levels of uncertainty for managers)
Organisational culture	• rule-based • emphasis on authority • task focus • mistakes punished	• shared values • emphasis on problem-solving • customer focus • learning from mistakes
Organisational structure	• layered hierarchy • top-down influence • centralisation • mechanistically bureaucratic (rigid)	• flat hierarchy • mutual (top-down/bottom-up) influence • decentralisation/devolution • organically bureaucratic (flexible)
Work/job design	• de-skilled, fragmented jobs • doing/thinking split • individual has single skill • direct control of individual by supervisor	• whole, enriched jobs • doing/thinking combined • individual multi-skilled • indirect control within semi-autonomous teams
Performance expectations	• objectives met to minimum level • external controls • external inspection • pass quality acceptable	• objectives 'stretch' and develop people • self-controls • self/peer inspection • continuous improvement in quality sought
Rewards	• pay may be varied to give individual incentives • individual pay linked to job evaluation	• pay may be varied to give group performance • individual pay linked to skills, 'mastery'
Communication	• management seek and give information • information used for sectional advantage • business information given on 'need to know' basis	• two-way communication initiated by any party • information shared for general advantage • business information widely shared
Employment relations	• adversarial • collective • win/lose • trade unions tolerated as inconvenient constraints • OR unions used as convenient intermediaries between managers and employees	• mutual • individual • win/win • unions avoided OR unions increasingly by-passed in the hope of their eventual withering away • OR unions involved in *partnership relations* with employers to give a 'voice' to employees in working towards employment security, innovative work practices, fair rewards and investment in training
Employee development	• training for specific purposes • emphasis on courses • appraisal emphasises managerial setting and monitoring of objectives • focus on job	• training to develop employees' skills and competence • continuous learning emphasis • appraisal emphasises negotiated setting and monitoring of objectives • focus on career
HR department	• marginal, and restricted to 'welfare' and employment administrative tasks • reactive and *ad hoc* • staffed by personnel specialists	• integrated into management, and working as 'partners' with other managers • proactive and strategic • staff interchange with the 'line' or other functions

Activity 1.6	Analysing HR strategies for consistency and fit

Analyse the human resource practices of an organisation of your choice using the scheme set out in Table 1.3 to assess the extent to which, in your opinion:

1. There is consistency within the various components of the HR strategy, so that they support each other rather than contradict or potentially undermine each other.
2. There is an appropriate level of 'fit' between the overall human resourcing strategy followed by the organisation and the broad context in which it operates – a 'fit' which means that it is more rather than less likely to survive healthily into the long term.

Summary

In this chapter the following key points have been made:

- Strategic human resourcing issues arise whenever human enterprises are set up to complete work tasks cooperatively.

- Human resources are best understood as the capacities that people bring to work situations, these resources including both capabilities that reside in individual workers and the shared capacities and cooperative potential created by those people when they work together organisationally.

- Strategic human resourcing challenges arise at various levels: from the tendency of human beings generally to resist control by others to the way modern societies and economies are organised.

- Organisational strategies are best understood not as big corporate plans but as patterns that emerge over time as strategy-makers – all of whom have their own personal and sectional priorities and interests – cope with the changing circumstances of the organisation to enable the enterprise as a whole to continue into the future.

- Strategic human resourcing is not necessarily something that simply follows from or supports corporate strategy-making. Human resource factors can themselves influence and sometimes significantly shape an organisation's broad strategy.

- The fundamental strategic human resourcing choice for an organisation is between a *low commitment* HR strategy (which tends to be appropriate where organisational circumstances require human resources are that relatively unproblematic, in the sense of creating low uncertainty for managers) and a *high commitment* HR strategy (which tends to be appropriate where organisational circumstances require human resources are that relatively problematic, in the sense of potentially creating high uncertainty for managers).

- HR strategies do not simply arise in automatic reaction to organisational circumstances but emerge from political processes of managerial debate and argument and from the way managers *interpret* the circumstances or 'contingencies' affecting the organisation.

- Human resourcing practices need not only to 'fit' the organisation's business circumstances and the political contingencies of managerial choice but need also to be consistent with each other and have a coherence in either 'high commitment' or 'low commitment' terms.

Discussion questions

1. Is the author of the chapter being too ethically sensitive in objecting in moral terms to the notion of 'managing people'?

2. What examples can you think of from your experience of work of the ways in which people tend to 'resist' organisational efforts to 'manage them'?

3. Think of any work organisation you know something about. To what extent has its broad strategic approach to HR issues (its overall 'strategy', that is) come about as a result of the particular people in charge of it, as well as the circumstances of the organisation?

4. With regard to the same organisation, or another one if you like, does its HR strategy lean towards the low commitment or the high commitment end of the continuum set out in this chapter?

Further reading

The most appropriate further reading for this chapter is indicated in the text, where readers can follow up citations that are most helpful to their particular interests. General texts that deal helpfully and broadly with matters of human resourcing strategies are those by Bamberger and Meshoulam (2000), Boxall and Purcell (2003) and Boxall et al. (2007). To locate some of the key arguments of this chapter in broader debates about the academic study of HRM, see Watson (2004).

2

Managing uncertainty or managing uncertainly?

Colin Bryson and Luchien Karsten

'The best-laid schemes of mice and men gang aft agley'

Robert Burns, 1786

Learning outcomes

Having read this chapter and completed its associated activities, readers should be able to:

- Assess the choices available to the manager and HR practitioner in trying to balance requirements for human resources in a context of uncertainty
- Understand the issue of 'flexibility' and so-called flexible employment practices
- Evaluate which theoretical and conceptual frameworks may be appropriate in the analysis of this topic
- Assess competing explanations about why flexible employment is introduced and practised at an international, national and organisational level
- Understand several flexible employment practices with reference to empirical evidence, the facilitating and constraining factors and apparent advantages and disadvantages to employers and employees
- Compare and contrast 'new' forms of employment practice against traditional approaches such as redundancy and overtime
- Assess the implications for using these approaches in detail within the organisation – issues of management for HR strategies, and outcomes for individuals
- Have some understanding of the implications external to the organisation, on labour markets, public policy and society

Introduction

Predicting the future is not something at which human beings have been particularly successful. Even if we have some rough idea about likely trends, the plans we make to cope with them may not work out the way we intended. The more we learn about human resourcing in organisations, the more we understand how difficult it is to manage the present, far less the future. It is readily apparent that human resource planning has limitations. In the *laissez faire* markets of global capitalism organisational survival is perceived to depend on two imperatives:

1. alignment of outputs with demand,
2. sufficient adaptability to cope with change.

Every organisation is subject to these imperatives. Even organisations in the public and voluntary sectors which, by tradition, were not exposed directly to market competition, have been forced to comply. It is currently a norm and expectation of society that organisations deliver services and products with maximum efficiency and at the lowest cost. Human resourcing has been at the forefront of this consumer and market-oriented philosophy and great emphasis has been placed on the concept of *labour utilisation*.

The traditional approach in the factory system has been stereotyped as *hire*: when additional labour or new skills are required, and *fire*: shed workers when there is no longer demand for their labour or particular skills. Short-term increases in demand were met by using overtime. As Clawson (1980) has shown, however, inside contracting gave skilled workers the opportunity to arrange for themselves working patterns based on an agreement with the general superintendent or the owner of the firm to make a part of the product and receive a certain price for each completed unit. With the advent of industrial capitalism, the role of craft workers to control both the technical details of the work process and the social order of the workplace in terms of inside contracting and working time arrangements withered away. In British textile factories owners marked the beginning and close of the daily cycle of production by subjecting the workers to rigid controls of entry and exit from the factory. The doors were locked at the start of the workday, compelling latecomers to return to their homes. In German textile factories, however, time discipline placed more emphasis upon the duration of production itself than on its precise starting and finishing times. German textile directors could shift hours among the days of the week, as long as the total remained the same. German textile mills introduced punch-in clocks on a wide scale at the turn of 1900 (Biernacki, 1995).

A new era of modern factory production started in 1908 when Henry Ford launched the full-scale American production of the Model T. The new car cost $825, the equivalent of a teacher's annual salary (Grint, 2000: 197). Taylor and Gilbreth brought the stopwatch and the film camera (time and motion studies) into the modern factory, speeding up work through the piece rate system. In 1914 Ford fixed the daily working time to eight hours for all employees, introducing a three times eight shift system and based simple work activities on the running speed of the assembly line. Workers saw their contributions reduced to one identical movement, repeated indefinitely, and were expropriated of their own know-how. Between 1880 and 1915, no fewer than 15 million new immigrants were recorded in the USA, many of whom were willing to accept a job at Ford.

Within the modern factory system the balance between skilled and unskilled workers was destroyed and managerial capitalism asserted itself. Managers and directors, who were also simply wage earners of the company, took over direction of the business. Their sole objective was to make companies as large as possible in order to attain economies of scale. Planning departments were installed to secure a stable production process. Their forecasts provided certainty about supply and demand and security of jobs. Short-term decreases in demand were met by laying off part of the workforce. Uncertainty due to fluctuations in production and exploitation of employees strengthened the unionised struggle for a general reduction of working time to eight hours a day in order to share work and unemployment as well as obtaining free leisure time. Demonstrations and strikes for the eight-hour day were finally successful after the end of the First World War in 1919. It marked either by law or by general labour agreement a clear distinction between time for the boss and time for personal development.

In the twentieth century Taylorism and Fordism developed an intrinsic logic of mechanisation favouring standardisation and uniformity to facilitate the mass production processes. They remained unchallenged well into the 1970s as the best practice of organising human work. Within that context a general trend prevailed to reduce working hours (like the free Saturday in the 1960s and more holidays) and to standardise working hours. The typical full time, permanent, nine to five, Monday to Friday job with one employer as the dominant work arrangement prevailed. But during the 1970s economic recession this trend became challenged by two distinct developments.

The Toyota plants in Japan underwent great transformations which eventually challenged the Fordist production system. Toyotaism was offering workers much more *flexibility* in performing tasks while promoting just-in-time (JIT) production. This form of production gained its power from the fact that inventory holding costs are cut down by reducing stock to a minimum through sophisticated systems or demand-oriented supply. The result was the development of lean production with teams of highly qualified members, flexible production facilities and a well-coordinated flow of information (Womack *et al.*, 1991). In this system, a worker reporting any defect could immediately appeal to his colleagues instead of to his supervisor and prevent any breakdown. This team-work model pushed decision-making authority as far down the managerial ladder as possible (Rifkin, 1995). Workers were even asked to reprogramme the production line when needed. Toyotaism's objective was to obtain the assent of the worker, humanise the austere Taylorite message and thereby implicate the worker in the organisation of work (Tsutsui, 1998). Japanese lean management made its manufacturing system ideally suited to take advantage of the new computer-based information technologies (CAD-CAM), which spread throughout the globe with lightning speed (Biesebroeck, 2007).

The digital revolution began to mark a definitive break with the manufacturing economy. With the pervasive use of information technology (IT) by banks, insurance companies, hospitals, clinics, warehouses and retail stores, the era of industrial mass production began to fade into the past. To survive in response to rapid technological advancements and increased global competition, firms downsized, eliminating many jobs. At the same time, however, there was a slowing down of productivity growth rates in spite of a substantial increase in technology inputs and acceleration in the pace of technological change (Castells, 1996). To change this downward trend of productivity growth, flexibility in the organisation of labour became advocated as a means of utilising labour more efficiently. Castells estimated that the social costs of flexibility might be high but he was positive about 'the transformative value of new work arrangements for social life, and particularly for improved family relationships, and greater egalitarian patterns between genders' (Castells, 1996: 267). Firms started to be populated more and more by knowledge workers who primarily work with information. However, they do not necessarily have to execute their knowledge work at their offices but can work in more flexible contexts such as their own homes. The 'electronic cottage' (Toffler, 1980) solves a large range of organisational issues through home-based production.

Standard versus non-standard work

Castells demonstrates a positive outlook and perceives the future flexitimer from a technology driven perspective. In the same vein, Bridges (1994) forecasted that IT would change the workplace dramatically: more flexibility would lead to more part-time work, more freelance work, work on commission, and consequently less certainty and predictability.

Firms take decisions that affect the way they organise their workforce and that may eventually lead to a fragmentation of the labour market. Companies have begun to use people only as they need them leading to just-in-time employment. 'Temporary workers and outsourcing make up the bulk of today's contingent workforce' (Rifkin, 1995: 194). Over the period 1985–95, the European Union has shown a 15 per cent increase in flexible employment. In the USA nowadays one out of five employed people work mostly at non-standard times, i.e. during the evening, at night or on rotating shifts (Presser, 2003; Golden, 2005; Presser *et al.*, 2008). The largest single employer is no longer Ford, General Electric or General Motors, but a temporary employment agency called Manpower Inc (Sturgeon, 2002). Since 1976 Canada has shown a 44 per cent increase in total employment growth but this was mainly due to growth in non-standard jobs (Gonzales-Rendon *et al.*, 2005). However, Bosch (2006) points out that Bridges' and Castells' views sound compelling but are not convincing. Contrary to what is forecasted about more flexibility and less security in the information society, in Europe the standard employment relationship is still the predominant employment pattern. The proportion of employees with fixed-term contracts rose between 1992 and 2003, from 11.1 per cent to 12.8 per cent, and the proportion of fixed part-time employees rose from 14.2 per cent to 18.2 per cent. Galin (1991) gave the following reasons for the growing international need for *non-standard* or *atypical work*:

- To increase productivity and competitiveness. For most firms this creates pressure to cut labour costs and the size of the labour force – downsizing. This results in a consequent need to seek optimal utilisation of the human resource.
- Adapt organisations to accelerated technological changes. This requires continuous revision of skills and organisational structures but enables new forms of organisation.
- Increasing employment opportunities. There has been growing pressure from groups who find it hard to comply with a full-time 9–5 routine. There has also been a reduction in working hours from social developments.
- Improving the ability of organisations to cope with peak workloads. Fluctuations may be seasonal or even daily.
- Adapting to fluctuations in availability of workers. Demographic trends have affected labour markets and social/legal changes have facilitated family and other leave.

- To meet workers' aspirations. People now aspire to more interesting jobs and more leisure time.
- There is evidence from several countries that certain factors are combining to force change.

The discourse on flexible working time arrangements seems primarily to be driven by a dominantly managerial language about the flexitimer. 'The gruelling schedules that used to be typical only for top corporate management and self employed people are becoming more common in one occupation after another' (Perlow, 1998: 331). But it is also said that flexibility may alter one's starting and ending times of work on a daily basis to such an extent that it helps employees to balance their work and family responsibilities. However, not all forms of flexible policies developed by employers can be considered 'family friendly' (Peper *et al.*, 2005; Tietze *et al.*, 2006). Flexibility has an ambivalent connotation. It is therefore necessary to look closer at what is meant when we talk about flexibility, so that at the end of this chapter you can draw your own balanced judgement concerning the discourse about flexibility and the flexitimer. Under the aegis of the impact of IT, there is a central concern as to whether the division between traditional permanent employment and increasing non-standard employment introduces a two-tier system in the labour market with good and bad jobs. Destandardisation of labour may indicate an emerging risk society and a further commoditisation of labour.

Conceptualising flexibility

Flexibility has many meanings. The concept was initially introduced in the 1960s. The American strategy author Igor Ansoff suggested that Fordist-structured firms needed to develop external and internal flexibility to cope with unforeseeable contingencies. Ansoff (1965: 55–7) linked external flexibility to 'the maxim of not putting all of one's eggs in a single basket'. Concerning internal flexibility, he stated that this issue 'is as old as business itself . . . it seeks to provide a cushion for response to catastrophe'. While striving for efficiency had dominated management science until the 1970s, being replaced in the 1980s by quality, in the 1990s flexibility became the dominant topic to cope with uncertainties. Flexibility was seen 'as an organisational potential, created by flexible configuration strategies and broad strategic schemas' (Volberda, 1998: 73). It therefore came as no big surprise that very soon flexibility also became an integral part of human resource management, providing a way to manage time, space and people more effectively within the upturns and downturns of a global economy. Flexibility became seen as a way 'to attract and retain good employees in a labour market that is steadily becoming more competitive' (Olmsted and Smith, 1989: VIII, 1997). However, the concept itself faced a plethora of definitions. Every commentator tended to adopt a definition suited to the line of argument he proposed. Boyer's (1987) comment that flexibility is 'a multiform and particularly ambiguous generic term' is therefore very apt. Blyton and Morris (1991) gave three reasons why the concept of flexibility has often been misused or misunderstood:

it has been employed as a *summary* concept for a wide range of developments, the assumptions made about the *homogeneity* of the nature, pace, causes and consistency of these developments, and the tendency for it to be discussed as a *unitary* concept embodying no essential conflicts of interest.

(Blyton and Morris, 1991: 2)

At the most abstract level we could say that flexibility refers to the capacity to adapt to change. As mentioned, this was not a much debated topic during the era of Taylorism and Fordism. Market developments could be clearly forecasted and rigid planning policies secured deliveries against low prices. Some authors, however, pointed out that Taylorism and Fordism did not prevail in all industries. Piore and Sabel (1984) underlined that in Northern Italy geographically localised networks of small and medium-sized enterprises manufactured a wide and changing array of customised products in short runs. These industrial districts with their *flexible specialisation* were characterised by flexible production, differentiated and segmented consumption, and operated a restructured welfare state (Hyman, 1991). Uncertainty, fragility and mutability as constitutive features of economic life strengthened the capacity to adjust the volume and composition of output flexibly and to introduce new products rapidly in response to shifting demand and business strategy (Sabel and Zeitlin, 1997; Zeitlin, 2003). A number of alternatives to mass standardised production have since been detected: customised production which assumes a certain reduction in volume; diversified quality mass production which purportedly combines the benefits derived from product differentiation with significant quantities of production; and adaptive or reactive production which builds upon the constant redefinition of market niches and the fastest possible use of new technologies (Boyer and Hollingsworth, 1997; Giles *et al.*, 1999).

Flexibility also became perceived as a means for employees to balance or integrate their work and family responsibilities. Flexible scheduling performs a potentially dual function for employers as both an employee benefit and a productivity enhancing tool. More flexible scheduling of work may address workers more as whole persons seeking work-life balance and satisfaction through their multiple roles (O'Reilly and Fagan, 1998; O'Reilly *et al.*, 2000; Tietze and Musson, 2005; Boulin *et al.*, 2006). As the OECD (2004: 48) has pointed out 'the greatest difficulty in finding a balance between work and family life is very significantly linked to the presence of children in the household, to being younger and working longer hours or in more demanding jobs, or being self employed'. The European Working Time Directive of 1993 had set targets to limit the working hours to adjust work to the wellbeing of mankind (Supiot, 1999; Supiot, 2001), but it had not explicitly set an objective to improve the balance between work and family life. Recently, the European Union has taken up the topic of flexibility to provide a European wide institutional development which favours positive forms of flexibilisation.

The European Union

In March 2000 the European Council declared in Lisbon that its main objective was 'to become the world's most dynamic and competitive knowledge based economy with greater social cohesion in 2010' (quoted in Giddens, 2006: 15). The Council intends to improve competitiveness by promoting flexibility and attaining greater social cohesion by developing a European civil society. It tries to do this by pursuing a proactive labour market policy based on lifelong learning and a 'destandardisation' of the life course. It also targets increased participation of women by getting 60 per cent of European women into the labour market by 2010. For the social cohesion aspect it has taken important steps to address the issue of the balance between work and family life.

From the almost 6.8 million new jobs which have been created between 1994 and 1999 across the European Union, two-thirds went to women but they accounted for 80 per cent of part-time workers and 13 per cent of them were employed on short-term contracts (European Commission, 1999; Webster, 2001). Despite the fact that many of these jobs had flexible work arrangements, they did not restore a proper balance between work and family life for both sexes. In the late 1990s, the European Foundation financed a study on employment options and labour market participation which indicated that over half (54 per cent) of the European workforce (both self-employed and employed) would prefer to work fewer hours if they had the choice, and to balance their work with care responsibilities thus reducing the average working week to 34.5 hours (EFILWC, 2003; Doorne-Huiskes *et al.*, 2005). More recently the European Commission (2004) has underlined again that a Working Time policy should improve the balance between working and family life. On 5 December 2007 the Employment and Social Affairs Council adopted some common principles about flexicurity. Flexicurity is a new way of looking at flexibility on the labour market. It starts out from the awareness that globalisation and technological progress are rapidly changing the needs of workers and enterprises. Flexicurity promotes a combination of flexible labour markets and a high level of employment and income security. The concept moves away from a job security mentality to an employment or employability security mentality (Flexicurity Pathways, 2007; Business Europe *et al.*, 2007).

The most recent report of the European Commission, *Equality between Men and Women* (2008) concludes that although flexicurity principles have now been embraced and the female employment rate has reached 57.2 per cent in 2006 – which brings the objective of 60 per cent by 2010 within reach – there are still large gaps between men and women when it comes to the reconciliation of professional life and private life. The European Commission supports the roadmap for 'equality between women and men' which intends to 'encourage men to take more part in family life' (European Commission, 2008: 5). It stresses that equality between women and men is an essential quality component of work and requires for its realisation innovative and flexible work and leave arrangements. The European Union, however, is a supranational institution that can only pursue its goal if it receives effective support from the European members. National policy-makers can promote the balance issue amongst the younger generations by eliminating gender inequalities in the professional sphere of life, promoting an equal distribution of time over the life course which enhances the quality of the life of its citizens.

Although Europe reflects a large variety of approaches concerning standard working time arrangements and flexibility (about which we will say more later in this chapter), the overarching image is that its employees prefer to live under conditions that prevent the blurring of the boundaries between work and life.

National European configurations show that the flexitimer has not yet become a dominant feature.[1] Many employees focus on flexible working and part-time work as a means to accommodate family demands. They look for adequate combinations of flexibility *of* the worker with flexibility *for* the worker.

The Lisbon agreement has put forward that an appropriate work-life balance for European citizens is basic to the EU policy guidelines. European citizenship includes men and women adhering to gender equality and a fair sexual division of labour but the European Commission has observed that 'the greater commitment of women to paid work has not been accompanied by any significant redistribution of household labour, with women performing more than 80 per cent of household tasks in all but the Nordic members states and the United Kingdom' (European Commission, 2000). In order to change this situation and further the shaping of a truly European civil society, the notion of European citizenship has lately taken on greater prominence in the face of pressures towards an increase in integration amongst the 27 members of the EU and the desire to foster a stronger identification with Europe.

Organisational perspective

Such macro-level frameworks and issues as suggested above are useful in shedding light on changes in the nature of work and work organisation. They may help to explain why there are some apparent differences between what is happening in different countries. We are concerned, however, with human resourcing and our focus is at the level of the organisation and particularly with management.

For some years, the notion that management might seek to manage flexibility, particularly through strategies of labour utilisation, was debated around the concept of the flexible firm. This model was advanced by Atkinson at the Institute of Employment Studies (Atkinson, 1984; Atkinson and Meager, 1986). The model of an ideal organisational design that could cope with all the contingencies of an uncertain world may have been superficially attractive, but drew a host of criticisms. These criticisms were on a number of bases: that researchers found little evidence of this type of organisational form (Marginson, 1989); that it was not sought by employers (McGregor and Sproull, 1991); that the promotional factors led to alternative consequences/strategies (Prowse, 1990); that the central concept of core and periphery was ambiguous in practice (O'Reilly, 1992); and that the whole concept was deeply flawed in being prescriptive and static (Pollert, 1991). Proctor *et al.* (1994) struck a counterpoint by suggesting that much of this criticism was ill-founded, particularly if the processual view of the organisation was taken.

Although few would now support Atkinson's narrow use of core and periphery, the forms of flexibility he suggested have been adapted by later authors such as Blyton and Morris (1991) to form a common parlance for the subject and have left a strong legacy of terminology and concepts.

One dimension that certainly needs to be considered is the essential difference between *external* and *internal* flexibility. External flexibility refers to the ability of

---

[1] Flex-workers in the European Union increased from a mere 36 per cent of the working population in 2001 to almost 40 per cent in 2005 (Spidla, 2007).

employers to call in flexible personnel from outside the company for which short-term employment relations are initiated and can be easily broken. External flexibility has to do with contingent work in the sense that there is a lack of attachment between the workers and the employer. Two common examples of this type of work are temporary workers employed by temporary work agencies and employees on temporary or fixed-duration contracts without the prospect of a regular employment contract. Other specific forms of external employment are subcontracting, employees on call, temporary substitutes, contracts with unspecified but variable hours and earnings (zero-hours and min-max contracts), outsourcing, labour pools and a further range of 'casual' employment (Visser, 2000).

Internal flexibility, on the other hand, refers to maintaining flexible relations with current permanent personnel, including aspects such as transferral, or making changes to an employee's responsibilities or working hours. Internal flexibility relates to an increased variation in working hours and flexible working-time arrangements of regular workers employed on standard contracts offering alternative work scheduling and multi-skilling.

The concept of allowing employees some individual choice as to starting and quitting times was first introduced in Germany in 1967 (Olmsted and Smith, 1989: 12). At that time it was seen as a means of relieving transit and commuting time problems. The Hewlett-Packard Company is generally credited with introducing flexitime in the USA in 1972 after having tried it first in its German subsidiary. Compared to external flexibility, workers are less uncertain about the continuation of their employment and earnings, whereas the employers have fewer worries about the quality of their staff. Purcell and Purcell (1999) have used the descriptive terms of 'outsourcing' to refer to external flexibility and 'insourcing' to refer to internal flexibility.

If the variability of labour input concerns the content of the job, we use the term (drawn originally from Atkinson) 'functional flexibility' such as multi-skilling, job rotation, team-work and similar forms. This refers to the facility with which an employee can be moved from one task to another. 'Numerical flexibility' has much more to do with varying the size and the structure of the workforce. An important issue in this context is the variety of working-time arrangements. Many authors (e.g. Deery and Mahoney, 1994) have used the term 'temporal flexibility' to refer specifically to employment arrangements where the working hours and pattern may be varied. This form may occur within both external and internal flexibility arrangements. The external forms are often associated with a more 'unstructured' (Purcell *et al.*, 1999) and one-sided approach, i.e. the employer has total control over when the employee works and may vary this at short notice. This may be contrasted with internal flexibility arrangements such as flexitime when working hours are subject to mutual control within an agreed framework. Studies on organisational learning and technological innovation apply temporal flexibility by drawing a distinction between exploration and exploitation. Exploration includes things captured by terms such as variation, experimentation, innovation and flexibility. Exploitation includes such things as refinement, implementation, execution and efficiency. These two concepts require different organisational structures and patterns as well as capabilities, and complicate the precise implementation of temporal flexibility (Li *et al.*, 2008).

Part-time work requires some care in categorisation because some arrangements are highly secure (located in internal flexibility) and others highly temporary and precarious (located in external flexibility). Some part-time work may not be subject to variation at all (just simply a contract for fewer weekly or annual hours) and therefore not be considered to be flexible employment!

Next to functional flexibility (task and role) and numerical flexibility (contract duration and security, and 'out-workers') we can distinguish financial flexibility (varying wage costs). The latter form now tends to be subsumed into discussions concerning reward strategy and employee resourcing but the terms of numerical and functional flexibility are still prominently used and form one dimension of the description of flexible employment. Some authors have put forward further categorisations of flexibility. Sparrow and Marchington (1997) propose no fewer than seven categories. However, we suggest that these additional forms do not provide conceptual clarity as more categorisation leads to more overlap and more ambiguity.

Resource-based view of the firm

The increasing share of skilled knowledge workers in the twenty-first century business community has increased the interest in the sources of a firm's competitiveness. The resource-based view of the firm (RBV) has provided human resource management with a powerful analytical perspective connecting HR with firm-specific advantages. RBV stresses that the capacity of a firm to improve its performance depends on its ability to acquire, combine and redeploy resources (Conner, 1991; Foss, 1996; Peng, 2001). It follows from this that any flexibility chosen by a firm strongly depends on its competence base. These competences encompass its knowledge, its ways of doing things as well as its ability to react and adapt. A firm's competences are contained within its routines which differ from firm to firm and incorporate the knowledge accumulated within the organisation. These competences are dynamic and constructed in the course of learning processes (Nelson and Winter, 1982). Human resource management is likely to sustain the key processes of improving competences. Individuals are the driving force in the accumulation of competences which they then embody in a tacit form. Tacit knowledge, according to Nonaka (1994), can only be acquired through experience (learning by doing). It is intuitive, not articulated and difficult to codify or transfer. Competences related to this tacit knowledge are embodied in the individual employee. However, the spreading of IT has for some time shifted the attention away from tacit to codified knowledge which the firm itself stores. This knowledge is defined as explicit when it can be easily codified and communicated by formalised and systematic language. It can be acquired through study without lengthy practical experience being necessary. It is contained in media such as documents, computer programs, and in procedures and routines which generate dynamic organisational competences that are not directly linked to an individual. While learning processes are in essence social and collective, Teece and Pisano (1994) noted that learning involves both individual and organisational capacities. Thus competences, like learning, have two dimensions, one individual and the other collective. This dual nature of competence is important when it comes to selecting a labour flexibility strategy. When competences lie more with individuals, internal labour flexibility will be preferred. When competences are more explicitly linked with the organisation, its sustainability will be promoted by external labour flexibility. Of course, the body of knowledge of a firm is never completely tacit or completely explicit (Caroli, 2007).

There are other conceptual approaches and dimensions that could be drawn upon. The availability of new technology has created the opportunity for employees to work away from the office or the factory, either in the field or at home, or even, it is claimed, in cyberspace. This encompasses the highly ambiguous notion of 'telework'. This has profound implications for the organisation and the individual, but we do not have the scope to discuss these here, except to say that this development creates the potential for the greater use of functional, numerical and temporal flexibility. The question is whether the top-down management approaches and tight control of work, that have been developed since Taylorism and Fordism, will disappear with the transformation to more flexible work time arrangements.

Now that we have established a conceptual framework for flexibility we can move on to examine the ways in which organisations deal with these issues and how managers may attempt to manage the uncertainty caused by flexibilisation. The approach we have taken in this book has been to be cautious of the orthodox approach to thinking about 'organisational strategy' and how this may be 'implemented'. Watson in Chapter 1 has advocated a more *processual* approach to thinking about organisations. Understanding this type of thinking allows us to appreciate that different conceptual frameworks may all be useful, at least in part because they tend to be reflections of different ways of looking at the issue rather than necessarily competing explanations.

Factors promoting a different approach in human resourcing

In 1992, Brewster *et al.*, who studied human resource policies, found evidence of the increasing use of flexible employment in 9 out of 10 European countries (the exception was Sweden), although a considerable diversity in the forms was prevalent. Two years later they came to the conclusion that this diversity had to do with differences in social contexts (Brewster and Hegewisch, 1994). Lewis (1997) stresses that there are in principle two different arguments to clarify these differences:

1. The presence of public facilities makes it less likely that employers introduce their own additional provisions to promote flexibility.

2. Public provisions which reinforce flexibility will stimulate employers to provide supplements.

Institutional differences

To study the validity of either argument, researchers have used Esping-Andersen's (1990, 1999) typology of welfare state regimes. He has distinguished between liberal, conservative-corporatist and social-democratic regimes. Based on this typology, den Dulk (2001) compared the UK (liberal), Italy (conservative/corporatist), the Netherlands (conservative-corporatist) and Sweden (social-democratic). Her conclusions indicate that employers in all four countries offer flexible hours to make it possible for employees to balance work with care activities. In Sweden, however, it is more common to be flexible, have opportunities to do telework, have a compressed working week or work occasionally at home. Many Swedish employers allow working parents with young children to work shorter hours. Although Italian and Dutch societies are both called conservative-corporatist, Dutch and Italian employers offer different kinds of arrangements for parents to be flexible. Dutch employers more often provide childcare and flexible work arrangements, whereas Italian employers mainly offer leave arrangements (den Dulk, 2001).

One issue, however, in particular stands out in the development of flexibility. Throughout the 1990s flexible employment grew, especially among women who took up part-time jobs (Delsen, 1998). A leading example of a major increase in flexible forms of work is the Netherlands with 42.9 per cent of the working population in part-time jobs (Sels and Van Hootegem, 2001). Temporary employment agencies also began to play an important intermediary role in the labour market in the Netherlands. In 1997 this sector, with around 18,000 agencies, constituted the second largest employer in the Dutch private sector. This rise in temporary labour must be seen as part of an increase in flexibility in the labour market in general (*Temporary Agency Work: National reports*, 2002). Based on an agreement with the social partners in April 1996 (Flexibility and Security), the government placed pressure on employers to adhere to a package of basic requirements to protect the interests of flexible workers, which is similar to those of standard workers (Visser and Hemerijck, 1997). At the same time an exchange was agreed of a shorter working week (36 hours) for increased working-time flexibility in sectors like department stores, banking, insurance, railways, the dairy and food industry, and chemicals and printing. Increasingly, working time became annualised with a corridor of 32–40 hours per week. Industrial unions introduced 'vari-time' or 'working hours corridors' and in the service sector unions negotiated *à la carte* collective agreements. In 1999 further legislation (the Flexicurity Act) was enacted to adequately match employers' demand for flexibility and employees' demand for working life security and income. Nowadays almost 70 per cent of working women have part-time jobs (SCP/CBS, 2006).

Studies comparing countries have offered further and competing explanations for differences between countries. Temporary work is very unevenly distributed, much higher in Spain and also high in France and Italy compared with Scandinavia and the UK. Anxo and O'Reilly (2000) differentiated three forms of flexibility which are determined by different national regimes. Sweden, Germany and the Netherlands are examples of *negotiated flexibility* countries because they have an extensive involvement of the social partners through negotiations and a moderate level of statutory working-time regulation. France, with its statutory working-time norm and the state's ubiquitous regulating role is an example of *statist flexibility*. Britain has an industrial relations system where statutory working-time regulation is still absent. Unions have a right to free collective bargaining but employees may have either very long- or very short-hour jobs. This regime is an example of *externally constrained voluntarism*.

A major problem for macro-level research and explanation is that it is based on aggregate measures and secondary data which may have been collected on different bases and using dissimilar definitions. In the next section we shall seek to adopt a coherent framework to use for analysis at the organisational level.

Activity 2.1	Applying concepts to examples of a national context

1. Consider the explanations presented in this section about comparative differences between countries and offer a rationale for why the Netherlands appears to have so much flexible employment.
2. Has the Dutch government legislated in favour of external or internal flexibility?
3. What is the explanation for the high incidence of long working hours in Britain?

A working definition of flexible employment and managing uncertainty

In an earlier section we noted some useful descriptive terms which are now shared between commentators internationally. We shall use that common terminology as a basis here.

Our approach is to present the issues as a set of options from which managers may choose the way they both employ and utilise human resources. Within the UK context it is clear that for some of these options there is no legal contract of employment, although there will always be some form of employment relationship.

As we already discussed, not all forms of flexibility are clearly distinct from each other and it is important to remember that an individual worker may be subject to several forms at the same time. Many of these forms are not new; indeed we have included forms that are not even described in the literature as *flexible*. This highlights the nonsensical aspect of the flexibility debate that all aspects of flexible employment must be new and different.

What has become clear, however, throughout the past 20 years is the fact that employers and employees have different interests when it comes to flexibilisation. In some situations these interests can coincide, in others they cannot all be realised at the same time – they may even conflict. In general, we can differentiate between four forms of flexibility:

1. *numerical flexibility*
   - temporary contracts
   - agency work
   - labour pool
   - part-time (insecure)
   - outsourcing
   - subcontract
   - freelance
2. *temporal flexibility*
   - shiftwork
   - rostering
   - annualised work

- part-time (secure)
- sabbatical leave
- variable working pattern
- compressed workweek

3. *ad hoc flexibility*
   - paid overtime
   - unpaid overtime
   - lay-offs
   - redundancy
   - casual work

4. *functional flexibility (qualitative)*
   - horizontal or vertical multi-skilling
   - team-work.

In order to indicate the different interests, let us recall the main reasons for organisations and employees to be interested in flexibilisation. For organisations in general there are two main arguments:

1. *Efficiency*, i.e. to obtain the highest result with the existing production capacity. This can be obtained by minimising labour, stock and production costs, making optimal use of capital goods, reduction of production, replacement and through-put time and increasing the availability of goods/services on the market.

2. *Quality*, i.e. by systematically innovating their products and services.

For employees, the two most important motives to favour flexibility are:

1. To increase the intrinsic motivations related to key characteristics of work, such as reinforcing challenges, variety, responsibility and success. Concepts such as empowerment and employability are popular within this context.

2. To promote the extrinsic motivation which refers to the results of work (earning an adequate income, prevention of unemployment). Related to flexibility and a reasonable income, employees will be eager to arrange their work with other activities such as caring, sabbatical leave, etc. The arguments of organisations and motivations of employees can sometimes be combined in such a manner that they favour both interests. See Figure 2.1 for an explanation.

This scheme can help clarify which forms of flexibility can address specific motives. The position of the ellipse in Figure 2.1 indicates which motifs of organisations and employees alike coincide with specific forms of flexibility. If, for example, a company focuses on quality or innovation, functional flexibility will be a preferred policy. Multi-skilling and team-work are forms of flexibility which correspond with highly motivated and well-trained employees. This functional flexibility is concomitant with the specific interest of employees when they are intrinsically motivated. This is associated with notions of relational employment relationships and an orientation to work predicated on the workers seeking meaning through their work and career.

If an organisation prefers to strive for efficiency three different options are available. If employees are externally motivated they value activities outside work

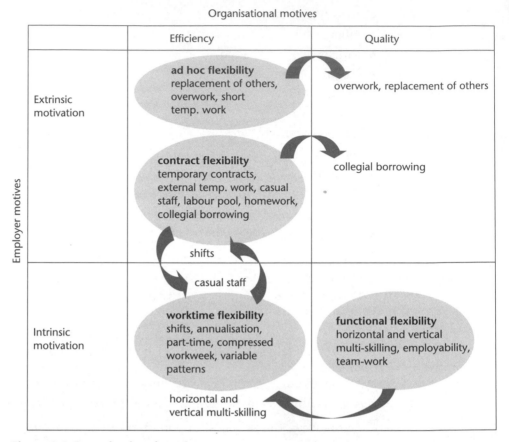

Figure 2.1 Organisational motives

Source: Oeij *et al.* (2002)

more than those at work. Free time becomes very important. Ad hoc flexibility and numerical flexibility favour that kind of motivation. This is associated with notions of transactional employment relationships and an instrumental orientation to work.

Worktime flexibility will be favoured by those employees who are not available full-time in the labour market but have a high intrinsic motivation. These employees are recruited by companies or, if they already work within the company, may be facilitated to get part-time or some other form of temporal flexibility while they support efficiency improvements the organisation may want to realise.

Of course, life is more complex than this! Motivation, orientation and employment relationships are much more heterogeneous. If employers could simply manipulate the motivation of the workers towards a particular type, or if workers could all find the ideal employment role that meets with their aspirations, there would be no need for books such as this. Nevertheless, there is some association between the intention to use, implement and take up these forms of flexibility and the outcomes we have indicated. However, much of the research evidence urges caution in assuming causal or simple relationships between approach and outcome (Bradley *et al.*, 2000; Storey *et al.*, 2002).

We shall now scrutinise some of these options more carefully to explore what they entail, and why and to what extent they are used. Options will be primarily selected on the basis of representing the most innovative (or extreme – take your pick) forms drawn from each category together with a contrasting, more traditional form.

Please note that although the discussion which follows treats each employment form in isolation, these options are not mutually exclusive. Employers often use many of these forms at the same time in combination, although use of some types may clearly reflect the need to use other forms to some degree.

Functional flexibility – multi-skilling

We are not going to include a discussion of the traditional alternative to multi-skilling because that alternative is the 'norm' of the great majority of working roles in an organisation, i.e. performing a more or less defined role. The reader should consider this norm as a counterpoint to the 'flexible form'.

Boyer (1987) defined *polyvalence* as key to the multi-skilling of employees. He argued that indicators of this would be:

- an ability to occupy varied posts;
- sufficiently broad general and technical training;
- the involvement of the workers in the maintenance of quality standards;
- the lack of any insurmountable barrier between manual worker, supervisor and technician.

Beatson (1995) sought to make inferences from the quarterly British Labour Force Survey to show that multi-skilling had significantly increased, but his methodology was highly dubious as it was based on an extrapolation of data rather than any direct evidence. Legge (1995) reviewed the evidence and found within the manufacturing sector movement towards *task* flexibility, but very modest progress. There was little evidence of *up-skilling* – the enhancement or increase of skills – with an emphasis instead on job enlargement. Greenfield sites, which might have been expected to yield more innovation, were little different (Leopold and Hallier, 1997). Legge concluded that the outcomes of initiatives have been more about job enlargement and work intensification leading to enhanced management control. Recently Kersley *et al.* (2006) have published a large survey on workplace employment relations with statistics that shed more light on the issue.

Sparrow (1998) argues for a different perspective to be taken by widening the focus to *jobs-based flexibility* which starts to bring in all the issues connected with design of work, jobs and even organisations, for example business process re-engineering (BPR). BPR advocates re-engineering business processes from functional departments to process teams or case teams (Hammer and Champy, 1993). Even so, Sparrow finds that the main approach in this has been downsizing. BPR, downsizing, de-layering and de-regulation are an effect of the brutal intrusion of financial markets in the management of companies that took place in the 1980s and 1990s. The game rules of capitalism were transformed and financial profitability became the golden rule. Downsizing of companies signalled the end of Fordist production and the entrance of lean production. Raiders broke up conglomerates and sold various subsidiaries piece by piece. Corporations therefore had to re-centre their activities on their core business. Concentrating on a single trade, companies began to prosper and merged with others that had the same core business. One of the main issues became the need to avoid all possible duplicate jobs by making one person do what otherwise would have been done by two or three (Cohen, 2003). Within our framework of options this would appear to be a functional and numerical flexibility option.

An alternative source of evidence about multi-skilling could be sought in all the research on processes such as team-working, JIT and TQM (total quality management). TQM programmes include employee involvement as an explicit component of their operations (Wilkinson *et al.*, 1998; Cole and Scott, 2000). Team-working is believed to increase an organisation's adaptability to dynamic environments while they can handle more complex and variable production processes, have more transparent control structures, show an improved performance and have fewer coordination costs (Molleman and Slomp, 2003). There is little space to discuss this here and one suspects that the conclusions would not be dissimilar to those of Legge (1995). Indeed a fruitful source of such evidence – and similar conclusions – can be found in the literature on Japanisation.

Some examples from non-manufacturing sectors may illustrate to what degree multi-skilling is used (Table 2.1).

Skill mix re-profiling can be illustrated by examples from the UK public sector, for example in the National Health Service. Within the ambulance service there has been a separation between paramedics and 'drivers'. Paramedics are highly qualified and have incremental pay scales and the prospect of promotion and a career, whereas many former ambulance staff have been downgraded to 'driver' on a flat scale determined by local market conditions.

Similarly, healthcare assistants (much cheaper to train and employ) have been introduced to take over the 'low skill' aspects of nurses' jobs and some nurses have been allowed to take on a few duties previously restricted to doctors. We may also find new generic grades for combined porter/cleaners (Grimshaw, 1999). Similar moves have occurred in the other emergency services, police and fire brigade, and in the probation service (Farnham and Horton, 2000). Functional flexibility can

Table 2.1 Examples of multi-skilling/functional flexibility

Retail (Neathey and Hurstfield, 1995)
One supermarket expected staff to work in all departments rather than be limited to, for example, a bakery role – to move people in the store 'depending where the need is'. Another gave staff training as relief till operators.
Move to 'generic shop assistant' in a department store.
A building society had moved towards generalisation of tasks so that a customer enquiry could be dealt with by anybody
Banking (O'Reilly, 1992)
By comparing the UK and France she found evidence in France that banks promoted functional flexibility in order to provide an integrated service policy facilitated by highly qualified staff using new technology. This strengthened the core position of such staff and increased job interest and career prospects. In the UK functional flexibility had been developed in an ad hoc way to meet staff shortages or to fill up slack times for staff.

contribute to the quality of service in healthcare by reducing the number of staff a user has contact with and a more holistic service can be provided (Kelliher and Desombre, 2005).

Facilitating factors promoting functional flexibility

1. Educational level of workers – more highly qualified workers should be more adaptable, particularly *knowledge workers* who may be expected to manage their tasks and take much of the responsibility for their own training and skills updating.
2. Decentralisation – acts against specialisation of function.
3. Fluctuations of workload – necessitates more efficient allocation of tasks to minimise 'idle' time.
4. New technology – enables a broader range of tasks to be carried out (although ambiguities about up-skilling and de-skilling).
5. Ability of staff to resist – this is paradoxical: the greatest use of multi-skilling seems to be in highly unionised workplaces. Professionals are strongly opposed to *managerial* attempts to increase functional flexibility or to reprofile skills.

Barriers against functional flexibility

1. Most workers are more interested in some areas of work than others.
2. Managers recognise that specialist knowledge is important and should be retained and used.
3. Commitment and achievement of high-quality work derives from a narrow 'ownership' of a particular area.
4. Cost and availability of training.
5. Skill retention – best maintained through regular use.
6. Tight staffing levels – staff could not be spared for training.

Note that the regulatory/legal regime in the UK neither facilitates nor constrains the use of functional flexibility – it is a 'voluntary' matter for the employer and employee to decide.

Advantages and disadvantages of functional flexibility

Employers apparently gain more flexibility (e.g. allows team-working), higher productivity and require fewer workers. The disadvantages could be through more and regular training (e.g. NVQs), more rewards (through either skill supplements or new grades) and in the cost of technology.

For employees the situation is more ambiguous. Up-skilling and empowerment may be illusory except for a small elite. For the others work intensification is more likely.

Overview

Much of the hype around functional flexibility (Beatson, 1995; Dyson, 1991) promises a panacea to employer and employee. Wickens (1987) talked of a 'tripod of success', through flexibility, quality and team-work. Legge (1995) presented an alternative 'tripod of subjugation', through work intensification, control and peer surveillance. Echteld (2007) questions whether current evidence on functional flexibility really justifies the discourse of a post-Fordist paradigm or HRM notions of strong internal labour markets.

Numerical flexibility – fixed-term contracts

In fact no employment contract is permanent – they are either indefinite or until the age of retirement. The term 'temporary' is rather an ambiguous term. Casey (1988) has identified 11 often overlapping categories of temporary workers:

1. consultants/freelancers;
2. labour-only subcontractors;
3. casual and on-call workers;
4. seasonal workers;
5. fixed-term contracts;
6. workers with a contract dischargeable by performance;
7. workers on training contracts;
8. temporary workers on indefinite contracts;
9. temporary agency workers;
10. employees of works contractors;
11. participants in special programmes for the unemployed.

Meager (1985: 11) avoids lists and focuses on *mutual recognition* by the employer and employee that the employment relationship is temporary:

> This applies irrespective of whether the individuals are employees of the organisation . . . and avoids the legal ambiguities surrounding the permanent or temporary nature of the employment contract.

The category of fixed-term contract has been chosen for coverage here because it is unambiguously temporary and involves a legal employment relationship (although there are examples of employees spending their entire career on fixed-term contracts for the same employer). In the UK fixed-term contracts (FTCs) are the most common type of temporary employment, making up about 51 per cent of the temporary group, some 850,000 employees (Labour Force Survey, 2002). The use of FTCs grew rapidly in the early and mid-1990s, increasing by 39 per cent between 1992 and 1996 (Industrial Relations Service, 1997). Before this, numbers of all types of temporary workers had been static for a decade or more. Subsequently, the numbers of FTCs have plateaued (Purcell *et al.*, 1999). The use of FTCs is unevenly distributed (found in about 44 per cent of organisations, Cully *et al.*, 1998); 3.9 per cent of the female labour force compared with 3 per cent of men (Beatson, 1995); particularly concentrated in the public sector (Sly and Stillwell, 1997) where clerical and professional jobs (15 per cent on FTCs) were most likely to be subject to FTCs (Cully *et al.*, 1998); for example, in higher education over 50 per cent of professional staff are on FTCs (Bryson and Barnes, 2000).

We can use British higher education as representative of the sort of context in the public sector which has seen such an increase in FTCs (Bryson and Barnes, 2000). The growth appears to stem from budgetary constraints and cuts made since 1980 and the unpredictable nature of future funding, leading to a very short-term cycle of planning. Universities have sought new sources of funding but this is strictly time-limited in nature, leading to a fourfold increase in the numbers of contract researchers. However, there has also been a sweeping casualisation of the core workforce, including academic teachers, technicians and support staff. Some institutions have even begun to recruit all new staff on FTCs. However, there is little evidence that such moves are strategic; they are more ad hoc and opportunistic. This follows Hakim's (1990) view about the advance of numerical flexibility but contrasts with Atkinson's (1984) thesis, but does not mean that this form of flexibility may not be enduring.

Facilitating factors promoting the use of fixed-term contracts

These are:

● the need to cover short-term absence – this is the traditional reason which has been sharpened through decreased workforce size and loss of a 'slack' capacity;

● staffing for short-term projects – particularly applies to management and professional staff;

● the need to bring in specialist skills for a project;

● to reduce pay bill/employment costs – by keeping the permanent headcount down and by offering temporary workers poorer terms and conditions and less staff development;

● the need to deal with variations in workload – seen as increasingly important by organisations;

● uncertainties about the future.

Barriers against use of fixed-term contracts

The regulatory/legal regime in the UK provided little constraint on the use of FTCs. However, after considerable delay and obfuscation, the UK finally adopted the Fixed Term Regulations in 2002 stemming from an EU Directive. This supposedly limits the ability of the employer to use serial fixed-term contracts, i.e. to keep renewing the employment of an individual again and again on temporary contracts, and offered full parity in terms and conditions between employees, i.e. discrimination on contractual basis was outlawed. However, this legal change has had little impact in the sectors that use such contracts. There are small indications that some employers are beginning to realise that using FTCs may not be the cheap, low risk option that they thought and that they will need to accord their temporary staff the same rights in terms of redundancy and other provisions such as pensions.

Advantages and disadvantages of fixed-term contracts

The advantages for the employers are closely linked with the reasons noted above. To these we may add (Leighton and Syrett, 1989) the perception that staff on fixed-term contracts are cheaper, work harder (because of insecurity), are not unionised or included in collective agreements and are easy to dismiss. The disadvantages of FTCs are perceived as: temporary workers are less reliable and less productive (Atkinson 1996); transaction costs (more recruitment, induction, redundancy) may be hidden, but much higher than expected (Bryson and Barnes, 1997); higher levels of absenteeism; lower commitment and loyalty; and increased management problems. Leighton and Syrett (1989) also suggest that 'temporary work is most effective where professional and occupational loyalty is marked and therefore a powerful motivator overcoming ambiguous feelings of loyalty to the firm'.

There may also be issues of integration with HR policies and relationships with other employees (see later in this chapter).

For employees there appear to be few advantages except that FTCs may offer a variety of experience or a foothold into a particular career; however, both of these can be gained through permanent posts in a fair labour market. For some, FTCs may suit their present needs – student employment, probationary period, training, or even higher earning potential (e.g. IT experts). Although firms that use agency workers may not be inclined to train these employees, temporary work agencies sometimes are willing to provide them with general training (Autor, 2000). However, much of the actual evidence shows that most employees experience (Bryson, 1996, 1997; Barnes, 1997) worse terms and conditions, lower status, exclusion from activities and governance, lack of career development and progress, insecurity and, particularly for women, segregation and discrimination.

Overview

There does appear to be a sharp increase and fundamental change in the use of FTCs taking place in the UK, although there is some evidence that it is restricted to particular sectors. The 'new rationales' are associated with a strategy to deal with uncertainty. There would appear to be a polarisation of use to most highly skilled, with the low skilled often being employed on an even more casual basis. The apparent advantages may be outweighed by the disadvantages. Although this type of external flexibility appears to provide a buffer against uncertainty, it heavily restricts the HR options available. The ability to recruit temporary employees relies heavily on a ready supply of appropriately skilled workers, and some organisations are now dependent on temporary workers for even core activities due to drastic pruning of the permanent workforce.

Numerical flexibility – redundancy

The traditional reason for making staff redundant was because there was no longer a requirement for their services. In the long period of economic growth after the Second World War, redundancies were comparatively uncommon. Indeed, there was considerable social and public policy pressure against making redundancies on any sort of large scale and generally a company would have to go bankrupt before jobs were lost. This all changed in the 1980s. There was to be no more government support for 'lame duck' industries and *downsizing, de-layering* and the even more euphemistic *rightsizing* became fashionable. Waves of redundancy took place, in recessions and in economic boom. The basis of selection for redundancy changed from last in, first out (LIFO) to performance. Companies sought to 'cut out the dead wood' and to sharply raise productivity. In practice, resistance to involuntary redundancy led to severance schemes being put in place semi-permanently and a swathe of early retirements. The latter policy has changed the whole age profile of the workforce, with many organisations now having no workers over the age of 50.

At the time of writing this new edition, the UK has enjoyed a long period of economic growth although future prospects are currently appearing much more pessimistic. However even in these 'good' years redundancies have still been made to the extent of between 400,000 and 500,000 per year. The last figures before the imminent recession were 492,000 redundancies in the year to July, 2008 (Economic and Labour Marker Review, 2008). Although a disproportionate share of redundancies continues to occur in the manufacturing and construction industries, and among the young and old, white collar workers have become increasingly vulnerable to redundancy (Heap, 2004). Moreover such professional occupations as university academic staff have not been immune to compulsory redundancies.

Facilitating factors promoting the use of redundancy

- Relatively easy to dismiss workers legally in the UK. An OECD study rated Britain at 2 on a 16-point scale of difficulty in dismissal, with most EU countries rated at over 10 (Lehman Brothers, 1994).
- Workers and unions appear to have accepted that redundancy is a legitimate management tool.
- Becoming more competitive. Pressure to reduce headcount where staff costs are high.

Barriers against the use of redundancy

- There are a number of legal constraints. Once workers have two years of service they are entitled to a statutory minimum redundancy payment. If numbers of redundancies are over certain totals, individuals and unions must be consulted and alternatives to redundancy sought. A test of reasonableness in procedures must be met for dismissal to be fair.
- Unions are very resistant to involuntary redundancies.
- There may be strong pressure from the local community and public agencies against its use.

Advantages and disadvantages of redundancy

Employers appear to be able to dismiss workers on permanent contracts with little difficulty and cost. The use of a broad-scale definition of performance as a selection indicator allows the dismissal of workers for all sorts of reasons consistent with optimising the use of human resources. It will certainly raise the profile of the HR function. There are many disadvantages: it is a fraught process to manage; it creates anger, distrust and industrial relations problems; it is inimical to 'soft'

HR practices; highly damaging to image of HR function; and it leaves a legacy of problems among the 'survivors'.

For employees, voluntary redundancy may offer opportunities for early retirement or a new career (with a large deposit in the bank). However, the problems of involuntary redundancy are well known and the subject of a large volume of literature. There are many detrimental psychological and sociological effects. There is evidence of discrimination against ethnic minorities (Casey, 1995) and older workers (Arrowsmith and McGoldrick, 1997). Turnbull and Wass (1997) have described the 'lemon' syndrome where a redundant worker becomes tainted and stigmatised. It is very difficult to get back to the same 'level' of employment, with many former employees ending up in even more precarious jobs, particularly if they are older. For the 'survivors' insecurity is an ever-present threat.

Overview

Redundancies remain a very common form of numerical flexibility; virtually everyone is vulnerable. Although, in a sense, other forms of numerical flexibility have been introduced to replace redundancy, these workers are often made redundant too, in more than a legal sense. Redundancies create a paradox; they are ostensibly for the purpose of making the organisation more competitive, viable and secure. It is arguable whether this is delivered but redundancies give exactly the opposite impression to the workforce. Whereas functional flexibility is associated with commitment-oriented HRM systems, numerical flexibility is usually related to a hard approach to HRM. However, companies do try to apply both approaches simultaneously and introduce a more varied HRM policy in the form of human resource portfolios combining seemingly contradictory kinds of flexibility (Carvalho and Cabral-Cardoso, 2008).

Temporal flexibility – part-time/variable time

With reference to working hours there has been considerable pressure from both employers and employees to vary the length of the working week. Employees seek a reduction of hours and/or a pattern of hours to suit their personal needs like balancing work and family life – therefore flexitime and part-time patterns have become more common. Employers seek a reduction of hours wherever the firm has to adapt to sudden external changes. In 1993 Volkswagen, one of Europe's largest car manufacturers, adopted a 4-day workweek to save 31,000 jobs that might otherwise have been lost. Stiff competition and new work technologies had forced the company to act in this way. The employees supported the initiative of management. Volkswagen became the first global corporation to move to a 30-hour working week. The shorter workweek was an equitable alternative to mass permanent lay-offs. In November 2003, Opel in Germany took the same initiative for a period of a year covering 21,000 employees to save jobs.

In the UK a quarter of the workforce are part-time. Most of this figure is accounted for by the large number of women working part-time (45 per cent of female employees) compared with just 10 per cent of men (Equal Opportunities Commission, 2002). However, the growth of part-time work in the 1990s among men (138 per cent) has been even more rapid than among women (28 per cent). The pattern of part-time working between the sexes shows that men tend to be part-timers at the beginning and end of their careers and women in the middle or throughout. Much of the growth of jobs has been in part-time work and many such jobs are also temporary.

In the Netherlands many part-time workers are on permanent employment contracts and, as a rule, the number of hours worked by part-time workers is fixed. Hence, part-time workers are not faced with the uncertainty of continued or reduced earnings of temporary workers or workers with variable hours contracts (Visser, 2000). Only a few new arrangements – next to part-time – have been introduced to differentiate between minimum and maximum labour time per day or week. Formal rostering of these working schedules is one of the stumbling blocks. In 2002, The University Medical Centre of Utrecht started an experiment with working hours in order to anticipate the ever more acute shortage of qualified staff. Staff members – being parents at the same time – have been recruited on a so-called 'mother contract' in which working times are synchronised with childcare and school hours. The wishes of parents with respect to working hours are taken as the point of departure (*Daily Routine Arrangements*, 2002). Inspired by Swedish experiments with the software program Time Care, which facilitates employees' self-rostering, the Utrecht hospital introduced a similar practice in 2007. Although ideologically the nine-to-five view is still around in the Netherlands, the percentage of people working irregular hours has increased from 53.9 per cent in 1992 to 64.2 per cent in 2000 (Delsen, 2001). In the service sector, such as consultancy firms, sabbatical leave has become a popular instrument to offer employees the opportunity for a period of rejuvenation.

However, as long as 'deregulation is occurring in response to high levels of unemployment and the political quest for more flexible labour markets, part-time employment is likely to be marginalised, even if full-time standards are also reduced' (Fagan and O'Reilly, 1998: 24). A few firms in the vicinity of Helsinki introduced a six + six-hour day-shift model comprising two six-hour shifts, one starting at 6 a.m., the other at noon. The daily working time dropped by two hours. Overtime was no longer necessary. The basic wages remained the same but total income decreased while extra overtime bonuses disappeared. The new model facilitated the proper combination of work and free-time activities (Kandolin and Kauppinen, 1996). This example is just one illustration of an increasing variety of patterns of part-time work across Europe.

Facilitating factors promoting the use of part-time/variable time working

- Demand from workers for better work–life balance and to meet caring needs. More widely, meets societal demand for choice.
- State encouragement and an EU regulatory regime which facilitates this. Temporal flexibility is seen as more balanced and employee friendly than numerical flexibility.

- Temporal flexibility enables firms to respond quickly to changes in market demand.
- Companies can use this type of flexibility to support training opportunities for employees, thereby reinforcing their intrinsic motivation.

Barriers against the use of part-time/variable time working

- Employers often see the support and structural costs of offering this form of work as more expensive and difficult to administer than full-time contracts. Legislative regulation now ensures that such costs cannot be offset by offering poorer terms and conditions to part-timers.
- There are alleged difficulties in providing staff coverage and staff availability.
- Managers argue that part-time workers are less committed.
- Employees may perceive themselves to have lower status (men seem to tend more to perceive this).

Advantages and disadvantages of part-time/variable time working

This form of contract may provide a key source of competitive advantage for employers. Temporal flexibility has had, for example, a positive impact in the liberalisation of shop opening hours in the Netherlands and Germany. There are also advantages in comparison with temporary contracts: employers may improve internal labour market flexibility and do not have to worry about the quality of the staff or deal with the financial and opportunity costs of managing a flux of contracts. Employees obtain the opportunity to determine when to start and end their working day. This can offer them much more control of their lives. But disadvantages are also present. Much part-time work is associated with the secondary labour market and 'women's work'. Therefore lower salaries, fewer development opportunities and poorer career progress are associated with part-time work. Even in professional work, the belief that part-time workers are less committed weakens their career prospects. This is exacerbated by part-time jobs and shorter/variable work often only being available in combination with temporary or casual work. This raises the issue that part-time work may be involuntary, for example the worker desires more hours but is not given them. Tam (1997) argues that part-time work may become a trap from which it is difficult to escape into better paid or full-time employment even if some part-time workers enjoy strong organisational relationships and long tenure (Purcell, 2000).

Overview

Part-time/variable contracts appear to offer the advantages of flexibility to both parties but for many workers can be a compromise. Traditional values and cultures in many countries have hampered to give part-time work an equal status. There have been legislative changes to end abuses and exploitation and the progress of equal opportunities has done much to enhance the rights of part-time workers. So although it is gradually becoming more widespread, many employers and employees show reluctance to embrace such forms of temporal flexibility.

Activity 2.2	Philips and flexibility

The notions of exploration and exploitation (see page 42) are widely used in the context of innovation. Original Equipment Manufacturers (OEMs) like Philips apply these concepts when they focus on effective knowledge creation (exploration) in combination with efficient knowledge application (exploitation). Interaction between design and production requires more and intensive coordination which has propelled temporal flexibility, in the form of cross-functional team-work and 'floating' employees dealing with different sets of peers on a regular basis, to the status of a critical success factor in the performance of the firm (Karuppan, 2004).

Recently Philips has embraced Operational Excellence as a combined effort to promote innovation (exploration) as well as optimise exploitation. The overall purpose of Operational Excellence is to create a flexible firm (infrastructure, systems and culture) with a flexible strategy and flexible employees on the shop floor as well as in middle and top management.

This requires

- product development with minimal time to market;
- supply chain management which guarantees optimal coordination of all the nodes in the value chain;
- assembling of complex systems.

The business unit Philips Domestic Appliances and Personal Care (DAP) is market leader in the area of electrical shaving. The mass production of its standard commodities has been outsourced to China. DAP has introduced knowledge centres to uphold its leadership in technology and product innovation, customer intimacy and well structured transformation processes. DAP embraces a processual approach and operates in a flexible manner by promoting customisation through modular design of its production process. The responsibility for operational excellence is shared in product design teams in which the designers are focusing on exploration, while the product engineers focus on exploitation.

The organisation operates in a flexible manner and synchronises exploration and exploitation by employing a large group of flex workers which makes it possible to cope with holidays like Christmas, Father's Day and Chinese New Year. For that purpose DAP has introduced an hour-bank system to use the available labour capacity as efficiently as possible. During a period when demand for labour input increases, employees work longer but earn the same salary per week. In a period when work capacity diminishes, employees work less and still earn the same salary. The pluses and minuses on the balance sheet of the hour-bank system are registered against the contractual annual working time arrangement with each individual employee.

DAP has also introduced a centre for mobility. Employees who may lose their jobs, due to outsourcing of particular activities or due to changes in the requirements of work performance, are assisted in finding a corresponding job within the firm or elsewhere.

1. Discuss the effectiveness of temporal flexibility like job rotation which DAP has introduced to cope with the combination of exploration and exploitation.

2. Discuss the effectiveness of an hour-bank system.

3. Is the 'centre for mobility' an adequate instrument to improve flexibility?

Source: based on Assen *et al.*, 2008

Temporal flexibility – overtime

Employers have traditionally responded to increased demand by using overtime. In response to the need to maximise the use of plant or offer round-the-clock service they have increasingly moved to more, and more variable, shiftworking. Employers' use of overtime, however, is 'gendered' in the sense that it is often used for full-time workers in male-dominated jobs, whereas part-time work is more common in female-dominated sectors (Delsen, 1998). Echteld (2007) emphasised that the persistent presence of overtime causes time pressure and reflects time greedy employment relations.

Overtime has traditionally attracted premium rates of pay and in order to avoid this, a new form of temporal flexibility has emerged – zero hours contracts. This is where the employee is not guaranteed any work at all but is required to be available as and when the employer requires them (unlike bank or relief workers who may choose whether to work). They are usually not paid any sort of retainer. The European Working Time Regulations (WTD) of 1998 has banned the use of zero hours contracts.

Overtime appears to have increased as the base working time has decreased. A study (Casey *et al.*, 1997) found that this was the most common practice to increase output. It was frequently operated on an informal basis in which case it was likely to be unpaid (particularly for managerial or professional staff). Over half of employees on fixed hours work overtime every week – a twofold increase over the last decade. Throughout Europe overtime is still a serious issue and hampers the balancing between those who have a job and those on the dole.

Facilitating factors promoting the use of overtime

- Fairly simple to operate. Can be varied at very short notice.
- Acceptance by employees – with many keen to take advantage of the opportunity to earn extra income.
- Little legal restraint on its use (but see below).

Barriers against the use of overtime

The WTD had set a limit of a 48-hour week to be averaged throughout the year. However, the averaging aspect and the exclusion of many groups of workers have meant that this has had little effect on informal overtime. It is possible for the workforce to agree to waive or vary this through a collective agreement. British trade unions have acceded to management's desire to avoid the 48-hour constraint as they have been reluctant to deny their members the ability to earn more.

Advantages and disadvantages of overtime

At first glance, overtime appears to offer many advantages to both employer and employee. For the employer, overtime is very flexible, offers a method of rapidly increasing output when required, and makes use of the existing workforce with no associated recruitment, training or lay-off costs. For the employee there is not only the key gain of earning more, which is often seen as a perk, but also the opportunity to demonstrate commitment 'over and above' normal which may lead to advancement in salary or grade.

There are some disadvantages. Overtime may increase costs for the employer, especially if it is offered – as was traditional – at premium rates (e.g. double time for weekends, triple time for public holidays). This can be mitigated by the employer not paying a premium and this has become increasingly common as the balance of power has shifted more to the employer from the unions. However, this approach may exacerbate an existing problem in that employees may be unwilling to undertake overtime. For some employees, and many women, it has never been an available option as they were unable to take up the offer because they had responsibilities outside work which precluded their availability. For those who work part-time, overtime work is not offered at a premium, unless they exceed full-time hours, which for most would obviate any advantage of being part-time in the first place. Overtime is often seen as an entirely voluntary activity (for the employee) but it should be recalled that it has often been used in a (unfairly) discriminatory way, with the offer only being made to those 'whose face fitted'. There is another disadvantage to employers because there comes a point when productivity will start to fall as staff become exhausted if they are working too much.

This point links to a major disadvantage for employees – too much work. Not only do workers become tired and stressed but there can be additional negative effects on their home life (or what is left of it). The UK has long been criticised for having a 'long hours culture', and the longest average working week in the EU. This stems from both paid overtime and *unpaid* overtime. For some workers paid overtime may be compulsory, as those who refuse are subject to harassment or first in line for redundancy. For professional workers, in particular, unpaid overtime has become much more common. Arguably, managers and many other professional jobs have no fixed hours and the 'norm' was to work sufficient hours to complete the job, this being especially the case for those who wished advancement in career and pay. This has created an opportunity for *work intensification* which has spread and increased far beyond the ambitious careerist to virtually all employees across a range of roles (Burchell *et al.*, 2002). This phenomenon has been blamed for many current social ills, not least the widening income gap between those in highly paid, if overloaded, job roles and those in low-paid employment, unemployment or non-employment.

Overview

Overtime (paid or unpaid) is the most common form of flexibility. Indeed Casey *et al.*'s (1997) analysis of LFS data shows that overtime shows the largest trend in the period 1984–94, with an increase in the number of workers with varying hours rising from 31 to 56 per cent. There is concern among many commentators that despite its apparent advantages to both parties in the employment relationship, in many instances advantages to employees have become less tangible, particularly if this leads to work intensification.

Activity 2.3	Flexibility in practice

Based on the example of an organisation you have worked for or know about, consider the forms of employment that are used there. You may find multiple forms, in which case you should try to address the forms in combination. Assess the reasons why such forms of employment are used in this context, and the advantages and disadvantages they present. Consider:

1. employers – particularly the issues that both HR and line managers face;
2. employees – the issues for workers on these types of contracts or terms and their colleagues on standard contracts.

Implications and outcomes of different approaches to managing uncertainty

Our focus on particular forms oversimplifies the real picture. Unfortunately, this is not captured in national surveys or statistics but case studies reveal that the pattern unfolding in many organisations is more complex. Several commentators have suggested that the pattern of labour utilisation is contingent on factors such as:

● Labour costs and fluctuations in demand (Rothwell, 1986).

- Organisations with high labour costs and high fluctuations in demand employ a small core workforce (including homeworkers and part-timers) and meet fluctuations with agency workers and subcontractees.

- Organisations with low labour costs and high fluctuations in demand employ average size of core, using overtime and/or a pool of internal temporaries to meet fluctuations.

- Organisations with high labour costs and low fluctuations in demand employ an average core using part-time and shiftwork.

- Temporary workers may be used to meet seasonal peaks. Organisations may need to respond to employee-driven demand for flexible work.

- Organisations with low labour costs and low fluctuations in demand have a large core, use overtime and part-time.

● Historical precedent, product demand, labour supply considerations, the nature of the product, overall managerial approach, and the complementarity and substitutability of practices (Casey et al., 1997).

- Fluctuations in product demand (which could be influenced by employer policy, e.g. using JIT or marketing approaches) create an unpredictable demand for labour.

- Labour supply is influenced by management stereotyping genders – assuming women will not work overtime but will tolerate part-time or temporary work and vice versa with men. Employers tend to combine complementary forms of non-standard employment to manage, for example, working time.

Smith *et al.* (1995) add technology to the equation. The findings of Casey *et al.* (1997) support the conclusion by Hunter *et al.* (1993) that employers prefer to use full-time permanent employees because they believe that they are easiest to manage, the most committed and the least likely to leave.

Evidence of this type lends considerable weight to the *processual* view – a blend of managers enacting decisions based on their perception of organisational needs. A lot of the debate around the flexible firm centred on whether organisations were adopting the model as a strategic choice. All the early evidence appeared to be against this, but that is unsurprising as strategy was viewed as top-down rationality. Interestingly, a study by Mayne *et al.* (1996) found evidence that high use of part-time/temporary workers was correlated with explicit human resourcing strategies. The finding that it was the larger organisations that are increasing the use of flexible work forms and that many smaller firms are unaware of the types of option available (Casey *et al.*, 1997) lends creditability to the notion that strategy has *emerged* and is now being taken up by senior management in organisations with sufficient resources to have a focus on HR. Unions have been slow to respond to new employment forms but could be the main champion seeking to balance employer flexibility with the types of flexibility sought by employees. Individual resistance has been very weak in times of high unemployment.

There are clearly wider societal effects of flexible forms of employment. Societal pressure may act as a constraint on employer policies such as redundancy or very insecure non-standard employment. There are major equal opportunities considerations in the widespread discrimination that currently takes place against women, ethnic minorities and the young and old – note the sort of stereotyping exhibited by employers above.

Are there indicators to help managers make more informed choices? Leighton and Syrett (1989) offer a checklist of advantages and disadvantages against almost every flexible employment option. Purcell *et al.* (1999) offer a more updated commentary. However, what does research tell us? Studies which attempt to link organisational performance with one aspect, such as the use of outsourcing, from a minefield of complex factors occurring at the same time are invariably fruitless. There are a host of studies focusing on the effect on the individual. An interesting debate has arisen around the concept of the psychological contract – the *implicit* contract between employee and employer and the changes that have been taking place in the 1990s (see Table 2.2 based on Reilly, 2001). A group of commentators have stretched the concept of *new deals* (Herriot and Pemberton, 1995a). This does not involve a relational contract of trust, commitment and security but is much more transactional. Some (usually consultants and politicians) go so far as to argue that organisations should not offer any sort of career but, instead, the commodity of *employability*. It is dubious whether these new deals are what most employees seek and there may be serious resultant damage to the employment relationship. This could create problems and costs for employers (Bryson and Barnes, 2000).

Watson, in Chapter 1, suggests that organisations may pursue dual human resourcing strategies. Empirical evidence suggests that this could be problematic. Geary (1992) examined three firms which used a dual strategy with permanent and temporary workers and noted that the managers were averse to this policy because of all the problems that arose. One of these was tension between temporary and permanent workers, which has been noted in other studies (Filipzcak,

Table 2.2 **The changing psychological contract**

	1980s	1990s
Employer's offer to employees	• good pay • no lifetime employment guarantee • severance and outplacement • role of change minimised by company	• performance-driven pay • personal development support • constant business change • frequent role transition necessary
Employees' response	• work harder • work smarter • take more initiative • be cost-conscious	• be flexible • be self-accountable • perform

1997). There are similar problems with freelancers (Lewis, 1995). Bryson and Barnes (2000) found problems that seemed beyond the capability of being 'managed' away. Indeed, when dual strategies are used, the problems in the 'direct control, low commitment' group seem to spill over into the 'indirect control, high commitment' group. It is difficult to assess whether there are *managerial* solutions because so often the peripheral groups are virtually ignored by HR policy-makers and line managers seem to be just left to cope, often with reluctance and frequently without much success.

This raises another issue about 'new style' HRM practices and flexibility. The rhetoric of HRM is full of references about the need to be flexible and adaptable. The problem is that the types of flexibility that are extensively used seem to be very far from the high trust, high commitment models, in fact they undermine them. The rhetoric about new-style HRM practices and flexible employment share similar contradictions and paradoxes (Blyton and Turnbull, 1992). Walby (1989) has pointed out, echoed by others (Geary, 1992; Legge, 1995), that many of the so-called flexible forms of employment actually create *rigidities*; the very thing they are supposed to prevent. These organisational rigidities may still force women to step out of a full-time job when their children are young and return to work part-time when the children are older (Mainiero and Sullivan, 2006). Sustainable flexibility could prevent these rigidities by:

- designing organisations not only as totally flexible learning systems but by focusing on prevailing stable company structures too;
- effectively combining company-wide standardisation (coherence) and local differentiation (diversity);
- making organisations lean in terms of the fit between resources and tasks, while not endangering their capacity to adapt to changing environments (Mayerhofer, 1997).

This occurs both within the organisation and in the labour market. There appears to be a considerable weight of evidence to support this.

One problem with the flexible firm is that it is a tight model suggesting an optimal final configuration for organisations. This is somewhat paradoxical in a dynamic, uncertain world; surely adaptability entails being able to manage transitions – to be in a permanent state of *transition*. However, the reason organisations are successful is because they are, at least to some extent, *organised*. They seek to provide some stability and predictability and a measure of control over uncertainty. Nevertheless, securely organised companies may enhance flexibility. This is the point Streeck (1988: 417) made while writing:

> In human society, the substructure of flexible action is provided by institutions. A society without institutions, i.e. a totally flexible society, is anomic and anomy frustrates successful adaptive behaviour, of individuals or organisations, as much as total ritualistic regulation.

An obsession with immediate responsiveness to markets is a recipe for chaos and confusion, but unfortunately reflects the patterns and policies we observe.

Despite all the recent evidence that non-standard work forms are ever increasing – with populist predictions towards a jobless future – we do observe considerable continuity with traditional approaches: Casey *et al.*'s (1997) finding that overtime was the most common form of flexibility, the continued use of redundancy, and recently Dex and McCulloch's (1997) claim that the tide has turned. The latter points to the fact that British figures showed that full-time standard employment were increasing and temporary work declining. However, it must be the British private sector that is decreasing the use of non-standard forms because in the public sector they are ever on the increase. Although the main ideological imperative may have decreased – or has simply now become the standard view – cost-cutting and uncertainty remain very high in the British public sector. In other countries, however, such as the Netherlands, the job machine is based on an expansion of part-time employment.

The actual development of flexibilization is a challenging one. The creation of the flexible firm (a rather different version from Atkinson's), with its automated production processes which allow for small-scale production almost reaching near-personalisation of products can certainly have more positive effects: the opportunity to apply new organisational principles to labour and to innovate technology. Literature begins to show that the use of IT can be associated with centralisation and/or decentralisation in firms, with more flexibility and/or more rigidities leading to electronic scientific management. The more malleable the IT becomes, the less technical management and the more people management is required when thinking about the firm's organisation. All will depend on how the firm will turn human capabilities into competencies (Hagström, 2002). Sennet (2000) notices that corporations are shifting from being dense, often rigid, pyramidical bureaucracies to more flexible networks in a constant state of inner revision. The command lines are changing and the de-regulation of the workplace shifts responsibilities downward. At IBM this practice 'marks a stark contrast to the paternalistic tightly organised chain of command which orchestrated the corporation for most of its history' (Sennet, 2000: 187).

The drive for flexibilisation makes the tension between flexibility *of* and *for* the employees clearly visible. This requires new forms of employment relations where a flexible balance between work and care activities can be respected. Because, 'as women move in ever-increasing numbers into the dominant world of paid employment (bound time), they face norms and practices that seem to conflict with the responsibility and pleasures associated with unbounded, more subjective sense of time' (Bailyn, 2002: 263). Castells warns that the information society may turn into a world driven 'by individualization of work, destructuring of civil society and de-legitimization of the state'. To prevent this happening he calls for the rebuilding of families under egalitarian forms. 'Yet the transition to new forms of family implies an essential redefinition of gender relationships and society at large' (Castells 1998: 349).

Conclusion

As we have tried to show, the permanent, full-time, weekday, daytime-hours arrangements are in decline – albeit more slowly than politicians and management gurus would have us believe. Due to technological as well as social innovations which are rooted in a frantic drive for greater organisational efficiency and flexibility, either through quality, customer satisfaction or cost reduction, a greater diversity in working-time arrangements has been introduced in the industrialised world. The decentralisation of working-time arrangements reflects the increased popularity of the concept of citizenship as an active membership of the European community and willingness to participate in the various spheres of society, i.e. the state, the market and the family with all their interdependencies.

The desire for a stronger social Europe stimulates the social dialogue about the necessary balance between work and family as a precondition to promote flexibility. Europeans show a keen interest in more flexible working time regimes (EFILWC, 2003). While time is an essential resource for citizenship, a European citizenship influence may encourage a shift in the domestic division of labour (Lister, 2003). Citizenship puts the spotlight on care issues and pulls the private domain into the discussion on the importance of care to society (Kremer, 2005). Cass, however, argues that 'men should not be accorded full citizenship if they do not fulfil their responsibilities for care-giving work' (Cass, 1995: 60). She wants to reach beyond the constant struggle between the sexes. To do so, a language is needed which is common to both sexes. European citizenship can be the building block for this common language. In that sense Giddens (2006: 85) proposes a radical shift by saying that the EU can only establish the objective of economic development and social cohesion if it seriously promotes a further reduction of working hours: 'No country has yet come close to what we might take as a guiding ideal, both of gender equality and lifetime flexibility – a situation in which, as measured over the lifespan, both men's and women's jobs would converge around, say, a thirty-hour week (with periods of longer and shorter working hours for both)'.[2] In a similar vein, the European Trade Union Confederation argues that a limitation on working hours can provide flexibility to both workers and companies and so contribute to economic sustainability (Pillinger, 2006).

Working atypical hours and weekends will change the temporal structure of family life, constraining the time that family members spend with one another and threatening the quality and stability of relationships. Working non-standard hours is associated with greater health risks due to changes to an individual's circadian rhythms (Presser *et al.*, 2008).

---

[2] Thomas More believed six hours to be enough to live a happy life and wrote in *Utopia* that the enjoyment of a civil life is 'the virtuous object of all human efforts' (More, 1978 [1516]: 92).

We have attempted to make some sense of the concept of managing flexibly by examining the sort of options that managers have available when conventional human resource planning fails to provide solutions. There would appear to be a whole host of flexible employment forms to choose from. In practice the choice is not so simple and managers do well to avoid prescriptive advice and consider all the implications of their possible choices. They must be aware of the implications of integrating multiple forms of flexibility. We have introduced several theoretical frameworks which seek to analyse flexible employment and provide explanations. There is no overarching conceptual framework which is adequate for the task. In order to gain a broader understanding we need to synthesise concepts from diverse social sciences sources. Study at the individual level and in the context of case studies appears to be more useful than macro-surveys and national statistics for understanding what is unfolding at organisation level, although the wider external environment is clearly important.

There may be evidence that managers are using flexible employment options as part of a strategic approach, at least from a processual perspective, but too often it reflects an expedient approach to make short-term cost savings – more 'muddling through' than managing and planning for long-term viability. Such cost saving might, in fact, be illusory. Very rarely do the choices exercised reflect a balance between the needs and imperatives of the employer and the needs and aspirations of the employee. Arrangements of mutual flexibility, however, still are a realistic option. They are based on the principle that both parties have different interests, but that these can be reconciled through acknowledging the differences and working to find common ground between them. One specific characteristic of this mutual flexibility is that 'it addresses more than the economic needs of the person – it concerns itself with psychological well-being' (Reilly, 2001: 78). This is not just about the absurdity of using overtime and making redundancies at the same time but about a proactive response to workers to gain long-term productivity and quality. This is very unlikely to be based on numerical or reward flexibility but rather on functional, temporal or locational forms. A few organisations appear to have achieved some stability by respecting and seeking this balance. The search for greater flexibility may lead to a range of hybrid mixed and intermediate forms of productive organisation with more fluid forms of contract codification but workplace changes also reflect significant continuities and have hardly shaken the basic structure of hierarchically organised patterns of authority in productive organisations. Our main conclusion is that management will be challenged to deal with uncertainty but will have to manage flexibility not uncertainty.

Summary

In this chapter the following key points have been made:

● Organisations have struggled to cope with uncertainty due to the apparent inability of human resource planning to cope.

● New forms of employment flexibility have been utilised in addition to traditional methods in order to manage the size, costs and skills components of the labour force.

- Conceptualisations of flexibility have been provided through an examination of the ambiguity of the term. Several theoretical frameworks have also been outlined that may be used to clarify the issues.

- There would appear to be a set of factors that may combine to force changes in the way labour is utilised.

- There is evidence to show that non-standard employment is increasing internationally and there are competing explanations to explain this.

- A typology of employment and contract forms (including those where there is no legal employment contract) has been introduced that employers could use.

- Five contractual forms/strategies have been analysed in depth – multi-skilling, fixed-term contracts, redundancy, part-time/variable time contracts and overtime. This included an examination of the context and prevalence of use, promoting and constraining factors, and pros and cons for employers and employees.

- An assessment of the types of patterns emerging at organisational level.

- An assessment of whether there are management strategies of labour utilisation or whether it is ad hoc.

- An examination of the relationship between flexible employment and human resourcing.

- Finally, an assessment of the implications of using such employment forms at the level of the individual, manager, organisation, labour market and society.

Discussion questions

1. Are flexible forms of labour utilisation genuinely *new* or just variants on old themes?

2. Discuss which conceptual frameworks may be used to analyse flexible employment and for what type of analysis they are most useful – for example, national comparisons, impacts on society, impacts on the individual, employer strategy or the employment relationship.

3. To what extent are flexible forms of employment substitutable for each other?

4. To what extent is non-standard employment supplanting standard jobs, both currently and in the future?

5. Outline a form of flexible employment and discuss the advantages and disadvantages of its use to employers *and* employees.

6. Is the use of a dual strategy to utilise human resources consistent with new-style HRM practices?

7. What evidence is there to support the notion that managing uncertainty through labour utilisation is a strategic activity?

8. Has UK public policy and legal regulations had any influence over the use of non-standard employment?

9. Does flexible employment actually deliver flexibility and adaptability?

Further reading

The chapter has covered a broad range of issues around the general topic of flexible employment. The reader who wishes to follow up on specific points is advised to obtain and read the references identified in the text. There are some more general texts that are useful. Sparrow and Marchington (1997) cover a broad and similar range of issues on this topic but from some differing perspectives. Felstead and Jewson (1999) also offer a range of perspectives, more detailed explanations and international comparisons. Heery and Salmon (1999) focus on the issue of insecure and precarious employment. Proctor (2003) focuses on issues of managing and the management of flexibility. Zeytinoglu (2005) provides interesting empirical material about actual flexible practices in workplaces in different countries. New trends in working-time arrangements have been detected by Boulin *et al.* (2006).

3

Employment law and human resourcing strategies

Lynette Harris

Learning outcomes

Having read this chapter and completed its associated activities, readers should be able to:

- Understand the way in which the legal framework relating to employment has developed over the past 50 years
- Recognise how employment legislation can influence human resourcing strategies
- Analyse the impact of employment regulation on the extent and nature of line managers' responsibilities for human resourcing issues and decisions
- Appreciate how the degree of employment regulation impacts on the organisational role and contribution of the specialist HR function
- See why the level of employment regulation and litigation can shape the nature of the relationship between line management and the specialist HR function
- Evaluate the advantages and disadvantages of external employment regulation for the development of positive employment relationships
- Recognise that individual rights for designated groups may lead to feelings of inequity among others

Law and employment strategies

The key theme of this chapter is to examine the impact employment law has on human resourcing strategies. Owing to the nature of the subject, it particularly considers the development of employment law in the UK but the discussion will extend to a wider consideration of the nature of the responsibilities of the human resource specialist *vis-à-vis* those of the line manager for interpreting and implementing HR policies within the prevailing regulatory framework. It is not the purpose of this chapter to discuss the detail of individual statutes which Taylor and Emir (2006: 17) label as 'micro-debates'; there are many excellent textbooks which do just that. Nor is it the intention to explore the various merits of the ongoing 'macro-debates' about the degree of legal intervention seen as appropriate to support 'orderly industrial relations' at either an individual or a collective level (Collins, 2001: 17). Rather, the aim is to consider the influence of external regulation in shaping human resourcing policies, practices and approaches to the employment relationship.

Why regulate?

Collins *et al.* (2000) suggest that the justification for specific law focusing on the regulation of the employment relationship is based on two central arguments which may well overlap and contradict each other. These are:

1. The failure of ordinary market rules leading to a perceived need for regulation to facilitate competition, for example the introduction of legislation by the UK government during the 1980s requiring mandatory competitive tendering for certain services provided by local authorities.

2. When market rules are perceived to have unacceptable outcomes against some criteria resulting in legislation to address identified issues and inequities, for example minimum wage or anti-discrimination laws.

Let us consider for a moment how introducing a law to address unacceptable outcomes for one group can lead to less favourable outcomes for others by returning to the Aynshent tribe we met in Chapter 1.

Case Study 3.1

New tribal law with the Himnals and Aynshents

The Aynshents have addressed their shortage of labour by a series of successful alliances with the women from their closest neighbouring tribe, the Himnals. While the Himnals have gained land through these alliances, they have become increasingly concerned that the tribe's ability to cultivate their own land has reduced due to the numbers of their young women who have left to live with Aynshents. Only two Himnal women have returned to live with their own tribe and they did not stay for long before going back with their children to the more physically attractive and peaceable Aynshents. They say their workload with the Aynshents is less arduous and it is easier to produce a good maize crop as the soil in the lower valley is more fertile. Traditionally the Himnals have relied on the women to grow the tribe's food while the men hunt, so the continuing loss of skilled female hands has had a devastating effect on the cultivation and harvesting of their crops. As a result, the remaining women of the tribe are constantly complaining that their tasks are endless which means they neglect the children and work much harder than the men. After a full meeting of the tribal leaders, the Himnals decide to introduce a new law which is to take immediate effect and applies to all their womenfolk who have left to live with other tribes. This demands that for a period of time every year all Himnal women must return to help the tribe with the cultivation and harvesting of their crops.

If this law is not complied with, the Himnals have decided to take direct action, starting with the Aynshents. They plan to recapture their womenfolk living with the Aynshents by force through the night raids favoured by their forefathers. The younger women of the tribe are unhappy about the new law, saying it will deter other tribes from seeking them out as partners and mothers of their children. They are particularly concerned about their position in the present hierarchy of the tribe; as single childless women, they are expected to carry out the most menial tasks and have the heaviest workloads of all.

> ### Activity 3.1 New tribal law with the Himnals and Aynshents
>
> 1. Identify the arguments for and against the introduction of the Himnal's new tribal law.
> 2. What are the implications of the Himnal's new law for the Aynshents, in particular the tribe's present strategy for addressing its labour shortages?
> 3. What are the implications of this new law for the Himnals, in particular the tribe's existing negotiated order and its long-term survival?

Regulation and approaches to human resourcing

Views on the nature and degree of legal intervention deemed appropriate and acceptable clearly change over time and our approaches to legislation do not operate in isolation from the prevailing, and often conflicting, economic, political and social trends and theories (Jefferson, 1997). Taking a historical perspective of the dominant concerns in human resourcing in modern work organisations provides insights into how the focus on internal rules, traditionally agreed through collective bargaining, and external rules imposed by legislation can alter. One example of this in HR practice is the fluctuating level of organisational interest in job evaluation which was frequently introduced in the 1970s to address pay relativities and union concerns about demonstrating internal equity. By the 1980s it was seen as a source of workplace inflexibility and an outmoded intervention in a competitive labour market but there has been a resurgence of interest in recent years, largely as a means of resolving issues of equal pay for work of equal value and to provide a defence against equal pay claims.

The presence of employment rights is a critical factor in the selection of human resourcing strategies and it can lead to radical shifts in employment practice. The intensification of competition and economic uncertainty, in many instances due to globalization, has led employers to adopt employment practices which focus on adaptability and responsiveness to change rather than stability and continuity (Blyton and Turnbull, 2004). It has been particularly evident in the growth of 'core/periphery' employment strategies (Atkinson, 1987; Robinson, 2000) even in areas of public sector employment previously characterised by a large permanent core with a minimal peripheral workforce. Yet, as an approach to achieving workforce flexibility this is increasingly challenged by the extension of employment rights to workers not employed on full-time permanent contracts.

The two alternative resourcing principles of direct control/low commitment and indirect control/high commitment discussed by Watson in Chapter 1 (p. 31), are directly reflected in the nature of the employment contract. The combination of an uncertain external environment, a reduced trade union presence and minimal employment regulation in the 1980s led UK employers to 'hedge their bets' by offering a variety of flexible employment contracts. Increased direct control was achieved by employers offering reduced levels of job security, reflected in the ease with which employment could be terminated. It resulted in a proliferation of non-permanent employment contracts such as fixed-term appointments, 'zero hours' working and the use of subcontracting. These provided the organisational flexibility to deal with future uncertainties, albeit at the risk of reduced employee commitment. By the mid-1990s it was projected that one-third of the UK workforce would be on other than permanent contracts by the end of the century. But the predicted trend did not materialise owing to the impact of European Union (EU) legislation, particularly after the 1997 signing of the Social Chapter of the Maastricht Treaty, which widened the application of employment rights. As Bercusson (1999) observes employment statutes stemming from the EU are aimed at addressing the failure of 'market rules' to provide equitable outcomes for all workers in the labour market. Differing perceptions about the part employment regulation plays in creating labour market rigidities have long been at the heart of the flexibility debates among European member states (Hakim, 1990). Indeed the impact that employment protection legislation has on labour market performance continues to be the subject of 'heated policy debate' (OECD, 2004: 61) and there is a visible tension between the articulated EU's employment strategy of greater job creation and its pursuit of a proactive policy of common EU employment rights (Ball, 2001). Dual aims that are similarly reflected in the International Labour Organization's (ILO) objective to promote employment stability whilst maintaining a sufficient level of labour market flexibility.

The evidence that legislation acts as a deterrent to flexibility in employment practice is far from conclusive and often appears contradictory. Although successive Conservative governments in the 1980s and 1990s viewed minimal regulation of employment as a key factor in achieving organisational competitive advantage, studies by Brewster *et al.* in the 1990s (1996) into working-time and contract flexibility in the European Community did not lend support to the assumption that this led UK employers to demonstrate the greatest flexibility in their working practices.

Whilst OECD (2001) research suggests that the UK by the end of the 1990s was the most lightly regulated of the EU member states, Taylor and Emir (2006: 10) observe that the UK system now increasingly resembles that of France, Germany and Italy. Although this is largely as a result of workplace regulation created by EU laws it is also due to a Labour government's commitment to family friendly employment policies. The OECD's (2004) examination of employment protection legislation (EPL) and organisational performance supports the view that a process of convergence is taking place even though the relative position of countries in terms of the strictness of EPL has remained unchanged since the late 1980s.

Non-standard work patterns tend to be not only more frequent but also more popular in those EU countries with less strict EPL. This is particularly evident in levels of part-time working in countries with greater freedom over the choice of hours worked, for example the Netherlands, the UK and Denmark. While there is some evidence that more protective employment legislation reduces diversity and dynamism in the labour market, the OECD's analysis recognises that employment legislation alone does not explain national differences, which are highly influenced by a variety of labour market institutions and traditions. Leaving aside the debates surrounding the impact that levels of regulation may have on the development of flexible employment practices, we can with reasonable certainty predict that despite the ever expanding volume of employment legislation and related case law across EU member states, employers driven by ever increasing competitive pressures, will continue to seek out those human resourcing strategies that minimise their costs and maximise productivity.

The changing legal framework

Bach (2005: 31) observes that the combination of legalisation arising from EU initiatives and the Labour government's domestic commitments has led to the most far-reaching changes in the UK's regulatory framework since the end of the First World War. This has both positives and negatives for approaches to the employment relationship and for the role of the specialist HR function. What it undoubtedly does is keep HR policies and practices high on the organisational agenda, as Gratton *et al.* (1999) found in their longitudinal study of HR strategies in nine 'leading edge' companies. A Chartered Institute of Personnel and Development Survey (CIPD/Lovells, 2005) into the organisational impact of employment legislation found that 35 per cent of employers reported employment law as the key driver of change in their employment practice and behaviour and more than three-quarters rated it in their top five priorities, as illustrated in Table 3.1.

To trace how the UK's legislative framework has developed requires an examination of the key phases in its development during the post-war period. Table 3.2 sets out the principal labour law statutes enacted from 1960 to the present time to illustrate the expansion of employment law during this period.

In considering the thrust and direction of labour law, Kahn-Freund (1972) suggests it can be categorised as

- *auxiliary law*, which provides support and a framework for collective bargaining;
- *regulative law*, which provides employment rights;
- *restrictive law*, which specifies what is allowable in the conduct of collective bargaining.

Table 3.1 The main drivers of organisational change in employment practice/behaviour

	Employers (%) ranking this as the most important driver of change	Employers (%) ranking this as a top-five driver of change
The introduction of new employment	36	76
The need to improve business performance	25	72
Changes to the top management team	9	34
Customer expectations	4	33
Skills shortages/the need to become an employer of choice	3	42
Corporate image/reputation	2	36
Staff turnover levels	2	29
Threat of legal costs for non-compliance	2	20
Marketplace competition	2	14
The corporate social responsibility (CSR) agenda	2	13
Employee attitude surveys	1	23
National standards awards	1	17
Changes to labour market demographics (e.g. ageing workforce)	1	15
Trade unions	*	15
Staff councils/forums	*	9

* Less than 1 per cent

Source: *Employment and the law – Burden or Benefit?*, Survey Report 2005, p. 9 http://www.cipd.co.uk/NR/rdonlyres/3359BAC2-5A40-43D0-B3A0-3A55C32EA477/0/emplawsro605.pdf, Chartered Institute of Personnel & Development/Lovells, with the permission of the publisher, the Chartered Institute of Personnel and Development, London (www.cipd.co.uk)

Table 3.2 Key legislation impacting on employment from 1960 onwards

1963	Contracts of Employment Act	1995	Employment Tribunals Act
1965	Redundancy Payments Act	1996	Employment Rights Act
1965	Trades Disputes Act	1998	The Employment Rights (Disputes Resolution) Act
1970	Equal Pay Act	1998	National Minimum Wage Act
1971	Industrial Relations Act	1998	The Data Protection Act (replaced 1984 Act)
1974	Health & Safety at Work Act	1998	Human Rights Act
1974	Rehabilitation of Offenders Act	1998	Working Time Regulations
1975	Employment Protection Act	1998/9	Maternity and Parental Leave etc. Regulations
1975	Sex Discrimination Act	1998	Disability Rights Commission Act
1976	Race Relations Act	1999	Transnational Information and Consultation of Employees Regulations
1977	Safety Representatives & Safety Committees Regulations	1999	Employment Relations Act
1978	Employment Protection (Consolidation) Act	1999	Sex Discrimination (Gender Reassignment) Regulations
1980	Employment Act		
1981	Transfer of Undertakings (Protection of Employment) Regulations	2000	The Part-time Workers (Prevention of Less Favourable Treatment) Regulations
1982	Employment Act	2000	Race Relations (Amendment) Act
1984	Trade Union Act	2002	Employment Act
1984	The Data Protection Act	2002	Fixed-term Employees (Prevention of less favourable treatment) Regulations
1986	Sex Discrimination Act	2003	Employment Equality (Sexual Orientation) Regulations
1986	Wages Act	2003	Employment Equality (Religion or Belief) Regulations
1986	Employment Act	2004	Employment Relations Act
1988	Access to Medical Records Act	2004	Information and Consultation of Employees Regulations
1989	Employment Act	2006	Work and Families Act
1990	Employment Act	2006	The Employment Equality (Age) Regulations
1992	Trade Union & Labour Relations (Consolidation) Act	2004	Employment Relations Act
1993	Trade Union Reform & Employment Rights Act	2004	Information and Consultation of Employees Regulations
1994	Sunday Trading Act	2006	Work and Families Act
1995/99	Collective Redundancies and Transfer of Undertakings Regulations	2006	The Employment Equality (Age) Regulations
1995	Employment Protection (Part-time Employees) Regulations	2007	Sex Discrimination Act 1975 (Amendment) Regulations 2008
1995	Disability Discrimination Act		

Although these distinctions become blurred in practice, they do provide a helpful initial framework for classifying developments in this area of the law. As you will have noticed, most recent legislation has been regulative in nature and largely concerned with the provision of individual minimum rights.

Activity 3.2   Legislative cycles

Consider the regulations set out in Table 3.2 then attempt the following short activity.

1. Identify those periods when more employment legislation has been introduced and others when there has been little activity and provide an explanation for cycles of legislative activity or inactivity with reference to the political, economic and social context of the time.

2. Select any recent employment regulation you are aware of and provide reasons why you think such legislation was introduced.

To understand the direction and extent of employment regulation in recent years, we will begin with an overview of how the legislative context for organisations has changed during the post-war period in the UK.

Minimal intervention

Until the 1960s there was little in the way of legal intervention in the relationship between employer and employee. Wedderburn (1986: 1) suggests that at the time the prevailing view in British industrial relations was that 'most workers want nothing more of the law than that it should leave them alone. A secure job is preferable to a claim to a redundancy payment; a grievance settled in the plant or the office is better than going to a court or to an industrial tribunal.' This observed preference for non-intervention by a third party appears to contrast sharply with the growing numbers of UK workers who now seek redress for employment related differences through the Employment Tribunal system; a trend considered in more detail later in this chapter.

During the era of full employment in the 1950s there was a continuance of the approach taken since the First World War, namely a broad support for a voluntarist system. Dickens (2008) points out that at the heart of the voluntarist system is relative legal abstention with support for regulation through collective bargaining; statutory support being provided in those sectors where collective bargaining was insufficiently developed. These took the form of 'props' such as Wages Councils and the Fair Wages Resolution which enabled government to ensure contract compliance among contractors. The 1960s saw the beginnings of a minimum floor of individual rights for all employees, regardless of the existence of workplace collective bargaining, with the Contracts of Employment Act 1963 and the Redundancy Payments Act 1965. State intervention was further evident in the Industrial Training Act 1964 aimed at encouraging employers to train through a grant/levy system operated by Industrial Training Boards for different occupational sectors.

A growing concern about the impact of the country's high levels of industrial stoppages on the UK's economic performance led to the setting up of the Donovan Commission to investigate the country's industrial relations problems. While the Commission's report (Donovan, 1968) supported the continuance of the voluntary system of bargaining it recommended reform based on 'properly conducted, collective bargaining' with a greater formalisation of the process at company level which was to include the professionalisation of personnel specialists.

An election defeat for the Labour government heralded a radical change in direction with the new government's Industrial Relations Act in 1971. Based on American collective bargaining models, key concepts introduced by the Act were legally enforceable collective agreements and 'unfair industrial practices'. These met with resistance and failure because, as Hepple observes (1995: 308), the Act tried to bring about too drastic a change in behaviour by the means of law. It was repealed by an incoming Labour government, although the provisions on individual rights to seek redress for unfair dismissal were re-enacted in the 1974 Trade Union and Labour Relations Act. The almost universal unpopularity of this piece of legislation makes for an interesting comparison with the lack of objection a decade later to a 'step by step' approach to laws aimed at reducing trade union powers.

The era of the social contract

The period from 1974 to 1979 saw a rapid expansion of employee rights in the workplace, the majority of which are still on the statute book today. Compared to the present growth in regulation stemming from the EU, the impact of EC law was minimal at this time, although the Equal Pay Act of 1970 was intended to reflect the provisions of Article 119 of the Treaty of Rome. The basic purpose of the new legislation was 'to restore and extend the legal base for voluntary collective bargaining together with an improved "floor of rights"' (Wedderburn, 1986: 6) for workers and unions. This period has been labelled the 'social contract' because it was based on trade union cooperation with the government's policies on wage restraint in return for increased employment rights. The Employment Protection Act 1975 promoted and expanded collective bargaining and included new rights to time off for maternity, trade union activities and public duties. Further interventions were introduced by the Sex Discrimination Act 1975 and the Race Discrimination Act 1976. The social contract finally came to an end with the widespread pay disputes in the public sector in 1979, known as the 'winter of discontent', which culminated in the election of a Conservative administration with a very different ideology about the role of state regulation than previous post-war governments.

The market rules

The major break with the voluntary system was made by the successive Conservative governments committed to a monetarist, free market ideology between 1979 and 1997. Dickens (2008: 5) observes that employment law reforms at the time 'constituted a decisive shift away from a long-standing public policy view that joint regulation of the employment relationship through collective bargaining was the best method of conducting industrial relations'. De-regulation was seen as a key means of achieving the low-cost and highly flexible workforce held to be essential to greater competitiveness and lower unemployment (Deakin and Wilkinson, 1996). This resulted in the passing of successive Acts to reduce regulation viewed as unnecessarily restricting business and a steady dismantling of trade union immunities through the Employment Acts of 1980 and 1982, the Trade Union Act of 1984 and the Employment Act of 1988. The 'golden formula' providing immunity for acts in contemplation or furtherance of a trade dispute was limited to disputes directly between workers and their employers with picketing lawful only at the place of work of those engaged in the industrial action. The restrictions on industrial action were accompanied by increased penalties for unlawful action and compulsory union membership was finally rendered illegal in 1990. The freedoms of trade unions in conducting their internal affairs were constrained by provisions on balloting, union elections and the rights of members against their union.

The changes did not stop at reducing trade unions' powers. There was also a reduction of certain individual rights which increased the freedoms of UK employers in the processes of 'hiring and firing' (Beatson, 1995: 31). The qualifying period for claiming unfair dismissal increased to two years in 1984 and protections for certain groups of workers disappeared with the dismantling of Wages Councils (Trade Union Reform and Employment Rights Act, 1993). By the late 1980s there was a growing gap between the level of regulative law experienced by UK employers in their employment practices and their EU counterparts (Grubb and Wells, 1993), with the UK having the least stringent employment laws. But as Fredman (1997) points out in the period since 1979 there have been two different forces moving within the law; one driven by the ideology of a free market with minimal restrictions and the other from the European Community based on reducing divisions and inequalities through protective legislation. What changed after 1997 in the UK was the balance between these two forces in favour of increased individual rights.

New rights and the impact of EU legislation

The arrival of a Labour government in May 1997 with a manifesto commitment to make changes in the area of employment marked a new direction in legislative activity. This was evident in the introduction of a statutory minimum wage and new procedures for the recognition and de-recognition of trade unions. The most major influence on the UK's domestic legal development since 1997 has, however, been the growing impact of EU labour and social policy laws after a period of low activity in the 1980s (Hepple, 1995). In an examination of the symbiotic relationship between national and EC labour laws, Bercusson (1995: 3) observes 'it is not merely that UK labour law is required to incorporate EC norms. EC norms are themselves the reflection of the national labour laws of member states'.

The importance of a social dimension of employment was recognised by EU states other than the UK in 1992 in the adoption of the Protocol and Agreement on Social Policy of the Maastricht Treaty on European Union. In 1997 the UK government agreed to the removal of its opt-out from the 'social chapter'. The result has been the introduction, through domestic legislation, of a range of new individual and collective employment rights. To date, the greatest impact on employment matters in the UK has probably stemmed from EU legislation on equal treatment and the rights of individual employees in redundancies and business transfers. Since 1998, EU directives which have impacted on the UK's domestic employment legislation have included the regulation of working time and leave, equal employment rights for part-time and full-time employees, increased protection for employees on fixed-term contracts and in the transfer of undertakings, new rights on maternity, parental leave, time off for domestic incidents as well as statutory processes for providing information to and consulting with employees Many of these provisions had their roots in the Employment Relations Act of 1999 but the Employment Act 2002 introduced a range of family-friendly rights for men and women which extended to maternity leave, paternity and adoption leave and the right for employees with young children to request flexible working arrangements. A statutory right that was extended in April 2007 to include carers of dependent family relatives. The 2002 Act also saw the introduction of statutory disciplinary and grievance procedures under the Dispute Resolution Regulations (2004) in a perceived attempt to reduce the escalating number of tribunal claims and address employers' concerns about a 'compensation culture'. The unintended consequences of these procedures and their proposed repeal after operating for only a short period of time are returned to later in the chapter.

A comprehensive raft of new domestic legislation has been introduced to comply with the EU's Anti-Discrimination Framework Directive 2000 which extended existing law beyond sex, race and disability to sexual orientation, religion or belief, and age. The growth and range of anti-discrimination law led to the three equality commissions – the Commission for Racial Equality (CRE), the Disability Rights Commission (DRC) and the Equal Opportunities Commission (EOC) – merging into the new Equality and Human Rights Commission from 1 October 2007. Potentially the most far reaching of the new anti-discrimination laws on employment practice are the Equality Age Regulations of October 2006. These make discrimination against any employee on the basis of their age unlawful. The UK government's controversial decision to set the current default retirement age at 65 has been the subject of considerable debate, as is evident in Exhibit 3.1.

This default retirement age means that employers can retire employees after their 65th birthday without giving any reason and refuse to employ someone over 65 years of age, which has become the policy following the legislation in a number of organisations. Adopting such a policy does seem at odds with legislation introduced to address age discrimination, the UK's workforce demographic profile and a government commitment to widen labour force participation among older workers. Indeed a case has been brought against the UK government claiming that a mandatory retirement age is illegal under age discrimination law and this was referred to the European Court of Justice in August 2007. The majority of employers do, however, appear to be granting requests to work beyond retirement age according to the Confederation of British Industry (CBI), although it is concerned that 59 per cent of workers claim to have witnessed ageist behaviours in the workplace (Croner, 2007).

> ### Exhibit 3.1
>
> ### A default retirement age – wasting resources?
>
> Research by an offshoot of Age Concern reveals that nearly 60 per cent of people approaching retirement age want to continue working but it is up to employers and some businesses don't want to hire older workers and many refuse to hire anyone beyond the age of 65. Yet Alan Beazley of the Employers Forum on Age says that a mandatory retirement age is irrelevant in an era of longer life expectancy and better health and prevents companies from using a valuable resource pool. Graham White, HR Director of HR at Westminster Council, agrees that there is no reason to keep the mandatory retirement age calling it a ridiculous piece of legislation. Meanwhile Richard Port, a partner at law firm Clarion Solicitors, sounds a note of caution. He explains the practical implications of keeping staff on, particularly in relation to pension and employee benefits, insurance premiums and health screening. But the overall message is why force a skilled and willing employee to leave their job when they reach an arbitrary birthday.
>
> *Source*: Editorial comment, *Employers' Law*, June 2008: 3

An emergent and challenging area of legislation for HR practice and policy is employee rights to privacy at work in the light of new laws on data protection, investigatory powers and the Human Rights Act 1998. From October 2000, UK employers, courts and tribunals have had to take into account the provisions of the Human Rights Act. The full implications of the Act for HR policies are taking time to assess but it has had an impact on employment practices such as workplace monitoring and surveillance practices.

A more litigious workforce?

Not only has the UK experienced a growth in 'regulatory law' but employment tribunal (ET) statistics over the past decade suggest individuals are more likely to resort to the law to resolve work-based disputes and grievances. Whereas in 1990 ACAS received a total of 52,071 cases for individual conciliation with 26 per cent of these proceeding to tribunal, this case load had increased by 2007 to 132,577 cases although the proportion of cases proceeding to an employment tribunal had remained virtually unchanged at 25 per cent. A frequent complaint from employers about the tribunal process is the cost to business. The average tribunal case is currently estimated to cost an employer £9,000 to defend and to take up some 9.85 days of the business's time (Gibbons, 2007: 4). But this growth in ET claims needs to be viewed in a wider context. Although the total number of dismissals in the UK each year has almost certainly risen from a workforce of just over 29 million, the total number of claims each year is still less than 1 for every 200 workers, or just 0.4 per cent of the working population. By way of contrast, in Germany around 1.5 per cent of the working population submitted an employment claim in 2002 while in France the figure was 0.7 per cent (Gibbons, 2007: 15).

Whilst it is worth noting that the percentage of claims actually proceeding to tribunal has not changed significantly (ACAS, 1991, 2007), the sheer number of cases has caused consternation among government and employers. One interpretation of these statistics is that individuals are becoming more litigious but the escalating number of tribunal claims may well be better explained by the increase in jurisdictions that can now be considered by Employment Tribunals compared to 20 years ago. These more than doubled in the years between 1981 and 2001 and ETs now deal with more than 70 jurisdictions which provide a more likely explanation for the increase in tribunal cases than the suggestion of a US-style 'compensation culture' being imported to the UK. On closer examination, there is little direct evidence of an increased individual propensity to litigate. Hepple and Morris (2002) suggest that published research evidence suggests several underlying reasons for the rise in tribunal applications associated with the introduction of new statutory rights, for example the growing rate of female workforce participation and the lack of formal procedures in small firms.

In common with several other European countries, the UK government is trying to limit the cost of this expansion in individual rights and stem the seemingly 'irreversible demand for their enforcement' (Hepple and Morris, 2002: 245). The aim of the statutory procedures introduced by the 2002 Employment Act was to place the emphasis on employers and employees establishing and exhausting internal organisational dispute resolution procedures before referring issues to a tribunal. Although the statutory provisions were widely criticised at the time, it was estimated that the improvement in 'management controlled' workplace procedures would reduce costs by cutting employment tribunal claims by up to an estimated 31 per cent a year. In practice this has not been the case and the provisions were identified in the Gibbons Review of workplace dispute resolution as an impediment to early resolution and as having increased the likelihood of premature legal intervention in employment relationships (Renton, 2008).

What does appear to have happened is that tribunal statistics have grown as internal collective bargaining has declined in importance. Dickens, presenting the 2008 Warwick/ACAS Lowry lecture, pointed to the fact that over 50 per cent of claims to the Employment Tribunal Service are multi-claimant cases as evidence of essentially collective concerns coming to tribunals in the guise of individual cases. Nowhere is this more apparent than in the number of equal pay claims stemming from job evaluation in local government discussed in Chapter 8.

Other attempts to reduce legal claims can be found in the move towards relying on what is sometimes termed 'soft regulation' over legislation. This is where there are no formal sanctions for non-compliance but instead a reliance on the provision of a framework or a code of practice to inform and guide the development of employment policies and practice. One such example was the Telework agreement signed by the European social partners in July 2002 which is implemented voluntarily by member states; an approach which constituted a departure from previous developments in EU employment law which have had to be enacted domestically through binding Council directives. The 2007 Arbitration, Conciliation and Advisory Service report (ACAS, 2007: 15) confirms that a key aim of ACAS's work is 'to enhance the awareness and take-up of dispute resolution and conflict management techniques in the workplace'. Yet the ACAS arbitral alternative scheme introduced in 2001 to offer a more informal, non-legalistic and speedier alternative to having a complaint of unfair dismissal heard by an employment tribunal has had very little take up, possibly partly explained by a lack of understanding of the potential benefits to the parties of a less adversarial and costly approach to dispute resolution. Following pilot mediation schemes for smaller businesses, ACAS has developed and expanded the mediation services it offers over the past few years which have included accredited mediation training. There has been a healthy growth in the cases it deals with and a good success rate: its prime objective being to promote internal workplace mediation by training individuals to handle internal disputes.

In the light of the recommendations of the Gibbons Report for additional support for workplace mediation and the emphasis on workplace resolution in the 2007 Employment Bill, it will be interesting to see whether this leads to an organisational focus on developing internal mediation skills. Research under-taken for ACAS (Harris *et al.*, 2008) on dispute resolution in SMEs suggests that in the smaller business context an independent third party is frequently likely to be more acceptable than an internal mediator because of the close working relationships that characterise small business. The same research identified a lack of awareness of what mediation involved or the other options for alternative dispute resolution in the workplace. The findings also suggest the likelihood of a strong adherence to the present organisational emphasis on ensuring a well documented defence is in place as being less risky for employers unless there is a significant investment in building up employers' and employees' awareness of the positive benefits for both parties in adopting alternative means of dispute resolution than seeking legal remedy through the tribunal system.

In addition to these general developments, there have been some specific new laws which have impacted on employment practices. These have included, from July 2007, a smoking ban in all workplaces and new rules on the employment of migrant workers. At the time of writing there are proposals in a new Equality Bill for mandatory pay audits and positive discrimination which have already led to considerable criticism, not least on the grounds that these will create a recruitment and discrimination minefield for employers (Quinn, 2008: 9).

Organisational responses

The expansion of employment rights in the UK has re-addressed the balance of power between employer and employee. After a period in which the employment deal was more strongly weighted against the employee (Herriot and Pemberton, 1995a), an immediate interpretation of this growth in regulation is that it provides a means of restoring greater humanity in the relationship between employer and employee. It potentially creates opportunities to revisit and apply what Edwards (1979) describes as 'enlightened managerialism' through the development and enforcement of good practice across the range of human resourcing activities.

A growth in employment regulation can act as a catalyst for more proactive personnel policies. Two-thirds of employers in a CIPD survey (CIPD/Lovells, 2005) found employers identifying employment law as a driver of good practice and one that carried significant weight in their organisations. Family friendly legislation and the right to request flexible work is seen by government as having successfully supported the work-life balance.

Exhibit 3.2

Is the work-life balance battle won?

According to the government, more than 14 million employees, including part-time workers, work flexibly. Over 90 per cent of workplaces that received requests to work flexibly approved them all. Around six million employees – parents with children under 6 or with disabled children under 18 and carers of certain adults – currently have the right to request flexible working. The government recently announced plans to extend this right to all parents with children under the age of 16 which will open it to a further 4.5 million parents. . . . The survey evidence suggests that flexible working arrangements are becoming more popular. The Department for Business, Enterprise and Regulatory Reform's Third Work-Life Balance Employer Survey revealed that 95 per cent of workplaces in 2007 offered some form of flexible working. It also recorded sharp increases in arrangements such as compressed and reduced hours of working between 2003 and 2007. Some organisations that formed to push for change now think that their argument is all but won. For example the Work/Life Balance Trust disbanded on the eve of the 2005 General Election. Shirley Conran, the President of the Trust, said that the decision had been taken because it had 'accomplished what it had set out to do. Most people in Britain now know what work-life balance means: everyone knows whether they've got it or not: everybody wants it.'

Source: *Work-Life Balance*, IDS Study 873, p. 11, July 2008

Activity 3.3   Work-life balance and family friendly legislation

1. Based on your own organisational observation and personal experiences, do you feel the work-life balance battle has been won?

2. If not, why do you think this is the case?

3. To what extent do you think maternity leave and parents' rights are 'sabotaging women's careers' as suggested by the Chief Executive of the Equality and Human Rights Commission (*The Times*, 14 July 2008)?

4. What are the arguments for and against legislation supporting a more equal sharing of parental leave between men and women in the UK?

The new flexible working laws do present fresh challenges and potential pitfalls for employers in terms of developing consistent but constructive approaches to employment relationships and will take up increasing amounts of managerial time as these are expanded. There are inherent tensions and conflicts between the imperatives of the market, external levels of regulation, organisational demands for the control of employees and the needs of individuals at work (Keenoy, 1990) which can be at their most acute in the small businesses and the service sector (Harris and Foster, 2005). The balance is a delicate one which can alter quite quickly whenever the level of influence of these recognised regulators of the employment relationship changes. While a favourable economic climate prevails, one outcome of a combination of more legislation and skills shortages is a reduced emphasis on organisational control and autonomy. Another is that capital–labour substitution through increasing automation becomes more attractive and cost effective when labour costs rise, due to a growth in law and litigation (Hammermesh, 1987). Such a situation is presenting problems for the Gourmet Division of Moddens Foods in the light of the agreement reached in 2008 between the UK government, employers and trade unions on the rights of agency workers in advance of any agreement being reached among EU member states over the Agency Workers Directive.

Case Study 3.2

Temporary workers at Moddens' Gourmet Division

The Gourmet Division has been performing very well indeed and has become an independent trading company with a strong brand image for hand-finished high-quality products. It is renowned for its personalised seasonal hampers at Christmas time, which are particularly popular as corporate gifts. These hampers have become one of the best-selling lines of the business but are currently available only to customers in the UK and mainland Europe. The plan is to develop the overseas market to countries outside mainland Europe. This will mean increasing the number of temporary staff the company takes on each year to help with the seasonal increase in orders for a period of four months from September to the end of December each year.

The company prides itself on the individuality of the hampers and its ability to meet customers' specific requirements. These have been a major factor in its success and there is a heavy reliance on local, predominantly female, workers keen to earn extra income before Christmas returning year after year to work for four months. They have become a very loyal and committed team who are very familiar with the company's requirements and the work involved but Jean Frear, the HR director, is concerned that this mutually beneficial arrangement may not be able to continue. She has just learnt that in future after 12 weeks' employment, temporary and agency workers will be entitled to the same pay as permanent workers. This will increase the costs of Gourmet Foods' hampers and these will have to be passed on to the customers. Jean Frear's particular concern is that temporary staff will also have an entitlement to the Christmas bonus that the permanent staff receive annually based on the company's performance. This has been sizeable in recent years.

At the next board meeting the expansion in new overseas markets is under discussion and Jean mentions that temporary/agency workers will have to receive the same pay as permanent staff. She is taken aback by the heated response of the managing director who seems to feel she has personally elected to sabotage Gourmet's expansion plans. He actually accuses HR of 'always putting a spanner in the works'. Banging on the table, he shouts at Jean: 'How on earth are we expected to run a business let alone expand it?' and 'Why have you only just told us about these new rules?' and 'We will just have to employ migrant workers on two-month contracts'.

> **Activity 3.4   Temporary workers at Moddens' Gourmet Division**
>
> 1. In the light of the new rights for temporary and agency workers:
>   a. consider what the different human resourcing options are for the Gourmet Division
>   b. identify the advantages and disadvantages of the different options in terms of growing the business and maintaining the desired quality standards.
> 2. How can the responsibility for ensuring that employment regulation is complied with shape the nature of the HR function's contribution to the business?
> 3. What does this situation tell us about the tensions inherent in the HR specialist's organisational role?

While it is important not to overstate the impact of litigation on individual organisational experiences (Kersley *et al.*, 2006), the expansion of employment rights has meant that UK employers, regardless of employment sector, are having to review and amend their existing HR policies and practices. The author's own research (Harris, 2001b, 2002b) conducted in two highly contrasting employment sectors of local government and small business, revealed there were a number of common responses to an increasingly regulated employment relationship. Figure 3.1 identifies the key responses which were identified from the perspective of line managers and HR specialists.

Increasing regulation does present particular challenges for smaller businesses who are disproportionately represented in the employment tribunal statistics (Edwards *et al.*, 2003). In the absence of internal HR expertise, they are more dependent on external sources for legal advice, and lose more cases owing to procedural inadequacies and a lack of managerial capability in dealing with employee

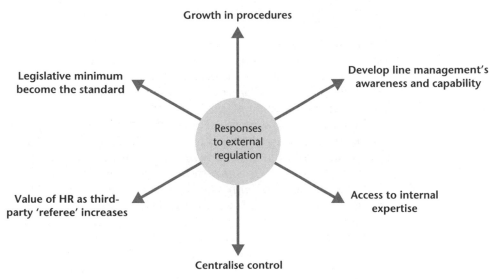

Figure 3.1 **Responses to regulation**

relations issues (Goodman *et al.*, 1998). An evaluation of the DTI's HR pilots in small firms (Emmott and Harris, 2004) revealed an SME propensity to seek advice from lawyers as a crisis measure when a specific problem arose. This raises questions about the internal capability of smaller businesses to develop proactive HR practices that not only comply with but also reflect the spirit of the law.

Internal expertise

The relationship between levels of regulation and the HR function's organisational role goes to the heart of some of the tensions and ambiguity long identified as inherent in professional personnel management. Bach (2005: 33) points to the growth of legal regulation as a dominant feature of HR practitioners' working lives and for the HR function, claiming it as a source of expertise as one rationale for the development of the occupation as a distinctive specialism (Legge, 2005). It helps to address a difficulty long associated with personnel work (Watson, 1977), namely identifying its particular organisational contribution.

To understand the influence employment law has had on the HR specialist's role, we need to trace briefly the function's development over the past 50 years. During the initial post-war period of full employment its organisational purpose was described by the then Institute of Personnel Management (IPM) in 1963 as one of administering and internally regulating the employment contract. This implies a dual responsibility (potentially conflicting) of achieving both efficiency and justice. In the workplace climate of the 1960s and 70s, its expertise was seen to lie in industrial relations. In practice, any ideal of professional neutrality appeared increasingly compromised by the need to represent the organisational position and prevent industrial disruption.

Despite initiatives to 'professionalise' the function, it was still difficult to identify a specialism that distinguished the occupation from other managerial groups until the significant expansion of labour law in the mid-1970s. A knowledge of the new legislation potentially offered to the personnel function a source of influence and a power-base more self-evident and transparent than anything that had gone before (Harris and Bott, 1996). It complemented the industrial relations expertise still seen as the function's key contribution. Furthermore, the new legislation was not a body of knowledge it seemed other managers actively sought to become involved in; most appeared far too daunted by its perceived complexity to become engaged in its intricacies through choice.

For the majority of larger organisations, the solution was to identify a named person with a specific responsibility for interpreting the new legal requirements in the workplace and membership of the IPM grew by 59 per cent between 1971 and 1981. The Warwick IRRU survey of 1978/79 (Brown, 1981) reported personnel specialists attributing the increase in the importance of the function over the previous five years to the growth in employment legislation.

When the rights of employees and trade unions expanded significantly in the 1970s, it led to a period Torrington and Hall (1987) describe as dominated by legal wrangling. The interpretation of collective agreements and individual contracts could readily subsume a personnel practitioner's working week. The need for fire-fighting skills and the ability to agree a 'quick fix' to keep production or services going were the order of the day. It resulted in the function having an operational responsibility unconnected with strategic management and undertaking a 'game keeper role where the prime function is to keep threats at bay' (Purcell, 1995: 78). This led to the view that, as the identified 'industrial relations experts' (Legge, 1988) corporate personnel departments had become overly controlling bureaucracies, resulting in the removal of ownership of the conduct of the employment relationship from the line manager (Millward and Stevens, 1986). The theory was that moving 'day-to-day' personnel responsibilities to line management would provide the opportunity for the HR function to make a strategic and specialist contribution.

In practice the HR function experiences a double bind in its responsibilities for ensuring legal compliance (Watson, 1986; Legge, 2005) which has been exacerbated by the ongoing trend to devolve HR responsibilities to line management (Kersley et al., 2006). If line managers only pass those employment issues with complex legal implications which they are unable to resolve on to HR practitioners then, as the 'acclaimed specialists', they will constantly be faced with the most problematic situations to resolve and run the risk of being scapegoated when there are no quick or acceptable solutions. This is particularly the case where earlier actions taken by line managers may have made the issues more difficult to resolve because of procedural lapses. One response of the HR function to increased devolvement is to place a stronger emphasis on compliance with centralised organisational rules and procedures to avoid inconsistencies in decision-making and unequal outcomes for employees. As a result, other managerial groups may well see the function as undertaking an essentially negative role owing to its perceived preoccupation with regulation and the compliance element of its role. The result is a focus that is heightened for the specialist function by the present emphasis on measuring performance outcomes, evaluating the contribution of different services and the growing trend towards outsourcing and centralising HR into shared services (Reilly and Tamkin, 2007).

Increasing line management's responsibilities

The political, economic and industrial relations climate of the 1980s lent further support to organisational initiatives to return responsibility for the conduct of the employment relationship to line management. These were reinforced by the concept of 'human resource management' as an alternative approach to the employment relationship compared to traditional personnel management; the shift of responsibilities for the employment relationship to line managers being identified as one of its defining characteristics (Guest, 1987). The reallocation of HR responsibilities to the operational manager was assisted by the erosion of legal protection and a reduction in workplace bargaining in the UK. This has provided greater scope for the exercise of managerial prerogative (Dickens et al., 1995) and emphasised the vital role line managers play in carrying out activities that Hutchinson and Purcell (2003: 6) describe as 'the bread and butter of the personnel and HR department'. By the second half of the 1980s line managers reported spending more of their time on personnel activities (Millward and Stevens, 1992), and by 1998 the Workplace Industrial Relations Surveys found that their portfolio of employee relations responsibilities had significantly widened (Millward et al., 2000); this has been a continuing trend reported in the 2004 WERS Survey.

The raft of new individual and collective employment rights was predicted by Sisson (1999) not only to change approaches to employment relations in the UK but also to reduce the scope for managerial discretion to agree individual solutions. This is particularly likely to be the case where there is new law and it has encouraged an increasing emphasis by the HR function on developing centralised HR policies to support a consistency of approach (Harris, 2008). Increased regulation is a likely constraint on the extent of devolution of HR responsibilities seen as advisable by both the HR specialist and line manager. Hope-Hailey *et al.* (1997) found a reluctance among line managers to take on personnel responsibilities in the light of their increasing legal complexity. Hard-pressed managers challenged the wisdom of expanding their responsibilities in an area where they lacked both specialist knowledge and the time to devote to issues seen as 'too hot to handle'.

Increased proceduralisation

The expansion of employment law and workplace litigation intensifies pressures on employers to demonstrate consistency and procedural fairness in their human resourcing policies and practices. It can lead to the specialist HR function concentrating its efforts on the consistent application of the rule book as the most tangible means of achieving demonstrable fairness in managerial decision-making (Legge, 2005). The devolvement of HR responsibilities to line managers is then accompanied by an increase in corporate procedures which they are expected to apply in a highly uniform manner (McGovern *et al.*, 1998). Where this descends to managing by 'systems control' (Watson, 2002: 382), it conflicts with any concept of empowerment through a developmental approach to employment management.

The emphasis on systematic employment processes also leads to the familiar criticisms from other managers about the bureaucracy, inflexibility and lack of appreciation from HR staff of operational issues, as experienced by Jean Frear at the Gourmet Division. Increased regulation brings to the fore the ambivalent attitudes many managers have towards formalised employment policies and procedures. Greater freedoms to exercise discretion in HR decisions may, in theory, be the preferred approach of many managers but, in reality, when faced with the possibility of a personal decision leading to litigation, well-developed rules become more attractive. The prospect of their individual judgement and behaviours being closely scrutinised can be a daunting prospect to managers, particularly for the less experienced (Sheppard *et al.*, 1992; Harris, 2008).

As the pressures mount for the specialist function to demonstrate its organisational contribution, the avoidance of litigation can provide a very tangible form of measurement. If this becomes the dominant measurement it is likely to have negative consequences by reinforcing a compliance and penalty avoidance approach to employment relations (Dickens, 2000) at the cost of more strategic developmental activities. Where the devolution of HR responsibilities to managers has been accompanied by staff reduction in the specialist function there may well be a lack of resources to do more than initiate procedures. More positively, it can encourage the growth of clear policies for managers to implement but these need to be accompanied by a proper understanding of their purpose and the supporting managerial behaviours.

Case Study 3.3

Handling long-term illness

Peter Wren was a driver for a transport company with 28 years' service. Mr Wren lost his licence for a 12-month period after suffering a stroke but unfortunately suffered another stroke during this period which meant he was unable to return to work as a driver. Under his terms and conditions of employment he qualified for an enhanced ill health retirement if he was permanently incapable of performing his duties. The manager, Jim Eyatt, was in charge of the section where Peter Wren worked and made all the decisions relating to employment issues although he had not received any training on employment law or in the company's different procedures. He had also never had a long-term health issue to deal with. Most of the others drivers were young. There was some turnover in the section due to buoyant labour market conditions for drivers in the area although the company was regarded as a good employer. After a period of nine months Mr Eyatt found he had no alternative but to find a replacement driver for Mr Wren although his latest medical certificate was for a period of three months. When this certificate expired Mr Wren applied for ill health retirement. Mr Eyatt came to the conclusion that Mr Wren was not permanently incapable as required under the ill health retirement scheme but that he was unable to return to his job as a driver so he should be dismissed on the grounds of capability. The decision to dismiss him was communicated by letter to Mr Wren who at no point met with this manager to discuss his situation, nor was medical advice sought about his condition. Informed by the manager's judgement in the matter, the company turned down Mr Wren's application for ill health retirement. Mr Wren decided to take his case to a tribunal who found that he had been unfairly dismissed.

Activity 3.5   Handling long-term illness

1. Identify the reasons why you feel the tribunal would have decided this dismissal was unfair.
2. What should have taken place in this situation to ensure Mr Wren was fairly treated and to avoid the case going to a tribunal?
3. What are the key learning points for good organisational practice that emerge from this case?

Developing line management capability

As illustrated by the case of Peter Wren, managers all too often receive insufficient training to handle the legal implications of the employment matters they have to deal with although such training needs to be handled with care (Harris *et al.*, 2002). The danger is that procedures are passed on to line managers for implementation with plenty of 'health warnings' about the legal considerations but with inadequate advice on how to actually respond when faced with a diversity of employment issues. Where training is heavily orientated towards ensuring procedural compliance and stressing the potential costs of getting it wrong, it can lead to managers, already hesitant about their HR responsibilities, abdicating their involvement by referring problems back to the 'experts' in personnel (Cunningham and Hyman, 1999; Whittaker and Marchington, 2003). It requires an approach to development that does more than just raise line managers' awareness of what must be avoided. To have the desired effect, training and development must strengthen the real capability of operational managers by deepening their understanding to improve their knowledge and the consistency of their HR decision-making. One organisation's approach to developing such consistency is outlined in the following exhibit.

Exhibit 3.3

Consistency and training pays

The fact that Sharon Benson, heralded as HR director of the year in the 2007 Personnel Today awards, has never experienced any tribunal proceedings during her 11-year career in HR speaks for itself. Benson who joined pharmaceutical company Trinity-Chiesi three years ago says 'the majority of grievances are usually raised by employees who are unhappy with the way they are managed by their line manager'. She argues that you can have the most robust policies but if they are not flowing through correctly and consistently employers are at risk of being led down the tribunal path. At Trinity-Chiesi, managers attend a rigorous induction course where they are taken through all the policies and procedures and then issued with 'manager guides' on how to implement them. Every 18 months all managers attend a three-day legal training course or a shorter refresher course to keep up with employment law. The company has also just launched a coaching master-class where role plays are carried out so that managers learn how to steer away from the legal pitfalls. . . . Her advice is to adopt policies that suit the company culture. 'It is all about consistency', says Benson, 'Objectives and expectations can be made crystal clear though policies and managers need to follow them in a way that its consistent across the business to eradicate any ambiguity, so that everyone knows where they stand, helping to eliminate the risk of tribunal'.

Source: 'Avoiding Tribunal Trouble', Natalie Cooper, *Employers' Law*, February 2008: 12–13

Despite line managers' increased HR responsibilities, there is frequently a shared belief among line managers and HR specialists of the value of the HR function acting as a third-party arbiter of workplace fairness as a means of monitoring consistency in decision-making (Renwick, 2003; Harris, 2002a). This is particularly the case in the handling of disciplinary and grievance procedures where the presence of other parties, such as an employee representative and an HR specialist, is important as a means of demonstrating fair procedure and the transparency of decision-making.

Regulation and the employment relationship

The ability to demonstrate fairness in employment procedures has grown in organisational importance not only in terms of avoiding 'rule violation' (Bierhoff *et al.*, 1986) but also because of its influence on the likelihood of an individual claiming unfair treatment. The organisational rationale for focusing on the development of strong procedures and ensuring a clear document trail appears well justified. In the context of legal dispute resolution, control over the process is identified as a key determinant of procedural justice (Thibaut and Walker, 1975: 78) as well as the essential means of employers proving the 'reasonableness' of their decision-making. It is an approach supported by research that suggests that violating dimensions of procedural justice can have a greater impact on feelings of fairness than the justice of final outcomes (McFarlin and Sweeney, 1992). Put another way, fair procedure can result in an individual perceiving a decision as just even when there has been an unfavourable personal result, but there are other important dimensions of perceived fairness to consider (Folger and Cropanzano, 2000).

Concentrating on procedures can be at the cost of investing in the quality of interpersonal relationships which are just as, or arguably more, important in creating positive employment relationships in the longer term. Regulation and fear of litigation can result in an overly 'proceduralised' approach where HR practitioners and line managers alike place the emphasis on adhering to processes developed to demonstrate moral neutrality as a means of defending managerial decision-making. If a growth in labour law and associated litigation results in employers feeling threatened or 'under siege' it can encourage the adoption of a defensive approach to the employment relationship which descends into 'a destructive spiral of ever greater checks and controls followed by more sophisticated avoidance tactics' (Liff, 1989: 32).

Such fears are evident in concerns about a growing 'appellant culture' and a focus on the 'rules of the game' rather than the fairness of the final outcomes. Paradoxically, the very rules developed to promote equality of treatment and reduce litigation can then become the sources of discontent by creating an impression of a lack of concern for the individual in the process. As the cost of legal compliance grows, employers with limited resources are likely to concentrate on ensuring minimal compliance rather than generating solutions which might be more suited both to the needs of the organisation and to a wider range of employees. Consider the problem Chris Ewe is facing in his new role as the Head of Parks and Recreation.

Case Study 3.4

Equal treatment in practice?

Chris Ewe works for a large local authority as its Head of Parks and Recreation. He has two administrative staff, Margaret, an older woman who works full time, and Ruth, a young mother who works four days a week from Monday to Thursday from 9.30 a.m. to 3.00 p.m. to fit in with childcare. Margaret has been with the Authority for over 30 years, has a vast amount of knowledge and everyone relies on her. Ruth has just told Chris that she wants to reduce her hours to three days a week to devote more time to her children. After referring to the Council's family-friendly policy booklet, it is agreed that Ruth will now work Tuesday to Thursday each week but do an extra hour every afternoon as she can arrange for someone else to collect her children from school on those days.

Chris is taken aback when Margaret asks to see him about the new arrangements. He has never seen her so irate. 'No one gives a thought to my needs,' she tells Chris. 'I may not have young children but my elderly mother takes up more and more of my time when I am not working and I can never get a long weekend off. What if I want holiday on Fridays or Mondays, how will we manage then? I am also totally fed up with all the time Ruth spends outside the building having smoking breaks. I know smoking is banned in the offices and I fully support the "no smoking" policy but what about my non-smoking breaks? I am always manning the phones with never a minute to myself and I am not getting any younger you know. What about a bit more real equality around here and proper recognition for those people who really put in the hours and hard work? I am half minded to put in a grievance about the extra cover I am expected to provide without any recognition or extra pay.'

Without waiting for a reply, Margaret then rushed out of the office on the verge of tears, leaving Chris wondering just what had gone wrong and what could be done.

Activity 3.6   Equal treatment in practice?

1. What issues do the problems Chris Ewe is experiencing with Margaret raise?

2. Identify how Chris could have approached these for a better outcome?

3. How could some of the issues you have identified in your answer to question 1 be addressed through organisational policies?

4. What are the implications of any further development of family friendly rights for consistency and fairness in managing employment relationships?

5. How should employers approach the issue of competing needs of employees, for example childcare versus caring for an elderly relative, whilst meeting the needs of the business?

On of the difficulties illustrated by this case study is that benefits offered to one group may adversely impact on another, leading to feelings of inequitable treatment. One organisation which has tried to create a more level playing field of entitlements for all staff to avoid the potential for unfairness is ASDA.

Exhibit 3.4

Flexible working at ASDA

ASDA, the supermarket giant, is pioneering a flexible working scheme and hopes to encourage all of its 165,000 UK staff to take advantage of it. ASDA Flex features six flexible working options including an unpaid 3-year career break and up to 12 weeks' paid leave for staff who wish to make an organ donation. The six categories are

1. Shift swap
2. Me time
3. My lifestyle
4. Family first
5. Career break
6. My health.

Colleague relations manager Chris Stone explains: 'We've always prided ourselves on being ahead of employment law and I hope this programme reflects that. We already had a number of flexible working schemes available but we wanted to simplify and broaden them. . . . The new scheme has broken down any barriers that may have existed between different staff groups. Although it has only been a few months since the scheme was introduced, the response has been encouraging. The feedback has been amazing and store managers have been really pleased with the response.'

Source: Fuller, G., *Employers' Law*, July/August 2008: 19

Conclusion

The challenge for the architects of HR policies is how to develop systems that are sufficiently robust in terms of demonstrating procedural fairness and objectivity to withstand potential litigation but that are also sufficiently flexible to accommodate other important factors conducive to positive employment relationships. A judicial orientation in resolving issues in the employment relationship has encouraged an emphasis on demonstrating impartiality with less attention to the role of feelings and emotion in the employment relationship. Winstanley and Woodall (2000: 19) suggest that this is an approach reinforced in human resource management by the concentration on the 'resources' aspect to the detriment of the 'human' and that greater attention to an 'ethics of care' agenda would help to address this imbalance. The dilemma is that increased employment rights are likely to lead to the avoidance of potential legal claims being valued more highly by HR specialists, line managers, senior managers and owner/managers than taking the risk of a more individualistic approach, particularly if it could erode a defence of equal treatment.

Edwards (2007) argues for a new public policy initiative for workplace justice. He points to the impact of increased statutory rights having, in practice, resulted in a widespread approach to the employment relationship based on minimum standards and a preoccupation with procedural compliance rather than exploring the mutual benefits for employers and employees. The experience of employment regulation on human resourcing strategies to date contains two essential messages for approaches to the employment relationship. Firstly, the importance of developing processes which not only meet legal requirements of procedural justice and equality of treatment but also allow for sensitive personal interactions which take account of individual need. Secondly, that management behaviours in the application and interpretation of organisational rules are the most significant factor on individual perceptions of fair treatment (Hutchinson and Purcell, 2003); a major consideration which needs be reflected in any training and development interventions. For the majority of employees, evidence of an empathetic management responsive to their individual needs could lead to a greater tolerance when mistakes do occur. The likelihood of individuals seeking redress for alleged injustices through legal claims could reduce if it is perceived that there are genuine internal attempts at the level of the individual manager/supervisor to address their personal concerns.

A growth in employment rights does provide opportunities for the development of more innovative solutions to the resolution of individual grievances and problems. A positive perspective is that, as the personal and financial costs associated with litigation increase, there will be a greater recognition of the benefits to both employer and employees of resolving their differences internally. This would require line managers and HR specialists to develop and hone their skills of conciliation, mediation and arbitration, which could lead to a greater sensitivity to individual feelings of fairness within the workplace. A more negative perspective is that increased legislation and litigation is already 'tipping the balance' in favour of concentrating on processes designed to demonstrate procedural justice at the potential cost of developing a more individualistic and 'caring' approach to employment relationships.

There still remains the fundamental question of whether the courts are the best place to resolve issues of the legitimacy of workplace practice or whether it would be more beneficial for working relationships to place more emphasis on seeking out alternative forms of dispute resolution of a less adversarial nature. Commenting on the case for a Workplace Commission, Mike Emmott (2008: 5), Employee Relations Adviser for the CIPD, acknowledges the growing government recognition that the scope for reducing the impact of employment regulation on employers is limited and argues that a different approach is needed if employment law is to be seen as something other than a burden on their activities. Certainly, the present level of external regulation of the employment relationship suggests that the pendulum has swung in the opposite direction since Lord Wedderburn's observations (1986) about the preference of British workers for minimal legal intervention in workplace dispute resolution.

It remains to be seen whether an ever-expanding volume of legislation and litigation in the UK workplace will encourage a return to seeking internal organisational remedies on the grounds that these are more likely to create trust and confidence in employment relationships than the pursuit of external legal redress.

Summary

In this chapter the following key points have been made:

- The degree of legislation regulating the employment relationship is heavily influenced by the prevailing political, economic and social factors and is a significant factor in the development of human resourcing strategies.
- Employment law is a major factor in the focus of the specialist HR function's activities, the nature of its relationship with line management and the degree of devolution of HR responsibilities to line managers.

- Despite the increasing HR responsibilities of line managers, HR specialists are still essentially regarded as the 'guardians of the rule book' who act rather as 'general practitioners' (Torrington, 1989: 65) responsible for an initial diagnosis when it comes to the provision of legal services on employment issues.

- Increasing external regulation of the employment relationship may place significant constraints on the ability of managers to exercise strategic choice in their human resourcing decisions and raises new challenges for the development of management HR expertise.

- Legislation can lead to a preoccupation with formal procedures as a demonstrable organisational defence against litigation resulting in a perceived depersonalising of the employment relationship at the level of the individual. This can actually work against the delivery of organisational justice and mutual benefits for both employers and employees.

- Employment law provides a valuable specialism and a potential source of influence for the specialist HR function but it has its disadvantages. It can create or reinforce negative perceptions about the nature of its organisational contribution.

- Increased employment rights provide opportunities for greater innovation in the development and application of human resourcing policies and practice but can also reinforce the adoption of a minimal compliance approach rather than developing practices more tailored to the needs of an organisation and the people who work in it.

- As litigation grows, largely due to expanded employment rights, so will the seeking out of new ways of dispute resolution that are less costly and more organisationally focused.

Discussion questions

1. Select any piece of employment legislation to investigate further. Having done so, consider how it has impacted on HR policy and working arrangements in any organisation you are familiar with.

2. Having read this chapter and reflected on your own experiences, to what extent do you feel greater regulation of employment practices is leading to increased workplace fairness?

3. What is the likely impact of increasing employment regulation on the devolvement of HR responsibilities to line management and the services provided by the specialist HR function?

Further reading

Further reading relating to the content of this chapter is provided in the text and readers can follow up the citations on particular aspects of the discussion. A text that considers the legal regulation of the employment relationship in considerable depth is by Hugh Collins (2003). A general text which provides a particularly useful introduction to the subject for non-lawyers and explores the major debates about employment law is by Stephen Taylor and Astra Emir (2006).

4

Ethics and strategic human resourcing

Diannah Lowry

Learning outcomes

Having read this chapter and completed its associated activities, readers should be able to:

● Understand that ethical issues are a fundamental yet complex aspect of strategic human resourcing

● Recognise ethical issues underlying strategic human resourcing activities, and identify potential ethical implications of both low commitment and high commitment HR strategies

● Understand a number of normative and descriptive ethical theories and be able to analyse the activities of strategic human resourcing against the backdrop of such theories

● Appreciate that HR managers and HR practitioners have a range of options with regard to the ethical stance they may (or may not) adopt

● Understand that management decisions concerning ethical issues do not just affect organisations, they also have potential wider societal implications

Introduction

Activities associated with strategic human resourcing have an inherent tension associated with the often mismatched goals of the organisation and the diverse needs and concerns of workers. In simple terms, the instrumental activities and priorities of the global marketplace tend to retard a serious and practical consideration of what is 'human' about strategic human resourcing. This chapter explores some of the ethical issues that underpin much of the activity associated with strategic human resourcing. With the focus on the *human* aspect of strategic human resourcing, it is emphasised throughout the chapter that workers are *social* actors with moral sentiments and commitments, embedded in relationships, networks, community, organisations and society.

A common mistake made by many business students is to assume that the organisation of work in advanced economies in the twenty-first century is without problems for vast numbers of the workforce. This is indeed an easy mistake to make from the standpoint of the comfortable position of employment that many of us may enjoy. But according to findings from the TUC's Commission on Vulnerable Employment (2008), millions of workers in Britain are subjected to intolerably poor working lives where mistreatment is the norm and where workers are trapped in low-paid and insecure work, facing daily exploitation from employers; overall findings which led the Commissioners to state: 'We take an unashamed *moral* stand [emphasis added] in urging people to challenge various types of (vulnerable) employment' (CoVE, 2008: 8).

But what does it mean to adopt a moral stand in the context of how work is organised or to investigate work from an ethical standpoint? The subject of ethics and morals is potentially complex, and when analysed within the context of 'work' or 'business', and more specifically here within the context of 'strategic human resourcing', the complexities can appear magnified. Some theorists use the metaphor of a moral maze to illustrate the nature of the journey that we take when we enter the realm of ethics (see, for example, Jackall, 1988; Ackers, 2001). This chapter will navigate around the maze and, consistent with the underlying framework of strategic human resourcing throughout this text, the emphasis here is on presenting each turn of the maze as a type of negotiated choice.

In order to enter the maze you need some understanding of why a consideration of ethics is important within the context of strategic human resourcing. Moreover, before considering the issue of ethics and strategic human resourcing, it may help to explore what is meant by the terms 'ethics', 'morals' and 'values'. The words 'ethics' and 'morals' have similar etymological roots – 'ethics' has its origins in ancient Greek in the word *ethikos* meaning the authority of custom and tradition, while 'morals' is derived from the Latin word *mos*, which also refers to authority associated with tradition and custom. In this chapter, the terms are used interchangeably, although some theorists do ascribe different meanings to the terms (interested readers should refer to Crane and Matten, 2007).

In addition, what do we mean when we talk of ethical and moral concerns? Grace and Cohen (2000) consider that there are four points to be considered in trying to describe what ethics 'is'. First, they suggest that thinking ethically requires us to go beyond our self-interest alone in the decisions we make. Moral (ethical) opinions then are not based on the promotion of self-interest alone – they are impartial. Second, an ethical or moral judgement can be 'universalised' (Grace and Cohen, 2000: 4). It is a judgement that can apply to everyone in similar situations, not just to one's self. Third, ethical perspectives must be able to be defended with reasons. In this way ethical views are distinct from mere biases and preferences that have no ultimate 'reason' (e.g. I don't have a reason for liking lemon sorbet better than raspberry sorbet; I simply prefer the taste of lemon sorbet). Finally, ethical opinions are not only of academic or theoretical interest, rather they are essentially 'action-guiding' and thus centrally concerned with behaviour. Ethical perspectives and philosophies provide the means to describe, evaluate and prescribe human behaviour. To some extent, this requires that we examine the consequences of actions taken.

How then do ethics and values differ? We can see from the four points raised above that ethics (and moral considerations) are likely to be 'drawn from the books and debates in which philosophical theories about right and wrong are proposed and tested' (Fisher and Lovell, 2003: 16). This is somewhat distinct from the notion of 'values', which are informally and socially acquired. Nevertheless, there are areas of overlap between values and ethics:

> The processes through which values are formed, adopted or modified within groups and societies may be influenced by debates between philosophers. Equally the rational discourses of ethics may be swayed by the emotional undertow beneath the participants' arguments. Within a group of philosophers social learning, conforming to the group's norms, may be more emotionally comfortable than challenging it. Conversely, critical study and the reading of books may challenge the values people have acquired through life.
>
> (Fisher and Lovell, 2003: 16)

Thus, while values are socially acquired rather than studied, they can both impact on, and be informed by, ethical and moral views.

A fundamental premise of this book is that 'human resources' can be seen as human 'capacities' necessary for task performance and sustainable organisation. It follows from this that how well or badly employees are treated will make a significant difference to the release of such human capacities. Chapter 1 established that the main relationship between employees and employers is one of exchange, both economic and social. This notion of exchange is crucial – workers' perceptions of fair treatment significantly impacts on the quality of work and the commitment they are likely to 'release'. Additionally, other constituencies such as the state or the communication media are also likely to monitor (inadvertently or otherwise) the treatment of workers. Cases where workers are viewed as being treated 'badly' may result in 'informal' (and initially 'invisible') action such as customers and clients rejecting the organisation and its services or products, as well as more 'formal' (and visible) action such as legal punishment.

In simple terms, the fair and ethical treatment of workers is an important *strategic* concern, since the way employees perceive the way they are treated potentially impacts on the *long-term* concerns of an organisation. If we consider the concepts of high and low commitment HR strategies, we may initially think that ethical choices made by employers in each type of commitment strategy are likely to be different. A high commitment HR strategy suggests an orientation towards carefully considered ethical choices, while a low commitment HR strategy may be more confined to calculated and instrumental 'ethical' decisions. But is it really this simple?

Throughout this book it is argued that HR strategies are not simple automatic reactions to organisational circumstances. Rather, HR strategies emerge from political processes of debate, negotiation and argument among strategic decision-makers, and from the way that managers interpret the circumstances affecting the organisation. Figure 1.1 (p. 28) reveals that such debate and negotiation is informed by (and contributes to) the values and interests (both personal and group interests) of the strategy-makers. Included in such values and interests are inherent ethical 'positions' and different types of ethical stance. At times, there may be competing ethical positions, even within a firm pursuing a high commitment HR strategy. We can see this in the case of CityGroup, a finance company that has a strong 'commitment' culture.

Case Study 4.1

Long working hours at CityGroup

This scenario illustrates that even within a particular commitment HR strategy, in this case a high commitment HR strategy, managers will have different values reflected in different ethical positions. Robyn Hillsdon-Smythe believes that by encouraging her employees to work long work hours she is providing benefits to her employees and the organisation. She believes she is doing the 'right' thing for her employees by providing high levels of financial reward, and feels she is doing the 'right' thing for CityGroup since her employees are providing high levels of productivity. Also, by encouraging her employees to stay longer in the office she feels she is helping to ensure that competitor organisations have less access to CityGroup's valued staff, thus ensuring CityGroup's long-term survival. Laura Dunlop, however, also feels that she is doing the 'right' thing by considering issues related to the work–family balance as well as important gender issues. Both Robyn and Laura feel that their own views have long-term (strategic) implications. As a result of increased opportunity for rewards, Robyn is convinced that her future employee retention rate will be high, ensuring CityGroup's continued success. On the other hand, Laura feels that if the issue of long working hours is not addressed, over time those working the long hours may be prone to burnout and staff turnover, while morale may decrease among the numerous female employees who cannot work the long hours owing to other commitments. Laura feels that such outcomes will be detrimental to the health of CityGroup and its employees.

By now hopefully you are able to see that strategic human resourcing involves ethical considerations, and that such ethical considerations can give rise to considerable complexity for practitioners, academics and students alike. In the following sections of this chapter, as we weave our way around the foggy maze of ethics, we will address (and in a sense, embrace) this complexity. An assumption here is that we can shift our level of *ethical sensitivity* (Winstanley and Woodall, 2000: 8), in other words, our ability to reflect on strategic human resourcing to be able to identify the ethical and moral dimensions and issues associated with it. A second assumption in this chapter is that we can continually develop our *ethical reasoning* or, in other words, our 'ability to identify appropriate ethical frameworks with which to explore the ethics of those dimensions and issues' (Winstanley and Woodall, 2000: 8).

It is important to note that ethics have always been a concern of those involved in personnel and the human resources movement, although arguably the extent of this concern has gone through various phases. Early social reformers during the industrial revolution and Quaker industrialists such as Cadbury and Rowntree were the first to implement dedicated factory welfare officers. This was the genesis of the Welfare Workers' Association in 1913, which was the foundational organisation for the current Chartered Institute of Personnel and Development (CIPD). The earlier welfare focus has changed in focus over time; however, there still remains an ethical concern in HRM for the reasons discussed in the section above – 'unethical' strategic human resourcing is considered to be detrimental to the release of the human capacities so vital for organisational survival and success. This is not simply an instrumental view. The position adopted here both encompasses the view that the ethical treatment of employees is important since employees are most usefully seen as resourceful humans *in their own right*, and addresses the concern of various other constituencies who are concerned with long-term organisational survival and success.

The ethical responsibilities of HRM have come under considerable scrutiny in recent times. Some writers have attempted to unravel ethical issues in HRM by posing questions such as 'is HRM ethical?' or 'can HRM ever be ethical?' (see, for example, Legge, 1998a, 1998b). This chapter takes a different form of exploration since it rests on the notion that strategic human resourcing involves the establishing of principles and practices which facilitate the carrying out of work tasks that enable sustainable organisation. The concepts of mutuality and reciprocation thus become fundamental, as do dignity and respect. This poses a huge, although hopefully not insurmountable, challenge to strategic human resourcing, given that it is operating in (some would say *contributing to*) an environment of instrumentalism and inequality (see, for example, Francis and Keegan, 2006; Bolton and Houlihan, 2007).

This means a complete rethink of the context in which strategic human resourcing operates. Sayer (2007b) usefully adopts an approach of 'moral economy', whereby economic life is structured by peoples' rights and their responsibilities, and 'both relies upon and influences their motivations, character and moral or ethical dispositions' (Sayer, 2007b: 22). Against this backdrop, Sayer (2007a) reminds us that people are essentially needy beings, capable of flourishing or suffering. By acknowledging the essence of people as social actors with needs, it is possible to explain how organisational practices, such as strategic human resourcing, affect actors within organisations. He goes on:

> As people, employees have multiple needs and concerns which fit uneasily alongside the narrow and instrumental priorities of the organization. The need for recognition and participation on a par with others is a condition of flourishing that is in tension with the instrumental and unequal character of organizations, especially capitalist ones subject to the pressure of competition and the upheavals of market forces. Although their motivations are influenced by the characteristics of the organization for which they work, employees' concerns and interests go beyond it, and attempts to narrow these down to those which can be manipulated to suit the organization are likely to damage employee morale and well-being and be counterproductive for organizations.
>
> (Sayer, 2007b: 38)

Strategic human resourcing is not a homogenous activity – there is a wide range of principles and practices (options), as is evident in the consideration of high and low commitment strategies and the multitude of variants that exist in between these two extreme types. To examine whether or not HRM is *inherently* ethical or otherwise is therefore somewhat redundant, since it is not entirely clear what 'HRM' actually *is*. What can be explored, however, are specific aspects in terms of the principles and practices of strategic human resourcing. In this way we can explore the ethical implications of, say, a long-hours work culture, or the ethical implications of flexible labour or the flexible organisation of work, as well as ethical issues associated with training and development, performance management and reward practices. We can also explore the role of the human resource specialist, since arguably they make a significant contribution to strategic human resourcing and any associated ethical concerns.

It is not possible in a single chapter to explore the ethical issues associated with every conceivable principle and practice of strategic human resourcing. Thus, this chapter will be confined to an exploration of the ethical dimensions of the practices just mentioned, including discussion of the role of the HR specialist, as well as an examination of certain relevant ethical theories. The ordering of the ensuing sections in this chapter is somewhat unusual. A standard way of approaching ethics and strategic human resourcing is to initially discuss the various relevant ethical theories, and then proceed to analyse the ethical dimensions of 'HRM' against the backdrop of those theories. The approach taken here is slightly different – we will examine some of the ethical dimensions of strategic human resourcing, in other words some of the issues which surface as potential ethical issues in a pragmatic sense, and only *then* go on to examine the relevant ethical theories by which to analyse such issues. This is considered by the author to be a more useful way of developing our ethical *sensitivity*, before progressing to develop our powers of *ethical reasoning*.

We shall enter the 'maze' with an overview of some of the ethical dimensions of strategic human resourcing. Following on from this we'll go deeper into the maze, and explore some of the different ethical positions available to an HR manager. Finally, we'll enter the inner realm of the maze, and examine some of the relevant ethical theories or 'codes' which an HR manager would use (usually implicitly), which determines their ethical 'positionings'.

Ethical issues associated with strategic human resourcing

Against the backdrop of an ageing workforce and skill shortages, organisations are becoming aware of the need to embrace practices that will serve to attract and retain their workforce. The extent to which various strategic human resourcing practices or 'bundles' of practices can be considered *inherently* 'ethical' is a contentious issue. What is less contentious however, is the notion that that how well or badly employees are treated will make a significant difference to the release of their capacities or talent(s). Some firms clearly acknowledge the need to 'humanise' the appearance of their human resourcing activities, as evidenced by Bristol-Myers Squibb in Exhibit 4.1.

Exhibit 4.1

A pledge of 'humane leadership' at Bristol-Myers Squibb

Bristol-Myers Squibb (BMS) is a global biopharmaceutical and related healthcare products company. The company employs around 2,000 people in the UK and for the second year running has been recognised in the *Sunday Times*' 'Best Companies to Work For' awards. Keen to foster a culture of 'total reward' incorporating both financial and non-financial aspects across the organisation, BMS re-launched its total reward package in 2008 with the aim of increasing employee awareness across the company. This holistic approach to people management is reflected in the Bristol-Myers Squibb pledge which states the following:

> To our colleagues we pledge personal respect, fair compensation and honest and equitable treatment. To all who qualify for advancement, we will make every effort to provide opportunity. We affirm our commitment to foster a globally diverse workforce and a company-wide culture that encourages excellence, leadership, innovation and a balance between our personal and professional lives. We acknowledge our obligation to provide able and humane leadership and a clean and safe work environment.

The original total reward model implemented at BMS six years ago established a traditional hierarchy of elements with compensation at the top, benefits in the middle and 'your life at work' at the bottom. But BMS were concerned that the way this original model was presented led to a perception among some staff that compensation was more important than benefits and similarly, benefits were more important than 'life at work'. The new revised model implemented by BMS in 2008 adopts a more pyramidal structure by positioning 'life at work' as the foundation on which the other elements of total reward are built, thus highlighting the importance of less tangible elements.

Source: IDS, *Total Reward*, Study 871, June 2008

This section presents you with a selection of activities and contemporary pheno-mena associated with strategic human resourcing, with the intention of drawing your attention (raising your ethical sensitivity) to the ethical dimension(s) of such activities and phenomena. Please note that the list of ethical issues and activities included in this section is by no means finite, and you are indeed encouraged to reflect on other issues and activities that you experience or observe in your own organisation.

Ethics and training and development

Training and development as a strategic activity in organisations is an area that is not typically put under an ethical microscope. Wilcox (2006) however presents a strong case for a consideration of ethical issues associated with both macro and micro training and development strategies, arguing that the interconnection between the two, combined with broader labour market policies, is ultimately reflected in matters related to social exclusion. Poorly developed training and development policies (again, both macro and micro) lead to a vicious cycle, whereby workers marginalised by their lack of appropriate skills or competencies are unlikely to be in a position to bargain for the enhancement of those skills. Wilcox (2006: 191) further argues:

. . . one of the most significant HRD ethical issues remains the issue of equity and access to the range of developmental opportunities necessary for full participation in society. A right to employability has important implications for HRD, not the least of which is that learning and development programs need to go beyond narrow job-related outcomes. Other concerns relevant to HRD include elements of career and succession planning, mentoring and the availability of the social networks necessary for full development of one's occupational potential.

Ethics and performance management

It is repeatedly emphasised throughout this text that successful strategic human resourcing rests on creating the conditions (through certain principles and practice) that enable the release of the human capacities required so that work tasks can be enacted that ultimately lead to organisational survival and competitive success. The monitoring of such enactment of human capacities as they manifest in required behaviours can be viewed as an important component of strategic human resourcing. Seen in this way, performance management then contains something of a paradox: how can performance be 'judged' at the same time as it is 'developed'? Put differently, is strategic human resourcing more concerned with *developing* human capacity, or is it concerned with monitoring (and controlling) desired behaviour?

Ethics and reward

In recent years we have seen significant changes in reward systems, most notably in the area of performance-based pay systems and other contingent reward systems. Aside from the critique that such systems don't achieve their aim of improving performance where it is most needed (see Chapter 8), a number of related ethical issues can also be identified. Contingent pay systems may lead to economic insecurity, especially if employees have little or no control over what performance measures are used and how such measurement occurs (Heery, 2000). In addition, performance-based pay operates under an assumption of a commonality of interests between employer and employee. As a result, a feature of such reward systems is that they neglect the issue of employee rights and provide little scope for the representation of employee interests (Heery, 2000).

Ethics and equality

Issues associated with equal employment opportunities are an important aspect of strategic human resourcing, and there is much debate as to how such equality can be encouraged and maintained (refer to Chapter 5). A number of different perspectives underlie such debate, and each has ethical implications. The 'business case' argument stems from a different perspective, arguing that it is in the interest of organisations to fully utilise all existing and available resources, hence equality can serve organisational ends. The social justice perspective rests on the assumption that men and woman are fundamentally the same, and as such they should be treated the same. The social justice perspective then sees that equality is simply *morally right* and should be pursued for this reason. A 'merit' approach to equality encompasses aspects of both the social justice perspective and the business case. The 'merit' approach agues that equality can be achieved by judging individuals on their particular merits against the same standards. This approach assumes that men and woman are fundamentally similar, *and* that it is in the best interest of the organisation to determine those with the most 'merit'. 'Diversity' approaches, however, explicitly acknowledge differences. Such approaches argue that inequality is partially the result of the failure to accept differences and to respond to them. Strategic human resourcing activities will be different according to which perspective is adopted, although some theorists have argued convincingly that many organisations tend to integrate the approaches in their policy and practice (see, for example, Liff and Dickens, 2000).

Ethics and long working hours

Over the past few years there has been much debate over the 'work-life balance' (see for example Guest, 2002; Shorthose, 2004; Fleetwood, 2007) stemming from a larger concern with the impact of long working hours. Case Study 4.1 introduced you to some of the issues associated with long working hours, or what is known as 'presenteeism'. Competitive pressures, downsizing, new technologies and takeovers have fuelled the phenomenon of presenteeism, since such activities serve to heighten employees' sense of job insecurity. Simpson (2000) found a number of interrelated reasons for working excessively long hours. First, employees cited increased job demands, either as a result of downsizing or of some other restructuring exercise. These restructuring exercises also led to feelings of job insecurity, and so in order to be *seen* to be committed and valuable, employees stayed at work longer. A second and related reason was that over time in prone organisations, a culture of competitive presenteeism seems to emerge. Given that career progression is limited in restructured and delayered organisations, long hours becomes a central means by which to compete for career progression. This serves also to put pressure on aspiring employees lower down the hierarchy, in turn assisting presenteeism in becoming an endemic aspect of the organisational culture. In some cases this results in employees working later into the night, not taking time off when they are ill, and not taking holidays. Leisure time and recuperation time are thus sacrificed. A further issue arises when we consider the gender implications of presenteeism. In a study of managerial practices, Watson (1994) found that working long hours into the night served to marginalise many female employees. Other studies have suggested that men have actively created cultures where women are prevented from reaching their full potential, or at least prevented them from being recognised as 'star' performers (see, for example, Cockburn, 1991; Maddock and Parkin, 1993). The issues of increased pressure to work excessive hours resulting in a sacrifice of leisure and recuperation time, as well as serving to marginalise a group of workers on the basis of gender, present us with problems that involve a number of ethical concerns. These will be further examined during our exploration of some of the relevant ethical frameworks in a later section of this chapter.

Ethics and 'flexible' labour

Flexible labour is an umbrella term that encompasses a wide variety of different types of employment relationship. Flexible work can thus take many forms, such as part-time work, temporary work, fixed-term contract work and casual work. For our purposes here, rather than getting sidetracked with the technical definitions of flexible work forms (for a discussion of such definitions refer to Felstead and Jewson, 1999), it can be argued that such arrangements involve elements of precariousness and job and wage insecurity. It should be noted that aside from various groups of skilled and 'knowledge workers' who choose to enter into flexible work arrangements, many so-called flexible work arrangements are in the lower-skilled segments of the labour market. Arguably many workers in precarious, flexible arrangements can be considered both 'captive and disposable' (Wilcox and Lowry, 2000). They have little job mobility, yet are relatively easy to dispense with according to the ebb and flow of product or service demand. Such workers typically receive little training, which serves to exacerbate their entrapment. Since they experience wage insecurity and resultant fluctuations in income, as well as 'working-time' insecurity, they often have difficulty in obtaining bank loans for housing, and can experience difficulties in financially 'making ends meet' if working hours are reduced during low demand times. Additionally, 'flexible' workers who are on call for the majority of the time are likely to experience a loss of control over their personal time, since they are unable to plan ahead owing to uncertain work requirements.

Ethics and downsizing

Over the past decade there has been a dramatic increase in organisational restructuring efforts such as mergers and acquisitions and, in particular, downsizing. The ethical impacts of downsizing are considerable, regardless of the type of downsizing strategy that is used. Workers who are made redundant are likely to experience a considerable sense of uncertainty before and after the downsizing exercise. For many workers, redundancy involves the loss of income and work-related status, not to mention self-esteem. In mass lay-offs involving thousands of workers from regions dependent on a sole employer, entire communities potentially experience significant economic and social hardship. In addition, those workers who escaped redundancy (the 'survivors') potentially experience changed work conditions, including work intensification, not to mention other factors such as work insecurity, and guilt or anger over the way that targeting and selection of redundancies was carried out.

Activity 4.1	Thinking about ethical issues

Reflect on the activities associated with strategic human resourcing in your own organisation or in one in which you have worked (use the type of activities discussed so far as a starting point). Can you identify any issues that may be considered ethical issues associated with such activities, and if so, what are they?

We've now reviewed a number of areas of strategic human resourcing which highlight the potential areas of ethical concern. We will revisit some of these areas again when we explore certain ethical traditions and frameworks later in the chapter. For now, let us turn our attention to the role that the HR manager or specialist may (or may not) play in ethical strategic human resourcing.

The HR manager and ethics

Issues related to human resourcing specialists and ethics are a growing area of interest. Most typically this interest has surfaced in professional/practitioner HRM journals, which have from time to time addressed the issue of the HR manager as the provider of ethical stewardship by prescribing certain ethical activities that an 'effective' HR manager should adopt. This includes such activities as providing training in ethics, communicating codes of ethical conduct, managing compliance and monitoring arrangements, and establishing and maintaining principles of corporate social responsibility (see, for example, Arkin, 1996; Johns, 1995; Pickard, 1995; More, 2002).

Academic literature has, however, highlighted the difficulties faced by HR managers despite the type of prescriptions in practitioner journals. Foote and Robinson (1999), for example, found that HR managers are able, in varying degrees contingent upon circumstance, to exert some influence on ethical practice in organisations, but at some risk (Macklin, 2006). When we consider that strategic human resourcing involves the *values* of the strategy-makers which then inform, and are informed by, processes of debate, negotiation and choice, we need to examine the ethical role of the HR manager more closely. Furthermore, there is a need to incorporate other factors such as the *personal* orientation of the HR manager (their own ethical standards and how they 'sit' with the values of the organisation) as well as their views towards the way other decision-makers in the organisation treat employees.

The discussion here will attempt to unravel the nature of the range of options or choices available to the HR manager concerning the ethical stance they may take. It is important to note here that choice does not imply a complete 'free play' with regard to ethics, rather, it suggests that 'moral choice proposes an oscillation between possibilities, where these possibilities are determined situationally' (Clegg *et al.*, 2007: 111). Before going on to look at such options, let us first explore the organisational context of the HR manager. Like any other actor in an organisation, the HR manager is a part of a complex and emergent set of structural, political and symbolic aspects of organisation. HR managers are expected to both conform to and devise rules and procedures, and they must debate and negotiate their activities in a way which is politically and culturally acceptable. This context suggests that the ethical stance adopted by an HR manager is likely to be affected by *more* than personally held moral convictions. In other words, on one level we all like to think of ourselves as autonomous moral agents, yet in organisations we become engaged by bureaucratic models of practice, which involve us (in varying degrees) in manipulative relationships with others (MacIntyre, 1985). An important point here is that manipulative relationships do not necessarily involve active manipulation, for manipulation can also take a passive form. Jackall (1988: 6) puts it eloquently in stating the following (emphasis added):

> . . . bureaucratic contexts typically bring together men and women who initially have little in common with each other except the impersonal frameworks of their organisations. Indeed, the enduring genius of the organisational form is that it allows individuals to retain bewilderingly diverse private motives and meanings for action as long as they adhere publicly to agreed-upon rules. Even the personal relationships that men and women in bureaucracies do subsequently fashion together are, for the most part, governed by explicit or implicit organisational rules, procedures and protocol. As a result, bureaucratic work causes people to *bracket*, while at work, the moralities that they might hold outside the workplace or that they might adhere to privately and to follow instead the prevailing morality of their particular organisational situation.

As we shall see, 'bracketing' is a potential form of manipulation, and the concept of bracketing provides an extremely useful means by which to explore the level of ethical involvement exhibited by the HR professional. Recent critical studies that explore the dynamics behind the process of bracketing provide some clues as to the range of options available to the HR manager in terms of adopted ethical stance. Based on empirical research, Fisher (2000) identifies three main forms of ethical *inactivity* among HR managers. The most extreme form is what Fisher (2000: 68) terms 'quietism'. This refers to an enforced (through the pressure of other organisational strategic decision-makers) process of total bracketing, whereby an HR manager is likely to be punished in some way (perhaps through termination of employment) unless organisational requirements are met. With this form of enforced bracketing, the HR manager is forced to internalise organisational values and activity, even if they are unethical. The position of quietism is an extreme position in the case of all decision-makers in the scenario. As Fisher (2000: 69) comments:

> The assumption is that if (the HR manager) is not with the organisation they are against it. At this stage, in the dialectic of inactivity, tolerating an act while retaining the right to let your true feelings show, through the whispered aside, is not acceptable. Neither is an agreement to disagree and say nothing about the subject. The failure to take action against an unethical act must be reinforced by committing oneself to the act. The threat, real or implied, is that if they do not volunteer a positive compliance they will be punished.

A second form of inactivity identified by Fisher is referred to as 'neutrality'. This is a less extreme form of inactivity, since there is no requirement to internalise or offer voluntary positive compliance to an unethical act. With this sort of stance, the HR manager chooses to be mute. In Fisher's research, HR managers gave a number of reasons for such moral muteness, ranging from a lack of opportunity to 'blow the whistle', to the pace and political nature of organisational life as well as a sense of a lack of positional power. The third form of inactivity is the situation where an HR manager may tolerate unethical organisational activity (such as, say, poorly executed redundancies, or unfair recruitment and selection in providing 'jobs for the boys'), but may vent their dissent in the form of ironic comments or facetious humour. Again, the underlying dynamic involves 'bracketing' their personally held moral convictions from their work life, although in this case the bracketing is self-generated and temporary rather than externally enforced (as it was with quietism). The rationale for such tolerance of unethical activity offered by HR managers in Fisher's study was that they could see the business case for acting in a certain (unethical) way.

So far, we have only discussed the HR manager as being ethically inactive, based on the assumption that HR managers operate within a certain interpersonal and hierarchical context. As emphasised throughout this text, however, managers (including HR managers) are also caught up in wider institutional patterns involving the notions of resource dependence, resource trading and strategic exchange. In other words, HR managers may also need to reconcile ethical pressure being exerted by the various groups with which an organisation exchanges or trades. Thus, if HR managers offend employees or future employees, they risk the loss of the labour resources and associated commitment and competencies that the organisation requires to survive. We need then to consider the options for the ethically active HR manager.

Indeed, we may at this point consider that the scope of ethical choices available to an HR manager may be usefully conceptualised as a continuum. Figure 4.1 illustrates the available options of ethical stance that an HR manager may adopt. Using the concept of bracketing (separation of public and private domains), we can chart a set of ethical positions that an HR manager may take, depending on the ethical issue or dilemma in question, ranging from an extreme ethically inactive stance through to an ethically active stance. If we turn our attention to the ethically active end of the continuum (having already dealt with inactivity), we see that ethical activity involves a lessening of the bracketing activity discussed so far. The ethical active HR manager is one who is likely to consciously address any discrepancy between the public and private domain. Watson (2003) suggests that there are two broad positions from which such ethical activity can arise. The first of these is termed 'ethical reactivity'. Here the HR manager may 'choose' to deal with ethical issues, but does so because of a need to respond to pressures from the 'various resource dependent constituencies with which their organisation exchanges' (Watson, 2003: 182). In this stance, the public domain may be dominant, as it is with the 'quietist' inactive stance, but in this case it also encompasses a *wider* public domain that goes beyond the public domain of the 'interior' organisation. The second stance identified by Watson (2003) is termed 'ethical assertiveness'. Here, we have no separation between public and private domain. An HR manager acting in this way has managed to 'bring together such

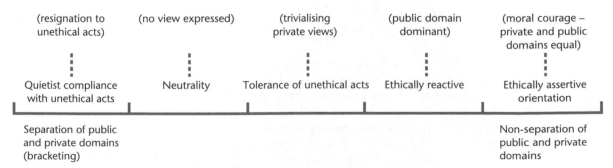

Figure 4.1 **Range of ethical choices for HR managers**

(internal and external) pressures with their private moral concerns and act in a way which is both corporately expedient and satisfies private moral concerns' (Watson, 2003: 187).

How is such ethical assertiveness achieved? Satisfying both private and public domains is no easy task. If we refer back to the Moddens Foods case study in Chapter 1, we can see that there is a certain amount of ethical ambiguity in most organisational activity. Why, for example, not employ workers in the cheap labour countries, when 'home-grown' labour works unsocial hours for a fairly low national minimum wage (refer to Case Study 1.2a, p. 17)? It would appear that the ethically assertive HR manager is one who can successfully *translate* private moral concerns into a form of business parlance (emphasising, for example, the long-term implications of various forms of HR policies etc.), and then proceed to debate and negotiate on those grounds. This stance thus involves considerable *practical* skill, and also involves the somewhat sophisticated understanding that the reconciliation of public and private domain (personal and organisational moral interests) is likely to involve (in varying degrees) the consideration of the implications of certain ethical choices. At the extreme end of the continuum, the ethically assertive HR manager is likely to possess what Mahoney (1998) terms 'moral courage'. This is defined as 'the capacity to do what one judges is ethically called for in spite of one's instinctive reaction to the perceived dangers and difficulties in which such action will result' (Mahoney, 1998: 189). In addition to the practical skills of debate and negotiation, Mahoney suggests that moral courage is characterised by confidence, patience and perseverance.

HR managers at the ethically assertive end of the continuum are likely to make certain ethical decisions in different circumstances using different types of rationale to justify those decisions. Consideration of such 'rationales' or 'reasons' leads us now into the inner realms of the foggy maze as we now explore some of the available ethical traditions or 'theories'.

Activity 4.2   The range of ethical choices continuum

1. Refer back to the Moddens Foods Case Study in Chapter 1. Where would you place the HR director, Jean Frear, on the continuum in Figure 4.1? What are your reasons for placing Jean at that particular point on the continuum?

2. Reflect on an ethical issue with which you have had to deal in the past within the context of your organisation. Where would you locate yourself on the continuum in Figure 4.1? Is this point on the continuum one you would consistently locate, or would it change according to the issue and circumstances involved?

Ethical traditions

Philosophers have been grappling with issues related to ethical theories for centuries. This section will explore some of the main principles in ethical thought. In order to make our navigation around our 'moral maze' more manageable, the main ethical theories have been grouped here into two main camps – normative ethical theories and descriptive ethical theories (Goodpaster, 1995). Normative ethical theories tell us what actors in organisations *should* do, while descriptive ethical theories tell us what organisational actors *actually do*, and *why*. It is important to have some understanding of both normative and descriptive frameworks since organisational actors may adopt and use normative frameworks in order to justify the *basis* of their moral (or otherwise) decision-making and associated strategic human resourcing activity.[1] This first cluster of 'normative' theories or frameworks will be further divided into *traditional* theories and *contemporary* ethical theories. Traditional normative ethical frameworks are concerned with what is right or wrong for *any* given situation, claiming that there are eternal and universally applicable moral principles, while more contemporary approaches more or less refute this assumption of absolutism.

'Traditional' normative ethics

If we refer back to the Moddens Case Study 1.2c (p. 24), we can see that Sam Modden and Jean Frear are grappling with issues associated with what is 'right' and 'wrong'. In particular, they are wrestling with the idea that while some managers perceive the human resources of an organisation to be the 'means' by which business opportunities and strategies are fulfilled, an alternative perspective is that human resources are in themselves an important business opportunity – in other words, they could also be considered, in a long-term strategic sense, to be the 'ends'.

This type of reasoning brings us to the consideration of a group of ethical theories that are concerned with rules and principles that attempt to inform what is 'right' or 'wrong' for a given situation. Because such theories are concerned with what is right or wrong for *any* given situation, traditional normative theories are considered to adopt a position of 'absolutism'. In other words, traditional normative ethical theories claim that there are eternal and universally applicable moral principles. Normative ethical theories begin with an assumption about the world and about the nature of human beings, and can be broadly classified into two groups. First, there are theories that explore moral judgement against the backdrop of the underlying principles of the actor's motivation. So, an action is either 'right' or 'wrong' depending on whether the underlying principles are morally right. Such ethical theories have as their starting point a focus on the rights and duties of individuals, and they do not take into account the consequences of moral decisions or acts. Because of this, this group of theories is termed 'non-consequentialist'. Included in this group are deontological theories, based on the Greek word *deon* or duty, as well as justice-based theories. A second group of theories are those that do consider the consequences of certain actions – if the consequences of an action are desirable, then the action is morally right. This group of theories are termed *consequentialist*.

Each of these traditional normative groups will now be explored in turn.

---

[1] In other words, the dualism between descriptive (or positive) and normative frameworks is useful for certain types of analyses but can arguably be construed as false in action.

Non-consequentialist theories

As just stated, 'non-consequentialist' frameworks do not take into account the consequences of moral decisions or acts. Within this camp, 'duty-based' ethics and 'justice-based' ethics will be examined here.

Duty-based ethics

This ethical theory has its origins in the German philosopher Immanuel Kant (1724–1804), who thought that morality involved eternal and unchangeable principles which humans must apply to their lives. Thus, he devised his 'categorical imperative' which consisted of three parts or 'maxims' (cited from Crane and Matten, 2007):

- Maxim One: Act only according to that maxim by which you can at the same time will that it should become a universal law.
- Maxim Two: Act so that you treat humanity, whether in your own person or in that of another, always as an end and never as a means only.
- Maxim Three: Act only so that the will through its maxims could regard itself at the same time as universally lawgiving.

The first maxim explores whether an action can be performed by everyone, and thus focuses on the notion of consistency. The second maxim asserts that human dignity must not be ignored, so, for example, while employees are paid to elicit effort and performance in order to achieve wider organisational goals, they should not *just* be treated as means. We can see such reasoning in the social justice approach to equality which argues that men and women should be treated equally as ends (rather than means). The third maxim emphasises the notion of universality or acceptability by other rational actors. Trevino and Nelson (1999: 89) explain this more simply by referring to it as the 'New York Times' test – if you would prefer that your actions regarding a particular issue not be reported in your local newspaper then it is likely that such actions are of dubious moral status.

Kant's theory is appealing, with its emphasis on principles and intellectual self-scrutiny. It has, however, been criticised on the basis that is somewhat overly optimistic. The view of man as rational actor who acts according to self-imposed duties could be considered more of an ideal than a reality with regard to business actors (Crane and Matten, 2007).

Justice-based ethics

In addition to duty-based ethical frameworks, there also exist justice-based theories, a notable proponent being John Rawls (1971). In similar fashion to Kant, Rawls asserts the golden rule of 'do unto others as you would have them do unto you'. More specifically, Rawls essentially advocated two criteria in order to ensure justice. First, each person has an equal right to the most extensive system of basic liberties compatible with a similar system of liberty for all. Second, inequalities in distribution should be to the benefit of all or to the least advantaged.

Associated with Rawls' emphasis on justice are three particular forms of justice which have relevance in the context of strategic human resourcing. These are:

- distributive justice;
- procedural justice;
- interactional justice.

'Distributive justice' has its focus on fair *outcomes*, especially in regard to economic *fair outcomes*. The fair distribution of reward, work scheduling and training is related to such broad economic distribution issues. We can see then that 'New Pay' systems could be seen to have negative ethical implications if we consider such systems through the lens of distributive justice, as discussed in an earlier section of this chapter. Similarly, in the context of equal employment opportunities, the issue is one of how jobs and opportunities can be equitably shared between different social groups. Likewise, when certain 'flexible' labour forms are analysed through the lens of distributive justice we may see that certain minority groups do not have access to the type of economic advantages and opportunities (for example, property ownership) provided by more secure forms of employment, nor do they have access to mobility-enhancing opportunities such as training. Downsizing also has issues associated with distributive justice if we consider the way that redundancies are distributed, in other words, the fairness of the targeting and selection methods in terms of who was selected for redundancy and which divisions and levels of the organisation are most affected.

'Procedural justice' highlights a necessity for *fair processes*. From this vantage point we can see that the range of processes and activities associated with strategic human resourcing would require careful consideration. For example, processes associated with recruitment and selection would be required to be 'fair', free from, say, nepotism and unfair discrimination. Likewise, pay systems and performance management systems would need to operate under principles of due process and with a certain degree of transparency. Procedural justice also has implications for the way that downsizing is conducted. For example, the level of employee involvement and consultation in the process is associated with fair processes, as is the way that management justifies the downsizing effort in terms of the quantity and quality of the communication associated with it.

Finally, we have the notion of 'interactional justice' with its focus on *fair interpersonal exchange*. This also has implications for a range of strategic human resourcing activities. In recruitment and selection, for example, it implies that the interview process be conducted in a manner which facilitates a fair interpersonal exchange. Likewise, interpersonal processes associated with pay negotiations, on an individual or collective basis (bargaining 'in good faith'), as well as interactions that form part of a performance management scheme, should facilitate fair exchange and facilitate employee 'voice'. Interactional exchange also has implications for downsizing in terms of the fairness of interpersonal treatment of those made redundant and fair interpersonal treatment of survivors.

Consequentialist theories

This group of theories emphasises the consequences of a certain action. Consequentialist theories are thus based on intended consequences or goals of a certain action.[2] For our purposes here we will examine two main consequentialist theories, notably egoism and utilitarianism.

---

[2] For this reason this group of theories is sometimes referred to as 'teleological' ethics based on the word *telos* which is the Greek word for 'goal'.

Egoism

Egoism focuses on the outcomes for the decision-maker – an action is morally right if the actor freely decides it in order to pursue his or her short-term *desires* or long-term *interests*. It is important to note at this point that we are not discussing egoism in its day-to-day 'common-sense' usage or as a psychological opposite to the notion of altruism (see, for example, Baier, 2002). Adam Smith (1723–90) in particular presented egoism as an important feature in his formulation of liberalist economics. Smith's (1776) proposition was that the economic system rendered self-pursuit as acceptable since it produced morally desirable outcomes through the 'invisible hand' of the marketplace.

Of interest is this later conception concerned with egoism based on the pursuit of (long-term) interests, a notion referred to as 'enlightened egoism'. This is considered by many to be a feasible ethical stance in business ethics, and much of the literature on corporate social responsibility could, arguably, stem from this position of enlightened egoism. In fact, the position adopted by this book could be seen to adopt *aspects* of enlightened egoism, since an implicit argument throughout this text is that for sustainable organisational survival and success, decision-making actors in organisations must take into account the outcomes of their decisions on all relevant constituencies.

Egoism is appealing since it appears to be a concept of humans that is fairly well confirmed by conventional patterns of actors and decision-makers in organisations. One of the main limitations to egoism, however, is that there is no assurance that 'egoists' will not pursue their interests at other egoists' expense. In Adam Smith's way of thought, the mechanism of the 'market' would provide such assurance. However, we need only look around us to see that the global market does not function 'perfectly', and that there does exist an unequal distribution of wealth across the globe.

Utilitarianism

Perhaps one of the most easily recognised ethical traditions, utilitarianism rests on the principle that the goal is to achieve 'the greatest good for the greatest number', as well as the principle that 'an act is right if it results in benefits for people, wrong if it damages or harms'. Such reasoning is commonplace in organizations, but this does not mean it should be accepted without question or criticism. The 'business case' for equality is distinctly utilitarian, resting as it does on the assumption that it is in the interest of the organisation as a whole to fully utilise all existing resources. We often also see evidence of a utilitarian rationale in downsizing. For example, managers often justify the 'goal' of downsizing by asserting that downsizing is the only way for the majority of employees in a particular organisation to keep their jobs.

But the utilitarianism approach is beset with problems and suffers from simplistic assumptions related to the costs and benefits of certain actions. But how do we measure 'good' or 'benefit'? Economists promote the idea of cost–benefit analysis, but this type of reasoning is dubious in the realm of ethics. For example, there may be a rationale for downsizing, but how do you compare organisational survival with increased unemployment and associated welfare costs? What is the effect of downsizing on organisational survivors who in some circumstances must cope with significantly increased workloads?

Activity 4.3   Identifying traditional ethical theories

1. Identify which traditional ethical theory (or theories) best accounts for the actions of Robyn Hillsdon-Smythe and Laura Dunlop in Case Study 4.1 (p. 99).

2. Refer back to the Moddens Foods Case Study in Chapter 1. Identify which ethical theory (or theories) discussed so far best accounts for the actions of Sam Modden (company chairman); Jean Frear (HR director); Juan Poort (managing director); Frank Angle (operations director); Hal Selz (marketing director); and Ivan Kelp (finance director). Provide justification for your answer(s).

Critique of traditional ethical theories

It should be noted that the contemporary social and economic context in which we find ourselves, particularly as that context relates to the realm of business ethics, renders the exploration of moral concerns as perhaps involving a different set of assumptions to those addressed by the classical philosophers and their traditional ethical frameworks. As MacIntyre neatly articulates:

> We all too often still treat the moral philosophers of the past as contributors to a single debate with a relative unvarying subject matter . . . (and) as contemporaries both of ourselves and of each other. This leads to an abstraction of these writers from the cultural and social milieus in which they lived and thought so the history of their thought acquires a false independence from the rest of the culture.
> (MacIntyre, 1985: 11)

The traditional theories discussed above are largely absolutist theories that are based on objective reason. Such theories present a series of problems in their usefulness for exploring issues associated with business ethics. One problem lies in their reductionist approach; in other words, each theory tends to focus on one aspect of morality to the exclusion of other factors (Kaler, 1999). Why choose 'rights' or 'duties' or 'consequences' when all such considerations are important? Another criticism and one that you as a student may relate to, is that traditional ethical frameworks are simply too theoretical for the practical operational concerns of managers (Stark, 1994). Related to this is the criticism that by focusing on abstract principles, traditional ethical theories discount the human bonds and relationships which inform our thoughts and feelings and intuitions about what is 'right' or 'wrong' (Gilligan, 1982). Not only are such traditional theories impersonal, but they also attempt to define the essence of right and wrong in terms of reference to codified rational rules of behaviour. Again, this has the effect of lessening the importance of our feelings and emotions which, according to Bauman (1993), are a crucial factor in our moral behaviour. A final criticism lies in the objective and elitist nature of much traditional ethical theorising. Parker (1998a, 1998b) proposes that traditional ethical theories attempt to assume the high ground – moral philosophers and ethicists who understand such theories can then adjudicate on the rights and wrongs of others, with little subjective experience of the situation under scrutiny. We can see then that there are some problems with traditional ethical theories. By no means is this to suggest that this entirely detracts from or negates the worth of traditional moral philosophy as it relates to the business ethics and more specifically to the ethics of strategic human resourcing. Rather, it suggests a 'rethinking' of how such theories may be used to understand the complex ethical dilemmas that confront us in the context of contemporary organisations. Let us now turn our attention to some contemporary theories that assist our understanding of the range of ethical choices in the context of strategic human resourcing.

Contemporary normative ethics

Over the past few decades, a number of different ethical frameworks have emerged, which are being seen to have increasing relevance within the context of business ethics, and more specifically within the context of strategic human resourcing. Whereas the traditional frameworks reviewed tend towards absolutism, contemporary ethical frameworks are inclined toward a more relativistic stance. In other words, morality is more subjective and is context dependent, and as a result is unable to be 'rationally determined'. In short, many contemporary frameworks assert that there is no notion of 'right' or 'wrong' which is universally shared. Let us now turn our attention to briefly examine a selection of contemporary ethical frameworks.

Ethics of virtue

This approach is a modern interpretation of Aristotle's notion of virtue ethics, and emphasises the state of character of actors rather than their actions *per se*. At its simplest, this approach rests on the fundamental assumption that good actions come from good people. Virtues can be intellectual (for example, 'wisdom'), or they may be moral (for example, courage, honesty, patience, modesty, to name but a few). Such traits are acquired by learning, and in the virtuous person are exhibited on an habitual and continuous basis. According to MacIntyre (1985), in the context of organisations such traits are acquired and visible by being in relationships with other organisational actors in a community of practice. From this perspective, all stakeholders are seen to be equally important. An important concept in this framework is that of the 'good life'; however, it is not the 'good life' in a hedonistic sense, rather it is a broader, more holistic sense of the phrase that is intended. The 'good life' does not involve the mere achievement of success, it also involves relishing the pleasures of a virtuous manner of attaining success (Crane and Matten, 2007). Thus for managers in organisations it is not just profits that are most important, it is the *way* profits are achieved. The satisfaction of all stakeholders is thus considered *equally* important. This begs two questions, however; is it possible to satisfy all stakeholders equally, and how is such satisfaction to be achieved? Such questions highlight yet again the importance of processes of negotiation, debate and choice, processes that are addressed in the frameworks discussed below. Before exploring these frameworks, however, let us look more closely at the idea of 'virtue' and 'virtuous manners of achieving success'. Regardless of whether a virtue is a disposition or is learned, the endurance and congruence of a virtue or 'virtuous manner' is questionable. The reality of 'bracketing' (where people separate their values and beliefs from their private and public domains) has already been discussed in this chapter, and lends some scepticism to the notion of the virtuous organisational actor or manager. Moreover, any definition of what counts as a virtue within the organisational context is likely to change from one organisational actor to another and from one level of the organisational hierarchy to another.

Discourse ethics

Ethics of virtue assumes a natural and shared set of meanings as to what constitutes a particular virtue. Discourse ethics rests on the assumption that such 'natural' sharing of meanings is unlikely. This approach focuses on the reality that ethical conflicts in organisations require attention on a day-to-day basis, and that the 'ideal' way to go about this is to provide practical *processes* and procedures so that issues can be debated. Under this framework, such debate is both rational and consensus enhancing, with actors from morally diverse backgrounds engaging in a discourse aimed at conflict settlement. While the approach is certainly to be applauded, it is arguably optimistic in its assumption about rational human behaviour, and downplays the inevitable power relations that exist *both within and between* various organisational stake-holding groups.

Ethics of care

A similar 'processual' approach is found in an 'ethics of care'; however, in contrast to the rational approach emphasised in discourse ethics, an 'ethics of care' focuses on personal and subjective reasoning, with a particular emphasis on intuition and feeling. In the organisational context, actors are seen to be embedded in a net-work of interpersonal relations, and the care and maintenance of this network is seen to be a responsibility of organisational actors. The emphasis is on social processes which aim to achieve empathy and integration with regard to moral and ethical issues (Gilligan, 1982). A criticism of this approach is that its emphasis on 'care' resembles a paternalist 'parent–child' metaphor with the 'parent' (manager) deciding what is 'best' for the 'child' (employee). From a strategic human resourcing perspective, regardless of whether a high or low commitment strategic direction is being followed, this could involve managers making so-called 'caring' decisions on behalf of employees as a device for safeguarding their own managerial interests. As Winstanley and Woodall (2000) point out, however, an 'ethics of care' goes beyond a simple view of people as 'human resources', and incorporates the notions of respect and empathy for the individual. This approach is not entirely at odds with the view expressed throughout this text. 'Human resources' can be seen as human *capacities* necessary for task performance and sustainable organisation – how well or badly employees are *treated* (this includes notions of '*care*' and how well employees are *respected and understood*) will make a significant difference to the development and 'release' of such human capacities.

Activity 4.4   Identifying contemporary ethical theories

1. Identify which contemporary ethical theory (or theories), best accounts for the actions of Robyn Hillsdon-Smythe and Laura Dunlop in Case Study 4.1 (p. 99).

2. Refer back to the Moddens Foods Case Study in Chapter 1. Identify which contemporary ethical theory (or theories) discussed here best accounts for the actions of Sam Modden (company chairman); Jean Frear (HR director); Juan Poort (managing director); Frank Angle (operations director); Hal Selz (marketing director); and Ivan Kelp (finance director). Provide justification for your answer(s).

Descriptive ethical theory

While normative ethical theories tell us what actors in organisations *should* do, descriptive ethical theories tell us what organisational actors *actually do*, and *why*. We have already touched on descriptive theory in our exploration of the role of the HR specialist and the different ethical 'positions' they may adopt (see also Lowry, 2006; Clegg *et al.*, 2007). Throughout this chapter it has been argued that strategic human resourcing involves the *values* of strategy-makers which then inform, and are informed by, processes of debate, negotiation and choice. Ultimately such values influence the ethical decision-making process. There is thus a need to understand the factors that impact on values, which in turn lead to a particular ethical orientation of actors in organisations. The ensuing discussion will explore the *interaction* of individual and situational factors that may impact on the ethical values and ethical decision-making of actors engaged in strategic human resourcing.

Moral development, moral awareness and ethical decision-making

Much of the research into moral awareness uses the framework of Kohlberg's stages of moral development as a starting point. Synthesising the work of Piaget (a developmental psychologist) and Rawls (a philosopher concerned with moral philosophy), Kohlberg proposed three levels of moral development, with each level subdivided into two stages. Each stage is considered to be qualitatively higher in both cognitive and moral terms. The first level of moral development (the '*pre-conventional level*') is characterised by ego-centrism and a self-centred ethics of convenience. In other words, at this stage there is an overriding concern with self-interest and external punishments and rewards. The second level of moral development is the '*conventional level*', and relates to the ethics of conformity. Here, the individual has a basic understanding of conventional morality, and reasons with an understanding that norms and conventions are necessary to uphold society. More simply, this stage involves doing what is expected of you by others. The final stage of Kohlberg's model is the '*post-conventional level*'. This stage involves the development of autonomous decision-making, based on principles of justice and rights rather than conformity to external influences. Here a principled-centred ethics of conviction is (according to the theory) evident. Kohlberg's model (especially the final stage in level three) has been criticised by a number of philosophers. The grounds for such criticism are numerous and beyond the scope of this chapter. In overview, the critique centres on issues such as Kohlberg's erroneous assumption of a 'Foundational Principle', the overly individual orientation of the model, and that the model emphasises rational aspects of morality while neglecting emotional aspects (for a full discussion of these issues see Rest *et al.*, 2000).

In the final stage of level three, there is an understanding that elements of morality transcend particular cultures and societies and are to be upheld irrespective of other conventions or normative obligations. In essence Kohlberg characterised the developmental change of adolescents and adults in terms of a shift from conventional to post-conventional thinking.

Rather than explore the development stages of individual actors, other models have attempted to map the stages of the *process* of ethical decision-making. Such models typically view that there are a series of steps that contribute to an ethical decision or action (see, for example, Rest, 1986; Jones, 1991; Weber, 1992; Trevino, 1992; Butterfield *et al.*, 2000). Moral awareness, or recognising the moral nature of a situation, is considered to be the first step in ethical decision-making. Deciding what is morally right and making a moral judgement then follows. The third step involves the establishment of moral intent, in other words, deciding to give priority to moral values over other values. The final step is engaging in moral action. This is depicted in Figure 4.2.

Figure 4.2 A model of the moral decision-making process
Source: Adapted from Rest (1986)

Each stage in Figure 4.2 is distinct; in other words, an organisational actor may reach one stage in the model but this does not mean that movement to the next stage will necessarily or automatically follow. In this way, the model does distinguish between knowing what is the 'right' thing to do and wanting to do the 'right' thing, and actually doing something about it or knowing what the best course of action is (Crane and Matten, 2007).

If we refer back to our discussion of the role of the HR specialist and the different ethical positions they may adopt, we can see that there is some commonality between the continuum presented in Figure 4.1 and the model described in Figure 4.2.

Quietism, tolerance and neutrality can be linked to the first two stages of Figure 4.2. For example, an HR specialist may recognise, say, that the selection and targeting of employees for downsizing is dubious (recognition of a moral issue), and may decide that such methods unfairly disadvantage a certain group of workers (a moral judgement). The HR specialist may choose, however, to remain mute on the issue, for a variety of reasons. As we discussed earlier in this chapter, the HR specialist may 'bracket' their personal ethical values from their organisational ethical values (separation of private and public domain). As discussed earlier, such bracketing could be a result of the potentially 'alienating' effect of authority or bureaucratic structures. The HR specialist may in this case know what is the right thing to do and may even want to do the 'right' thing, but has either chosen not to follow this impulse or lacks the method or *power* to do so. The ethically reactive and ethically assertive HR specialist can be located in the final stages of Figure 4.2. In the case of the ethically reactive HR specialist, moral intent is fuelled by a felt need to respond to pressures from the various resource-dependent constituencies with which their organisation exchanges (reaction to wider public domain). The ethically assertive HR specialist, however, manages to combine internal and external pressures (private and public domain), which results in ethical decision-making and moral action, ultimately leading to ethical strategic human resourcing.

Summary

In this chapter the following key points have been made:

- The fair and ethical treatment of workers is an important strategic concern, since the way employees perceive the way they are treated potentially impacts on the long-term concerns of an organisation.

- HR strategies emerge from political processes of debate, negotiation and argument among strategic decision-makers and such debate is informed by, and contributes to, the values and interests of the strategy-makers. Included in such values and interests are inherent ethical 'positions' and different types of ethical stance. At times, there may be competing ethical positions.

- The ethical 'positions' adopted by actors in organisations (implicitly) stem from different types of ethical theories or codes.

- HR practitioners and other organisational actors have a range of options concerning the ethical stance they adopt, from being ethically 'mute' to being 'ethically assertive'.

- Management decisions concerning ethical issues affect organisations *and* have wider societal implications.

- Normative ethical theories tell us what actors in organisations *should* do.

Discussion questions

1. In what way(s) are ethical concerns a fundamental aspect of strategic human resourcing?

2. In this chapter a range of ethical issues associated with the activities of strategic human resourcing were identified. What are some of the other areas of strategic human resourcing activities that may have an ethical dimension?

3. How do contemporary ethical theories differ from 'traditional' ethical theories?

4. How do normative and descriptive ethical theories differ, yet complement each other?

5. What are some of the potential ethical issues associated with low commitment strategies and high commitment strategies?

6. What factors affect the range of ethical stances that organisational actors may take?

7. In what areas may management decisions concerning ethical issues have wider societal implications?

Further reading

Readers wishing to further explore a variety of issues associated with ethics and strategic human resourcing are strongly encouraged to read Bolton and Houlihan (2007) and Winstanley and Woodall (2000). For some informative and interesting reading on the general area of business ethics, readers should consult Crane and Matten (2007). Readers interested in the wider subject of corporate social responsibility are encouraged to read the collection of excellent chapters by Crane *et al.* (2008).

Part II

Human resourcing policies in practice

Introduction to Part II

In the first part of this book we considered a number of the main contextual factors that inform the strategic directions chosen by managers in human resourcing matters. The second part explores how these are reflected in human resourcing policies and practices when addressing diversity and equality issues, in assessment, selection and evaluation, managing performance and rewarding individual contribution, handling employee exits and in approaches to international human resourcing in a variety of organisational contexts. The discussion and supporting activities contained in these chapters identify and illustrate some of the challenges and tensions these areas of HR responsibility present for line managers and HR specialists in terms of meeting both organisational needs and those of employees.

The content of these chapters is intended to encourage readers to reflect on the intended outcomes of particular human strategies and the actual outcomes these can have when put into practice. A central theme is the importance of trying to achieve organisational 'best fit' as well as 'best practice' in the design, development and application of human resourcing strategies. This is based on the view that, while best practice provides guiding principles for the development of HR policies and procedures, the managers responsible for implementation need to see them as relevant, appropriate and workable. Where this is not the case, they are likely to be regarded as unnecessary, time consuming constraints on their managerial effectiveness and lead to a growth of informal processes which can erode and even contradict the intentions of formal policies.

A number of these tensions are considered in Chapter 5 through an exploration of the issues that can arise for employees, managers and employees in the development and application of human resourcing policies with the stated aim of promoting equality of opportunity through diversity management. Changes to the political, economic, social and technological environment reinforce the importance of organisations utilising fully their available resources; for example, through human resourcing strategies which maximise the capability of the internal and external workforce through diversity initiatives. Yet an examination of the responsibility placed on line managers to demonstrate fair treatment in a visible, consistent manner that can be defended if legally challenged as well as promote a 'diversity perspective' of equality, suggest this can frequently be problematic in practice.

A key point made throughout the book is that an essential part of managing is about making choices. This is particularly evident in organisational approaches to the assessment, selection and evaluation of individuals to decide who is to be employed, promoted, reassigned, trained or even dismissed. Chapter 6 examines these activities through two different lenses: the traditional 'systematic' view of selection based on the principle of getting the 'right' people in particular jobs and 'the exchange or process' view of a negotiation between the employer and the potential recruit. Both approaches are informed by the notion of achieving a fit between the individual and the job environment but, whereas the 'systematic' tradition emphasises that the process is one of matching the applicant with the fixed dimensions of the job, the 'exchange' view emphasises a focus on the matching of the expectations and needs of the individual with the values, climate and goals of the organisation.

Although the traditional approach dominates practice, the processual alternative has much to offer, both theoretically and practically, to rapidly changing work environments. Through an examination of a range of selection methods, it is acknowledged that there is simply no 'one best way' to undertake assessment but that to overlook the subjectivity of selection decision-making is to ignore the inevitable. As organisational competition for talented individuals intensifies, the processual approach gains in relevance through its recognition of recruitment and selection as a two-way decision-making process and as a critical first stage in any future employment relationship. It is not being suggested that what has been learnt from past research into selection is abandoned but rather that moving from the traditional view of selection as one of management decision-making to one based on a series of exchanges with prospective candidates helps them develop greater realism about their future with an organisation and makes them less likely to leave due to unmet expectations.

Chapter 7, following Walters' (1995) definition of performance management as the process of improving the quality and quantity of work done and bringing all activity in line with an organisation's objectives, identifies the actual practice of performance management as more akin to a corpus of folk prescription and remedy. Its examination and critique of the various methods and techniques of performance management reveals the difficulties in clarifying through perform- ance processes how an individual's work contributes to the written objectives and goals of the organisation. As in Chapter 8, the essential problem is identified as the application of systems which are intended to measure past performance but also encourage future development; the end result being that these become overloaded or even try to achieve contradictory things. While the evidence that formal performance review processes can contribute to improvements in overall organisational performance is still insufficient, it is concluded that individuals may find these helpful in defining and evaluating their own organisational roles. This suggests that whilst people continue to be critical of aspects of their organ- isation's performance management schemes and the time these consume, they still find a value in them.

The impact of linking any evaluation of employee performance to pay is discussed in Chapter 8 which considers the variety of factors that can influence different organisational approaches to rewarding employee contribution. The problems associated with individual, output-based performance pay have led employers to use a combination of different compensation techniques. But the evidence is that these are growing alongside rather than taking the place of such performance pay schemes in those organisations where it is applied.

The contradictions between commitment and reward in the pursuit of human resourcing strategies which try to make a visible link between individual contribu- tions to organisational performance are examined with particular reference to the two motivational theories of expectancy and goal setting and their limitations in terms of providing a complete picture of the complexity of human motivations. Although the principle of paying people for their contribution appeals to a sense of fairness in most of us, it is concluded that performance-related pay can actually act as a demotivator where there are unrealistic goals, unrecognised achievements and/or insufficient rewards to motivate individuals. In practice, problems are identified in establishing what should be rewarded and the perceived equity of the assessment processes even where the rewards are designed to recognise collective as well as individual achievement.

While Chapter 6 focuses on the processes for selecting people to enter an organisation, Chapter 9 examines the different organisational strategies for exiting from the employment relationship either through redundancy, performance-related dismissal, the end of a fixed-term contract, retirement (early or statutory) or employee resignation. An examination of the processes for terminating employment provides insights into how diminished expectations of job security in employment may have contributed to increased voluntary and involuntary labour turnover.

Selecting exiting strategies that comply with legislation, are cost effective and minimise any adverse effects for the remaining workforce is one of the most demanding human resourcing responsibilities required of managers. Achieving a balance in exiting strategies that will minimise conflict but also support future organisational success is no easy matter. It is also an area of human resourcing activity where 'getting it wrong' can prove expensive both financially and in human terms. Recognising that the selected approach to employee exiting is heavily influenced by the organisational context, managerial ability is identified as the crucial factor in reducing any negative consequences for the organisation, and frequently for the individual as well.

In Chapter 10 the discussion surrounding issues of choice, chance and circumstances in the adoption of human resourcing strategies is extended to the management of the employment relationship in firms operating internationally. Globalisation, viewed as the growing economic interdependence among countries reflected in the increasing cross-border flow of goods, services and know-how, provides the critical context for exploring organisational approaches to international human resourcing. The key argument is for the use of a framework of contingent factors to analyse any set of employment circumstances as a means of providing a set of principles to inform a contingency approach to human resourcing decision-making in both domestic and multinational companies. By taking this approach, international human resourcing can be considered in a way that builds on, rather than replaces, our understanding of strategic human resourcing as described in the discussion and illustrations provided in previous chapters.

The differences and similarities between national and international human resourcing are identified to be frequently differences of degree rather than of substance with those responsible for managing across national boundaries being likely to encounter a greater range and a less familiar set of contingent factors. It is concluded that the essence of managing human resources in the overseas organisation is best served by acknowledging a shifting balance between universal HR concerns and those that differentiate the host country location.

5

From equal opportunities to diversity management

Carley Foster and Lynette Harris

Learning outcomes

Having read this chapter and completed its associated activities, readers should be able to:

- Understand how issues of equal opportunities and managing diversity inform and influence human resource strategies and strategic human resourcing

- Identify the principles underpinning the differing approaches to equality issues in organisations

- Recognise that the interpretation of these concepts may vary in different organisational contexts

- Evaluate the respective responsibilities of HR specialists and line managers for managing diversity and equal opportunities policies and practices

- See why there can be potential problems in the shift from the traditional approach of equal opportunities to one of diversity management and how these may be addressed

- Appreciate the challenges in developing and delivering equality and diversity strategies in practice

Introduction

The increasing diversity and changing demographics of the UK workforce, the expansion of anti-discrimination legislation, legal rights for individuals with caring responsibilities and a government policy commitment to the work-life balance have created new challenges for employers across employment sectors. This chapter explores some of the issues and dilemmas that arise for employers, managers and employees in the development and application of organisational human resourcing policies which are intended to promote equality of treatment and recognise diversity in the workforce. The 2004 WERS survey (Kersley *et al.*, 2006) found that 73 per cent of workplaces had a final written equal opportunities policy or a policy on managing diversity compared to 64 per cent in 1998. This figure increased to 98 per cent in the public sector (97 per cent in 1998) with the incidence of formal policy being higher in large workplaces which means that most employees work in establishments with a formal policy. The existence of a written policy does not, however, indicate the presence of a strategic approach to diversity. This was evident in the 2007 CIPD annual recruitment and retention survey which revealed that only half of the 905 participating organisations had a formal diversity strategy although again the public sector is more proactive with 83 per cent reporting a strategic approach to diversity (CIPD, 2007a).

The purpose of this chapter is to explore the concepts behind approaches to diversity and equality and discuss how these are enacted within organisations rather than examine the detail of the anti-discrimination legislation set out in Table 3.1 (p. 74). Approaches to employment inequalities are informed by two main principles, equal opportunities and diversity management, which present managers with the challenge of how to demonstrate equality of treatment in a consistent manner whilst accommodating individual needs stemming from differences such as disability, gender, age, sexual orientation, race and religious belief. A recurrent theme in the discussion will be the extent to which individual differences are recognised in human resourcing strategies and how this impacts on perceptions of fairness in the workplace. In particular, it will consider the role of line managers as the crucial interpreters and arbiters of organisational equality policies, and the principles that inform their decision-making. It will be argued that not only is the concept of managing diversity open to different interpretations but its application will vary according to the prevailing organisational environment; for example, the role of the HR function, the extent of anti-discrimination legislation, the image of the industry, sector or organisation as a place to work and the composition of the available workforce. The chapter concludes by considering the challenge presented by diversity issues in the development of human resourcing strategies.

Examples of diversity management in practice are provided throughout the chapter. Many of these illustrations are taken from the public sector which has frequently led the way in its approaches to diversity management and from the retailing industry which has tended to address diversity issues as a means of broadening the appeal of its products and services to a wider customer base.

From equal opportunities to managing diversity

Since the 1970s successive UK governments have introduced anti-discrimination laws to address workplace inequalities with the stated aim of reducing disadvantage for particular social groups through statutory regulation (Collins, 2000). This regulatory approach was informed by the use of the law in the US to rectify the social injustices which gave rise to the Civil Rights movement in the 1950s and 60s. The UK adopted, in common with most other European countries, a legislative approach which concentrated on redressing the inequalities experienced by identified disadvantaged groups, for example women, ethnic minorities and the disabled (Johnson and Johnstone, 2000: 127). The argument for legal intervention is that without it groups of workers who have been traditionally discriminated against in the labour market (such as women, ethnic minorities and the disabled) are totally vulnerable to market forces and unable to move out of the secondary labour market segments considered in Chapter 2.

The UK's legal framework has developed around a view of inequality in the labour market which Chryssides and Kaler (1996: 89) describe as *discriminating against people on grounds that are irrelevant to the jobs they are doing or for which they are applying* – a definition that is evident in the UK's anti-discrimination law on sex, race, equal pay, sexual orientation, religious belief, age and disability which reinforces the concept of equal treatment through the removal of prejudice and supports selection on merit. It is essentially based on a 'liberal' perspective of achieving equality through the application of a principle of neutrality to provide fair treatment (Jewson and Mason, 1986). In employment it has led to a focus on eradicating disadvantage where it has been identified that discrimination has occurred in recruitment and dismissals as well as in other workplace practices.

The primary means of achieving equality of opportunity has been through the adoption of procedures designed to avoid a consideration of social group characteristics, such as gender or ethnicity, in the decision-making process. One of the limitations of this approach stems from its underlying assumption that individual characteristics such as gender and ethnic origin can be and should be discounted in workplace resourcing decisions.

A long-standing criticism of the traditional 'equal opportunities' approach is that it reinforces a negative view of difference because it is based on the promotion of sameness of treatment to reduce inequalities (Elmuti, 1993; Wilson and Iles, 1999). In contrast, central to the concept of 'managing diversity' is the belief that all individual differences should be valued and recognised. Furthermore, an approach based on neutral treatment and negative rights – key values underpinning the anti-discrimination legislation (Fredman, 2001) – does not actually reflect changes in the political, economic, social and technological environment in which many organisations operate. Changes in the composition of the working population, patterns of workforce participation and consumer markets mean that the contemporary UK workforce looks very different and has other needs and values compared to the workforce of only 20 years ago (Mavin and Girling, 2000).

A report on 'Diversity in Britain's Labour Market' (Taylor, 2002), commissioned by the Economic and Social Research Council as part of its Future of Work series, identifies the challenges an increasingly diverse workforce presents to government, employers, trade unions and employees. To use just one example, women's participation in the labour market, particularly those with young children, has continued to grow across the EU countries with the European Commission (2007) reporting that six of the eight million jobs created in the EU since 2000 have been occupied by women. In the UK, the proportion of women of working age either in employment or seeking employment has risen from 66 per cent in 1984 to 73 per cent in 2003 (Hibbett and Meager, 2003). In contrast, the number of economically active men in the UK has declined from 88 to 84 per cent over the same period. But although the UK has one of the highest rates of women's participation in Europe, it is also among the most gender segregated (Hibbett and Meager, 2003). According to the Equal Opportunities Commission (2006) for example, only a quarter of senior managers in the Civil Service are female, only 10 per cent of senior police officers are women and only one in nine university vice chancellors are female. This is despite the existence of workforce demographic changes and skills shortages which have meant that organisations have had to widen their recruitment activities to include people they may not have traditionally employed. Severe nurse shortages in the UK, for instance, forced the NHS in 2002 to recruit

14,000 new nurses from Europe and the Philippines (Hall, 2003); skills shortages that have continued with over 11,000 doctors, nurses and midwives with overseas training registered to work in the UK health industry in 2007 (Dreaper, 2008).

An International Labour Office report (2002) identified that millions of new jobs will be needed to sustain the growing population who are aged 60 and over in the EU member states. It warns that employment policies will be required which can attract the reserve labour force identified among women, the old and the young and people with disabilities on the grounds that their workforce participation will be essential to financing social benefits in the future. Yet Taylor (2002) reports continuing differences in the work experiences of men and women, older and younger workers and those employed in small businesses in the UK, despite the widespread adoption of equality policies. Dickens (2005: 181), commenting on this continuing employment disadvantage despite the signs on the surface of progress towards greater workplace equality, points out that 'progress in terms of significant aggregate distributional outcomes is at the best slow and often difficult to identify'. Nowhere is this more evident than in the enduring earnings gap between men and women in the UK. Women working part-time still earn around 40 per cent less than men working full-time per hour worked and the lack of quality part-time work is identified as a major constraint on their career opportunities (Women and Work Commission, 2007). These findings have profound implications for employers if an adequate supply of workers is to be recruited into the active labour force to sustain future economic growth. Whilst increasing numbers of employers are declaring that they encourage diversity or an equal opportunities approach there does appear to be an enduring gap between such statements and the actual experience for many in the UK workforce or, put another way, an enduring gap between the rhetoric on equality and diversity and workplace realities.

Activity 5.1 Adopting a diversity strategy

1. What could be the main advantages to your organisation of encouraging greater diversity when recruiting staff?

2. Identify, in descending order of importance, the main obstacles in your organisation to recruiting a more diverse workforce.

3. What organisational HR policies exist or may be needed to address the barriers you have identified?

Undertaking this activity may well have suggested that employing a more diverse workforce could enhance an organisation's ability to broaden the appeal of the organisation's services or products to a wider range of clients or customers. Certainly changes to the composition of the working population, patterns of workforce participation and consumer markets have prompted the emergence of the 'business case for diversity' (Johnston and Packer, 1987) as an approach which departs from an earlier rationale for equality in employment practices based solely on the provision of social justice. It addresses an objection which tended to dominate the equality debates in the 1980s and early 1990s in the UK, namely that, while laudable, equality legislation presents just another constraint on business operations. This is an issue that continues to dominate discussions about managing diversity and flexible working arrangements. For example, a study undertaken for the then Department of Trade and Industry (Harris and Foster, 2005) into flexible working in small service sector businesses found that, whilst such employers had no principled objection to family friendly legislation, their concerns were about the significant burden upon the business of any extension of these rights, particularly in relation to maternity leave and pay.

Changes in the characteristics of the economically active workforce leading to the increased spending power of minority groups and women (Valdiserri, 2002) has increased interest among employers who perceive that adopting diversity management strategies which take into account the proliferation of individual differences in consumer markets, could bring business benefits. In recognition of the thousands of new Polish workers in Britain, Asda, Tesco and Sainsbury's, for example, have all recently decided to stock Polish food ranges in their supermarkets for the first time (BBC, 2006).

What is managing diversity?

A review of the diversity management literature reveals the absence of a universally accepted definition of the term 'managing diversity'. One interpretation is that managing diversity is something radically different from equal opportunities (Kandola and Fullerton, 1994), another that it is a reconfiguration of equality initiatives (Ford, 1996). Consider what it means to you and to an organisation with which you are familiar by undertaking the following activity.

Activity 5.2   Organisational policy and practice

1. What is your understanding of the term 'managing diversity'?
2. How do you think this differs from equality of opportunity?
3. Compare your definition with how managing diversity and equality of opportunity are described in any equality and diversity statement provided by your organisation.
4. Examine how managing diversity is reflected in your organisation's practices; give examples.
5. What, in your view, are the explanations for any gaps you have identified between observed organisational practice and policy statements?

Undertaking Activity 5.2 is likely to have identified that defining diversity management is far from straightforward. The lack of a common understanding of managing diversity contributes to the frequent variance in what is intended in a policy statement on diversity and what happens in practice. This was found to be the case in a study undertaken by Foster (2003) of diversity and equality in one large UK retailer. The study revealed that there was a lack of a common understanding of the term 'managing diversity' and that it meant different things to different people in different work contexts. Nevertheless, there is some consensus among commentators over the general principles that characterise the approach; for example, as identified, the business case rationale for adopting a managing diversity approach rather than one of equality based solely on a notion of social justice. Kandola and Fullerton's (1998: 8) definition of diversity management highlights its main concerns:

> The basic concept of managing diversity accepts that the workforce consists of a diverse population of people. The diversity consists of visible and non-visible differences which will include factors such as sex, age, background, race, disability, personality and workstyle. It is founded on the premise that harnessing these differences will create a productive environment in which everybody feels valued, where their talents are being fully utilised and in which organisational goals are met.

Put another way, the key principles that inform diversity management can be summarised as:

● valuing, recognising and harnessing a wide range of individual differences;

● the business advantages that stem from recognising individual differences;

● the benefits to the employment relationship of responding to individual needs.

Advocates of managing diversity propose that organisations should recognise all the ways in which *people* differ and not just those recognised in anti-discrimination legislation which can be described as the inclusive approach. This is reflected in the Chartered Institute of Personnel and Development's (2005b: 2) interpretation of diversity management as 'valuing everyone as individuals – as employees, customers and clients'. Commentators define these individual differences in a number of ways. Gill (1996), for instance, lists age, personal work preferences and personal and corporate background as characteristics to be considered in addition to those identified in the anti-discrimination legislation. Thomas (1991) points out that an 'inclusive' definition of diversity should also consider the needs of white able-bodied males – employees who have typically not been the focus of past equality initiatives.

Categorising the differences in a managing diversity approach as being *visible* and *non-visible* is one way of defining these characteristics (Kandola and Fullerton, 1998). In contrast, Wilson and Iles (1999) classify the differences as *primary* (e.g. gender, age and disability) and *secondary* (e.g. class and sexuality). Caution needs to be exercised, however, when defining differences in this way. Categorisations into visible/non-visible or primary/secondary differences fail to recognise that, in reality, people possess a combination of characteristics; for example, an individual could be female, Asian, university educated and an extrovert. Moreover, some aspects of individual difference, such as disability and religion, can be both visible and non-visible. Another approach is reflected in the CIPD's position (2005b: 7) on diversity management which argues that not only should account be taken of social category diversity (demographic differences) but also informational diversity (organisational-based differences) and value diversity (psychological differences).

The business case for diversity

The business case argument for diversity frequently emphasises four main reasons for its promotion in organisational human resourcing strategies. These can be summarised as:

- maximising the resources available in the labour market;
- maximising the potential within the organisation's workforce;
- creating business opportunities through the employment of a diverse workforce by gaining insights into new customer markets and enhancing appeal to a wider customer base;
- organisational sustainability in different cultures which is of particular significance with the increasing globalisation of business.

The changing demographics and patterns of workforce participation already referred to have led migrant workers, particularly from Eastern Europe, being seen as the solution to persistent skills shortages (CIPD, 2007a; Dench *et al.*, 2006). In terms of human resource management outcomes, a central argument in support of adopting a management diversity strategy is the one put forward by Robinson and Dechant (1997), namely that employees will be more committed to employers who recognise and value their individual differences and, consequently, the costs associated with turnover and absenteeism will be reduced. Developing this line of thought, Cox and Blake (1991) suggest that organisations which have adopted such an approach will position themselves to be 'employers of choice' by enhancing their employer brand and thus their ability to recruit the most talented applicants from the labour market. In terms of marketing outcomes, the managing diversity literature suggests that organisations with visible diversity in their staffing can attract a wider customer base and be more sensitive to different customer needs in their products and services (Thomas and Ely, 1996; Whitehead, 1999; Foster and Harris, 2005). This was evident at Ford of Europe where senior managers sought advice from their committee of Asian workers to help with the marketing of Ford Transit vans to Asian shopkeepers (Eglin, 2002).

Research carried out by Johnson-Hillery *et al.* (1997) found that older customers viewed sales staff of the same age more positively than younger personnel. The DIY retailer B&Q was an early pioneer of a recruitment policy targeting the over-50s. One rationale for this was that older customer-facing staff who were more likely to have carried out home improvements, would be able to offer better DIY advice to customers. This policy was identified as leading to higher profits, lower staff turnover and absenteeism and improved reported customer service compared to other stores (Hogarth and Barth, 1991) but it has had to be revisited in the light of the UK's age discrimination legislation although B&Q continues to be a market leader in its diversity policies. This is reflected in its current diversity mission statement which states: 'We like to employ people from every kind of background. It gives us different perspectives – and a much richer mix of experience. It also means we're better equipped to understand the needs and priorities of all our customers' (B&Q, 2008).

Proponents of the managing diversity approach argue that diverse workgroups generate richer ideas and solutions than homogenous groups. Further reported benefits of diversity management include a greater concern for socially responsible behaviour in organisations (Wentling and Palma-Rivas, 1998) and more flexibility in organisational policies since recognising the different needs of employees will demand that policies are less rigid and more innovative (Cox, 1993).

Although Linehan and Hanappi-Egger (2006) suggest that in practice diversity management for European employers has a tendency to focus upon activities such as recruitment and selection rather than marketing, a central message from a study of 500 UK and European organisations conducted by Rajan and Harris (2003) is that employers see diversity management as being about more than just conventional HR issues. It is identified as a means of improving organisational resilience by creating new customer segments aided by developing a diverse workforce that is representative of their customers. Indeed there is some evidence that UK organisations are adopting a wider interpretation of diversity management. Research by the Roffey Park Institute (McCartney, 2007) claims that, although approximately three-quarters of the 74 employers they surveyed had diversity initiatives relating to staff, just over half had diversity strategies relating to their customers.

A broad interpretation of diversity management is illustrated in the corporate diversity statement of Goodyear, one of the world's largest tyre companies which has operations in most regions of the world. Consider how this compares with any organisational policy statement you identified in Activity 5.2.

Exhibit 5.1

Diversity is a business imperative at Goodyear

Diversity makes good business sense for a global company such as Goodyear that is committed to continued growth and maintaining its position as the world's tire industry leader. Goodyear has embraced diversity throughout the organization – from its world headquarters in Akron, Ohio, to all its facilities and markets around the globe.

As the workplace and technology bring associates together in pursuit of common objectives, personal bonds are created beyond whatever racial, ethnic or cultural differences exist in society. A diverse and inclusive workforce provides the strategic advantage to successfully conduct business in multi-cultural marketplaces globally, and Goodyear's diverse mindset has enabled it to respond to change much quicker than its competitors.'

Goodyear's Chairman, President & Chief Executive Officer Bob Keegan also adds,

> 'Our most important asset is the people of Goodyear. Being committed to maintaining a diverse workforce, reflective in large measure of our diverse marketplace, is an important part of what we must do to grow our company . . . So, for us, an inclusive environment is a business imperative. I believe diversity is a competitive advantage for this great company. Bringing that diversity together and building the right team of leaders breathes success into an organization.'

Source: http://www.goodyear.com/careers/careers_diversity.html 20/11/08

Whilst in theory it is relatively easy to identify the business-related advantages of diversity management, the approach is not without its limitations. Dickens (1994: 11) suggests that organisations are not always responsive to arguments that state an effective approach to equality will enable them to compete in the labour market because '. . . *employers operate in different labour markets and . . . labour market and skills shortages are not experienced everywhere the same.'* An example of this variation is evident in the degree of multiculturalism in UK cities. It is anticipated that by 2037 at least 12 British cities will no longer be dominated by one ethnic group and Leicester, Birmingham, Slough and Luton are all set to become 'superdiverse' cities in less than 20 years (Hill, 2007).

Despite many reported diversity initiatives, Mavin and Girling (2000) point to the lack of empirical evidence demonstrating a direct link between diversity management and competitive advantage. This can be partly explained by the difficulties of systematically measuring its impact on an organisation due to the different experiences of those at the receiving end of such policies but also because some of the advantages claimed for the approach, such as improving job satisfaction and creating a better corporate image, are indirect benefits (Kandola and Fullerton, 1998). But it can also be the case that employing a diverse workforce can present managers with new conflicts of interest and increase the complexity of their problem-solving and decision-making. One way of reducing such tensions is not to limit benefits to one defined social group. This is evident in the approach taken by the retailer Asda, nominated in the top 10 companies in the UK to work for by the *Sunday Times* newspaper for three successive years. It has adopted a diversity strategy based on 'opportunities for all'; for example, in support of cultural tolerance the company operates a policy of Religious Festival Leave which allows colleagues to take up to two days' unpaid leave to attend any religious festival – an inclusive approach which avoids the perceived unfairness created by one group enjoying a benefit not available to another. It is acknowledged that this is less likely to be a practical option for smaller, less well-resourced organisations.

Such experiences are not an argument for denying that benefits can be achieved from adopting a strategic approach to managing diversity. It is rather to recognise that by addressing the needs of one group there is frequently the potential to create a disadvantage for another, with resultant feelings of unfairness. The following fictional case study draws upon research conducted by the authors (Harris *et al.*, 2007) in the retail industry. It reveals some of the tensions experienced by store managers in meeting their performance targets as well as the needs of part-time workers.

Case Study 5.1

Career progression at Freshfoods Ltd – whose flexibility?

Store managers working for the Freshfoods supermarket chain are under pressure to meet store performance targets set by head office. Their individual performance bonus and any group bonus based on each store's sales figures depends on it, so the management team is constantly looking for ways to increase profits and turnover whilst reducing costs such as those associated with high staff absenteeism and attrition rates. One way of achieving this is to rely on the availability of part-time staff as a means of providing a low-cost, flexible and efficient solution to staffing sales assistant roles.

Whilst part-time workers are a key factor in each store's staffing arrangements and cost effectiveness, there are no real opportunities for their progression and promotion. This is evident in the absence of part-timers in any management or supervisory roles which may be explained by the difficulty of accessing opportunities for development for those working part-time and a company policy requirement that anyone taking on a managerial role has to be prepared to move to another store. Part-time staff find that they are frequently unable to undertake the training events that are essential to progression because they require a full day of attendance, are scheduled for a time when they are not working or are held at a location that is not manageable due to childcare arrangements. Where there are requirements for self-development using web-based learning, part-time staff find they do not have the time to complete these during their limited working hours.

Whilst managers, full-time and part-time staff identify that career opportunities are in theory available to all staff, they all recognise that, in practice, part-time staff would find it difficult to take on management responsibilities in an environment which requires a great deal of flexibility from individuals in the hours they are available to work. As a result it is widely felt such opportunities can only realistically be taken up by full-time staff. As one female part-time sales assistant remarked 'promotions go to those working full-time. I'd like to be a supervisor but would have to work to look after my children so taking on responsibilities might be too much'.

Unsurprisingly the tension between the business case for employing part-time workers and recognising the developmental needs of such staff has led to feelings of unfairness amongst those part-time workers who are eager to progress. These workers feel that they should have the same developmental opportunities as their full-time colleagues and store managers can see that the talents of many part-timers are not fully utilised in their current roles. Those managers who are more aware of the challenge of balancing work and home life and have childcare commitments of their own are keen to seek ways of addressing the issue of career progression and more development for part-time staff. They are also aware that staff in managerial roles are required to offer flexibility in the hours they work in this fast moving and customer focused retail working environment.

Activity 5.3   Career progression at Freshfoods Ltd – whose flexibility?

1. What do you see as the main arguments for addressing the lack of opportunities for career development for part-time staff at Freshfoods Ltd?

2. Identify the key constraints on the career progression of part-time staff at Freshfoods Ltd.

3. Consider to what extent equal rights legislation for part-time and full-time staff can overcome the issues raised in this case study.

4. Suggest ways in which the issue of career progression for part-time staff could be addressed taking account of business needs.

Sameness or difference to achieve equality?

As already identified, a key assumption of diversity management is that individual differences should be valued, recognised and harnessed in order to achieve business-related advantages. This implies that people should be treated differently rather than similarly in organisational practices but, as we have seen with the part-timers at Freshfoods Ltd, in practice there is likely to be a price to pay for accommodating individual needs. Fredman (2001) sees a clear distinction between an approach that encourages differential treatment for individuals and one that emphasises neutrality through 'sameness' of treatment to provide fairness in workplace decision-making. Recognising the limitations of attempting to provide any such classifications, Table 5.1 summarises a number of the main differences in the principles associated with the two approaches.

One interpretation of these differences is that, in order to maximise their potential, the two approaches have to operate in isolation from each other, which has led to some concern that promoting diversity initiatives could actually erode the achievements of equal opportunities programmes if it resulted in a reduced awareness of group-based disadvantage (Overell, 1998a). Ford (1996) argues that to avoid this, equality and diversity policies should be regarded as interdependent, a position long supported by the Chartered Institute of Personnel Management (then IPD, 1997) who view managing diversity as a progression from and not a rejection of earlier equal opportunities principles. Yet the suggestion that managing diversity is a logical development of equal opportunities may well be overlooking the complex reality this presents particularly for those required to put policies into action. Liff (1999), for example, observes that, analytically, the combination of an approach that claims the cause of equality is best served by ignoring differences with one that claims it is better served by acknowledging and responding to difference looks odd and recognises the importance of preserving the benefits stemming from established equal opportunities processes in any move to a less tested diversity orthodoxy.

In practice, research findings suggest that many HR specialists and line managers see no distinction between equal opportunities and promoting diversity (Mavin and Girling, 2000). Foster's research (2003) suggests that for most employees and managers the approaches do not meaningfully differ, with 'managing diversity'

Table 5.1 **Key differences between managing equal opportunities and managing diversity**

Equal opportunities	Managing diversity
Addresses inequality through rights	Promotes diversity for organisational benefits
Neutralises individual differences	Recognises individual differences
Treats people the same	Treats people differently
A narrow view of difference	An inclusive view of difference
A focus on HR processes	Concerns all functions of the organisation
Promotes assimilation	Promotes variety
An emphasis on procedures and regulation	An emphasis on organisational objectives

being seen as simply a new name for 'equal opportunities'. A US study by the Society for Human Resource Management and the American Institute for Managing Diversity Inc found that, despite employers recognising that workplace diversity is important, a common diversity management language to help organisations in their efforts to establish a shared organisational understanding of what it involved did not exist and only 30 per cent of the businesses surveyed had an official definition of the term (HR Focus, 2008). This may help to explain why, despite a growing interest in managing diversity and the recognition of individual differences, well-developed, proactive diversity management strategies are not more widely in evidence in UK workplaces, despite the claims that these can lead to competitive advantage. For example, a major survey of diversity management in 445 organisations found that only 7.5 per cent provided diversity training to their staff and just fewer than 10 per cent conducted diversity training specifically for managers (Kandola and Fullerton, 1998). A further explanation is that the real difficulties with diversity management lie in its organisational implementation. For busy line managers it may be just that it is viewed as being more likely to present dilemmas than offer potential advantages; for example, how to accommodate individual differences but still ensure compliance with anti-discrimination laws which equate workplace 'fairness' with neutrality of treatment.

Anti-discrimination legislation and approaches to workplace equality

The anti-discrimination legislation framework in both the UK and the EU has developed in an essentially fragmented way as a result of a series of laws providing individual rights against discrimination in relation to certain specific characteristics; for example, race, gender and disability. These statutes permit individuals who feel that unfair discrimination has taken place to seek redress through the employment tribunal system, but there is still no overarching legal right under the equal opportunities banner that guarantees equal treatment for all as there is in the human rights approach of the US or Canada. This is despite the UK's Human Rights Act 1998 which incorporates all the articles of the European Convention on Human Rights, including Article 14 prohibiting discrimination. But at present this is not a free-standing right as it can only be invoked in conjunction with an allegation that another Convention right has been infringed – a situation that will change in the future when Protocol 12 to the European Convention is adopted across EU member states as it will provide a free-standing individual right not to be discriminated against.

The UK's Race Relations Act (1975) and the Sex Discrimination Act (1975) introduced the concepts of direct and indirect discrimination. These concepts continue to be present in recent anti-discrimination legislation, for example those prohibiting discrimination on the grounds of religious belief or sexual orientation implemented in 2003. Direct discrimination involves treating someone unfairly, for example because of their gender, race, religious beliefs or disability, whereas indirect discrimination occurs when a requirement condition applies to all but in actual fact means that certain groups are placed at a disadvantage. This may not always be obvious and requires an ongoing assessment of established HR practices. So, for example, advertising for a middle management post stating that applicants need to have a minimum of three years' relevant managerial experience and be aged under 35 will be likely to discriminate against women who are less likely than men to have gained the required managerial experience within the prescribed age limit because of time out of the workplace to raise children.

In the UK, the individual statutes until recently have been supported by the Commission for Racial Equality, the Equal Opportunities Commission and the Disability Rights Commission. In 2007 these three bodies merged to form the Commission for Equality and Human Rights (CEHR). The Commission has a duty to help eliminate unfair discrimination in the workplace, review legislation and promote equal opportunities in organisations. Furthermore, through Codes of Practice, the Commission is required to provide practical assistance and good practice guidelines to support compliance with equality law.

To address identified inequalities, the UK government has implemented a range of individual anti-discrimination rights aimed at the promotion of equal treatment in obtaining and retaining employment as well as workplace practices. This legislation has resulted largely from the EU's Anti-Discrimination Framework Directive 2000 which was fully implemented in domestic legislation in 2006 and which extended existing law beyond equal pay, sex, race and disability to sexual orientation, religion or belief and age. To avoid the singling out of specific groups, some organisations made provisions in their employment practices to encompass different religious beliefs across their workforces. For example, one local council in London has abolished their previous flexitime system requiring staff to work core hours; instead, staff can now work from home or job share. For Muslim employees it means that they are not forced to work on Friday, their holy day (Cooper, 2003). The law on sexual orientation has required organisations to reassess their HR policies. For example, employers providing pension schemes and health insurance to unmarried heterosexual couples are required to make provisions to ensure that such policies are also available to same-sex couples (Hayfield, 2003). Similarly, the recent introduction of age discrimination legislation has raised a number of new issues for employers and employees prompting a recent article in *Personnel Today* to declare that ageism is set to be the 'most common form of discrimination' (Vorster, 2008). With the government setting 65 as the default statutory UK retirement age, employers can still uphold the retirement age of 65 and refuse an individual's request to work beyond this age. This seems at odds with stated government policy encouraging individuals to have longer working lives to alleviate skills and pension shortages.

Unsurprisingly this has led to criticism of a rigid adherence to the statutory retirement age by employers and there is some evidence that the setting of the default retirement age will encourage some employers to retire all workers at 65 to avoid the complexity of making decisions in individual cases and any entitlements to redundancy pay. It has already led to cases such as the professor whose request to work part-time after 65 was refused by Manchester University prompting student protests (Braid, 2008). Recent findings from the Recruitment Confidence Index (Williams, 2008) have also suggested that despite the age discrimination legislation, stereotypical views of old and young workers continue to exist. The study also found that 25 per cent of the senior UK managers they surveyed were aware of the existence of an ageist employment practice in their organisation although the full organisational impact of the legislation has yet to become evident and there is still very little case law. Furthermore many employees welcome retirement and the desire to work longer is still not evident among the majority of the workforce although it is argued that pension shortfalls will increasingly become a driving factor.

Achieving equality and diversity

Fredman (2001: 154) observes that, traditionally, equality laws have been informed by three principles: *neutrality*, *individualism* and the *promotion of autonomy*. The first of these, the principle of neutrality, aims to ensure that people are treated in the same way and appears to be the most dominant consideration in the UK anti-discrimination framework. It is an approach to workplace equality based on achieving fairness through consistency of treatment. Second, the principle of individualism refers to the notion of judging people on their merits rather than their social group membership. The intention is that individuals are judged on their talents and not treated less favourably as a result of characteristics such as disability, race or gender. Finally, the principle of autonomy is concerned with the idea that individuals should be free to make their own choices.

An important consideration in the way the European workplace equality agenda has developed in practice is that the legislation has been based on the provision of negative rights; in other words, individuals should *not* be discriminated against. Organisations have not been required legally to promote the *positive* rights of staff to achieve equality in the workforce. But there are specific statutory duties placed on public sector employers in the UK to eliminate discrimination on the grounds of sex, race and disability and to promote positively equality of opportunity. The positive duty on public sector employers to promote racial equality, for example, was introduced by the UK's Race Relations Amendment Act 2000 resulting from the MacPherson's Commission's finding of institutional racism in the police force. Employers can elect to use positive action initiatives as a supplement to the anti-discrimination legislation. These are initiatives, voluntarily adopted by organisations, which aim to encourage applicants from minority groups and can also involve implementing training programmes to help under-represented groups compete more favourably in the workplace. 'Opportunity Now', for example, was launched in the UK in 1991 to increase the number of women in senior management positions with the aim of ultimately improving the balance of genders at all levels within the workplace (King, 1994) but progress has remained slow. Walsh (2007) in her analysis of the 2004 Workplace Employment Relations Survey findings points out that women's representation in senior management in UK workplaces had only marginally improved by 2 per cent between 1998 and 2004. Similarly the Women's National Commission (2002) reported that, despite women constituting half of the population, they still occupy only a third of all public appointments in the UK. This has become of such concern to some employers, particularly in the public sector, that they have taken positive action to address the under-representation of certain groups in the workforce. The term 'Positive Action' refers to a range of measures and development initiatives that employers can lawfully take to help people from under-represented groups to compete for jobs and career opportunities on equal terms with other applicants as shown by the following illustration of positive action at the Devon and Cornwall Constabulary.

Exhibit 5.2

Positive Action at Devon and Cornwall Constabulary

Devon and Cornwall Constabulary has a strong commitment to equality and diversity both within the organisation and in the service we provide. We are committed to ensuring that our workforce reflects the community, by providing a high quality service which meets the needs of your community, and the people who live within it. We are currently underrepresented by some groups. As an equal opportunities employer we use lawful provisions in order to positively address this. In order to provide a high level of service, Devon and Cornwall Constabulary endeavour to encourage applications from underrepresented groups and we are proud to pursue a policy of Positive Action in an attempt to achieve this.

Source: www.devon-cornwall.police.uk/v3/recruit/diversity

Positive discrimination (also referred to as reverse discrimination) which proactively sets out to compensate individuals for past discrimination should not be confused with positive action which aims to encourage rather than regulate. Positive discrimination may involve targeting selected minority groups in order to fulfil quotas that define the profile of the workforce and making selection decisions based on the visible diversity of the candidate (typically race and gender). Positive discrimination, unless allowed for by the under-representation provisions of the legislation or where there is a genuine occupational qualification for a particular characteristic, is illegal in the UK but legal in the US. It reflects a 'radical' approach to equal opportunities in that it focuses on altering the outcome of a decision rather than the procedures (Jewson and Mason, 1986). It has its roots in the notion of distributive justice in that it is concerned with how fairly rewards are allocated, which in the workplace particularly relates to the outcomes of human resourcing decisions.

Positive discrimination has been heavily criticised. Research conducted by Singer and Singer (1991) in the US suggests that positive discrimination may be viewed as contradicting the notion of merit-based selection, a central principle in the UK's anti-discrimination legislation. Reverse discrimination aimed at rectifying past under-representation can heighten feelings of unfairness and harden attitudes to particular groups (who might well have preferred to attribute their recognition to merit); for example, where a quota exists and more qualified 'majority' candidates perceive that they have been rejected in favour of less qualified 'minority' applicants.

Activity 5.4   The anti-discrimination approach

The 'anti-discrimination' model has prevailed in European Community law on equality, the duty of the courts being to determine whether individuals belonging to a particular group have been adversely affected in the distribution of certain advantages or disadvantages.

What are the advantages and disadvantages of the traditional anti-discrimination model in legislating for equality in employment in terms of:

1. Reducing inequality in the labour market?
2. Developing organisational approaches to equality of opportunity and promoting diversity?

This activity helps to illustrate that, whilst the legal framework has supported an approach to fair treatment in workplace practice based on ensuring consistency, consistency is a relative principle and its pursuit alone will not act as a stimulus for progressive employment practices. Provided that sameness of treatment is demonstrated, the quality of the employment practice is not at issue. This leads Fredman (2001) to observe that the consistency principle does not require individuals to be treated well, only alike, which in reality could be equally badly.

Furthermore, anti-discrimination laws have meant that claims of discrimination can be pursued only through litigation on the basis of an individual being able to demonstrate less favourable treatment compared to the norm. This reinforces the requirement to refer to a comparator to demonstrate that discrimination has taken place, which neither challenges the accepted norm nor promotes the seeking out of creative alternative employment practices. As a result, the usual comparator for demonstrating gender neutrality has been the male standard (Mackinnon, 1987) and for ethnic minorities it has meant neutralising differences stemming from their own cultures if they wish to be treated like the rest of the community (Parekh, 1998). In practice this can lead to an equal-treatment approach reinforcing past or ongoing discrimination, as it fails to challenge the established standard.

We have identified that findings from Foster's retailing study (2003) suggest that managing diversity means different things to different people; a lack of conceptual clarity that, it is suggested, leads line managers to interpret it in a variety of ways according to the pressures and dynamics of a range of contextual factors that impact on the design and interpretation of a diversity strategy. The most frequently identified of these are illustrated in Figure 5.1.

A consequence of the way in which the present UK anti-discrimination legislation is framed, specifically in terms of how it defines 'fair' treatment, is that it has led to an emphasis on procedural justice in organisations (Harris, 2000). This is because formal policies that stress procedural fairness are the most visible means of defence if an organisation is accused of discriminating unfairly. So, for example, advice provided by the Equality and Human Rights Commission states that when recruiting female staff, assessors should not ask questions about a woman's plans

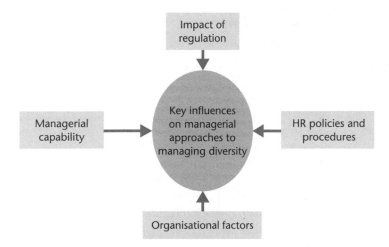

Figure 5.1 **Key influences on managerial approaches to managing diversity**

for starting a family and that when advertising jobs, employers should not include any age limits.

The expansion of individual rights relating to discrimination further heightens the preoccupation of both human resource specialists and line managers with procedural fairness. This is largely driven by the dominant concern of defending potential legal claims by demonstrating 'that justice has been done'. It has encouraged approaches based on sameness of treatment which may be at odds with the wider aim of increasing workforce diversity or promoting positive action to address identified under-represented groups (Barnes and Ashtiany, 2003). Yet much of the organisational justice research reinforces the value of focusing on procedural justice on the grounds that violating dimensions of procedural justice is likely to have a greater impact on feelings of fairness than the distributive justice of final outcomes (Dipboye and de Pontbriand, 1981; McFarlin and Sweeney, 2001). In other words, fair procedures can result in an individual perceiving a decision as just, even when there has been an unfavourable personal result (Greenberg, 1987; Leung and Li, 1990). This helps to explain the organisational emphasis on 'getting the procedures right' which is the essence of much of the equal opportunities training received by line managers rather than changing their beliefs and attitudes, but it is an approach that acts as a constraint on really moving the equality and diversity agenda forward. Not only does it encourage a compliance/defensive approach to equality in employment practices but it can actually become destructive (Liff, 1989) if controlling the processes and avoiding potential litigation become the ultimate aim rather than promoting greater diversity and equality of opportunity in the workplace.

Treating everyone the same irrespective of group identities ignores the importance of that identity to the individual and challenges the extent to which the norms of the dominant culture are embedded in workplace processes. The absence of role models for individuals in management roles who have been able to work flexibly or at some stage work part-time was evident in the Freshfoods Ltd case study (p. 134). This is an issue that is being specifically addressed by the UK retailer John Lewis.

Exhibit 5.3

John Lewis Partnership – creating flexible career paths

The John Lewis Partnership aims to create a culture that values difference and makes the most of the talents of all employees, who are known as partners because they are co-owners of the business. To this end, the right to request flexible working is extended to all. But a gender forum of partners found that there is still a perception that it is difficult to combine a career with parenthood. In response, the Partnership has continued to develop its work-life balance policies and promotes senior role models who work flexibly. For example, a career break scheme allows up to 12 months unpaid leave with continued service and a job to return to. Case studies of senior managers working flexibly are highlighted in the staff magazine.

Source: Women and Work Commission (2007), *Towards A Fairer Future*, Executive summary, Crown Copyright: 11

In contrast to the approach at John Lewis, the following experience of a small IT company shows how tensions can occur in employment relationships where there is a lack of understanding of differences and other cultures in the workplace.

Case Study 5.2

Promotion at Venture Services

Venture Services is a rapidly expanding small company providing a range of IT services to businesses with a specialism in developing dedicated systems for libraries and higher education establishments. The staff have always been a close-knit group and good teamworking has been a vital ingredient in the company's success and growth. In the past year, two staff of the Muslim faith have been recruited. They are beginning to be regarded as poor team players and even unfriendly. They do not come to any social events and have never joined the staff who meet after work to celebrate the start or finish of a contract or birthdays. Recently a promotion opportunity arose and one of the new staff, Imran, who has excellent technical qualifications, applied. He was unsuccessful and, identifying that he was better qualified than the applicant who got the promotion, Imran complained on the grounds of racial discrimination. The manager making the selection was anxious to clarify things so decided to provide feedback to Imran on the reasons for the decision, namely that despite his high level of specialist knowledge, he is not regarded as a team player whereas the successful candidate has a proven track record of excellent and productive working relationships with other colleagues. Imran is completely taken aback by this explanation, especially as, to his knowledge, he has worked very well with everyone in the team, and is even more convinced that the decision not to select him was due to his ethnicity.

Activity 5.5   Promotion at Venture Services

1. What are the likely explanations for the different perceptions of the parties?
2. Identify the issues in managing diversity that this scenario raises.
3. How could Venture Services avoid or minimise similar difficulties arising in the future?

This short case study shows how a lack of consideration of diversity issues has meant that it has simply not occurred to the established staff group that, rather than feeling uncomfortable in socialising at events where the consumption of alcohol plays a central part, colleagues belonging to the Muslim faith have decided it is better just not to participate. Yet by not explaining the reasons for their absence to their colleagues or reflecting on how their absence might be interpreted, the decision not to join in has contributed to their work colleagues' lack of understanding.

Developing awareness and managerial capability

On a more positive note, new legislation can act as the catalyst for creating greater awareness of diversity issues and reviewing practices to ensure that existing processes do not disadvantage those who are different. If the pursuit of uniformity and neutrality erodes managerial discretion and the willingness to seek out different solutions to fit different circumstances, then employment law aimed at addressing identified individual needs may encourage the adoption of more proactive and innovative personnel policies, for example flexible work patterns for parents of young children. But it also presents fresh challenges and potential pitfalls in terms of their managerial interpretation and application. There are inherent tensions between the imperatives of the market, external levels of regulation, organisational demands for cost-effective HR practices, employers' ethical responsibilities to attend to the needs of individuals at work (Keenoy, 1990) and perceptions of workplace fairness (Harris, 2002a). The balance is a delicate one which can alter quite quickly whenever the level of influence of these recognised regulators of the employment relationship changes. Drawing upon research conducted by the authors (Tansley *et al.*, 2007), the following case study explores the issues faced by UK public sector line managers required to identify individuals suitable for talent management programmes in a working environment which encourages open access for all.

Case Study 5.3

Developing future leaders at Westwood County Council

An ageing demographic profile, particularly in its present middle and senior management, and an identified shortage of managerial skills when recruiting from the external labour market led Westwood County Council to introduce an internal leadership development programme. This is a two-year programme that is partly externally delivered by a university business school but is predominantly project work based as a means of developing both the breadth and depth of participants' experience. It has been a successful development initiative which has been very popular with those individuals who have completed it and Westwood Council has now developed a talent pool of 60 employees.

Great emphasis is placed on self-development, mentoring and coaching as a way of developing individuals into future leaders. Consequently, there is an expectation amongst staff that if they successfully complete the programme they can expect fairly rapid promotion. The senior management of the Council have been highly supportive of the programme but are very aware that an expectation of progression has been created among a particularly enthusiastic and motivated group who are very committed to the organisation. They also recognise that if their expectations of progression are not met, it is quite likely that these individuals will seek opportunities elsewhere. The Chief Executive has made it clear that having such talented individuals within the organisation is critical to its future success.

As a public sector employer with a strong trade union presence, the Council has a firm commitment to creating open access to any job opportunities that occur as well as taking positive steps to address the under-representation of specific groups in its workforce to reflect the diversity of the community it serves in its employees. These approaches to achieving greater equality and diversity appear to be at odds with the provision of specific career progression to those who have completed the leadership programme. So, whilst the programme has started to tackle succession planning issues, it has raised another set of problems associated with equality of treatment and the Council's commitment to positive action to promote diversity across the organisation.

The leadership programme has been one of open access for individuals in junior or middle management roles provided their line manager supported their application and was able to release them. There has been no formal selection process and some individuals, mainly those with personal commitments, such as women with childcare responsibilities, have tended not to apply. The result has been that the programme has not assisted the Council's strategic aim to address the issue of women's under-representation in middle and senior managerial roles, in fact it has made it possibly more difficult to address.

There are growing concerns among employees and managers about the fairness of selection onto the programme and that individuals who have not completed it will be disadvantaged when it comes to promotion in a managerial role. Line managers are also concerned that valuable but limited resources are being focused on those employees seen as 'future talent' which means reduced resources to develop other staff they are responsible for. At the same time, individuals who have been on the programme feel it would be unacceptable after the investment in their development if their qualifications and abilities are not properly recognised. Some are already growing frustrated with their lack of progress and are seeking opportunities outside the organisation.

Activity 5.6   Developing future leaders at Westwood County Council

1. What are the arguments for and against differential treatment in terms of career progression for those on the talent management programme?

2. How could the leadership development initiative be better aligned to existing equality and diversity policies and aims?

3. Suggest what could be done to address feelings of unfairness amongst those staff not on the leadership management programme. What role should the line manager play in this?

This case study has illustrated some of the workplace equality issues busy line managers are increasingly experiencing. One response to such issues is for these managers to adhere to the tried and tested approach of treating staff the same rather than seeking solutions to meet individual circumstances, particularly where such an approach may be easier to justify to the majority of staff. Indeed, Foster's research (2003) into diversity management found that, although in theory employees were supportive of differential treatment, in practice, actually achieving workplace fairness was equated with treating people the same by both managers and employees. Managers experiencing increasing levels of HR responsibilities as a result of devolved decision-making are likely to find this aspect of their role growing in its complexity largely due to the growth in individual rights. On the one hand, moving away from the sameness of treatment principle in favour of treating people differently, as diversity management advocates, may increase the potential for claims of preferential treatment and feelings of inequity among others. For example flexible working arrangements create new issues for line managers to address, as illustrated in the following activity.

Activity 5.7	The request for full pay

Susan is a senior financial manager with the media giant Trojan and has reduced her hours to four days a week. She has reached an agreement with her employer that she will receive 90 per cent of her salary to reflect the decrease. The reality of the arrangement is that she finds she is fulfilling the same number of tasks and actually achieving more in the four days than when she worked a full week, by working longer days and doing a considerable amount of paperwork at home. She approaches Trojan's remuneration committee and asks it to reconsider her package on the grounds that she should receive 100 per cent of her pay.

1. What issues does this request raise?
2. How will a decision *not to grant* the full salary be viewed by Susan?
3. How will a decision to *grant* the full salary be viewed by other employees?

Managers will increasingly have to decide not only *what* but *when* they need to know more about the staff for whom they are responsible. This is highlighted by the conventional wisdom in recruitment processes that those selecting are best advised not to ask about an applicant's family circumstances so that such information cannot affect a decision to employ the candidate. Yet it can be argued that a diversity management approach might be better served by encouraging those selecting to ask about an applicant's personal circumstances to enable them to provide working arrangements adapted to their individual needs, examples being employees with caring responsibilities, or selecting staff to work from home (Harris, 2003). Once managers have gained knowledge about the diversity of their staff, it is likely that they will have to adapt their behaviour accordingly. Research carried out by Foster (2003) suggests that the leadership capability of line managers is an important element of being able to manage employee diversity effectively. Altering management styles according to a subordinate's personality, such as adopting a nurturing approach to ensure that a more introvert member of staff contributes to the department, was regarded by line managers as an essential element of managing diversity on a day-to-day basis.

As the potential grounds for claiming discrimination have grown and the associated costs of litigation escalate, so will the importance managers attach to risk avoidance by adhering to safe solutions in their HR decisions. Harris's findings (2000) suggest that when balancing the pressures of demonstrating care for the individual and defending the robustness of their decision-making, managers opt for the 'safety-net of the sameness of treatment' approach.

One response is that the devolvement of HR responsibilities to line managers is accompanied by an increase in corporate procedures which they are expected to apply in a highly uniform manner (McGovern *et al.*, 1997), the danger is that it will descend to managing by 'systems control' (Watson, 2002: 382). While greater freedoms to exercise discretion in HR decisions may, in theory, be the preferred approach of many managers, faced with the possibility of a personal decision leading to litigation, well-developed rules become more desirable. The prospect of their individual judgement and behaviour being closely scrutinised can be a daunting prospect to many managers, especially the less experienced (Sheppard *et al.*, 1994; Harris *et al.*, 2002) who are therefore less likely to feel comfortable with exercising discretion in decision-making to accommodate individual circumstances. Centrally developed personnel procedures with training in anti-discrimination and employment rights is frequently regarded as the best way of minimising internal grievances and reducing the risk of litigation. But this also reinforces the wisdom of compliance and discourages managers from exercising discretion to accommodate individual circumstances (Harris, 1999). As Dickens observes (2000: 150) 'handling equality in the workplace is dominated by compliance-avoidance pressures, to the detriment of moving to more flexible, proactive approaches aimed at promoting diversity'. Equality and diversity training also relies on case studies as a method for exploring how staff might handle sensitive issues arising from managing individual differences. The CIPD professional qualification, for example, utilises case studies as a principal method of examination. However, there are shortcomings to this method of training. It is unlikely that managers will fully appreciate the real-life tensions associated with managing different employees by simply considering a series of case studies. This point is illustrated in Foster's (2003) study which used a series of short fictitious scenarios to explore how respondents might interpret and implement diversity management. The scenario responses were then compared to what managers actually did in practice. It was found that, in theory, managers believed that recognising differences in employment practices could bring business benefits to the organisation. However, the reality was that differential treatment was costly, risky and difficult to manage, and therefore many of the business advantages of treating staff differently were not viable.

It has been argued throughout this chapter that an approach to equality which places the emphasis on adhering to processes to demonstrate their moral neutrality leads to an overly 'proceduralised' approach at the cost of investing in inter-personal relationships and more flexible diversity policies. Yet the organisational rationale for focusing on the managerial application of corporate procedures and ensuring a clear document trail can be well justified (Harris, 1999). In the context of legal dispute resolution, the process remains a key determinant of procedural justice. It is not only the essential means of employers showing the 'reasonableness' of their decision-making but a major influence on the likelihood of an individual claiming unfair treatment (Bierhoff *et al.*, 1986). The negative outcome can be that the priority in organisational approaches to equality becomes one of 'ensuring visibly fair process', with the very procedures becoming the sources of conflict and even grievances between HR practitioners, line managers and individual employees.

Organisational factors

Managerial approaches to diversity will inevitably be informed by the specific organisational context. Attracting different types of people to an organisation will be determined by, for instance, people's perceptions of the industry/sector in which the organisation operates.

Exhibit 5.4

Industry image – the Lloyds TSB experience

'Back in the late nineties, we identified that only 3 per cent of our graduate intake came from ethnic minorities when 12 per cent of people graduating at that time were from these groups', says Andrew Wakelin, a senior manager for equality and diversity at Lloyds TSB. 'We did a huge amount of work that started with focus groups across universities with undergraduates and the lessons learnt have enabled us to become far more inclusive.' The biggest lesson was that many ethnic minorities didn't see banking as the dynamic career their parents hoped they would go into, he says. 'So the first thing we had to do was not only sell Lloyds TSB brand, but also banking as a career to both graduates and parents.'

Source: adapted from Hilpern, K. (2003) 'The rich rewards of racial equality', *The Independent*, 30 October

The image and reputation of the organisation as an employer will affect the types of people attracted to the organisation (Markwick and Fill, 1997). These images are further influenced by elements such as the products sold, services offered and the behaviour and visible diversity of front-line staff. All of these factors help to reinforce the employer's brand and position in the labour market, in other words how they are perceived by potential applicants as a place to work compared to the competition (Barrow and Mosley, 2005). The maternity and children's specialist retailer Mothercare who came 18th in the 2008 *Sunday Times* '20 Best Big Companies to Work For' list attribute their ranking to a number of factors relating to their employer brand. These include an emphasis on work-life balance, flexible working, better than average maternity pay and leave, and a generous staff discount. This, they argue, helps to attract and retain staff, particularly female employees who make up 90 per cent of the workforce.

Some organisations may be perceived as having an 'inclusive' identity; others may have an image that discourages patronage from diverse job applicants and customers. The ability to attract different types of employees also assumes that the appropriate and available pool of labour is diverse. If this lacks diversity, the chances of employing different types of people will be greatly reduced, although it may well be that other sources of labour supply need to be considered (as discussed elsewhere in this chapter) or specific strategies for encouraging more diverse applicants generated.

If an organisation is able to employ a diverse workforce, the extent to which these individual differences are recognised in employment practices will be significantly affected by the size and structure of the organisation. The larger, more bureaucratic and spread out the organisation, the more likely it is that prescriptive, formal procedures will exist. For example, due to public accountability, a strong trade union presence and ideology, it is argued that public sector employers will be predisposed to pay greater attention to issues of demonstrating procedural fairness in their HR practices. This approach is further reinforced by a traditional inclination in this sector to a bureaucratic, administrative and regulatory approach to the employment relationship (Farnham and Giles, 1996). In contrast, smaller organisations with lower levels of union membership and trade union recognition are less inclined to have in place formalised employment procedures that define how people should be treated and are more likely to enter into 'ad hoc' arrangements to meet circumstances as they arise (Matlay, 1999; Harris and Foster, 2005).

The impact external stakeholders might have on approaches to diversity within an organisation is also worth considering. Customers may demand new products and services according to their specific needs. In response to a changing customer profile, British Telecom and the HSBC bank have developed tailored services for customers in the UK Asian business community (Race for Opportunity, 2002). While some external stakeholders, such as customers, may help to promote diversity management, others may hamper its adoption or not fully understand its aims. One well-publicised example of this was the unfortunate experience of Ford Motors who used an external advertising agency to generate company literature for a Polish promotional campaign. The agency changed the faces of the ethnic minority workers to white in the Polish literature because they argued that the original picture used in the UK, depicting ethnic minority staff, did not reflect the ethnic mix of Poland (Siler, 1996). As a result, Ford had to issue compensation and an apology to their ethnic minority workers.

Activity 5.8   Contextualising diversity

1. Referring to Figure 5.1 (p. 141), examine how these elements impact on your organisation's ability to implement a managing diversity approach.

2. Amend Figure 5.1 to reflect your own organisational context, removing those factors that do not apply and adding those you have identified as having more impact.

3. If working in a group with representatives from other industry sectors, compare your amended figures. What are the major differences, if any, between the factors identified for private and public sector organisations?

Future challenges

We have argued that adopting a more radical approach to promoting workforce diversity is complex since it requires careful evaluation of the different elements that may impede or promote its adoption. Does this mean, then, that diversity management, particularly in relation to treating people differently, is often found to be unworkable for organisations, or is this to oversimplify the situation (Foster, 2003)?

What the available evidence does suggest is that 'home-grown' solutions to managing diversity are the best way forward. It supports Boxall and Purcell's

(2002) wider message for strategic HRM to focus on 'good practice' which reflects external and internal organisational 'fit' rather than pursuing the best practice approach which may be at odds with the organisational and environmental reality. This allows for proper account to be taken of the many and varied factors affecting its implementation, some of which may be organisationally specific and even unique, but it is an approach which challenges the advocated universalism of the best practice model. This is not to argue that identifying best practice in equality and diversity employment strategies is not of value. As Boxall and Purcell observe, identifying best practice provides guiding principles for employers which can then be contextualised to what is appropriate for a particular organisation. What it does mean is that the best fit approach suggests that there is not just one model of 'good diversity management' and that the possibilities for innovative practices are both richer and more varied than frequently considered.

Conducting an audit addressing basic questions such as 'where are we now?', 'where do we want to be?' and 'how do we get there?' is a useful starting point for employers seeking to develop relevant and achievable diversity practices. Although these questions may suggest an oversimplistic framework, they do apply an element of rationality to the implementation process that is useful for what is frequently an underdeveloped and under-regarded aspect of strategic HRM. The aim is for employers to gain a much more realistic and integrated view of diversity management than is all too often depicted in equality literature and which is frequently viewed in isolation from other strategic choices in HR decision-making.

Despite this argument for more organisationally-based diversity strategies, there still remains the fundamental challenge for managers of how to recognise individual differences, comply with anti-discrimination legislation and promote a general feeling of fair treatment among the workforce. Companies reporting on the benefits of diversity advocate a culture of inclusion through implementing employment policies which reflect corporate values such as 'respect for individuals, the right to be heard and the need to balance work with personal demands' (Rajan and Harris, 2003: 19). The research suggests that the vast majority of organisational procedures continue to adhere to the sameness of treatment approach as a safer and less demanding option although this approach is increasingly being challenged by the growth in rights for specific groups in the workplace.

Conclusion

In this chapter we have explored why there is an increased interest in managing diversity, the different interpretations of diversity management, the antidiscrimination legal framework and the implementation of managing diversity. We have suggested that putting the concept of diversity management into practice is complex, particularly as equality legislation has reinforced approaches to equality that are informed by a notion of 'sameness of treatment'. The implications of an absence of clarity surrounding the concepts of 'managing diversity' compared to those informing the provision of 'equal opportunities' and the variable mix of contextual influences suggest that for many operational managers managing diversity means whatever is deemed to be the most expedient approach at the time. The danger is that this is likely to result in inconsistencies of treatment which will undermine progressive HR policies intended to actively promote diversity.

Recognising that there are some inherent difficulties in operationalising managing diversity (Maxwell *et al.*, 2001), line managers have the pivotal role in the advancement of innovative workplace diversity policy and practice and are the gatekeepers for training and development opportunities (Hutchinson and Purcell, 2007). This reinforces the importance of not only developing policies which reflect an interpretation of diversity and fair treatment that is understood and shared by those who apply and experience the processes, but also of how managers are trained in equality and diversity issues. As previously suggested, relying on prepared scenarios or case studies as the main method of exploring people's attitudes and behaviours is likely to result in an unrealistic view of how diversity management will really be approached. Furthermore, it is unlikely that a positive view of difference, as diversity management advocates, will be realised if the emphasis on training is on 'what not to do' to ensure demonstrable legal compliance. What this chapter has tried to illustrate is that the way forward relies on an approach based on managers and employees supported by HR specialists examining diversity issues from the perspective of their operational reality to achieve more durable and relevant work-based solutions.

Summary

In this chapter the following key points have been made:

- Changes to the political, economic, social and technological environment in which organisations operate combined with a rising concern for the individual have prompted interest in the business case for diversity management.

- Although there lacks a universally accepted definition of managing diversity, the approach is informed by a notion of recognising, valuing and harnessing many individual differences in order to achieve competitive advantage. This implies differential treatment at an individual level.

- A dominant principle in the anti-discrimination legal framework is one of neutrality of treatment. This has led to an emphasis on approaches to workplace equality based on procedural fairness and consistency of treatment.

- Implementing diversity management is problematic. The design and interpretation of diversity management is dependent on a number of factors and their interrelationship.

- Line managers have the crucial role in the advancement of innovative workplace diversity policy and practice but frequently lack a clear direction and an understanding of the organisation's diversity agenda.

- A key challenge for employers is how to develop HR policies that are sufficiently robust in terms of demonstrating maximum procedural fairness and objectivity to withstand potential litigation but are also sufficiently flexible to accommodate different individual circumstances.

- Diversity management requires employers to develop an approach that best fits the unique requirements of their organisation.

Discussion questions

1. Identify examples drawn from your own experience where there have been potential conflicts between promoting the interests of a specific group and the rights of the individual not to be discriminated against.

2. It has been suggested that the recent age discrimination law will have the greatest impact on employers of any anti-discrimination legislation. Why do you feel this may be the case and what are the implications of such legislation for an organisation with which you are familiar?

3. In the light of the discussion in this chapter, design an outline for a managerial training programme on managing diversity where the main aim is to change the behaviour of the participants.

4. In your opinion, who could be responsible for creating and implementing a diversity management programme in an organisation? Present an argument for and against, for each suggested individual/group of people.

Further reading

Further reading is provided by the references in the text and readers can follow up citations relating to any particular aspect of the discussion. A text that considers managing diversity in more depth and from a critical perspectives is Kirton and Greene (2005). A general text particularly aimed at individuals studying equality and diversity as a unit on a wider programme of study is Daniels and Macdonald (2005).

6

Assessment, selection and evaluation

Sue Newell

Learning outcomes

Having read this chapter and completed its associated activities, readers should be able to:

- Emphasise the centrality of assessment, selection and evaluation processes to strategic management in general and strategic human resourcing in particular
- See assessment, selection and evaluation as a learning process, which is inherently emergent and subjective
- Review, briefly, epistemological options in the field of behavioural science
- Critically consider the importance of the validity of different methods of selection
- Consider the importance of different levels of criteria in assessment
- Emphasise the importance of individual perceptions and constructs in all assessment processes
- Develop a 'healthy scepticism' regarding both management theory and received HR wisdom

Introduction

A manager has to make many decisions every day. These decisions are the underlying building block of strategy-making. Assessment, selection and evaluation are fundamental aspects of the decision-making process:

- We first *assess* a number of choices we have in relation to a particular problem/opportunity that we face, for example, what university and what programme to apply to, if we want to study for a degree.
- We *select* the option that looks the best for us, for example, based on the content of the degree programme given our career goals, and the location of the university, given our preferences for location.
- We then subsequently *evaluate* our chosen option on the basis of the criteria that seem appropriate given what we were trying to achieve, for example, the enjoyment and rewards we perceive once we have started the chosen degree at the chosen university.

This chapter concentrates on assessment and evaluation in relation to human resourcing selection decisions. That is, decisions about who to employ, whom to promote, whom to reassign, whom to train, and sometimes even whom to dismiss, for example when a company is going through a redundancy programme or when someone's annual review suggests that they have not met performance expectations. These kinds of decisions will fundamentally influence the achievement of the organisation's strategic objectives. Hiring someone who does not have the competencies that are required for a particular job or who does not suit the culture of the organisation is likely to have serious negative consequences. While this chapter tends to focus on selection decisions in respect to the employment of new personnel, many of the issues which are discussed are relevant to the other types of human resourcing decisions and indeed to assessment, selection and evaluation in the broader management domain.

Throughout our lives, we continuously have to make selection decisions. This evening you may well have to select what to eat for dinner, select whether to go out or stay in, select what time to go to bed etc. The decision that you make will be based on your assessment of the likely outcomes of each potential choice. Many of the selection decisions which we make on a daily basis involve selecting between people – whom to date, whom to go to lunch with, whom to ask for help etc. Therefore, we have to make assessments about other people – which of these potential 'others' will be friendly, interesting, sympathetic, fun, a source of useful knowledge, trustworthy and so on. The problem of *assessing* people, their competencies, actions, motivations and satisfactions, is very important to understanding behaviour in organisations. As we will see in this chapter, it is full of problems and potential pitfalls. Moreover, once we have made a decision (selected a particular person for a date, for example), there is also the issue of *evaluating* how effective that decision was (Was the person whom we thought would be fun and interesting actually like that on the date?). Again, however, as we will see, evaluation is often very difficult if we are going to do it effectively. The aim of this chapter, then, is to critically consider these issues of assessment, selection and evaluation in the context of strategic human resourcing decisions within an organisation. In doing this, we raise issues, which should encourage critical questioning of many of the assumptions implicit in current managerial teaching and practice in relation to assessment, selection and evaluation.

There is an extensive literature on the subject of 'personnel or human resource selection', but before exploring this literature *per se*, we first look at the field through two different lenses – the traditional 'fit' approach and what we describe as the processual approach. This provides an introduction to alternative ways of examining the bundle of techniques, which we commonly think of as personnel selection.

Two perspectives on selection

The 'traditional' view regarding recruitment and selection is that there is a 'right' person for a particular job for which we need to hire; the aim of recruitment and selection is thus to ensure that we find the person who will be the best fit, given the job requirements. A corollary of this perspective is that, if we get the wrong person, there will be problems, manifest, for example, in high labour turnover, absenteeism, disciplinary problems, low productivity, poor customer satisfaction and so on. In other words, there are 'right' people, and 'wrong' people for a particular job, so that understanding and assessing differences between people are crucial for organisations. Indeed, our daily observations of other people provide us with ample evidence of the many ways in which individuals differ. At the most obvious level people differ in their physical appearance, but we also recognise psychological differences – in terms of personality, abilities, motivation, emotions and so on. It is also very obvious that jobs and organisations differ and that therefore some individuals will be more suited to some jobs/organisations than others. The traditional view is that, given these differences in individuals and jobs/organisations, recruitment and selection should be thought of as a process by which the organisation (or at least its managers) strategically matches the individual to the job.

The objective, then, as perceived from the traditional approach, is to get the right person in the particular job. The emphasis here is usually on the word *right* – 'too good' may pose as many problems as 'not good enough'. Given this objective, the traditional approach focuses on ensuring that the recruitment and selection processes are done systematically. This is achieved by following a sequence of activities, as follows:

1. Define the job (the job description) – in terms of tasks and responsibilities.
2. Define the ideal candidate (the person specification) – in terms of the competencies (knowledge, skills and attitudes) the person would need to be able to effectively carry out the defined tasks and responsibilities.
3. Attract good applicants (recruitment) – that is applicants who can demonstrate the required competencies.
4. Measure applicants (prediction) – using a variety of assessment techniques which provide data that can be used to evaluate differences between applicants in relation to the required competencies (these measures of relevant individual differences are referred to as the *predictors*).
5. Selection decision – chose those candidate(s) who has the competencies most similar to the defined ideal candidate profile.
6. Evaluation (criteria) – measure selected employees' performance on-the-job and decide whether the predictors which have been used are in fact related to job performance (this measure of job performance is referred to as the *criterion*).

In other words, the traditional approach assumes it is possible to define an 'ideal candidate', based on a systematic analysis of the job demands, and then to measure potential employees in order to choose that candidate who most closely 'fits' this ideal profile. Selection thus involves a number of logical steps, with objective assessments being made at each step, which results in a rational decision, where the 'best candidate' is offered the job. Hiring the 'best candidates' will ensure that the organisation is able to achieve its strategic objectives.

In this chapter it is argued that this systematic approach to selection oversimplifies the process of making decisions about people and assumes a level of objectivity that is not attainable in practice. As an alternative, we present a processual perspective, which not only provides a more accurate picture of what happens in practice, but which can also improve the effectiveness of selection decisions (for a fuller comparison of a systems and process perspective, see Chapter 2). Next, the systematic and the processual perspectives on selection are examined in more detail.

The traditional 'fit' approach to selection

In the traditional approach the focus is on *the* job, which is portrayed as a set of discrete tasks and responsibilities. Job performance on these tasks is the criterion, which we are attempting to predict. Prediction is based on identifying individual competencies that are considered likely to influence this criterion behaviour. Another term for this traditional approach to selection is thus the 'criteria-related predictive validity' approach because the goal is to achieve a high correlation between the predictors (the measures of individuals' competencies) and the criterion (the measures of job performance).

In metaphorical terms, the traditional approach attempts to select a square peg (the 'right' individual) from a set of non-square, multi-shaped pegs (the 'wrong' individuals) to fit a square hole (the job) (see Figure 6.1). So, in Figure 6.1 we have a range of different candidates (A–D) each with a different profile of competencies, and we have a job with a particular profile because of the tasks and responsibilities associated with it. Selection involves measuring candidates' competencies so that we find and select the candidate with the nearest matching competency profile to the job profile (candidate C in this example). Another way of thinking about this approach is to visualise it as a hurdles race between the candidates: the organisation puts up increasingly high hurdles over which the candidates must jump. Each hurdle represents a competence, which is deemed necessary for the job incumbent. The first, lower hurdles, are those competencies that are deemed essential. If you can jump these, you are assessed on other, desirable competencies. The individual who can demonstrate the greatest number of competencies that are deemed essential or desirable (that is, can jump the most hurdles, with the greatest clearance) is given the job. For example, if the job involves gathering numerical data from various internet sources and manipulating these in complex mathematical ways to arrive at business forecasts, the 'right' individual is likely to have high numerical ability, to have computing expertise through previous experience or education, and to be a fairly introverted personality (as there will be little personal contact in the particular job). Assessment will focus on measuring candidates in terms of these desired characteristics and competencies.

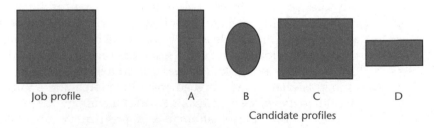

Job profile   A   B   C   D

Candidate profiles

Figure 6.1 The traditional 'psychometric' view of the selection process: fitting a square peg to a square hole

The problem with this view of selection is that it assumes that there is 'one best way' to do a particular job – hence the person specification. A previous job incumbent did the particular job a certain way (he was a 'square' not 'round' peg), and it is assumed that it is necessary to find a similar 'square peg' to replace him. This can result in unfair discrimination. So recruitment and selection is about making discriminations between individuals, but based on relevant and so fair criteria like ability and knowledge, rather than irrelevant criteria like sex, race, age, sexuality, religion or disability. However, given the 'one best way' assumption, unfair discrimination and prejudice can occur even when focusing on seemingly relevant criteria like ability and knowledge. To take the example above, the job involved forecasting but whether this had to be done, or was indeed best done, in the way described, is problematic. Recruiting a less numerically biased, more extroverted individual, might mean that the person has a very different approach to carrying out the tasks – talking to people for example about what they predict will happen rather than basing it on the manipulation of remotely accessed published data. In other words, the traditional approach to selection tends to perpetuate the status quo. The problem with this is that it can restrict certain groups who have been previously under-represented in particular jobs. For example, research has shown that women often have a different management style to men (Eagly and Carli, 2007). If senior management positions in the past have always been held by men, women may therefore be disadvantaged.

This traditional approach to selection also presents a very static picture of the job and of individuals and underestimates the degree of change within organisations (Worley and Lawler, 2006). Jobs continuously change in response to changes in the environment so that the 'square hole' today, may be a 'round hole' next year, requiring very different knowledge, skills and attitudes, and individuals can and do change as a result of job experiences (Illes and Robertson, 1997). Moreover, the traditional approach overestimates personal influences on job performance, and underestimates the role or situational demands. Thus, in many jobs role expectations are so strong that the individual has limited flexibility in how they behave so that individual differences have less relevance. Finally, this approach assumes that it is possible to objectively measure relevant differences between individuals in the same kind of objective way as physical differences between individuals can be assessed. Thus, I can measure my height accurately with a tape measure and the assumption is I can also measure my verbal or numerical ability or my personality accurately with a test of some kind. All of these assumptions can be questioned and this is precisely what adopting a processual perspective achieves.

The processual approach to selection

While the traditional approach continues to dominate, in this chapter we argue that the processual approach has a lot to offer both theoretically and practically. Herriot (1984) was one of the first to explore this processual alternative. His view of selection presents a very different metaphor of the process – as a process of exchange or negotiation between two parties, the employing organisation and the potential recruit. We have already seen in Chapter 1 how the employment relation is best characterised as a relationship of exchange and how work organisations develop through a process of negotiation. The traditional approach to

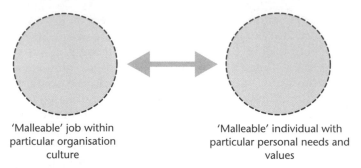

'Malleable' job within
particular organisation
culture

'Malleable' individual with
particular personal needs and
values

Figure 6.2 **Recruitment and selection as a process of exchange and negotiation**

selection, however, tends to ignore this aspect of exchange and views selection as a management perogative and as a one-way decision-making process – the recruiting manager selects between a number of passive applicants. From the exchange perspective, both parties (the recruiting manager(s) and the candidate(s)) have a set of expectations related to their current and future needs and values. Selection involves a series of episodes in which increasing amounts of information are exchanged to determine whether there is indeed compatibility between the organisation and the individual. Negotiation is possible because neither the job/organisation nor the individual is seen as having fixed characteristics, although the underlying values and needs of both sides are seen to be more stable. The outcome of this process, if successful, is that a viable psychological contract (Rousseau, 2004) is negotiated which encapsulates congruence between the expectations of both parties. However, if the process of negotiation breaks down because the parties are unable to develop congruent expectations, this is also positive – or in Herriot's terms, 'valid negative' – because in this way the organisation avoids employing someone who will not strategically align with it and the candidate avoids taking on a new job for which they are not suited (see Figure 6.2).

So both the traditional and the processual approaches emphasise 'fit' between the person and the job environment (Morley, 2007). However, in the traditional approach the fit is between the fixed dimensions of the job and the person, with the organisation's management determining the 'fit'. While from the processual perspective, 'fit' is the outcome of a process of exchange and negotiation in which both parties make decisions. Moreover, in the former case, 'fit' is between the competencies of the individual and the technical demands of the particular job (person-job fit). In the latter, the 'fit' is between the expectations and needs of the individual and the values, climate and goals of the organisation (person-organisation fit) (Ostroff and Rothausen, 1996).

This contrast between the traditional and processual views of selection mirrors the difference between the planned and emergent views of strategy-making discussed in Chapter 1. Thus, the view of strategy-making as about producing plans, which are subsequently implemented is similar to the traditional view of selection, which involves producing specific job specifications (the plans) and then finding the person to 'fit' this specification. On the other hand, the emergent view of strategy-making is aligned to the exchange view of selection. Thus, the exchange view sees selection decisions as emerging from complex processes of interaction between the candidate and organisational representatives. Indeed, we could use the same words to describe the processes. Thus, exchanging the word 'strategies' for 'selection decisions' from p. 27 we could write: '*selection decisions* are outcomes of human interpretations, conflicts, confusions, guesses and rationalisations rather than clear pictures unambiguously traced out on a corporate engineer's drawing board'.

Case Study 6.1

Jenny's role

Jenny works as a project manager for a small biotechnology company. She manages projects that involve organising and running early stage clinical trials for new drugs. She has a biology degree from a UK university and became a project manager by chance, when her company moved to run its first clinical trial for a development drug (prior to this the company had always outsourced its clinical trials). Jenny has no training in project management but is very good at building relationships. She talks to the various people involved in the project to understand what is required in terms of sample size, criteria for sample selection, environment for conducting the trial, testing resources to evaluate the trial results, and clinician involvement. She then builds very general plans for the project and goes to negotiate with her clinician contacts to find ways to recruit the needed sample. When the trial is actually being run, Jenny stays on-site so that she can answer any questions that crop up, as well as ensure that the agreed protocol is stuck to. The trials that she has managed to date have generally been very successful, although to date she has only run four and these were all very small, first-phase trials that have been focused on establishing the safety of the new drugs. In the future, the organisation will also need to do trials on much larger samples that test for efficacy as well as safety of the new drugs.

Activity 6.1   Jenny's role

Jenny is leaving the company and so needs to be replaced. Write a person specification for her role. In other words, identify the competencies (skills, knowledge, attitudes) that you think the organisation should be looking for to find someone to replace Jenny.

1. Did you base this specification on Jenny's competencies? What are the limitations of doing this?

2. Do you think there could be people with different competencies who might be equally, if not more effective, in this role? What might be the advantage of having someone with this different set of competencies in this role?

3. If you were the manager responsible for this hiring decision, how would you deal with this idea that there might be two very different people who could do this job equally well?

4. Based on this activity, what do you see as the strengths and limitations of the traditional and the processual views of the selection process?

Selection and the learning process

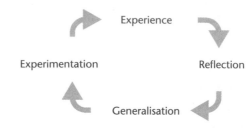

Figure 6.3 Kolb's learning cycle

One key difference between the exchange/processual and traditional approach to selection is that only the former recognises the learning involved in the process. We can explore this by identifying the problems associated with the traditional approach through the lens of learning.

When a manager assesses somebody in order to make a decision about his or her suitability for a particular job, the manager is, in effect, attempting to learn something about this other person – his or her attitudes, abilities, personality, motivation etc. The manager then uses this information to decide whether they fit the job requirements. We can think about this using Kolb *et al.*'s (1974) 'experiential learning cycle', which views learning as a perpetual process with the output of one cycle (testing or experimentation) providing the experience that begins the cycle again (see Figure 6.3).

The core idea is that people are cognitive beings who learn from experience and make assumptions regarding the world in which they operate. We can apply this model to the learning that takes place during the selection process:

- *Concrete experience*: This refers to any experience, either planned or unplanned. In selection this would include the manager's experiences of interacting (directly or indirectly) with candidates during the various selection episodes, including for example, reading about candidates from application forms, listening to their responses in interviews, reviewing their responses to psychometric tests, observing their behaviour during group exercises (these will be discussed in more detail later).

- *Reflective observation*: This refers to the cognitive process of thinking about or reflecting on the experience – trying to make sense of the experience (Weick, 1995) and trying to understand the causes of what was experienced. In selection this would include the reflection by managers of the candidates' behaviour during the various selection episodes. However, it also includes the candidate's reflection on what happened during an interview, for example.

- *Abstract conceptualisation and generalisation*: This relates to the conclusions that are drawn from the reflection process. The manager will generalise from his or her reflections about each of the candidates involved as to their suitability for the particular job and then make the selection decision. At the same time, the candidates will also draw conclusions about whether they would want to work for the company, if they received a job offer.

- *Experimentation and evaluation*: This involves evaluating the decision to test whether the generalisations were appropriate. In selection this relates to evaluating whether the person actually chosen for the job has met expectations. To the extent that the person has not been successful, a new cycle will be activated perhaps using different selection methods so that a different range of experience is provided about the candidates. From the candidate's perspective, he or she will evaluate whether the job actually lives up to expectations.

Kolb's learning cycle provides a useful vehicle for considering the problems involved in assessment, selection and evaluation. First and foremost, considering assessment, selection and evaluation as a learning process reminds us that there are two parties involved, both making decisions – the manager and the candidate. So the candidate is also: gaining experience about the job and the organisation from the different selection episodes; reflecting on what that experience means in terms of what the job will be like and the culture of the organisation; generalising as to whether they feel that this meets their own expectations for a job or career; and then subsequently evaluating whether their expectations have actually been met on the job. Since the traditional approach to selection tends to ignore the learning process of the candidate, it presents a limiting view of the whole process. Thus, candidates make decisions throughout the selection process – choosing whether to apply for a job, choosing whether to turn up to an interview to which they have been invited, choosing whether to take up a job that they have been offered. Additional limitations of the traditional approach to selection can be considered by looking at each step in the learning cycle in more detail.

Experience and impression management

Decisions made about candidates during selection depend on the concrete experiences that are provided. These experiences of the 'target person' (i.e. the candidate) may be indirect (e.g. information from an application form or a personality test) or direct (e.g. behaviour exhibited during an interview or a group exercise). The assumption of the traditional view is that this 'experience' should be systematically designed so that it provides an accurate picture of *the* person being assessed. That is, the various recruitment and selection methods employed need to be specifically designed to gather information about the target person that will be relevant to the particular job. Thus, if the candidate does not make much of a contribution to a group discussion it is assumed that this is typical behaviour. The problem with this is that it ignores the fact that candidates are attempting to create a certain impression of themselves during the selection process, which coincides with what they believe the assessor is looking for. Thus, to some extent at least, the manager only sees what the target person wants him or her to see. This is referred to as *impression management*, defined by Gilmore *et al.* (1999: 322) as 'conscious or unconscious attempts to influence images during interaction'. A variety of techniques can be used to convey a particular impression, such as ingratiation ('I have always wanted to work for this organisation'), selective description of events (candidate ignoring details of failed assignments they have been involved in and only giving information on the positive ones), positive descriptions of self ('I am a very self-motivated person') (Arnold *et al.*, 1997).

Not surprisingly, the 'high stakes' nature of the selection situation makes it a setting particularly ripe for impression management (Rosenfeld, 1997). Moreover, it is the manager as well as the candidate who engages in this behaviour – the candidate because they believe it will help them get the job and the manager because they want to attract the best applicants. For example, Varma *et al.* (2006) found that ingratiation tactics used in application letters significantly improved evaluators' assessments of candidates. Other research has found that impression management tactics can be overused (e.g. Baron, 1989), alerting us to the fact that using impression management is not easy during selection because the applicant must balance being 'confident but not brash, polite but not sycophantic, lively and interested but not voluble and manic, sufficiently nervous to show an appreciation of the importance of the occasion but not visibly anxious throughout' (Fletcher, 1989: 273).

Individuals differ in terms of their use of these impression management techniques. Snyder (1974) distinguished between high and low 'self-monitors' to reflect the extent to which individuals use cues from the situation to guide their own self-presentation. High self-monitors are those individuals who can more readily adapt their own behaviour to suit the particular situation. On the other hand, low self-monitors tend to behave in ways that coincide with how they feel. While these differences in self-monitoring ability were expected to influence the outcomes from an interview, research has actually found that this ability is only moderately and non-significantly related to interviewer outcome evaluations (Anderson *et al.*, 1999) and that whether self-monitoring has an impact depends at least partly on the assessor's personality (Lazar *et al.*, 2004). These findings demonstrate the complex nature of the interactions that occur during a selection situation.

The key point is that impression management is inevitable in selection situations. Rather than try to eliminate, or at least minimise, impression management, as the traditional approach might advocate, the alternative is to recognise it as inevitable. The processual perspective recognises the inevitability of impression management because selection is viewed as an inherently subjective process of interaction. This perspective would then advocate that attempts are made to level the playing field by providing all candidates with more information about how they are expected to present themselves during the various selection episodes (Herriot, 1984; Fletcher, 1989), and recognising and trying to understand how both parties (candidates and managers) are interacting to influence the process (Posthuma *et al.*, 2002).

Reflection and attribution theory

Once the manager as assessor has some kind of concrete experience of the candidates, she then reflects on that experience to form a view of each candidate. While structured checklists can help here so that all candidates get assessed using the same criteria, the process is by definition, subjective. One way of considering this process of reflection is to relate it to attribution theory (for a good overview of the usefulness of considering attributional processes during selection, see Silvester *et al.*, 2002). Attribution theorists begin from the premise that we naturally try and look for the causes of either our own or other's behaviour. These theorists (dating back to the work of Heider, 1958) have sought to uncover the principles we use in deciding the causes of what happens. Basically, these causes can be narrowed down to three kinds:

1. *Internal-controllable causes* – where the outcome is explained in terms of the individual's own behaviour, that he or she can control, i.e. effort.

2. *Internal-uncontrollable causes* – where the outcome is explained in terms of the individual's own behaviour, that he or she cannot control, i.e. basic aptitude.

3. *External causes* – where the outcome is explained in terms of something outside the individual him or herself (e.g. luck, other people).

For example, supposing mathematical aptitude is considered to be an important predictor of job success and a candidate provides information that he failed his high-school level mathematics exam at the first attempt. The assessor then looks for explanations of this. She can decide that the failure was either due to internal factors – the candidate lacked ability or did not try hard enough. Or she may decide that it was due to external factors – the candidate's teacher was not very good, for example. The type of attribution made will significantly effect what the selector feels she has learnt about the candidate. An external attribution excuses the failure because it was 'not his fault' and so does not reflect on his abilities. The internal, controllable attribution (that it was due to a lack of effort) is not taken as an indication of underlying mathematical ability, although it may still reflect negatively on the overall impression if self-motivation is considered to be a key predictor of job success. The internal uncontrollable attribution (that it reflects a lack of mathematical ability) will lead to the conclusion that this candidate is deficient in a required ability. So the same information can lead to very different assessments depending on the attributions that are made.

Attribution theory is relevant to selection, because during a selection process assessors will inevitably find out information about the past performance of candidates. The candidates may be given the opportunity to explain this past behaviour and in doing this they will make statements that indicate how they attribute the causes of that performance. Silvester *et al.* (2002) showed that interviewers have a better impression of candidates who, when asked about previous negative events, provided internal-controllable attributions. Where attributions were made that suggested either internal-uncontrollable or external-uncontrollable causes, interviewers had more negative impressions of the candidates.

The problem is that research evidence demonstrates that there are regular biases in the attributions we make. The *fundamental attribution error* refers to the strong tendency to attribute responsibility to the actor – i.e. infer an internal attribution. We tend to ignore situational factors, at least in Western society with its strong emphasis on individual responsibility (Morris and Peng, 1994). The one exception to this is when we are looking at our own behaviour when we are likely to make the *self-serving error*. That is, when things go well, we accept personal responsibility, but when things go badly, then we find 'excuses' in the external environment. So if I do well in my exams then it is because of my own effort and ability, but if I do badly then it is because of the bad teacher, the lousy textbook, the poor library facilities, the fact that the teacher does not like me etc., etc.

In terms of reflecting on candidate information, it is the fundamental attribution error that is more pertinent. Assessors will tend to assume that the 'data' they have about an individual candidate can be attributed to the personal qualities of the individual, rather than seeing it as a reflection of his or her situation. Thus, candidates may wrongfully get credit for successful performance, either during the selection episodes themselves or from previous history, or may wrongfully get the blame for failures. For example, in an interview situation, the candidates' behaviour is strongly influenced by the behaviour of the interviewer (Dougherty *et al.*, 1994); or in a group discussion exercise, a normally fairly shy person can appear to dominate because she is working with others who are even more shy than she is, while a fairly dominant person may appear reticent because he is working with a group all high on assertiveness.

These biases in perception clearly, therefore, influence what we believe we learn about candidates in a selection situation (Posthuma *et al.*, 2002). There are also other biases in perception, for example the halo effect. This is where we decide we like a person, for example because they attended the same school as we did, and then view all other information about the candidate through 'rose-tinted spectacles'. The opposite, horn effect, is also possible, where we decide we dislike someone and then view all subsequent information about this person through 'dirty spectacles'. This led Dipboye (1997: 459) to conclude that 'the outcome of these biases in the conduct of the (interview) session is that the information gathered reflects more on interviewer behaviour in the session than the applicant's knowledge, skills, and attitudes'. These biases can never be totally eliminated, but acknowledging them as part of the inevitable, subjective process of assessment, we can attempt to minimise the extent to which they have an unfair discriminatory impact on decisions. One way of doing this is to consciously build in to the selection process a consideration of the attributions that are being made (Herriot, 1989).

Generalisation and personal construct theory

Once we have obtained information about candidates and reflected on its meaning we then make the actual decision, generalising from the specific selection situation to predict future job behaviour. The traditional approach assumes that past and present behaviour will predict future behaviour. The processual approach assumes the relationship is not quite so straightforward. We can contrast the two approaches by considering the difference between the nomothetic and idiographic views of personality. The nomothetic approach to personality (e.g. Eysenck, 1953; Cattell, 1965) seeks to identify the core characteristics of personality. There are two main nomothetic theories: type and trait. The trait theory uses bipolar, trait continuums, with individuals fitted somewhere along each continuum, for example somewhere between extreme introversion and extreme extroversion (Cattell, 1965). The type theory 'pigeon holes' individuals into particular personality categories, for example you are either 'an introvert' or 'an extrovert' (Eysenck, 1953). Trait theories are much more common today, with much research converging on the idea that there are five key personality traits that can be measured (Costa and McCrae, 1992). Nomothetic theories of personality make the following assumptions:

1. Personality is relatively fixed, being determined at least in part by hereditary, so you are born more or less extrovert.

2. Behaviour is a reflection of underlying personality, so you behave in an aggressive way typically because you have an extrovert personality. Obviously it is recognised that the situation will influence the display of this trait, but if

comparing two people in the same situation (e.g. a board meeting), differences in extrovert behaviour are seen to be the result of underlying personality.

3. It is therefore possible to predict future behaviour on the basis of past behaviour. So, if you have tended to exhibit extrovert behaviour in the past, then it can be assumed that you will demonstrate this again in future. So, if the organisation is looking for an extrovert manager, they can predict this on the basis of behaviours exhibited during the selection episodes and from accounts of past behaviour.

Cattell's Trait Theory of personality is perhaps the best exemplar of this method, and his 16PF is still used to measure people's personality during selection. Cattell used statistical analysis (specifically factor analysis) to reduce the 100s of trait words that we use in everyday language to a small number of what he called 'source traits'. He believed that these source traits affect the pattern of behaviour that is observable in day-to-day activities. He developed the 16PF to measure the 16 most important source traits. The 16PF is a questionnaire which asks a number of questions (e.g. 'People don't often get the better of me in an argument') which the respondent has to answer on a likert-type scale – 'agree', 'uncertain' and 'disagree'. Based on answers, a 'sten' (standard 10) score is calculated, which places the subject in relation to a normal distribution of respondents. Interpretation is relatively complex (although computer programs are now available which reduce the time and effort involved) and training and proven competence to British Psychological Society (BPS) (or its national equivalent in other countries) standards is a requirement for using personality instruments.

Given the complexity of this 16-factor model, together with research that indicates that there are significant correlations between some of the dimensions, it is now more common to focus on the so-called 'Big-5' personality traits. The dimensions composing the 5-factor model are neuroticism, extraversion, openness to experience, agreeableness and conscientiousness. Each of these dimensions is measured along a continuum, so that an individual is more or less neurotic, more or less extraverted and so on. The five dimensions can be defined as follows:

1. *Neuroticism* – this refers generally to the degree of positive psychological adjustment and emotional stability. Neurotic individuals are anxious, hostile, prone to depression, self-consciousness, vulnerable and impulsive.

2. *Extraversion* – this refers to the degree of sociability. Extraverted individuals are sociable, active and impulsive and not introspective and self-preoccupied.

3. *Openness to experience* – this refers to the degree of curiosity. A person scoring high on this trait exhibits high levels of intellectance (philosophical and intellectual) and unconventionality (imaginative, autonomous, and nonconforming).

4. *Agreeableness* – this refers to the degree of cooperation a person exhibits. Agreeable persons are cooperative (trusting of others and caring) as well as likeable (goodnatured, cheerful, and gentle).

5. *Conscientiousness* – this refers to the degree of self-control. Conscientious individuals are very achievement orientated (hardworking and persistent), dependable (responsible and careful), and orderly (planful and organised).

In each case, the opposite end of the continuum represents a person with the opposite characteristics (see Figure 6.4).

Low-score description	1	2	3	4	5	6	7	High-score description
Anxious and prone to depression								Not anxious and emotionally stable
Sociable and impulsive								Not sociable and self-reflective
Curious and always willing to learn								Apathetic and not willing to learn
Cooperative and likeable								Uncooperative and not likeable
Dependable, orderly, hard-working								Not dependable, disorganised, not hard-working

Figure 6.4 'Big-5' personality factor model

For a good recent review of the usefulness of personality assessment, and in particular the effectiveness of the Big-5 model, see Ones *et al.* (2007).

Activity 6.2	Completing a personality profile

1. Complete your own profile on the Big-5. So, if you see yourself as high on 'anxious' you might place a cross in box 1 or 2 on this trait.

2. You could then ask someone who knows you well to complete a profile as they see you. Then you can compare the difference. Where there are differences, especially where these place you on a different side of the continuum, why do you think this happened?

3. Now ask someone who knows you in a different context to complete the profile for you (e.g. a parent as opposed to a friend). Again, where there are differences, why do you think this happened?

In reflecting on your experience with the Big-5 and the questions it hopefully raised, it is helpful to consider the alternative approach to personality. The idiographic approach starts from the premise that the assumptions of the nomothetic approach are problematic. Personality is not fixed, certainly not fixed from birth. Rather, personality is the outcome of our interactions with other people. So it is the way people treat us and respond to us that leads us to develop a particular self-image (Mead, 1934, reproduced in Clark *et al.*, 1994; Rogers, 1970). We then strive to behave in accordance with this self-image. But as our interactions change, so our self-image may change. Moreover, as our interactions differ in different situations, so our 'personality' can be expected to differ. So, for example, just imagine what your parents would think if they 'caught' you in certain situations! They may be shocked because your personality 'at home' is somewhat different to your personality when 'out' with a group of friends. For example, when football hooligans are exposed there is sometimes surprise among those who know them in a different work context, because such behaviour would not have been expected from them based on their behaviour in work. The idiographic approach attempts to capture the wholeness and uniqueness of personality as it functions in a diverse range of situations. An example of this idiographic approach is Kelly's Personal Construct Theory.

Kelly (1955) suggests that people are fundamentally inquisitive and wish to make sense of their world – we all conduct our lives rather like scientists, exploring, hypothesising, experimenting, explaining our experiences and predicting the future via developing strategies and procedures (very similar to the ideas underlying management and this book). The term that Kelly uses to describe the unit of meaning we develop in order to make sense of the world is *personal construct*. He suggests that we have personal constructs about all aspects of our lives (including ourselves). These constructs define and help us make sense of our existence and, once formed, will be the basis on which we interpret events, experiences and future possibilities.

The idiographic approach focuses on how we construct meaning from our experiences. This is considered to be an active sense-making process (Weick, 1995). The basic insight to emerge from this approach is that no two individuals ever share an identical construct, and so their experiences of 'reality' will be unique. For example, if I use the word 'father', this will immediately trigger the reader's unique personal construct of 'father', a construct that will have been formed over a long period of time, based on the reader's experience of fathers. If they have a good, positive relationship with their own parents their construct would be very different to that of a person who had been regularly beaten and abused by their father, which in turn may be very different from that of a person who was orphaned at an early age. In other words your construct of 'father' is uniquely your own, and this will influence the perceptions, reactions and responses every time the word is used.

To explore constructs, Kelly devised what is called the Repertory Grid Technique. A series of cards is used, which relate, for example, to occupations. These are referred to as the elements – so there may be cards with job titles written on them such as Barperson, Teacher, Accountant, Doctor, Librarian, and so forth. The experimenter chooses three of these at random, shows them to the subject whose constructs are being elicited, and asks 'which one is different?' When the subject has identified the 'different' one, the next question is 'in what way is that occupation different to the other two?' thus eliciting a personal construct about occupations. A personal construct always has two poles (or is bi-polar): two elements are the same (e.g. teacher and nurse are both 'caring') and different from the third element (e.g. as opposed to an accountant who is 'cold'). Next another three cards are chosen at random and the process repeated with the sole proviso that the same construct can not be used a second time – in other words an alternative way of recognising 'difference' between jobs has to be found.

Once the jobs have all been compared and the constructs elicited, they can be placed in a matrix of elements (jobs) against the bi-polar constructs. Each job can then be assessed in terms of each of the constructs. In this way a grid can be developed which allows examination of the ways in which constructs relate or overlap, or of the similarities and differences in perceptions between elements. Clearly such a technique could be used to establish the dimensions (constructs) which managers use to assess applicants for jobs (or assess existing staff) and the extent to which competing candidates are similar or different. For example, Harris (Harris, 2001a) used the technique with managers selecting for international appointments to elicit their personal constructs and assess how this was influencing the appointment of women to these roles.

Activity 6.3 Repgrid exercise: developing personal constructs

It is useful to try an exercise to look at your own constructs regarding different people:

1. Across the top of the grid you see a number of 'people-types' – yourself, your partner, your parent, your boss, a colleague you like, a colleague you dislike, yourself as you would like to be. Pencil in the space provided the names of the real people who fit those descriptions in your life.

How 1 different	Yourself	Your partner	Your parent	Your boss	A colleague you like	A colleague you dislike	Your ideal self	How 2 the same

2. You will see that three boxes have been picked out in bold print in the first horizontal row – corresponding to the characters 'yourself', 'your partner', 'your parent'.

3. Think of the three people you have identified – which one is different?

4. Write in the right-hand column the characteristic that makes that person different from the other two.

5. Write in the left-hand space what you perceive as being the opposite of that characteristic. It will help if you avoid using 'closed' constructs such as male, female, bald etc.: wherever possible and use more open, adjectives that you use in thinking about differences between people.

6. Now work along the next three people (partner, parent, boss) you have identified and again think about which one is different and identify the characteristic on which they differ from the other two – complete the bi-polar construct.

7. Complete the rest of the grid, row by row, following the same procedure – the only limitation is that you should not use the same construct more than once.

8. To score the grid, imagine a rating scale between each bi-polar construct from −3 at one end (how the one person was different) to +3 at the other end (how the two 'other' people were the same). Go through each bi-polar construct for yourself and give yourself a score from −3 to +3 on each construct.

9. Repeat the exercise for the other people in the grid.

10. Now you can look at the grid and see the relationship between the different constructs that you use to describe other people.

Questions

1. What do the relationships look like in your grid?

2. What does that tell you about the way you perceive other people?

3. What might the implications be for you if you were involved in a selection process?

4. Do your constructs suggest certain jobs that you might be well-suited for and others that you might not be suited for?

5. Share your personal constructs with someone else who has done this exercise – are differences in the constructs reflective of differences in the ways you relate to other people?

Doing this exercise, hopefully encourages you to consider how your interpretation of 'reality' is different from others, which is the essence of the idiographic approach to personality. The idiographic approach is obviously fundamentally different to the nomothetic approach, since the latter assumes there is a fixed reality that can be measured using systematically developed psychometric 'tests'.

Experimentation and validity

The final step in the learning cycle is to test out the conclusions from the earlier steps. While most of the literature and practice focuses on validating the selection process, it is also important to validate the recruitment process. Recruitment refers to the activities used to attract people to apply for jobs in a company, while selection refers to the process of actually choosing between the attracted candidates. If recruitment is not effective then there will not be good candidates to select from. Barber (1998) points out that actually there are different phases in recruitment. He identifies three phases – generating applicants (i.e. persuading people to apply to the company), maintaining applicant status (i.e. encouraging people to stay interested while the company goes through the selection process) and influencing job choice (i.e. encouraging a person to take a job if offered). Carlson *et al.* (2002) argue that the first of these phases is most important in determining the applicant pool and suggest that it is very important to evaluate the effectiveness of this recruitment activity. Attraction activities establish the pool of applicants – if an organisation is unable to attract talented applicants it will suffer, hence the current emphasis on talent management (Cappelli, 2008). For example, Huselid (1995) demonstrated a positive relationship between low selection ratios and organisation financial performance. Lower selection ratios are achieved by attracting larger numbers of applicants (so that you have more applicants to choose from). Given the importance of recruitment, Carlson *et al.* (2002) recommend that organisations assess attraction outcomes using estimates of the job performance potential (i.e. quality) of each applicant, rather than simply in terms of the quantity of applicants received, so that organisations begin to understand how attraction is influenced by different recruitment practices.

In terms of selection, the key is whether the people selected are indeed the competent employees that were predicted. The traditional approach sees this in terms of job-related (or criteria-related) validity. In other words, were the measures (the predictors) used able to accurately predict successful job performance (the criterion). This is referred to as *predictive validity*. So does our assessment of people during the interview as either potentially 'good' or 'poor' employees actually match (or correlate) with their subsequent performance on the job? One difficulty with this is the length of time which might need to elapse before such studies can be undertaken. We would need to measure applicants, but then ignore this evidence so that a follow-up study could be conducted at a later point to establish whether initial ratings on the selection methods (the predictors) accurately predicted future job performance (the criterion). Ideally, we should employ people randomly so that we have a normal distribution, from those predicted to be 'no-hopers' right through to those predicted to be 'stars'. If we only employ those predicted to be 'stars', we can never know for certain whether those predicted to be 'no-hopers' actually would fail on the job. However, managers are, understandably, very reluctant to employ people who have been predicted to fail. As a result predictive validity, although of great importance, is rarely established in practice. The exceptions are in those jobs where large numbers are recruited, such as the armed forces.

An alternative approach is to establish *concurrent validity*, which involves establishing the relationship between the predictor measure (e.g. an in-basket test) and some criterion of job training or performance that may be obtained at the same time, using current employees. So current employees are asked to complete the proposed in-basket exercise (the new selection method) and then some measure of their job performance is obtained. If there is found to be a relationship between performance on the new selection method and job performance for current employees, then it is assumed that this will also be the case for prospective employees. So, if those people who score highly on the in-basket test also obtain high job performance ratings, while those who score poorly on the in-basket test get lower performance ratings, then the test can be considered to have concurrent validity. Establishing concurrent validity is obviously more attractive to organisations as it allows judgements as to the validity of a selection measure to be established relatively quickly. Its weakness is the assumption that an existing relationship will predict accurately for the future. Also, it ignores the fact that current employees do not represent a full cross-section of potential employees, since they have already been selected using past methods. Establishing concurrent validity may, therefore, create an overly homogeneous group of employees. Given the increasing need for innovation this may be a problem, because creativity is stimulated by heterogeneity rather than homogeneity.

There are other types of validity, which can be established, but the one that is most important for contrasting the traditional and processual views of selection is *face validity*. Face validity refers to whether a measure 'looks right'. The traditional approach would not really consider this important – it does not matter whether candidates believe a particular selection method can (or cannot) predict future performance; the only real question is whether or not it does (i.e. whether it has criteria-related validity). However, from the exchange perspective face validity influences how candidates respond to the various selection methods. For example, graphology (analysing handwriting to assess personality) is a popular selection method used in France but is very uncommon in the UK (Shackleton and Newell, 1994). A British candidate asked to provide some handwriting for personality analysis may well find this rather strange and this may lead her to take a negative view of the organisation. The point is not about whether or not graphology can be used as an accurate measure of personality (in fact the evidence about the predictive validity of graphology is that it is no better than chance). Rather, it is about how candidates' perceptions of a selection method can influence their interpretation of the job and the organisation. As seen, this is considered essential from the processual perspective. Thus, candidates' reactions to a particular method of selection can effect their commitment to the organisation and their personal self-esteem (Illes and Robertson, 1997). From the exchange perspective, therefore, the narrow focus on predictive (or concurrent) validity is restrictive because it ignores how selection methods themselves influence the process of interaction between the candidate and the organisation.

The other problem from adopting the narrow criteria-related predictive validity approach relates to the issue of the criteria used. Thus, much research on selection has focused on establishing the validity of various selection methods, and there is now a wealth of information about the relative validity of different methods (these will be considered when we look more specifically at the different methods of selection). However, the other issue that is important when we are attempting to evaluate selection decisions, is to consider the criterion used (Guion, 1997). One evaluation model that is helpful here was developed by Kirkpatrick (1967). Kirkpatrick argued that we need to distinguish between what people do in their particular jobs, and how this impacts on organisational performance. The problem is that the criteria-related predictive validity model tends to focus almost exclusively on predicting job performance. However, we might select someone who can carry out the individual tasks of the job very effectively (job performance criteria or 'behaviour'), but who does this in such a way that he antagonises or disturbs people in other jobs who therefore perform less effectively, so that overall organisational performance is inhibited (organisational performance criteria or 'ultimate outcomes').

So, the reality is that evaluating something is very difficult to do, partly because the criteria we choose can affect the evaluation we arrive at (Ibbetson and Newell, 1998).

| Activity 6.4 | Evaluating an academic course |

If you were asked to evaluate your course:

1. What criteria would you use?
2. Is it likely that students will all have the same objectives?
3. Are your objectives the same as your tutor's objectives?
4. Are they the same as the university's objectives?

Normally there is a wide divergence between responses to this exercise. It becomes clear that the criteria used are likely to determine the evaluation. For example, students may use the criterion of whether the course leads to a good job, while tutors may use the criterion of whether the students can write what is judged to be a good dissertation. Both criteria are actually important even though they may not always be correlated. Similarly, in looking at selection validity, we also need to think about different levels of evaluation. Smith (1994) distinguished between three types of individual characteristics that relate to job performance: 'universals' which refer to characteristics that are relevant to all jobs; 'occupationals' which refer to characteristics relevant to particular jobs or occupations; and 'relationals' which refer to characteristics relevant in a particular work setting. This typology suggests that it is important to match characteristics of people with the characteristics of particular work settings and not just with characteristics of the particular job to be undertaken. Research has demonstrated that this is particularly important in small and medium-sized firms (Stewart and Knowles, 2000) as well as in knowledge-intensive organisations (Robertson and O'Malley-Hammersley, 2000). Thus, Robertson and O'Malley-Hammersley found, in a scientific consultancy, that the selection process was dominated by subjectivity. Many of the consultants were involved in the selection process, assessing whether they felt the individual candidates was 'the right stuff' for the organisation rather than any specific job.

From the exchange or processual perspective, therefore, the focus on criteria-related validity is too narrow because it treats selection and job performance as discrete entities, rather than as mutually interacting. For example, a very competent individual may be selected for a position but then not given opportunities that she had been led to expect, leaving her feeling demotivated in the job and uncommitted to the organisation. Her performance is likely, therefore, to be evaluated as poor. Focusing on narrow criteria-related validity may obscure the reasons for the poor performance and lead to the assumption that the methods used to select the individual were not valid (Fogarty, 2000). In recognition of this, a growing body of literature is considering selection and performance in a more holistic sense, using the concept of socialisation to understand the entire process. For example, Anderson and Ostroff (1997: 413) argue 'We contend that selection and socialisation are facets of essentially the same overarching process – the screening and integration of newcomers into an organisation and their learning of specific knowledge relevant for work role performance'. That is, both are stages in a longitudinal process of 'newcomer integration' into both the job and the organisation. They argue that adopting this perspective takes the focus away from narrow job performance prediction to the establishment of a set of congruent expectations between the parties. The concern is, thus, not so much about how far a particular selection method predicts job performance, but about how far this method impacts the attitudes and behaviours of candidates (Illes and Robertson, 1997) and how far different methods are perceived to be fair by the applicants (Anderson and Witvliet, 2008). Baker and Jennings (2000) provide a good example of this need to see recruitment and selection as part of an ongoing process of socialisation in their account of why Riddick Bowe (the world champion boxer) joined but then subsequently left the United States Marine Corps (USMC). They argue that in this particular case, the recruiters ignored indications that Bowe had unrealistic expectations about what it would be like to be in the USMC because of his celebrity status.

		Organisational message	
		Accurate	Inaccurate
Candidate perception	Accurate	Quadrant 1 Realistic – correctly construed	Quadrant 2 Unrealistic – correctly construed
	Inaccurate	Quadrant 4 Realistic – misconstrued	Quadrant 3 Unrealistic – misconstrued

Figure 6.5 **Typology of selection methods**

Anderson (2001) develops a typology of selection methods, not dependent on their predictive validity but on the accuracy of the information they convey (see Figure 6.5).

The most useful selection methods, from this perspective, are those that allow candidates to develop realistic expectations about the job and the organisation. A selection method may have low predictive validity in the traditional sense, for example the unstructured interview, but may encourage negotiation, which promotes the development of commitment and adjustment to the organisation. On the other hand, a selection method with a very high predictive validity, for example a structured interview, may actually present a misleading picture of the organisation or even the job so that unrealistic expectations are promoted. The person selected may then possess the narrow competencies for the job, but because of unmet expectations, may quickly leave the organisation.

This is not as far-fetched as it may seem. For example, it is estimated that up to 50 per cent of graduates leave their first job within five years, despite the fact that this group are perhaps the most rigorously or 'systematically' selected group within many organisations. The most common reason for leaving is because of unfulfilled expectations. They leave, not typically because they are not competent at the job, but because they do not feel committed to an organisation which they feel has misled them. So companies spend vast amounts of money ensuring their selection methods have good predictive validity, ignoring the fact that such predictive validity (especially if measured in terms of narrow job performance criteria) does not necessarily translate into long-term commitment to the organisation. Considering selection as part of the socialisation process provides a more holistic way to evaluate the effectiveness of selection decisions. A good example of the limitations of focusing in isolation on the selection process is provided by the BellSouth case (Leopold and Hallier, 1998). BellSouth was a new telecommunications company in New Zealand. As with many greenfield sites at the start-up phase, it had loose management structures and so wanted to recruit employees who could work in an uncertain, ambiguous, fluid environment. It used a very rigorous selection process in order to select people who were intelligent, flexible and high on energy. Employees who had been selected viewed the selection approach adopted very positively as it had made them feel 'special individuals on whom a lot of time and effort had been expended'. The problem was that nearly a quarter of new staff left the company within six months and 50 per cent in the first year. Analysis of why this was occurring demonstrated that it was because the job had not turned out as expected. So although they had been made to feel 'very special' during the selection process, they reported that thereafter they had received much less individual attention and support. In other words, the socialisation that had begun during selection, was not carried through to their initial experiences on the job, where they felt they were 'thrown in at the deep end'.

Nearly 30 years ago Wanous (1980) criticised recruitment practice based on *attracting* applicants on the grounds that it was often at the expense of honesty about the position to be filled. Recruiters, he argued, regularly painted an overly rosy picture of the job, which created unrealistic expectations, inevitably leading to disappointment when the opportunities were not as promised. Wanous argued for *realistic job previews*. It is a depressing observation that these criticisms would still appear relevant to much current practice.

A critical exploration of 'traditional' practice

Having considered selection as a learning process, it is now possible to consider how selection is generally carried out within organisations and the problems associated with this, again comparing the traditional and processual approaches.

Defining the job and the ideal candidate

It was argued in the earlier part of the chapter that 'best practice' from the traditional approach begins with a thorough job analysis. This seeks to identify the knowledge, skills, abilities and other characteristics required to carry out the defined tasks involved in a particular job. If this stage is carried out superficially then any subsequent judgments and decisions could well be flawed (Algera and Greuter, 1993). So the demanding and time-consuming process called job analysis is used to identify functions, tasks and sub-tasks (the job description) that, in turn, determines the characteristics and competences of the ideal candidate (the job specification).

Traditional methods of job analysis focused on collecting documents (e.g. from training analyses), interviewing the job-holder or the line supervisor about the job, observation of someone in the job, and sometimes, attempts to do the job by the analyser. Other methods include using group interviews (a form of job-based focus group); holding a technical conference with 'experts'; or asking job-holders to keep a diary record. The critical incidents method can be used in an attempt to focus interviews or observations on those aspects of the job which are critical, as opposed to those aspects which are more mundane (Flanagan, 1954). There have also been attempts to develop questionnaires and checklists, which simplify the job analysis process. Examples include the Position Analysis Questionnaire (PAQ) (McCormick *et al.*, 1972) and Saville and Holdsworth's Work Profiling System (WPS) (Saville and Holdsworth Ltd, 1995). Dierdorff and Wilson (2003) provide a good review of the evidence related to the reliability of job analysis methods, demonstrating for example that while raters had fairly high consensus in relation to tasks involved in a particular job, there was much less consensus with regard to generalised work activity requirements.

Having clarified what the job entails the person specification (ideal) is drawn up. This identifies such issues as attainments, aptitudes, physical requirements, personality characteristics and any possible external constraints such as the need to travel or work shifts. The model developed by Rodger (1970) has been a popular framework for considering these personal characteristics (Mackay and Torrington, 1986). Rodger's Seven Point Plan groups these personal characteristics under seven headings:

1. physical make-up
2. attainments
3. general intelligence
4. special aptitudes
5. interests
6. disposition
7. circumstances.

Under each heading, those characteristics considered to be essential and desirable are identified, along with any disqualifiers – characteristics, which would make it difficult for the person to do the job effectively. More recently, the focus has been on competences, what the person can do, rather than characteristics or attributes, what the person is like (Heinsman *et al.*, 2007).

When developing a competency profile it is worthwhile considering employing a variation on the repertory grid technique discussed earlier in the chapter, for example, comparing 'stars' and 'failures' in a particular role in order to isolate and clarify the factors which seem to be important to job success. This may sharpen the specification by avoiding bland and trite statements and focusing on the real discriminators between good and less good performers. This is more likely to lead to the identification of specific behaviours or competences that are relevant for effective job performance.

It might be argued that as the nature of work changes from predominantly physical work to an increasing emphasis on knowledge or conceptual work, the job analysis process becomes very much harder as less of what makes people effective in the job can be seen by external assessors as much of the activity goes on inside the job-holder's head. Moreover, with the increasing emphasis on team-work there is a need to incorporate a broader analysis of competences than those directly related to the particular job. Even more significant is the move towards flexibility and continuous change. All these changes suggest a need to broaden the scope of traditional job analysis. Analysis needs to be done at different levels:

● person-job fit (job analysis) – which is the traditional approach and considers the competences necessary to fulfil the specific job;
● person-team fit (team analysis) – which considers the competences necessary to work within a multi-disciplinary team (West and Allen, 1997);
● person-organisation fit (organisational analysis) – which considers the competences necessary to work effectively within the particular organisational culture (Schneider, 1987);

● Person-environment fit (environmental analysis) – which considers what kinds of competences will be needed in the future, given the changes in society generally, and in markets in particular.

Once these different levels of analysis are undertaken, they might well highlight contradictions between what is required at different levels (Herriot and Anderson, 1997). For example, at the job level there may be a requirement for an aggressive approach, but this may conflict with the organisational culture, which values compromise and discussion. Or, the environmental analysis may demonstrate a need for creativity and innovation, while the current organisational culture rewards caution and low risk-taking. The traditional, criteria-related validity approach misses these contradictions because it focuses exclusively on job analysis. While this appears to look neater and more systematic, it ignores the real-world complexity where such contradictions are commonplace. Adopting a processual perspective helps us to recognise complexity and, therefore, the need to go beyond the overly-simplistic focus on job analysis. Perfect 'fit' is unlikely at all levels, but from the processual perspective this is considered to be inevitable. The focus will be on negotiation, in order to arrive at some kind of compromise, which can allow both the organisation and the individual to grow and develop. This may mean purposively employing individuals who are not the best 'fit' for the job, but who are brought in because they have good team-working skills. Or it may mean employing a person for a particular job who is more creative than most others within the organisation because this is felt to be particularly necessary for the future. But there would be open discussion about these 'misfits' during the selection process, so that individuals are aware that they are going to be seen as different and so do not start with unrealistic expectations. The emphasis in the more recent talent management literature also recognises some of these tensions (Mucha, 2004).

Measuring candidates

Once the analysis has been completed and there is an understanding of the requirements (which as seen, may involve recognition of contradictory requirements), the next step is to decide how individuals are going to be measured or assessed against these requirements. There are a variety of methods which can be used here and research provides an indication of their predictive validity. The predictive validity has been established on the basis of meta-analysis, which brings together the results from a number of individual studies in order to provide a more robust calculation (Hunter and Schmidt, 1990; Hermelin and Robertson, 2001). However, from a processual perspective it is also necessary to consider how these methods are used in practice and how they are perceived by candidates. Next we consider different methods, concentrating on those that are used most commonly.

Application forms and biodata

Application forms and biodata are methods that are used to screen out unsuitable applicants and so leave a pool of applicants for further investigation. Such pre-screening is especially necessary where there are a large number of people applying for a limited number of jobs. Application forms ask candidates to provide information on a range of topics. Some of this information is, at least in principle, verifiable (e.g. last salary or qualifications obtained), while other information requested is non-verifiable (e.g. the reasons for wanting to apply to the company). As Marchington and Wilkinson (1996) state 'the most effective application forms ensure that the information provided ties in with the person specification and core competences required for the job . . .'. However, research has demonstrated that this is, in practice, not in fact the case. For example, Keenan (1995) found that very few of the 536 organisations in the UK included in a study of recruitment practice, actually designed their application form around selection criteria, with over half relying on off-the-shelf products. It has also been shown that the information on application forms is not used in a systematic way, with, for example, different individuals within the same organisation actually basing their decisions on different information (Knights and Raffo, 1990). This occurs despite the fact that the information on application forms appears significantly to influence selection outcomes, at least in graduate recruitment (Keenan, 1997). Such random pre-screening can not be considered ideal from either a traditional or a processual perspective.

Biodata is a highly structured and detailed example of the application form and consists of demographic and lifestyle questions, which have been found to be sound predictors of job performance. So, for example, if past data demonstrates that first-born children do better than those who have older siblings, then this question is asked and those who are first-born score points for this fact. If data also demonstrates that those with a first-class honours degree do better than those with poorer degrees then, again, points will be awarded to those with this qualification. A whole series of data is then collected about candidates, where this has been shown to link to performance criteria. The items are weighted appropriately and scored according to the strength of the link with performance. Armstrong (1995) observes that the approach is most useful when large numbers of applications are received for a limited number of posts. The predictive power of biodata is comparatively high. For example, Harvey-Jones and Taffler (2000) demonstrated that adopting a more systematic approach to pre-screening, based on mapping basic aspects of a candidate's past experience, such as grades achieved in school and college, could substantially improve the pre-selection process. However, by its very nature the use of biodata is particularly vulnerable to charges of unfair discrimination. If we have an organisation where successful managers are predominantly white, male, middle aged and middle class, and then we construct our criteria based on their responses to demographic and lifestyle questions, it seems highly probable that we will select even more white, middle class, middle aged males. To overcome this Cook (1993) suggests that cross-validation with independent assessment is necessary and goes so far as to assert that 'an inventory that has not been cross-validated should not be used for selection'.

Biodata is not very widely used despite the good predictive validities that can be achieved (Shackleton and Newell, 1997). Application forms are much more common as a pre-screening device. However, as seen, application forms are often used unsystematically. It is also interesting to consider candidates' reactions to the different methods of pre-screening. On application forms, especially on the free-format, unverifiable questions, both potential candidates and recruiters assume that candidates will 'fake' answers (e.g. to a question about the reasons they have chosen the particular company to apply to). Even on biodata questions Stokes *et al.* (1993) found that job incumbents responded differently to items compared to actual job applicants, with the latter responding in more socially desirable ways. In other words, real applicants were using impression management tactics to respond to the questions, especially those questions where answers were non-verifiable. Moreover, biodata has been found to engender negative reactions (Robertson *et al.*, 1991), especially among candidates rejected by this procedure. These rejected candidates expressed doubts about its accuracy, validity and usefulness.

Perhaps one key point in terms of this pre-selection stage is for organisations to be more open and honest about the likely opportunities available. At present, this early stage in selection is little more than a ritual dance, with organisations presenting limited 'real' information, so that candidates are not able to self-select out. Instead, glamorous or glossy information is presented, which would attract almost anyone. This encourages potential candidates, in turn, to present themselves in unrealistic ways, trying to pre-empt what they think the organisation is looking for. Research has indeed shown that offering potential candidates a realistic preview can improve selection decisions. For example, Wang and Hinrichs (2005) showed how realistic assignment previews increased the success rate of expatriate assignments.

Psychometric measures

There are a variety of different psychometric measures although the two most commonly used in the context of selection are ability tests and personality questionnaires.

Ability tests

Intelligence testing has a long history, starting with the work of Alfred Binet and Theodore Simon in the early years of the twentieth century. Reber (1985) observes that 'few concepts in psychology have received more devoted attention and few have resisted clarification so thoroughly' as intelligence. Thus, it has been defined as 'that which is measured by intelligence tests' by the delightfully named Boring (1923). Nevertheless, there is general agreement that intelligence involves: an ability to adapt to a variety of situations; an ability to learn; and an ability to employ abstract concepts. There are also different aspects of intellectual activity, for example, logic and creativity – roughly equivalent to ideas such as convergent and divergent thinking. This is not the place to rehearse the work of Binet, Guilford, Spearman, de Bono etc., suffice it to observe that there are a number of tests, which purport to measure these qualities.

Aptitude tests are also measures of ability but concerned with more specific abilities. They commonly measure specific areas such as:

● verbal
● numerical
● perceptual or diagrammatic
● spatial

- mechanical
- clerical, and
- sensory or motor aptitudes.

It is common to administer batteries of aptitude tests such as those published by Saville and Holdsworth, ASE, The Psychological Corporation, EITS (Educational and Industrial Test Services), and Oxford Psychologists Press. These tests are designed to measure an individual's propensity to acquire a particular skill or set of skills at some future point. Both general intelligence and specific ability tests are typically presented as multiple-choice questions with right/wrong answers. In both cases it is essential that the tests are administered consistently (e.g. with exact time limits) and scored and interpreted by qualified individuals (in the UK this means being BPS accredited). These kinds of tests will provide standardised norms for the relevant population, for example if a test is being used for graduates then graduate norms will be used. Individuals are given a percentile score, which compares their result against this population norm. For example, if someone scores at the 10th percentile this means that 90 per cent of the comparative population score higher than this.

The key issue from the traditional perspective is predictive validity with respect to the job being filled. Here intelligence tests and aptitude tests do very well, having a relatively high predictive validity across a range of jobs, although they predict better for jobs that are more complex (Hermelin and Robertson, 2001). They also have high face validity, and are relatively easy to use. However, there is a question about how much additional information intelligence test results provide, over and above that obtained from already accessible information, like qualifications obtained.

Personality questionnaires

The majority of personality questionnaires used during selection follow the nomothetic tradition, at least in the UK. Thus, they are concerned with a stable element of people, which could be thought of as dispositions of behaviour. The measures in use currently are self-report instruments. This raises immediate issues of faking (sometimes referred to as motivational distortion or the social desirability effect) or alternatively, self-delusion. We may safely assume that in work situations of selection, promotion etc., faking will be a probable occurrence and this must be borne in mind when contemplating the use of personality questionnaires (for a good discussion of these issues see Morgeson et al., 2007). We can relate this back to our earlier discussion of impression management. So we immediately have validity issues surrounding assumptions about personality predicting work performance and the reliability of the measures. This is confirmed by research which demonstrates that personality questionnaires generally have a rather low predictive validity. For example, in terms of the Big-5 dimensions of personality, conscientiousness has the highest predictive validity, followed by emotional stability (Hermelin and Robertson, 2001). Extraversion, openness and agreeableness, on the other hand, are not good predictors of overall work performance, although they can provide some predictive validity in relation to specific criteria or specific occupations (Barrick et al., 2001). Indeed, it is clear that personality measures are better at assessing specific aspects of job performance than job performance per se.

For example, Borman *et al.* (2001) demonstrated that conscientiousness was a better predictor of citizenship behaviour than of general task performance.

More recently, attention has been devoted to developing tests that are specifically constructed to measure personality constructs that are work related, rather than simply using general measures of personality such as a Big-5 measure. Examples include tests to measure integrity or honesty, violence, stress-tolerance, and customer service. These have been defined as criterion-focused occupational personality scales (COPS). While the development of such tests is still in its infancy, preliminary evidence suggests that these can be valid predictors of the specific aspects of job performance that they are targeted to measure (Ones and Viswesvaran, 2001).

Aside from these validity issues there is also a more fundamental problem. The traditional approach begins from the assumption that there is a particular type of personality or a particular type of ability required for a focal job. Individuals would then be chosen who demonstrated that particular profile. Hopefully, having read the rest of this chapter the reader can begin to think through the limitations of this. Specifically, it does not allow for the fact that someone with a different personality or a different range of aptitudes might do the job equally effectively but in a very different way. Nor does it allow for individuals to change and 'grow' in to their jobs.

From a processual perspective, these ability tests and personality measures might still be used during selection but in a rather different way. Rather than looking for individuals with the 'ideal profile' and rejecting those who have different abilities and personalities, the results might be used as the basis of discussion. Thus, if I apply for a job as an operations planning manager and a personality measure demonstrates that I am a relatively 'unconscientious' person, this could be used during an interview to discuss whether I am in fact suited to this position, given that the previous job incumbent took a very methodical and conscientious approach to the job. This discussion might well encourage me to decide that I am not in fact suited. On the other hand, I might feel that I could do the job effectively and with personal satisfaction, because I recognise that I am not that thorough but have developed coping strategies for dealing with this. Moreover, I may convince the interviewer that actually this is a benefit, because the manager being relatively disorganised means that the subordinates will have to plan more for themselves so that they will develop valued skills and experience. Meanwhile, my high level of creativity can be used to bring in new ideas to solve some of the routing problems within the department. In other words, I might do the job very differently from the last incumbent but be equally, if not more, effective. Such a discussion would encourage the kind of realistic recruiting that leads to increased role clarity and expectations that can lead to the start of successful socialisation (Baker and Jennings, 2000).

Performance tests

These are of particular value when specific job activities can be set up as tests of performance. Keyboard or driving skills could be assessed relatively easily and, for some occupations, such as musicians and actors, they are well established as 'auditions'. Within academia, for example, candidates are often asked to present a lecture as part of the selection process. Such methods are relevant when we are seeking persons who already possess a skill or competence, and trainability testing (attempting to measure an applicant's ability to *develop* the required skills) could be considered a sub-set of this type of measure. It is also possible to attempt to design exercises such as the 'in-tray' which seek to replicate job skills. The 'in-tray' exercise involves giving candidates a range of different correspondence (e.g. memos, faxes, letters, minutes of meetings etc.). Candidates must then respond to these different items, typically having to state what action they would take and why and with what level of priority.

These types of tests can have high levels of predictive validity, but most importantly they can provide candidates with a realistic understanding of what the job involves. Clearly, the closer to 'real life' the exercise is the greater this level of understanding and therefore the more likely are candidates to develop realistic expectations. However, while it is possible to emulate the job tasks in this way, it is much more difficult with this type of method to provide candidates with an insight in to the organisational culture. Probation periods and/or internship opportunities can be useful for gaining this understanding.

Group selection methods

Group selection exercises are used in an attempt to assess the social, interactive and influencing skills of the subjects. Typically the group is given a task to tackle – this may be a business problem such as budget allocation, devising strategy, generating ideas for marketing initiatives, designing structures to achieve some goal with limited material or building a specified structure with 'lego bricks'. The exercises may involve candidates being given roles to play (managing director, sales manager, accountant etc.) or alternatively the task may be set to the group without any roles either being assigned or indicated. The participants are observed and assessed while tackling the group exercise. The assumption is that behaviours demonstrated will be typical of 'real life' responses. However, validity tests have not yet confirmed how effective these measures are. This is at least partly because this would depend on establishing team-level criteria against which to judge the outcome from these exercises. Such criteria have rarely been used. Nevertheless, these exercises may still be useful if they involve activities, which have some resemblance to the team-working that will be expected on the job. The problem may be that, since few organisations undertake any team-level analysis in identifying the requirements for the job, the actual tasks involved in these activities may bear little relation to the actual team-working environment.

References

References are very common in the UK (Shackleton and Newell, 1994). References may be used to check on the accuracy of factual details given by the applicant, and/or they may seek opinions to predict success in the job. However, predictive validity is low. There are a number of factors which influence this:

● The stage in the process at which they are sought. Commonly in the world of education, references are demanded as part of a short-listing (i.e. before interview) process. However, it is more common for references to be taken up after a job has been offered, simply to check that there is nothing in the individuals' history to suggest they are not suitable (e.g. a criminal record).

- Referees are normally asked to comment on generalities of personality such as honesty, cooperativeness and social adjustment. Such vague personality constructs are likely to be interpreted very differently so that the basis of comparison is limited. Using structured reference forms can improve their validity (Dobson, 1989).

- Who chooses the referee? If it is the applicant who selects the referee, we should not be surprised if the result is a favourable observation. The alternative, which is only practicable if it occurs later in the process, is for the assessor to determine what information is required and then demand of the applicant a question such as 'who, in your current organisation, could we contact in order to get a realistic opinion of . . . ?'

- The specificity of the questions asked of the referee. Generalised questions are likely to get generalised replies. This generality, together with a reluctance of many to be critical, can lead to a very unhealthy practice of 'reading what is not included' in the reference.

Interviews

Interviews are used almost universally in the UK (Shackleton and Newell, 1994) but the predictive power of unstructured interviews, as still used in many organisations, is depressingly low. Much of the difficulty arises from issues of interpersonal perception (for a review of interviews in personnel selection see Posthuma *et al.*, 2002). The traditional interview suffers from being unstructured, self-reporting and open to bias. The subsequent rating of applicants is bedevilled by halo and horn effects, leniency (an unwillingness to give poor ratings) and central tendency (using the middle of the scale). The low validity and openness to bias has led to criticism under the banner of equal opportunities. The response has been to attempt to make the interview more structured by using standard questions with scaled pre-rated responses. There are several different types of structured interviews, but the two most common are:

1. The 'situational interview' poses hypothetical situations to candidates and asks them how they would react to this situation – i.e. what would you do if. . . . These hypothetical situations are based on a critical incident job analysis (Latham *et al.*, 1980). In the interview itself, interviewers ask each question in turn, using exactly the same words for each candidate, with no follow-up or variations allowed. The applicant is then rated on each question according to a predetermined set of dimensions that were identified from the original critical incident job analysis. Each of the dimensions is anchored with behavioural rating scales, which depict what are good, mediocre and poor answers.

2. The 'behavioural interview' asks applicants to identify situations where they have had certain, job relevant, experiences. The interviewer then probes to establish what the applicant actually did in that situation. So rather than ask the candidate, 'what would you do if . . . ?', the candidate is asked, 'what did you do when . . . ?' (Janz *et al.*, 1986). The questions asked are, as with situational interviews, related to those job dimensions considered important in the particular job. The assumption here is that past behaviour predicts future behaviour. During the interview, the interviewer is encouraged to take concise notes and to use follow-up questions to probe answers. After the finish of the

interview, the interviewer rates the candidate on predefined rating scales, again derived from job analysis.

Both these approaches have been shown to improve criteria-related validity basically through increasing job-relatedness, providing limited access to ancillary data which may bias impressions of interviewers (interviewers do not view data from the application form prior to the interview), and standardising questions (Dipboye, 1997). That is, these techniques limit questions to those which have direct relevance to the knowledge, skills and attitudes required on the particular job. Yet despite the clear evidence that structured interviews have a higher predictive validity than unstructured interviews, evidence of actual use suggests that the unstructured (or at best semi-structured) interview remains the norm. There are a number of reasons for this:

- The flexibility of the unstructured interview allows the interviewer to shift from assessment to recruitment when it is clear that the candidate is well-suited to the job (Dipboye, 1997).

- Unstructured interviews are preferred by both candidates, possibly because this gives them more control over the situation (Schuler *et al.*, 1993) and interviewers (Meehl, 1986).

- While structured interviews may encourage a good fit with the particular job, they may be less effective at selecting for the organisational context (Bowen *et al.*, 1991). As Judge and Ferris (1992: 23) comment: 'calls for structured interviews as a way to improve the validity of the interview may be misplaced if the true goal, and utility, of the interview lies not in selecting the most technically qualified, but the individual most likely to fit into the organisation'. Similarly, the unstructured interview may allow more scope for the candidate to explore, through the interviewer, more about the job and organisation thus allowing them also to make a better assessment of fit.

What this suggests is that the interview has multiple functions, only one of which is to assess the direct fit to the job (Palmer *et al.*, 1999). In addition, it can be used as a basis for negotiating a mutually agreeable psychological contract and serve as a preliminary socialisation tactic (Anderson and Ostroff, 1997). A structured interview will be severely restricted in facilitating this negotiation. This does not mean that good practice should abandon all the evidence of the past 50 years and revert to totally unstructured interviews, which are not based on any understanding of the job to be done or its context. Rather, adopting a processual perspective recognises the multiple functions of an interview, with job prediction being only one of these. A semi-structured interview, which allows exploration and negotiation on both sides, can meet these multiple functions and be satisfying to both parties involved.

Assessment centres

Assessment Centres (AC) are not a method *per se*. Rather they operate as an amalgam of previously discussed selection methods and operate on a multi-trait, multi-method basis. ACs have been shown to have high criterion-related validity (Krause *et al.*, 2006) and face validity (Macan *et al.*, 1994). Fundamental to the design of an AC is the notion of a matrix of dimensions against which candidates are assessed in a variety of exercises/methods. The AC allows a group of candidates to be assessed at the same time – this has a number of advantages, particularly in terms of the cost effectiveness of test administration. It also allows group dynamics to be examined via group exercises etc. On the other hand it is also expensive and time consuming, demanding trained (and expensive) observer/assessors for a period of time, which may be as long as three days. The predictive power of ACs is impressive, but there is an irony in that as Cook (1993) observes 'the fact is that psychologists don't know why ACs work so well'. Thus, despite the good overall validity, the actual ratings of candidates on the individual dimensions across exercises within an AC are problematic (Hoeft and Schuler, 2001). Thus, numerous studies have shown that ratings on different dimensions within a particular exercise correlate highly with each other (thus demonstrating low discriminant validity) while measures of the same dimension across different exercises do not correlate very highly (low convergent validity) (Kauffman *et al.*, 1993). Part of the problem here concerns the design of ACs and it is now clear that there are a number of things that can be done to improve AC construct validity (Lievens, 1998). In particular, it is advocated that:

- a small number of dimensions be used – say three or four;
- dimensions are used which are conceptually distinct;
- dimensions are defined in concrete and job-related ways;
- training is given to familiarise assessors with the dimensions;
- dimensions are revealed to the candidates so that they know what they are being assessed against – this will reduce the advantages to high self-monitors (see above).

Most importantly, not only do ACs demonstrate good predictive validity it is also clear that they are generally favourably regarded by candidates and perceived to measure job-related qualities accurately and fairly (Anderson and Witvliet, 2008). Interestingly, therefore ACs fulfil both the systematic requirements for good predictive validity and they also fulfil the process requirement of providing a good opportunity to develop realistic expectations and to begin the process of organisational socialisation. However, it should always be remembered that ACs are only as good as their designers make them. While research has demonstrated good predictive and face validity, this can only be achieved through a careful design process. The AC design should be specific to the job being filled and to the organisation – it is not satisfactory to throw together a rag-bag of tests and exercises, often 'borrowed' or taken off the shelf. Each element should be purposeful and there should be plenty of scope for candidates to find out more about the organisation as well as for the organisation to find out about the candidates. ACs should also be evaluated to establish how far the people actually selected are, in fact, effective at the various levels that may be relevant – effective in the job, in the team, in the organisation and in relation to the changing environment.

Selection decisions

Once the selection methods have been used, decisions are made – the organisation decides to whom to offer jobs and candidates decide whether to take a job that is offered. From the point of view of the organisation one would hope that decisions were based on a careful weighing of the evidence. However, the organisational literature is replete with studies that have shown that decision-making in organisations typically deviates from this rational model (Pfeffer, 1981; Hickson *et al.*, 1971). Beach (1990: 13) suggested that most decisions are made 'quickly and simply on the basis of "fittingness", and only in particular circumstances are they made on the basis of anything like the weighing and balancing of gains and losses that is prescribed by classical decision theory'. This is consistent with the finding that interviewers typically make their decision well before the end of the interview and at times very early in the process. In other words, despite efforts to make selection 'objective' and 'scientific', decision processes are inevitably affected by human subjectivities, as shown by the exhibit below.

Exhibit 6.1

Best practice recruitment!

One of the authors had been involved in designing an assessment centre for graduate trainees for a genuinely internationally famous organisation. Analyses were conducted, competences identified, exercises designed and matrices justified. Managers and staff underwent the experience for themselves and were trained in interviewing and assessing behaviours. Finally, the great day arrived and the first set of applicants who had survived the short-listing process were invited to central London.

No expense was spared – the chief executive greeted them, videos of organisational plans were shown, the HR director wished everybody well. The assessment centre progressed with exercises, tests and interviews.

At lunch the high and mighty returned to mingle with the troops. On arrival, the HR director sidled up and inquired, *soto voce*, 'How is the girl in the red coat getting on? I really like the look of her!'

'Best practice' recruitment and selection

Activity 6.5   Best practice recruitment and selection

Referring back to the case of Moddens presented in Chapter 1, the tensions within this company were resolved by setting up two separate divisions, each focused on a very different market – the Gourmet division and the Volume division. Design a recruitment and selection process for each of these divisions.

1. What are the similarities between the recruitment and selection processes that you have suggested?

2. What are the differences between the recruitment and selection processes that you have suggested?

3. Why have you suggested that the two divisions use different approaches to recruitment and selection?

Hopefully, you have recognised that the two divisions are likely to use different approaches to recruitment and selection. For the Volume division, with its emphasis on low commitment human resourcing strategies, the traditional approach to selection is likely to predominate – fitting the person to the job, having little regard for the individual's commitment to the organisation and so not particularly concerned with how the recruitment and selection process is viewed by the candidates. For the Gourmet division, with its emphasis on high commitment human resourcing strategies, there will be more emphasis on finding people who fit the organisation and using recruitment and selection processes which can effectively start the socialisation process that will help to develop the high commitment employees that they are looking for. Thus, even if the same methods are used in these two divisions, they are likely to be used in rather different ways.

This reiterates what has been said previously in this book – that there is no simple 'best practice' here in relation to recruitment and selection that can be followed in all circumstances. Thus, while in this chapter we have emphasised the differences between the traditional and processual approaches to selection and have portrayed the exchange approach as being more realistic, it is nevertheless the case that the traditional approach will better describe what is happening in some organisations. Organisations may then adopt a traditional approach to recruitment and selection, ignoring the inevitable human processes that will influence this. In some circumstances this may be the cheapest and easiest approach to adopt, even though it may lead to unfair discrimination and lead to the recruitment of employees with unrealistic expectations who do not fit the broader organisational context. This may not matter in organisational contexts where employees are treated as disposable resources that can be substituted relatively easily by others, as perhaps in the Volume division of Moddens. However, in contexts where an organisation is attempting to recruit and retain talented workers with high levels of knowledge, skills and expertise, and where commitment to the job and to the organisation is paramount, this approach would not be effective. In such contexts, understanding and emphasising the processual aspects of recruitment and selection is likely to be both more realistic and more effective in terms of attracting and retaining the kind of high commitment employees that are sought.

Conclusion

The literature and research on recruitment and selection is well-established. However, this has been dominated by a particular perspective, which we have called the traditional or criteria-related validity approach. While this 'looks' very objective and scientific, the reality is that in selection we are dealing with human judgements, which are inherently subjective – judgements by managers as to the suitability of candidates and judgements by candidates as to whether they would like to work for a particular organisation. To try and overcome or minimise this subjectivity is to ignore its inevitability. Instead, we have advocated adopting an exchange or processual perspective, which recognises this subjectivity. Selection is then a process of two-way negotiation in which both parties attempt to make sense of the other to determine whether there is any mutually beneficial fit or accommodation. This process approach, therefore, recognises that applicants are also making decisions and that the impact of the selection process on these individuals may have a significant bearing on their future involvement with the organisation. Adopting the processual view thus recognises that recruitment and selection are strategic decision-making processes that are emergent. Assuming this processual perspective does not necessarily change the selection methods that are actually used, rather it changes the ways in which they are used. Nevertheless, in some organisational contexts the traditional approach may suffice, even though it ignores the inevitable negotiation that underpins any selection decision.

Summary

This leads to the following conclusions in relation to adopting a processual view of selection:

- Understanding and theorising from the processual perspective requires an approach that captures dynamic processes through time, as the individual and the organisation negotiate a strategically compatible fit through the 'messy web of reality'.

- The focus needs to be on how individuals create their own environments through the processes of interaction, rather than simply studying individuals as if they were determined by their biological trait structures. Adopting the processual perspective, therefore, requires moving away from the positivist epistemology that has dominated to date.

- Adopting a processual perspective, however, does not mean abandoning all that we have learnt from past research on selection, but it means building on this base.

- Understanding predictive validity is important, but we need to expand this to focus beyond the individual job level, to think also about this strategically at the team, the organisation and the environment levels.

- Recognising these different levels of analysis will highlight inconsistencies within organisations. Selection is then seen as the process through which such contradictions are openly negotiated with prospective candidates.

- In particular, we need to move from the current situation where prospective candidates are wooed to work for an organisation by promises that cannot be fulfilled, so leading to disillusionment when they confront the often less than glamorous reality.

- Instead, prospective candidates should be encouraged to develop realistic expectations so they can actually begin the process of organisational socialisation 'up front'.

- In some contexts, however, the traditional view of selection as a management decision-making process to find the 'best' candidate for a specific job is likely to dominate, and can lead to unfair discrimination and to the recruitment of employees who will show limited commitment to the organisation because once they start work they realise that they have unrealistic expectations of the job and the organisation.

Discussion questions

1. In what ways might the traditional approach to selection result in decisions which discriminate against minority groups?

2. How far, if at all, does the processual view of selection overcome this problem of unfair discrimination?

3. Can managers make informed selection decisions, given the subjectivist view, which sees 'knowing' as dependent on social and cultural forces that shape the process of interpretation?

4. Adopting the traditional and processual perspectives in turn, what might be the respective roles of personnel/HRM specialists versus line managers in assessment, selection and evaluation?

5. Consider any two selection methods and compare and contrast how they might impact on a candidate's view of the organisation.

6. In your view, what makes an effective selection method? Consider your answer in relation to a small family firm and then a large multinational firm.

Further reading

For a comprehensive general overview of issues to do with assessment, selection and evaluation, see the books edited either by Anderson and Herriot (1997) or by Campbell and Knapp (2001). For a good practical text on recruitment and selection see Dale's (2006) book or the book by Taguchi (2002), which focuses specifically on the recruitment and selection of MBA graduates and Rosalind Searle's (2004) book. For a book that focuses on the role of headhunters in the recruitment process, see Finlay and Coverdill (2002). For more detailed discussion of the role of personality testing in selection decisions, see Blinkhorn and Johnston (1990) and as a counter to this viewpoint, O'Reilly *et al.* (1991) and the paper by Posthuma *et al.* (2002). For a comprehensive review of personnel selection at the beginning of the new millennium see the two special issues of the *International Journal of Selection and Assessment* edited by Jesus Salgado (vol. 8, 3–4, 2000 and vol. 9, 1–2, 2001).

7

Performance management and performing management

Colin Fisher and Anne Sempik

Learning outcomes

Having read this chapter and completed its associated activities, readers should be able to:

- Point to the fundamental strategic options that face human resource strategy-makers when developing performance management systems, especially the choice between high commitment performance management approaches and low commitment performance management approaches
- Describe and critique various methods and techniques of performance management so that the practices followed in its name are clearly understood
- Analyse the performance management practices of an organisation and assess the extent to which they are consistent, one with another, and are appropriate for the general environmental business conditions of the organisation

Introduction

Judges are supposed to be free from interference from others to maintain their independence. But it is proposed by the government that even they should not be able to avoid performance appraisal. This issue was raised in 2003 (Susskind, 2003) and some judges saw appraisal as unnecessary and worrying but Susskind argued that it would be beneficial for judges to have their competences and practices reviewed. If they are working well they can be reassured by this knowledge; if there are some problems they can be helped. But who should judge the judges? (other judges probably), should their judgments be appraised? (probably not) and should the durations of their summings-up be measured? (also probably not). The issue was still alive in 2007 when it was reported that some lawyers, who appeared before judges, argued that judges should be subject to 360° appraisal that would allow a range of interested parties, including the lawyers to comment on the judges' performance (Gibb, 2007). The story shows how performance management has become near universal but also that each performance management system has to be right for the particular situation.

There are many ways in which performance management can be conducted and in this chapter the following methods will be reviewed:

- clarifying and publishing programme structures which attempt to show the links between staff's activities and the objectives of the organisation;
- the use of performance measurement and performance indicators;
- target-setting and monitoring;
- the use of competency frameworks;
- 360° appraisal;
- personal development planning;
- dealing with problem staff;
- staff appraisal interviews – which are often the arena in which all the above activities are played out.

Performance-related pay as part of performance management is discussed in Chapter 8.

Performance management is seen as an important issue in many organisations. It is often seen as part of 'hard HRM' and defined as a bundle of HR practices that influence organisational performance and so justifies HRM's claim to have a strategic impact (Guest, 2007: 54). In its 2005 survey, of 506 companies, the CIPD reported that nearly 90 per cent of the sample said they had performance management systems. Overall between the survey in 1997 and that carried out in 2005 there had been some significant changes; team assessment featured for the first time in the 2005 survey, individual annual appraisals and objective setting and review were less popular, and once more 360° appraisal had increased in organisational popularity. Competency frameworks as a basis for performance management are used by just over 30 per cent of the sample (CIPD, 2005a); this focus on a developmental role for performance management is underpinned by 71 per cent of the respondents.

Performance management as managerial folklore

Insecurity is a common phenomenon in organisations and it is often expressed in the stories, jokes and anecdotes people at work tell each other; in other words, in an organisation's folklore. Senior managers, for example, may be concerned about their lack of grip on what is happening in the organisation and on what it is achieving. Team leaders and middle managers might be told by management trainers that their role is to 'achieve things through others' but are unsure about how this can be done. People in personnel and HR departments argue that their function is critical to the performance of the organisation but worry about whether they have instituted enough programmes and policies to convince others of their work's worth. Staff at all levels worry about whether they can prove to their bosses that they have met, or exceeded, the organisation's expectations of them.

Performance management is often the vehicle for quelling such anxieties and demands. As a consequence, performance management systems, and in particular the appraisal component of them, can become overloaded. This may happen on occasion because, as Silverman *et al.* (2005: 59) argue, elements of performance management, such as 360° appraisal, can be introduced 'on a whim'. Strebler *et al.* (2001: 24, 29, 55) studied performance management systems in a number of organisations and discovered that many of their performance management systems had multiple objectives and multiple contents. For example the system might be linked to business objectives to developing employees' skills and competences. Such a system might incorporate setting and reviewing objectives and competences, planning training and development, and succession planning. A large number of tools would have to be employed in such a scheme, such as:

- performance-related pay;
- 360° appraisal, sometimes implemented through an intranet;
- learning resources and knowledge management systems;
- team bonuses;
- forced choice rating schemes (see p. 215);
- quarterly appraisal interviews;
- personal development plans.

In the conclusion of the report the authors question whether such complicated schemes can work. They ask whether:

- line managers can keep abreast of such all-encompassing performance management schemes;
- the cost of the management and development time needed to implement such schemes might not be too great;
- the human resource specialists will be able to provide speedy and appropriate support for large schemes;
- the costs of designing and running large integrated schemes are justified by their benefits.

Some performance management systems are designed as integrated wholes. Many are formed by bringing together many different components that had been introduced into the organisation at different times and to meet different needs. Performance management could thus be seen as a collection of folk prescriptions and recipes, the purpose of which is to reduce people's anxieties about their problems by giving them something to do. In seventeenth-century England, for example, people would visit the local cunning woman or man for help in finding a missing belonging or for a charm against ill-luck or curses (Thomas, 1973). In a similar fashion the models, homilies, procedures and techniques of performance management help people feel that they are doing all that can be done to do their job well. Managers may be assured that they are meeting their targets by checking the monthly metrics (the performance measurement information that their organisation produces). Team leaders can bring forward, as evidence of competence, their exemplary records in conducting staff appraisals and in mentoring the personal development plans of their staff. Personnel and HRM staff may reinforce their perception of their worth to the organisation by redesigning the staff appraisal scheme. Staff attend at cascade or team briefings to understand their role in the organisation. This emphasis on performance management as a loose body of knowledge used to help people make sense of their organisational experiences is a mark of the processual approach to understanding management that is described in Chapter 1.

Like any heap of ideas, the body of performance management methods and folklore will contain things of value and things of doubtful origin and usefulness.

Some of the remedies and prescriptions will be based on rigorous research and sound theory such as expectancy theory and goal-setting theory (Mabey and Salaman, 1995: 190). Goal-setting theory claims that people work better when they have clear, realisable and significant goals. Expectancy theory takes a more sophisticated tack and argues that people will put more 'E' (energy, effort, enthusiasm, excitement and so on) into their work if they believe their efforts will result in tangible achievements that will help them fulfil their personal needs.

Other performance management remedies will be commonly held beliefs that have developed, through the accretion of anecdote and experience, until they finally emerge in a textbook and acquire authority. Many prescriptions will be the result of cumulative plagiarism, as when, for example, a samizdat copy of one company's 360° appraisal questionnaire is used as a starting point by someone with the task of designing such a scheme in another organisation. Some of the prescriptions are communicated by myths (case studies, pub stories, corporate and training videos and newspaper stories) of organisations that have, as the story goes, increased turnover by 200 per cent by introducing target-setting.

Within this matter there is an undercurrent of contrary stories and theories that challenges the validity of performance management methods. Some of these emerge in the proceedings of academic conferences and others are found in the office ephemera people put on their notice boards at work (see Exhibit 7.1).

Exhibit 7.1

The canoe race: an example of the stories told about performance management

Once upon a time it was resolved to have a canoe race between a Japanese team and a team representing an NHS Trust.* Both teams practised long and hard to reach their peak performance. On the big day they were as ready as they could be. The Japanese won by a mile.

Afterwards the Trust team became very discouraged by the result and morale sagged. Senior management decided that the reason for the crushing defeat had to be found and a working party was set up to investigate the problem and recommend appropriate action.

Their conclusion was that the Japanese team had eight people paddling and one person steering, whereas the Trust team had eight people steering and one person paddling.

Senior management immediately hired a consultancy company to do a study on the team's structure. Millions of pounds and several months later they concluded that 'too many people were steering and not enough paddling'.

To prevent losing to the Japanese next year the team structure was changed to three 'assistant steering managers', three 'steering managers', one 'executive steering manager' and a 'director of steering services'. A performance and appraisal system was set up to give the person paddling the boat more incentive to work harder.

The next year the Japanese won by two miles. The Trust laid off the paddler for poor performance, sold off all the paddles, cancelled all capital investment for new equipment and halted developments of a new canoe. The money saved was used to give higher than average pay awards to senior management.

Source: Anon
* Various versions of this story, naming specific companies, are extant.

If you are inclined to dismiss this story as a piece of unrepresentative mischief-making it is worth noting that in their 2005 survey the CIPD reported that a minority, just over a quarter, of respondents believed that performance management was time consuming and bureaucratic; and this was a reduction on the number who believed this to be the case in 1997. Such stories illustrate people's tendency, identified in Chapter 1 (p. 12), to resist the control that endeavours such as performance management seek to impose on them. The stories, anecdotes and myths in which people tell of their experiences of performance management, as designers, managers or subjects of such schemes, are as much part of the corpus of performance management as the contents of textbooks, organisational policies and procedures.

The uses and abuses of performance management

The uses of folk remedies should not be trivialised or dismissed because of their apparent irrationalism. In the context of the processual approach taken in this book, folk remedies can be seen as part of the process by which pattern is identified in, or imposed on, the flow of organisational activity (Chapter 1, p. 25). Folk myths are a resource for the *enactment* of contingencies by organisational actors. In other words, it may be argued that the body of performance management material is important because of the rhetorical and practical resources it provides for the performing of management. For example, the stories about the benefits of macho target-setting, which originated in the private sector, appear to have affected how ministers in the Labour government understood, and enacted, their understanding of social problems. In health for example, many problems were to be tackled by setting targets such as maximum time to wait before being seen in a hospital accident and emergency department. As the Institute for Employment Studies report on performance management (Strebler *et al.*, 2001: 53) noted, performance management became politicised. However, in 2002 the government failed to meet some of its own targets for primary education and subsequently withdrew some of its targets in other areas such as drug misuse. This can be interpreted as government using the stories told in the mid-1990s of the effectiveness of private sector techniques to enact those practices in the public sector, only to modify their position when the stories of how private sector organisations, such as Enron and WorldCom, manipulated their targets and performance measures were told in the 2000s.

It follows from the discussion above that performance management is inevitably a matter of controversy and argument. It is not a simple matter of knowing the right and the wrong way of doing performance management. The issues for debate include:

● Whether performance measurement systems measure the right things and whether managers are sufficiently skilled at interpreting the statistics.

● Why it is that most staff appraisal schemes fall into disuse within three years and need to be relaunched. In relation to 360° appraisal schemes Silverman *et al.* (2005) note that after a period of initial enthusiasm response rates and commitment decline, schemes undergo local 'tailoring' and personal agendas are perceived to undermine the integrity of the scheme. Wilson and Nutley (2003:

309) researched appraisal schemes in universities and identified 'appraisal fatigue' that led to great effort being necessary to keep the scheme alive. Bowles and Coates (1993: 9) suggest that appraisal schemes are long lived but their survey did not investigate the frequency of relaunches of companies' performance management schemes.

● Whether personal development plans are seen by staff as a genuine aid to growth; or are seen as part of a developmental liturgy that people first acquire at schools, preparing their records of achievement, and which they then repeat by rote as they proceed to the production of continuous professional development portfolios.

● Why it is that most staff seem to dislike appraisal, or do they?

The methods of performance management are intended to clarify managers' roles, but, from a processual perspective, this is a vain task because organisations are ineluctable and messy. The tension between clarity and ambiguity can be illustrated by a common problem of performance management. The difficulty concerns the level at which performance management should operate. Should the focus be on the whole department or organisation, on teams, on individuals or on a combination of all three? In a hierarchical structure it should be possible to specify targets for the organisation as a whole and then disaggregate these into targets for sub-units, teams and individuals. In practice this can be difficult. A survey from Saville and Holdsworth (1997) reported that less than 40 per cent of the sample used appraisal to set team objectives and only 11 per cent thought the process was effective. There can be overlap between targets. It may be that an individual is charged with a target that can only be achieved through a team effort or that a senior manager's targets are achieved when all his or her subordinates have achieved their goals so that it is uncertain wherein lies the particular contribution of the senior person. In such circumstances a traditional view of organisations and management cannot explain the situation. A processual view is needed because it emphasises the adjustments and negotiations that are required to deal with the consequences of the overlap of responsibility for targets. These accommodations could include, when targets are reviewed, for example, much retrospective rationalisation to explain why, in the illustrations just given, it was a lack of cooperation from team colleagues that led to a failure to meet the target, and why the senior manager should be rated highly because his or her staff have done their jobs. In the appraisal interview the appraisee will create stories to convince themselves and their interviewer of a favourable interpretation of their performance against the targets. Jacques (1992) argued that an appraisal is an occasion when appraiser and appraisee make sense of their organisational experience by creating stories that interpret and justify their actions.

If the reader has detected a sceptical (some may say a cynical) tone in this chapter so far they may be assured that the intention is not to advise people to avoid performance management, because it is ungrounded and uncertain, and to cultivate their gardens instead. Rather the objective is to help readers towards an understanding of the purposes of the remedies and recipes discussed so that they can learn how to use them in an exploratory and experimental way. To this end the next section of the chapter will take the main activities of performance management, describe them and evaluate them. How these approaches might be contingently adapted in organisations following a high commitment and in those adopting a low commitment approach will also be considered. These two terms were introduced in Chapter 1, p. 27.

Clarifying and publishing objectives

It is a common view among managers that staff will perform better if they understand the contribution that their work makes to meeting the written objectives and goals of the organisation (Hackman and Oldham, 1976). Walters (1995) defined performance management as a process intended to improve the quality and quantity of work done and to bring all activity in line with an organisation's objectives. It follows that anything that makes this connection clearer to staff should enhance performance. This insight has encouraged organisations to publish documents that show, through the medium of a programme structure, how all the myriad jobs undertaken contribute to meeting the organisation's objectives. An example, based on the work of a district council, is shown in Figure 7.1. By studying this document a person who was employed, in this case, to survey

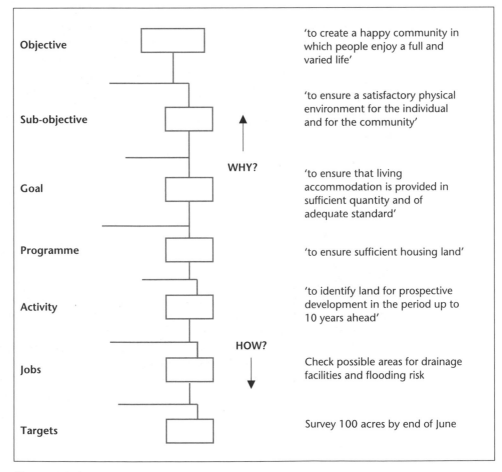

Figure 7.1 **A programme structure**

drainage and assess the risk of flooding, could see in the programme structure how their work contributed to the council's wider purposes.

Programme structures, like the one in Figure 7.1, are often at the core of performance management schemes (Lowson and Boyce, 1990). It is worth noting that the example illustrates the uncertainty of performance management jargon. In many textbooks (Walters, 1995: 9), unlike in Figure 7.1, a goal would be higher than an objective in the programme structure. In the vocabulary of performance management the terms goals, aims and objectives are often used interchangeably.

Similar methods have been used in private sector organisations. One proprietary package, for example CALM (n.d.), suggests that managers should first identify intent objectives. These are general and woolly statements that describe the purpose or focus of an organisation. Once this generality is stated, managers should identify their direction objectives. These indicate, by using active verbs such as improve, decrease and increase, the broad direction in which the managers should lead. Direction objectives, like the intent objectives, are not measurable. At the next level down in the structure managers are required to produce measurable result objectives. These state a precise result measured against at least two of the following criteria: quantity, quality, time and money. The achievement of these result objectives is dependent on fulfilling task objectives, the lowest element in the structure, which specify which jobs have to be done, by whom and by when. The hierarchy between intent objectives and task objectives links the broadest intentions of the organisation with the particular jobs of each employee.

The hierarchical nature of programme structures, including the CALM approach, gives them a mythic value to organisational management. It locates employees to a particular place and status in a great chain of organisational being and so reduces the threat that individuality might pose to organisational good order (Legge, 1995: 115). This at any rate is probably the function of a programme structure in an organisation with a low commitment strategy where it would form part of the rule-based culture that emphasised authority and a task focus. Employees' roles in the programme structure would be non-negotiable. Employees' involvement would not stretch beyond watching the corporate video presenting the organisation's objectives and reading the detailed documents that explain their contribution to them. That the role of cascading objectives may be more mythic than practical is reinforced by Strebler *et al.* (2001: 530) who doubt whether organisational goals can in practice be easily broken down into individual objectives. Despite this the CIPD's 2005 survey reports that 44 per cent of its respondents put their faith in this process (CIPD, 2005a: 4).

In an organisation with a high commitment strategy the value of programme structures to performance management would lie less in their power to fix people than in the encouragement they give to questioning the value and contribution of particular activities. In other words, it is the process of constructing a programme structure that is important because, in creating it, people have to review whether each activity undertaken in the organisation does make a contribution towards its objectives or whether the activity could safely be dropped. To be effective the programme structure needs to be a constantly reinvented document that emerges from the dialogue between all staff on the strategy of the organisation. Once the programme structure has been published as a final document and stored in filing cabinets, it probably reinforces the inevitability of existing activities rather than acting as a challenge to them.

Performance measurement

In Hackman and Oldham's (1976) model of job satisfaction, feedback is as important as understanding the significance and contribution of one's work. Many managers believe that feedback should be based on measurement (Watson, 1994: 136) and consequently much of the effort under the heading of performance management is used to develop systems for measuring performance.

Identifying appropriate measures

Most measurement methods are based on a systems model that attempts to measure the input to an organisation, the uses to which those resources are put and the activities and benefits that arise from that activity. In Table 7.1 two examples are given that show how such a model might be applied in public and private sector organisations.

Performance measures only have value, as information rather than data, if they are constructed as ratios that put one piece of statistical data into the context of another. All of the performance measures in Table 7.1 meet this criterion. But more information can be obtained by comparing one level in the systems model with another. If a final output measure is divided by a measure of input then the result is a cost-effectiveness figure that purports to show how much good was achieved per unit of resource. If an activity statistic is compared with an input statistic the result is a measure of efficiency.

Table 7.1 A systems approach to performance measurement

Stages in a systems model	Public sector example: hospital physiotherapists	Private sector example: pharmaceutical sales person
Inputs	• Unit costs of staff and materials • Conformance and variance on cost budgets	• Unit costs of staff and materials • Conformance and variance on cost budgets
Activity	• Number of patients treated per month • Quality of treatment judged against professional standards	• Number of GPs visited per month • Number of conferences and exhibitions attended per month
Intermediate output	• Patient satisfaction with service as measured by questionnaire compared with the same time period in the previous year • Improvement in patients' clinical condition assessed on a rating scale	• Orders taken as a percentage of orders for the same time period the previous year • Percentage change in market share for each category of product compared with the same period in the previous year
Final output or outcome	• Improvement in patient's quality of life (in terms of relief of distress and improved mobility [Gudex, 1986]) and expectations of longevity	• Company growth rate • Profitability as a per cent of capital employed

The complexities of performance measurement

There are a number of issues that arise out of the use of performance measures. They can be expressed as a syllogism. A syllogism is a form of argument in which a conclusion is drawn from two or more premises. The first premise is that important things about an organisation's performance are more difficult to measure than the less important things. The second premise is that managers and staff will only give their effort to achieving those things for which they have been set targets and objectives or for which they will be rewarded. Therefore, the conclusion can be drawn that performance measurement systems can undermine the achievement of an organisation's objectives by encouraging people to achieve lesser objectives at the expense of greater ones. This argument is clearly a generalisation and it needs to be considered in more detail.

The problem of devising valid measures of the important issues, the first of the two premises, is considered first. In the public sector, for example, the objective of a service is often to bring about an improvement in the state of society. This normally means studying the impact of a service on individuals and aggregating the results to arrive at an overall assessment of the services' impact. This is a technically difficult trick because the impacts may be intangible, such as in the case of social services where an improvement in a person's state of well-being might be part of the aim. Assuming that such a thing can be validly assessed by the use of a rating scale of some kind there remains the problem that well-being may have several dimensions. This raises the question of the weightings to be used to integrate all the different aspects (Challis, 1981; Smith, 1995). A further problem is that it would be impracticable to assess the benefit to all clients and so sophisticated sampling procedures would have to be used. If equity were to be taken into account then it is arguable that the disutility of people who need services, but do not receive them, should be discounted against the benefits to those who do.

The mismatch between the desirability and the practicability of performance measures is well expressed in the results of a small survey of hospital consultants (Table 7.2). The majority of consultants were of the view that indicators of clinical outcome were important but difficult to measure whereas indicators of patient satisfaction were easier to measure but less important. Pollitt (1985: 4) also attested to the difficulty of defining measures of the effectiveness of medical (clinical) interventions.

Table 7.2 The desirability and practicability of performance indicators in hospitals: hospital doctors' views on the desirability and practicality of two types of performance measure

Indicators clinical outcome	Percentage		Percentage
Very desirable	88.6	Reasonably practical	11.5
Fairly desirable	11.4	Difficult but possible	81.4
Undesirable	0	Impractical	7.1
n = 113			
Indicators of patient satisfaction			
Very desirable	57.5	Reasonably practical	23.7
Fairly desirable	38.1	Difficult but possible	50.9
Undesirable	4.4	Impractical	25.4

It is normally reckoned that, because the important objectives of a private company relate to growth and financial returns, they are easier to measure. But even in private companies many common performance measures are of doubtful validity because of the discretion available in calculating them. An example is given in Case Study 7.1.

Case Study 7.1

The validity of financial measures in the private sector

The examples of Enron and WorldCom show how companies can use improper means to manipulate their financial results. Enron used offshore companies to keep debts off its balance sheet and WorldCom classified current costs as capital. The following examples show how financial results may be manipulated legally and within the accounting rules.

The public utilities in the UK work under a regulatory regime that controls the rate of price rises. A formula is used, RPI – x, which states that for a given time period prices may only rise by the rate of inflation minus a figure for x which is determined by the regulator. The regulator is obliged to allow the companies a reasonable rate of return when calculating x. The utilities therefore attempt to maximise their costs and minimise their profits in ways that will ensure that the regulator's price controls are lenient.

An illustration of the tendency to maximise the reporting of costs in the accounts occurred in the case of British Gas Transco's calculation of the value of its capital assets (Vass, 1996: 159). Transco wished to value its assets at current replacement cost, which would be higher than a valuation, closer to the costs that the shareholders paid for the assets, that the regulator wished to use. The advantage of a higher capital valuation was that the company's rate of return would appear lower and its costs higher and the figures could be used to justify a lower value for x. At various stages during the negotiations, between the regulator Claire Spottiswoode and British Gas, the regulator argued that British Gas had valued its assets at £17 billion when a figure of between £9 billion and £11 billion would have been more appropriate, that its forecasts of capital expenditure were too high and that its depreciation mechanisms were excessive (Barnett, 1996; Beavis and Barrie, 1996). British Gas countered by saying that if it had to cut its prices at the rate demanded by the regulator it would have to make up to half its workforce redundant. The two sides could not agree. The issue went to the Mergers and Monopolies Commission who found, in 1997, in favour of the regulator.

Activity 7.1 — Questioning the validity of performance measures

1. How much do accounting practices affect the validity of financial performance indicators?

2. Can you find in press reports examples of similar accountancy manipulation in non-regulated or private sector organisations?

The balanced scorecard and a stakeholder approach to performance measurement

The second premise of the syllogism is characterised by the work of Kaplan and Norton (1992: 71). They argued that 'what you measure is what you get'. In other words, people in organisations will work to achieve those things for which they have been set targets and will ignore other things even though they may be equally as important. As most organisations give priority to measuring financial performance, this suggests that performance measurement systems distort managerial effort by privileging the achievement of financial targets. In particular, they argued, it is important for organisations to maintain their competitive advantage in the marketplace by encouraging innovation and continuous improvement. But, when there is a premium on achieving a measurable rate of financial return, it is tempting to achieve it by squeezing out of the system the time and resource necessary for innovation and experimentation. In local government, for example, there was an anxiety, which turned out to be unjustified because the targets were never enforced, that the introduction of the Citizens' Charter performance indicators, which focused on input costs and on such things as the speed with which phones were answered (Audit Commission, 1993), would drive out interest in the measurement of more important aspects of local government services (Ball and Monaghan, 1996). Performance measurement can lead to sub-optimisation, which means that one goal is achieved, but only at the expense of another. In a supermarket, for example, managers might successfully reach the goal of reducing costs per square metre of sales floor but only at the cost of annoying customers by reducing the number of checkouts that are open at any given time.

Kaplan and Norton's solution to this problem was the balanced scorecard. This was a proposal that companies should collate performance information from four viewpoints:

1. the financial perspective;
2. the customer perspective;
3. the internal business perspective;
4. the innovation and learning perspective.

The ability to inspect trends and developments in all four areas would make it easy to spot whether achievement in one area was at the cost of a worsening in another. The balanced scorecard is discussed further in Chapter 8.

The balanced scorecard technique implicitly recognises that the various stakeholders of an organisation will have different ideas about which measures are the important ones. This can make an apparently simple question such as 'how well is the organisation doing?' a complex one to answer unless it is doing either extremely badly or well. In an evaluation study of a psychogeriatric day hospital, Smith and Cantley (1985) developed a pluralistic approach to service evaluation and performance management. In the investigation, the perceptions of different groups about how well the service met their needs, as they interpreted them, became the key information in deciding whether the hospital was doing a good job and how services needed to be developed. A number of interest groups concerned with the hospital were identified, such as doctors, nurses, social workers, patients, patients' relatives, administrators and so on. Then six different criteria of success, used by the interest groups, were isolated. They were:

1. free patient flow – preventing blocked beds and 'silting up';
2. clinical cure – improving the patients' clinical condition;
3. integrated service – good communication and liaison with other related services;
4. impact on related services – provision of support to other agencies concerned with this client group;
5. support of relatives – the relief of the strain put on relatives who have to care for aged people;
6. quality of service – concern for ethos and excellence in the way the service is actually delivered.

The criteria have been simplified. However, within the developing argument, the important fact is that the different interest groups viewed the six criteria differently.

> Some groups of staff and relatives employ some criteria and some others. Some employ several criteria and some adopt a more single-minded stance . . . In practice different criteria are used in different ways by different groups at different times in different contexts for different purposes with different effects.
>
> (Smith and Cantley, 1985: 44)

In short, the researchers found disagreement amongst the stakeholders about the relative weighting between the six criteria. They could produce a very useful evaluative analysis of the hospital, but could not produce an overall, objective evaluative judgement about it. It all depended on who you were in the system. This perspective places a significant limitation on the usefulness of performance measurement.

Approaches to performance measurement

A conclusion that can be drawn from the review of the two premises about performance management is that managers in particular take metrics very seriously while harbouring doubts about their validity. The use of management metrics creates an appearance of measurable and fixed purpose while the difficulties implicit in performance measurement, suggested by a pluralistic or postmodern view of organisational evaluation, challenge as illusory any hope of an ultimate purpose for organisations. In such a situation, massaging the measurements may appear a necessity. Most examples of manipulation are, of course, anecdotal, and Colin's example relates to an occasion when someone tried to steal his car from his drive. The policeman who came to register the crime complained that, because of new regulations, the incident would no longer be registered as a crime. The thieves had set off the alarm when they broke open the car door and had run away before they could steal it. As the car had not been taken from his property, no recordable crime had been committed. The policeman expected that there would be a noticeable drop in recorded car crime in the coming year. The folklore of the manipulation of metrics suggests that managers are highly skilled at using and abusing statistical information. But there is also a contrary theme in the literature which either suggests that managers are insufficiently numerate to understand

and benefit from performance information, or they are provided with information that is so poorly presented that it is impossible to discover the patterns and trends skilfully buried in the spreadsheet or the half-inch thick, A3 sized, blue ruled, computer printout (Meekings, 1995).

Organisations adopting a low commitment approach would deal with this problem in different ways compared with those following high commitment practices. They would impose tighter rules and checks on the production and interpretation of the statistics. This would, of course, simply be seen as an interesting challenge by some staff and a vicious circle may well develop in which increasingly sophisticated sabotage of the metrics would lead to the imposition of more draconian rules, and so on. One consequence might be the loss of any capacity for innovation and creativity in the organisation as staff become ever more focused on meeting an increasing number of ever more specific targets.

Organisations adopting high commitment approaches would not see metrics as definitive and would seek to avoid the regressive cycle just described. The measurement systems would be seen as an aid to employees who were capable of self-development and of accepting stretching objectives. The measurements would not be seen as a method of control but as part of a matrix of, sometimes ambiguous, information on the performance of the organisation that participants have to make sense of in ways that help them work better. Measures would be seen as helpful but not the absolute arbiter of success. A case study that describes how such an approach might work is provided by Winstanley and Stuart-Smith (1996). They argued on ethical grounds that potential conflicts over identifying corporate objectives and associated performance measures should be resolved by fair and transparent procedures and dialogue. Where conflicts existed in the case study organisation they were presented as competing claims that had to be balanced against each other rather than as sectional interests that had to be either supported or rejected. Once these issues were resolved the staff identified the measures that would best evaluate the organisation's achievement against the objectives. Performance measures were the material of debate and agreement in the organisation and were not seen as imposed and unbending demands.

These two approaches to performance measurement, of course, are extreme positions. The approach of most organisations will lie between the two.

Target-setting and monitoring

Performance measurement can provide the basis for target-setting. Once it is possible to measure an activity or outcome it is a small step to set or agree a point or level on the measure that an employee must achieve. There are three issues that need consideration in judging the usefulness of target-setting. The first is the motivational impact of target-setting; does it encourage staff to perform better than they otherwise would? Second, how equal and open is the process of agreeing targets when a member of staff and their boss meet to discuss these things? Third, how skilled are people at setting appropriate targets?

Targets and motivation

Intuitively it might seem that setting targets should increase the standard of people's performance. The chances of our finishing the writing of this chapter were much improved by the knowledge of a deadline drawing ever nearer. Hofstede (1984: 148–50) analysed research about the motivational effect of targets in the context of budget management. Building on experimental and survey research he considered the impact of loose and tight budget targets. There must, in his analysis, be an equilibrium point where the amount of the budget is perfectly balanced with the level of resource needed to do the job. A loose budget is one that provides the budget holder with more resources than he or she could possibly need to do the job. Hofstede's research showed that when a very loose target is set the budget holder is aware of the fact and plans to spend rather less money (their aspiration level) than is available. When the budget is in balance with resource needs the budget holder will be relaxed and probably spend up to the budget limit but not beyond. When the budget is tight (i.e. the budget is below the equilibrium point) there will be a significant motivational effect and the budget holder will both aspire to, and probably achieve, a level of expenditure lower than that defined by the equilibrium point. As the budget becomes tighter, however, the budget holder will try to reduce their costs to the budget level, but the chances are the task is not achievable and they will overspend on budget but probably still spend less than the equilibrium level. A point will be reached, however, when the budget is so tight that the budget holder recognises it as impossible, and not only ceases to try to restrict expenditure, but, in a glorious cocking a snook at the situation, will spend money with abandon. The conclusions of Hofstede's research are that tight targets can produce better than expected performances; but targets that are too tight or too loose do not.

A further finding of Hofstede's work is that where there is good upward communication, where a boss is open to the ideas of their subordinates, people are less likely to see the targets as tight. Departmental meetings help budget holders to internalise external targets into personal aspirations. The implication of these findings is that effective targets are arrived at by an open and consensual process. This is not always the case in organisations, either because of the temperaments of the people involved or because of the systems of the organisation. In one organisation, in which one of the authors was involved in setting up a performance management system, staff appraisals were held in March when it was expected that the appraisees would negotiate and agree their targets for the coming financial year. But in practice the planners in the finance department had been working on their budgets for the coming year in October and November the previous year. By the time of the appraisals a detailed sales and revenue budget had been constructed for the whole organisation and, in effect, appraisees were presented with their targets as a *fait accompli* at their appraisal. To have adjusted the targets at that late point in the year would have caused too much disruption to the organisation's plans.

The skills of target-setting

Setting targets involves forecasting and judgement. This is a difficult craft and people's forecasts are often mistaken. These errors can be compounded by poor calibration. A well-calibrated person knows what they know and is conscious of their limitations (Wright, 1984). Poorly calibrated people are either over-confident (they think their targets are fair and sensible when they are not); or underconfident (they are so uncertain that they find the act of fixing a target intimidating). To make an assessment of your target-setting skills try the exercise in Activity 7.2.

Activity 7.2 Setting time deadlines and targets

Your appraisee's task is to put a specified number of staff through a customer care programme. The first stage towards this goal is to get top management support for the idea and to obtain agreement to fund it. This will most likely take 3 weeks of lobbying and persuading but if their luck is in it could be done in 2 weeks. If their luck is bad it could take 12 weeks. The second stage in the task, which can only be started when formal approval has been obtained, is to research existing customer care practices. This will take a minimum of 4 weeks, a maximum of 9, but will probably be completed in 6 weeks. The other stages of the project are listed in the table below with their time estimates.

Phase of project	Most likely time estimate	Pessimistic time estimate	Optimistic time estimate
3. Identify a training provider organisation	4	10	2
4. Design the programme	2	5	1
5. Run the programme	6	10	5

1. How many weeks would you give this appraisee to complete this project?

2. How certain are you that the target is fair?

By using a critical path network and the PERT technique (see www.netmba.com/operations/project/pert/ if you want a brief description of the technique) it can be calculated that the probability of the task being completed in 24 weeks or less is 50 per cent. To set a target of less than 24 weeks therefore is tough. But when this exercise is used in training programmes people commonly set targets that are less than 24 weeks. The distortions to which judgements are prone do not always favour the boss. Anchoring and adjustment, which is a well-researched heuristic of judgement, can favour the appraisee (Hogarth, 1980).

Target-setting and management control

One of the debates about performance management is whether its core purpose is to support employees in their work or to control them. Target and performance measures are often the focus of this debate. The idea of the panopticon (see Exhibit 7.2) is used, by those who think the function of performance management is control, as a metaphor for the role of targets in performance management.

Exhibit 7.2

The panopticon as a metaphor for performance management

Jeremy Bentham was a philosopher and reformer who published in 1791 *Panopticon* (or *The Inspection House*) in which he described a design for a circular prison where it would be easy to keep all prisoners under surveillance from the central point. An image of the panopticon can be seen at http://cartome.org/panopticon1.htm. (Bentham can currently be seen embalmed, wearing his own clothes but with a wax head, in a cupboard in University College London.) The panopticon is a metaphor for subtle management control much discussed in management literature. It had a physical existence, for example, in the Victorian round wards of Nottingham General Hospital. Once under the gaze of the nurses at the centre of the circle, the Victorian patients would, as would staff in modern organisations who have to meet their performance targets, be obliged to conform, albeit reluctantly, to expected standards of behaviour.

Activity 7.3   Performance measurements and targets as a panopticon

1. Discuss whether the following statement is true of the organisation you work in: 'The purpose of target-setting is to make employees visible to the controlling (panoptic) gaze of management.'
2. If it is true, do you think this is good, bad or both?
3. Is it appropriate to use performance management as a panopticon in a low commitment strategy context?

Control by targets can be the subject of disputes between management and professional staff. In a solicitors' practice, in which one of the authors with others acted as a consultant, there was a partner who had used his professional autonomy to develop a specialism in Spanish conveyancing law. This subject was of great interest to the partner but it detracted from his ability to meet the billing targets that were imposed on him by the performance management system we installed. Targets were the mechanism used to distract him from his professional interests towards the interests of the management of the partnership (of which he of course was a part). If he had given priority to his professional interest, his status in the firm, as well as his personal share of the partnership's profits, would have diminished. As Townley argues, performance management systems allow management to 'measure in quantitative terms and to hierarchise in terms of values the abilities, level and the nature of individuals' (Townley, 1993: 533–4).

The visibility of individuals that comes from performance management is not always contrary to the perceived self-interest of staff. An insurance broking firm, for which we devised an appraisal scheme, differentiated between 'inside staff' who did all the backroom work and 'outside staff' who did the selling and had the contacts with clients. In response to feedback an appraisal scheme was designed which focused on development for the inside staff but which also incorporated target-setting and monitoring for outside staff. However, there was a provision that any inside staff who wished to agree targets for themselves could do so. A few took the opportunity because they were ambitious for promotion and valued the increased visibility that came from target-setting. They thought it improved their promotion prospects. In organisations where managers seek a high commitment approach to strategy, targets can be seen to be mutually beneficial to management and employees. Targets sensibly negotiated and monitored can be an aid to developing shared values between employees and their organisations.

Competency frameworks

Performance management systems are not necessarily restricted to concern with outcomes and targets. They may also, reflecting the theme of strategic competence mentioned in Chapter 1, p. 10), be concerned with developing staff. Competency frameworks have been developed to assist this process by providing a 'map' or inventory of the competences (including knowledge, skills and behaviours) that are needed in a job role. Once this map has been identified employees can be assessed against it to decide what further training or development they may need.

Two broad research techniques have been developed for identifying competences; one is known as functional analysis and the other as the critical incident or event technique. Each produces a different kind of competency map and the suitability of each may be contingent on whether managers in organisations think they are following a high or a low commitment strategy.

Functional analysis is the form of job analysis that was used to develop the occupational standards which are the basis of the system of National Vocational Qualifications (NVQ) in the UK. A functional analysis has to be done for every job role. It begins with a statement of the functions of the job, which are the outcomes that are anticipated if the job is done properly. The analysis is then taken to the level of the tasks that have to be done to achieve this standard by defining units and elements of competence. The system produces very detailed accounts of how a job should be done. For example, there are occupational standards for custodial healthcare, which deal with nursing roles in prisons and immigration detention centres and other similar institutions. There are 17 units of competence within this role, one of which requires the employee to 'contribute to the protection of individuals from abuse'. The elements of competence go on to explain what staff have to do to fulfil this element (Custodial Care Training Organisation, n.d.). In addition, the occupational standards define the performance criteria that will be used to judge competence as well as the knowledge requirements and the various contexts in which the competences should be exercised.

Functional analysis produces detailed and job-specific accounts of competences. They are often available as software-based checklists that employees can use for self-assessment, or their managers can use to appraise employees' competence levels and development needs. It may be that in organisations where it is thought that only a low commitment approach is necessary, any investment on competences would be thought wasteful. But if a competency framework were to be regarded as a good idea (and it could be helpful where an organisation has a high staff turnover and needs to assess and train many new recruits) then a functional competency approach would be the best option. It is specific to the job and can be bought in from the stock of national occupational standards and would not have to be expensively produced to suit the particular conditions of the organisation.

The other research method for identifying competences, critical event interviewing, is associated with the work of Boyatzis (1982). He was interested in establishing the competences of effective managers and (this is rather a simplification) he interviewed managers and asked for examples of when they had dealt well with issues at work and when not so well. From this he was able to identify a series of generic competences that he defined as 'an underlying characteristic of a person which results in effective and or superior performance in a job' (Boyatzis, 1982: 21). Competences derived by this method tend to be behavioural and cover such areas as leadership, customer focus, results orientation, problem-solving, communication skills and teamworking (Abraham *et al.*, 2001: 850). They are more likely to be favoured by organisations seeking to adopt a high commitment strategy because they can be employed in a range of situations and do not constrain people within a tight job specification. Many organisations use both kinds of competence (usually distinguished as core/behavioural and technical/functional competences) for addressing training needs, performance management and career development. In one survey, all the companies questioned used behavioural-type competences for some if not all categories of staff, and a quarter used technical competences drawn from the NVQ system. The survey reported a move away from occupational standards in the 1990s (CIPD, 2001; IDS, 2001). Abraham *et al.* (2001: 848) also noted that although many (American) companies developed competency frameworks for managers, many did not use them for appraisal purposes.

360° appraisal

Interest in and application of 360° appraisal as a performance management practice continues to grow. The CIPD's 2005 survey reports that it is used by 14 per cent of employers, whilst Silverman *et al.* (2005) suggest that the figure could be much higher with up to 50 per cent of medium-sized to large UK organisations employing this practice. It is sometimes called multi-rater assessment and that perhaps is a more accurate name for the activity. The term appraisal evokes the image of an interview between appraisee and appraiser. However, face-to-face contact is a rarity in 360° appraisal, which is mostly conducted through the use of questionnaires (Ward, 1995). The questionnaires are normally designed around a competency framework or a psychological instrument (such as Leadership Impact [Human Synergistics, n.d.]). A range of people are asked to assess an individual against the competency framework. The feedback can be from the subject's bosses (90° appraisal), from their staff (180° appraisal) and from colleagues and clients or customers (the full 360° appraisal).

If you were to design a 360° appraisal scheme you would construct a questionnaire that asked people to rate the subject of the appraisal on certain dimensions or competences that were essential to the subject's job. The questions might ask the respondent to judge the subject's effectiveness on these dimensions. The questionnaires would be gathered together and the replies abstracted and formed into a report to the subject that would say such things as (and here we caricature such feedback) 'your staff believe you are a competent team worker but your peers believe you to be incompetent'. There may well be an interview in which a member of personnel or HRM explains the results of the opinion poll (which is what 360° appraisal essentially is) to the subject and helps them develop an action plan in response to the 360° feedback.

There are several difficulties in the implementation of 360° schemes. The questionnaires can be large and cumbersome because their designers are too anxious to obtain feedback on every aspect of managerial performance. In an extreme, and out of date, example a scheme in a factory in Soviet Leningrad asked a great many questions, mostly about the political consciousness of the subjects (Redman and Snape, 1992: 39). Some organisations have chosen not to use questionnaires as the basis of their 360° scheme. Instead they use an ongoing narrative system. Typically these systems use an organisational intranet and appraisal scheme. For each appraisee a number of different appraisers are identified. During the year these appraisers can go online and make a report about the appraisee's work behaviour. If the appraisee, for example, has shown a great deal of effective skill in running a difficult team meeting then a member of his or her team might go online and report the fact. The appraisee's boss can access these reports at any time but at regular intervals will review all the postings and use this information to draft an appraisal report that is then discussed with the appraisee. This system has the advantage that information on the appraisee's work behaviour is reported while it is still fresh in appraisers' memories and it gives the boss much richer information than can be provided by tick box questionnaires on which to base an appraisal judgement. One disadvantage identified by Kutzberg *et al.* (2005) might be that people are more prone to make negative judgements of people when using electronic means of communication (in the case of this research e-mail) than when communicating using paper and pencil.

Managers are often only willing to accept multi-rater appraisal within certain constraints (Redman and Snape, 1992: 40–1; Silverman *et al.*, 2005: xi). They accept its use for development purposes but are less willing to see it used as a basis for judgements concerning pay, performance or promotion. This may be the basis for different attitudes towards multi-rater feedback in organisations pursuing high and low commitment strategies. In the former it would be used for developmental purposes alone; in the latter, if it were used at all, it would be the basis for hard-nosed judgements on reward, promotion and permanence.

Managers are often wary of the feedback from their staff. They question whether the staff are in a position to judge their competency in parts of their job that the staff do not witness. Conversely, staff may be chary of giving honest feedback on their managers if they think their anonymity might be insecure. For this reason some schemes only operate when a manager has, in different cases, at least four, five or eight people reporting to them. With small numbers it may be difficult to maintain the raters' anonymity and their judgements may be sweetened to avoid any danger of reprisals. In a full 360° system there is also a problem of the weighting to be given to the various perspectives; should the views of subordinates have the same value as those of senior colleagues and how seriously should the assessments of customers or clients be taken?

It can be argued that upward, 180°, appraisal (if not the full 360°) is an appropriate balancing of the power relations between appraisers and appraisees. Appraisees may see their appraisal as an occasion when they have to accept whatever their appraiser says, and it can take them a long time to get over the experience (Kay *et al.*, 1965). Upward appraisal can be an attempt to empower appraisees to reciprocate by judging their appraisers. It can certainly be a painful experience for the subjects. Edwards (1995) mentions the case of a (apocryphal?) senior manager who unwittingly upset people by standing too close to them and by spraying them when speaking words containing sibilants. Upward appraisal, together with a backward step and a visit to the dentist, made him a more effective manager. Another manager was observed coming out of his office, having received his appraisal feedback, and loudly proclaiming 'I'm a bastard. I know I'm a bastard. You know I'm a bastard. So why should I change!' (Brewerton, 1997).

The intention of 360° appraisal is to give a broader and more objective assessment of people's competence, although, from another angle, it must multiply the biases and distortions of judgement to which all appraisal is prone. As Stewart (1998) points out, much assessment procedure in organisations accepts a logical fallacy, that the sum of many subjective judgements is an objective one.

Personal development planning

The personal development plan (PDP) is a document and a process that encourages employees to:

- undertake a systematic diagnosis of their development needs;
- present their development plans in a form that will encourage line managers and training specialists to provide the resources and support needed to achieve them;
- keep a record of their learning achievements against their learning targets;
- provide others with a systematic profile of their competences and achievements.

One would normally only expect to see PDPs adopted in organisations with high commitment HR practices. Even in these cases PDPs are often introduced as a discretionary task. Staff are encouraged to write them but it is not insisted on. However, in many professions, such as nursing, PDPs have become obligatory as part of the process of continuous professional development, which practitioners have to undertake in order to maintain their professional registration (UKCC, 1996; Jones and Fear, 1994). In their study of performance management in five companies, Data Services (IDS, 2003) found that PDPs were becoming central elements of the systems for both high-potential staff and for poor performers.

The impact of both 360° appraisal and personal development plans is to individualise the employment relationship. They focus responsibility for personal development on the employee and remove responsibility from the organisation. In one banking company, the PDP was presented to staff as their personal business plans that would make them more employable in the labour market.

> As with any product, if they [the staff] became out of date, no longer met their customers' requirements or ceased to offer a competitive product they would lose their share of the market and their ability to attract customer interest. Learning logs were also encouraged in this way – 'Who would buy a second-hand car without the service history and the logbook?'
>
> (Floodgate and Nixon, 1994)

This quotation recognises that although PDPs are individually driven they are often positioned within organisational processes of performance management. A dialectical tension can emerge. Multi-rater appraisal and PDPs make an individual confront, and take responsibility for, their own limitations but the limitations are defined by comparison with a competency framework designed to express the needs of the organisation. In developing themselves to conform to this framework the individual might be distorting or denying their own ethical values and positions. The formal benefits of appraisal and PDPs – the right to personal growth and development – can be contradicted by the manifold and contingent organisational demands placed on the competency frameworks by their corporate designers. In the policy document of one organisation, staff were given a 'right' to receive feedback on their work performance; but if they chose not to exercise this right then they would be subject to disciplinary proceedings. In a similar vein the ubiquity, and relentless nature, of the action plan and the development portfolio can convert them from personally significant learning activities to bureaucratic hoops to be leapt through.

Case Study 7.2

Developing a new performance management approach for Greenfields Pharmaceuticals

Greenfields Pharmaceuticals (GP) is a medium-sized pharmaceuticals company based in the south-east of England. It is one of only a handful of businesses operating in a niche market developing and manufacturing novel drug delivery systems, for example inhalers and injection kits and various dosage units. The company was established as a management buy-out in the 1990s, part financed by venture capital.

Greenfield's customers are major pharmaceuticals companies based principally in the UK, Europe and the US. There are three strands of business; the first is the design and development of bespoke drug delivery systems, known as 'Response'; the second is the manufacture and testing of a customer's own system and the third is highly speculative designs for which customers have to be sought. This latter strand of business is high-risk but has huge potential returns as the designs are patentable; it is known in GP as 'Innovation'.

Overall GP employs just over 300 people with 250 of these in manufacturing and testing being under the responsibility of the operations director. He also has responsibility for the packing team of 25 whose services are sub-contracted from a specialist packer. There is a 15-strong sales and marketing group all of whom are experienced in the pharmaceuticals industry; 10 cover Europe from the UK HQ and 5 are based in the US (the US team is retained on a self-employed basis). In R&D there are 30 employees – 20 working in Response and 10 in Innovation. These individuals are very specialised scientists with scarce skills in the labour market. Finance and Admin employs 3 people. The Finance Director has responsibility for HR and has recently appointed you as the HR manager.

GP has a performance appraisal scheme and all employees, except the manufacturing operatives, are supposed to have an annual appraisal. You are aware that this does not happen consistently, except within R&D,

and you have heard grumbling among all groups that some appraising managers are more lenient than others. You have also discovered that when the company was established the MD of the venture capital company had just attended a seminar on the balanced scorecard and insisted that this was implemented to guide strategic development of Greenfields. Performance indicators were developed for the financial perspective of the balanced scorecard but no further action was taken.

The manufacturing process is necessarily high-precision and the manufacturing and testing operatives are highly skilled individuals; their specialist skills are in great demand in the south-east. Manufacturing and testing was recently re-organised into self-managed teams. Since this time production quality has improved and the reject rate across manufacturing as a whole is now less than 2 per cent. Amongst the manufacture/testing groups there is dissatisfaction that no mechanisms exist to recognise excellent performance or to provide development opportunities. Turnover amongst this group has begun to increase.

The sales and marketing team are paid a basic rate and are bonused on a complex range of sales metrics which include calls made, calls to conversion ratio, value of sales, and new or repeat business. On target earnings can be 30 per cent of the base rate. The US team are paid a per diem rate with equivalent bonuses. Whilst the sales and marketing people seem to earn bonuses each month, sales growth has slowed down in the past nine months.

Research and development, whether Response or Innovation, requires the scientists to work in teams and to share information amongst themselves. The scientists are paid well according to market rates and there is an individual PRP scheme which is based on the outcome of the annual performance appraisal. Five years ago the MD, under pressure from the venture capital company introduced targets for individual scientists within Innovation to each produce a certain number of patentable products every two years. This caused outrage amongst the scientists concerned who objected to targets being set for a research process in which, they said, serendipity played a large part. These targets have generated additional work for the patent lawyer but have not resulted in an increase in successful patent applications. The director of R&D has recognised that the current arrangements are detrimental to team-working and morale and he wants to make changes.

| Activity 7.4 | Analysing performance management in Greenfields Pharmaceuticals |

You will be meeting with the finance director in the next day or so and she would like you to discuss with her:

1. Your perception of the key performance issues affecting Greenfields Pharmaceuticals.

2. The features of a performance management system that you would recommend that would meet employee and organisational requirements.

What will you suggest?

Dealing with poor performance

Managers may consider that some of their staff are 'problems' and others may feel that some of their staff present problem behaviours. Whilst such labelling may in itself be problematic, poor performance is an organisational reality and, if not recognised and dealt with promptly, may translate into poorer organisational performance. Strebler (2004) notes that although dealing with poor performance is low on the agenda of many organisations, the failure to do so has a negative impact on the motivation of other staff and may contribute to higher labour turnover.

Management 'how to do it' books and seminars try to give puzzled managers bullet-pointed techniques. Very often these devices draw their inspiration from the clinical psychology technique of behaviour modification (Honey, 1980; Miller, 1989) or counselling. Many training videos (Gower, n.d.) on appraisal skills tell appraisers to use a counselling approach, not to jump in with solutions to the problems presented by the appraisees, but to encourage the appraisees to recognise and articulate their own problems and to identify their own solutions. The two sources of technique carry very different implications for the relationship between superior and subordinate. Behaviour modification places the responsibility for change on the appraiser whereas a counselling approach places it on the appraisee. Only, it is suggested, if these techniques bear no fruit should recourse be made to the disciplinary procedure.

Neither technique, however, considers the factors that may contribute to poor performance; whether it is the capability of the individual concerned, the personal or organisational circumstances in which they find themselves, their attitude to work or whether the poor performance is a consequence of misconduct. It seems entirely unreasonable to expect an employee, themselves, to find a solution to infra-structure problems that are causing their poor performance and, in organisations adopting a high-commitment approach, performance problems might trigger a review of processes or systems. However, in organisations that do not require high commitment from their staff, and do not expect to give much commitment to them, the disciplinary process may be more readily used to solve people problems.

A final point to consider in relation to poor performance is the issue of how it is defined and how judgements are made about individuals in relation to the definition.

Staff appraisal

The appraisal interview is the occasion when many of the practices already discussed are acted out. Judgement of an employee's abilities and contribution, as assessed through performance measures and personal development plans or whatever, is the central act of appraisal. But judgement is suspect. As well as the possibility of an appraiser responding to malice or prejudice when they make an assessment, there is the possibility of more insidious distortions of judgement. An

Table 7.3 **The purposes of staff appraisal**

	Accountability	Development
Peer	Peer accountability	Peer review and development
Hierarchy	Performance target-setting and review	Competence assessment and development

Source: Fisher (1995)

assessor may, for example, give more credence to a recent failure than to a whole string of successes in the more distant past. The halo and horns effect may still cause someone to be given a better or worse assessment than their performance might justify. (The halo and horns effect is when one feature of a person, whether they have a moustache or not for example, is focused on and the judgement made of the individual as a whole is just a projection of the appraiser's like or dislike of moustaches.) How to minimise the consequence of inaccurate or biased judgements is central to the task of designing appraisal systems.

Designers of appraisal schemes have many options to choose from and their task should be seen as one of strategic choice (Chapter 1, p. 28) in which the contingencies they see around them are enacted. The first choice facing designers concerns the purposes of appraisal, the varieties of which are shown in Table 7.3. The first of the two dimensions shown in Table 7.3 concerns whether the intention of appraisal is accountability or development. The former is concerned with results achieved and resources expended whereas the latter focuses on behaviour, competence and knowledge. The second dimension concerns the person who conducts the appraisal and whether they are the appraisee's line manager or a peer. The two dimensions lead to the identification of four purposes of appraisal.

1. The purpose of the first type of appraisal, *peer review and development*, is to give supportive feedback to the appraisee and help them plan their self development. It focuses on helping a person make sense of their work experience and it does not give any priority to the needs of the organisation. As a commentator on one such scheme reported, 'It [the interview] was not seen as a management exercise but as a personal opportunity to reflect and plan' (Oxford Polytechnic Educational Methods Unit, n.d.)

2. *Competence assessment and development* appraisals are also focused on development but they are designed to integrate the individual's development with the competency requirements of the organisation. It follows, therefore, that the organisation requires appraisers to make ratings of the appraisee's knowledge, competency and qualities against an organisational framework. The framework may be purpose designed for the organisation (Glaze, 1989) or use generic standards such as lead body occupational standards. The assessments are entered into an organisational database to give management an inventory of the skills available to them.

3. The next form of appraisal is *peer accountability* and it is often found in professional contexts. Medical audit of clinically significant events (Marinker, 1990: 120), in which clinicians conduct 'a systematic, critical analysis of the quality

of medical care', is a good example of the genre. Such appraisals take place in the context of external professional standards rather than the imperatives of the organisation. In some cases, such as the hospital consultants' merit scheme, peer review was the mechanism used to allocate financial awards (Department of Health, 1989). This scheme has since been reviewed and changed.

4. The final type of appraisal is concerned with *setting and monitoring targets*. In this approach appraisal becomes a cascade process in which targets are set for the whole organisation and are then disaggregated and allocated to people throughout the organisation.

The designers of appraisal schemes also have a range of design features that they can choose to include in their schemes. The main choices are shown in Figure 7.2. They are not disconnected. A choice of one option may affect or limit the designers'

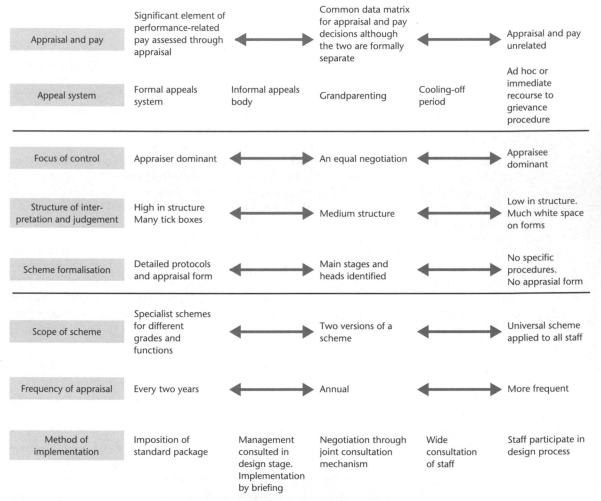

Figure 7.2 Design options for designers of appraisal schemes

Source: The differences between appraisal schemes: rhetoric and the design of schemes, *Personnel Review*, 24(1), pp. 51–66 (Fisher, C.M. 1995) Copyright 1995 by Emerald Group Publishing Ltd. Reproduced with permission of Emerald Group Publishing Ltd in the format Textbook via Copyright Clearance Center

choices in other areas, but it will be helpful to describe the options separately. The first issue is whether appraisal should be linked with performance-related pay. This subject is discussed in more detail in Chapter 8. The next choice is whether the scheme should include arrangements for dealing with appeals against the ratings or decisions made during appraisal and the degree to which legal or formal process should be used in any appeal mechanism.

The next three areas of choice all concern the degree of formalisation of a scheme. The most important issue here concerns appraisal documentation. One option is to have no pro-formas and to let the participants write reports of appraisal interviews in any way that seems suitable to them. Another possibility is to have an appraisal form which had a few headline questions to guide discussion but which gave much white space to allow the form to be completed in a variety of ways.

The most formal possibility is to have an appraisal form entirely composed of rating scales and tick boxes. Rating scales have sometimes been seen, mistakenly, as the whole of performance management. Many people have struggled to produce objective and accurate rating scales using such techniques as the following:

- Forced comparison – where appraisers' ratings of their staff have to fit a defined distribution so that, for example, no more than 15 per cent of the staff can receive the top rating.

- Distributional appraisal – in a traditional rating scheme a Likert scale might be used by an appraiser to show whether he or she strongly agrees, agrees, is uncertain, disagrees or strongly disagrees that the appraisee exhibits a particular competence or feature. In distributional appraisal the appraiser records the percentage of occasions on which he or she thinks the appraisee shows a particular competence. It may be, for instance, that on 60 per cent of occasions the appraiser strongly agree that the appraisee is displaying a particular competence but on 5 per cent of occasions he or she strongly disagrees and thinks the appraisee is not exihibiting that feature (Kane, 2000; Fox *et al.*, 2005).

- Paired comparison – where each appraisee is compared to every other appraisee (e.g. Darren is better than Zoe on interpersonal skills) and each is ranked according to the number of times they are judged better than their peers.

- Behaviourally-anchored rating scales – see Exhibit 7.3 for an example.

Critics have continued to point out that the political and contextual factors that surround the rating process probably account for the failure to design valid rating scales (Fletcher, 2001: 474). There appears to be increasing objection to rating, especially among staff in organisations that aspire to a high commitment approach to performance management (IDS, 2003).

There are also different degrees of formality and standardisation that can be applied to the procedure for conducting appraisals. In some organisations, for example, the procedure might specify the time of year when the appraisal has to take place; in others this is left to local discretion. The formality of an appraisal scheme can mostly be judged by the thickness of the appraisal procedure manual and its associated paperwork. The thicker it is, the more formal the scheme.

Exhibit 7.3

Behaviourally-anchored rating scale

There are six stages in developing a behaviourally-anchored rating scale.

1. Identify examples of effective and ineffective job behaviour. This is often done by using the critical incident technique.

2. Use a group of people experienced in the job to sort the collected behaviours into clusters. These will be the dimensions that people will be rated against, *e.g. team working skill*.

3. Develop brief behavioural statements (descriptors) from the critical incidents, *e.g. 'Is aggressive and defensive when working in a team'*.

4. Ask experts to allocate the descriptors to the dimensions. If people do not agree on which dimension a descriptor belongs to, it should be taken out of the analysis.

5. Scale the remaining descriptors by asking the panel of experts to rate each descriptor on a scale of effective to not-effective behaviour using a convenient numerical scale. For example, 5 might equal highly effective and 1 represent highly ineffective. Average the scores from each expert to find the descriptor's position on the scale, *e.g. the experts give the following statement, 'Is aggressive and defensive when working in a team' a mean rating of 1.5 with a standard deviation of 0.2.* Reject any descriptor that the experts rate too variously and that consequently has too large a standard deviation.

6. Use six or seven descriptors to create the scale for each of the dimensions.

The last three areas of choice listed in Figure 7.2 concern:

- The frequency of appraisal (some people argue that preparing for an appraisal is such a major task that once every two years is more than sufficient, whereas others argue that appraisals should be six-monthly or even quarterly).

- Whether one scheme should suit all or whether there should be different schemes for different categories of staff.

- The method of design and implementation. This concerns the degree to which staff should be involved in the design of the scheme. In some cases the scheme may be imposed by management, in others the employees may be consulted and sometimes the employees may be directly involved in designing the scheme.

The success of an appraisal scheme will, in part, reflect the contingent fit (as negotiated by managers and staff) between, to use Mohrman *et al.*'s (1989) terms, appraisal schemes and organisational realities. The notion of fit in this context refers, not to some technically correct, or necessary, solution to the design problem, but to the degree of acceptability that a scheme has among all the parties with an interest in it (Fisher, 1995). As in our discussions of other aspects of performance management practice, the options available can be seen in terms of their 'fit' with high and low commitment strategies and a possible analysis is shown in Table 7.4. Bear in mind that this table is not intended to be definitive. It is simply one way in which scheme designers might interpret the contingencies.

Table 7.4 Designing an appraisal scheme: possible design preferences for managers seeking to follow high and low commitment strategies

Low commitment	High commitment
Focus on job-specific competences	Concern with long-term employee development and with generic competences
Targets and performance indicators used as a means of control; less likely to use elements of peer review or 360° appraisal	Targets and performance indicators used as a means of development; more likely to use elements of peer review or 360° appraisal
High element of individual commission or piecework pay	Performance-related pay based on merit assessment or on team or organisational performance
Formal appeals system	Grandparenting; The appraisee's boss resolves any conflict between appraisee and appraiser
Appraisal interviews high in structure with the appraiser being dominant; heavy use of tick boxes and rating scales	Appraisal interviews low in structure with the appraisee being dominant; either no appraisal forms to fill in or the forms ask mainly open questions and leave lots of white space
Highly formalised appraisal scheme; lots of rules and procedures determine how the system should be implemented	The appraisal scheme will be of medium or low formalisation; the procedures are brief and allow much discretion to appraisers and appraisees
Appraisals more frequent	Appraisals less frequent
Appraisal scheme bought in off-the-shelf from consultants	Appraisal scheme developed locally with the involvement of staff

The suggestions in Table 7.4 might be helpful when tackling Case Study 7.3.

Case Study 7.3

Designing an appraisal scheme for a university

Skegmouth University introduced its appraisal policy in 1993. It began by declaiming:

> Appraisal is the process by which as accurate a picture as possible of staff performance and staff professional needs is obtained. It is concerned, therefore, with developing the abilities, strengths and aspirations of all staff and working positively with them to fulfil their needs. Skegmouth University appraisal scheme is focused on staff development. The whole emphasis of the scheme will be to offer positive opportunities to staff.

The university has performance-related pay for managerial staff but the operation of this scheme is formally separate from the appraisal scheme that applies to management grades, the 800 academic staff and the 1,600 support staff.

Appraisal, according to the policy document, has three features: firstly the analysis and determination of objectives, secondly the measurement or judgement of the quality and quantity of work and thirdly the operation of effective staff development. Appraisals should be carried out by heads of departments (HoD) or by colleagues nominated by heads. Staff can express a preference or a concern about who may appraise them. It is up to heads to decide when appraisals shall take place but everyone must have an interview at least once a year. The appraisal interview 'shall be a two-way process' and include a review of the past year and the setting of targets and objectives for the forthcoming year. There is no pro-forma on which to record the results of the appraisal. The appraiser must write a draft summary after the interview on which the appraisee can comment. Heads must prepare an annual staff development plan based on the summaries of the appraisals and the plan must be sent to the personnel office.

Staff were wary of the scheme. Many of the manual, clerical and administrative staff found the scheme's obsession with setting targets irritatingly irrelevant to their jobs. They pointed out that, when they had achieved competence in their jobs, it was only required of them that they maintain the standard. The setting of annual targets, such as 'to maintain last year's error rate at 0.25 per cent' would become monotonous. The scheme also implied a fixation on personal growth that seemed almost insulting given the narrowness of their job roles.

Academic staff tended to harbour suspicions about the real purpose of the scheme. Academics value their professional autonomy (although as Skegmouth is a new university the idea of academic tenure has no contractual validity) and they saw the appraisal scheme as an attempt by management to replace collegial relations between staff with a hierarchical and managerial line relationship. The chain of argument leading to this conclusion was complex. Until the introduction of appraisal it was assumed that all academic staff reported directly to their HoD. Such a large span of control gave lecturers a deal of freedom from managerial interference. It was also practically difficult for HoDs to interview all their staff and many appraisals were conducted by principal lecturers (PLs), a post which in the past had not been seen as a line managerial post. In some departments an appraisal conducted by a PL was seen as a peer appraisal. But a difficulty could arise. Appraisals, under this scheme, involved setting targets and agreeing expenditure on staff development. As these could be seen as managerial functions, the fact that they were being carried out by PLs could be seen as, *de facto*, converting the PL post into a line management, or team leader, post. The argument could then be developed that appraisal was a device for undermining professional autonomy and replacing it with a centralised and hierarchical chain of command in which PLs ceased to be the academic colleagues of the other lecturers and became their managers. Indeed some academics, from other institutions, had written academic papers on the role of appraisal in the proletarianisation of the academic labour force (e.g. Wilson, 1991; Townley, 1991).

If PLs were not seen as line managers then they had the problem, when conducting appraisals, of not having any managerial discretion with which to agree or pay for staff development activities.

Other issues were raised. A substantial lobby argued that the lack of formality in the appraisal reports and procedures meant that the scheme could easily allow discrimination and prejudice to seep into the system. There is much opportunity for people to be treated unequally and there was certainly no standardised documentation that could be used to prove otherwise. Many staff were afraid of biased or incompetent appraisers, and the trainers who carried out the appraisal training were surprised at how many of the latter there were. A further problem emerged when the university failed in its first attempt to become accredited as an *Investor in People*. The reason given by the assessors was that there were parts of the organisation where appraisals were not being carried out. There were two factors that made the implementation of the appraisal policy difficult, according to the personnel manager. He thought that getting academics to accept university policies was like 'herding cats'. There were also many detached parts of the university, science parks, research centres and so on that were largely self-contained and were separate from the mainstream activities of the university. University policies on such things as appraisal tended to pass them by.

The Appraisal Steering Group is charged with monitoring the workings of the appraisal scheme and they are meeting to consider changes to the scheme.

Activity 7.5   The university appraisal scheme

1. What are the expectations and anxieties of staff and management concerning the existing appraisal scheme and about any changes that might be made?

2. Would your assessment of the contingencies of this organisation lead you to think it was an organisation in which human resources tend to create high or low levels of uncertainty for managers?

3. Which of the two basic approaches, high commitment or low commitment strategies, would you adopt?

4. What changes to the appraisal scheme would you recommend and why?

Conclusion – does performance management work?

We have now reviewed the elements most commonly found in performance management systems. In conclusion we shall consider their value. The first issue to consider, which picks up on the issue of horizontal integration mentioned in Chapter 1, is whether all the components in a particular organisation sit easily together or contradict each other. In practice many performance management schemes are developed piecemeal and so there is a high probability that they are not internally consistent. In one company observed by one of the authors, the staff were paid a commission if they met their sales targets and a bonus if they met their objectives (which were different and negotiated separately). They were subject to an onerous performance measurement regime and received weekly reports on up to 20 performance indicators. This left them little time to develop the creativity and the 'out-of-the-box' thinking that the generic competency framework their company had adopted insisted they should do. They had all been provided with portfolios in which to maintain their PDPs but few found the time to keep them up to date. They tended to be soft in their judgements of their colleagues when they did their peer review as part of a 360° scheme that the organisation had recently commenced. In this organisation the various components of the performance management scheme, which had all been introduced at different times, contradicted each other. Sensible performance management activities can become silly when combined thoughtlessly. If in Activity 7.5 you used the high and low commitment model to help you arrive at your conclusions you should be assured that the various component parts of your appraisal scheme fit with the external circumstances as well as being internally coherent.

We will now return to the broader question of whether performance management works. If performance management is seen as a body of lore then the task of deciding whether it works is a difficult one. The answer would depend on what function the lore fulfils. The Saville and Holdsworth (1997) report argued that the problem with performance appraisal is that there are too many stakeholders who want it to do contradictory things. Most schemes therefore fall between several stools. Some might see performance management as a way of creating a false consciousness among staff, which blinds employees to the ways in which they are being manipulated and exploited (Buglear, 1986). Bowles and Coates (1993: 15) argued that, as organisations experience difficulties with their performance management schemes, they try to create good impressions of them: '. . . those actions they take [in relation to the schemes] appear to be aimed at maintaining an idealised view of PA [performance appraisal] in their organisation, and not at the actual realities of the problems involved'. The implication is that management is in danger of believing its own propaganda. But staff are not necessarily convinced by impression management and can knowingly use schemes to manipulate their bosses into having a good impression of them as employees (Wayne and Ferris, 1990).

Some people would argue that the value of the lore of performance management lies in its effectiveness in helping organisations achieve their goals. This conclusion is not entirely supported by research evidence. The IPM (1992) surveyed 500 high-performing private companies (with a consistent profits performance over five years), 750 private companies selected at random and 538 public sector organisations. They reported:

> The most important conclusion is that organisational performance is not associated with the pursuit of formal performance management programmes. Such programmes are as likely to be introduced by poor performers (in relative terms) as high performers and even more likely to be adopted if the organisation is in the public sector (where performance measures are difficult to compare).
>
> (IPM, 1992: 17)

In a subsequent, interview-based, survey of a smaller sample of organisations only two respondents claimed, without any evidence, that performance management had improved their companies' overall performance. But many managers in the sample did claim that it had made a difference at individual and team level. In particular, respondents in public sector organisations claimed that it had made staff 'output conscious' (IPM, 1992: 98).

It can, finally, be argued that the function of performance management lore and myth is to provide people with the rhetorical raw material from which they can craft personally relevant interpretations of their organisational and personal roles. There is much evidence that, even when people are critical of aspects of their organisation's schemes, they can still find value in them. In one confidential survey of a performance management scheme in a county council, 67 per cent of the respondents agreed (strongly or slightly) that the process of reviewing their accountabilities and assessing their performance helped to clarify their sense of purpose and the direction of their job, even though they had many detailed criticisms of the scheme. It is as if staff want performance appraisal to work even when they are worried about the fairness of the assessments made and about the amount, and usefulness, of the training and development that will emerge from the process. Performance management in this regard will generate myths and stories that can be used to help people to come to terms with the ambiguities and dilemmas of their roles, which is the traditional function of myths (Kirk, 1976: 82). The corpus of performance management includes both contradictory views of performance management and the stories and myths that palliate them.

Summary

In this chapter the following key points have been made:

- Performance management can be seen as a body of lore and recipes, some based on good research and theory, some based on symbolic resonance and workplace myths.

- The main elements in the corpus are programme structures, performance measurement, target-setting, competency frameworks, 360° appraisal, personal development plans, performance-related pay and techniques for dealing with 'problem' staff. These activities wax and wane in popularity.

- The key issue concerning programme structures is the maintenance of their currency and accessibility.

- The main managerial concern in performance measurement is designing schemes that do not lead to organisational sub-optimisation.

- The problem of pitching targets at an appropriate level is the main area of difficulty in target-setting.

- Competency frameworks can be developed in two different ways with each having different implications for the functioning of performance management schemes.

- The problem of the sensitivity of managers' egos, especially in relation to evaluative, as opposed to developmental, multi-rater feedback (McEvoy, 1990), and the difficulty of weighting the feedback from different groups are critical issues in designing 360° appraisal schemes.

- Personal development plans can be a powerful tool for individual learning but they can degenerate into bureaucratic chores.

- Appraisal schemes need to be carefully designed to be broadly acceptable to appraisees and appraisers, which is to say performance management schemes should be designed to enact people's understanding of the organisation's strategic circumstances.

- There is no objective evidence that performance management improves an organisation's performance but there is evidence that people can find it helpful in interpreting and evaluating their organisational roles.

Discussion questions

1. In what ways do people in your organisation attempt to manipulate, sabotage or avoid performance measures and indicators? How might this situation be changed?
2. Should performance management focus primarily on the organisation/department, the team or the individual?
3. Compare the advantages and disadvantages of peer and hierarchical staff appraisal.
4. How useful is staff appraisal when dealing with 'problem' staff?
5. Is 360° appraisal a necessary counterweight to staff appraisal?

Further reading

The main book on the subject of performance management is still Armstrong and Baron (2005). Boxall and Purcell (2008) is also a useful adjunct. Chapter 7 considers managing individuals' performances and Chapter 8 looks more broadly at the links between HR systems and organisational performance.

8

Reward strategies and paying for contribution

Lynette Harris

Learning outcomes

Having read this chapter and completed its associated activities, readers should be able to:

- Recognise the importance of context in organisational approaches to rewarding contribution
- Understand the impact that paying for contribution can have on individual performance and performance management processes
- Analyse the extent of linkages between pay, employee performance and organisational performance in different situations
- See why issues, tensions and contradictions can arise in the application of performance-related pay
- Identify the respective responsibilities of the line manager and the HR specialist in balancing the relationship between pay, the job role, performance and the individual
- Appreciate that both financial and non-financial incentives form part of a total reward strategy

Introduction

This chapter is primarily concerned with how employee contribution is recognised through monetary rewards, with an emphasis on the use of pay as a strategic means of aligning individual efforts to organisational priorities. Performance related pay (also described as variable or incentive pay schemes) as an addition to basic salary has been the most significant of the systems developed to measure and reward performance since the 1980s. It has been the defining characteristic of the externally focused 'New Pay Agenda' which is based on a logic of pay being explicitly linked to business performance (White and Drucker, 2000). Here pay is used as the means of forging a partnership between the organisation and its employees on the premise that they have a shared interest in achieving high organisational performance (Zingheim and Schuster, 2000). Although, as Reilly (2003) points out, this can no longer be regarded as a new agenda, financial incentives linked to business and/or individual performance continue to capture the attention of both practitioner and academic commentators. Kessler (2007:

325) sees this as probably attributable to textbook orthodoxy which advocates pay linked to achieving business objectives, which may be the performance of the entire company, a unit, department, team or individual, or a combination of these. But reward systems designed to offer employers flexibility and encourage individuals to maximise their contribution by 'outperforming their contracts' can give rise to tensions for both employees and their managers. The issues that can arise in implementing incentivised pay will be the subject of this chapter's activities.

A more strategic approach to paying for contribution?

A major debate in reward management is to what extent employers have, in reality, moved away from an 'essentially reactive and ad hoc approach to rewards to one that can be described as strategic in character' (Taylor, 2000: 12). One interpretation is that the growth in performance-related pay (PRP) since the 1980s constitutes evidence of a shift towards a more strategic approach to rewards (Armstrong and Murlis, 1998). Another is that there is a lack of evidence of any radical change towards reward strategies linked to organisational objectives and that contemporary incentive and bonus schemes are not really different in substance from the blue-collar incentive schemes that were the preoccupation of the 1960s and 1970s (Smith, 1993). CIPD annual rewards management surveys reveal little change in the numbers of employers reporting a rewards strategy. In its 2008 survey of 603 employers across all industrial sectors, only one third of respondents had a reward strategy and this number may have even reduced since its 2003 survey when two-thirds of employers reported having a strategic approach to reward, although this apparent decrease could have more to do with the framing of a survey question.

Fashions in pay change over time and are often easier to identify retrospectively. They reflect employers' pursuit of pay systems that address specific organisational problems, such as internal equity, recruitment and retention or economic and political pressures. To illustrate how the prevailing business context influences pay systems, Kessler (1995) points to the widespread use of piecework for production workers as a means of boosting production after the Second World War and resisting the influx of cheaper foreign goods. These payment-by-results schemes for manual workers were predominantly output driven and remained the major consideration in remuneration until the late 1970s. By then many of the wage and salary systems in Britain were observed to be in a depressingly chaotic state due to 'ad hoc adjustments to pay in response to immediate pressures' (Smith, 1983: 53).

A perceived weakness in reward systems at the time was the frequent lack of association, particularly in larger organisations, between wages and organisational performance which insulated employment from competition and external labour markets. Capelli (1995: 585) argues that this resulted in a psychological contract based on exchanging employee commitment, loyalty and adequate performance in return for job security and predictable improvements. This can partly be explained as an outcome of collective pay bargaining where the concern is internal rather than external relativities and with establishing system and order to accommodate a collective view on the allocation of rewards – an approach still in evidence in those areas of the public sector which still have incremental salary scales within grades and where an employee's position on the scale is likely to reflect length of service rather than the quality of individual contribution.

The search for more flexible reward strategies linked to business performance grew out of a rejection of the rigidities identified in such traditional approaches to pay. For employers seeking ways of responding to increasingly competitive and rapidly changing markets variable pay offers a 'practical and appealing alternative' to pay arrangements which take no account of individual contribution (IDS, 2003). Its introduction was encouraged by the market-based ideology of the 1980s, combined with economic, societal and technical changes which altered the context for organisational reward policies. In summary, its growth can be attributed to:

● the search for human resourcing strategies that link the efforts of individuals to corporate objectives;

● it is viewed as a key means of attracting, retaining and motivating key staff;

● attempts to improve a sense of company and commercial awareness particularly where there is a financial share in success;

● the political ideology of a market economy which emphasises the importance of pay systems that are sufficiently flexible to take account of market forces and promote the philosophy of an enterprise culture;

● a belief that linking rewards more closely to individual performance is more motivating and equitable than providing identical rewards for dissimilar levels of contribution and standards of performance;

● the devolution of HR responsibilities to line managers who are required to discriminate in the allocation of rewards between different levels of employee performance;

● the move away from collective, trade-union-dominated pay bargaining;

● a belief that rewarding the 'right' behaviours assists cultural change and reinforces the desired organisational values by providing a visible means of recognising achievements and behaviours that support organisational goals.

As the degree of integration between human resourcing strategies and business strategy is increasingly identified as a vital ingredient in organisational success (Pfeffer, 1998; Boxall and Purcell, 2008), demonstrating the relationship between pay and individual contribution has grown in importance for employers. Employers see their reward systems as a vehicle for conveying organisational objectives and rewarding the outcomes and behaviours they seek from the workforce. Such initiatives have been assisted by the reduction in trade unionism in the workplace particularly in the private sector where the latest WERS survey (Kersley *et al.*, 2006) found only 26 per cent of employees have their pay determined through collective bargaining. Moving away from having a common rate for the job, which Marsden (2004: 130) observes characterises a joint regulation approach to pay, has led employers to seek out performance-related pay as a means of achieving a more direct relationship between employer and employee (Hendry *et al.*, 1997: 23).

Promoting the link between organisational performance and employee commitment has been a strong and enduring theme in the strategic human resource management literature (Walton, 1985; Guest, 1987; Marchington and Wilkinson, 2008). For Kessler (1995: 260) this has explicitly informed the use of various systems linking pay to indicators of company performance and, in particular, the growth in individual performance-related pay (IPRP). If, as Lawler (1973, 2000) argues, reward systems are one of the most influential of all human resourcing strategies on employee behaviour, using pay to link employee contribution to corporate objectives seems a demonstrable way of identifying and reinforcing these through the setting of personal objectives. IPRP has been one of a number of HR initiatives implemented to progress and reinforce organisational 'culture change' and this was particularly evident in the privatisation programmes of the public utilities. Dismantling the bureaucratic controls that supported the operation of internal labour markets (Edwards, 1979) was viewed as an immediate way of signalling a break with past practice and led to an early focus in the newly privatised companies on their rewards policy. Yet the complexities of making the change from a collective to a more individually based approach to pay are not always fully appreciated and place a heavy reliance on the quality of the performance review process and line management. This is illustrated by the experience of one electricity supply company, post-privatisation, which implemented individual performance-related pay.

Case Study 8.1

Pay strategy at Eastern Power plc

Prior to becoming a privatised electricity supply company, pay awards at Eastern Power PLC were across-the-board annual pay increases and personal progression through salary grades until the maximum of the grade was reached. Annual pay awards were based on cost of living indexes nationally negotiated between the employers and trade unions on an industry-wide basis. With the formation of independent and competing electricity supply companies, the pay system was identified by senior management at Eastern Power as an important means of demonstrating the company's new, more autonomous, market-driven nature. Furthermore, it provided a tangible mechanism for reinforcing the cultural change required of individuals accustomed to working in a large public utility.

Performance-related pay was introduced with no real preparation of the workforce and minimal training of line managers about either its intended purpose or application. After several years of operating PRP, the reported employee and managerial experience was far from positive. Complaints of inequitable treatment grew and employee surveys revealed a patchy experience of performance review. Many managers were uncomfortable with their increased discretion and pay decisions were frequently viewed as unfair, subjective and over-dependent on personal managerial preferences. Line management reported feeling unclear about what was expected of them in the new organisation, which was reflected in the difficulty they had in setting clear and measurable targets for the employees for whom they were responsible.

| Activity 8.1 | Pay strategy at Eastern Power plc |

1. Why do you think individual performance-related pay was viewed as a more appropriate pay system at Eastern Power plc than the 'across the board' pay rises which had applied prior to privatisation?

2. What would be the main arguments for and against the retention of performance pay in terms of what it is likely to have achieved from the perspective of

   a. senior management

   b. supervisory management

   c. employees

   d. the trade unions?

As seen at Eastern Power plc, moving to performance-based pay can strengthen the power and influence of line managers in the employment relationship but it also increases their responsibilities for demonstrating fairness and consistency in their decision-making. In a rapidly changing organisational context, incentivising pay may well provide an immediate means of 'signalling a changed organisational climate' but clarifying mutual expectations of the wage/effort bargain at the level of the individual remains of paramount importance in the employment relationship.

The process of achieving the desired alignment is widely recognised as complex and 'reward management can be seen as indicative of the contradictions that exist within the discipline labelled human resource management' (Kelly and Monks, 1998: 113). In part this is due to the very tangible nature of pay compared with many other human resourcing strategies. The contradictions observed in reward systems certainly provide plentiful illustration of the dilemma long identified in implementing human resourcing strategies which have both 'hard' and 'soft' dimensions; how to elicit organisational commitment through the development of employee potential while optimising the use of human resources just as any other factor of production (Storey, 2007: 11).

What is performance-related pay?

Performance-related pay is a generic term used to describe a variety of variable payment systems which rewards employees on the basis of performance (Milkovich and Newman, 1987). It can be applied to individual, team based, departmental, site level or company wide bonus payments which are to be distinguished from financial participation schemes, such as share incentive schemes intended to encourage employees to invest in the business. Such schemes are not the focus of this chapter. They are frequently viewed as not being particularly effective as individual motivators because the link between effort and reward is not sufficiently visible or direct (Armstrong, 2002) although the employee ownership model operated by the John Lewis partnership since 1929, is identified as considerable factor in the company's strong performance in the retail sector

(De Vita, 2007). The most commonly applied performance-related pay schemes are described briefly below.

Individual performance-related pay

Traditionally, individual performance-related pay (IPRP) was the outcome of payment-by-results schemes or piecework for hourly paid employees but in the past 20 years the emphasis has been on individual performance-related pay for managerial and other 'white collar' workers. Although a number of organisations have introduced pay-related appraisal schemes for manual workers as part of a move to single integrated pay structures (Brown, 2000), they have been largely excluded from the growth of performance-based pay. In IPRP schemes an assessment of individual performance leads to a level of bonus which can be paid as part of basic salary or as an additional lump sum that is not consolidated with basic pay. Widespread practice is for the level of pay to be decided through a formal appraisal system, in contrast to traditional discretionary merit payments which frequently had no links to a review process.

Team-based performance-related pay

In situations where good team-work is a key factor in organisational success, pay linked to a team/group performance may be more appropriate than IPRP which can lead to detrimental levels of competition between individuals (CIPD, 2008b). The usual approach to team pay for managerial, professional, technical and other office staff is for a cash bonus to be paid to members of a defined group (Suff, 2001) which may extend to a whole department. Shop floor schemes usually operate in the same way but schemes do show a large variation from one organisation to another in how such bonuses are calculated and then allocated among the defined pool, and again whether they are paid as part of basic salary or as an additional lump sum which remains unconsolidated for other pay calculations.

Competence/skills-related pay

An alternative to performance pay based on measured outputs has been competence and skills-related pay which Armstrong (2002) defines as a method of rewarding people wholly or partly by reference to the level of competence or skill they demonstrate in carrying out their roles. Implied in the concept of competence is the development of individual capability to meet both present and future roles (Boyatzis, 1982). It is frequently regarded as a more appropriate way of assessing performance than achieved 'outputs' as it encourages a focus on the continuous development needed to grow human resourcing capability in organisations experiencing rapid change. But relating pay to competence presents difficulties in measuring levels of competence with any real accuracy requiring an identification and shared understanding of the behaviours or 'inputs' individuals need to demonstrate to achieve what is organisationally required of them.

Site-based performance pay

Particularly in manufacturing and retailing, a bonus payment may be linked to the performance of store or site, for example at Asda, Boots the Chemist or BMW Engine Manufacturing. The rationale is that this encourages greater cooperation from staff who all stand to benefit from increased performance but the limitation is that some individuals may contribute more than others whilst the reward is equally distributed.

Company-wide performance schemes

Taking variable pay to the next level is the payment of a bonus linked to the performance of the whole business that is only paid when the company is doing well. There are also company or factory wide schemes, know as gainsharing, where there is a formula for employees sharing in an organisation's financial gains as a result of improved productivity. Profit sharing is based on more than just productivity and will include factors which are beyond the workforce's control, for example increased world prices for raw materials, which is why Armstrong (2002) observes that as a motivational tool, its motivational impact is likely to be less than IPRP.

A combination approach

To reduce the limitations of different types of performance pay, many organisations choose to reward performance across a number of levels, as illustrated by the approach taken at BT. The advantage of such arrangements is that they provide the flexibility to tailor the incentivised elements of pay for different groups but they also lead to increased complexity and, potentially, a dilution of the amount available to reward individual contribution.

Exhibit 8.1

The management bonus scheme at BT

BT, a provider of telecommunications, broadband and internet services has operated a multi-factor bonus scheme for all its non-sales managers (around 28,000 in 2007) for a number of years. A bonus under the scheme depends on four factors, namely the performance of the BT Group, the operating unit, the team and the individual, although the weighting and targets for each factor varies according to an individual's role, occupational unit and status. Managers assess performance at an individual level and within teams against a number of weighted personal objectives and there are minimum levels for individual and company performance that must be met before any payments are made. Maximum amounts vary according to grade and performance and can range from 0–15 per cent of salary for first level managers, 0–20 per cent of salary for second level managers and 0–25 per cent of salary for third level managers. Payments are made annually and are not pensionable. The scheme is reviewed annually and adjusted according to the company's objectives. Whilst the scheme is not subject to negotiations with the trade unions, they are consulted about the bonus arrangements.

Source: IDS, *Bonus Schemes*, Study 843, April 2007

Motivational principles and PRP

A fundamental assumption in support of all performance-based pay is that a monetary incentive linked to performance acts as a motivator to increase performance although the research evidence on the motivational impact of performance pay continues to be limited (Kessler, 2000). Much of it relates to studies done in specific public sector contexts such as local authorities (Heery, 1998), the National Health Service (Dowling and Richardson, 1997) and education (Richardson, 1999; Atkinson *et al.*, 2004).

In terms of the principles that inform systems that link pay and performance, those motivational theories that are particularly pertinent are expectancy theory (Vroom, 1964), goal-setting theory (Locke *et al.*, 1981; Locke and Latham, 1984, 1990) and agency theory (Jensen and Meckling, 1976). In its application to performance-related pay, expectancy theory's linked concepts of expectancy, instrumentality and valence suggest that only if rewards are valued will individuals adjust their behaviours to attain them. Put another way, unless the financial rewards available are perceived by individuals to be sufficiently attractive and worth the effort needed to achieve them, they will not act as a catalyst to encourage higher levels of performance which was the experience of the Managing Director of Gourmet Foods.

Case Study 8.2

The Christmas bonus at Gourmet Foods

After several difficult years with no Christmas bonuses due to the expansion of the business and weak European sales, Gourmet Foods has had a better trading year. The newly appointed managing director, Andrew Straw, has decided to pay a bonus to the workforce of 120 employees in post on 1 December and announced his intention to express his appreciation for the staff's contribution in this way at a meeting with employee representatives in early November. As a result, the pay slips to staff circulated the Friday before the Christmas break revealed that everyone had received an extra £100 in their pay packet. Much to the MD's disappointment, his gesture was not received with the universal approval he had expected. Most employees appeared to be disappointed with the amount they had received and Andrew Straw began to wish he had not bothered with the bonus at all but put the money to a more productive use by investing in new packaging equipment.

Activity 8.2   The Christmas bonus at Gourmet Foods

1. To what extent does what we know about motivational theory explain the staff's reaction to their Christmas bonus?

2. What lessons can be learnt about rewarding performance from Andrew Straw's unfortunate experience?

3. What do you think Andrew Straw should do about a Christmas bonus next year?

The basis of goal-setting theory is that the goals employees pursue are a significant factor in achieving superior organisational performance. But for these to be motivating, Mento *et al.* (1987) identify that the set goals need to be specific, demanding but realistic, accepted by employees as desirable and the subject of subsequent feedback. Looking at these requirements, it is not difficult to see why the 'SMART' (specific, measurable, agreed, realistic, and timed) formula for targeting-setting is in evidence in so many organisational performance management schemes (IDS, 2003). It is an approach seen as providing a means of achieving greater objectivity in assessing whether or not a target has been achieved, which is particularly vital if reward is linked to performance.

Lawler and Porter's motivational model (1968) recognises that individual abilities and role perception have to be taken into account in the wage/effort bargain. The essential argument is that what individuals believe they are required to do or believe they should be doing plays a crucial part in the process of establishing mutual expectations and goal-setting – a dimension which is easily underestimated in the application of performance-related pay, particularly in the public sector where the beliefs of individuals may be at odds with the growing influence of the marketplace in the provision of public services.

Another perspective is that if the job itself is the true source of motivation (Herzberg, 1966) then offering incentives to do it better may at best be regarded as an irrelevance by occupational groups whose loyalties are more closely linked to the attainment of high professional standards than to specific organisational objectives. Such a response is exemplified by the reported case of a senior police constable who memorably declined a Home Office appointment because it included an element of individual performance-based pay on the grounds that 'the notion I will work harder or more effectively because of PRP is absurd and objectionable, if not insulting' (Hogg, 1998).

A central tenet of agency theory is that employers should seek out ways to ensure employees will act as agents in the best interests of the organisation. As Grimshaw and Rubery (2007) point out, bonus payments linked to higher performance which benefits the organisation are seen as a key means of achieving this, but there are many contingent factors which shape the motivational impact of any performance pay system. For example, the influence of any incentive pay erodes over time as employees begin to expect to receive a certain level of variable pay, or the amount paid reduces as a result of a downturn in trading beyond the control of individual employees.

Performance pay and the rewards agenda

Increased competitive pressures have encouraged employers to adopt variable or 'at risk' pay elements as a means of reducing fixed costs, for example by linking any 'payout' to either individual performance or organisational performance, or to both. IPRP has been the most popular of these approaches and its application grew rapidly in the UK from the mid-1980s to the mid-1990s. By 1992 Bevan and Thompson were reporting, in a major survey undertaken for the then Institute of Personnel and Development, that 'Performance pay has become increasingly central to the personnel agenda in recent years' (1992: 41). However, when some of the initial schemes failed to deliver the promised results, there was a reported backlash against the earlier enthusiasm of employers for individual performance pay and more emphasis on development rather than past performance (Strebler and Bevan, 2001: 6). The CIPD's 2008 survey on performance management found that 55 per cent of employers did not see linking pay to performance as an essential part of performance management (CIPD, 2008c). Nonetheless, some form of performance pay is used by a significant number of employees, although its rapid growth ceased by the end of the 1990s, at least in the private sector (Suff, 2001). It does appear that performance pay has become an established feature of many organisational payment systems but there are significant sectoral differences. The 2004 WERS survey (Kersley *et al.*, 2006) revealed that the number of workplaces using performance pay (differentiated in the survey from profit-related pay or bonuses) had increased since the last survey in 1998. But whilst it was in operation in 44 per cent of workplaces in the private sector – and particularly in evidence in private manufacturing companies and financial services, where 82 per cent of workplaces had such incentives – only 19 per cent of public sector workplaces used performance-related pay.

The CIPD reward management survey (CIPD, 2008a) reported 70 per cent of employers using some form of variable incentivised pay but again revealed that this was more popular in the private than the public sector where its usage had dipped since 2007, possibly explained by concerns about equal pay in the sector. Most organisations operated more than one scheme, the most popular arrangement being IPRP combined with a bonus linked to business results. The various approaches adopted by the main economic sectors are set out in Table 8.1.

Despite its lower adoption in the public sector, there is renewed interest in variable pay in parts of the public sector to support the modernising of the public services agenda. For example, the Makinson report (2000) 'Incentives for Change' reviewed four government offices (the Employment Service, the Benefits Agency, Customs and Excise and the Inland Revenue) and recommended the introduction of performance bonuses to be measured against operational targets and paid separately from the rest of the compensation package (IDS, 2003). But there can be particular issues in putting IPRP into practice in the public sector which may be due to problems associated with performance review processes

Table 8.1 **Types of cash-based or incentive plans on offer by sector (%)**

	All	Manufacturing/ and production	Private sector services	Voluntary sector	Public services
Individual-based	60	53	61	65	72
Schemes driven by business results	51	57	54	26	19
Combination	50	46	57	35	25
Ad hoc project-based	27	24	30	26	16
Gainsharing	3	3	3	–	2

Source: CIPD 2008 *Reward Management Survey 2008* p. 12 (2008), CIPD, with the permission of the publisher, the Chartered Institute of Personnel and Development, London (www.cipd.co.uk)

which Stiles *et al.* (1997) found were often regarded as bureaucratic processes detracting from getting the job done. Davidge (2007) points out that whilst the tools of performance management were identified by a Treasury and Cabinet Office audit in 2005 to be pivotal to the ability of local authorities to deliver on their aims and objectives, the CIPD's 2007 reward management survey shows that the level of government funding, pay guidelines and union pressures seriously constrain local authorities from introducing performance-related pay (CIPD, 2007b). There is also the question of whether performance pay is actually appropriate in a public sector context which is likely to attract individuals motivated by a public service ethos and where it can be difficult to identify the range of factors that would properly measure their contribution. Burgess *et al.*'s (2007) study of public workers found that, whilst they do respond to incentives, it can be difficult to evaluate the benefits of such schemes in terms of improving performance and found evidence of 'game playing' to meet targets which did nothing to improve productivity.

Yet schemes linking pay to performance continue to be an enduring method of reward and the economic context of low inflation has encouraged the use of non-consolidated performance-linked payments to overcome the problem of pay awards that are too insignificant to motivate employees. The UK's tight labour market conditions in recent years have led to employers facing difficulties in recruiting and retaining staff (Philpott, 2008), and examining the rewards package they offer compared to those of competitors. This has resulted in market rates and external equity becoming dominant considerations in rewards with variable pay arrangements providing a mechanism to adjust the rewards package. But internal equity in rewards is increasingly an issue in variable pay arrangements due to public policy concerns about the continuing gender earnings gap in the UK (Women and Work Commission, 2006) and the experience of equal pay claims in the public sector. At the time of writing, a major preoccupation for UK councils is resolving equal pay claims arising from the bonus payment arrangements for certain occupations implemented in the 1970s which it is estimated will cost them a staggering £5 billion (Fuller, 2008). This raises the issue of whether the private sector is sufficiently prepared to meet potential equal pay claims and address issues of internal equity in its incentive pay schemes.

Variable pay has operated alongside graded pay structures, 'broadbanding' (described by Armstrong and Brown (2001) as 'the process of compressing a hierarchy of pay grades or salary ranges into a number of broad pay bands'), individual job ranges and pay curves, which provide for different rates of individual progression. It has also provided flexibility in flatter, more devolved organisational structures where there is increasing likelihood of lateral rather than hierarchical career moves. In the public and voluntary sector where service rather than performance was traditionally recognised by incremental salary scales, there is a greater focus on linking pay progression to individual contribution. Individual performance is the most frequently reported basis for deciding pay progression leading Charles Cotton, the CIPD's adviser on pay, to observe that in the private sector 'the traditional annual, across the board pay increase is becoming a thing of the past' (CIPD, 2008a: 33).

Substituting IPRP with competency-related pay, team pay and other incentivised approaches to reward is still rare and these are likely to be used in conjunction with individual performance pay (Thompson and Milsome, 2001). Recognising the limitations of performance pay schemes dominated by solely rewarding achieved outputs or levels of competence, a mixed model has emerged described as 'contribution-related pay' by Brown and Armstrong (1999). It is a mixture of paying individuals on the basis of achieved objectives and the competencies needed to achieve them. In theory, such an approach should help to address the subjectivity associated with assessing behavioural competences as well as the inflexibility of systems that encourage a concentration of effort on outcomes that will attract financial reward. The intention is to reward past achievement but also promote the development needed to support future success. Examples of organisations that have adopted the mixed model of contribution are American Express UK, HSBC Bank, Xerox UK and Littlewoods Retail (Suff, 2001).

The increased diversity of the workforce and the pursuit of a greater work-life balance has been the catalyst for another trend in pay, namely the growth of flexible benefits which can be highly significant in terms of forging employee commitment to the organisation if these offer choices that suit individual employee circumstances. Although Kessler (2005) observes there is some evidence that employees tend to undervalue the fringe benefits they receive, it seems that such benefits are becoming mainstream organisational practice as a result of new statutory entitlements, a greater preoccupation with the work-life balance and as a support for recruitment and retention (Thorpe and Homan, 2000; IDS, 2007c).

The needs of a more diverse workforce, labour market pressures and the constraints for some organisations in providing additional cash incentives to reward employee contribution, for example in the voluntary or public sector, as well as a recognition that pay is not the only motivator have set the scene for the concept of 'total reward'. This is defined by the CIPD as 'a reward strategy that brings additional components such as learning and development, together with aspects of the working environment, into the benefits package. It goes beyond standard remuneration by embracing the company culture and is aimed at giving all employees a voice in the operation, with the employer in return receiving an engaged employee performance' (CIPD, 2007b).

Whilst the concept of 'total reward' may be identified as the next step in terms of recognising wider employee contribution, in practice, employers report difficulties when it comes to integrating fully the financial and non-financial aspects of pay. Yet there is a growing awareness among employers and employees of the value of non pay benefits in the rewards packages on offer. For example, with the closure of many final pension salary schemes, pension provision has increased in importance in the reward package. As Purcell et al. (2003) identified in their research into the 'People and Performance' link, offering work-life balance and family friendly benefits is important in strengthening employee commitment to an employer. Offering an attractive benefits package alongside a competitive salary is one way in which an organisation may seek to position itself as an employer of choice but the total rewards approach is much broader. It also embraces issues of personal development, recognition, career progression and the flexibility to meet individual needs. This is illustrated by the approach at Denplan, a dental insurance company employing some 317 people, which was one of the winners of The Sunday Times Best Companies awards in 2007 and listed as the sixth best small business to work for in the UK.

Exhibit 8.2

Rewards and recognition at Denplan – Dental health insurer

With holiday allowance starting at 29 days a year, rising to 41 with seniority and job tenure, staff at Denplan have plenty to flash their pearly whites about. But a job at the UK's leading provider of private dental payment plans is about more than the fringe benefits. Staff get a lot out of their working lives, with communication and line managers coming in for particular praise. Employees say their managers talk openly and honestly with them, giving this question the top score in the survey at 86 per cent positive. They also think their managers care about how satisfied they are with their jobs (82 per cent and the second highest result) and share important information with them – rating this point 84 per cent positive, another top score.

The company gives managers plenty of support via a leadership development programme as well as a mentoring system linking all new managers with more experienced hands. Training is available in a range of areas to everyone, from short workshops in career management to two-day courses on presentation skills. No courses start before 9.30am so parents can do the school run and still get there on time. Staff say their job is good for their personal growth and 85 per cent rated this question 83 per cent positively.

Source: The *Sunday Times*, 9 March 2008

Problems of application

The principles that inform paying for performance appear both logical and straightforward until we begin to examine their application in practice. An incentivised pay element in rewards strategy frequently presents those responsible for its interpretation with dilemmas. Criticisms frequently levied at pay related to individual performance are:

- Individuals are motivated differently, pay is not the only motivator and whilst performance pay may motivate some it may even demotivate others, particularly if they are not the best performers and see little value in expending effort for unlikely returns. In this way, it may only reward those who, without performance pay, would still be the best performers so does little to progress the general level of employee performance.

- Expectancy theory suggests that people will not respond to incentivised pay if the potential reward is not seen as worth the effort. Yet incentive pay increases are often small, and in times of low inflation and pay increase inflation they decrease further. The reward offered just may not meet the expectations of the individuals concerned, as we saw in the payment of the Christmas bonus at Gourmet Foods.

- Individuals focus on those activities that will bring financial reward to the detriment of pursuing innovation if a 'tried and tested' way of working is more predictable in terms of achieving tangible rewards.

- It breeds short-termism and can be detrimental to team-work as individuals focus on those personal goals most likely to deliver financial reward.

- There is less transparency in how pay progression is arrived at and it may hide discrimination and inconsistencies in managerial decision-making.

The tendency is that in solving the dominant issue of allocating pay according to contribution a host of other problems are created. All too often incentivised pay systems end up rewarding short-term achievement and can result in goal distortion and displacement of other important requirements in the longer term (Kessler and Purcell, 1992: 17). Kerr (1991: 485) argues that this can lead to certain behaviours being rewarded that the organisation may be seeking to discourage. He provides the example of US university teachers who it is *hoped* will not neglect their teaching responsibilities although they are *rewarded* for their research and publications – a situation familiar to academics in many UK universities where it is rational for staff seeking promotion to concentrate on their research activities rather than teaching.

The potential for dysfunctional outcomes of the operation of individual performance pay are illustrated in the following case study.

Case Study 8.3

The new performance bonus at Homeserve Ltd

Homeserve Ltd is a key supplier of major electrical household appliances that offers a comprehensive installation and maintenance service to both its new and existing customers. Traditionally, the engineers have worked Monday to Friday, with Saturday and Sunday work paid for at premium overtime rates.

To become more competitive it had been critical to negotiate new working hours and a pay agreement which reflects the needs of dual-earning families who require weekend and evening delivery and installation times for items such as washing machines and cookers. This led the new HR director, Jo Fern, to spend a great deal of time during her first six months working on the implementation of a new rewards structure based on an annual hours payment and the removal of overtime premiums; an arrangement that worked well at the food processing company she previously worked for as it accommodated the seasonal fluctuations in work.

In order to reach agreement with the union over the removal of overtime payments, the senior management at Homeserve agreed to the introduction of a bonus payment related to the number of household calls per week made by an engineer during each four-week period. The intention was that this would improve individual levels of productivity and encourage more flexible working. At the end of its first full year of operation Jo Fern was asked to review the effectiveness of the new scheme. This revealed some interesting trends. Whereas previously the installation engineers had demonstrated flexibility in their daily scheduled routes to cover for colleagues who were on holiday or unwell, now they were only willing to take on these duties if they fell within their immediate geographical area. There had also been an increase in the number of return calls, often due to missing parts, being made to the same household and a growing difference in the earnings between the engineers working in the south-east and those in the northern regions of the country. In fact, looking at the figures paid out over the past year in bonus payments, Jo Fern is concerned to see that the overall salary bill is higher than it had been under the previous flat rate and overtime arrangements. In contrast, the actual volume of completed work has remained at very much the same level as before.

| Activity 8.3 | The new performance bonus at Homeserve Ltd |

1. Identify the impact of the new performance bonus system at Homeserve Ltd and explain what has happened.

2. How, if at all, could the present reward system be improved to both support company performance and recognise individual contribution?

The Homeserve performance bonus illustrates a classic performance pay problem; the distorting effect of an overemphasis on one measure when rewarding performance. Encouraging engineers to concentrate on the specific measurable outcome of call rates has led to wider business aims, for example the quality of customer care, being neglected or even ignored. It has led the engineers, who as a peripatetic work group have a lot of autonomy in organising their schedules, to create work to maximise their earning power. It has also reduced flexibility as they are now less willing than hitherto to accommodate unforeseen work demands or calls in other geographical areas if it could adversely impact on their overall call rate.

Conflicts between development and measurement

There is a central tension in many approaches to performance management between reviewing past performance and encouraging future development. Wood's (1995) research suggests a distinction in human resourcing strategies and practices between those designed to promote high commitment and those aimed at controlling performance in circumstances of low mutual commitment. The first approach focuses on progression, training and development and internal forms of flexibility whereas the second is dominated by a bought, more instrumental commitment to organisational aims through financial incentives. Contemporary wisdom is that a mixed model of rewarding contribution, already referred to, can reflect both aims (Suff, 2001). But a source of confusion for many employees is that whilst many employers talk the language of development, their workplace reality is one of increasing targets and pay progression based on the achievement of set goals. Personal development will then take second place to maximising individual earnings.

The balanced scorecard (Kaplan and Norton, 1992), discussed in more detail in Chapter 7, is one process designed to address the 'twin vices of subjectivity and inconsistency' and the short-termism of performance pay (Kessler, 1994: 485). Its intention is to encourage a long-term as well as short-term planning perspective through promoting a balanced selection of measurements which are developmental and not just based on short-term financial gains. Another approach is reflected in the design (and redesign) of performance management schemes which aim to broaden the basis of evaluation by setting 'stretch' objectives to encourage future personal development as well as measuring past achievement. For example, line managers at Microsoft are required to consider how goals are to be achieved as well as what needs to be done in the goal-setting process which will identify personal development needs. As a result, at Microsoft the acronym SMART has been extended to become SHMART to include the 'how' (IDS, 2003). Openness about individual development is, arguably, constrained by having one performance review process that considers issues of development and past achievements to decide pay at one and the same time. As a result, some organisations operate a separate review process to consider personal development and career progression and Cannell's performance management survey (Cannell, 2005) found 46 per cent of private sector employers adopting separate review processes.

Issues of felt fairness

Once pay is introduced into the performance review process it is argued that it rapidly becomes a dominant element in the review of performance. Strebler and Bevan (2001) found it to be the major outcome of the review process for most of the respondents in their study into organisational problems and issues in balancing the objectives and content of performance reviews. This places the consistency and fairness of decisions on how performance ratings are arrived at and pay allocated under close scrutiny. Whilst a 1998 IPD study of performance pay (p. 4) reported the majority of participating employers viewing IPRP as a source of increased fairness in pay matters it also commented 'this is a perception not usually echoed in evaluation studies directly measuring employee opinions'. The available evidence is certainly less than conclusive about the extent to which pay linked to performance is viewed as a fairer system of reward. For example, only half of the employees in Guest and Conway's study (1997) into the psychological contract reported that performance-related pay actually motivated them to work harder. But consecutive employee attitude surveys across two NHS Trust Hospitals revealed the majority thought pay based on individual contribution would be more equitable than the present system and viewed this as more important in their pay system than rewarding team-work (Fisher *et al.*, 2003). These findings add to the confusion as to whether a seemingly fairer reward process is also likely to be motivating one and Torrington and Hall (1998: 627) suggest that 'the growth in performance-related pay undoubtedly owes as much to the appearance of fairness as to its supposed incentive effects'.

At face value, the concepts underlying performance-related pay would appear to be self-evidently fairer than paying the same rewards to everyone regardless of performance. The logic that it is only right to pay more to those who make the greatest contribution or, to reverse the argument, less to those who contribute the least, feels intuitively right. Yet the application of this principle in practice repeatedly shows it to be problematic. One explanation for this may lie in the inadequate attention paid in the design, implementation and operation of performance-related pay schemes to equity theory (Adams, 1965) which is concerned with *how* individuals perceive they are being treated in comparison to others. It reinforces the importance of the 'felt fair' principle in reward systems (Jacques, 1961) which suggests that the concept of fairness in pay systems depends to a very considerable extent on whether or not they are seen as equitable by the individuals who apply them and those who experience their outcomes.

A major consideration for line managers lies in deciding not only how any performance pay should be allocated within the terms of a scheme but also how it will be viewed from the perspective of the employee at the receiving end and by other employees. This is the dilemma facing Helen, an office supervisor in implementing an output-based IPRP scheme.

Case Study 8.4

Applying the 'felt fair principle'

Marie and George are the two shipping clerks who work in a busy agricultural machinery export office. Marie is tireless. She works demonstrably harder than George, is more punctual, extremely helpful and is always observed as giving of her best effort, frequently staying late in the office for no additional payments. George, on the other hand, achieves just as much as Marie and is actually more accurate so satisfactorily completes more orders but he is nowhere near as hard-working. He never stays beyond finishing time, is regarded generally as having a rather uncooperative manner and getting away with the minimum of effort.

This poses a problem for their supervisor, Helen, when it comes to deciding the performance-related element of pay appropriate for the two staff in her section. In all the training sessions on the new performance management scheme it was emphasised that achieving the set goals was the crucial measure she must apply in assessing individual levels of performance.

Activity 8.4   Applying the 'felt fair principle'

1. In applying the new scheme, to which shipping clerk should Helen award the higher level of performance-related pay?
2. Taking account of the 'felt fair principle' in pay, what would the implications of your answer to Question 1 be in terms of improving both Marie's and George's performance?
3. What measures of performance should be applied in this case to improve the performance of Marie and George in the future?

In this scenario Helen is being asked to decide whether it is the performance of Marie or George which best meets the criteria for allocating performance pay. Fundamental to the operation of performance pay, whether it is team or individually based, is a requirement for managers to discriminate between different levels of performance in their allocation of rewards, by recognising good performance (Cannell and Wood, 1992) and sending out negative signals about poor performance. The problem for Helen lies in the definition of what constitutes good performance in terms of acceptable fairness. A scheme that is purely output based which ignores the means of arriving at these outputs, may actually reinforce behaviours the organisation wishes to discourage, for example George's uncooperative behaviour. Increasing managerial involvement and autonomy in pay decisions can bring such tensions to the fore, as Gratton *et al.* discovered in their longitudinal study (1999: 64) of eight high profile companies who reported difficulties in operationalising performance management systems because of 'the presence of mixed messages and employees' perceptions of fairness and accuracy'. The result is that allocating IPRP can all too easily lead to supervisory managers like Helen finding themselves placed between the proverbial 'rock and a hard place', with managerial responsibilities for transmitting the desired corporate messages but who also view the fairness of the process from the perspective of an employee. The natural inclination may be to opt for the simple option of treating

Marie and George the same, possibly by giving neither a performance pay award but for different reasons. One difficulty is that this can lead to an individual feeling and claiming unfairness in terms of having met a scheme's targets.

A study into middle managers' values and beliefs on paying for performance (Harris, 2001a) revealed that managers faced with the dilemma of being unable, due to insufficient resources, to reward both employees who maintained high performance as well as those who had shown the most improvement, saw maintaining harmony as a high priority. It was viewed as more important than risking alienating a number of good performers by deciding 'whose turn it is' regardless of actual performance that year. Mindful of the need for future cooperation and trying to keep their own trustworthiness intact, the majority revealed a preference for a collective approach by singling out no one individual for a higher pay award, at the risk of criticism from senior management for failing to operate the scheme properly. As a survival mechanism for managers trying to achieve high levels of trust and reciprocity, this seems a justifiable means of achieving what Watson (2006: 54) describes as 'productive cooperation'. Such an approach can, however, still lead to employees feeling aggrieved about a process which, in practice, has neither delivered tangible rewards nor a fair process in terms of discriminating between different levels of contribution.

A distinguishing feature of PRP is that it operates largely outside collectively agreed procedures. This results in reduced openness about pay decisions, heightened by decreasing the trade union involvement which previously provided procedural checks and balances. The lack of a developed or independent appeals process can aggravate feelings of mistrust about the process. Standard practice for appeals arising from IPRP decisions is for these to be dealt with outside existing grievance procedures, with one stage of appeal to the next level of management – an approach that hardly encourages perceptions of impartiality. If the 'correctability' of decisions is taken as an essential measure of fairness (Sheppard et al., 1992) then most IPRP schemes fail to encourage employee optimism in their neutrality.

The combination of reduced pay transparency and the increased discretion of line managers about IPRP provides more scope for discriminatory practices and can be viewed as detrimental to addressing the long-standing issues of pay equality already referred to. This is the basis of Rubery's argument (1995: 637) that performance pay can pose a potential threat to greater gender pay equality in pay determination. Although concerns about equal pay have intensified in recent years, the level of awareness of equal pay issues is generally found to be low among private sector employers where the 'equality proofing' of systems frequently lack robustness. Certainly the lack of demonstrable internal measurement systems other than the use of appraisal lends weight to a key criticism levied at IPRP by employees – that it is too subjective and overly reliant on the quality of the relationship with the line manager.

It is interesting to note that a study into contingent pay by E-Reward (2004) found that the factors rated most important by organisations in the design of variable pay schemes were that they were 'easy to understand' and 'equitable and consistent'. Factors, as Kessler points out (2007) that were rated considerably higher than aligning pay to business goals or being able to differentiate pay according to performance. One conclusion to be drawn from this examination of fairness and performance pay is that if both employers and employees believe that it leads to greater equity in distributing rewards according to actual contribution it may well be a more motivating system. Yet Strebler and Bevan's study (2001) points to the size of the rewards making more difference to PRP's motivational impact than the issue of internal equity and found that managers wished PRP would differentiate more, even though it was not seen as a motivator for the majority of employees.

Changing the psychological contract

Using pay for performance as a key determinant in creating the framework within which the relationship between employer and employees is to operate has placed a heavy reliance on line management to develop a different form of employment contract. One interpretation is that by introducing or increasing an element of 'at risk' pay based on performance, there is a move away from a relational psychological contract built on long-term relationships to one that is more transactional (Rousseau, 1996) owing to a focus on outcomes and distributive justice. The argument is that the introduction of PRP may well be a signal that an employer is withdrawing from a longer-term form of mutual commitment in the pay/effort bargain based on loyalty and security to a more short-term instrumental form of exchange perceived as more appropriate in an increasingly uncertain environment.

Creating a climate where the old securities have gone and reinforcing a message that continued employment is contingent upon individual contribution can be intended to reduce complacency, as we saw in Case Study 8.1, by bringing a level of anxiety and reducing certainty in the working relationships. To Stiles *et al.* (1997: 65) the emphasis on linking pay to performance and short-term pressures has led to contradictory messages by making 'the employment relationship more transactional' despite a 'company rhetoric' stressing commitment. This can be exacerbated where there is a lack of clarity about what the employers' expectations are and what is needed to 'exceed expectations'. The absence of any parameters or specificity in performance ratings reinforce perceptions of an ongoing and unstoppable escalation of organisational expectations which leads to an erosion of trust in the employment relationship. Using performance pay as a control mechanism and a means of intensifying work is described by Hendry *et al.* (2000: 53) as the 'dark side' of performance management. It is reminiscent of the alleged speeding up of the assembly line in mass production systems, without the agreement or knowledge of employees, to reach new production targets which were such a regular cause of past industrial discontent and conflict (Beynon, 1984).

PRP and line managers

Getting the implementation process right has long been recognised as a vital success factor in payment schemes (Bowey *et al.*, 1982), and incentivised pay alongside decentralisation has increased the responsibilities of line management in pay decisions (Millward *et al.*, 2000). It means they play a vital role in PRP schemes (other than company, divisional or plant-wide bonuses) in transmitting the desired corporate messages about pay to the workforce and ensuring that there is the desired 'line of sight' between individual objectives and organisational priorities. As Kessler and Purcell (1992: 23) observe, performance pay provides 'opportunities for the greater exercise of managerial control' and herein lies one of its central problems. The actual process of introducing performance pay, how it is communicated and managed, can be as significant as the amounts paid out in terms of employee perceptions of its motivational impact and acceptability. For example, Dowling and Richardson's (1997: 360) survey of performance-related pay for managers in the National Health Service revealed that the money available was less important as a motivator than the clarification of objectives by their managers. The author's own research (Harris, 2001a) found that organisational constraints, workforce values and their personal experiences of what motivates the majority led middle managers to have a far greater belief in the importance of demonstrating trustworthy behaviours as a means of encouraging employee commitment than singling out individual performance for reward. In some instances perceptions of IPRP's value as a motivator among the middle managers, particularly where the 'pay pot' is limited, reflected a collective view of equity that is arguably closer to those they supervised than the principles senior managers sought to promote by incentivising an element of pay. This was illustrated by one compensation manager for a high street bank who complained: 'the trouble with our branch managers is that they are too close to the staff they supervise; they are in the trenches fighting with the troops'.

There is tendency for the discussion on IPRP in both the academic and practitioner literature to focus on rewarding the high performer who, arguably, will be self-motivated to achieve high standards regardless of financial reward, but at the other end of the axis is the impact that withholding performance pay has on the under-performer. The concept of 'rewarding the goodies and punishing the baddies' has always been one of the intended outcomes of performance pay (Lewis, 1991), although it is an understated element of the performance management agenda. The intention is, nevertheless, that the results-orientated nature of many schemes will make identifying underperformance clearer for the line manager. This aspect of the process frequently creates particular difficulties for supervisory management. While using IPRP to reward the high performer is an approach most managers are comfortable with, there is a discomfort for many about its use to essentially punish the lower achiever for a variety of reasons. Not least of these is the observed reluctance of line managers to be the imparter of bad news to employees (Stiles, 1999).

This may reveal a lack of belief that such action will have little if any impact on underperformance – a view that was confirmed by an IPD survey (1998) which reported 52 per cent of employers feeling that PRP had made no real change in poor performance and that 10 per cent saw it as actually leading to deterioration. A further managerial concern can be the need to substantiate the grounds for such action, particularly if the situation is a long-standing one which may reflect badly on the capability of present or past supervision. Managers may lack the skills of feedback or feel unable to undertake the coaching role needed to address the situation. There is also the potential for an individual to challenge their judgement and even litigate if it is claimed that some form of discrimination has taken place. This is not helped by a frequent lack of transparency in the links between performance review and pay and that 'most managers do not feel well equipped to explain how it works' (Strebler and Bevan, 2001: 51).

The difficulty is that the manager is invariably identified as the weak link in the application of performance management systems (Hendry *et al.*, 1997; Harris, 2001a). For many managers the urgent and measurable is their prime consideration at the cost of the longer-term development of organisational capability, particularly where the measurement of their own performance is judged against achieving set targets which are highly dependent on the achievements of their staff. Implementing IPRP can present line management with very real conflicts in terms of pursuing their own short-term self-interests, reinforcing the objectives of the scheme and ensuring the 'collective good'. The argument is not that these goals are mutually exclusive but rather that the level of emphasis placed on each one will impact significantly on a scheme's outcomes.

Harris's study into the values and beliefs of line managers about performance (Harris, 2001a) revealed widespread support for the principle of financially rewarding employee contribution but for 'hard pressed' managers the outcomes of individual performance pay did not justify the amount of time taken up by performance measurement and evaluation. Notwithstanding this, concerns about the reliability of measurement processes have tended to lead to the introduction of more sophisticated, time-consuming processes which, as Thompson (2002) observes, erodes the benefits of variable pay costs. It also supports Strebler and Bevan's (2001: 55) conclusion that performance review processes are frequently so overloaded in terms of being actually deliverable by line managers that employers 'cannot implement what they design'. The bureaucracy of performance management processes are a major source of discontent (Gratton *et al.*, 1999; Thompson and Milsome, 2001). This increases where there is the practice of forced distribution through centrally imposed parameters on the allocation and distribution of rankings for performance pay, an approach that was abandoned, for example, by Network Rail to the appreciation of its union membership as part of its 2007 pay award (TSSA, 2007).

It is argued that the twin trends of devolving HR responsibilities to line management and the distancing of HR professionals involvement from operational issues has impacted detrimentally on the integration of performance strategies with organisational strategies. Faced with other, more immediate, operational demands a 'task orientated' line manager will focus on getting the 'job done' in the shortest possible time particularly if it leads to personal reward. Organisationally this can mean the erosion of a scheme's wider objectives, for example, developing new skills in individuals or encouraging innovation in the workforce. Such factors highlight why their understanding of a performance management process and how it is part of approaches to employee reward is so important. Anglian Water recognised this in the implementation of its new performance processes in 2005 and invested heavily in training its managers.

Exhibit 8.3

Training line managers at Anglian Water

Every line manager at Anglian Water and AWG central services (400 in total) was given comprehensive training on the new performance development process. This training covered the whole performance cycle, from agreeing SMART objectives to giving performance ratings. . . . During January 2006 there was a company wide roadshow focusing on the new pay deal and the link with the PDR process. This was supported by a series of more detailed surgeries for groups of 10–20 line managers.

Source: IDS, *Performance Management*, Study 839, February 2007

Keeping to a 'tried and tested' route to achieve personal goals is a less time-intensive and more predictable route to achieving targets than coaching, mentoring and the team-building required by a more developmental approach. Whitener *et al.* (1998: 525) observe that this can lead to a 'potentially tragic outcome' for organisations which are seeking to encourage a more trusting organisational climate and greater flexibility that will never be properly realised because of the reluctance of managers and employees to take the risks involved.

Few organisations report involving their line managers in the design of their performance and related rewards systems and this can lead to a subsequent lack of ownership among managers. Hutchinson and Purcell (2007), in their study of the line manager's role in rewarding work, identify the importance of this happening as it does at the John Lewis Parnership. The danger of a lack of line management involvement is that such interventions are regarded as the 'brainchild of the HR function', driven by senior management and the board (Harris, 2001a).

A further challenge for the HR function is that devolving the implementation of schemes to line managers means that the scope for inconsistencies is heightened, but HR practitioners still carry a wider organisational responsibility when things go wrong, for example a claim of sex discrimination over the level of bonus received. Textbook wisdom is for the HR function to play an active role in developing and supporting managers so they are better equipped to handle the processes involved – a familiar facilitating role that can consume large tracts of HR practitioners' time but produce no measurable outcomes for the assessment of their own contribution. The issue for the specialist function remains how to achieve some consistency of application across the organisation while playing no active part in pay decisions, which becomes even more problematical when HR services are geographically distanced from the actual workplace. What is evident is that employees are most likely to be influenced positively or negatively by line manager behaviours in the implementation of rewards policies but these will be influenced by the approach taken by senior management. As Purcell and Hutchinson point out (2007: 14) senior management has an important part to play in 'establishing an organisational climate that supports, recognizes and rewards people management behaviours'.

Current challenges

Whilst variable pay has provided the flexibility employers seek to reflect the market value of certain employees, it has contributed to an increasing earnings gap within organisations but also within occupational groups which can erode collective spirit and team-work. Furthermore concerns about equal pay and potential litigation are placing the spotlight on the issue of internal equity and pay transparency. A major challenge for employers lies in designing processes to reward contribution that are appropriate for the increasing diversity of the workforce. Employers' rewards strategies need to motivate the growing numbers of part-time and temporary workers, as well as the full-time worker, and be sufficiently flexible to recognise the different motivational patterns of an increasing older workforce (Parry, 2008) and those at the start of their working lives. To meet the challenges of creating a high-performance workplace, HR professionals need to consider how attractive their reward packages are to all their employees and undertake pay audits to check how well they recognise the contributions of different groups of workers (Thompson, 2002).

Not only has demographics changed who works, but technology is changing how, when and where work takes place, presenting fresh complexities in deciding how to measure and reward performance. An obvious example has been the growth of call centres which share many of the characteristics of the factory production assembly line with similar problems in finding reward systems that will not only boost productivity but also address issues of employee commitment (Malhotra *et al.*, 2007).

Technology has enabled growing numbers of employees to work from home and LFS statistics identify this as a trend in EU countries and the US (Hotopp, 2002) leading to a need to re-evaluate the concept of working time (Karsten and Leopold, 2003). Rewarding a less visible workforce presents new challenges in terms of fairly identifying contribution, particularly for line managers responsible for variable pay decisions based on individual performance. One interpretation is that this will actually reinforce the use of pay against quantitative targets as the simplest, most accessible means of measuring productivity and maximising performance (Bibby, 2002) based on task time rather than clock time. The nature of jobs continues to change, with the growth of the service sector increasing the importance of social skills, creating problems of measurement which will reinforce a continuing interest in competency frameworks to develop skills and reward performance.

The communication of pay systems is an identified weakness in CIPD reward surveys yet there is a heavy reliance on line management to deliver the pay messages the organisation is seeking. Involving managers and employees in the design of pay policies would encourage their engagement as well as their understanding of what is offered but they continue to report a low level of involvement, if any, in their design and development. Some of the challenges of developing rewards strategies to meet the needs of different groups of workers are evident at Mid Western Bank.

Case Study 8.5

Reward policy at Mid Western Bank

Mid Western Bank has a long and successful history of retail banking but like many other organisations in the sector it has a mixed history of success when it comes to rewarding employee contribution. It has not had a comprehensive review of its reward policy and practice in recent years although there was one in the 1990s largely prompted by concerns about equal pay legislation. The bank employs 30,000 full- and part-time employees throughout the UK of whom 65 per cent are women. The ratio of male to female employees in managerial roles is 4:1 but a lot of women are employed in high street branches where 60 per cent of them work part-time. A current concern of the bank is that it is not retaining its graduates once they have completed two to three years of service and interviews have revealed that they are largely going to other employers in the sector, some of whom pay significant bonuses to their high performers. Feedback from managers in the high street branches was that individual performance pay was not encouraging the team-work essential to high performance in the branch network and the company ceased to operate IPRP in 1999. Since then employees have received, in addition to annual pay increases which have been minimal due to low inflation, an annual performance bonus related to the performance in their division of the business together with a wider company bonus linked to profitability which has fluctuated considerably in recent years. These is some confusion about how these bonuses have been calculated and the recent company-wide bonuses have been low whereas divisional units have varied significantly. Some employees have enjoyed good bonuses whereas others working in other divisions have done less well, which has been demotivating as they feel they have worked as hard as other colleagues in different areas of the business. There is a view that these areas have been better resourced or experienced less turnover of high performing staff. Generous family friendly benefits were introduced at the same time that flexible working legislation was introduced but take up has been quite low: there is concern among employees that working reduced hours will impact negatively upon their career progression.

Line managers would like to do more to reward high performing individuals and complain that it is the most talented that are leaving to go to other employers. Overall there are many employee benefits to working for the bank but some of these are just not known.

Activity 8.5   Reward policy at Mid Western Bank

A new chief executive has arrived who wants to promote the organisation as an employer of choice to new talent into the bank. You have been asked to review the bank's rewards system, particularly in terms of attracting and retaining employees and recognising individual contributions.

1. Identify the key issues that Mid Western Bank needs to address in its rewards policy.

2. What changes would you recommend to:

   a) support the employer of choice agenda and the recruitment and retention of talented individuals

   b) reward contribution and motivate staff

   c) ensure that any new reward strategies are fully implemented by line managers.

Conclusions – does performance pay improve performance?

Whilst the trend towards variable pay is evident to differing degrees across countries in the Western economy, the scope for national differences in reward systems is considerable and will be shaped by a 'complex set of influences' (Sparrow, 2000: 203). Underestimating these factors, combined with a visible lack of congruence between employment practices which use the language of development yet apply hard measures when it comes to the allocation of rewards, can erode rather than improve levels of employee commitment.

Despite the limitations of performance pay and of its most popular application, IPRP, there is little evidence that employers are substituting it with alternatives. A brief glance through the managerial remuneration packages offered in the appointment pages of the national press confirms the enduring popularity of using performance pay in the search for top management capability. For example, an examination of senior management jobs advertised in just two editions of the *Sunday Times* (April, 2008) revealed the majority offering a remuneration package with a performance bonus payable in addition to basic salary. What does appear to be emerging is a greater use of a combination of different compensation techniques to reward team or individual performance or competences (CBI/William Mercer, 2000; CIPD, 2008a). This supports the view of Brown and Armstrong (1999) that practices such as team and competency-based pay grow alongside, but do not replace, individual performance-related pay.

The principle of paying people according to their contribution appeals to a sense of fairness in most of us but, in practice, there are very real problems in establishing what should be rewarded and the perceived equity of the assessment process. Boxall and Purcell (2008: 192) point to the limitations of expectancy theory in telling us about the full 'content of human motivations (for example, pay, status and intrinsic job satisfaction)' but point out that it tells us three quite important things. These are that unrealistic goals will frustrate rather than motivate; goals that are not rewarded will be ignored; and finally that the rewards available must be those that will motivate the individuals concerned, for example access to interesting work as well as meeting pay expectations.

The debate about PRP's effectiveness in improving employee commitment and contribution to organisational performance looks set to continue. There are claims that performance pay can actually be demotivating if expectations are not met (Pfeffer, 1998) and Tyson and York (2003) comment on the absence of evidence that performance pay improves performance in the longer term. Faced with such arguments, it is difficult to explain why performance-related pay is quite so enduring or as widespread in its application. But those employers who invest heavily of their time and effort in applying performance-related pay as part of their performance processes reveal a marked reluctance to abandon it, despite the fact that its effectiveness in contributing to organisational performance remains something of an 'act of faith'. One explanation is that reward packages which help employers to attract and retain talented individuals and may provide the means of motivating employees to align their efforts with organisational aims will continues to be a high priority. In addition, talented individuals also expect their pay to reflect their individual contribution so that in a competitive labour market performance pay continues to be viewed as an aid to recruitment for certain types of appointments. Its disadvantage is that it can also act as 'golden handcuffs' for individuals seeking to move on but who are reluctant to do so because of the risk of losing an attractive bundle of incentivised pay arrangements.

Summary

In this chapter the following key points have been made:

- Although the relationship between pay and performance is complex and problematic, performance pay remains of central interest to employers as a human resourcing strategy aimed at improving organisational performance.

- Performance pay continues to be significant as a variable element of reward strategies within organisations but it is increasingly recognised that there is no 'best way' and that processes have to be appropriate and relevant to organisational requirements.

- A tension between developing the individual and rewarding past achievement is ever present in approaches to rewarding contribution; a mixed model based on rewarding performance and behaviours is increasingly popular as a basis for pay progression.

- The available evidence suggests that performance pay's impact as a motivator is highly questionable. It is more likely to have a more positive impact on the high performer than the average performer and little or a negative impact on the underperformer.

- Where there is a paying for performance element in a performance management process it will become the dominant influence. It can obscure the other aims of performance review processes which are often so overloaded that, in practice, they cannot be effectively implemented.

- An emphasis on the link between pay and performance makes the employment relationship more transactional. It can lead to a focus on short-term achievements at the cost of longer-term commitment which may result in individual behaviours that employers are seeking to discourage rather than reward.

- The principle of paying people according to their individual contribution seems fair but, in practice, measurement and rating processes are full of contradictions about how to reward fairly and what constitutes good performance. It has also resulted in a widening of the earnings gap and reduced transparency about pay decisions.

- As the interpreters of individual performance pay schemes, line managers are vital to their success or failure but they need to play an active role in process design and development if they are to develop a sense of ownership. Many managers will ultimately resort to a collective approach if they feel it will reduce friction and 'get the job done'.

- HR specialists have a particularly difficult role in the development and maintenance of reward policies and practices that are linked to performance. Whilst decentralisation and shared service arrangements are diminishing their operational role and workplace presence, they are still expected to oversee PRP processes in terms of problem avoidance and ensuring a consistency of approach.

Discussion questions

1. Taking account of these summary points, why do you think performance-related pay has an enduring interest for employers despite its unproven motivational qualities?

2. Why is it frequently difficult to establish what constitutes good performance and what should be rewarded?

3. How effectively has this been achieved in work roles that you have undertaken and how could this have been improved?

4. Identify two organisational contexts where you feel that linking pay to performance would work well and two where it would not, with reasons for your suggestions.

Further reading

Specific reading material relating to the content of this chapter is provided in the text and readers can follow up the citations on a particular aspect of the discussion. A comprehensive practitioner-orientated text that provides a great deal of information on reward systems and processes is by Armstrong and Murlis (2007). For those seeking a broad overview of rewards and an analytical perspective on the topic is a new book by Perkins and White (2008). In terms of other specialist texts, a less recent book but one that considers reward strategies in significant depth is by Thorpe and Homan (2000).

9

Parting company: the strategic responsibility of exit management

David Walsh and Edward Lugsden

Learning outcomes

Having read this chapter and completed its associated activities, readers should be able to:

- Explain how management-initiated and employees' voluntary terminations of employment are critical components of human resourcing

- Appreciate the potential contribution, towards broad corporate strategy, of 'managing' all types of employment exits

- Understand that exits from employment involve not only the loss of an employee's particular capacities and their contribution to organisational knowledge but also the need for the organisation to manage consequential human resourcing and human relations issues

- Recognise that issues associated with employee departure can be especially understood in terms of human beings, individually or collectively, resenting and resisting management control

- Examine critically high commitment approaches to exit management

- Analyse the exit management practices of any organisation to assess the extent to which they are consistent with each other and are appropriate to the relevant business context

Introduction

'Parting company' refers to the severing of the relationship fully and finally between the employer and the employee. It signifies the termination of the contract of employment that hitherto has bound both parties in a work-based relationship of mutual obligation and responsibility. Both employers and employees can terminate the contract of employment, but in practice the majority of labour turnover is employee initiated. In the UK, for example, of the 4.4 million who left their jobs in 2006 (almost 1 in 5 employees) 3 million left voluntarily. The most obvious exception to this is when employers have to make large numbers of employees redundant. In 2006 this numbered well over half a million (CIPD, 2007a: 38). Either way, employers have a choice in managing such employee exits from the organisation, whether these are management initiated or employee initiated.

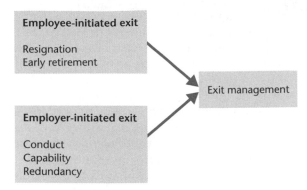

Figure 9.1 Types of employee exit

The central argument of this chapter is that the exercise of choice in how exit is managed is strategically significant to organisations. The chapter additionally serves to critically examine the main reasons for employee exit, using a framework that distinguishes between employee-initiated and employer-initiated exit as shown in Figure 9.1. This model also provides the basis for a simple classification of employee relations implications for the various forms that exit can take.

The chapter begins by outlining the concept of exit management, followed by analysis of employee-instigated and employer-instigated exit. We then examine the extent to which 'blame' for each of the main types of exit can be attached to the other party. For example, management would blame an employee it had to dismiss for gross misconduct; and an employee would lay blame against a management that had failed to deal with a grievance, leading to the employee's decision to resign. For each type of exit we also consider the advantages of using a high commitment approach to exit management.

Dismissals of employees by management can be categorised in two main ways. First, an employee might be dismissed by reason of their deficiency or failings through, for example, their conduct, performance or capability. Second, dismissal of an individual may be the outcome of a management decision to eliminate certain work activities, leading to a reduced requirement for certain jobs or posts. This process of redundancy invariably arises from a perceived business need that management decides is best served by, for example, plant closure, relocation, reorganisation or transfer of business ownership.

We should not be surprised by the relentless nature of organisational redundancies, which is closely associated with 'job turnover', as distinct from labour turnover. Job turnover encompasses the evolution or creation of new forms of work, leading to changes in job content and often to the loss of jobs. This and today's emphasis on labour market flexibility, a typical component of our global capitalist economy, have diminished employees' expectations of, and aspirations for, jobs for life. However, job turnover does not always result in a reduction in the workforce, since strategic human resourcing implies a more considered approach to workforce utilisation. For example, an advance in technology, resulting in a need for fewer workers of a particular type, may provide an opportunity to redirect existing workforce capabilities through retraining and redeployment.

At the same time, we have already identified that a reduction in the workforce can be the result of more than simple job turnover. Management's assessment of economic slowdown or the need to align the skills profile of the workforce with changing business needs can lead to decisions on plant closure, relocation, reorganisation, merger or even takeover. In essence, 'making people redundant is usually a last resort for companies trying to balance the books' (IDS StudyPlus, 2001). In turn, these decisions can all contribute to a need to manage employees' exits from the employing organisation.

It is clear from Watson's treatment of strategic human resourcing (see Chapter 1) that a consideration of the management of employee exits – 'exit management' – is as significant as all other components of the human resource function. Yet this crucial area of HRM is invariably regarded as an employee resourcing problem rather than as a key component of HR strategy. The decision by an employee to leave an organisation means more than ending or breaking their contractual arrangement. It also means withdrawal of their capacities: 'efforts, knowledge, capabilities and committed behaviours' (Chapter 1, p. 9). This is especially significant when it involves employees critical to the success of the business, as in the impending departure of the top food and cookery experts at Moddens Foods, which is threatening the company's long-term future. In these circumstances management can seek to safeguard the organisation's position by taking urgent remedial action. Furthermore, in addressing employees' immediate concerns, management might also be able to introduce measures designed to prevent or minimise staff turnover in the longer term.

Invariably, however, the occurrence of 'natural wastage' in line with a labour turnover rate that is regarded as the 'norm' for the industry means that management may need to replenish its stock of corporate capacities in terms of employee knowledge, skills and physical effort. As such, the replacement of lost human resources might be through a combination of redeployment and recruitment, supported by training or retraining.

We have already noted that it can be management that decides to dispense with the capacities offered by particular employees. If the removal of human resource capacities results from a management evaluation concerning employee shortcomings or inadequacies, it will usually follow that management will need to replenish these capacities. By contrast, in a redundancy situation management is obliged to operate in line with its deliberate reduction of the organisation's capacities. However, it does have the choice of specifying the jobs that are redundant and ideally which employees are to be dismissed and which are to be retained. Furthermore, redundancies often require organisational restructuring, entailing, for example, management's interventions in areas such as redeployment, retraining and rewards.

Our analytical framework suggests that management can take responsibility for managing all forms of employee exits in a strategically beneficial way and Figure 9.2 illustrates how data on leavers can be used to inform other key aspects of the HR system. In particular each leaver has the potential to provide valuable feedback on both their experience as an employee and their reason for leaving. Too often, however, this information is either not collected or not used to best effect in informing management's decision-making on aspects of the HR system. This is shown in the case of FleetBoston Financial (see Exhibit 9.2), which also raises important issues about the validity of data gathered from departing employees.

Sound analysis of data on leavers might identify possible shortcomings in HR systems and practice. For example, ineffective recruitment and selection processes

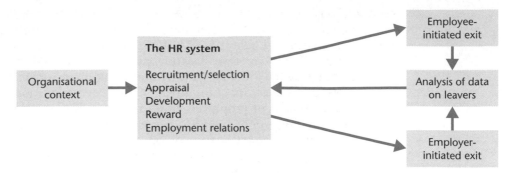

Figure 9.2 **Linkages between employee exit and the HR system**

could lead to unsuitable employees either resigning or being dismissed. As well as the time, cost and effort of replacing such employees this situation can also have serious consequences for the business due to a loss of productive capacity. It follows that unless recruitment and selection procedures are reviewed the likelihood is that poor selection decisions will continue to be made.

It could be, of course, that a problem of an employee's capability to carry out their job may be linked to the quality and level of training; or that it is unsatisfactory rewards that may convince some staff to resign. All of these examples of HR systems and practice illustrate that it is management that bears considerable responsibility for employee exits and highlight the need to take a strategic approach to the issue of exit management.

In addition to considering the loss of employees' productive 'capacities' we need to recognise that in severing the employment relationship emotions and motives almost inevitably come to the fore. As Watson reminds us, 'Human resources are essentially problematic because they are supplied by human beings' (Chapter 1, p. 12) but, as we shall see later, dismissal by management (and perhaps the loss of a person's livelihood, status and routine) may be especially traumatic for the employee, inviting feelings of rancour against the company. Even when an employee determines to leave of their own choice they may well be touched with feelings of bitterness or anger about the reasons that 'pushed' them towards that decision. From this perspective the *voluntary* nature of the decision can appear less recognisable to the leaver. As such, we may view staff turnover rates not only as a cost to the business, but also as a broad indication of employee resentment and an expression of resistance against the employing organisation.

These human relations issues are clearly a factor in managing the exiting process, but not only with regard to the departing employees. All forms of exiting can potentially have an adverse impact on *remaining* staff in terms of their morale and job satisfaction. This is particularly relevant in the case of redundancies and any corresponding occurrence of 'survivor syndrome'. This is where remaining employees experience feelings of guilt because co-workers were chosen for redundancy and not them; as well as a sense of loss over the departure of their colleagues (Brockner, 1992; Doherty and Horstead, 1995, cited by Redman and Wilkinson, 2006: 359). It may also mean increased levels of job insecurity as aspects of their psychological contract come under threat (Rousseau, 1995).

From a human resourcing perspective it is important, therefore, that attention is paid to employee reactions and attitudes if management is to secure the full contributions of its workforce. As Watson notes (Chapter 1), 'Strategic human resourcing . . . has to involve itself in such matters as trust building and the seeking of . . . "committed behaviours".' The individual worker, as a seller of labour services in a capitalist economy, has the right to sever the employment relationship and therefore take the initiative in leaving the employing organisation. However, it is in losing one's job involuntarily that the essence of modern capitalism is illustrated. Although in propitious times the employment relationship may be generally calm, cooperative and acquiescent, when a business decision requires dismissals, because of redundancy or on the grounds of employee deficiencies (conduct or capability), human resources are removed in much the same way as any other factor of production. Management has the right to manage and therefore to dispose of human resources as and when it feels it necessary. This right to manage is made easier when the balance of power lies clearly with management. Even so, management is obliged to conform to a legal definition or interpretation of 'reasonable' standards of management conduct in its handling of exit processes. In many economies to transgress is to invite litigation.

With regard to dismissal related to redundancy, and using an example from the UK brewing industry (Exhibit 9.1), the closure of Scottish & Newcastle's 148-year-old brewery illustrates management's right to manage, the nature of the capitalist enterprise and a climate for collective employee resistance expressed as a 'coalition of interest'. Immediate reactions to the loss of 170 jobs are typically hostile and in such a situation management may see the need to manage the exit process cooperatively with, for example, the employees' trade union. Moreover, a choice for management is to manage the exit process itself sensitively and with care, because it makes business sense to minimise employee opposition and resistance and to maintain goodwill with retained (i.e. 'surviving') employees in other parts of the group. An alternative option for management would be to manage these exit processes in a manner that is not too concerned with retaining goodwill and trust because of, say, a docile workforce and where the balance of power lies with management.

Exhibit 9.1

Redundancy through closure

Tony Froggatt accelerated his restructuring of Scottish & Newcastle yesterday with the announcement that its landmark Fountainbridge brewery in the centre of Edinburgh was to close in December with the loss of 170 jobs. The decision to streamline its core UK business comes amid speculation that S&N could be a candidate for a takeover or a merger. The reluctant decision to sell the site of S&N's home-town brewery has underlined the pragmatic sense of urgency that Mr Froggatt has sought to bring to the company after taking over as chief executive last year.

A plan to continue production of some S&N beers elsewhere in Edinburgh was not enough to defuse angry criticism. One Transport and General Workers' Union representative called the closure an 'absolute outrage' motivated by 'sheer corporate greed'. Camra, the real ale lobbyist, said it was 'concerned' for the future of S&N's McEwan's 80/- and 70/- ales, questioning the company's past commitment to keeping breweries open.

John Dunsmore, chairman and managing director of Scottish Courage, S&N's UK beer business, said unit production costs at Fountainbridge had become twice the level of the brewer's lowest-cost operation at Tadcaster, North Yorkshire. Its location in an increasingly residential part of Edinburgh's city centre had left it uncompetitive. 'You wouldn't put it there today', said Mr Dunsmore.

Edinburgh property experts suggested that the 10-acre Fountainbridge site – which includes a unique stretch of canal frontage – could command between £40 million and £75 million.

Mr Dunsmore would not comment on plans for the Tyne Brewery in Newcastle, which produces Newcastle Brown Ale. 'We've not come to decisions on what we're doing', he said of the Tyneside brewery. 'We're just not commenting on any speculation.'

Neither would Federation Brewery in Gateshead comment on suggestions that it might brew Newcastle Brown Ale should the Tyne brewery be closed.

S&N estimated that closing the brewery at Fountainbridge would save £10m a year. It said it would cost £25 million to achieve these savings, but this sum would be offset by site sale proceeds. Alex Oldroyd, an analyst at Morgan Stanley, was unimpressed by the expected savings. She said S&N had been seen as a 'restructuring story', adding: 'Here they have announced a major part of it and they have only given us £10m cost savings.'

Source: 'S&N to close its landmark Edinburgh brewery', The *Financial Times*, 18 February 2004

It can be interpreted that the decision by Scottish & Newcastle to close its Fountainbridge brewery has been driven by pragmatism born of economic and financial reasons, fuelled by takeover speculation. In such circumstances we should not be surprised if we learn that human resourcing ramifications and considerations of 'exit management' are not uppermost in the minds of the group's senior decision-makers. A tradition of nearly 15 decades of production at the one plant would appear to form only a minor part of their thinking, which seems dominated by their assessment of the dynamic imperatives of a globally competitive product market. However, this revelation does not invalidate our hypothesis that effective exit management can play a strategic role in a corporation's long-term success. As such, we need to examine the issues arising from the ending of the employment relationship – as well as the different ways in which that relationship may end. Whether it is the employer or the employee who takes the initiative in 'parting company', we need to consider how the organisation manages the exit process and its consequences. If at all possible, organisations need to have in place a strategic approach to managing and controlling exits from employment, whatever the type, and bearing in mind the likely ramifications and repercussions of getting it wrong. Ideally, organisations need to manage the process so as to minimise conflict and promote the success of the concern.

We argue that a high commitment HR strategy, which subscribes to and reinforces a 'best practice' HR model, is probably the preferred approach in managing employment exits. In turn this requires an investment in time and management skills, as well as an appreciation of human values and ethical choice. Furthermore, we will need to consider critically the possibilities or outcomes offered by management's adoption of such an approach towards the various forms of exit. Are there not features inherent to the termination of the employment relationship that severely limit the extent to which high commitment can go hand-in-hand with exit management? Can such an approach actually do any more than paper over, rather than repair, any cracks? In light of the deep-seated conflicts of interest and tensions that are fundamental, paradoxically, to both the contract of employment and its termination, can sensitive and ethical measures achieve substantially more than the 'hire and fire' of the low commitment school? We cannot ignore, therefore, the existence of a low commitment approach. This tends to abide by the legal minima set by the state. Sometimes, however, it might not even do that: where, for example, management makes a conscious decision on pragmatic grounds to summarily terminate someone's employment and is prepared to offer that individual a financial settlement.

Employee-initiated termination of employment

Since a voluntary termination of employment is usually initiated by the employee, its occurrence might not be foreseen by management and can therefore have a particularly disruptive effect (ACAS, 2006). It is also likely to be unpredictable in terms of the types of skilled worker and actual *capacities* that might be lost to the organisation. In this sense human resource planning can be a somewhat ill-equipped management tool since such exits are unplanned (by management, at least) and so difficult to anticipate. However, using historical labour turnover data, management may be capable of making fairly accurate predictions in terms of anticipating *numbers* of voluntary leavers. Hence, extrapolations of labour turnover and staff survival rates can make this aspect of human resource planning relatively straightforward. Planners may also be guided by the 'norm' for their industrial sector. The median rate for call centres, for example, is 25 per cent. The highest rate of 32 per cent is in the hotel, catering and leisure industries. By comparison, central and local government have rates at less than 15 per cent, similar to that for many specialist manufacturing companies (CIPD, 2007a). We need to recognise, however, that such headline turnover figures can mask the significance of losing those employees that are critical to the success of the organisation. For example, if an acute hospital loses a number of orthopaedic surgeons in a short period of time it will be unable to meet client demand. Waiting lists will lengthen and ultimately patients and money may go elsewhere, with the result that the jobs of a wide range of staff will come under threat.

In reaching the decision to leave the organisation many employees will leave quite amicably, by mutual consent, some to move on to 'better things'. Others will leave 'voluntarily' on reaching the requisite retirement age. Though the specified age can vary between employers and across nations, most employees regard retirement, which is usually covered in their terms and conditions of employment, as an inevitable outcome. They may find the event tinged with sadness, even trepidation, but most employees leave with good grace, particularly those who are granted early retirement on favourable terms.

However, there will always be situations where employees will leave, or threaten to leave, because of an acrimonious breakdown in the employment relationship. This could be, for example, when an employee, whose grievance (on pay, unfair treatment, promotion etc.) has not been addressed, leaves under protest. This can be interpreted as a response to the company's failure to act, whether through oversight or more deliberate omission. In some instances the employee may feel justified in claiming 'constructive dismissal' at an employment tribunal, on the grounds that it has been management's unreasonable behaviour that has forced their departure. The rancour resulting from such episodes, if not dealt with by management, may have an adverse impact on the contribution of the remaining workforce.

Figure 9.3 encapsulates the essential dynamics at work when an employee decides to leave their employing organisation. In the same way that an employer can initiate an employee's termination on the basis of laying blame or not, an employee can hold their employer responsible for their decision to leave. Where an attribution of blame is levelled at the employer, we suggest that an employee chooses (either explicitly or implicitly) to 'disengage' from the relationship. This option entails a psychological as well as a physical departure. In this way, the parting is likely to be most unpleasant or at the very least marked by a degree of ill-feeling. The most obvious occurrences are when an employee perceives the 'cause' of their leaving as being their employer's deficiencies. If management persists in unjust or unacceptable treatment (acting 'by commission'); or fails to attend to a grievance (by deliberate omission); or simply appears oblivious to unsatisfactory conditions of work (through oversight or implicit omission), then the employee will most probably feel justified in showing their resentment and opposition by severing the employment relationship. In especially grave circumstances the employee may perceive that they are obliged to leave: that they have no alternative. They may feel that the behaviour of management or that of fellow employees, whose respective conducts are ultimately the employer's responsibility, has given them little option but to exit their work situation. In turn they may reason that they are fully entitled to claim 'constructive dismissal' on the basis

Employer deficiency		No employer deficiency	
'disengagement' *(blame)*	'moving on' *(no blame)*	'disengagement' *(blame)*	'moving on' *(no blame)*
Examples:	*Examples:*	*Examples:*	*Examples:*
Employer's behaviour by:	Change of career	Employer unable to grant employee's request for:	Retirement
omission or commission (including constructive dismissal)	Promotion outside the organisation	• part-time working • deferred retirement • a reduced workload	Family requirements
Outcome: ↓ Parting company with *ill-feeling*	Outcome: ↓ Parting company *on good terms*	Outcome: ↓ Parting company with *ill-feeling*	Outcome: ↓ Parting company *on good terms*

Figure 9.3 **Employee-initiated termination of employment (resignations)**

257

that the circumstances are so intolerable that they are leaving 'under duress'. In so doing, the employee is indicating that, rather than leaving voluntarily, it is management that has to take responsibility for their departure. In this sense, an employment tribunal may conclude that the termination of employment is *de facto* 'employer-initiated'.

This framework permits us to recognise that, even when it is the individual (and not management) who has instigated the departure, 'blame' and 'ill-feeling' on the part of the employee are also possible outcomes. This resentment can build from the view, for example, that management is unable to accommodate an employee's request for a change of hours or an extended contract. Management has not initiated this development but, in being seen as not responding helpfully or in refusing to act, it can be blamed for the individual 'having to leave'.

A high commitment approach to employee-initiated exits

It is difficult to envisage how management can fruitfully prevent such negative sentiments and steer the inherent tensions associated with the process of exiting towards the 'goodwill' that is a hallmark of *high commitment* employment relations. How can it bring about the harmony typically associated with the 'no-blame' scenarios, in which employees perceive that they are not so much 'pushed' by factors from within the organisation as 'pulled' by external factors? Even so, in these 'no-blame' circumstances it is still possible for the company to be comparatively deficient. For example, it may not provide the kind of career opportunity obtainable elsewhere. However, if the employee is enthusiastic about 'moving on', then the parting is more likely to be 'on good terms', especially if the company has a policy of investing in an individual's future 'employability'. Similarly, when the reason for leaving is very much outside the company's control, as in the individual's desire to retire or to look after family members, management can be perhaps more confident in safeguarding goodwill.

In aspiring to adopt a *high commitment* approach, management will need to demonstrate that it can deal fairly, consistently and sensitively in relation to any of the situations illustrated in Figure 9.3. This is because current staff may well form a judgement on management's response when an employee has opted to leave the organisation. Has management shown its consideration of the impact on remaining staff by, for example, seeking to provide cover for the vacated post? How is management tackling any fundamental expressions of discontent associated with the individual's decision to leave? In dealing constructively with such issues management could be seen to be acknowledging that the loss of particular human resource *capacities* is inextricably bound up with less tangible qualities such as employee *commitment*. A high commitment approach, following Watson (see Chapter 1), will engage with both dimensions, based on the supposition that such an investment will be recouped in the more effective contribution of employees towards broad corporate objectives in the long term. Such a position will also endeavour to do more than simply break a 'vicious circle' of low morale, which would cause other workers to leave and thus increase the dissatisfaction of those who remain (ACAS, 2006). It will seek to move beyond this by adopting an appropriate response to voluntary turnover that helps build morale and hence increases worker commitment.

However, our analysis provokes serious doubts about the possibility of securing such high commitment at the very point at which employees are 'parting company' with their employing organisation. First, by definition, this approach to exit management might be seen as largely irrelevant to the departing employee, since the severing of the employment relationship signifies an end to the mutual self-interest that has bound both parties. Just as dismissal implies that the employer has reached a judgement that the employee has no further value to the business, in relation to voluntary termination the employee has reached a conclusion about working for the employer and decided to withdraw their capacities, including any commitment that they might have offered. On the other hand, were both parties to 'part on good terms', there is the basis for a mutually agreed return to employment at a later date, should this possibility arise. More prosaically, from an employee's viewpoint 'a tactfully worded resignation letter with friendly goodbyes to all the right people, however insincere, is likely to make a better impression than a two-fingered salute as you head out of the door' (Donkin, 2003).

The prime focus for a high commitment approach to exit management inevitably turns, therefore, to its impact on those employees who remain employed by the organisation. It is their contributions that remain fundamental to the performance of the firm. As such, anything that diminishes or detracts from the current employees' effectiveness and efficiency is critical to strategic human resourcing. We have established that issues of blame, resentment and resistance are likely to accompany most dismissals and departures, whether or not these are management or employee initiated. The extent to which these recriminations affect and are felt by remaining staff is, therefore, of significance in a high commitment approach to exit management – as is their impact on potential new recruits. A company that needs to replenish its human resource capacities from outside the organisation can find its efforts hampered by an unfavourable reputation for its management of staff. Cases of unfair treatment of employees or judgements of their unfair dismissal, which enter the public arena, are perceived as damaging to the employer, especially one seeking to recruit in a competitive labour market.

It should now be very clear that the process of 'parting company' presents 'high commitment' management with a huge challenge, in view of the ill-feeling and acrimony that can accompany such events. However, the litany of professional advice on offer seems to convey a view that an emphasis on cooperation and shared interests is possible, even for the most testing of situations.

We have indicated our view that from a management perspective it is helpful to appreciate that where the employee voluntarily leaves the organisation, the individual has made a decision to sever the contract of employment that has formally regulated their mutual work relationship with the employer. We have also observed that, from a more subjective viewpoint, it is likely that this decision has involved and given rise to a mixture of emotions and feelings linked to a multiplicity of purposes and causes. Yet we ought not oversimplify this last point, bearing in mind our recognition of the existence of more dispassionate types of worker characterised by an instrumental orientation to work, including the incessantly mobile 'portfolio' careerist. These are more likely to have a calculative attitude towards the employer; and can be expected to be drawn towards rival organisations that are more competitive in the relevant labour market. This is especially so for employees who are confident they possess competences that are in demand. A CIPD survey suggested that staff retention problems in the UK 'are most noticeable in the categories of staff who could work anywhere and thus could easily find other jobs' (CIPD, 2003b: 28). The survey also identifies 'movers and users' who are quite prepared to leave a company in order to progress elsewhere (p. 30).

However, where the employer and other firms are largely comparable in the rewards they offer, we ought not to underrate the influence of *inertia* on the individual. Objectively speaking, the effort required to make a 'fresh start' elsewhere invariably exceeds the impetus needed by the individual simply to instigate a 'parting of the ways'. The 'intention to quit' can be interpreted as a cognitive rather than a physical 'disengagement strategy'. In turn, it 'instigates tensions concerning finding another job and giving up present responsibilities and relationships with co-workers' (Begley and Thomas, 1998: 4). The prospect of completing applications, attending interviews and adjusting to a new regime can all weaken the appeal of a new employer. In other words, the 'pull' of a more attractive position elsewhere or the need to 'try something new' does not necessarily culminate in an employee's departure. Indeed, relatively satisfied employees may routinely scan job advertisements without ever moving on to a 'focused search' or 'contacting prospective employers' (Steel, 2002).

It is for this reason that management can most usefully explore those factors that cause exit behaviour and 'push' employees away from the organisation. For leavers with fewer than six months' service the CIPD survey (2003b: 30) identified the significance of a mismatch between employees' initial expectations and what they then experienced. For those leavers of longer service it is more likely that other sources of work dissatisfaction have arisen or occurred. Whatever the cause, it is through an appreciation that leaving employment voluntarily is the outcome of a decision-making process, however unaware of this the employee may be, that exit management can be best applied. Employees can respond in several ways. They might voice their concerns and seek to improve their conditions. They might decide to do nothing and to accept their plight. They may 'disengage' psychologically and neglect their duties and reduce effort. Or, they may decide to leave the organisation (Zhou and George, 2001). Whichever of these responses applies (and they can also manifest as a combination or a progression), a high commitment approach to exit management would seek to 'connect' with employees by encouraging an open dialogue and responding to any expressions of discontent. In displaying concern, as well as fairness, management is seeking to minimise staff turnover. Moreover, in the event of an employee's decision to leave, management is better placed to defuse any acrimony and help ensure that the departure is 'on good terms' and without the attribution of blame.

However, the model we are proposing requires that management does more than attend to the seeds of employee discontent. The employee's decision to leave or stay can also be affected by:

- there being an available and acceptable alternative to their present employment and the individual's thoughts as to its value, and
- the ease with which the individual can move to another job by having those attributes and transferable skills attractive to a new employer.

By identifying both 'pull' and 'push' factors and their interdependence, we can investigate more than why dissatisfied workers might leave. We can also start to appreciate why dissatisfied workers might want to stay and why relatively satisfied workers might decide to leave.

The influence of moderating factors can help explain these outcomes (Beard, 2003). For example, dissatisfied workers may decide to stay if there is a lack of viable alternatives open to them. This might be because of a generally depressed labour market or because the employee does not have the necessary competences to move to another employer. On the other hand, workers who possess attributes considered attractive to recruiting employers and are on the lookout for new opportunities are more likely to find leaving their current employment an easier option.

For the most part, though, managements are mainly concerned with identifying those factors that prompt employees to leave, irrespective of the latter's employability elsewhere, which is perceived as more outside the employer's control. However, it is a company's investment in training and development (a crucial feature of a high commitment approach) that ironically can promote a higher level of staff turnover. To counter this outcome, a firm could deliberately restrict its training to non-transferable skills, thus minimising employees' marketability to other employers. At the same time, however, it would also need to establish a meaningful promotional or developmental structure to avoid sowing its own seeds of staff discontent. This is not easy, especially when the number of staff that are eligible for internal promotion and development opportunities greatly exceeds the posts available.

At the very least we would expect a high commitment approach to exit management to identify and deal with those reasons for labour turnover that are levelled against the company and that attract employer blame. These can be categorised (see Figure 9.3) as the result of either *employer deficiency* or *no employer deficiency*, related to the employer's inability to grant an employee's request for a change in working conditions. The most common of these factors for the UK are 'lack of development opportunities' (39 per cent) and 'level of pay' (39 per cent) (CIPD, 2007a). Other prominent 'blame' issues include 'working hours' (12 per cent), 'level of workload' (11 per cent), 'stress of the job' (14 per cent) and 'lack of support from line managers' (16 per cent). However, 'change of career' (52 per cent) and 'promotion outside the organisation' (47 per cent) figure more strongly and might reasonably be connected more to a 'no blame' situation in spite of an *employer deficiency* in not offering these opportunities. The implication is that the workforce is especially responsive to opportunities beckoning elsewhere and not overly committed to staying with a single employer. On the *no employer deficiency* side of Figure 9.3 'retirement' (27 per cent) and 'leaving to have or look after children' (18 per cent) are also prominent in the CIPD survey (2007a: 33).

In spite of the robust arguments above, the actual benefits for management of taking a proactive stance on curbing voluntary labour turnover are open to debate, acknowledging the view that the replacement of leavers by 'new blood' can bring fresh energy to a place of work. However, cost savings on minimising labour turnover are potentially very significant. The average cost of labour turnover for the UK in 2007 was £7,750 and £11,000 for managers (CIPD, 2007a).

Yet, Taylor reflects that the true costs associated with the departure of an individual are likely to be much higher:

> When management time is taken into account, as well as time spent by the new recruit being inducted and trained, and direct recruitment costs, the total can easily amount to half of a year's salary. More sophisticated approaches also add in opportunity costs . . . and account for the fact that new recruits take time to operate at full effectiveness.

(CIPD, 2004: 25)

Despite such compelling evidence, Taylor suggests that most organisations 'are not seeking to reduce their labour turnover in a systematic or strategic way', but in 'an informal and relatively perfunctory manner without any great expectation that turnover can be brought down significantly in the future' (2004: 24). One reason for this is that, as this CIPD survey makes clear, the vast majority of UK organisations do not attempt to calculate the costs of voluntary resignations. Indeed most organisations seem wholly unaware 'of just how significant a saving they could make, were they to reduce turnover levels by a few percentage points' (2004: 24).

We suggest that only by adopting the type of all-embracing model we have outlined can a management effectively tackle the issues associated with employee-initiated exits. However, the basis for management being equipped to resolve such issues has to be its accurate collection of valid information, notably the reasons for employees leaving. In the CIPD annual survey of 2007, 9 in 10 of the 800 organisations use exit interviews and 1 in 4 also relies on word of mouth. The latter method suffers from not being systematic and relying on hearsay. To this end it is generally unreliable and not an entirely safe foundation for management action. Conversely, its inclination towards informality may have the merit of occasionally gaining privileged access to an employee's actual complaints and feelings. Whatever approach is taken to collecting and analysing labour turnover data, 'organisations are still unlikely to drill down to uncover the level of turnover among their identified high-performing staff' (CIPD, 2007a: 32).

By contrast, the exit interview seems a more structured and methodical technique for gaining relevant information. While its success undoubtedly relies on the interviewer's interpersonal skills, it would appear to offer an open and relevant opportunity for impending leavers to explain the reasons behind their imminent departure. It appears to provide a straightforward forum for getting to know why a member of staff is leaving. The justification is that a departing employee with no remaining vested interest 'will be more candid than one who is still in place' (Donkin, 2003). Unfortunately, this argument is flawed. The exit interview is much more likely to result in individuals offering reasons or motives that are considered socially acceptable, bearing little relationship to what they are thinking (Nalbantian *et al.*, 2003). As Donkin (2003) notes, the employee does not want to burn bridges or create bad feeling. Indeed, Taylor reminds us that the exit interview has long been considered to be a highly unreliable tool to use: 'The truth is that people lie in exit interviews' (CIPD, 2003b). They are unwilling to criticise the company or its managers when it is much easier to offer a safe, innocuous explanation that will minimise ill-feeling and perhaps safeguard a good reference.

Exhibit 9.2

The fallibility of exit interviews

FleetBoston Financial, a regional bank in the US with more than 40,000 employees, carried out an employee survey five years ago to find out why people were leaving in large numbers. Its employee turnover rate was twice the industry average.

Exit interviews had suggested that excessive workloads and poor pay rates were causing people to leave.

The company increased its pay rates and brought in policies designed to help people cope with stress but people were still leaving. It then took a deeper look at turnover patterns over a period of time and found that a series of factors was involved, of differing degrees of importance. Pay levels were found to have the weakest impact on employee turnover.

The biggest source of retention was promotion. Other factors were the transfer of employees from hourly pay rates to salaried positions and giving staff the opportunity to change jobs frequently. Most people who left had been in the same job for more than two years. People were also more likely to leave if they lost a good manager.

This new information persuaded the company to do its utmost to keep good managers, to focus on career development and opportunities for good employees and to provide career streams into salaried posts. The company estimated that the measures saved it $50m a year.

Surely such management policies are a matter of best practice? Job variation is a classic way of avoiding staleness and who does not warm to a good boss? The authors insist, however, that they are not pointing to best practice.

Source: extract from 'How to learn a lesson from the leavers' by Richard Donkin, *The Financial Times*, 11 September 2003

The example above raises serious questions about exit interviews and suggests that their inadequacy should disqualify them from being the basis for an exit management or retention strategy. The exit process is inherently wrought with issues of 'cancellation': the cessation of the employment relationship. Even when the interviewer is a 'neutral' from the HR function and a good listener who shows empathy, the employee is perhaps justified in questioning management's motives in this rather contrived reaction to a resignation. Furthermore, the interviewee has no obvious vested interest in being candid when disclosing the reasons for 'parting company'. The leavers at FleetBoston Financial indicated through their exit interviews that poor pay was an issue. Had the company known that pay was in truth a very weak factor behind staff turnover, it might have saved on the amount spent on increasing pay. Similarly, had it known what the 'real issues' were, it would have recouped the annual savings of $50 million much earlier. The lesson is that an essential, if not sufficient, condition of 'managing' employee-initiated turnover is to obtain reliable data and to interpret them accurately. For FleetBoston this meant 'a deeper look at turnover patterns' and responding astutely to its analysis.

Notwithstanding this telling example, the challenge for management is to adopt a methodology that can elicit the 'truth' *from* or *about* its leavers. The former is more likely if an open and trusting employment relationship exists. However, since the capitalistic relationship is essentially a mutually exploitative one, misgivings are likely to persist no matter what method is used. The choice of a confidential questionnaire to leavers *after* they have resigned is also likely to founder, unless a way can be devised that provides a motive for the respondent to complete the survey and to do so honestly. As this is probably unlikely, an alternative approach is to conduct a positivist analysis of employees' data, which seeks to infer 'reasons' from the patterns of their leaving. Critics of this approach could contend that this implies that management thinks it knows its workers better than they do themselves, because it presumes that behaviour patterns are more significant indicators than the motives ('reasons') themselves. It also follows that patterns are less discernible when applied to a varied or small number of leavers.

It can be further argued that voluntary terminations of employment are by and large unanticipated events that management can at best only attempt to predict. Paradoxically, however, certain management-initiated terminations can also be unanticipated, since dismissals as a result of indiscipline and lack of capability, or aptitude, are essentially unplanned events. Moreover, we can suggest other conceptual links between the voluntary and involuntary forms of job separation. In the voluntary form (resignation) it is the employee that is leaving, whereas in the involuntary form (dismissal) the employer has decided to 'leave' the employee by discharging him or her. Finally, both forms of job separation can be incorporated in the concept of 'employee churning', which is the result of 'a mismatch in skills and/or expectations held by the employer and/or employee' (Weir, 2003). Having drawn attention to certain points of interconnection between these two sources of 'parting company', we now direct our attention to an analysis of *management-initiated* employee terminations.

Management-initiated termination of employment (dismissal)

Under UK employment law all terminations by the employer are categorised as 'dismissals' and we use the term in a similar way, in that it is not intended to be pejorative. Dismissals in themselves are not necessarily wrongful (from a breach of contract) or unfair. However, to the extent to which there is an emphasis on 'blame' levelled against the employee by the employer, there would appear, *prima facie*, to be significant limitations to managing this form of exit by means of a high commitment approach. As mentioned previously, management-initiated termination can be usefully looked at under two main headings:

1. resulting from *employee deficiency*, and

2. resulting from *no employee deficiency*, typically as a consequence of a management decision to initiate redundancy action.

The potential dynamics of these distinctive actions are outlined in Figure 9.4, identifying the additional possibility in each case of 'no blame' being attached to the leaver, which in theory permits their 'parting company' to be amicable.

Employee deficiency		Redundancy	
'exclusion' (blame)	'release' (no blame)	'exclusion' (blame)	'release' (no blame)
Examples: Discipline: • gross misconduct • persistent complaints	*Examples:* Capability Long-term sickness	*Examples:* Selection criteria: • attendance record • disciplinary record • job performance	*Examples:* Short service Voluntary
Outcome: ↓ Parting company with *ill-feeling*	Outcome: ↓ Parting company *on good terms*	Outcome: ↓ Parting company with *ill-feeling*	Outcome: ↓ Parting company *on good terms*

Figure 9.4 Management-initiated termination of employment (dismissals)

Employee deficiency

Management's assessment that an employee should be dismissed can be based on an employee's behaviour problems (conduct) or issues relating to an employee's performance (capability). While both can ultimately lead to dismissal, we make a distinction between how management needs to handle each type of problem, as can be observed from Figure 9.4. The former is governed by the assignment of blame. By contrast, the latter is based on a management decision that the employee lacks the ability to undertake the tasks expected by the employer. No blame is attached to the employee, as it would not be considered fair to expect someone to perform above their innate capacities. However, this simple, 'blame-free' view would be altered were the employee's lack of ability to be perceived, rightly or wrongly, as an outcome of their lack of motivation or application.

Rollinson and Dundon (2007) identify three different managerial approaches to discipline at work; punishment, deterrence and rehabilitation. While there is a tendency among some managers to equate discipline at work with punishment, which may as a result serve as a deterrent to others, a human resourcing perspective would adopt a rehabilitative or 'corrective' approach towards both conduct and capability problems. This has the intention of providing the employee with an opportunity of improving and ultimately benefiting the organisation. However, the 'correction' of *gross misconduct* (as in fighting, stealing or sabotage), or *repetitive misconduct* (as in lateness, insubordination or disobedience), may ultimately result in the *exclusion* of the employee – and with blame attached to that individual. By contrast, management's lack of success in trying to remedy an employee's *incapability* to perform certain tasks satisfactorily may ultimately result in the *release* of the employee – and with no blame attached. However, situations might arise in which an employee is seen to ignore management's request, encouragement and support to improve, in which case the termination is more in the nature of *exclusion* – and with blame attached as in dismissals for misconduct.

The significance of whether or not blame is attached to the dismissed individual relates to the *messages* that management wishes to convey to its workforce, in pursuit of the control that it seeks to maintain over that workforce.

With regard to *misconduct*, the dismissal declares management's view on standards of behaviour and that the employee is responsible for meeting them. It also demonstrates management's position on failure to meet such standards, and that dismissal is an appropriate outcome for an employee who is shown to be culpable of a serious enough misdemeanour. The apportionment of blame against that employee is important if management is to ensure the exclusion of the individual, uphold its right to dismiss future transgressors and sustain its workers' adherence to the organisation's rules of conduct.

By contrast, dismissal on the grounds of *capability* is a decision that should ideally be seen as in the interests of both the organisation and the employee who, in spite of remedial training and support, has shown an inability to do the tasks that they are paid to undertake. By taking this corrective approach management can show other staff that the company has undertaken all steps to assist the employee's work performance. It seems to be saying that, unfortunately, through no fault of either party it has been necessary to 'part company'. This style of presentation depicts management as caring and is designed to ensure no stigma is attached to the hapless individual. Increasingly, organisations find that a 'probationary period' provides a practical and explicit mechanism for implementing the exit process for those who fall short of their expected performance.

A high commitment approach to discipline and capability dismissal

We have already stated that the dismissal of an employee on disciplinary grounds is an enforced separation or 'exclusion' by management from the employing organisation. Under most circumstances this is likely to lead to an acrimonious departure and might, therefore, seem to run counter to a high commitment exit management strategy. However, we have also noted that such a strategy will need to direct its attention to the effects on the remaining staff. Put simply, it is quite feasible that the eviction of the 'bad apple' from the workplace may come as a welcome relief to those who had to suffer their misdeeds. Furthermore, staff are likely to feel reassured if management's conduct of the disciplinary process is perceived as consistent, fair and reasonable. Such a correctly managed process should ensure that dismissals would only occur when they are warranted and that lesser transgressions will be dealt with proportionately, through an oral or a written warning. This will encourage staff to accept that management can be trusted to carry out its own judicial process. This is important for management, since an employment relationship based on trust would appear to be an essential basis for an employee to 'buy in' to management's appeal for high commitment. Conversely, any 'perceived unfairness may create resentment and militate against compliance' (Farnham, 2000: 422).

With this in mind, management is advised to demonstrate its adherence to the principles of 'natural justice' when reaching its 'verdict' and dispensing its 'sentence'. This is especially so because it is the same management that is responsible for overseeing the company's rules and regulations, which are drawn up to primarily protect management's interests over those of its employees. Management must convince employees, therefore, that the disciplinary process is in safe hands: that it adheres to the checks and balances that will ensure that any dismissal is a fair and sensible outcome. Employees must perceive that their rights are safe-guarded by the principles and practice of natural justice, which are governed by a procedure that is conducted fairly. In practical terms, all managers engaged in action that might culminate in a dismissal should, in order to allay employees' anxieties and meet their expectations, conform to a number of essential features, as follows.

It stands to reason that employees will expect management to notify the person concerned of the complaints against them, but that no specific allegation of a disciplinary breach should be made unless a *prima facie* case has been established from a thorough preliminary investigation. Also, employees will consider it fair only if the individual is given a full opportunity to put their side of the story at an impartial hearing. However, this meeting would appear to be less than impartial unless the individual is encouraged to be accompanied. This is in management's interests, as attending management's disciplinary hearing unaccompanied could be easily interpreted as tantamount to victimisation. Yet, no matter how commendable the fairness of the process, employees' opinions are likely to be affected most by their perception of whether or not the penalty (e.g. dismissal) corresponds to the offence, taking into account any extenuating factors. Employees' suspicions of persecution or unfair treatment by management will effectively destroy the trust required for a high commitment approach, even if, for example, an appeal to a more senior level of management leads to a change of decision in favour of the individual.

It can be argued that in a high commitment approach to disciplinary dismissals it is an essential but insufficient condition that management practises the principles of natural justice. It is essential since employees' perceptions on management's treatment of the person dismissed will impinge on their view as to whether management can be trusted or not. It is insufficient because, when it comes down to it, management is following a structure and process that ultimately assigns to it the roles of prosecutor, jury and judge. In so far as a management seeks to depict itself as an impartial arbiter by, for example, adopting a reverential attention to natural justice and procedural correctness, employees might just accept this at face value. However, the perennial issue for employee relations professionals is the problems that line managers seem to have with the discipline process. According to Gennard and Judge (2005: 272) many managers believe that the disciplinary process is 'cumbersome and ineffective'. As a consequence, a system that is designed to bring consistency and fairness may in effect be carried out in an inept, haphazard or precipitate way, which might not only damage any goodwill, but also leave the company open to litigation over the employee's dismissal.

It would appear that it might be easier to avoid this unwelcome pattern of events in those instances where an employee is delivering a less than adequate performance as a result of 'incapability': not having the ability to do the job properly (Gennard and Judge, 2005: 291). Figure 9.4 indicates that no blame need be attributed to this form of employee deficiency. An individual simply lacks the inherent ability required to carry out their work. Unfortunately, it would appear that when it comes to poor performers, it is 'natural that managers *assume* that the blame for such a situation lies with the employee: the employee is the problem and the only satisfactory way of dealing with the problem is to dismiss the "useless" worker' (Lewis *et al.*, 2003: 302).

The inclination might be to launch into a formal disciplinary process, whereas this situation gives management an opportunity to present a positive and supportive stance in helping an employee remedy such poor performance (Gennard and Judge, 2005: 291). A careful analysis of the evidence may determine that the best way forward will be the provision of training and advice. In return, the employee is required to improve and meet performance standards. With this approach, dismissal would only occur after it is quite clear that, even after appropriate support, the employee is still not going to reach the standards required within the expected time-scale. Yet, can this eventual dismissal be successfully 'packaged' as a mutually beneficial parting of the ways, devoid of any blame? Perhaps this can be claimed if both sides have made an honest effort to resolve the employee's performance problem, but genuine incapability renders this unattainable. Furthermore, remaining staff are likely to have seen and understood this remedial process and accepted its outcome, especially if they think they have been 'carrying a passenger' who would be better off elsewhere. We might conclude, therefore, that dismissal for incapability can indeed produce a positive response from the workforce, essential for its high commitment.

However, we must view this with caution. The dismissed employee may feel stigmatised by the label accorded them after their failure to improve, in spite of management's constructive role. Ultimately, the employee is conforming to management's stereotype of being 'useless' and of no further value to the employer. Furthermore, it is quite feasible that the remaining workers may still view dismissal as an ill-judged decision, especially if they perceive that redeployment would have been a valid option. If so, their allegiance to the company may well be adversely affected.

Our model of management-initiated dismissal seems reasonably robust in that disciplinary exits, being associated with exclusion and blame, are generally at odds with a high commitment strategy. By contrast, a dismissal of an employee for incapability might be construed by work colleagues as a legitimate release that benefits all concerned. However, any management pronouncement as to an individual's lack of value and worth to the company could also invalidate a constructive, caring approach to exit management. It is for this reason that dismissal on the grounds of ill-health requires special consideration. Generally speaking, ill-health dismissals fall into two categories. The first, regular periods of absence of short duration, tends to be extremely disruptive. They are often unpredictable and management may find it difficult to organise cover for the absentee. Moreover, if such absences are perceived not to be genuine they are likely to cause resentment among other workers. Consequently, managers are recommended to take a firm but fair line, which could ultimately result in dismissal.

The second category relates to longer-term absences for medical conditions. These are more likely to be seen as genuine, so how management treats such an employee may well have an effect on other workers. Management's good intentions towards a long-term sick employee may be seen, for example, in its use of an occupational health professional; seeking out alternative employment; and allowing the employee's entitlement to paid sick leave to expire before moving to dismissal. If workers judge that the organisation has done everything possible to assist a colleague, then they are likely to perceive management's treatment as fair and well meaning. This could also promote a feeling of security for those facing similar ill-health.

Redundancy

The process of redundancy involves management identifying those human resource capacities seen as surplus to the organisation's requirements and the selection of employees for dismissal. In this form of job separation, rather than people leaving the job, jobs are 'leaving' people (Weir, 2003: 121). However, dismissal may not always be the outcome, because redeployment and retraining is considered sometimes a more effective human resourcing solution.

Where dismissal is seen as the only option managers have a choice between implementing compulsory redundancies and asking for volunteers. Compulsory redundancies are invariably less costly and usually take less time to implement. Yet they can harbour other, less manifest, costs. Being a source of conflict they may produce employees' resentment, provoking workers' collective resistance or more usually leading to patterns of behaviour associated with 'survivor syndrome' (see above). Voluntary redundancy, on the other hand, is initially more costly in that managements typically offer financial inducements to attract sufficient numbers of volunteers. At the same time, inviting volunteers can overcome most of the negative factors associated with compulsory redundancy. Indeed, reference has been made to 'happy leavers' (Lewis *et al.*, 2003: 389) for whom a sizeable redundancy payment and, in some cases, early access to pension benefits can be very attractive.

Given the strategic basis of management's decision, dismissal on the grounds of redundancy should be regarded as a 'release' rather than 'exclusion' since no blame is attached to the redundant employee. However, as depicted in Figure 9.4, the predominant use by management of 'objective criteria' in the selection process for identifying those to be dismissed might imply some blame. The use of some factors, such as absence, disciplinary record and job performance, might be interpreted as management holding the employee to account and judging them to be partly responsible for their dismissal. Hence, the employee might well feel that the employer has, through the use of selection criteria, attributed blame in some way. In these circumstances the onus is on management to demonstrate its consistent and fair application of the criteria, if it is to defuse the ill-feeling that may result. In other words, management's actions to dispense with the human resource capacities that the business no longer requires, ought not to be undermined by the human relations issues that a selection process can exacerbate.

Redundancy is, for many employees and managers alike, one of the most stressful and traumatic experiences in working life. The very announcement of redundancies will 'invariably have an adverse impact on morale, motivation and productivity' (CIPD, 2003a: 1). Giving the bad news is 'unpleasant and needs careful handling. Common faults include being brutally abrupt or too vague' (CIPD, 2008d).

The fear of losing one's job creates uncertainty. This can undermine an employee's cooperation and commitment to an organisation that is proposing to expel a proportion of its workforce. Furthermore, even where there is no blame implied against those finally chosen, there might still be a feeling of resentment, bitterness and a perception of unfair treatment. One interpretation of this is that management's decision constitutes a violation of the psychological contract, which could be perceived by the workforce as a betrayal. Whether or not such a view will be manifested in collective opposition and some form of resistance by the workforce can depend on:

- the way that the company manages the process, and
- the ability of the workforce to mobilise its power, which depends on its organisational capabilities, willingness to engage in some form of protest, and the perceived balance of power between itself and management, including its potential ability to inflict damage on the company while being able to contend with any cost to its members.

These factors help our explanation of employees' strike threats over planned redundancies at Royal Mail, the UK's postal service, an episode that is covered later in Exhibit 9.3. The redundancies formed part of a three-year plan by the newly appointed chairman to restructure the postal network and cut 3,000 jobs, in response to losses of as much as £1.7 million a day.

It is to minimise these emotionally charged reactions that management is advised to adopt a considerate approach towards its employees. But, how realistic is it to 'manage' human relations issues while giving notice of dismissal to employees regarded as surplus to organisational requirements?

A high commitment approach to redundancy dismissal

It should be easier for the employer *to retain goodwill* if employees perceive that the reduction in jobs is inevitable and is outside management's control. After all, in today's competitive environment redundancies seem increasingly commonplace, cover all levels of employee and are an imperative of business life. Attributing cut-backs to the global economic slowdown in general and the 'credit crunch' in particular, businesses in the relatively prosperous county of Nottinghamshire in central England have experienced a loss of 100 jobs every week since the start of 2008. Amongst others, this has seen 200 call centre jobs move to Bangalore in India; a major electronics company closing its plant with a loss of 160 jobs; and the liquidation of an IT firm with 120 jobs disappearing (*Nottingham Evening Post*, 31 March 2008).

In such an environment the declared redundancies are more likely to be perceived as 'genuine', which also ought to minimise the question of 'blame' against management. This is more likely if, for example, employees have observed a reduction in their workloads or are aware of a decline in the order book. More proactively, the employer can further help to minimise employees' negative reactions if there is a clear commitment to limit the number of redundancies and a programme is in place to help redundant employees find alternative employment or training opportunities elsewhere.

It also makes the outcomes seem less contentious if management is able to clearly identify the surplus positions along with their occupants. However, in a more complex situation management might need to select a percentage of employees from a particular category or role. If so, it might be less contentious if this were to be done without recourse to any 'personal' selection criteria. However, the use of so-called 'objective' criteria – based on personnel records and a systematic points system – still requires management's interpretation, judgement and evaluation. Not surprisingly, therefore, the deployment of these criteria can arouse suspicions regarding management's manipulation. Hence, the transparent objectivity of an employee's length of service, normally used to operationalise redundancy on the basis of last in, first out (LIFO), could act to defuse employee misgivings about consistency and fairness. The LIFO criterion is readily understood and is more likely to be accepted as being uncontroversial.

Following the 'blame-free' route for managing redundancy, the outcome may well be one of parting company 'on good terms', but this is likely to gain little more than an employee's acceptance of their 'release' and being resigned to their lot. However, one could argue more positively that LIFO is not only cheaper to use but that it may strengthen the commitment of those who remain: staff with longer service and probably greater experience, whose loyalty would appear to afford them greater job security. Nevertheless, employers are increasingly dispensing with LIFO, being more concerned to retain those staff, irrespective of service, who will contribute most to the business – and to rid themselves of those who will not. In terms of our framework, the decline in the use of LIFO can be related to management's increasing emphasis on retaining optimal human resource capacities, even if at the expense of achieving a standard of human relations conducive to high employee commitment.

This tendency moves us back into that area of our model that smacks of 'exclusion' and which may well incur ill-feeling and employee hostility, at least from those selected. This approach to selection identifies surplus jobs, but then examines individuals and their overall credentials. As such, it is open to accusations of management favouritism and a chance to target 'troublemakers' for exclusion. However, it could also be argued that simply the experience of being put out of a job is sufficient to traumatise some individuals. Indeed, Redman and Wilkinson refer to 'the intense damage to self-esteem, failure, loss of confidence, decreased morale, anxiety, bitter feelings of betrayal, debilitating shock and sense of loss' (Redman and Wilkinson, 2006: 368).

But what of those staff *remaining*? Can management's use of a more caring, considerate approach to its employees' redundancies form a meaningful part of a high commitment HR strategy? Is it possible to promote goodwill among the remaining staff while managing a workforce reduction? This is the key question because 'such employees are, by their very nature, now much more important to the employer' (Redman and Wilkinson, 2006: 359). This has prompted a concern with 'survivor syndrome', which alludes to the adverse impact on the business of workers' decreased morale and motivation allied to their cynicism towards, and distrust of, the organisation. Is a decline in morale inevitable, with pressure on employees to work harder in order to survive the next cut?

To promote the best interests of the organisation, redundancies could be managed in such a way that employees perceive the employer as acting in good faith in seeking to provide long-term job security through the survival and success of the company. This would convey the 'big picture' of business economics and the need to relinquish the services of some employees for the benefit of those who remain. Then, during the process of redundancy decisions, management could demonstrate that it is acting in a socially responsible manner that goes beyond simply the dismissal of employees.

If employees are to be convinced that this stance is more than pretence, management will need to be consistent and resolute in both its words and deeds. A good starting place might be a redundancy agreement reached with the employees or their trade union. Ideally, this would have been agreed when the issue of redundancy was more hypothetical than actual, producing a more considered procedural document, less affected by any emotional intrusion. Also, working towards a 'job security agreement' rather than a 'redundancy agreement' might further strengthen the rationality of this approach. Furthermore, it would enable management to place an emphasis on its commitment to protecting jobs and avoiding redundancies except as a last resort. Such a document could very easily link management's strategic and social responsibilities in a coherent way: appealing to the unitary notion of the greater good alongside a caring approach to a loss of jobs. However, when the need for redundancies arises, the test for management will be to ensure that the fine words and intentions of the agreement are acted on.

Whether there is an agreement or not, management will need to ensure that it communicates its messages effectively, if it is to have the intended impact on employee attitudes. First, it would need to notify workers of potential redundancies and to do so in a consistent way. Collective meetings with staff or with trade union representatives, a circular letter, the use of a notice board or a general e-mail will all help to ensure the message is uniform. Even so, a general announcement of forthcoming redundancies 'will require managers to be well briefed to respond to questions that arise' (Lewis *et al.*, 2003: 383). However, the use of individual letters or meetings from the outset may provide a more personal, and hence empathetic, means to indicate possible redundancies.

The law also emphasises the need for consultation and directs a collective approach. Employment law in EU countries is influenced by the EC Directives on Collective Redundancies (EC 75/129 and 92/56), which require management to notify and consult the workforce, through either a recognised trade union or elected representatives. This requirement applies even where there is only one employee involved. In all cases consultation has to begin 'in good time', but there are also minimum statutory periods of notice. In the UK, for example, collective consultations with recognised trade unions or elected representatives must start at least 90 days beforehand for proposed redundancy dismissals of 100 or more employees, and at least 30 days before notification of redundancies for 20–99 employees. In cases where collective consultation is required, it must be completed before notice of dismissal is given to any of the employees concerned.

The law requires meaningful consultation – it is not enough only to inform. The purpose of such notification and consultation is to discuss and if possible find ways of avoiding or minimising redundancies. In order for this process to be meaningful, UK law dictates that notification should be in writing and should detail:

- the reasons for the proposed redundancies;
- the numbers and descriptions of jobs under threat;
- the method of selection of employees;
- the proposed method for implementing the dismissals; and
- the method of calculating any redundancy payments in excess of the statutory scheme.

It can be seen that, in the case of redundancy handling, employment laws constrain management's freedom to act quickly and decisively. This would seem reasonable when one considers that employees are liable to lose their livelihood. Although this legal constraint might frustrate management in some situations, the law may help to facilitate a high commitment approach since it promotes employee consultation at a time of considerable uncertainty and anxiety. Good communication and meaningful consultation can stem rumours and assist a smooth implementation. Indeed, anything that 'does not focus on the specific concerns and interest of those affected will not alleviate their inevitable sense of concern, uncertainty and perceived powerlessness' (Lewis *et al.*, 2003: 383). It is important, therefore, that employees do not perceive the process as little more than a 'token action' by reluctant managers who have to comply with the law.

In practice, however, redundancy consultation is often not complied with in the UK. The maximum compensation that can be awarded an employee if an employer fails to consult is 90 days' pay. Although in essence the law is advocating a joint problem-solving forum, the decision on the need for redundancies has often already been made. Furthermore, managers choose to make additional payments in lieu of notice 'so as to shed workers quickly via a short sharp shock approach of a sudden announcement and a quick lay-off' (Redman and Wilkinson, 2006: 367). Such a method would certainly hamper any attempts to retain good-will and trust, which once lost are difficult to rebuild.

For a more considerate approach to be effective, employees should be made fully aware that management has sought to help them by avoiding or at least minimising the need for redundancies through, for example:

● 'natural wastage',
● 'freezing' recruitment,
● disengaging contract workers and other flexible workers,
● reducing overtime working,
● organising career breaks,
● the introduction of flexible working practices such as part-time working.

Then, if it transpires that some staff will still need to leave their current roles, management might be able to offer alternative employment within the organisation. Redeployment of staff to available jobs can be presented to employees as a new opportunity. On the other hand they may perceive moving to another job or department as an unwelcome necessity. Indeed, Lane (1988) identifies a sense of loss that can prove problematic for such workers, who may exhibit symptoms more associated with displacement or disruption than redeployment. Such painful reactions are likely to be worsened by any reluctance shown by receiving managers, who might well regard the transferee as another manager's cast-off, implying that any employee selected for redundancy is probably mediocre or second-rate. This perception applies equally to those searching for jobs with a new employer, with the outcome that 'those most likely to be made redundant are least likely to follow a smooth path to re-employment' (Redman and Wilkinson, 2006: 369).

For the older worker a more attractive option might be to apply for voluntary early retirement. However, management needs to be aware of the possibility of 'corporate memory loss' as a result of key staff leaving. More dramatically, the loss of 'organisational memory' can be responsible for major incidents such as the horrendous fire at the Buncefield fuel depot, north of London (Hackitt, quoted by Chubb, 2008). According to Judith Hackitt, chair of the Health and Safety Executive in the UK, accidents can occur because organisations fail to embed a culture of sharing lessons learnt from mistakes. She goes on to emphasise the importance of 'the learning and experience of 50-something employees to be transferred to younger people' (Hackitt, quoted by Chubb, 2008).

The company may, of course, encourage other, younger workers to volunteer for redundancy, perhaps by offering additional payments. The implication here is that the company is confirming that the compulsory form of redundancy is seen as a last resort. Also, in placing its emphasis on staff volunteering to leave, there is the potential to reduce grounds for conflict and feelings of resentment. By shifting the 'leaving' decision to the employee the loss of their job is, to some extent, de-stigmatised (Redman and Wilkinson, 2006: 360). However, the job loss remains one that is initiated by management and, as such, the employing company is unlikely to escape being blamed, even by its volunteer leavers. Indeed, this is even more likely when individuals' decisions to volunteer are the result of managers 'leaning' on targeted employees (Redman and Wilkinson, 2006: 360). This accusation formed part of the employees' grievance against the Royal Mail's efforts to secure 3,000 redundancies through volunteers (Exhibit 9.3).

It seems that management is hard pressed to win any employee appreciation, even from those who are required to stay. In seeking volunteers to avoid compulsory redundancies, management may also insist on its right to select from those applying. Consequently, it might well demoralise those volunteers it turns down, having initially raised their expectations in terms of the compensation package and a new start. Management's decision could be on the perfectly sensible grounds of expense, organisational needs or both, but such a refusal may also be to the detriment of goodwill and cooperation.

In due course, management may find that it has not enough of the 'right' volunteers to meet its job reduction targets. It may be obliged, therefore, 'as a last resort', to instigate compulsory redundancies. This places the employer, as the perpetrator of employees' *exclusion* from the organisation, in a situation that would seem to run counter to a high commitment strategy. Rather than relief or acceptance, outrage and anger would seem more probable reactions from those directly affected: an aspect that is exemplified by Royal Mail employees in Exhibit 9.3.

Exhibit 9.3

Collective reactions to compulsory redundancy

Middle managers at Royal Mail are threatening to go on strike over plans to cut 3,000 jobs, claiming they are being bullied into agreeing to voluntary redundancies.

The postal group is slashing its headcount in non-operational management areas such as marketing and finance. It said yesterday that more than 2,000 staff had signed up to a voluntary redundancy package. 'We want to do everything we can to deal with surpluses on a voluntary basis', Royal Mail said. But it added that it had 'always been the case' that compulsory job cuts would be necessary if there were not enough people taking voluntary redundancy. It is likely that about 650 managers will be forced to leave over the next few months.

Amicus, the union representing the group's non-operational management, is considering a strike ballot over Royal Mail's handling of the cuts. The union said staff were being threatened with less generous redundancy terms if they did not agree to the voluntary package by 25 March. The group had not tried hard enough to redeploy staff, it said.

Peter Skyte, Amicus national officer for Royal Mail, said: 'Royal Mail has been duplicitous. At the same time as they have been saying to us that they are seeking to secure changes by voluntary means, they are drawing up plans for compulsory redundancy. There is now every prospect that Royal Mail's managers may be balloted on industrial action for the first time in 20 years if the company seeks to impose compulsory redundancy or reneges on the terms of the job security agreement with us.'

Source: extract from: 'Royal Mail managers threaten strike over job cuts postal services', *The Financial Times*, 16 March, 2004

The prospect of 650 middle managers being made compulsorily redundant (in addition to those volunteering) has led to battle lines being drawn. The first salvo from the trade union against the company's intention to impose compulsory redundancy is a threat of industrial action, which would be the first time in 20 years for this group of employees. In such circumstances, we ought not to be surprised by a decline in employees' morale and their trust in their employer.

A voluntary redundancy strategy has certain advantages, including reducing: a) conflict in a unionised environment, b) the likelihood of adverse media coverage and comment, and c) any damage to the commitment of the survivors (Lewis *et al.*, 2003: 389). However, it has its obvious limitations when certain volunteers are not accepted or there are insufficient numbers of volunteers. Accordingly, management may need to instigate compulsory redundancies from among those who did not volunteer, with 'equally negative consequences for morale' (Lewis *et al.*, 2003: 390).

By demonstrating the employer's appreciative, supportive side towards its employees, could a well-managed process help to minimise a decline in morale and a loss of trust? This was certainly an outcome reported by HR professionals in the CIPD survey on redundancy (2002). The employer can demonstrate social responsibility by offering 'dedicated' post-redundancy support to those losing their jobs. In addition to providing compensation that exceeds that required by law, a package of such post-redundancy measures might include: counselling to help those suffering from shock and anxiety; access to outplacement services specialising in finding alternative employment; and professional financial advice. More tangibly, perhaps, companies might permit its more senior employees to keep their company car or laptop computer. All of the above, as features of the compensation package, could be presented as gestures of sincere management support. If effectively communicated to, and then accepted by, the workforce, this message may help to bolster the organisation's reputation as a caring employer. In essence it has the characteristics of a high commitment approach to handling a redundancy situation.

Case Study 9.1

A high commitment approach to redundancy?

Credit Marque (CM) is an American-owned credit card company employing a global workforce of 30,000, including 2,000 at its European headquarters in Sunbrough in the north-east region of England. Most Sunbrough staff are engaged in call centre work, and quite a few have been with the company since the opening of its UK operation 10 years ago. During that period, however, work at Sunbrough has been shared with outsourced operations in India and the Philippines, where labour costs are significantly lower.

Management style at Sunbrough has been based on a predominantly unitary view and an intention to be seen as an 'employer of choice'. No trade union is recognised. Staff are referred to as 'associates', and are to be shown the utmost respect. They receive above average pay and occasional treats such as Christmas gifts and free dinners. Crates of sweets are used as rewards for 'best month ever'. In tune with the company's team values, staff are also encouraged to participate in 'fun days'. Moreover, the company wishes to be recognised for its contributions to community projects, involving all levels of staff in very practical ways, and reaping positive local publicity. Even more high profile is CM's sponsorship of the city's football team, which is seen to complement the company's desired image and brings with it free tickets for staff from time to time.

Company's jobs loss announcement

Staff were told at a number of meetings held in September that Credit Marque is to make 925 people in Sunbrough redundant. Call centre and IT jobs will go as the company seeks to improve 'cost competitiveness'. In addition, several group posts will be eliminated, notably in the human resources and risk management functions. CM has also advised that there will be a three-month consultation process about the redundancies.

The company has been hit by the economic downturn, with its US parent massively increasing the amount of money it had to set aside for bad debts. In all there are 2,200 planned job cuts across the company's global workforce. These job losses are to be seen in the context of a longer-term restructuring of the business. The pressure on companies in the financial sector has increased, leading them to 'offshore' certain operations to countries with lower labour costs.

In a letter handed to all Sunbrough staff that afternoon, the Managing Director of CM Europe, Ralph Scott, included the following points:

In recent months my team and I have been giving very careful consideration as how best to effectively compete in the credit card market and doing so at the right cost. As we continue to build our presence in the UK, and balance this with reducing our cost base, we have reached some difficult decisions, which we have not made lightly. This includes our looking to further develop our relationships with third party call centre and technology providers.

Earlier today we have announced our intentions to reduce the number of roles we have across Operations and IT and our group functions in Human Resources and Risk Management. We currently estimate that up to 925 associates will be made redundant across those four areas, including associates who have performed well and have made many valuable contributions to CM. It is our intention to complete the programme by the end of the year.

Focusing on business efficiency is not new for us. We've been leveraging outsourcing, making process improvements, and reducing costs for many years. These were significant efforts, and we pulled them off thanks to the hard work of our associates.

In recent months, as a prudent measure pending a decision on our sourcing plans, we have restricted recruitment as far as possible in order to minimise any potential redundancies; and will continue to do so over the coming months.

As we implement our plans, we must stay true to our values and treat every associate with the greatest dignity and respect.

As we have in the past, we will support those made redundant during this transition with financial support, job placement services, retraining assistance and enhanced severance payment. We will ensure all associates have access to the information they need regarding their own personal circumstances via access to one of your Directors for questions or concerns. Responses to frequently asked questions and all announcements relating to these changes will be provided through the Personal Development website.

I am confident that the business model we are moving towards will allow us greater opportunity to bring our costs in line with our competitors so that we are able to compete more effectively and efficiently in the UK credit card market. I appreciate your help as we implement this important programme.

Employee reactions to job losses

Taken from dozens of contributions to the Sunbrough Evening Mail's on-line message board, what follows is a representative sample of employees' comments following the newspaper's headline 'Credit Marque Sunbrough Bombshell', revealing that the company had announced that afternoon its decision to make 925 people redundant. The Mail broke the news before the official announcement. Unfortunately, some employees first discovered their plight from this external source.

- 'Yes I found this news out from the Evening Mail first! CM didn't even have the decency to ensure I'd find out before the rest of Sunbrough.'

- 'A massive thank you to the editor of the Mail for letting us know in the contact centre.'

A minority of respondents were relatively sanguine about the announcement; and reacted in a way that Ralph Scott would have wished, showing appreciation of the company's predicament and supportive efforts.

- 'I have worked at CM for nine years and today had confirmation that my role is one of the ones to no longer exist after November. Rather than over-reacting with anger and hurt, I have chosen to view this as an ideal opportunity to make a life-changing choice about my future. I don't know what that is yet, but I know that CM are providing extremely generous severance packages as well as expert support from an outplacement company and a re-training budget. I thank CM for all they have taught me and how this will set me up for the future.'

- 'I'm also about to lose my job, but I can honestly say CM is the best job I've ever had and I've had a few. The company are in business to make a profit – they are not a charity and if we are not competitive then there wouldn't be a job for anyone. Those people moaning in the call centre are being given a golden opportunity to train for another job. I'm sure most of them hated working in the call centre anyway – all I ever heard was people moaning about the job anyway. Plus they will receive an enhanced redundancy package to ease the next few months.'

Most employees, however, indicated their profound dissatisfaction, though one or two writers to the message board were displeased at *not* being selected for redundancy.

- 'I just found out I'm not being made redundant and am disappointed. I would gladly swap my call centre hell job with someone who actually wants it. A severance package with a retraining money award would give me the chance to get a real skill rather than having to listen to ungrateful rude customers moaning in my ear all day.'

From a company perspective the great majority of employees tended to respond in a less 'constructive' way. It seems that the employees' *reality* was not in accord with management's *rhetoric*. Hence, reactions are highly charged and emotional. Anger and bitterness are typical. Staff feel ill-served after devoting themselves to the CM cause; and cynical about the company's decisions to axe their jobs, whilst outsourcing them overseas.

- 'I was in one of the meetings at 3pm, not a total shock to be fair, but 925! Has the world gone mad? They made £34 million profit last year – over 20 of it came from operations and that's where all the redundancies have come from. I feel cheated and let down. £27 million spent on new IT, just for our jobs to be outsourced to India, Philippines and South Africa. Cheers CM. That's what you get for eight years hard service. These decisions haven't been taken lightly they said. Yeah right-o! It's all money money money. If they can get ten workers for the price of one Sunbrough associate they'll do it. We've got families, mortgages for god's sake! Truly sickening; I thought I had a job for life. Turned out that was all lies as well, but it will get worse before it gets better.'

- 'What a sad sad thing to do to all those loyal staff that have been busting their guts for this company, working overtime, learning the new systems, explaining to customers when alls gone wrong behind the scenes, fronting the lies to our customers, telling them we are doing our best, living the values, believing we mattered. Putting the customer at the heart of everything we do – bull! It's all about more profit.'

● 'I remember last month taking calls with my head on my desk as I was so sick and managers asking me to stay as there was calls in the queue, which resulted in me being more ill, and then having the next few days off to return to be told I'm put on a plan (which means if your sick again, your out). They don't care; that's why they can treat so many loyal employees like this.'

Some employees also feel this is the time to criticise some of the company's efforts, including its ongoing recruitment freeze and even the community projects.

● 'I was hired by CM one month ago along with lots of others. I've just got through training and actually know what I'm doing now. Now they are telling us that we will be made redundant, it's pathetic. They would've known many months ago if they were going to have to fire people, so what was the point in even hiring us?'

● 'I'm appalled. I have given this company my all. I have a mortgage, a family and now no job. They have sucked the life out of this city 'Working within the community' – whatever. It's always been about getting the public onside for the inevitable. Funny thing is they tried to brainwash us into believing they care about the community too!'

Some employees raised the issue of how unlikely they were to put in their usual effort and commitment at work during the three-month notice period. Several turned their attention to encouraging collective action in protest.

● 'There'll be loads of tears on the day we all leave, but CM don't care. I think it is going to be weird going into work now. I just don't think people will care less and will now sit around till October to get their redundancy pay. I can't see anyone bothering to hit targets. I mean who really cares anymore? I can see a mass walk out though, depends how many have the balls to do it. What have we got to lose? We've already lost our jobs.'

● Every single day I receive calls from India and the Philippines when a nervous and incompetent associate asks for help. The line we were fed by a certain senior manager was 'please help them so they can help us!' And surprise surprise they are now replacing us. If they want help from me they will be disappointed. WALK OUT AT NOON! I know I will be.'

● 'I'm definitely with you on that one. Let's get an email out to everyone but sales managers to spread the word. ALL OUT TOMORROW AT NOON! If enough people walk out at noon tomorrow then the management will see that we won't have it.'

Without any established form of collective organisation and with the knowledge of what the implications might be, the suggested walkout never materialised. Perhaps the following e-mail is indicative of employees' fears.

● 'My thoughts are that if you want the redundancy pay then protesting or walking out isn't really going to do anything other than get you dismissed without pay, I can't afford that.'

Ralph Scott's words to the Sunbrough workforce may be unpalatable and at the same time point towards a high commitment approach to handling this redundancy situation. There is a harsh reality in his announcement. He is clear and certain about the scale, timetable and location of the job cuts. Management would have to dismiss 925 employees, even those who had performed well and contributed to previous changes for competitiveness. Moreover, redundancies would occur alongside the need for additional cost improvements through further outsourcing overseas of call centre and IT work.

Even so, on behalf of the company he is seeking to soften the employees' reactions. First, he seeks to absolve management from direct blame. The future of CM in Sunbrough is sustainable only through being more competitive by reducing costs. Also, management has reached these decisions only after considerable deliberation; and they are the first to recognise the hard work and contributions of 'associates' over many years. Management really has no option other than these redundancies. The implication is that this is the only way to secure future jobs at Sunbrough.

Against this rather bleak outlook for associates' jobs, Scott asks for employees' help to implement this important programme. This implies continued efforts from those who have only three months to go (who could be excused for interpreting this request as 'please cooperate even if you are losing your job') and from the 'survivors', who have not been selected for redundancy. Scott seeks, therefore, to demonstrate the company's good intentions towards the workforce at this unfortunate time.

Attributes of a high commitment approach can be seen in management's honesty and transparency; and in their resolve to keep lines of communication open during the three-month consultation period, including the promise of individual consultations from those at director level. Furthermore, there is the offer of enhanced financial compensation. Professional support in training and in seeking employment elsewhere can be seen as a sign of the company's good intent to its workforce. Such an approach is also consistent with CM's corporate values of treating 'every associate with the greatest dignity and respect'.

Employees' reactions to the job losses are mixed, but lend support to our model (Figure 9.4) in revealing the tendency for workers' responses to include statements that are either critical of management and lay blame or choose not to blame management. A small minority accept management's interpretation of the exigencies of business that demand redundancies; and are appreciative of 'generous severance packages as well as expert support from an outplacement company and a re-training budget'. Such individuals are more likely to lay no blame at management's door, to part on good terms and remain ambassadors for the company's reputation as an employer of choice. Also, like-minded survivors may be reassured by the manner in which the company is treating their redundant colleagues. The exception would be those disappointed by being neither selected for redundancy nor invited to volunteer.

From the company's viewpoint the great majority of workers chose to adopt a more critical, even cynical, attitude towards the impending redundancies, in spite of the recompense and help on offer. As such employees exhibit a strong inclination to react in a hostile and antagonistic way. Feeling 'cheated and let down' respondents target their enmity against management's duplicity, pouring scorn on any caring sentiments towards them and showing contempt for CM's decision to move jobs overseas in search of cheaper (and 'less competent') labour. Such reactions will unsurprisingly see leavers harbouring ill-feelings and having the potential to undermine CM's reputation as an employer of choice.

Whilst resentment and bitterness are evident, the desire to translate these emotions into industrial action and protest are not realised. A non-union organisation that has always encouraged team-working and camaraderie is hardly the seedbed for such a radical possibility. Yet, CM's management has no grounds for complacency. The high commitment approach to redundancy handling has, by and large, achieved little more than grudging compliance. The challenge for management is how to organise and deliver normal working and productivity during and after the three months' notice period. It is worth reiterating that in principle this period is intended for management's consultation with the workforce, including an exploration of ways to avoid or alleviate the redundancies. In reality it is most unlikely to alter the company's decisions on redundancies. Moreover, rather than helping the company's operations, management might view the three months as an expensive and unwanted constraint.

Management's desired effect of a high commitment approach to redundancy is that remaining staff will appreciate that their employer has, in adverse and difficult circumstances, sought to do the 'right thing' by its workers. The premise continues that such staff are more likely, therefore, to respond positively to such an approach, being favourably impressed by the exemplary treatment extended to redundant staff by their employer. Less altruistically, surviving staff may well regard management's approach as an indication of their own possible redundancy treatment. However, even if we accepted this highly debatable contention, such a management tactic is unlikely to be enough. Redman and Wilkinson cite considerable evidence that 'remaining employees feel shocked, embittered towards management, fearful about their future and guilty about still having a job while colleagues have been laid off' (2006: 369).

Indeed, if the predominant mood amongst those selected for redundancy at Sunbrough continues to be one of low morale and distrust of management, it seems very likely that survivors will be adversely affected by ill-feeling in the company and any strains between the parties. This may well, at least in the foreseeable future, undermine the company's rhetoric and practice of unitary, paternalistic employee relations and diminish the goodwill that the company has sought to sustain in its handling of this situation.

If the *survivor syndrome* of lowered morale and an inherent distrust of management are to be resolved, therefore, management's attention to human resourcing and human relations issues must also extend more directly to its remaining staff. For that reason, we can conclude that it is essential but insufficient for the employer to have followed the caring or compassionate approach. Employees' acceptance of the necessity for job reductions; a recognition of the fairness in selection for redundancy; and an appreciation of the assistance offered to redundant staff may fall short of addressing the post-redundancy concerns and uncertainties felt by the survivors. Consequently, the organisation's human resource capacities are doubly diminished. First, survivors are likely to face intensification and restructuring of work as they cope with fewer staff. Second, any emotional turmoil they experience could adversely affect their contribution to the firm.

This analysis leads to us to conclude that relevant communication links between management and remaining staff should continue well into any post-redundancy phase. Managers should be trained to handle the effects of redundancy, both in terms of adjustments to work restructuring and the human relations consequences. The company might extend its counselling support to its survivors and seek to transform their mindset towards one of individual opportunity and corporate success. However, this would be very reliant on the employees' perception that this future is one based on employment security. It would require an interpretation that the recent workforce reductions were necessary for the organisation's future and hence their own employment. Accordingly, it is difficult to conceive of a high commitment strategy without employees' certainty in their own job security.

One might argue that redundancy is no more than the legal termination of a contractual bond and, as such, is best seen as a formal and impersonal matter. If people were to take this view then redundancy might not be an issue and much of the above discussion would be irrelevant. However, workers invest themselves into their jobs; and to be made redundant is to lose one's job rights, one's livelihood and perhaps one's self-respect. No matter how well an employer manages the redundancy process, it is most unlikely that these economic and social realities can be hidden, even from the 'survivors'. As such, a litmus test of a high commitment HR strategy could be the extent to which management can incorporate this approach in handling employee exit resulting from redundancy.

Case Study 9.2

Managing redundancy and beyond

The Robinson Group is a multinational retailer of furnishings, clothing, foods, general household goods and financial services. It operates through some 200 retail outlets, which for the most part are department stores in the UK. The company has some 60,000 employees in the UK, with its large head office situated in the north-west of England. In addition, Robinson's trades in more than 30 countries worldwide, including several in the European Union.

The company has an outstanding reputation for its caring and sensitive approach to its employees, based on the paternalistic and benevolent principles applied by its nineteenth-century founders, who were counted among a group of like-minded reforming employers with a social conscience. Today, Robinson's is known as a company offering good terms and conditions of employment, as well as providing quality goods at value for money.

Recently, however, share prices have fallen in response to declining sales and falling profits. As a consequence, shareholder pressure has resulted in the resignation of the managing director, who had been with the company all his working life, to be replaced by a new MD, Tom Evesham. Evesham has been headhunted from another part of the retail industry to make Robinson's more profitable, and was expected to bring with him a more dynamic style of management.

Evesham's view is that he needs to 're-energise the company' by looking at costs and sales, and one of his early pronouncements is that Robinson's would be making 900 people redundant from its Head Office in England, reducing the numbers there from 2,000 to just over 1,000 employees. He also set out plans for a management review of all stores, with the clear signal that this would mean reorganisation and further redundancies. By contrast, previous redundancies have been a rarity. When they have occurred, the company has always seemed to minimise any acrimony and resentment by managing the process in keeping with its benevolent image.

On this occasion the announcement first appeared on radio and television and then in the local press, and before the workers or their union representatives had been informed. Evesham was reported as saying, 'Robinson's operates in an extremely competitive environment, where the pace of decision-making and speed of implementation are fundamental to success. It is essential that organisations respond quickly and flexibly to rapid workplace change. These redundancies will reduce costs and improve our ability to compete.'

The immediate result of the MD's press announcement is a strong reaction from the trade union, which is quick to condemn the company for not first informing and then consulting the staff. More specifically it attacked the company's new 'autocratic approach to employee relations'. The trade union is recognised by the company for the purposes of collective bargaining and represents in-store sales personnel and the clerical and administrative grades at HQ.

After reluctantly discussing matters with the union, Robinson's subsequent approach to managing the redundancies is to invite volunteers and then, through line managers, select the remaining candidates by using a points scoring system. Scores are attributed to such factors as service, qualifications, capability issues, age and attendance and disciplinary records.

Some line managers have taken this opportunity to give extra weighting to their more 'troublesome' members of staff on account of their disciplinary record or lack of capability and aptitude. Furthermore, in many cases there is no formal personnel record of alleged indiscipline or lack of capability.

The whole redundancy process is to be carried out in a three-month time span.

> ### Activity 9.2   Evaluating redundancy handling at Robinson's
>
> 1. How is the Robinson Group's human resourcing strategy affected by the new managing director's action?
> 2. To what extent is management's ability to exercise a high commitment approach 'constrained' or 'enabled' by external factors?
> 3. Discuss the employee relations implications of the selection of employees for redundancy dismissal on account of their disciplinary records or alleged lack of capability or aptitude.

Robinson's has a new managing director, Tom Evesham, whose main objective is to reverse the company's decline in sales, profits and share values. In order to create an immediate impact his strategy is to identify short-term opportunities to reduce costs, with headquarters' headcount being an obvious target. In keeping with his reputation as an energetic and forceful business leader, Evesham resolves to move quickly and wastes little time in announcing plans to almost halve the number of jobs at head office. However, the first that staff know about this is from reports and bulletins in the news media. This method is unlikely to address employees' concerns and interests. It also conveys a clearly identifiable low commitment approach, which is likely to increase employees' feelings of uncertainty, anxiety and helplessness. More particularly, for Robinson's staff, this method of communication sits uneasily with their employer's long-established benevolent management style and is, therefore, likely to have deleterious effects on a hitherto loyal and devoted staff.

Evesham's rationale in terms of the company's reliance on 'speed of decision-making and implementation' is conducive to a cost-conscious, low commitment strategy. It is also indicative of a view that since redundancies are bound to have an adverse effect on staff morale, decisions are best taken and announced as soon as possible. However, this 'hard-nosed' approach is just as (if not more) likely to encounter those strong negative reactions that lead to lower morale across the workforce. Given management's tactic of a short, sharp shock through its use of the media, staff are more liable to be *sympathetic* towards those earmarked for redundancy and *negative* towards the organisation (Lewis *et al.*, 2003: 392). As such, Tom Evesham has sacrificed an opportunity to win the support or allegiance of the survivors, especially in view of the clear signal that further redundancies are intended.

It is important from the managing director's perspective to improve Robinson's trading position as quickly as possible, but this short-term perspective is unhelpful in promoting the trust and goodwill that seem to have served the company well. Furthermore, Robinson's has disregarded its legal requirements to consult meaningfully with its staff and their trade union representatives. From the company's perspective, employment law constrains management's freedom to act quickly and decisively on its redundancy plans. The messages transmitted to its employees seem, therefore, doubly duplicitous and certain to incite the trade union to speak out against this newly 'autocratic' management.

Evesham's apologists might argue that his 'refreshing directness' will address the company's worsening financial situation and drag the company into a new era of competitiveness. Those inclined to a high commitment human resource strategy will look upon his 'reckless impatience' as damaging to employee relations in the longer term. A more critical view might suggest that, since redundancies always have the potential to generate uncertainty, fear of change and a dip in staff morale, it is debatable whether management can ever achieve a high commitment solution when managing such an exercise. Certainly, Robinson's concession to the trade union in inviting volunteers is unlikely to make good the damage already inflicted on the organisation's employee relations.

Robinson's subsequent use of the points system appears, *prima facie*, to satisfy the requirement to apply objective criteria when selecting personnel for redundancy. Nevertheless, whereas it might be legitimate to take account of disciplinary, capability and aptitude issues when selecting employees, Robinson's would be at risk from litigation at employment tribunal were it to have no supporting evidence in the form of personnel records. Decisions based on managers' short-term recollections can be called into question in terms of fairness and consistency. Also, it is important for the company's credibility that 'redundancy remains the reason why the dismissal is to occur, rather than the subsidiary reason for choosing who is to lose their jobs' (Lewis *et al.*, 2003: 382). More seriously for Robinson's, there is clear evidence that managers have been both subjective and manipulative in applying those criteria to shed any so-called 'troublemakers'. This situation has been used as an opportunistic solution for dispensing with what line management see as inadequate personnel. This occurrence perhaps underlines the tensions that sometimes exist between line managers and human resourcing specialists and their respective inclinations towards low and high commitment approaches. While the former are probably grappling with the new realities of Robinson's business performance, the latter may well mourn the loss of employee allegiance as a result of management's somewhat precipitate handling of job cuts.

Conclusion

Taking our lead from Watson (see Chapter 1), strategic human resourcing refers to the general direction that an organisation adopts to secure, develop, retain and dispense with the human resources it requires to ensure its long-term success. Consequently, it is of strategic importance that the organisation can not only employ the people it needs, but also jettison those it does not. In the capitalist system management is, therefore, entitled to initiate the departure of employees that do not fulfil the company's requirements, whether this is dismissal on the grounds of indiscipline, incapability, or redundancy – as a result of occupying a job that is no longer required. We also acknowledged that employees too, have the right to initiate their own departure from their employing organisation, but that it is important for organisations to retain those staff it really needs. Consequently, this places emphasis on the need to 'manage' employee-initiated decisions to leave, so that the right people stay rather than quit.

By relating these decisions of 'parting company' to an organisation's strategic need for human resource capacities, we introduced the notion of 'exit management'; and within this we also emphasised the importance of human relations issues. We then offered the view that in a high commitment strategy, management would want to ensure that those personnel the organisation continues to employ remain well disposed towards their employer, if they are to give of their best. Hence, we suggested, the organisation would need to attend to the manner in which it managed employee exits in order to ensure that remaining staff recognised and appreciated management's efforts in treating leavers and survivors fairly, consistently and considerately.

While exit management does have a strategic coherence, we have also charted the variety of ways of 'parting company', with as many differences as similarities. Thus, in seeking to bestow some structure to these decisions and events, our starting point was to differentiate between the perpetrators or initiators of the exit process in terms of management or employee. Then, in order to encompass the human relations issues, our exploratory framework used the notion of attributing 'blame' (or not) between employer and the departing employee. This provided us with a workable, if perhaps rudimentary, mechanism for determining whether reactions were likely to be acrimonious or not. It also enabled us to reason that the extent to which the outgoing employee left 'on good terms' or 'with ill-feeling' would affect the attitudes of remaining employees towards their employer and their work.

A high commitment approach would emphasise the importance of working towards promoting positive employee attitudes through effective exit management. However, our model presents the view that in certain types of dismissal or resignation, high commitment employee relations is contradictory to the underlying dynamic associated with the termination of the employment relationship. However, this is not to argue that an employer cannot manage employee exits effectively in order to promote goodwill. More accurately, it is to indicate the significant constraints on achieving much more than the allegiance (rather than the commitment) of the remaining staff, especially when management initiates the process.

It may well be that an approach to exit management that shows consideration towards employees might maintain the full commitment of certain individuals, but, generally speaking, this is unlikely for most types of exit. Management might usefully adopt a coherent approach to exit management as it has a strategic contribution to make. At the same time, however, exit management is more likely to be effective if managements appreciate the inherent limitations in their use of 'good practice'.

Summary

In this chapter the following key points have been made:

- Both management-initiated and employees' voluntary terminations of employment are critical components of human resourcing.

- The effective management of all types of employment exit has the potential to make an important contribution towards human resource and corporate strategies.

- Exits from employment, of whatever type, involve not only the loss of an employee's particular capacities and their contribution to 'organisational memory' but also the need for the organisation to manage consequential human resourcing and human relations issues.

- Depending on the nature of employee departures, both voluntary and enforced exits have the potential to result in resentment and resistance towards management, either individually or collectively.

- Employee exit, especially voluntary exit, sends important signals about the way employees feel about an organisation. Managers should collect and make sense of these data to inform other aspects of the HR system.

- Our exploratory model helps our understanding of the impact of various types of employee exits on employment relations by reference to the attribution of blame or not, by one party against the other.

- A critical examination of high commitment approaches to exit management reveals that management can go some way towards maintaining a degree of goodwill with staff that remain in employment.

- Since dismissals and resignations signify the termination or dissolution of the relationship between employer and employee, there are likely to be major human relations issues, which in turn place significant limitations on the achievements of a high commitment approach to exit management.

- The exploratory framework that we propose for the various types of 'parting company' can help our analysis of exit management practices in any organisation, including the extent to which such practices are consistent with each other and are appropriate to the relevant business context.

Discussion questions

1. How valid is the assertion that the strategic management of employee exits can significantly benefit the organisation?

2. What push–pull factors might influence employees in deciding whether or not to leave an employer?

3. What is the value of exit interviews as a tool in exit management?

4. How useful is the 'attribution of blame' model in understanding strategic exit management?

5. How might a high commitment approach to exit management help survivor effectiveness and organisational efficiency?

6. In what circumstances might management find it preferable to adopt a low commitment approach to exit management?

7. What conflict and tensions might arise between line managers and human resourcing specialists in managing redundancy and why?

Further reading

Although the term 'exit management' does not appear in the *Dictionary of Human Resource Management* (Heery and Noon, 2001), the phrase has entered the lexicon of today's human resource managers. However, its use seems to concentrate on grouping together the various forms of management-initiated dismissals. By contrast, in focusing on the theme of 'parting company', we have sought to identify connections between management and employees, which logically adds employee-initiated departures to our view of exit management.

Since this conception relates precisely to the management of human resource capacities for the achievement of organisational ends, we have explored the strategic dimensions of exit management. Unfortunately, in terms of suggested further reading, we have not found a text that adopts this kind of framework. This is not to suggest that authors are unaware of this approach, but that someone has yet to put it all together in a comprehensive way. Consequently, our suggestions for further reading refer to the different forms of dismissal.

A book that deals with employee turnover from a management perspective is Taylor (2002). Starting with measuring, predicting and explaining staff turnover, Taylor then offers prescriptions for improving retention rates. As he notes, 'Employers often devote huge resources to recruiting staff – and far too little effort to retaining them.'

Basic texts that provide management guidelines on redundancy are Fowler (1999) and Lewis (1993). A useful, critical counterpoint to these is Noeleen Doherty's chapter on 'Downsizing', which appears in Tyson (1997). In contrast to most HRM textbooks, this gives the topic prominence by placing it at Chapter 3.

An appropriate book on disciplinary dismissal is not immediately obvious, but a useful theoretical treatment of discipline can be found in Edwards' chapter on discipline in Bach, S. and Sisson, K. (eds) (2000). For an analysis of the practical issues involved in discipline and dismissal see Rollinson and Dundon (2007). A very useful guide for UK managers concerned about the legal implications of dismissal is Barnett (2002).

10

Human resourcing in international organisations

David Walsh and Dave Doughty

Learning outcomes

Having read this chapter and completed its associated activities, readers should be able to:

- Make informed judgements on the management of human resources in different types of multinational organisation
- Understand the similarities and differences between national (domestic) and international human resourcing
- Demonstrate an understanding of the process of globalisation and its significance for organisational approaches to international human resourcing
- Recognise the variety of factors that constrain and influence the operation of human resourcing in transnational companies in the context of different local cultures
- Address the organisational issues, tensions and contradictions associated with managing human resources across national boundaries
- Advise on key considerations for staffing the international organisation
- Appreciate the human resourcing implications of different approaches to staffing
- Analyse contingent factors for host country employment arrangements
- Appreciate that human resourcing priorities, challenges and interventions are likely to change as the overseas subsidiary moves towards a more mature phase of existence
- Understand that the essence of managing human resources in the international organisation entails an adjustment between universal HR concerns and those that differentiate the host country location

Introduction

For some, a discussion of managing human resources across the globe invites enticing images of employees working in corporate outposts, where the customs, language, food, climate and laws are different from those of the parent company's national base. However, for those practitioners involved with the administration of international work assignments, the topic is more likely to suggest organising travel and accommodation arrangements; devising intricate reward packages; and attending to all manner of bureaucratic and legal formalities.

While these impressions may help to convey something about the nature of international human resourcing, they are plainly incomplete, and it is the aim of this chapter to provide a comprehensive framework for understanding the *essentials* of managing human resources across national boundaries. It will do so by concentrating on human resource strategy-making from the viewpoint of the parent (home-based) company, and by seeking to apply Watson's proposition that strategic management processes involve active management choice in the context of the influence of constraining and enabling factors. 'We need to recognise the existence both of the scope for managerial choice and the limitations on that scope that arise from the various circumstances of the organisations within which those managers are working' (Chapter 1, p. 25).

We will need to explore, therefore, the extent to which the choices and the circumstances associated with international human resourcing are different from those encountered by the human resourcing function of a domestic-only organisation. If we discover that the strategic management of human resources operates in much the same way, whether intra-national or international, the practitioner will be able to build on what they already know about human resourcing in general and to focus more intently on any crucial characteristics of the international version of human resourcing that make it distinctive.

As this book has been written to help the reader make informed judgements on the practice of human resourcing, this particular chapter aims to concentrate on what might be distinctive about managing human resources internationally. In so doing we may be able to discover principles that are likely to be *peculiar* to this area of work, and avoid replicating those that have a more general application. Our initial approach, however, is to identify the general features shared by national and international human resourcing in order to highlight differences that might be significant. This might then provide a way of thinking to help the practitioner tackle any *international* human resourcing issue, including the ability to assess the appropriateness and utility of human resourcing practices covered elsewhere in the book.

From domestic to international human resourcing

There can be few organisations that have not been affected to some extent by the increasing intensity of competition which comes from the globalisation of the economy. Business decisions taken by managers on behalf of their organisations are influenced by the exacting competition from foreign as well as domestic companies. Increasingly, domestic companies are part of the 'global market'. Businesses whose products become more expensive to export and which struggle to compete at home against a flood of cheaper imports can readily suffer from falling profits and a loss of jobs. Understandably, therefore, managers are placing even greater emphasis on winning custom and growing or sustaining their business through attending to customer satisfaction through the provision of a quality service and product at an attractive price. In so doing they have often sought to minimise costs by reducing the wage bill, typically through redundancy and restructuring exercises. However, pressure on costs seems unrelenting and the lure of relocating overseas has become increasingly attractive.

A prime example is the move of British and American call centres to India. There is, of course, nothing new about corporations relocating their operations to countries where labour is cheaper. However, since the advent of broadband telecommunications and plummeting telephone charges, the choice of India is especially compelling. The wages of workers in the service and technology industries there are less than one-third of their counterparts in the UK, contributing to average cost savings of more than 40 per cent (BBC2, 2003). In addition, call centre jobs typically attract university-educated Indians who speak English. 'British call centres moving to India can choose the most charming, biddable, intelligent workers the labour market has to offer' (Monbiot, 2003: 25). Indeed, Indians have been answering bank, telephone and air travel enquiries from their British and American customers for some time now.

However understandable the rationality behind such decisions to relocate might appear, certain issues cannot be ignored. First, with the growing exodus of jobs to the cities of India, the damaging impact on those call centre workers who are losing their jobs is likely to severely test any Western support for the unfettered globalisation of business. There are certainly signs of anger, fear and resentment among British and American workers; and the case of Credit Marque, an American-owned credit card company based in the UK (see Chapter 9), is testimony to the bitterness and betrayal felt by those 'tossed on the scrap heap' by their profit-seeking global masters' desire to save costs by moving jobs overseas.

Watson addresses this theme of competing rationalities within global capitalism through his examination of Moddens Foods (Chapter 1). The strategic debate between the company's ambitious advocates of globalisation and those directors with a strong commitment to the company's home location and its existing workforce replicates the tensions detected as part of the jobs stampede to India.

The second issue relates to a tendency by commentators to either gloss over the task of establishing an effective workforce in an overseas operation or to underestimate the problematic aspects of managing people in Indian call centres. Initial research by the authors suggests that the unrelenting, pressurised nature of call centre work combined with issues of cross-cultural management present organisational decision-makers with significant HR challenges. As such, more research is needed to establish the relevant human resourcing aspects and dimensions of the 'flight to India', which represents a particularly prominent example of Western companies moving their operations overseas.

Available evidence of the problematic nature of transferring work to India is the decision by some companies to resist the 'bottom line' allure of overseas relocation. Even more visible are the actions of those employing organisations that have actually brought jobs back to their home country. The main rationale for this seems to be management's realisation that the quality of call centre responses to the customer is critical to the business. By way of example, a German-owned utilities company recently transferred its Indian call centre work back to its UK operation. This was in response to an appalling record on telephone response rates and to customers' overwhelmingly negative reactions to a perceived lack of effective communication. On returning to the UK the company also instigated a high commitment approach to managing customer requirements. Its UK staff are now recruited, trained and enabled to deal with a call 'through to completion'. This has replaced the fragmented structure previously adopted. Thus, instead of a customer having to be passed from one operative to another and being subjected to a number of separate responses, the aim is to permit a member of staff to spend as long as is necessary (typically half an hour) to deal with the customer's situation. Consequently, the company has found it uses its human resources more effectively and enjoys a marked improvement in its call centre outcomes.

Although we have acknowledged that overseas expansion is not necessarily an inevitable path for a multinational, there is little doubt that such organisations are powerfully attracted to 'lightly regulated labor markets' that provide comparative advantage and with that 'an economic rationale for globalization' (Frenkel, 2006: 397). This entails the tendency for multinational companies to enter overseas markets and more significantly to undertake foreign direct investment (FDI). In this way they establish a physical presence in a country other than their home economy, with the FDI relationship consisting of a parent enterprise with control over its foreign affiliate. Parent and subsidiary together form the multinational corporation, and it is this institution that presents us with compelling questions concerning its human resource management.

What are the implications of being actually engaged in employment relationships with the workforce of overseas subsidiaries? Is human resourcing so very different when it is international and carried out across several nations compared with when it is conducted in a domestic setting and confined to one nation? The answer is that *in all essentials* human resourcing should be no different whether it is conducted in a domestic or international context. In either setting, human resourcing ought to be shaped by the same corporate imperative: to deliver the effective contribution of an organisation's human resources towards that organisation's long-term success. At the same time, however, we should also expect to find significant differences, but these might be considered more as differences of *degree* rather than of essence. Indeed, the framework adopted in Chapter 1 by Watson serves to demonstrate both the essential similarity and the differences between domestic and international human resourcing. On the one hand, through his study of the Aynshents he reveals that strategic human resourcing issues arise whenever 'human beings organise themselves, or are organised, to complete work task' (Chapter 1, p. 1). As such, human resourcing applies to *any* organisation, whether national or international. On the other hand, Watson stresses the significance of constraining and enabling circumstances as they impact on human resourcing decision-makers. Consequently, the management of an organisation encompassing business units or divisions in foreign countries is likely to encounter an increased range (and perhaps complexity) of political economic contexts, cultural values, employment legislation and labour market conditions compared with those operating in only a domestic environment.

Human resourcing in the domestic organisation

In order to expand on this view of similarity and difference, we will briefly explore the human resourcing issues associated with various forms of *domestic-only* (i.e. national) business organisations. Our aim is to develop a way of thinking about international human resourcing that builds on, rather than replaces, our understanding of its practice in a national context. We can assemble a picture made up of the essential similarities between domestic and international human resourcing together with those characteristics which are shared yet perhaps differ by degree. Through a process of filtering out similarities we will be in a position to see whether there are any *additional* features which identify human resourcing in an international context as in any way distinctive.

The single business organisation

It has already been established that an organisation, whether national or international in scope, relies on 'the efforts, knowledge, capabilities and committed behaviours' that people contribute (Chapter 1); and that a human resourcing strategy depicts how managers tackle the problems of securing, developing, retaining and dispensing with these human resources to enable the organisation to continue into the long term. In theory, and hence putting to one side issues of the relative power, status, influence and ambiguity of the human resourcing function, the process of human resource strategy-making is at its simplest in the *single business organisation*. As such, it will provide confirmation of the features of human resourcing that ought to be essential for *any* employing organisation, whether international or domestic.

The human resourcing function of a *single site* organisation, whether it is a college, factory, hospital or software company, can operate as a centralised, corporate function that is mindful of the needs of the organisation and is also sensitive to local circumstances. Centrality and locality coincide. As such, the function is well placed to adopt a human resourcing strategy that fits the organisational context and hence secures a level of *vertical integration* to promote the organisation's goals. Being located on one site should also help the function deliver a coordinated and consistent approach within the organisation. In theory, then, there should also be fewer obstacles to *horizontal integration*, whereby human resourcing activities such as recruitment, selection, training and payment are managed in such a way that they are mutually supportive, compatible and consistent. In addition to the human resourcing function being centralised, employees are generally more accessible, so that communication is easier and change can be more readily instituted.

A human resourcing strategy exists to fulfil corporate goals, and management's choice of strategy for the single-site business organisation can be a relatively straightforward application of Watson's model (see Chapter 1). For example, in a medium-sized manufacturing company, a direct control/low commitment management strategy, exemplified through a no-nonsense macho style of workplace supervision and the hegemony of quality control inspectors, would 'fit' a situation of cheap and plentiful, non-unionised female labour hired on low wages to carry out repetitive machining and assembly tasks. As Watson points out, management's stance is feasible because in these circumstances employees 'are not a major source of strategic uncertainty for the employing organisation' (Chapter 1, p. 31). It follows, therefore, that a similar strategy might be appropriate in similar circumstances in another country. This suggests that this relatively uncomplicated model can operate in *any* country, and that one option for the management of a multinational corporation is to adopt a *multidomestic* approach where the human resourcing function of each foreign subsidiary adopts its own strategy in accordance with local circumstances (Hoecklin, 1995: 69). This *polycentric* approach may, however, rest uneasily with those responsible for advancing the merits of a *global* human resourcing strategy that can benefit from the expertise at the centre and across the company.

The multi-unit business organisation

It is clear that the nation-by-nation approach is only one option, and that we need to develop a comprehensive framework for understanding the essentials of managing human resources *across* national boundaries. To do so we will need to continue with the process of filtering out similarities with human resourcing in the domestic arena by now considering *multi-unit* business organisations. We aim to identify characteristics shared with international human resourcing, which clearly operates within a multi-unit business organisation, albeit one that is located in countries additional to its corporate home base.

Many domestic-only companies can be designated multi-unit or divisional business organisations. In addition to their corporate centre or head office, such companies may have several business units, each typically with its own location. Banks have branches, retailers have stores and supermarkets, leisure companies have hotel chains and clubs, logistics firms have warehouses, and so on. In any multi-unit business organisation, management choice can be represented in the form of a continuum: from employing a centralised, corporate-level human resourcing function through to having a decentralised function which operates at the business-unit level. This approach is outlined more fully by Hall and Torrington, based on their UK research (1998: 73–95). As we explore the implications for *domestic* human resourcing, the *similarities* shared with its *international* counterpart should become clear.

One approach is for the human resourcing function to be *centralised* with a manager given responsibility for several sites while being based at head office. This manager is well placed, therefore, to convey the human resourcing requirements of the parent company and to ensure a coordinated and consistent approach at each site. A centralised approach gives pre-eminence to the needs of the corporation as a whole and endeavours to deliver a cost-effective, standardised version of human resourcing based predominantly on expertise at the centre. As such, it is more likely in companies where the product or service is uniform across the different business units and relies on the management of each business unit translating corporate objectives into workable local activities. In such a situation, however, communication is typically more problematic and the personnel specialist may need to make regular visits to individual sites for face-to-face meetings to solve problems, deliver training, evaluate events and promote change.

The focus on corporate control by a central human resourcing function can expose the organisation to potential difficulties associated with a lack of responsiveness to local issues. For example, a standardised corporate approach to recruitment, including wage rates and issues of flexible working, can give rise to problems in more affluent regions compared with those where the supply of labour is plentiful (see Walsh, 1992). In addition, centrally imposed demands that are perceived as out of touch with the situation can provoke local resistance or avoidance. One option for larger companies is to adopt a *regional* structure, a sort of halfway house for meeting and aligning corporate and divisional or business unit needs.

At the other end of the continuum is the decision by corporate management to adopt a *decentralised* structure with the human resourcing function operating at business unit level. This approach to human resourcing is more attractive where the business units have diverse products or services, and there seems less need for standardisation across the group. Although there may be inconsistency between the business units in the way employees are managed, local autonomy can ensure a speedy response to specific issues and the development of systems that are engineered to meet the needs of the business unit. This may, of course, be at the expense of meeting corporate requirements, but local decision-taking can promote a feeling of ownership of tasks which in turn can generate greater staff commitment to the organisation.

In addition to the regionalised halfway house or its non-geographical variant of *clustering* related business units, what other measures can help to bridge the gap between the centre and the business unit in order to marry corporate coordination or integration with local responsiveness? The simple answer is to ensure a two-way flow of communication, but in practice this is never straightforward, especially in larger organisations where centre and unit can seem far apart. Another solution is to propagate and cultivate a distinctive corporate culture that can engender a strong sense of identification with the organisation; and evidence of this can be found in the fashionable statements of company vision, mission and shared values, indicative of new-style HRM practices. We should not be surprised to find, however, that 'attitudes are harder to change than behaviours' (Hall and Torrington, 1998: 32). The same authors then suggest that 'In developing corporate culture we have to start with trying to change norms of behaviour; over time those changed behaviours may lead to a change in the more deeply-held beliefs of shared norms' (1998: 32). This alerts us to another possible answer to the problem: the use of company-wide human resourcing policies, procedures and systems that are required to be followed. Again, it should not surprise us to find local human resourcing departments practising 'the art of keeping the centre happy while doing the right things by the business' (Hall and Torrington, 1998: 80).

Human resourcing in the international organisation

What can we draw from our analysis so far? It should already be clear that the international company is a type of *multi-unit* business organisation, one which has a corporate centre in its *home* country and its business units located in various *host* countries. We can also appreciate the added complications that a divisional or multi-unit structure creates for the strategic management of human resources of any international company. Parent company managers can, in theory, decide to operate somewhere on a continuum between two distinct choices of a decentralised or centralised approach. Managing human resources through a decentralised structure, with an emphasis on *local* systems and methods appropriate and responsive to that area, region or nation, helps promote a feeling of task ownership and the commitment of the staff to the local organisation. The alternative is to consider placing an emphasis on the policies, systems and methods associated with the company's base or *home*. This advances the needs of the corporation worldwide and encourages a consistent, coordinated approach utilising the expertise established at the centre.

A *local* solution would be favoured by those who adopt a perspective of *cultural relativism* where cultural differences and societal diversity are considered pre-eminent. This strategy for managing cultural differences is that of leaving alone the culture of each business unit (Hoecklin, 1995: 56–70). For present purposes a working definition of culture would refer to a community's shared values, attitudes and behaviour which are passed from one generation to the next. By contrast the corporate or *global* solution would appeal to those who are attracted to a *universal* outlook where work is considered to be such a fundamental activity that its management (in the hands of experts) is viewed as having a general and uniform applicability. As previously suggested, this rather stark choice can be modified by efforts to *combine* the two approaches, though we have noted that this can be difficult to sustain even in a domestic context. How much greater the human resourcing challenge is likely to be in an international context, no matter how appealingly simple the often quoted edict of *think globally, act locally* may sound! The task of attaining the vertical and horizontal integration of the human resourcing function across the companies of a global enterprise will always present difficulties, especially when managers believe they have to pursue local diversity and corporate integration simultaneously (Torrington, 1994: 101).

How then can the balance between the centre and its subsidiaries be managed in the international organisation? How might it be possible to think globally yet act locally? Taking in turn the same solutions proposed for the domestic, multi-unit organisation: a two-way flow of communication between the centre and its foreign subsidiaries will present the same obstacles but magnified by even greater differences of distance, time and perhaps linguistic expression. Great claims, however, are being made on behalf of today's telecommunications systems which have enabled cheap and convenient electronic mail to 'shrink the globe' into a more manageable entity. Even so, the use of international assignments by multinationals and of managers' regular visits to overseas subsidiaries reveals the continued reliance on face-to-face relations, which remain a critical aspect of communication across international organisations.

Effective two-way communication is probably an essential but insufficient condition for achieving a combination of corporate and local effectiveness. It is the medium for the message. This leads us to the second possible strategy, one that is said to require relentless communication: to build a strong corporate culture internationally, to promote shared values and to reinforce consistent behaviour (Hall and Torrington, 1998: 41). *Building* a corporate culture that is distinctive almost always means a need to *change* the culture of its members. This is to amend the values, beliefs and attitudes of individuals as applied to their work. We have already asserted that it is not easy to transform a person's taken-for-granted view of their world, but it is debatable that it will always be more challenging to inculcate a distinctive corporate culture in a foreign location. Our own observations tell us that the respective cultures of the churches and military organisations, for example, are probably more difficult to change than the work-related cultures of local staff employed by the foreign-owned businesses in countries like Malaysia or Azerbaijan. In this comparison national culture is less significant for human resourcing decisions than organisational culture. The indigenous language and culture of Malaysian or Azeri staff are usually reserved for outside working hours, and those charged with changing the army or the church will need to be as discerning about cultural factors as any international manager (Welch, 1997; Overell, 1998b).

Once again we seem to reach the conclusion that international human resourcing differs little from its domestic counterpart even in the apparently obvious area of culture. However, this is not to argue that culture, and especially national culture, is not a crucial factor in devising an appropriate human resourcing strategy. Work on multicultural teams reveals that the members' different nationalities (rather than their personalities) lie at the root of group tensions and misunderstandings (Adler, 1997). This should not be too surprising a revelation since for most people our nationality or national identity can be said to define our *lifelong* culture (Billig, 1995). However, there is a danger of emphasising the employees' national culture at the expense of their subculture, which might be more significant. Variety exists within nations as well as between them, as visitors to multicultural societies, for example, can testify. In addition, a focus on national customs and rituals may divert attention away from that part of the society's culture which is concerned with work and employment. It is this particular dimension that a strong corporate culture should be seeking to change. Yet, just as work can come to dominate one's life, so can a company's work culture be perceived as omnipotent and not always welcome: *you bind me to a constancy which is not my way.*

This discussion of a cultural strategy to bind centre to subsidiary raises doubts about its efficacy, though the chiefs of companies such as Hewlett Packard, IKEA and BP will no doubt attest to its part in their global successes. We have also confirmed the importance of taking into account relevant cultural factors when devising human resourcing strategies. This will apply equally to the design of human resourcing systems and procedures, which is our third possible way of bringing expertise, coordination and consistency from the centre to each local company. The thorough consideration of cultural and other contingent factors would seem to be a necessary component in shaping such procedures and systems if they are to work in each organisational context. However, this returns us to an earlier theme concerning the importance of the horizontal integration of human resourcing procedures and systems across each part of the global organisation, and the achievement of a high degree of internal 'fit' (Marchington and Wilkinson, 1996: 394–400). A contingent approach might appear not to deliver this outcome on an international scale and practitioners are often more attracted to models of so-called 'best practice'. These would seem to offer a uniform collection of human resourcing practices which, in addition to qualities of integrity and consistency, claim to have universal application and the promise of delivering competitive advantage (Pfeffer, 1994).

However, actuality is almost certain to prove disappointing unless best practice ideas can be translated into distinctly local solutions that ensure they are appropriate for the specific organisational context (Stopford *et al.*, 1994). This will apply to both domestic and international situations, and a study of local cultures, including employee expectations, will help management formulate those recruitment, selection, employee development and reward practices that are the most likely to work, and to avoid those that will not. For example, an individual performance-related pay scheme may prove ineffective if the workforce has a collectivist or group-centred outlook. Similarly, a sophisticated approach to recruitment and selection may be at odds with a societal preference for personal recommendation or where the candidate's family seek to be involved. While these may sit uneasily with professional notions of propriety and impartiality, a form of nepotism based on mutual obligation and respect, as well as self-interest, can offer the employer a guaranteed level of work performance which the recruit will feel personally obliged to honour. Finally, the case for a contingency approach to international human resourcing is demonstrated by the need to examine employment laws to determine which practices are permitted to work! This assumes, of course, that it is company policy to respect and operate within a country's laws, no matter how irksome or corrupt they may appear to be.

National and international human resourcing

The examples above illustrate our view that managers make human resourcing decisions based on their interpretation of societal and organisational factors: their choices are influenced by circumstances and their opportunities reined in by constraints. We have already seen that this process applies to national as well as international human resourcing; and both will be subject to a manager's *bounded rationality* whereby interpretations are made and decisions reached on the basis of less than complete information or understanding (Simon, 1977). It would seem reasonable to presume, however, that human resourcing managers are more likely to perceive a foreign set of circumstances as more complex and indeterminate than those encountered in their home country. Consequently, managers with international responsibilities will perhaps be more conscious of the inadequacy of their knowledge and of the need to act upon this by conducting investigations, taking expert advice, hiring a consultant and so on. It is ironic that a manager's assumption that they have sufficient knowledge about human resourcing issues in their national environment may lead to an inattention to detail and a neglect of significant factors.

Whatever the manager's level of awareness of the need to conduct a careful examination of contingent factors, the method of analysis outlined for human resource strategy-making is identical for national and international contexts. This has to be so, since the contribution of the human resourcing function to the enterprise and the dilemmas associated with a multi-divisional organisation provide a common agenda for practitioners, whether within or across national boundaries. As such, the decision-making model, emphasising management choice based on an evaluation of circumstances, is valid for any context and calls for a sensitivity to those contingent factors that might have an impact on the management of the organisation's human resources. It is true that the choices and contingencies found in international human resourcing may provide the practitioner with a host of novel and different situations, but it is equally true that those features which might be thought to define an *international dimension* are essentially those found in all human resourcing situations.

Torrington assembled 'The seven Cs of international HRM' – culture; cosmopolitans, i.e. staffing arrangements; compensation; communication; consultancy; competence; and coordination – 'to identify some activities that are different in nature when a business is international' (1994: 6). As will be evident from the preceding discussion, these seven activities are not exclusive to international companies, and the underlying principles of skilful human resourcing implicit in our analytical model should remain unaltered. However, we do need to acknowledge that these seven elements are likely to exhibit some differences in international companies. Though these are differences *of degree* and not of basic nature, they will visibly affect the tasks undertaken by those in the human resourcing function.

Furthermore, if our framework for understanding human resourcing across national boundaries is to be truly comprehensive, it will be necessary to incorporate any *additional features* that will complete our picture. In the next section, therefore, we will build on our way of thinking about international human resourcing and begin the process of providing more information on some of the choices and circumstances that practitioners may encounter. By focusing on the international dimension we are acknowledging that other chapters in this book will be dealing with key human resourcing activities in more detail. As such, they represent a valuable information source that supplements and supports our approach to international human resource strategy-making.

In general, management choice is restricted in effect by *constraints* which arise from the circumstances that exist. Constraints such as those imposed by demands from the legal system are self-evident and likely to be observed out of necessity. Other constraints may, however, present a degree of choice for management decision-makers who, in theory, will perceive their own self-interests as being best served by promoting the goals of the organisation. As an example, the technical and organisational skills required for a key position in a multinational company's foreign subsidiary may lead to the management decision to appoint an existing employee from the *home country*. Most of the workforce, however, is likely to be from the *host country*. Not only are they likely to be significantly cheaper to employ, such staff will also be attractive to the management if they are perceived to be malleable and conveniently recruited, trained and retained (at least in the short term). Ideally, if successful, this human resourcing strategy ought to satisfy both the decision-maker's self-interest and the goals of the organisation.

Case Study 10.1

Setting up a business in a host country: Elite Hotel

The 'Elite Group' is a well-established American multinational company that has its headquarters in New York, from where it directs the operations of its 80 wholly owned five-star hotels worldwide. The company has an enviable reputation as a leading player in the hospitality industry. Located in the major business and tourist centres of the developed world, it offers its business and tourist clientele outstanding service and facilities and is able to charge premium prices.

The company's senior decision-makers have recently been presented with an intriguing opportunity to set up an Elite hotel in Azerbaijan, a newly independent republic, formerly part of the Soviet Union and situated between Iran and Turkey. Intelligence from an influential oil executive has alerted the Group's directors to the recent influx of Western oil companies that are negotiating with the government of Azerbaijan, which is looking for inward investment in the development of its oil and gas industry that will rival any other in the world. This will mean, insists the source, a significant and long-term demand for hotel accommodation suitable for visiting oil executives, government leaders and their various officials. The country's few existing hotels are austere and very much part of the Soviet era. They would be unacceptable to this clientele.

An obvious location for any new hotel is Baku, the capital of Azerbaijan. Its population of one million is packed tightly into the city's margins, which adjoin the Caspian Sea. The city has a cosmopolitan reputation in an overtly Muslim country, which is marked by strong family values and social roles that tend to be clearly defined by traditional male dominance. However, Baku, like the rest of this less developed country (LDC), has an inadequate infrastructure. Frequent loss of water and gas, electricity and telephone services appears to be a normal feature of daily living. Communications with the 'outside world' are difficult and there is certainly no concept of a five-star hospitality industry.

The company's decision-makers can see an opportunity for furthering its corporate objectives of growth, market leadership and enhanced returns to shareholders. Furthermore, the country has a low-wage economy (the equivalent of $30 per month) and is experiencing high unemployment, so its well-educated population is likely to be grateful for any sort of employment. Set against this is the risk of venturing into a relatively under-developed host country with concerns about political instability, with an evening curfew that is rigorously enforced.

This presents a number of challenges, not least those involving the human resourcing function. An *equivalent 160-room hotel* in Geneva, for example, employs a total of 300 full-time staff across 7 departments. The main three: Rooms (comprising reception, reservations, housekeeping, security, fitness centre and swimming pool), Food and Beverage, and Maintenance, employ by far the most staff. The more specialist functions of Human Resources, Marketing and Sales, Purchasing and Accounting have relatively fewer personnel. However, as is typical of this industry, each department is headed by a director supported by two levels of management. All seven directors report to the hotel's general manager, who is charged with achieving the targets set by headquarters in New York.

At stake is the Group's international reputation, but it has a strong corporate culture and the experience of establishing itself in a variety of host countries, though none as 'challenging' as Azerbaijan.

Activity 10.1   Human resourcing in Elite Hotel – part 1

1. Taking account of the organisational context, what are the particular *human resourcing challenges or issues* that will need to be addressed in setting up a new hotel of international five-star quality?

2. What steps could be taken to ensure that the company meets these challenges and what people can the company draw on to undertake these tasks?

The Elite Group's corporate management will be keen to steal a march on its international rivals, but to do so it will need to invest heavily in the construction of first-rate accommodation and satisfactory utilities, such as power and water supplies. Above all, the company has to make sure that its clients experience the seamless qualities of five-star service throughout their stay.

Clearly, the human resources employed by the hotel will also be absolutely critical to the achievement of this aim. In securing people with appropriate capacities and attitudes to work, management can be reassured that the Azeri workforce is well educated, can speak some English and is likely to be most grateful for a position with a prestigious Western multinational and for only modest payment. Following Watson, such a set of circumstances appears to present employees who are not going to be a source of uncertainty for the employing organisation. Their tasks are relatively straightforward and the labour market would suggest 'easily obtainable and replaceable employees' (Chapter 1, p. 27). Consequently, a less experienced management might opt for a low commitment HR strategy, notwithstanding a need to consider the significance of employing mostly female staff in a male-dominated, family-oriented Muslim society. Indeed, such a marked balance of power in favour of the employing organisation would mean that Elite's management was able to ensure that the hotel's allegiance to five-star standards prevailed. Any initial unease or reticence on the part of Azeri employees, concerning their exposure to Western ways, was dealt with firmly through a constructive but autocratic style of management, which was consistent with a view that the hotel would always need to be run by expatriates.

However, the overriding importance of high-quality customer-facing service for the hotel's international residents and guests presented management with a particularly challenging set of human resourcing issues to resolve. The hotel's reputation is paramount, so how can amenable but inexperienced Azeri employees be transformed into effective human resources dedicated to the aims of the hotel? In this respect the multinational was able to call on its own international expertise. By appointing staff from across the group as the general manager and as directors of the seven departments, the hotel in Baku was provided with men steeped in the organisation's culture and equipped with the technical knowledge of five-star service. Such company men, especially chosen for their 'pioneering spirit', were excited by such a project. They would seem well placed to recruit and select and then initiate their untried employees and, by offering above the local rate of pay, the hotel was inundated with applicants. For the time being, such remuneration would be quite acceptable.

At the same time these expatriate managers would need to be mindful of, and alert to, any cross-cultural issues that might occur. How to appoint females in preference to males? How to handle the selection interview that has the female candidate accompanied by members of her family keen to vet the company's suitability as an employer? How to reassure their concerns about the safety of their daughter or sister, who is required to work in the company of foreign businessmen and until after the curfew? How to train staff to Western concepts of service?

Such is the stuff of international human resourcing. The basic elements typically differ only in detail from the domestic version, but it is this detail that can provide the tingle of excitement that comes from its challenge. That said, it is also true that international human resourcing involves dimensions that are worthy of particular analysis.

Globalisation and organisational approaches to international human resourcing

Globalisation at a worldwide level refers to 'the growing economic interdependence among countries as reflected in increasing cross-border flows of goods, services, capital and know-how' (Govindarajan and Gupta, 1998a). At an organisational level globalisation can refer historically to the extent to which a company has expanded its operations so that it engages in 'cross-border flows of capital, goods and know-how across subsidiaries' (Govindarajan and Gupta, 1998a). It can also be used to describe a corporate strategy, designed to reap the benefits of becoming a global company. Globalisation at all levels is, therefore, very much an outcome of corporate decision-makers who perceive globalisation as an attractive and feasible proposition. For example, in stark terms manufacturing has been outsourced to the developing world.

Yet, the process need not be an inexorable one. Economic uncertainties may drive national governments and corporate decision-makers towards the protectionism of defending a home market and away from the free-market ideology that has been synonymous with globalisation. Indeed, some would argue that 'ideology' is all it is. The European Union, for example, continues to give over $80 billion a year to its farmers. Critics claim that livestock in rich countries get more money than poor people in developing countries! In simple terms, the EU gives around $800 per year for each cow, which is more than matched by the $1,000 from the US and $2,500 from Japan for each animal. Frenkel (2006: 398) cites similar evidence for the United States. In 2002 around 25,000 US farming companies accounted for a third of total global output, even though their costs were twice the international price of cotton per pound (Stiglitz, 2003: 207). Monbiot explains that this was made possible by the use of subsidies worth around $4 billion. These reduced world prices by a quarter and at the expense of 10 million African farmers (Monbiot, 2003: 190). With regard to manufactured goods, the average OECD tariff is more than four times higher for developing countries than for other OECD countries.

Such protectionism serves to sustain the stark disparities between the rich and poor countries. Developed nations make up 20 per cent of the world's population but consume 86 per cent of the world's goods (UNDP, 2001). By contrast, the poorest 40 per cent of the world's population account for just 3 per cent of world gross domestic product (GDP). World trade is estimated to be worth $10 million a minute, but the world's 49 least developed countries account for only 0.4 per cent of this. The persistence of such inequities continues to fire unresolved debates on what can be done to prevent global capitalism destroying itself. Neither have the various rounds of ministerial meetings of the World Trade Organization produced a solution. Consequently, there is a continuing concern that 'global capitalism's blindness to anything but the bottom line and an apparent indifference to inequalities suffered in the poorest countries' make the system unsustainable, which in turn places in jeopardy the living standards in the developed world (Elliott, 1998). However, the collapse of the latest world trade talks in Geneva (the Doha round) is interpreted by Elliott with sanguinity more than pessimism (Elliott, 2008). He concludes that it does not mean that the world is 'going to be plunged into a new era of protectionism. It doesn't mean that there will be a retrenchment in world trade that will lead to a 1930s-style Depression' (Elliott, 2008).

However, commentators seem less sure about the impact of a likely global recession, which in 2008 has seen economic stagnation combine with rising inflation. As consumers find themselves overstretched, prospects for global growth and corporate earnings remain uncertain. Prices have risen steeply for oil, agricultural and metal commodities alongside the so-called 'credit crunch' that emanated from the US. This was sparked by that country's over-exposure to high-risk (i.e. 'sub-prime') lending for house purchases. Consequently, individual borrowers have been unable to pay their mortgages and have defaulted on their liabilities. The ensuing fallout extended far beyond the US, demonstrating the scale of financial globalisation. Major institutions (notably banks) have written off billions of pounds in bad debts and face 'continued financial distress' with equity investors and the banks themselves 'worried about the health of the banks' (Wolf, 2008). However, as 'the storm clouds of inflation, rate rises and pressure on earnings steadily accumulate' and both established and emerging economies face troubled waters, the implications for globalisation still remain unclear (*Financial Times*, 2008a). However, with the advantage of being witness to subsequent events and outcomes, including the demise of major commercial banks worldwide, the reader may be in a position to assess the implications of this unprecedented fiscal crisis of global proportions.

At the same time, analysts have detected that the credit crisis does seem to have 'now worked its way into the real economy, with individuals and companies struggling in almost equal measure' (Dey, 2008). Dey points to the fragility of both corporate and consumer confidence; and it is possible to identify even very successful companies that need to respond to a deteriorating business environment.

By way of example, in two decades Starbucks Coffee moved from a handful of outlets in Seattle to become the largest coffeehouse chain in the world: a corporate empire of more than 15,000 stores in nearly 50 countries, generating annual sales of about $10 billion (Cornwell, 2008). In view of its global ubiquity, the company could be said to have 'expanded too far, too fast' and certainly 'no retailer is immune from an economic downturn . . . and none less so than the sector that deals with discretionary expenditure' (Pukas, 2008).

Thus, just a year after the onset of the 'credit crunch' Starbucks reported its first quarterly loss in 15 years and announced store closures and job cuts worldwide. Six hundred stores across America were to be shut, with the loss of 12,000 shopfloor jobs and 1,000 in administration. Australia was to lose 61 of its 85 outlets and around 700 jobs. As Cornwell (2008) notes, the 'laws of the marketplace can bring even the mightiest low . . . consumers are cutting back on non-essential spending, with expensive coffee among the first things to go'. Moreover, premium coffee is a product others can easily imitate and in 'an age of belt-tightening' Starbucks' voguish coffeehouses are not as appealing (Cornwell, 2008). This is definitely so for Jan Moir, whose personal view is that Starbucks' coffee is 'ludicrously priced muck'. True to form, she seems thankful that a world recession had finally halted the company in its tracks: 'Where good taste failed, the credit crunch has prevailed' (Moir, 2008). The group seems also to have attracted the ire of anti-globalisation campaigners. They have condemned the corporation for its dominance over the Third World coffee producers as well as allegedly draconian employment practices imposed on its employees (Pukas, 2008).

Needless to say, Starbucks contends that its international expansion strategy remains in place. The company saw the cutbacks as the result of conditions specific to each location. The group continued to view Britain, for example, as a growth market, and planned to complete the opening of 100 outlets within a year, bringing its UK total to 700 (Walsh, 2008).

In spite of the above case study analysis there can be little doubt that, on balance, a global economy and global businesses remain very much a critical component of our existence. The best-known branded names – drinks, fast foods, sports equipment, motor cars, petroleum, computers, pharmaceuticals, electronics and other consumer products – can be found in the majority of the world's 200 countries. Popular statistics can also reveal the dominance of multinational companies. Fifty of the world's top 100 economies are not countries but companies. The largest 200 corporations control 28 per cent of economic activity, but employ only 0.25 per cent of the global workforce. Furthermore, the 10 biggest companies combined turn over more money than the world's smallest 100 countries, and the $104 billion profit of the top 10 firms exceeds the GDP of 29 African countries.

We can sense the impelling force of globalisation ourselves. We can also appreciate that the economic liberalisation of the world's developing countries and the technological advances in telecommunications and transportation have combined to make globalisation an enticing prospect for those corporations seeking to grow and survive. In the face of increasing international competition, multinational company chiefs have identified the opportunities afforded by the globalisation process as the means by which to meet the challenges. In turn, their business decisions help to sustain the process. These international opportunities, such as in China (today's leading recipient of FDI) and the former Soviet Union, include capturing new markets and realising greater economies of scale; the creation of extensive networks for the transfer of new ideas and know-how across the organisation; and the optimal allocation and relocation of resources. All of these set an agenda for an organisation's international human resourcing strategy. Attention to human resourcing activities and initiatives will be required to mobilise those resources which will best contribute towards growth and increased profits, leading ultimately to long-term corporate survival. In theory, a comparable agenda ought to be present in a domestic organisation, too.

Multinational companies are undoubtedly agencies for increasing global interdependence, but it would be wrong to assume that they were truly independent of any nation since, outside a handful of companies, the biggest corporations are owned by capitalists from a particular country and dominated by the culture of that country. Using *The Financial Times*' list of the world's top 500 companies, which is based on their market capitalisation, in 2003 the United States contributed 240 of the 500 followed in order by Japan with 47, the UK with 34 and France with 24. In the rankings for 2008 these have moved to the respective totals of 169, 39, 35 and 31 corporations (*Financial Times*, 2008b). This indicates a relative decline in the fortunes of American and (to a lesser extent) Japanese-based multinational companies.

However, the list may also serve as a pointer to even more significant developments. Familiar US names remain in the top 10 companies: Exxon Mobil (1), General Electric (3), Microsoft (7), AT & T (8) and Proctor & Gamble (10), but have been joined by PetroChina (2), which is a new entry to the Global 500; Russia's

Gazprom (4); China Mobile (5) and the Industrial & Commercial Bank of China (6). Making up the number is the UK's largest company, Royal Dutch Shell at ninth. Furthermore, the total of 39 companies in 2003 from Asia-Pacific countries (excluding Japan) has risen to 74 in 2008, represented predominantly by China (with 25 companies), India (13), Australia (11) and Hong Kong (10); and followed by South Korea (5), Taiwan (4), Singapore (4) plus Indonesia and Thailand with one each.

In terms of using the FT Global 500 as a snapshot for the evolving nature of business globalisation from 2007 to 2008, American companies still dominate but less so, and the number of Chinese companies has increased most, from 8 to 25, followed by Russia and India, each on 13. Another burgeoning international player is Brazil with 11 companies in the top 500. Perhaps even now China, Russia, India and Brazil can be regarded as the 'big developing countries' (Elliott, 2008), but to what extent are we seeing their part in the early stages of the changing contours of global business? In his piece on the failure of the Doha round of world trade talks, Elliott refers to the World Trade Organization as 'the cockpit of globalisation'. For him, 'the emerging powers of the East are no longer prepared to be pushed around by the Europeans and the Americans' and as such they 'saw no real reason to make concessions' (Elliott, 2008).

The structure of multinational companies

From the above analysis we can also conclude that our model, of a parent company controlled from its national home base and linked with its foreign subsidiaries, remains an appropriate one for nearly all multinationals. We can also pursue our contention that a key consideration of global business is operating effectively across cultural boundaries and balancing organisational integration with responsiveness to local demands. The issue is how business units in several different countries are to be linked through human resourcing policies and practices. In theory, a strategic decision-maker might select from among the several choices and alternatives that exist along a continuum of centralised and decentralised arrangements. However, practitioners need to be aware that the strategic choice that has been made or has emerged for their own employing organisation will constrain and guide the human resourcing activities that follow.

The first such constraint is defined by the *structural form* which the multinational company (our generic term for those companies operating in several countries, whatever their structural form) exhibits, whether by management design or not. Although individual multinational companies may display a set of arrangements that are specific to them, it is useful to employ a classification of the forms of organisation used to manage multinational companies. This will enable us to identify our own organisation's structure in relation to the alternatives. The most productive typology is probably that formulated by Bartlett and Ghoshal (1989), which shows multinational companies evolving from the 1960s to the present (Hendry, 1994: 72) and displaying four distinctive organisational patterns, identified chronologically as:

1. the multinational (1960/70s),
2. the global (1980s),

3. the international (1980/90s), and

4. the present-day transnational (1990s).

The details of these are as follows:

1. The *multinational* pattern is predominantly a collection of decentralised and fairly autonomous operating units that are directed towards their own national markets. It displays relatively low company-wide integration and can be regarded as a multi-domestic organisation. The head of an operational unit is typically an expatriate but one with a considerable degree of autonomy. Human resourcing focuses on the needs of the local operation and will usually be managed by a local national who will be familiar with local laws and employment practices. Control exercised from the centre may well be confined to financial targets and results.

2. The *global* pattern is distinguished by a high degree of integration managed from a corporate centre and designed to take advantage of the economies of scale from worldwide activities that are geared to distributing standardised products to global markets. The management of foreign operations is required to implement strategies determined at the centre, including decisions to switch resources between countries in the service of corporate goals. Consequently, in this structure human resourcing expertise and knowledge will reside at headquarters where policies, systems and schemes are formulated and issued to those in the subsidiaries for implementation. Those at the centre may need to ask whether formalised policies and practices will be sufficient in ensuring that local employees will carry out the directives or whether expatriate managers might be required to control the foreign units (Schuler *et al.*, 1993).

3. The *international* structure is best regarded as an intermediate type, combining the decentralised and centralised elements of the multinational and global types. This version is associated with managements' perceived need to be more responsive to distinctive local market needs without losing the global integration that generates so many competitive advantages. The outcome is an arrangement which affords autonomy to the overseas units on some matters while retaining central control over key areas like finance, product development and market development. The human resourcing expertise and knowledge developed at headquarters is transferred to the company's subsidiaries for local adaptation as appropriate. This requires the systematic development of umbrella policies and practices. However, where the foreign units exhibit considerable local differences an all-embracing directive on, for example, compensation, recruitment or performance appraisal may prove fairly meaningless. There seems to be a presumption in this type that the predominant flow of information should be from the centre, which is assumed to be the repository of good human resourcing practice. This idea and its shortcomings are challenged in the latest organisational type, the transnational.

4. The *transnational* structure provides an integrated network of highly interactive units that encourages all parts of the organisation, including the centre, to share and benefit from the expertise and knowledge that each possesses. As Hendry points out, it 'means transferring innovations from the centre to local markets, and from local markets to the centre and other localities' (Hendry, 1994: 74). It offers the synergies of cooperation with the autonomy needed for

staff motivation and the best decisions for the local conditions (Schuler *et al.*, 1993: 429). It has been suggested that the transnational type is an ideal towards which multinational companies will need to develop for long-term competitive advantage. Multinational companies are faced by 'the need to manage globally, as if the world were one vast market, and simultaneously locally, as if the world were a vast number of separate and loosely connected markets' (Schuler, 1998: 138). This may render the ideal solution unattainable since it means developing simultaneously the local responsiveness, the efficiency and the transfer of know-how associated with the multinational, the global and the international types of organisation respectively (Bartlett and Ghoshal, 1989: 12).

However, one might conceive of a transnational human resourcing function being managed in order that the best ideas and systems were shared company-wide, for consideration by managers with both local autonomy and an overall appreciation of corporate priorities. Understandably this transnational approach is likely to entail particular attention to recruiting and developing a certain kind of manager. Management development programmes and events will be organised, coordinated normally by the corporate human resourcing unit, as a way of providing the glue that 'bonds together otherwise loose and disparate entities' (Schuler *et al.*, 1993: 433). One suggestion is the development of a *global mindset*, which places a high value on sharing information and skills across the whole organisation (Govindarajan and Gupta, 1998b).

Increasingly, it is the transnational type that receives attention from commentators who assert that 'any structure must cope with what is likely to prove the 21st century's biggest management challenge: combining worldwide reach with the flexibility and speed of reaction of a local competitor' (Martin, 1998). The logic of this kind of thinking is that the success or failure of a multinational company will depend to a large extent on having an international human resourcing strategy that strikes the right balance between meeting corporate, i.e. company-wide, human resource needs, and the particular local needs of its subsidiaries.

We have now examined the first set of strategic choices on the *structural form* of the multinational company and how each can act as a major constraint on the subsequent operation of international human resourcing, which is shaped by the way in which the problematic relationship between central and local management is resolved.

The dominant management orientation of multinational companies

The second major set of strategic choices, which in turn will significantly influence the practice of international human resourcing, is defined by the *dominant cultural viewpoint or approach* adopted by the multinational company's management at headquarters towards its foreign subsidiaries. As this contingent factor refers to top management's attitudes and values it is not always the outcome of conscious choice but often the expression of a taken-for-granted view of the world held by individuals. As such, we are acknowledging that the human resourcing priorities and practices can be circumscribed by the Weltanschauung or world-view of corporate decision-makers through which they seek to make sense of things. In our analysis we will be able to illustrate some of the implications of a dominant management orientation for human resourcing activities by looking at staffing decisions (Hendry, 1994: 79) and appraisal criteria (Tung, 1998: 384).

Heenan and Perlmutter (1979) have provided a fourfold classification of such an orientation:

1. polycentric,

2. ethnocentric

3. geocentric, with

4. its regiocentric subset.

A particular orientation is identified through its *stance on different national cultures*. This is applicable to those at the helm of a multinational company, since their company is identified by its national home base in relation to foreign operations. It follows, therefore, that any orientation displayed by headquarters management towards their foreign operations may be heavily influenced by comparisons of national culture. In addition, it should soon become clear that, although the three main orientations have distinctive implications for human resourcing, they are also likely to correspond (though neither inevitably or precisely) to the forms of organisation as follows: multinational-polycentric; global-ethnocentric; transnational-geocentric.

1. The *polycentric* orientation recognises the validity, at least for business reasons, of each foreign operation's national culture and, as such, replicates a multi-domestic view of the organisation's subsidiaries. As a consequence, each business unit is afforded considerable autonomy with regard to local human resourcing decisions and activities, though strategic decisions are invariably controlled at headquarters. This means that subsidiaries are usually managed by local nationals with staff from the parent company occupying the key jobs at headquarters. There is a logical inclination to adopt local standards to evaluate staff performance, but this invites the problem of offering staff little incentive to adopt strategies that can maximise the firm's achievements globally.

2. The *ethnocentric* orientation of the dominant management coalition sees the world, including foreign subsidiaries, from the viewpoint of its own particular culture, which in turn is regarded as superior to any other cultural background. Unlike *parochialism*, which assumes that the home culture is best because cultural differences are unwittingly not acknowledged or recognised, *ethnocentrism* implies a conscious belief that the home culture is superior. This means that the organisational culture will mirror that of the home country and that little account is taken of the cultures of the host countries. It is not uncommon and quite understandable, therefore, for ethnocentric managers to see things from their own cultural perspective and to evaluate people in foreign subsidiaries against the standards and expectations of the parent country. The pre-eminent status of these standards is then confirmed by the human resourcing systems and procedures which are devised by the experts at headquarters for transmission to each locality. When applied to appraisal, this approach could lead to an unfavourable assessment of those managers who may be performing effectively in local circumstances, but who are not accorded sufficient consideration. Such a bias is further reinforced by a staffing structure that allocates key jobs, both

at home and overseas, to employees from headquarters. As Hendry notes, 'nationals from the parent country rule the organisation both at home and (as expatriates) abroad' (1994: 79).

3. A *geocentric* orientation, unlike the other two approaches, does not differentiate between employees on the basis of their nationality. Instead it endeavours to adopt a supranational view of the organisation in which a preoccupation with national cultures is regarded as a constraint on the global interests of the corporation as a whole. The only culture that matters is that embodied in the multinational company itself which, in demoting nationality *per se*, will espouse the value of the diversity of skills and insights that national differences can bring. The development of multicultural teams sits easily with this orientation. Furthermore, ability rather than nationality provides the basis for staff selection, development and promotion, which means that the top management team must also be international in composition and global in outlook if this approach is to have credibility across the organisation. One manifestation of such an outlook is the creation of global standards for staff appraisal. The assessment of staff performance is gauged in relation to the organisation's global position and advancement. This may entail, for example, the rationalisation of production activities around the world. The opening of plants in one location may be accompanied by the closure of others elsewhere.

The geocentric view is epitomised in Percy Barnevik's 'own words', which are as resonant today as they were when he first offered them in 1997 when interviewed for the *Financial Times* (see Exhibit 10.1). Speaking as an organisational decision-maker in his role as chairman of ABB, the Swiss-Swedish engineering company, he emphasises the importance of building a multinational cadre of international managers. Not only will this ensure having the 'best people in place', but it will also deliver the competitive advantages that accrue from a group of managers with diverse cultures. However, Barnevik counsels that such arrangements ought to be contained within an overarching set of corporate values that all managers adhere to and exemplify. In this way he offers his practical formula to resolve the global–local dilemma: the need to have global coherence alongside local receptivity. As such, it sets the foundations for the company to move towards a transnational structure.

Exhibit 10.1

Percy Barnevik, ABB and Investor: A multinational cadre of managers is the key

'Too many people think you can succeed in the long run just by exporting from America or Europe. But you need to establish yourself locally and become, for example, a Chinese, Indonesian or Indian citizen.

'You don't need to do this straight away but you need to start early because it takes a long time. It can take ten years. Globalisation is a long-lasting competitive advantage. If we build a new gas turbine, in 18 months our competitors also have one. But building a global company is not so easy to copy.

'ABB has virtually finished building its global structure. The main task now is to bring more executives from emerging countries in Eastern Europe and in Asia into the higher levels of the company. We have 82,000 employees in emerging economies. We have to bring the best of these to the top.

'This takes time. Building a multinational cadre of international managers is the key. It is one thing for a chief executive himself to be a global manager. It is quite another to persuade other executives to think and act globally. At ABB we have about 25,000 managers. But not all of these need to be global managers. We have about 500. Very rarely would you get a global manager from outside.

'Of course, companies such as Shell and IBM have such people, but there are relatively few available to hire. Also it's better if people grow up with ABB values. It's difficult to digest our culture if you have spent 10 or 20 years in another company. The difficulty is that bosses tend to attract clusters of people from their own nationality around them.

'They do this not because they are racists, but because they feel comfortable with people they know best. You get a German cluster or a Swedish cluster. So you must make sure that when a boss selects managers, he considers people from other countries. And you must make sure good people from other countries are available to him. Managers have to be asked to supply lists of potential candidates for work outside their countries.

'Then, if a German manager selects four Germans for a task, you will be in a position to suggest an Italian or an American and ask him to think again. There's a disadvantage in doing this because you lose a little since maybe they will all have to speak in bad English instead of in German or whatever. But the advantage is that you get the best people in place. And you build a global company.'

Source: A multinational cadre of managers is the key, *The Financial Times*, 8 October, 1997 (Wagstyl, S.)

4. A *regiocentric* orientation is best regarded as a subset of the geocentric orientation, replacing a global view with one defined by reference to a particular geographic region, such as Asia-Pacific or South America. This means that a corporate region is perceived by management as a microcosm of the corporate world. The policy will be to promote the company's own regional culture and to appoint and develop staff from within the region to manage its operations. As with the geocentric view, this orientation is probably the result of a deliberate strategy related to the parent company's business operations. The definition of a *region* may differ between companies and the perceived coherence of a designated region will depend significantly on the approach of the human resourcing function towards issues such as staffing, training, rewards and career progression. The movement of staff across the geographic region promotes this orientation, but would be at odds with the continued domination of the very top jobs by managers from the parent country (Hendry, 1994: 79).

We have now examined the second set of strategic choices on the *dominant management orientation* of multinational companies and how each can act as a major constraint on the subsequent operation of international human resourcing, shaped by the way in which organisational decision-makers approach national differences and cross-cultural issues. It is this latter dimension which distinguishes international human resourcing from its domestic counterpart. But in principle the practice of human resourcing will be constrained by *dominant orientation* as well as *structural form* in *both* types of environment. However, in focusing on the international aspects of human resourcing, we can briefly consider the function's contribution to an organisation where the move towards becoming a transnational business is regarded as the best strategy for survival in the global economy.

Changing the mindset

As argued above, the transnational organisation model is perhaps one that corporate decision-makers are more likely to aspire to than actually attain. Its attraction lies in its promise to deliver, to large and unwieldy multinational companies, organisational integration with local responsiveness: the capability of operating effectively across cultural boundaries without losing the essentials of good management within cultural boundaries. The slogan 'think globally, act locally' provides a simple lead; but how might those responsible for human resourcing assist in moving a company towards the transnational model?

One crucial ingredient appears to be the development of a *way of thinking* that will ensure that managers and other key employees operate in accordance with a geocentric organisational culture. This will embody a set of values, attitudes and behaviours that rests on a foundation of openness towards national cultures and 'operates on the premise that cultures can be different without being better or worse than one another' (Govindarajan and Gupta, 1998b). It then follows that staff should embrace the rationale and advantages of sharing ideas, information and work practices across the whole organisation and not just their small part of it. However, in practice multinational companies are much more likely to display an ethnocentric orientation (Govindarajan and Gupta, 1998b). So what are the human resourcing initiatives that might refashion this more closed world-view? How can the function help to create the new way of thinking, which we have labelled *geocentric* and others have termed (perhaps confusingly given the ethnocentric pedigree of the global structure) a *global mindset*? Assuming the adoption of an approach that is integrated by its reference to corporate goals and the need for mutually supportive practices, the human resourcing levers shown in Table 10.1 (Govindarajan and Gupta, 1998b; Pucik, 1998) may provide the basis of an answer.

It should be apparent that the task of managing change in a single-site domestic organisation is itself difficult; and that delivering cultural change will be even more difficult. The problems and barriers of doing the same for a multinational company, with its conglomeration of national cultures and multitude of employees, are bound to be immense. Not least, the levers identified above have to be enacted in a fairly coherent way in a very uncertain environment. It would appear that normative integration through the building of common perspectives, purposes and values is an attractive but complicated human resourcing strategy. Perhaps transnational coordination might be better achieved through bureaucratic control. Appealing to employees' self-interest through a consistent set of rules and procedures and supported with straightforward messages may generate the behaviour and eventually perhaps the mindset desired.

Table 10.1 Human resourcing levers in the multinational firm

Staffing	A mix of nationalities; international experience and language skills in senior and other key positions; the utilisation of cross-border business teams (multicultural project teams)
Development and training	Management development programmes with a mix of nationalities; international assignments; training programmes for cross-cultural awareness, language skills, IT applications and corporate information
Rewards	Career ladders that reward international experience and are open to employees worldwide; performance assessment and pay schemes that reflect global as well as local performance
Communications	The development of flexible networks of global relationships for the exchange of information; employing state-of-the-art communications media
The HR function	The corporate HR function will gain credibility to influence others only if it presents itself as an example of how a transnational organisation: – recruits, develops and rewards people – makes decisions that integrate global and local perspectives – stimulates global networks

Exhibit 10.2

Altering behaviour and attitude through bureaucratic control

We would like to illustrate this last point by reference to an analogy that affected one of the authors personally: a simple management decision that altered his behaviour and attitude towards what he had previously perceived as a trifling item, a twenty pence piece.

'The fare for the journey to work by bus was until recently £1.10 and my payment to the driver was constrained by the company regulation that no change could be given to passengers. This meant that my energies were continually directed towards having the exact amount to give the driver for both the outward and return journeys. Consequently, gathering £1 and 10 pence coins became a priority, with a couple of five pence coins being considered an acceptable alternative. From my perspective the twenty pence coin shared a low priority with the one and two pence coins in my pocket. At this point such coins were perceived as not only insignificant, but also mildly irritating.

'Then the management of the bus company decided to raise its fare to £1.20! My behaviour patterns and my attitude towards the much-maligned twenty pence piece have been transformed. It now plays an important and obvious role in my travel arrangements; it appeals to my self-interest and operates in an uncomplicated (exact fare) system.'

It would be simplistic to suggest that human resourcing systems can emulate such an approach, especially in a multinational company, since the control mechanism over the fare-paying passenger is face-to-face and immediate. However, it is worth postulating that the essence of effective human resourcing, international or otherwise, is one that has a direct impact on the perceived self-interest of the employee. The complication in a multinational environment arises because it is more challenging to establish how *self-interest* is perceived and interpreted by employees of diverse cultural backgrounds. *Self-interest* can be viewed in our framework as a contingent factor for human resourcing managers to consider, and we will briefly address the issue of national culture as a contingent factor shortly.

Staffing for transnational companies

'Almost everything else in international HRM flows from the way the firm manages its movement of staff . . . the overall approach to staffing determines the degree of attention given to each of three groups of employee – parent-country nationals (PCNs), host-country nationals (HCNs) and third-country nationals (TCNs)' (Hendry, 1994: 79). PCNs come from the country where the multinational has its head-quarters; HCNs are from the country where the subsidiary for which they work is located; and TCNs are from outside both.

Staffing policies represent our third set of strategic choices as represented by the various combinations of PCNs, HCNs and TCNs that might be employed in the multinational company. In theory, staffing arrangements should be determined through a systematic human resource planning process. However, this activity can only come into play in conjunction with the organisation's staffing policies which, as we noted above, are shaped both by the *structural form* and the company's *dominant management orientation*.

Most companies currently convey an ethnocentric approach to staffing, favour-ing PCNs for their headquarters staff and for the top jobs whether in the parent country or a host country. PCNs are often used for foreign assignments for their technical expertise and product knowledge, and to ensure adherence to standards by local staff as well as an allegiance to corporate goals. HCNs will figure more prominently in a polycentric approach, but predominantly in the host country where their local knowledge will be regarded as invaluable in dealing with local factors. Understandably, therefore, the human resourcing role, which needs to take account of employment laws and labour market conditions, is typically allo-cated to an HCN. Finally, TCNs are most likely to be employed by a geocentric, transnational organisation, which manifests a very pragmatic view in seeking to employ staff according to capability. Consequently, it does not differentiate between employees on the basis of nationality, and a TCN can additionally convey the international nature of the business.

Activity 10.2	Recruitment in an international humanitarian aid organisation

Consider the following advertisement for a Senior Manager of Programmes with a Danish humanitarian organisation in the Democratic Republic of the Congo (formerly Zaire), which appeared in the recruitment pages of a Kinshasa newspaper. Taking into account a) the duties and personal requirements described, and b) the following *fact file* on the country:

- A population of 50 million Congolese, comprising more than 250 ethnic groups, inhabits an area the size of western Europe that is not linked by roads or railways. An estimated 3 million people have been killed in Africa's bloodiest war, which lasted five years and involved at least six other African armies along with numerous rebel groups. A new power-sharing government is tasked with organising multi-party elections in two years' time. However, the country has always experienced either conflict or dictatorship since independence from Belgium in 1960.

- Average life expectancy is 41 years for men and 43 years for women. Average annual income is US $80. Currently, there are more than 10,000 United Nations military personnel in the country to monitor the peace process. Finally, with the improving situation, aid workers from various agencies such as the World Food Programme have access to areas that were too dangerous to enter earlier,

1. In general, what are the likely advantages and the potential limitations of employing an HCN in this post?
2. What would be the likely advantages and the potential limitations of employing a PCN in this post?

ADVERTISEMENT

Denmark's largest humanitarian organisation has a vacancy for a suitably qualified Congolese national to work initially on a major programme in the Democratic Republic of the Congo, in the challenging position of:

Senior Manager of Programmes

In this position you will work closely with our Danish Director of Operations in developing, directing and implementing comprehensive plans and programmes to ensure the most effective utilisation of the funding provided by the Danish government for achieving our humanitarian objectives.

You will be heading our team of fifteen local staff and take responsibility for the formulation and implementation of human resourcing policies and procedures, including recruitment and selection, performance appraisal, grievance and discipline, and staff welfare. Additionally, you will establish training and development policies and programmes, to achieve excellence for all levels of employees and to ensure their total commitment and the right attitude to work.

Requirements

- A degree qualification, with relevant working experience of at least four years.
- Fluent English speaker (the language used in all our operations).
- Highly developed interpersonal and organisational skills and an ability to interact with governmental officials and national and local representatives of non-governmental organisations (NGOs).
- Familiarity with national and local laws including employment or labour law.
- The appointee must be frank with staff at all levels and give all necessary support to the Director of Operations, to ensure all programmes are implemented effectively.

Remuneration

The right candidate will be given a very attractive remuneration and benefits package.

Interested candidates are requested to apply in confidence giving complete personal particulars including age, career record, educational background, present position, current and expected salary and contact telephone number and e-mail address. Please enclose a recent passport-sized photograph (n.r.) to

The Advertiser
P.O. Box 1234 (Ref. 664)
Kinshasa

Only short-listed candidates will be notified

It would appear to make sense that overall responsibility for the humanitarian organisation in the Democratic Republic of Congo (DRC), which is funded from Denmark and is ultimately answerable to its Danish government sponsors, should reside with a native Dane, who is more likely to have experience of the NGO's organisational culture and systems. Furthermore, the holder of the post of Director of Operations needs to be well placed to coordinate between the two countries and to manage activities accordingly. There needs to be an assurance that operations in the DRC comply with corporate objectives and policies.

Equally, for the vacancy of Senior Manager advertised above, there is a good case for appointing a national Congolese, especially in terms of ensuring the effective utilisation and motivation of the local staff. An inherent grasp of the national context and the ability to converse in a native language clearly give the HCN a tremendous advantage. As a result, the formulation and implementation of human resourcing policies and procedures are likely to be more relevant to this country's peculiar set of circumstances. One would also expect that the qualified local is more likely than an expatriate to be accustomed to government protocol and national employment law.

Nevertheless, underlying misgivings on the part of the Danish may persist, but these should be allayed by the requirement of the appointee to 'work closely with our Danish Director of Operations'. In particular, it is important that the HCN is capable of being open and honest with people from various stations in society and also follows the NGO's humanitarian agenda and not his or her own.

An obvious area for consideration in appointing a PCN or an HCN to this vacancy relates to the war-torn history, poverty and present political uncertainty in the DRC. An HCN is likely to be more resilient in such an impoverished environment. He or she is, therefore, the more likely to perform well and to manage staff effectively – and to stay in post for a longer period in spite of these immensely difficult circumstances. Furthermore, his or her salary costs are going to be significantly lower than those for an expatriate and, in a cost-conscious NGO, this may be another important consideration. By contrast, an expatriate may take too long to adapt to the host environment and even then may experience barriers of language and culture that invite misunderstandings. As such, expatriates are much more likely to meet with failure, incurring considerable costs for themselves and for their employing organisation.

Our humanitarian aid agency in the DRC is relatively small and employs just one PCN and a number of HCN staff. This is in contrast to the type of company classified as *transnational*, where a combination of all three groups of employee, PCN, HCN and TCN, is more likely to be evident. Furthermore, in tune with this approach to staffing is the quest for a *global mindset*. The logical outcome in the transnational organisation, therefore, is that all three groups of employee are unlikely to be limited to working in only one country. At various times during their employment, employees (as international transferees) might be classified as *expatriates* when working away from the company's parent country; *inpatriates* when working in the company's parent country but which is not their home; and perhaps *transpatriates* when operating in a country that is neither their home nor that of the parent company. For reasons of political correctness the management of a transnational company might prefer to play down the significance of employee nationality implied in the above classifications. But for reasons of pragmatism it is essential that the human resourcing function recognises and seeks to deal with issues associated with *employee relocation*.

International relocation

In addition to normative integration and bureaucratic control, *critical flows of staff* within and between the units of the organisation represent a third human resourcing strategy for achieving inter-unit coordination in the transnational (De Cieri and McGaughey, 1998: 631). The flow of people through staff transfers impacts on the corporate culture by helping staff in all locations to develop a broader corporate perspective and increase identification with the global organisation. Transfers also promote networks for the exchange of knowledge and the sharing of ideas and skills.

According to De Cieri and McGaughey, relocation involves 'the transfer of employees – and often families – for work purposes between two locations and for a period of time that is deemed to require a change of address and some degree of semi-permanent adjustment to local conditions' (1998: 631). Interestingly, the prevalence of expatriate transfers reflecting the traditional multinational and global structures is gradually being rivalled by inpatriate transfers, which are associated with developments towards transnational structures. However, this trend in international staffing points more towards disquiet about the escalating costs and 'added value' of employing expatriates. More recently, a growing unease about the danger of global terrorism has been included in the decision-making equation on whether or not to use expatriates. As a consequence, the increased use of HCNs in key positions means that the number of foreign nationals annually brought to corporate headquarters by their employers is rising. As inpatriate transferees they come for development assignments, technical training, to participate in project teams, and to absorb the corporate culture. Many are being groomed to return in place of expatriates. Human resourcing specialists in particular are trained so that they can use new skills on their return to their subsidiary unit.

The concept of international relocation draws our attention to the significance of the transfer to another country and the similarity of experience between the various types of international transferees. It seems reasonable, therefore, to confine our analysis to the expatriation scenario as a concise way to explore the relocation process, noting that a country that is not one's own might be experienced as foreign and strange whether one is an inpatriate or an expatriate.

The success of an international relocation can be gauged by the employee's work performance and contribution to the company's goals. All employee performance is clearly the remit of the human resourcing function and attention to human resource planning, recruitment, appraisal, development and reward activities, for example, can be found in other chapters. Work performance and staff retention also depend on an individual's adjustment to the new environment and culture, and establishing constructive relationships with new colleagues. Again this will apply to all employees, domestic as well as international. The main difference for the expatriate's experience is that typically such adjustments are likely to be more demanding and may revolve around the family's inability to adapt. Furthermore, the cost of expatriate failure is very expensive in terms of lost investment. The direct cost of maintaining an expatriate overseas may exceed four times normal salary. Indirect costs may include lost sales, reduced productivity and competitive position, and damage to international networks. It is crucial, therefore, for the relocation process to be managed effectively in order to reduce labour turnover and to enhance the expatriate's work performance. This management of the process can be usefully divided into the pre-departure, expatriation and repatriation phases (De Cieri and McGaughey, 1998: 633).

The pre-departure phase

Building on the firm foundations of a systematic approach to human resourcing will help to ensure that the selection, remuneration and training processes utilised in a domestic environment are applied appropriately to the international situation. The selection criteria, including proficiency in the host-country language, can be constructed from an analysis of the job to be undertaken. Individual characteristics such as cultural tolerance and the ability to learn in an alien setting can be added, and many organisations also consider partner and family factors. One key reason for the resistance of employees to international mobility is the disruption of a partner's career or children's education. This leads us to the variable nature of the *inducement–contribution equilibrium*, which describes the calculation that an individual makes before deciding to take up a post or not. The individual will need to perceive that the contribution, effort and sacrifices required will need to be balanced by the inducement or rewards on offer. Postings in either the Democratic Republic of Congo or Azerbaijan are, for example, likely to require additional inducement to compensate for the deprivations that are expected and will have to be endured. Another reason that employees might be reluctant expatriates is the uncertainty surrounding their career on their return. Transnational companies, however, are less likely to invite this concern since high office is often critically dependent on international experience.

The inducement–contribution equilibrium enables us to appreciate the significance of non-financial as well as financial rewards in the pre-departure phase. An expatriate remuneration package must attract the candidate in the first instance. Thereafter, it must motivate and retain the employee during the expatriation phase. It is important that the package is drawn up at an early stage, and the employee will probably be offered a package that includes base salary, expatriate premium, cost-of-living allowances and additional fringe benefits. Taxation advice is also of prime consideration (De Cieri and McGaughey, 1998: 635). However, a main issue will be that expatriate salaries may strain the organisational objective of fairness and equity for all categories of employees. Perceptions of inequity can demoralise employees. A home-based remuneration policy will ensure equity for the expatriate with colleagues at home, but will alert those in the host location who may be paid different amounts (Adams, 1963). The alternative host-based remuneration policy, however, may cause disquiet for the expatriate. It may well be that the incompatibility between the objectives of fairness and equity and motivation is insurmountable. However, it is perhaps the very complex structuring of expatriate remuneration that will enable a reward system to be designed so that it is perceived as respecting both host and home country relativities.

Pre-departure training and development can be equated to pre-assignment training in any domestic situation, and will therefore utilise the practices outlined elsewhere in this text on training needs analysis and programme design. Consequently, training interventions should enable managers to acquire the knowledge, understanding and skills to operate effectively in the host country. In addition, training opportunities might sensibly be offered for family as well as expatriate orientation. The expatriate may be required to conduct business in the host country language and to develop cultural awareness and interpersonal skills. Both language and cross-cultural training typically entail a huge investment in time and energy, especially if field experience through an initial visit to the host country is considered desirable. Intercultural experiential workshops and sensitivity training are other methods used in cross-cultural training programmes, but it would appear that many companies limit their training to information briefings and the provision of reading material (De Cieri and McGaughey, 1998: 636), thus tempting expatriate failure, which typically means cutting short the assignment.

The expatriation phase

Cross-cultural training in the pre-departure phase is designed to assist in the adjustment process during the expatriation phase, but further support mechanisms may also prove vital in ensuring that expatriates and their families can adjust to different organisational and societal cultures. This is important if the expatriate is to work effectively in the host environment, and introduces us to the possible detrimental repercussions associated with *culture shock*, which refers to 'the experience of psychological disorientation by people living and working in cultural environments radically different from that of their home' (De Cieri and McGaughey, 1998: 636). The set of psychological and emotional responses that people experience emanate from their being 'overwhelmed by their lack of knowledge and understanding of the new, foreign culture' (Black *et al.*, 1999: 47). The springboard for these negative feelings is likely to be the way in which a seemingly alien culture challenges the taken-for-granted assumptions that people hold. Furthermore, feelings of frustration, anger and anxiety are associated with the disruption of routines and an inability to handle everyday situations without great effort. 'The more basic the routine that is disrupted because of cultural ineptitude, the more severe the blow to the ego, and the more severe the resulting culture shock' (Black *et al.*, 1999: 49). Anger and frustration might even turn to anxiety and depression as the expatriate's 'positive self-image gets battered and their confidence crumbles' (Black *et al.*, 1999: 49).

Support through the appointment of capable and conscientious mentors at both the local and home sites, regular information from the parent company, and social gatherings may help; but assistance with practical problems and building host country networks will perhaps be more important as expatriates seek to establish a position in their new community. With appropriate support, the highs and lows of the initial 'honeymoon' and 'homesick' stages are more likely to lead to a realistic appraisal of the situation and an acceptance and adjustment to the new environment. The alternative is disenchantment and an inability to cope.

Culture shock and expatriate failure conjure up images of whisky-soused colonials depicted in the old black and white films. Yet this feature of the relocation process can also occur in a domestic environment. Adjustment can be painful when you are sapped by homesickness, whether or not you are 60 or 6,000 miles from home.

The repatriation phase

In a transnational environment a *repatriate* should ideally be perceived as a valuable member of the parent company and settled into a new position that benefits the organisation by calling on the knowledge, skills and contacts gained from overseas. In this instance human resource planning for career development has met the needs of both the company and the repatriate. In practice, however, insufficient attention is often paid to ensuring that the repatriate does not suffer from problems of readjustment (Forster, 1994). Having been away from the centre of activity for some time, repatriates may find that they have been quietly forgotten, that there is no clear role for them. Things have moved on and no one is much interested in their tales from overseas. This can obviously lead to feelings of disillusionment with work and the company, which will not be helped if the repatriated employee's family members find they are similarly placed in their home environment.

A planned and positive approach to re-entry is clearly preferable; and preparatory training, repatriation planning, written job guarantees and mentoring may all have a role in promoting this approach (De Cieri and McGaughey, 1998: 639). In contrast, initiatives aimed at patching things up after the event, such as counselling, are tackling the symptoms and possibly focusing on the individual rather than the deficient relocation systems. Inadequate repatriation management in particular would have adverse implications for a transnational's human resourcing strategy. Potential expatriates in the company are unlikely to accept an international posting if they perceive the diminished career prospects of repatriates and their indifferent reception. It is far better to create a virtuous cycle of a career structure that incorporates international postings. Effective human resourcing would ensure that such an approach would apply equally to host country and third country nationals, too. One outcome of this would be the creation of robust and purposeful international networks, which are the lifeblood of the transnational organisation. In practice, however, it is typically left to individual departments to initiate international assignments. As a consequence, more thought is given to filling the gap left by the expatriate than to that individual's return. In these circumstances it comes as little surprise that the repatriation process fails to incorporate the expatriate's return to a suitable job.

Host country employment – contingent factors

In this chapter we have sought to establish a way of thinking about human resourcing and to use a framework for analysing any set of employment circumstances that will equip us in making decisions about the management of an organisation's human resources. We have asserted that the principles underlying this contingency approach hold for both domestic and multinational companies, though we have also identified those additional features that strengthen our comprehension of an international version of human resourcing.

We have also seen the different ways in which a host country subsidiary can be viewed, and the various implications this has for the employment of host country nationals (HCNs). This depends partly on the degree to which any notice is taken of host country conditions and circumstances. Our framework suggests that human resourcing decisions should always rest on a careful and sensitive analysis of contingent factors; but the role of the human resourcing function is to neither defend cultural traditions nor to ignore them. The decisions themselves are matters of human judgement, subject to bounded rationality and, in balancing global business needs with local circumstances, human resourcing managers may have to decide 'where and how to push and where to give in to cultural differences' (Pucik, 1998).

The position taken in this chapter is that the analytical consideration of contingent factors is a process that applies equally to both domestic and international situations. It could well be, however, that domestic managers take for granted that their many assumptions about the local workforce are correct. They do not consider the need for 'careful and sensitive analysis of contingent factors'. International managers, on the other hand, may feel rather overwhelmed by the number of host country factors that are not known or just cannot be taken for granted. This may lead to a concerted effort to conduct an analysis, possibly with the help of a fact file on the country and its ways, and perhaps through a specialist consultant. Unfortunately, much of this analysis starts and ends with environmental factors. These clearly are important influences on human resourcing activities, but can lead unhappily to a concern with national characteristics that detract from the real focus of attention, the employee. By way of example, a traditional analysis of political and economic factors will examine the country's national systems and their influence on future business investment.

It is proposed, therefore, that human resourcing analysis concerns itself primarily with the employment relationship, since it is this reciprocal connection between employer and employee as buyer and seller of labour that is at the centre of all human resourcing activity.

The analysis of local conditions

The employment relationship

For students of the employment relationship this starting point generates a collection of important variables that together provide a significant insight into the *choices* available to human resourcing decision-makers (as outlined in Chapter 1).

The *legal* dimension of the employment relationship is in theory the most transparent of all factors yet also the most elusive and complicated. If you have experienced the confusion and nuances surrounding national employment law, then it is likely that other societies (such as Azerbaijan and the Democratic Republic of the Congo) will have regulations on contracts of employment and statutory rights that will warrant the advice of an expert. Decisions can then be made as to the level and nature of any legal constraints on the management of human resources.

The *economic* dimension of the employment relationship relates primarily to the terms and conditions of employment that prevail in the local labour market. A study of the financial and non-financial rewards on offer from other employers and the productive endeavour that might be expected from the employees in return may enable the subsidiary to recruit and retain suitable employees. Such analysis will have helped the management of both the Elite Hotel in Baku and the humanitarian agency recruiting in the Democratic Republic of the Congo.

The *political* dimension refers to the balance or indeed the imbalance of power between management and the workforce. While this is likely to vary between organisations, several factors can contribute to the general balance of power in the host country. Those that would generally favour management include: high levels of unemployment; low levels of trade union membership; and anti-strike legislation. A balance of power that works in management's favour will provide a greater range of options for the human resource decision-makers.

The *psychological* contract is defined by the unwritten, often unspoken, expectations that each side has of the other. For example, workers may be expected to give their employer loyalty and commitment in return for job security, recognition and mutual respect. Alternatively, an investigation into our host country may discover that the local workforce has relatively low expectations on the quality of working life and that the management can, as a consequence, make greater demands.

The *social* dimension of the employment relationship concerns the actual relations between and within the parties: are they typically detached, affective, informal, deferential, collectivist or individualist? Analysis may detect patterns that identify our host society and help determine how management might best interact with the workforce. In Malaysia, for example, informal relations may appear reasonably relaxed and familiar. However, when it comes to the use of their authority, managers are expected to be unequivocal and their subordinates efficiently acquiescent.

Finally, the *moral* aspects of the relationship define what is considered right and wrong. Some societies may exhibit very prohibitive outlooks on the use of child labour and sexist attitudes and behaviour; others may countenance both activities as acceptable. It is in such areas that those representing the company may be advised not to give in to cultural differences. Indeed, recent cases involving sweatshops and child labour in third world countries have damaged the reputations of certain manufacturers. Hasty retreats have served to demonstrate that *ethical* human resourcing is often the best strategy.

Through the analysis of these critical and complementary dimensions, the decision-makers of international organisations should be better equipped to make judgements on how best to manage the employment relationship in each of its foreign locations. However, such factors are subject to change and any analysis should be recurrent if it is to be effective. The management of the Elite Hotel is beginning to experience such change four years after the establishment of the hotel in Baku.

Case Study 10.2

Four years on – human resourcing issues at the Elite Hotel

Early success

Four years after the completion of building its new hotel in Baku, Azerbaijan, Elite's senior executives can look back with tremendous satisfaction that this hotel has outperformed nearly all others in the Group. It has an average 95 per cent occupancy rate and, with a room-only charge in excess of $300 per night, has consistently delivered high profits to its American owners and has hitherto added to Elite's international status.

Increasing numbers of oil company executives and senior politicians of all nationalities make regular visits to Azerbaijan, which is seen as a 'land of opportunity' for Western multinational corporations. Until now, Elite has been the only hotel offering acceptable standards of accommodation, in terms of both its facilities and its standards of service.

Much credit has been given to the original strategy established by Elite's head of corporate HR. Each of the hotel's seven departments is managed by an expatriate manager, as are the other managerial posts. Such managers have all had experience elsewhere in the Group and represent a range of nationalities: British, Swiss, German, Turkish, Moroccan, American and Malaysian. Some of these initial appointments specifically took into account individuals' experience of Elite's previous 'new openings' and their inclination to be 'trailblazers' and to champion Elite's corporate culture.

Almost all other employees are local and particular attention was paid to their training to ensure the hotel's five-star level of customer service. Initial recruitment was managed by the director of HR, a Malaysian who has been with the Group for over 20 years. There were over 50 applicants for each vacancy and female applicants were invariably accompanied at interview by a senior family member. Those appointed to customer-facing jobs were predominantly well-educated females with an excellent command of English. For most candidates the driving motivation seemed to be the status of working for a Western multinational, together with the relatively high earnings, which traditionally go to the employee's extended family. Status also accrued to specific departments, and locals most valued working on Reception and especially the 'door', which both have high visibility.

To a large extent the hotel's undoubted economic success can be traced back to the contribution of its human resources. Expatriate managers discovered enormous fulfilment from opening the hotel in spite of working long hours in very difficult and tiring conditions. A pioneering spirit and sense of achievement was evident, with local staff sharing in this initial sense of excitement and showing real enthusiasm for developing new skills. A genuine sense of belonging seems to have been generated in the hotel and guests commented on the welcoming and congenial atmosphere.

Surfacing problems

Four years have passed and three top-class hotels have opened in direct competition for Elite's business and conceivably its experienced staff. Human resourcing problems are beginning to emerge, though not especially related to the new competition.

The Elite Group's policy of moving its managers to new locations has meant that several expatriate managers have been moved on. Others are getting 'itchy feet' and replacements are not easily attracted by the prospect of relocating to Baku. At the same time, Group HR is under pressure to reduce expenditure by cutting back on 'excessive' levels of expatriate remuneration.

Similarly, the satisfaction of local staff has appeared to waiver. Hitherto, management has been able to achieve results through an autocratic style, tempered in some measure by the benevolence shown through, for example, the annual 'open day' for family members. Consequently, management has taken for granted the high levels of performance of local staff, reassured by low staff turnover that is typical of a national culture where people are meant to be content to stay in their jobs indefinitely.

However, staff now appear compliant in their work rather than committed. Increasingly exposed to Western values and encouraged by the support of a few individual managers, the expectations and aspirations of local staff have changed over the four years. For some there is disquiet over a lack of promotional opportunities. Many talented and capable staff are now seeking career development and management appointments, but feel their enthusiasm and ambitions are not being recognised. Staff feelings of gratitude are being further eroded by resentment against inequitable rewards offered to their expatriate 'betters'.

Such reactions have surprised many of the more seasoned managers and the first signs of Elite staff moving to a competitor and taking with them transferable, marketable skills have heightened their concern. The hotel's general manager has now turned to his director of HR for advice and Group HR has recently issued a discussion document on 'aligning HR with the business strategy by earning employee commitment'.

Activity 10.3   Human resourcing in Elite Hotel – part 2

The general manager of the Elite in Baku has identified the pressing need to resolve the hotel's human resourcing issues and to gain employees' high commitment to sustain market leadership in the long term.

1. What are these issues and why are they so critical to the hotel's future?
2. What strategic HR interventions would you recommend and why?
3. To what extent should your proposals be a corporate or a local responsibility?

For the Elite Hotel in Baku to continue its impressive business performance, its management has to redress those human resourcing issues that have emerged with the organisation's changing context. Externally, the arrival of three top-class hotels has posed a potential threat to the Elite's advantageous position in the local labour market. From Watson's perspective (Chapter 1) the hotel is facing an increase in uncertainty surrounding its local employees, which is manifested in the first signs of staff leaving to work for the competitors. Such departures can be costly as valuable personnel and their skills need to be replaced through recruitment and training. In addition, the uncertainty for the business is intensified by the growing discontent among those staff that remain. The initial aspirations and expectations of local staff have been transformed by their ongoing encounter with the hotel's ways of working and by the confidence shown in them by some of the expatriate managers. Hence, certain individuals have developed ambitions that seek promotion into management positions, and the recognition, status and intrinsic work satisfaction that this might bring.

Unless and until such aspirations and dissatisfactions are addressed, the hotel's local human resources can create increasing levels of uncertainty for its managers and potentially weaken its long-term success. Now, with management's increased confidence in the capabilities of its local workforce, the Group's original staffing plan of appointing only expatriates to management positions can be reconsidered. Furthermore, Group HR has advocated a move towards an HR strategy based on 'earning employee commitment'. This would seem to endorse Watson's model, which suggests that an uncertain environment is probably best served by a high commitment HR strategy, the components of which are spelt out from page 31. More specifically, the appointment of locals to supervisory or management posts would signal a move towards a high commitment approach, which will necessarily mean their receiving management training and development and enhanced rewards to match increased responsibility. This course of action and its underlying principles could also serve to inspire other staff, especially if it is communicated effectively throughout the hotel. Ideally it might be part of a planned succession programme, such as 'Pathways to Management'. The hotel's expatriate managers could coach and equip their Azeri protégés in management skills, handing over their Baku responsibilities before they depart to other parts of the Elite Group's global empire.

This particular HR strategy has the merit of being governed by the changing context of the organisation and its relatively unchanged business objectives. In so doing it also seeks to resolve some of the issues associated with the expatriate managers. The restlessness of key expatriates, the difficulty in attracting replacements to Baku and a directive to cut back on expatriate costs indicate that the appointment of some managers from the hotel's local workforce is very appealing. It is also feasible in view of the qualities demonstrated by those locals of high calibre, the encouragement from certain expatriate managers and the general support of Group HR.

On balance, the main responsibility for steering the proposed transition should lie with the hotel's general manager, advised by his HR director. They can be expected to share an understanding of the cross-cultural dynamics at work in their hotel. At the same time they will be fully aware of the twin instructions from HQ: to promote high employee commitment and to cut expatriate costs, with the need to enhance business performance being implicit. They can, therefore, call on corporate HR for broad guidance on implementing organisational change and to coordinate staff transfers group-wide.

For whatever reason, when the Elite Group opened its hotel in Baku there was an initial management conviction that no Azeri could or would ever take on a management role. This belief has since become ill-founded and the subsequent appointment of locals to junior management posts has proved so successful that, through further development, two people have now risen to directorial posts. However, just as the company changed over four years, it can change again. In HR continual vigilance is needed, not least in being sensitive to managing cross-cultural issues.

Cultural factors

It will already be evident that our schematic analysis of the various dimensions of the employment relationship can help to inform corporate strategists on how a subsidiary's human resources might be managed. It will also be apparent that *all* of the above dimensions both define and are informed by the culture of the subsidiary's local community. This partly explains the interest, both academic and practitioner, in studies designed to identify the relevant attributes of national cultures and in comparative frameworks based on a considered view as to the *key* cultural dimensions (Hofstede, 1991; Laurent, 1983; Trompenaars, 1994; Hall and Hall, 1990). Our approach, however, would be to go beyond (though not ignore) such broad characterisations of national cultures and to undertake a rigorous investigation into the actual situation affecting the host country subsidiary. In so doing we need to be sensitive to the particular values, beliefs, attitudes, expectations and patterns of behaviour as they relate to work and its management in a specific set of circumstances. Our aim, therefore, would be to unearth the relevant features of the host culture as it affects the employment relationship and hence the management of human resources.

As previously mentioned, human resourcing decision-makers may find it useful to adopt a perspective which has at its centre employee self-interest as it relates to work performance and staff retention. The analysis of the local culture and the consequent design of human resourcing systems (in recruitment, training and rewards, for example) would then be concerned with how employee self-interest is interpreted within that particular culture. By way of illustration, individual self-interest in Asian and Middle Eastern countries is typically (and outwardly paradoxically) promoted through *collectivism*, where any personal success relies on and is gained through an allegiance and obligation to others and to one's circle. This contrasts with *individualism*, which is more obviously indicative of self-interest and is evident in some Western societies. Self-interest can also be associated with *particularism:* a system that upholds the interests of friends and family. This is in contrast to one based on *universalism* where there is a shared understanding that individuals will succeed on merit through a procedure that evaluates everyone according to the same impartial criteria.

In designing systems that enhance work performance and staff retention in an overseas subsidiary, the human resourcing strategist might well decide to amend or modify parent company systems and practices. Any different interpretation of employee self-interest ought therefore to be borne in mind. For example, where it is the local norm to recruit through personal or government connections, as has been the case in China, it may be prudent to reconsider the exclusive use of impersonal selection criteria. Similarly, a reward system linking pay to individual performance is unlikely to be effective in an Indonesian subsidiary where 'they manage their culture by a group process, and everybody is linked together as a team' (Vance *et al.*, 1992: 323). Finally, that office with a window and the best view which we would expect to be earmarked for those with the highest status might not be welcomed in Japan. For a Japanese manager a seat by the window could imply that 'you have been moved out of the mainstream, or sidelined' (Schneider and Barsoux, 1997: 23).

Determining host country policies and practices

In recognising that the same policies will not produce 'the same effects in different cultural contexts' (Schneider and Barsoux, 1997: 128), we have suggested two broad approaches for human resourcing strategists to formulate policies and practices for host country subsidiaries. They can do so *ab initio* on the basis of an analysis of the local circumstances impinging on the various dimensions of the employment relationship (Schneider and Barsoux, 1997: 199–201), or by a critical examination of central or corporate human resourcing policies and practices with a view to local modification. It is perhaps this second of the two options which is most likely to appeal to decision-makers operating in a transnational organisation. Schneider and Barsoux envisage a management dialogue between headquarters and the subsidiary company, which would help to ensure 'a balance between global integration and local adaptation' (1997: 129). Needless to say, however, such a dialogue is in practice likely to be conducted within an inherently political relationship between the two parties, each with its own vested interests to pursue. Consider the following example (Exhibit 10.3) of the efforts by the headquarters management of a major American multinational to hold sway over its subsidiary managements. While ostensibly inviting host country managers to devise human resourcing practices suited to local conditions, there appears to be a clear steer in favour of adopting standards promoted by the centre. Hence, what might appear to be the actions of a well-meaning *transnational* organisation are more accurately interpreted as those of an *international* structure, where expertise and 'best practice' are considered to reside at the centre and be cemented in the intensive training provided. In this case it is more than implicit that subsidiaries will follow headquarters' lead.

Exhibit 10.3

Applying global standards?

Following the corporation's recent development of *best practices in leadership*, group management has sought to implement these globally by providing intensive training sessions around the world for the top managers of its subsidiary companies. The high profile sessions are designed to promote the new *standards of leadership* by driving home the importance of best practice in leadership, and by demonstrating how they can be applied in business situations for the benefit of subsidiary operations. This executive-level training is complemented by another series of leadership programmes aimed at the next layer of management and devoted to guiding individual behaviour. All of these training interventions are supported by high quality documentation and access to the various development guides on the company's intranet.

Promotional material for the initiative takes its lead from the group's worldwide house magazine, in which the corporation's group chairman notes that each business unit is being invited to take these best practices, comprising several competences, and tailor them to fit their own needs. The aim is to weave the standards into each business unit and to implement appropriate managerial behaviours translated for different cultures. In the same article, however, executives operating in the Asia-Pacific region commented that although some of the behaviours were expressed in different ways, their managers had been able to apply them with no major changes. In addition, the corporation's decentralised structure had allowed host country managements to apply the new standards to their recruitment and selection, succession planning, performance appraisal and culture training.

Maintaining favourable employee relations

In transnational organisations the intention is to ensure a satisfactory level of corporate consistency while avoiding the undesirable consequences of ill-considered or insufficiently modified human resourcing practices in the subsidiary company. This reflects an understandable management desire to attend to the quality of the employment relationship, so that it promotes rather than undermines the employee contribution that the human resourcing practices are designed to elicit.

From an employee relations standpoint, therefore, a human resourcing decision-maker will be concerned with maintaining sufficient goodwill and cooperation in the subsidiary company. This is likely to mean not upsetting local employees through transgressing their cultural norms or expectations. A reading of some illuminating examples of such violations (Schneider and Barsoux, 1997) reveals a host of employee sentiments that are potentially harmful to a constructive employment relationship. Distress, discomfort, frustration, friction, exasperation, alienation, demotivation and disruption are some of the similes used to convey the employees' adverse reactions to cultural infringements. Taken together they indicate the significance of cultural factors in maintaining favourable employee relations in a host country company. On the one hand, transgressions and misunderstandings ought to be avoided. On the other hand, management's sensitivity to a host country's work culture might be usefully developed and then harnessed to better advance the goals of the organisation.

Case Study 10.3

Cultural sensitivity?

The American manufacturing director of a multinational company in Kuala Lumpur continually affronts the sensibilities of his local Malaysian managers by his habit of putting his feet on the desk. This ignorance and transgression of a cultural taboo makes the managers feel awkard and uneasy in the director's presence, and less inclined to act diligently on his instructions. They have also had to get used to his more direct, argumentative and less diplomatic behaviour in management meetings.

However, for reasons of perceived self-interest employees *do* carry out his instructions and to some extent they seem prepared to eventually reconcile themselves to his 'foreign ways'. After all, the director represents the power of management on behalf of the parent company. He retains the authority and legitimacy of his position in spite of his unacceptable behaviour. Not surprisingly, therefore, our American director seems to remain quite oblivious to his impact on employee relations, even though his direct and blunt approach to appraising staff continues to engender hidden resentment from those on the receiving end of any critical comment. In Asia in particular, 'confronting an employee with "failure" is considered to be very tactless and even dangerous' (Schneider and Barsoux, 1997: 141). This is related to the need to 'save face' and to maintain an individual's self-esteem and overall reputation.

By contrast, a previous director from the UK was so conscious of the need to 'save face' that his diplomatically delivered criticisms of staff were often misinterpreted as praise. This did wonders for individual morale, if not for work performance.

Activity 10.4   Cultural sensitivity?

1. To what extent can we argue that, however inappropriate the behaviour of the American director, its consequences for the subsidiary company are likely to be negligible?

2. What kind of measures would you recommend for ensuring that both types of expatriate director manage their staff effectively?

This scenario raises questions about the significance of cultural factors in maintaining favourable employee relations in a host country company, and also about the importance of maintaining favourable employee relations *per se*. In this particular set of circumstances it is evident that Malaysian managers feel personally insulted whenever their manufacturing director rests his feet on the desk in their presence. Malaysians have learned that the act of showing the soles of your shoes in front of someone is both rude and ill-mannered. At the same time, these local managers judged that they were in no position to complain. Furthermore, their culture ordains overt deference to those in authority. They had, therefore, to come to terms with their emotions and continue to fulfil their work responsibilities.

Ill-mannered behaviour by the American director is unlikely to have a significant impact on the subsidiary company in so far as employees resign themselves to his different ways and continue to fulfil their work obligations. This submissive reaction follows the indisputable nature of managerial power. However, this does not mean that transgressing cultural norms can be safely ignored. Indeed, management would be wise to recognise and harness important work norms in order to promote productive employee relations. Hence, in certain Asian countries, for example, management should ensure that staff always 'save face' and be careful to avoid situations where there is a possibility of an employee feeling 'shame' when 'face' is lost.

This particular situation involves a potential loss of face and would appear serious enough for a Malaysian to harbour resentment against the perpetrator and to perhaps engage in forms of resistance against the company. As such, this transgression of cultural norms is significant and does have grave, rather than negligible, consequences for the company, all because of an expatriate's lack of cultural awareness in dealing with host country employees.

The American director seems insensitive to local work norms and oblivious to the damage he may be causing. This problem might well have been avoided had there been appropriate pre-departure training followed by support and advice from a suitable mentor in Malaysia. Cross-cultural training through experiential workshops may provide the essential knowledge and sensitivity, but such expensive interventions may be no guarantee of success. The American expatriate, for example, may have the knowledge yet lack the tolerance and behavioural skills required of him. In comparison, his British predecessor certainly possesses some relevant knowledge and shows an eagerness to respect Malaysian norms. However, his schooling in the importance for Malaysians of saving face has not equipped him to manage their appraisal interviews. Instead, his handling of the dynamics of this interaction has become too subtle and abstruse for it to be effective. Any practical solution is difficult to envisage other than through a mentor. This individual would need to be the eyes and ears of the expatriate and be capable of providing the director with appropriately constructive feedback.

Cross-cultural comparisons – the work of Hofstede

The case study above helps to illustrate our approach and preoccupation with

- identifying local organisational conditions, including relevant cultural factors, and
- establishing human resourcing practices for the host country environment.

As indicated previously (p. 325) our investigations and analysis would aim to go beyond those broader studies and typologies which seek to generalise comparatively about national cultures. However, such studies ought not to be disregarded. At the very least they are likely to increase our awareness of possible cultural dimensions, providing our own organisational research with a convenient starting point and a general guide as to what we might find.

In order to explore the nature and utility of these typologies, we will briefly consider the work of Hofstede (1991), a Dutch psychologist who has earned a considerable reputation as an international management scholar. By originally conducting a worldwide survey involving 116,000 employees of IBM, the giant American multinational company, Hofstede was able to show the enduring significance of national cultures in shaping employees' work-related values. Although IBM was renowned for having its own strong corporate culture, there remained 'substantial differences in work-related attitudes and values from country to country, revealed by his extensive and unique sample' (Barsoux and Lawrence, 1990: 8). The underlying national values espoused by the survey's respondents appeared to persist and the implication for management was clear: differences of national culture could not be ignored.

The four dimensions of culture

Through careful analysis based on the values held by people from different countries Hofstede was able to characterise the differences by reference to just *four key dimensions of culture*: power distance, uncertainty avoidance, individualism/collectivism, and masculinity/femininity. Furthermore, he was able to score and rank in order each of 53 countries against each of these key dimensions. This simplification of a potentially overwhelming number of cultural differences combined with the quantitative reassurance of league tables featuring many different countries might help to explain the attraction of Hofstede's typology. In addition, his value survey model appears to offer information that is sufficiently systematic, comprehensive and relevant for a managerial audience keen to make use of demanding yet accessible ideas. 'From a practical perspective, the cultural variables described by the model are intuitively appealing because of their apparent relationship to the management process' (Punnett, 1998: 20).

Through the work of Hofstede the human resourcing decision-maker can seek to locate a particular host country on each of the four cultural dimensions with a view to singling out the implications for management practices. A clearer indication is more likely where a country scores at the extreme end of a continuum, though it has to be acknowledged that most countries score neither very high nor very low on these indices.

Power distance

Power distance indicates the extent to which people in a particular culture accept and expect the existence of power differences in organisations and institutions. In a country ranked high on this dimension (Malaysia is ranked highest), organisations are likely to have more levels of hierarchy and greater centralised control, with little reference to employees for decision-making. Status and power would be viewed as appropriate reward mechanisms since those in authority are treated with the deference that is considered their due. At the other end of the spectrum (Austria followed by Israel), power differences in organisations are minimised and employees are more likely to participate in management decision-making.

Uncertainty avoidance

Uncertainty avoidance refers to the extent to which people feel uncomfortable with uncertainty and ambiguity. In a country where this sentiment is generally high (Greece is ranked highest, closely followed by Portugal), people look for certainty and predictability in their lives. In work organisations these might be secured through the precision of written rules and procedures, reliance on specialist expertise, and a preference for planning to minimise risk-taking. In terms of work motivation staff are likely to be especially interested in stability and security (Schneider and Barsoux, 1997: 79). By contrast, in a host country where uncertainty is seen as inevitable (Singapore exhibits the lowest levels of uncertainty avoidance, followed by Jamaica and Denmark), opportunities for innovation and change are typically welcomed and there is a greater acceptance of individual decision-making and risk-taking.

Individualism

Individualism relates to the degree to which people in a country accept the pursuit of individual self-interest, and value the effort and initiative associated with taking personal responsibility for decision-making and task completion. This contrasts with *collectivism* which is at the other end of the continuum, where the emphasis is on group cooperation and decision-making, and where group consensus and loyalty are valued. As an example, such cultural differences have clear implications for rewards management. Rewards based on individual effort should be more effective in the most individualist societies (the United States is closely followed by Australia and Great Britain). Those based on team effort should prove more appropriate for the most collectivist societies (Guatemala, Ecuador, Panama and Venezuela). At the same time, however, this particular cultural dimension is likely to affect most if not all facets of the human resourcing armoury.

Masculinity

Masculinity serves to describe a bias towards the values of assertiveness, competitiveness, performance, ambition, achievement and materialism. In Japan, which is ranked highest on this dimension, we might expect to find work organisations dominated by these task-centred characteristics and an emphasis on organisational success. However, such a generalisation is unlikely to prepare us for the various layers of etiquette and decorum which mark Japanese work relationships. *Femininity* refers to the opposite end of this continuum. It portrays those values which give priority to the quality of life, relationships and the environment; and it expresses a concern for those people considered less fortunate. Sweden, Norway, the Netherlands and Denmark (in that order) are ranked highest on this dimension, and managements in these countries might be expected to devote some of their attention to their employees' job satisfaction and the development of an agreeable work environment.

Using Hofstede's value survey model

Where the human resourcing decision-maker is most interested in a particular host country culture, this will be represented by a specific combination of its ranking and score on each of the four dimensions. Consequently, any interpretation of Hofstede's results may need to be more holistic than perhaps his model permits. Nevertheless, some conclusions can be drawn. If, for example, we recognise that Singaporean culture is broadly collectivist, does not avoid uncertainty, believes in power distinctions and is relatively low in masculinity, we ought not to be surprised if its managers display a paternalistic leadership style which expresses concern for staff and their quality of life, but without too much concern for job security.

While this type of national portrait is helpful in alerting us to possible cultural similarities and differences between host and parent countries, the human resourcing strategist would be well advised to assume that this represents no more than a general guide and a convenient starting point for further organisational research and analysis. This makes allowance for the cultural diversity that may reside in a single nation and recognises that 'any culture is far more complex than such models would suggest' (Punnett, 1998: 21). In just the same way that an organisation based in the city of Nottingham or Amsterdam, for example, might be characterised as *feminine*, so another Nottingham or Amsterdam company in a different industry could quite accurately be labelled as *masculine*.

A question can also be raised as to how representative and accurate are the model's descriptions of national culture as a whole. Since the study involved only IBM employees, there is a strong possibility that the scores reported by Hofstede for these particular respondents are 'an indication of the similarities and differences that one might expect to find among employees in this type of organisation in different countries' (Punnet, 1998: 19). Furthermore, any attempt to encapsulate all national cultures within just four key dimensions raises a concern as to whether important cultural variables might have been overlooked.

Notwithstanding these concerns, Hofstede's work should offer the discerning practitioner some useful concepts and insights. Furthermore, its focus on national cultures might well provide an appropriate *beginning* for the kind of organisational research that we have been advocating, leading to the comprehensive analysis of contingent factors and the subsequent establishment of host country employment arrangements. However, our approach should not be restricted to just host countries. As we have argued, domestic and international human resourcing are the same in all fundamentals. They also share the same essential methodologies and have access to the same portfolio of methods, techniques, systems and procedures – many of which can be gleaned from this book. It is on this basis that this chapter has directed its attention to those *international* aspects of human resourcing which might be considered as in some way distinctive.

Case Study 10.4

A global enterprise operating in a host country – HR strategy in practice

Premium Oil and Gas (POG) is the Dutch holding company of one of the world's largest petroleum and gas groups. The organisation employs over 80,000 staff in 80 countries and is best known to the general public through its 25,000 service stations.

POG's main activities are the exploration and production of crude oil and natural gas, together with the marketing, supply and transportation of these products. The company earns revenues of around £100 billion per annum based on its daily production of two million barrels of crude oil and eight billion cubic feet of natural gas, plus daily sales of six million barrels of refined products.

Over 90 per cent of POG's executives are Dutch nationals, of whom five per cent are women. This concentration can be explained by the company's Dutch origins and its consequent patterns of recruitment. Recently, however, POG's Chief Executive Officer, Ruud van der Zende, has pronounced that for the company to achieve its aspiration of being a 'truly great global company' it must work towards building a top management team that is visibly diverse. It should also continue to strive towards being 'genuinely meritocratic' at every level, attracting and retaining talent across the globe regardless of background, gender, nationality or sexual orientation. POG's stated intention is to respect different cultures and the dignity of individuals in all countries.

The company also aspires, says van der Zende, to be a 'modern, global learning organisation'. This will, he claims, enable success to be spread right across the company. The aim is to run a company that is responsive and flexible and that is distinguished by core values and objectives that are embedded everywhere.

This vision represents quite a challenge for a giant of a company that seeks to connect its central (group) headquarters with more than 120 decentralised business units. Business unit leaders are 'encouraged' to operate in many ways as if they are running their own separate business, but they are also 'required to comply with group policies and are absolutely accountable for the achievement of annual performance targets, which are subject to regular monitoring'. The rationale behind this management structure is its professed ability to 'facilitate rapid responses to new situations without the need for constant referrals to headquarters'.

One such business unit is POG Azerbaijan, enticed by the oil and gas reserves of the Caspian Sea, which are comparable to those in the USA and the North Sea. POG has been involved in offshore exploration in Azerbaijan for ten years, but has only recently begun actual production, delayed by political uncertainty and complex government relations. The development of offshore platforms and export pipelines represents for POG a £10 billion investment, which is critical to its long-term future.

The CEO of POG Azerbaijan is an experienced Dutch expatriate, Edwin de Boer. He heads up a company of almost a thousand employees, of whom 40 per cent are Azerbaijani nationals. However, over the next five years the workforce is set to double and de Boer is targeted to increase the local workforce to 90 per cent of the total. Privately, though, he thinks this is unrealistic. Recruiting qualified engineers (mechanical, electrical, production, instrument) and geosciences specialists will present particular difficulties, even though the company has an annual recruitment programme for graduates and trainees every spring. Other areas for active recruitment include drilling, commercial, health, safety and environment, public relations and human resources.

Interviewed recently for the company magazine, de Boer explained how one option for POG Azerbaijan would have been to rely on experienced expatriates to do the whole job, but that was not POG's way. His focus, he said, was on the recruitment of nationals, who could be developed so that they can ultimately manage the operation. Right now, 40 Azeri employees were undergoing technical training at POG's development centre in the Netherlands. For one thing, he continued, it costs considerably more to bring expatriates to Azerbaijan and it was important to employ those who understand the local environment, who know how to get things done. This fitted in with the company's belief in recruiting the best-possible staff to plan, build and operate the platforms and pipelines. A constant concern, however, was that Azeri standards were currently well below international standards on health and safety.

Recruitment and selection is a key function in a meritocratic company committed to employing the 'best of Azerbaijan's well-educated workforce'. Unfortunately, expatriate and local managers are known to 'turn a blind eye' to the nepotism and networking that secures employment. In order to combat such possibilities Group HR has instituted its assessment centre process for the Azerbaijani operation, including the use of standardised psychometric testing, designed to ensure consistency of selection worldwide.

However, the local HR services manager has expressed some reservations. Ongoing evaluation of the process has raised questions over the validity of westernised tests for the selection of nationals. In addition, candidates have shown their distrust of a process they see as impersonal and alien, at odds with more familiar face-to-face methods of recruitment.

With regard to training, Group HR, based in Amsterdam, is very much the champion of the 'learning organisation' advocated by van der Zende and is investing heavily in the Learning and Development (L & D) division of its Azerbaijani subsidiary.

The L & D team of five local staff, headed by a Dutch expatriate, is fully stretched. Its main responsibility is for the six months' dedicated training provided for each new intake of technician grade personnel, who are selected for their technical expertise and (preferably) previous experience with one of the national oil companies. In practice, L & D has to deliver three training and development programmes a year, covering a total of 120 entrants. Ominously, the planned expansion of POG's Azerbaijani operations will require future investment in the training of 600 over the next five years.

In addition to specialist modules in technical subjects and company procedures, English as a foreign language is taught every day throughout the six months. By contrast, the expatriates are not required to learn either of the local languages of Azeri or Russian.

Another key module is 'Communication and Team Working', which is seen by Group HR as a vehicle for promoting POG's corporate culture. Trainees find aspects of this module particularly alien. They are inherently suspicious of western multinational corporations, unlike their Azeri colleagues with several years' service, who appear to have internalised the POG 'mindset' and as a consequence tend to deride their newer co-workers' reluctance to follow suit.

In communication skills, trainees undertake activities that encourage them to adopt behaviour patterns that are consistent with the open and questioning culture of POG. Trainees are taught not to be afraid to ask questions, to raise issues with their managers and to learn from their mistakes. Trainees have found these 'simple' lessons problematic and the trainers have experienced initial difficulties engaging the trainees' active involvement.

For locals to ask a question is to admit to not knowing, incurring 'loss of face'. To raise an issue with a manager is also resisted. In a society typified by deference to authority there is a fear of undermining your superior's authority, with the danger of damaging relations with that manager. To learn from one's mistakes is also difficult, since it first requires admission of being responsible for an error!

Group HR has assumed that a collectivist society like Azerbaijan will be ideal for 'team-working', so that any skills training in this area should be fairly straightforward. Yet trainers have found this especially challenging, since Azerbaijan is also a status-conscious society. Group HR aims to promote team-working based on shared responsibility and equality of status, whereas in Azerbaijan team members are recognised for the status they bring with them. Hence, their teams inherently operate on the basis of the recognition of inequality.

Initial delivery of 'Communication and Team Working' modules has been by a visiting British academic, who is perceived by his trainees as an 'expert'. He shares each session with a local L & D officer, a highly qualified but young female, with the intention of eventually devolving the training delivery to her. Unfortunately, such a transition is proving impossible. The trainees resent being addressed by such a person, since Azeri male oil workers find it offensive to accept advice or instruction from a local female; and the head of the L & D team is reluctant to cause an upset.

There is no doubt that it will be the effective contribution of the company's human resources that will secure its future success at a time of significant expansion, but this case study raises some pressing HR issues and there remains a big concern over the degree of integration between Group HR and the HR function in Azerbaijan and a need to embrace the *rhetoric* from Amsterdam and the *reality* as seen in Azerbaijan.

Activity 10.5 | **Managing HR in a global enterprise**

1. POG can be identified as a MNC and a global enterprise, but how would you classify the Group's:

   a) organisational structure,

   b) orientation to national culture, and

   c) staffing arrangements?

2. What evidence is there to suggest that the senior decision-makers of POG *aspire* towards creating a 'transnational' organisation?

3. To what extent and why does POG fall short of being a 'transnational' organisation?

4. To what extent are the HR issues identified in POG Azerbaijan explained by a gap between Group's *rhetoric* and the locals' *reality*?

5. What steps would you recommend to secure and develop the effective contribution of the company's human resources towards achieving POG Azerbaijan's long-term success?

It is quite clear from the rhetoric of the company's chief executive that the senior decision-makers of POG aspire towards creating a transnational organisation. Van der Zende outlines his vision of a geocentric organisation where all staff are recruited on the basis of talent irrespective of background or nationality and where a diverse workforce is valued. He also looks towards a structure and outlook that can sustain a global learning organisation, enabling the spread of valuable knowledge right across its 120 business units worldwide. Through this approach POG should, in theory, be more capable of combining responsiveness to local conditions with a corporate outlook shared across the organisation.

Since the senior managers of POG aspire to the transnational model for their organisation, it follows that this particular multinational corresponds to a different structure and orientation. Although there is encouragement from the centre for the 120 business units to run their own separate businesses, there is plenty of evidence for the influence of group headquarters on operations and a requirement for each subsidiary to comply with group policies. More specifically, Group HR is responsible for initiating a variety of schemes and programmes in, for example, recruitment and selection and training and development. It appears that it is Group HR that is regarded as the repository of expert knowledge or, perhaps more accurately, is perceived to have control and authority over subsidiary HR departments. As such, we are looking at the *international* type of multinational structure.

While van der Zende's rhetoric demonstrates recognition of the importance of a corporate culture that transcends any one national culture, there is clear evidence of an *ethnocentric* orientation perhaps outstaying its welcome. The use of the company's standardised psychometric tests for selection and the introduction of western models of team-working and interpersonal communication run counter to those in Azerbaijan. In addition, expatriates are not required to learn the languages spoken by their Azeri employees.

Such ethnocentrism should not perhaps surprise us. In spite of the rhetoric and fine aspirations, 90 per cent of POG's senior executives are PCNs. Even in the

Azerbaijan operation only 40 per cent are HCNs, though this can be explained by a perceived need for expatriates with specialist skills and relevant experience. Certainly, there are plans to expand this proportion to 90 per cent of the total workforce, but the CEO of POG Azerbaijan does not consider this a realistic target in view of the particular competences being sought from this labour market.

It should be clear from the case evidence that there are several HR issues facing POG Azerbaijan, which impact adversely on employees' contribution to the business and illustrate a gap between the plans set forth by the centre and the reality experienced by those on the ground. To a large extent these problems are a consequence of differences between an ethnocentric corporate culture and that of the Azeri workforce. Hence, conventional methods of recruitment and selection are often at odds with the locals' personalised approach of networking and nepotism. Similarly, training programmes to change ingrained behaviour patterns are not always welcome. For example, being taught to ask questions, to raise issues with managers and to learn from one's mistakes can be construed as incurring the detrimental and undesirable outcomes of loss of face, undermining your manager's authority and admitting to one's error. The significance of the local work culture is fully exposed by the resistance of expatriate management to using a highly competent trainer, from whom local male workers would find it offensive to receive training solely because of her gender.

In analysing these HR issues there seems a huge perceptual and geographical gap between POG personnel at the centre and those in Azerbaijan. The ensuing problems are fundamentally associated with cultural differences and appear to inhibit the effective contribution of the company's human resources. Any resolution is likely to be multifaceted, but in simple terms one option is for the management of this multinational to invest heavily in achieving its transnational aspirations. However, this is a huge challenge for such a complex and gigantic firm. Alternatively, therefore, it might endeavour to become more sensitive to the realities experienced on the ground and adjust its prescriptions accordingly. As a consequence, the structures and arrangements for Azerbaijan are likely to differ in more than detail from those in other parts of this multinational's domain.

Host country employment in the mature organisation

There is indeed a fine balance to be achieved in establishing meaningful inter-unit integration between corporate centre and overseas subsidiary. As overseas operations reach greater maturity it is perhaps understandable that, in vibrant businesses, head office priorities and enthusiasm might shift towards the corporation's latest new enterprise. For POG this has been the development and protection of its Russian joint venture, mired in the intricacies of working with national officialdom and a trying Russian business partner. For the Elite Group of hotels, yet more exotic and lucrative locations are forever on the company's horizon. Thus, the pioneering talent of each of our case study companies is typically redirected towards the latest foreign undertaking, supported by corporate teams and resources.

It goes without saying that the decision-makers of any global business still need to ensure all of its overseas enterprises continue to flourish and that local managements need to take account of changeable conditions. Thus, for example, as industrialising countries like Azerbaijan become more developed, local labour markets are likely to present different challenges through increased competition. At the same time it is important that the global company's presence remains welcome and continues to receive support nationally. Frenkel (2006: 405) citing Klein (2000) notes that firms associated with global brands are especially vulnerable to adverse publicity. As well-known global brands it is important that Elite and POG steer clear of such calumny, and they might well take heed of Frenkel's observations. He refers to suspicion that has 'been fanned by illegal behaviour, allegations of exploitation of third world labour, environmental degradation, excessive senior management remuneration, and continuous restructuring that is often associated with large-scale lay-offs and subsequent employment effects' (Frenkel, 2006: 405–6).

Assuming our international organisations are untainted by such transgressions, it remains for their decision-makers to be alive to the shifting nature of their overseas businesses and to be equipped to undertake an ongoing analysis of factors critical to each location. Moreover, as we have explored throughout this chapter, the multinational organisation will still have to face issues and uncertainties associated with managing across national boundaries, including those related to governmental and institutional factors as well as with differences of culture and language.

By the same token, we have noted that certain human resourcing issues are not confined to the international arena and are likely to be familiar to most HR professionals. Pressures from head office to cut employment costs whilst delivering improved employee performance are the backdrop for many HR decisions. Difficult and changing labour markets have always challenged HR specialists, and organisational efforts to engender employee commitment through greater involvement are typically halted through problems with management's implementation.

To illustrate human resource issues associated with the maturing overseas organisation, the reader is invited to 'go back' to Azerbaijan. It is some five years after we last reported events at the Elite in Baku and at POG Azerbaijan. During this time both subsidiaries have employed considerably more local staff and fewer expatriates, including those at managerial and professional levels. Both companies are also beginning to find it more difficult to recruit people of the required calibre and competence. Moreover, for whatever reason both organisations are falling short of head office expectations and are under increasing pressure to address particular issues concerning employee performance.

Armed with your understanding of the essential aspects of international HRM, return to Azerbaijan and take stock of the changes that have occurred both within and outside the two organisations. Identify key HR issues and consider the extent to which they are resolvable. What steps would you advise each company to take to achieve its business goals, understanding that withdrawal from Azerbaijan is *not* an option in spite of a very tight labour market. First, in Case Study 10.5 we look at the present circumstances facing the Elite where management and staff are in a despondent mood. Then, we turn to POG Azerbaijan in Case Study 10.6. In spite of consolidating POG's sizeable presence in the Caspian region, management still has barriers to surmount.

Case Study 10.5

The Elite five years on

It is now a decade since the Elite hotel was the first to recognise its opportunity for opening in Baku during the first years of independence, when the government of Azerbaijan signed the 'contract of the century' promoting the development of its oil and gas reserves. Since that time, the government has also sought to develop other industries, including tourism, as part of its strategy for delivering substantial economic growth. Consequently, significant attention has focused on encouraging the improvement of the hospitality industry, catering for both tourists as well as business visitors.

It was within this context that, five years ago, the Elite opened the Elite Plus in Baku for its 'premier' customers. Situated across the road from its sister hotel, the Elite Plus has 159 rooms, 2 restaurants and 3 conference rooms. Primarily aimed at business travellers, each room has comfortable working areas with appropriate technical support. There is also a very impressive leisure centre, which is shared by guests from the Elite hotel.

The General Manager of the Elite, Imran Abdul, was also asked to take charge of the Elite Plus from its inception. Abdul, a Pakistani, had first worked at the Elite as finance director before his promotion to GM. At the opening of the Elite Plus, he advised his group of managers (all Azeri) that, 'the greatest challenge facing us is the need to build a strong team of trained staff who can run this complex operation without compromising the standards of Elite's reputation worldwide'.

This pronouncement was not unimportant or inconsequential. As a result of the government's supportive environment for the hospitality industry, the past five years has seen the development of over 200 hotels and guest houses. The vast majority can be classified as one and two star quality. However, in Baku alone there are now six globally-branded five-star hotels, and a newly opened hotel presents itself as exclusively 'six-star'.

Furthermore, allied to growth in the number of hotels there is also significant development in health resorts, restaurants, bars, clubs and entertainment centres. This expansion has been acknowledged with the recent 'Hotel Expo Azerbaijan', a specialised exhibition in Baku aimed primarily at potential investors. It is fair to say that such interest in the hospitality industry is unquestionably spurred by Azerbaijan's thriving economy. For the past two years GDP growth has been recorded at an astounding 30 per cent.

In such an increasingly competitive environment the Elite has sought to retain its market position by appealing to its customers' loyalty, relying on being the first global five-star hotel to operate in Azerbaijan. There are, however, certain issues that are having a major impact on the business of the hotel.

Since their opening, both the Elite and the Elite Plus have operated with very high occupancy rates, with yearly averages running in excess of 80 per cent. More recently, however, there have been major fluctuations in occupancy rates. For example, last year the Elite Plus had 86 per cent occupancy in September, which is to be expected during the annual oil and gas exhibition, compared with just 30 per cent in December. Its overall rate averaged only 60 per cent, yet was better than the average occupancy for the Elite, which has declined to 55 per cent!

A substantial proportion of this loss of custom can be attributed to its major client, a multinational that had regularly used the Elite hotels for its staff and visitors. Considerable dissatisfaction concerning the quality of service, accommodation and conference facilities had led to the withdrawal of this client's lucrative contract.

Such an opinion on the decline in standards is borne out by customer feedback. This indicates essentially a general sense amongst guests about both hotels no longer offering 'value for money'. Those guests whose stay is paid for by their respective companies are usually less sensitive to this aspect, such that their adverse comments have not been silenced by the hotels' senior management reducing room rates. This move was designed to arrest the decline in business. Yet room rates for both hotels remain higher than the majority of competitors.

For most guests price is probably less important than what the hotel offers them and anecdotal evidence indicates a relative decline in the service now being provided. By way of illustration, a business visitor from the UK arrived at the hotel to find confusion regarding prepayment by his company for his accommodation. As a regular guest of the Elite Plus and never before experiencing any difficulty over prepayment, our traveller found this extremely frustrating, not least because on this occasion he was checking in at 2.30 in the morning. Initially, he was told that he 'would have to settle his account by personal payment'. On then presenting the receptionist with his copy of the prepayment agreement with the hotel, he was then advised that 'this was irrelevant'. This was not what he wanted to hear after a very tiring journey.

Getting very annoyed and not a little upset, it required the duty manager to placate the guest and suggest it be sorted the following day. Unfortunately, a further two hours were spent the next day addressing the issue, which was resolved only when some missing paperwork within the hotel's system was located. Of particular concern to the visitor was the abrupt manner with which he had been treated. Not surprisingly, he has since stayed at a competitor hotel, even though over years of frequent visits to Baku he had grown attached to the Elite.

To some extent the demise of the hotel's fortunes might be linked to its changed labour market compared with the early years. Whilst the national unemployment rate continues to be around 14 per cent, the availability of quality applicants within Baku has greatly reduced. Although many people are now migrating from the rural areas into Baku in search of employment, they lack critical skills required within the hospitality industry: notably in the use of English and in 'customer care'.

In addition, the newly opened hotels have 'poached' key staff from the Elite. At the same time, there are growing employment opportunities within the rapidly expanding finance sector as well as the oil and gas industry. Moreover, the government's 'localisation programme' has created a very tight labour market for quality employees, whose aspirations and expectations have been raised significantly by an awareness of the economic boom within the country. Indeed, both within and outside the hospitality industry, talented Azeri's are looking to advance their careers internationally.

The overall situation within the Elite hotels in Baku is now worrying senior management at head office. From being the Elite Group's leading hotel its business performance is at best mediocre. Whilst acknowledging that the business context has significantly altered, head office's real concern relates to the hotels' human resources. This was encapsulated by the group's HR director who, at a recent meeting of the board at HQ, expressed concern and recalled the general manager's caution at the opening of Elite Plus that, 'the greatest challenge facing us is the need to build a strong team of trained staff who can run this complex operation without compromising the standards of Elite's reputation worldwide'.

In the group HR director's view, 'our Baku operation is a million miles away from meeting that challenge' and a decision has been made to send a troubleshooter to Baku to get a clearer understanding of the key issues – with a view to introducing an HR strategy that can improve employee performance and better support the business.

| Activity 10.6 | Managing HR in a developed overseas organisation: Elite Hotel |

You are required to assume this troubleshooter role and report back to the board of directors at head office.

As a troubleshooter experienced in the international management of HR you would be concerned to translate head office interests into pragmatic objectives for the Elite hotels in Baku. These are likely to be dominated by the need to obtain and retain suitably capable employees and to ensure that all staff are equipped and motivated to meet customer requirements of high-quality service. It would then be a question of assessing the challenges that the company would need to overcome to achieve such objectives; and the steps and resources required. Externally, for example, there is now severe competition for labour. Internally, the business has the added responsibility of running a sister hotel alongside customer complaints about staff competence and attitude.

In terms of taking a strategic view, a skilled troubleshooter would seek to integrate any specific HR proposals (such as actions in recruitment, rewards and training) in order to provide a coherent approach to improving employee performance and hence the business. A critical aspect is that there must be effective communication and coordination between the American head office and Elite management in Baku.

We should also expect to observe similar themes in the next case study, which takes us back to the oil platforms and distribution pipelines of POG Azerbaijan (POG Az).

Case Study 10.6

HR priorities at POG Azerbaijan

Five years have passed since we last reported on POG Azerbaijan (POPG Az). It remains one of the largest units and an important profit centre in the Exploration and Production (E&P) Division of Premium Oil and Gas worldwide, as well as Azerbaijan's biggest foreign investor. POG Az also continues to operate under the Production Sharing Agreement (PSA) signed with the Government of Azerbaijan, which obliges the company to 'nationalise' most of its workforce, thereby ensuring that staff are Azeri citizens.

Thus, under the PSA, the organisation needs to achieve 90 per cent nationalisation in its professional ranks within the next two to three years; but the company is finding it difficult to achieve further progress beyond the current proportion of 75 per cent. In particular, whilst the 60 HR and 100 finance control professionals comprise more than 90 per cent Azeri employees, the two operations divisions have only a little over 50 per cent. Well-qualified specialist engineers have not been as easy to recruit as those who opt to work in the company's support functions. While POG explicitly affirms its intention to be compliant with the legislation of the countries where it operates, the PSA does state that the company reserves the right to employ internationally recognised standards. This has implications for recruiting key personnel, especially when it comes to compliance with critical practices, including health and safety.

At the same time, to advance the nationalisation strategy of its professional grades, POG Az provides full funding of professional qualification programmes, usually delivered by visiting UK and Dutch universities. Professional qualifications are regarded as a core part of the learning offered for the development of national staff. Hence, company support is most enthusiastic and includes classroom attendance, study materials and study time.

Overall POG Azerbaijan now employs around 2,800 full-time employees and 2,000 contract workers. The largest group of staff is in Operations (over 40 per cent). The majority of these work in the Offshore Division, operating five offshore platforms in roles ranging from offshore installation managers – responsible for managing the production of large volumes of hydrocarbons – to operators – responsible for running day-to-day operations and maintenance activities at the sites. Those in the Onshore Division work on three terminals in Azerbaijan, Georgia and Turkey and with three oil and gas pipelines for transportation to Turkey and on to international markets.

The operations divisions are core to POG's business, since they generate the 'product' that the company sells to make profit. Quite simply, an average offshore platform in the Caspian Sea produces around 120 'thousand stock tank barrels per day'. At an oil price between $100 and $150 per barrel, the value of production every day from just one platform is between $12 million and $18 million. Yet, in spite of these exceptional figures, the POG Group has lost its competitive position as one of the world's leading energy companies. This is due largely to massive profit losses caused by the prolonged shutdown of refineries in the US for serious safety reasons, as well as delays in getting some major operating facilities on stream. This was two years ago and during that time, Dirk Van der Vaart, the new group chief executive, has embarked on a 'back to business' agenda, built on the three blocks of safety, people and performance – aimed at putting the company back on track. On these elements, POG is seeking progress in personal and process *safety* alongside the implementation of a common operating system; a focus on the capability and recruitment of *key people*; and a business *performance* that restores revenues, and cuts costs by reducing complexity.

In turn, POG Azerbaijan has seen its own share of major changes. The head of the business in Azerbaijan, Edwin de Boer, has retired from POG after 'eight successful years of building an excellent oil and gas business'. However, his successor, Bill Burroughs, has taken over as chief executive officer of POG Azerbaijan at the time of the POG Group's crisis. Consequently, Burroughs sees his challenge as 'managing a world-class business in the Caspian region, while providing our fair share of the returns and cost savings needed by the group to turn the company around – in line with the "back to business" theme'.

Thus, in relation to the focus on the nationalisation of the workforce, the new CEO is required to meet the commitment under the Production Sharing Agreement with the host government and to reduce costs to the business by replacing expensive expatriates with national employees. He is well aware that it is the expatriate members of staff – from Holland, the UK, the US and other Western countries – who fill most of the company's senior posts. Yet, the challenge – to tighten controls around expatriation and facilitate an accelerated departure of expatriate staff – is proving a difficult one. Above all, Burroughs has to be certain that any initiative is in a manner that is not detrimental to the safe operation of the business locally. He is well aware that only the highest standards of safety are acceptable in such a hazardous work environment. Yet that the attitudes of some local employees towards safe working continue to cause unease.

This concern is also related to Burroughs' other priority. In focusing on the basics, he has to demonstrate that the workforce of POG Azerbaijan is increasing its contribution to returns and cost savings. This is also proving to be a challenge, since a recent satisfaction survey (for which English, Azerbaijani and Russian translations enabled employees to respond in the language of their choice) reveals that operators' morale has fallen over the past two years. As Burroughs states, 'our policy is to create a work environment that is safe, productive and enables employees to contribute to the best of their abilities while pursuing rewarding careers with POG'. At the same time, he admits (off the record) that, 'the current climate is affecting employee morale, and can cause disruption, particularly when the company as a whole is in a state of turmoil and financial trouble'.

However, the sources of the low morale are likely to lie elsewhere, too. The workforce is non-unionised and POG's ultimate aim is to maintain and strengthen the individual relationship with employees and avoid collectivisation of this relationship through sound employee relations practices, essentially by gaining employees' engagement through establishing and strengthening processes for employee voice and involvement.

However, head of operations in Azerbaijan, Donovan Clifford (a Texan oilman) is wary of such processes. As far as he is concerned, 'Managers need to manage; labour needs to execute.' In his opinion management should never engage employees through a 'what should we do?' question, but rather through stating 'we are going to make changes for these reasons, how could we make this work better?' Moreover, his preference in discussing about 'how should your unit be working?' is to 'direct operators down the answer rather than asking what the answer is'.

In addition, Clifford seems quite content with the effectiveness of his performance reviews. He delivers these every quarter to all professional staff. Key points are then cascaded by project managers to the team leaders and on to the workforce.

By contrast, the staff survey has revealed that operations employees feel aggrieved that the company is falling far short of its ideals of employee involvement. They think that the company is not keeping them informed about what is happening in the organisation; senior and middle managers seem remote. On those occasions when they do speak to their managers, operatives feel management is not listening to them. Nor do workers have much opportunity to feed their views upwards or to make suggestions on helping to solve work problems.

Operatives consider that the key communication channel for them is their team leader. Irrespective of whether the team leader is an expatriate or an Azeri, some team leaders are considered to be very good at involving staff and mentoring their development, while others are seen as distinctly autocratic (even arrogant) and regarded as poor role models for POG's espoused open and questioning culture.

Burroughs is concerned that Senior Management must address this issue if the operations divisions are to contribute effectively in the areas of safety, people and performance. Moreover, in the longer term POG Azerbaijan needs to build a strong cadre of national talent for its current and future senior roles. To this end, two years ago a National Progression Programme was launched and 100 individuals selected, based on their strong performance and potential. Through support from the line manager, a mentor and the HR function each 'national leader' is being developed in terms of 'deepening their skills and confidence for their current and future roles'. However, Burroughs has doubts that this long-term programme will provide a sufficient influx of national staff to the most senior positions within the deadline set by the PSA.

Activity 10.7   Managing HR in a developed overseas organisation: POG Azerbaijan

You are Head of HR for POG Az and Bill Burroughs, Chief Executive Officer of POG Az, has asked you to set out your analysis of the HR issues in operations and their impact on the company's priorities around safety, people and performance.

Based on your analysis and understanding of the way that HR can contribute to organisational goals, what management actions will you recommend to Burroughs that will enable him to satisfy the various stakeholders?

Locally, POG Az is a much bigger operation than Elite hotels and it has made significant strides in moving towards its national staffing target whilst still providing valuable income for the POG Group. Yet expectations remain unmet; and your investigation is guided by the three broad priorities set by the group: on safety, people and performance. It is your role as head of HR for POG Az to interpret these for the operations divisions.

Issues over safe working and greater employee productivity seem to be paramount, as well as those positions in operations where there is a shortfall of local talent. In this latter aspect the company looks to have reached a plateau in its search for results. Other difficulties appear to be associated with low employee morale, which seems affected by and impacts upon management–employee relationships. This problem may well be a vestige of the local difficulties initially experienced in adopting the group's espoused open and questioning style of management, first highlighted in Case Study 10.3. Certainly, the pivotal role of team leader appears to be carried out in a somewhat patchy manner, irrespective of the incumbent's nationality.

Ideally, your recommendations to the local CEO, Bill Burroughs, should translate effectively in satisfying group senior management as well as those representing the nation-state of Azerbaijan. Furthermore, account needs to be taken of employee perceptions and, therefore, how POG Az deals with the apparent contradiction between the preferred communications style of its American head of operations (Clifford) and that avowed by group management and POG Az. This added complication is not untypical of organisational reality belying rhetoric; of line managers following their inclinations rather than toeing the company line. However, from Burroughs' viewpoint the decisions he makes and the actions taken by his cohort of managers are likely to be judged less by 'style' than by 'substance'. His priority lies in the sustainability of the POG Az operation and the returns and cost savings it delivers to the group.

Host country management

Both the Elite and POG Az case studies exhibit themes that relate to multinational organisations managing subsidiaries that have moved into a more mature phase of their existence. By contrast, different priorities ensued during the start-up phase (see Case Study 10.1). For example, it is quite typical for multinationals to initially employ a larger number of expatriates in key positions (management, professional and technical). The reasons for this should by now be clear, including a scarcity of appropriate skills amongst HCNs and the centre's need to establish corporate influence on standards and processes.

Then (in Case Studies 10.2 and 10.3), we looked at the more established overseas operation and how human resourcing interventions are designed to enable locals to replace expatriate employees – ideally without any loss in adherence to corporate values and principles. Needless to say, in the mature phase that follows (Case Studies 10.5 and 10.6) there appears to have been some 'slippage', though the reasons for this are more complex than simply the replacement of PCNs by HCNs. Indeed, the most ardent ambassadors for corporate ideals can often be the newer converts, who are seen to embrace their opportunities with relish.

In all of our case studies the business context, global and local, internal and external, has influenced and constrained the options open to those who run the overseas subsidiary. However, there may well be a tendency for the management of more mature companies to spend less time grappling with cultural and institutional differences. The significance of such differences will not have disappeared, but they are likely to assume less importance for managers more exercised by the everyday issues of running their part of a multi-unit business.

Such a view remains to be tested. However, it suggests that a robust understanding of the essence of managing human resources in the overseas organisation is best served by acknowledging a shifting balance between universal HR concerns and those that differentiate the host country location.

Summary

In this chapter the following key points have been made:

- The globalisation of the world's business economy has been particularly significant, resulting in an increase in the importance of, and interest in, international human resourcing.

- A comparative analysis of international and national human resourcing indicates that in all essentials they share the same characteristics. A grasp of international human resourcing builds on, rather than replaces, our understanding of the practice of human resourcing in a domestic environment.

- Our framework suggests that national and international human resourcing decisions should rest on a careful analysis of contingent factors.

- Those responsible for managing across national boundaries are likely to encounter a greater range and a less familiar set of contingent factors.

- International human resourcing is conducted within a multi-unit business organisation that gives rise to tensions and conflicts between managements of the parent company and its overseas subsidiaries.

- Parent company strategy-makers can decide to manage human resources somewhere on a continuum between a decentralised structure emphasising local autonomy and a centralised human resourcing function with its emphasis on global integration.

- Human resourcing strategists are showing more interest in securing the advantages of combining both of the above approaches by 'thinking globally and acting locally'.

- Measures that might contribute towards a global–local approach include: effective communication between the centre and its foreign subsidiaries; building a distinctive corporate culture; and the design of appropriate human resourcing systems and procedures.

- International human resourcing practitioners will be constrained and guided in their operational activities by the strategic choice that has been made or has emerged for their own multinational company.

- A contingency model suggests three sets of strategic choices in relation to the multinational company: its structural form; the dominant management orientation; and staffing arrangements.

- A useful fourfold typology of the structure of multinational companies shows a development from a decentralised *multinational* pattern to a centralised *global* pattern.

- Subsequent efforts to achieve a global–local structure are seen in the *international* form which has been superseded as the 'ideal solution' by the *transnational* structure.

- An analysis of the dominant management orientation towards different national cultures has produced a fourfold classification comprising the polycentric, ethnocentric geocentric and regiocentric orientations.

- The human resourcing function can help develop a geocentric way of thinking or *global mindset* across the multinational company through a mix of human resourcing levers. Attention given to their horizontal integration is essential.

- The overall approach to staffing the multinational company determines the degree of attention given to PCNs, HCNs and TCNs, and to the flows of staff within and between the units of the company.

- In the ideal transnational organisation all three groups of employee are likely to work in more than their own home country and will be subject to international transfers either as *expatriates*, *inpatriates* or *transpatriates*.

- The process of employee relocation must be effectively managed throughout the pre-departure, expatriation and repatriation phases.

- A careful investigation of host country conditions and circumstances will help determine how a subsidiary's human resources might be managed effectively.

- Human resourcing policies and practices can be formulated *ab initio* on the basis of an examination of cultural aspects of the local employment relationship.

- A second approach is to amend or modify parent company practices in the light of contingent factors.

- Where human resources (e.g. expatriate employees) potentially create high levels of uncertainty for managers, a high commitment HR strategy is preferable.

- In those situations of low levels of uncertainty (e.g. less skilled workforces in less developed countries) a low commitment HR strategy might be effective.

- Attention to cultural factors will help maintain favourable employee relations and avoid those negative employee sentiments and actions which can arise from transgressing local norms and expectations.

- Comparative studies and typologies of national cultures such as that by Hofstede are understandably appealing to a management audience, but need to be treated with caution.

- Hofstede's work may be useful as a general guide, but should ideally be no more than a starting point for a comprehensive analysis of specific factors and circumstances affecting the foreign subsidiary.

- Case study analysis shows that the decision-makers of international organisations need to be alert to the shifting nature of their overseas businesses. Human resourcing priorities, challenges and interventions are likely to change as the subsidiary moves from start-up towards a more mature phase of existence.

● Hence, a robust understanding of the essence of managing human resources in the international organisation is best served by acknowledging an adjusting balance between universal HR concerns and those that differentiate host country locations.

Discussion questions

1. How can we account for the increasing significance of international human resourcing in business organisations?

2. To what extent can it be argued that there are no essential differences between the international and national forms of human resourcing when the actual experience of working overseas is so obviously different?

3. What conflicts and tensions are likely to exist between the managements of a parent company and its overseas subsidiaries? How might they be successfully managed?

4. What is the attraction for a human resourcing strategist of working towards a transnational-geocentric approach for their multinational company? What practical measures can be taken to ensure that this approach is not just an unattainable idea?

5. How useful is the concept of the inducement–contribution equilibrium for human resourcing practitioners faced with identifying and posting staff to Australia and the Democratic Republic of the Congo respectively?

6. Employing a cost–benefit analysis, what assistance would you recommend for a group of design engineers who are scheduled to be 'inpatriated' to their European parent company from the United States for up to two years?

7. How useful is the fourfold classification by Hofstede for establishing the employment arrangements in an overseas subsidiary?

Further reading

This chapter set out to provide a framework and methodology to help practitioners understand and tackle international human resourcing issues, including the ability to assess the appropriateness and utility of human resourcing practices that are covered elsewhere in this book. The reader is encouraged, therefore, to refer to those chapters which deal with any pertinent human resourcing activities. These chapters represent a valuable and convenient source of information to supplement and support the contingency approach advocated for international human resourcing strategy-making.

A concise but informative text that covers the major human resourcing activities from an international perspective is that by Dowling *et al.* (2008). A comparative consideration of HRM can be found in Brewster *et al.* (2007). A comprehensive and critical account on the HR issues posed by internationalisation is the collection of chapters edited by Harzing and Ruysseveldt (2004).

Part III

Managing change and developing capability

Introduction to Part III

It is difficult to find a managerial text these days which does not refer to 'organisation change' and the need for managerial responses to meet the associated challenges. Indeed, it is a common observation of business school academics that the majority of both undergraduate and postgraduate dissertations, irrespective of their specific subject focus or research questions, begin with some descriptive account of the 'fast moving, global and ever-changing' context within which we all now live and work. The influence of managerial texts on readers' understanding of managerial work seems to be clearly demonstrated by those two statements. The growth and 'fashion' of specialist texts on managing change is probably another influence. There is a suggestion in the growth of such texts, and in the content of many of them, that change is somehow a new phenomenon. The Aynshents and Moddens case studies demonstrate that this is not the case. The Aynshents themselves were facing and responding to change. A comparison of the contexts of the two cases will reveal that change has been a continuous characteristic of human experience in the years that separate them.

The purpose and content of this part is not therefore to adopt or respond to a fashionable interest in the notion of organisation change, or its sister idea of managing change. Instead, it addresses three key assumptions. The first is that while change is continuous and inevitable, *particular* changes are of particular interest at particular times, and that certain ideas will arise through research and thought on how to respond to those particular changes. The second assumption is that change at all levels, global, societal, organisational and individual, is inextricably bound up with learning and knowledge. And that the two latter concepts are themselves inextricably bound up with each other. The final assumption is that it is a key, if perhaps self-imposed, purpose and task of managers to anticipate, create and respond to change to help ensure organisational survival into the long term. Therefore, the learning and development of managers becomes central to that survival.

These three assumptions provide the rationale for the inclusion and content of each of the three chapters in this part of the book. The chapter by Carole Tansley argues that changes in the business environment has led to the emergence of the 'knowledge economy' where individual and organisational knowledge is increasingly seen as vital to competitive advantage and the defining factor in achieving organisational success. However, these arguments are taken further than the usual managerialist perspective of such concepts through a detailed and critical analysis of the nature of 'knowledge' and the practices of knowledge development within an organisational context. Building on this analysis, the chapter examines the HR implications of these apparent changes, for example, the selection, motivation and retention of 'knowledge workers'. Another example is the connection between knowledge creation and learning through social processes engaged in by 'communities of practice'. This part of the content reflects the second assumption. This assumption is also relevant to the notion of 'knowledge sharing' which is another feature of the processes of communities of practice. It might be argued, though, that the importance of knowledge sharing is by no means a new phenomenon in organised enterprise. In training and development terms, it lies at the heart of the method known as 'sitting by Nellie'. This leads naturally to a consideration of what is now termed human resource development in Chapter 12.

Jan Myers and Sue Kirk, in Chapter 12, explore human resource development as a strategic intervention in an increasingly global business environment and the different approaches government and employers can elect to take in developing workforce capability. These are highly relevant to the achievement of effective 'knowledge management' as discussed in Chapter 11. A further connection between the two chapters is the analysis of international and national policies related to HRD in response to changing economic circumstances. Initiatives to promote investment in HRD and lifelong learning by the OECD, for example, as well as those by the UK government, are examined. Chapter 12 also argues that these issues are not the exclusive interest of for-profit enterprises, and that they are of equal concern to public sector and voluntary organisations. As part of this, the chapter also highlights the social, as distinct from economic, purposes of learning and development. The chapter clearly follows from and applies our second assumption. It also, though, reflects the first assumption in presenting arguments which suggest that many initiatives at government and organisational levels are often 'old' approaches in new forms. The central message of the chapter is that, whatever else it may entail, change requires learning to develop 'resourceful human beings' and that HRD needs to be a significant managerial activity.

Both Chapters 11 and 12 identify a central role for managers in achieving change and in promoting HRD. This then leads to the third assumption and the need for a chapter on management development. Chapter 13 meets this need. Following the purpose of the book as a whole, and the example set in particular in Chapter 11, the chapter approaches management development as problematic in both concept and practice. The central components of 'management' and 'development' are argued to be more complex than many conventional treatments of the topic allow. Based on this, the chapter then advances a number of frameworks to help deal with the complexity and to help inform decisions in and on practice. A number of ideas from Chapter 1 are applied to support some of the frameworks, in particular the idea of 'organisational contingencies' and that of 'high or low commitment HR policies and practices'. The arguments on 'emergent strategy' and the political nature of managerial decision-making from Chapter 1 are also applied to the particular example of formulating management development strategies. The key message of the chapter is that the notion of 'best fit' may have some relevance to management development, but the notion of 'best practice' is probably an irrelevant distraction.

The chapters in this part provide no easy answers to normative questions of HR policy and practice in relation to individual and organisational change and transitions. They do, though, provide much food for thought, which may well lead to better answers than the authors themselves could ever offer.

Knowledge organisations, strategies and human resourcing

Carole Tansley

Learning outcomes

Having read this chapter and completed its associated activities, readers should be able to:

- Understand the importance of strategically developing personal and organisational knowledge for the benefit of the organisation as a whole

- Critically assess the different ways in which particular terms used in the discourse of knowledge management are defined and used in practice, such as tacit, explicit and organisational knowledge and communities of practice

- Analyse the knowledge development practices of an organisation to assess the extent to which they are consistent with each other and appropriate for the general environmental or business circumstances of the organisation

- Consider what might facilitate and constrain knowledge development processes

- Understand how knowledge is the product of negotiated relationships arising from the processes of interaction between human beings operating in an organised work situation completing various work tasks

- Appreciate how human beings might resist knowledge-sharing processes

- Understand that managers might more usefully focus not so much on managing the knowledge resources people bring to the organisation but, rather, managing the HR aspects of knowledge development

- Understand that if knowledge and its development can be seen as essentially strategic practice, then appreciate how HR specialists can take responsibility for certain aspects

Introduction

Knowledge management has become a growing field of interest for managers in all areas of organisational life as we begin to understand the importance of strategically developing personal and organisational knowledge for the benefit of the organisation as a whole. However it is first important to have working definitions of key terms used in knowledge management, such as tacit, explicit and organisational knowledge and communities of practice. Next, plans must be made to develop policies and practices for knowledge-sharing and development, taking into account constraints such as resistance and the need for roles and responsibilities to be undertaken. Then it will be necessary to assess the extent to which such policies and practices are consistent with each other and appropriate for the general environmental or business circumstances of the organisation and make adjustments as necessary.

In the first instance, though, let us consider the vexed question of whether knowledge can actually be managed or not.

Can knowledge be 'managed'?

If we take a resource-based view of organisations (Barney, 1991), as discussed in detail by Tony Watson in Chapter 1, exploiting and developing the knowledge of employees is taken to be a core organisational competency (Hamel and Prahalad, 1994; Boxall and Purcell, 2003) which, if appropriately 'managed', can assist in the long-term survival of the organisation. While we are careful about suggesting that knowledge is a resource which can be 'managed', we do agree that there is a need for a strategic and critical appreciation (Prichard *et al.*, 2000) of how to organise in order to support knowledge development processes as a means of continuing the survival of the organisation into the future. As we shall see later on, although there is not a consensus about the characteristics of knowledge and the ways in which these knowledge resources might be used (Bhatt, 2001) and what to do when key employees threaten to leave (Hofer-Alfeis, 2008), what has become clear is that there is benefit from considering *how* people create certain forms of knowledge, particularly in their social interactions. But first, let us consider how one company, Moddens Foods (which we came across in Chapter 1), is beginning to feel a need to consider how a strategic focus on knowledge could be beneficial to the business.

Case Study 11.1

Knowledge as an organisational resource: knowledge management at Moddens Foods

Jean Frear generally enjoyed her role as vice president of HR for the Gourmet Division of Moddens Foods, which produces high-quality, broad range and 'premium' food products for European and North American markets. Today, though, she was not so sure. She was looking at item six on the agenda of the forthcoming company board meeting, as requested by Juan Poort, group managing director. It stated: 'Knowledge management for competitive advantage at Moddens.' Her heart sank. She knew he loved what she called 'consultantspeak' such as knowledge management and although she did recognise the advantages in attempting to utilise the personal knowledge of those who worked for the company, she knew that Juan would have taken the consultants' spin to heart.

The meeting moved swiftly through the items so when they reached item six there was plenty of time left for discussion. Sam Modden, group executive chairman and only remaining Modden family member left in the business, asked Juan to take them through the item. 'Sure. I asked for this because I have been hearing a lot about this lately and think it could be a way of making our human resourcing more effective than it currently is.' Jean did not respond so he went on, 'We must recognise that we now live in a knowledge economy and, as the company has grown, the recruitment of employees with key knowledge and skills in various parts of the world is a complex activity deserving serious, strategic consideration. We need to develop knowledge management as a core competence to succeed in tomorrow's dynamic global economy. In the knowledge management jargon our key people – for example our agricultural experts, chefs and food scientists – are called "knowledge workers". We not only want the right knowledge workers at the right time at the right place but these people seem to be able to pick and choose where they work. Once they do work for us, they then tend to work in their own disciplinary groups, so we must also ensure that we have systems in place to ensure that specialist knowledge in one part of the organisation does not "stick", but is used in other parts of the organisation for the benefit of the business. This is the only way to innovate, believe me.'

The finance director, Ivan Kelp, agreed with Juan. 'I do feel that harnessing the right sort of knowledge can improve competitiveness. If our competitors are taking the lead in moving towards a "knowledge economy", then we need to respond to this move. It might also lead to increasing profit levels which might help to fight off any future takeover bids by a certain large foreign-based international food company that is looking for a company like ours as a foothold in the country.'

Hal Selz, who had previously been marketing director but was now heading up the Gourmet Division, said 'I've always thought it was a pretty stupid suggestion that any aspect of human resources, knowledge or otherwise, could be used to improve our competitiveness.' Juan muttered under his breath, 'resistant, as usual'. Hal glared at Juan, 'I just don't think we should jump on the bandwagon of the latest managerial fashion, which this rhetoric about "knowledge economies" and "knowledge workers" seems to be.'

Jean, the human resources director, told the board that care needed to be taken before any initiative was developed. Taking knowledge as a key resource for strategic human resourcing activities would be quite a complex initiative and would take some thought to develop into a cohesive approach that linked with corporate and HR strategy. They must take care that they were not adopting what might later be deemed to be a managerial fad. She agreed to look into the whole area and produce a report on the value of taking such an approach for the Gourmet Division.

Activity 11.1   Managerial views of knowledge

1. We have seen in the Moddens' case how certain managerial concepts are viewed by particular managers. With regard to your own views, in a common-sense way, what do you think is meant by the term 'knowledge economy'?

2. Knowledge management has been referred to by many as 'just another managerial fad and fashion'. What other initiatives have been launched in your organisation which might fall under this description? What was the outcome of one particular initiative and why?

The discourse of knowledge management

Many managers are being seduced by the discourse of knowledge management. A *discourse* is a cluster of *discursive resources* (concepts, terms, ideas, images or expressions) which individuals such as Juan Poort or groups such as Moddens' directors can use as a means of talking about, writing or understanding particular issues (Watson, 1994) to make sense of their situations (Weick, 1995) and further their projects (Schutz, 1967). Juan is attempting to make sense of the Moddens' strategic and working environment and is enamoured of the notion of knowledge management (KM). He sees KM as a vital core competence for operating in the global economy (Skyrme and Amdon, 1998) and is attempting to persuade others to see how the knowledge 'held' in their organisation (both in the form of employees' personal knowledge and explicit knowledge inherent in organisational systems) is important for competitive advantage (Quinn, 1992; Drucker, 1993; Boisot, 1998). He does this by using the lexicon of knowledge management terms in his interest in developing the company. One such term is that of the 'knowledge economy'.

The knowledge economy

The idea that knowledge can be a source of economic wealth is not new (Penrose, 1959; Marshall, 1890: 1972) but it has recently become a major focus for academics and managers, consultants and policy-makers who feel that the development of 'core' knowledge and competences in organisations can be a key element of economic growth and organisational competitiveness (Hamel and Prahalad, 1994). One review of changes in the business environment (Stewart and Tansley, 2002) presents the knowledge economy as having the following characteristics:

- Individual and organisational knowledge is increasingly being seen as the most significant asset in achieving organisational success.
- With the importance of knowledge as its defining characteristic, the knowledge economy is a more accurate term than the 'new economy' to describe today's dominant economic environment.
- Globalisation and developments in information technology (IT) are the two most significant factors in the emergence of the knowledge economy.
- The emergence of the knowledge economy is not defined by the activities of dot.coms and goes further than the changes in the proportional and relative values of manufacturing versus service industries in the economy.
- The content and nature of production and consumption have been transformed.
- The rise of the knowledge economy has significant implications for the development of knowledge, learning and training for work.

Like many commentators, Ivan Kelp, Moddens' finance director, sees advantages for the firm to identify, value, create and develop their knowledge assets (Davenport and Prusak, 1998; Grant and Zack, 1999) and therefore 'gain competitive advantage'. This discourse is attractive to managers because it makes them feel that if the requisite knowledge is available within the organisation, then managers can have confidence in the face of uncertainty and difficulty. In turn, so the argument goes, this can have a positive effect on the way they take risks and help them not to have exaggerated beliefs in their ability to control complex situations. This could be criticised as being a naïve view of developing knowledge for organisational progress. Moddens' human resources director Jean Frear can see this naïveté clearly.

Case Study 11.2

Knowledge workers in practice

When Jean, Moddens' human resources director, returned to her office she closed the door and threw the papers from the meeting on her desk. 'It's OK Juan Poort bringing in his bright ideas about initiatives like knowledge management but it's me who has to figure out how to do it.' Sitting in her chair she stared out of the window at the grey skies and started to reflect on what aspect of knowledge management Juan seemed most interested in from an HR perspective. He seemed quite taken with the idea of knowledge workers. 'Wonder if he could give even a five-minute presentation on "knowledge workers"?' The thought of this made her laugh. If Juan ever did read anything remotely to do with management it would only be what she called 'airport lounge books for managers' with large writing, lots of white space and plenty of two-by-two matrices. His personal knowledge of knowledge management, knowledge work and knowledge workers would probably be very low!

Activity 11.2   What is a knowledge worker?

1. Note down your own understanding of the term 'knowledge worker'.
2. Would you say you could be described as one? How?

Jean has an interesting challenge ahead of her. The firm's managing director wants a knowledge management initiative, even though he might have little idea of the strategic and organisational implications of taking that route. He espouses the rhetoric of 'knowledge work' and 'knowledge workers', which he sees as a solution to current human resourcing difficulties. But is this necessarily the case? Let us analyse what these terms can mean in practice.

Knowledge work and knowledge workers

Knowledge workers have been described as qualitatively different from the occupational groups of the old industrial economy and characterised as individuals who have high levels of education and specialist skills combined with the ability to apply these skills to identify and solve problems (Drucker, 1993). As we saw in the case study above, there are many such 'knowledge workers' in the Gourmet Division of Moddens. It has been posited that their growing importance is associated with the emergence of a globalised, post-industrial economy in which knowledge displaces capital as the 'motor' of competitive performance (Scarbrough *et al.*, 1998: 10). It has also been suggested that if we take the position that our society is based on knowledge, then the 'knowledge worker' is the greatest asset of an organisation (Drucker, 1993).

From this perspective, the value of an individual's knowledge for the organisation is seen as a unique resource, which, if the organisation is to be competitive, needs to be inimitable. However, a practising manager trying to make sense of how writers describe this unique resource might have difficulty given the variety of terms. For example: distinctive competences (Andrews, 1971), core competences (Hamel and Prahalad, 1994), internal capabilities (Barney, 1991), intellectual capital (Stewart, 1997) and unique managerial talent (Penrose, 1959). Nevertheless, from this perspective, strategically managing the firm becomes an act of maintaining the uniqueness of the knowledge used in the production of its products/services.

Discussions about knowledge workers appear to be focused around three inter-related areas (Tam *et al.*, 2002): the cognitive nature of knowledge workers' (KWs') expertise and knowledge; the strategies KWs use to establish and guard exclusionary claims to their expertise and to maximise their economic and symbolic rewards and the management–employee relationships in which these workers are involved. KWs have been presented as a new expert group that adopt a *marketisation power strategy* to build up and maintain their expertise status (Reed, 1996) and who do not rely on conventional occupational or organisational credential systems to establish and gain economic and political advantage for their expertise, but instead make use of the esoteric and intangible nature of their knowledge to create market niches for themselves (Tam *et al.*, 2002). They are said to be located in external rather than internal labour markets, which, Reed (1996: 586) suggests, pushes them towards an organic or network organisational form, which is characterised by decentralised flexibility and autonomy.

Considering the challenges of knowledge management is important whatever the sector or type of organisation. For example, knowledge-intensive industries, such as management consultancy, pharmaceuticals, and IT (Mosco, 2008), are advanced in their adoption of a more systematic approach to learning and sharing knowledge, and seeing the benefits in improved technical capacity, efficiency, customer satisfaction and reduced risk. However, as Bartholomew (2008) found, sectors such as the construction industry lag behind. Here, design is a knowledge-based activity, and project managers, contractors and clients, as well as architects and engineers, have always learned from experience and shared their knowledge with immediate colleagues. However, the construction industry lagging behind other industries is potentially damaging to business, given the influx of increasingly sophisticated construction technology and more demanding markets.

In the more advanced sectors, such as management consultants who provide specific expertise, advice and management ideas and generally work in teams on client projects, their services inherently involve them either developing existing knowledge or creating new knowledge for their clients. Sturdy *et al.* (2009) studied consultancies and identified key aspects such as the importance of shared knowledge domains (e.g. sector knowledge and the complexity of social boundaries) to reveal a picture of complex and shifting insider–outsider relationships where different actors, roles and types of knowledge are involved in an interactive and dynamic process where various boundaries are constructed, reinforced, negotiated and transformed.

Knowledge workers within other types of organisations are often portrayed as being more psychologically complex than manual labourers, having greater powers of reflectivity than more 'primitive' employees and that, in spite of being relatively detached from corporate goals, are capable of preventing those goals being realised (Fuller, 2002: 8). It is also often presumed that KWs operate in ways that are mysteriously superior to management and that fathoming these ways would (presumably) lead to successful competitive advantage and increased profit margins. There are alternative views, though, namely that lack of commitment and ease of mobility among KWs can be used to management's advantage, as corporations increasingly shift to 'just-in-time' and 'outsourcing' production strategies, and otherwise flexibly adapt to changing market conditions (Fuller, 2002).

However, it does become more difficult to earn employees' loyalty because the old threats and bribes do not work well any more. If KWs have the ability to 'bite back' and interfere with managerial work (Fuller, 2002: 8), then managers need to provide a friendly 'self-organising' environment that enables KWs to report when they feel ready. Unfortunately, knowledge workers are no more likely to show solidarity with fellow KWs than with the managers who employ them, which gives union organisers difficulties when attempting to develop collective employee relations in order to ensure their welfare (Fuller, 2002: 8). To address these issues requires managerial consideration of the ways in which work commitment, effort and job satisfaction of knowledge workers are related and can be integrated (see Tam *et al.*, 2002 for suggestions) and for knowledge workers to consider strategies about how they can effectively respond when managers interfere with the conduct of knowledge work.

But what constitutes the knowledge of individuals such as knowledge workers in businesses such as Moddens?

The nature and processes of knowledge

Considering the nature of knowledge is no easy task. For one thing, 'knowledge' is often taken to mean data or information. It might be useful at this stage, therefore, to distinguish between data, information and knowledge. Data has often been defined as simple observations of states of the world that are easily structured and recorded by the appropriate technology on machines, often quantified and easily transferred (Davenport, 1997: 7). One example of HR data is the number of employees in full-time permanent employment in an organisation. Information, on the other hand, can be described as 'data endowed with relevance and purpose' (Drucker in Davenport, 1997: 9) and because a consensus is needed on meaning which involves human mediation, there is bound to be disagreement on what constitutes that information (e.g. time off work sick, holidays taken, overtime worked) and transferring it with absolute fidelity might be problematic. The process of changing data into information requires some understanding to take place because understanding is developed in the course of making meaningful connections between pieces of information, and involves an active and creative engagement with the content of what is being learned, which requires interpretation of relevance to a particular human endeavour (Knights and Willmott in Tsoukas and Vladimirou, 2001).

With regard to knowledge, however, there are a number of difficulties in the way that knowledge has been conceptualised. Let us first consider a typical working environment and the daily processes of the construction and reconstruction of knowledge.

Case Study 11.3

Knowledge development at work at Moddens' Gourmet Foods

Jean Frear, HR director of Moddens' Gourmet Foods division, decided that the best way to begin thinking about the knowledge management initiative was to actually sit in an area of the company and observe what knowledge development processes occurred during a normal day. She decided to sit in the Customer Enquiry department for two days. In this department there are four administrators who have responsibility for answering customers' queries on aspects such as price and range of goods.

Each administrator is expected to answer any enquiry but they each have in-depth knowledge about a particular set of Gourmet products, such as meats, fish, wine and confectionery items. Two of these administrators (Andrea, whose specialist area is wines, and Jimi, who has particular responsibility for fish) were highly experienced and had been in these roles for more than ten years. A third (Byron who deals with the provision of meat products) had been in the job a year and the fourth (Efi who has taken responsibility for in-depth knowledge about confectionery products) was a newcomer.

As well as answering e-mail and letter enquiries, the department can receive up to 200 telephone calls a day from all over the world, but this can fluctuate depending on annual, monthly and weekly events and busy times of the day in different time zones. The office is open for enquiries from 9 a.m. to 5 p.m. and there is an answer phone for queries received out of that time period. Jean decided to focus only on the administrators answering telephone queries.

Jean watched the administrators when they were on and off the phones as well as sitting with them in their coffee breaks. She spent both days taking extensive notes on their work practices. She asked them to describe what they were doing, and after they had taken a call she asked further questions if she needed clarification or wanted to probe on knowledge development issues.

Jean found that in order to answer queries, the administrators referred mainly to electronic databases and printed information, such as manuals on prices and recent price changes. Jean asked particularly probing questions when the administrators had to refer to a manual or ask each other for answers to a query. She also noted that each administrator had a personal notebook where they kept their own handwritten notes for guidance on particular aspects where they felt there was not enough information available elsewhere.

As might be expected, Andrea and Jimi were extremely fast in answering queries, listening for verbal clues about the 'mood' of the customer, tactfully getting them to get straight to the point of their query by asking specific questions and rarely needed to ask any other administrator colleague for additional information. Byron tended to ask questions only about non-standard items. The newcomer, Efi, took some considerable time answering each query because she could not stop inconsequential comments from the customer, sometimes losing the point of the query, did not always recognise what the query was about (cost or sales, for example) and she constantly had to ask the customer to wait while she asked the other administrators to help her answer the query. However, in spite of the pressure, there was a good working atmosphere and lots of joking and story-telling during the working day. The stories of the less experienced administrators were generally about difficulties they had had in answering strange queries and the two with more experience always had an answer on what they should have done. Even over the two days Jean saw a marked improvement in the quality of customer responses, especially from the newcomer.

Jean noticed that when she asked the administrators to describe how they knew how to answer a particular query they could never fully articulate what they had been doing. They had gained their original knowledge in an extensive induction programme organised by the HR department, but as they worked on the section they just learned from experience how to draw on different areas of knowledge to help them answer queries. As Jean said goodbye to the team at the end of the second day there were two things on her mind. The first was that all workers in Gourmet foods could be called knowledge workers and the second was that knowledge management was not a fad but had been going on since organisations were first created!

Activity 11.3 Knowledge and communication

1. In the process of taking a telephone call on the price of Moddens' Gourmet Division products, what might be considered 'data', 'information' and 'knowledge'?

2. What forms of communication would you say the four team members used to ensure that they developed their knowledge as a 'community' of current products and customer needs?

Personal or tacit knowledge

The knowledge of an individual is often portrayed as an 'entity' in the brain, that is, as some element 'that resides within the heads and motor neurone systems of employees and has not been codified or made explicit', with the danger being that 'such knowledge is not available to the wider organisation and managers may not be aware of its existence or its importance until employees leave the organisation' (Quintas, 2002: 10). This simplistic definition has been expanded on by calling individual knowledge 'embrained', which is made up of the analytical and conceptual understandings of that individual (i.e. 'know what') and also embodied in their practical skills and expertise (i.e. 'know how') (Blackler, 1995). Another term that is used to portray individual knowledge is personal or tacit knowledge (Polanyi,

1966). Many would define an individual's knowledge as *a justified true belief that increases an individual's capacity to take effective action* (see Nonaka and Takeuchi, 1995). Such knowledge, they say, is highly personal and hard to formalise, characterised as it is by subjective insights, intuitions and hunches and deeply rooted in actions, procedures, routines, commitment, ideals, values and emotions.

An individual's personal knowledge is said to be difficult to communicate and 'transfer' to others, since it is an analogue process that requires a kind of 'simultaneous processing'. However, such perspectives come from our thinking of ourselves and our interactions with each other as systems. The difficulty with this view is that it is reductionist, with human beings such as the Moddens' administrators in the case above being treated as mechanistic devices that respond to external controls and having no individual choice, aims or objectives in their actions.

Explicit knowledge

Polanyi (1966) suggests that knowledge can be explicit as well as tacit. Explicit knowledge has been characterised as consisting of formal and systematic language, with the potential to be codified and shared in the form of data, scientific formulae, specifications, manuals and similar, and processed, transmitted and stored relatively easily.

The codification and storage of knowledge

There are a number of key and related problems to codifying and storing knowledge (Newell *et al.*, 2002). First, in terms of the problems of actually codifying knowledge, it appears likely that some of the most valuable knowledge of a firm's employees may not be able to be captured and codified. Second, there is the problem that people may be reluctant to 'brain dump', given that knowledge is a key source of personal power in organisations. There are a number of reasons for this:

- *Difficulty*. Some knowledge may be just too difficult to explain in writing and so be more effectively communicated verbally or through learning by doing. For example, in order for Moddens' employees to gain security access to the site it is far easier to simply show the person how to swipe their personal ID card across the security machine rather than provide detailed written explanation about how the security system works.

- *Uncertainty*. Some knowledge may be too uncertain. For example, I may 'know' that certain customers might require information on the Moddens' wine list as well as answering their original enquiry about delivery times on fish. However, this is based on personal experience and intuition and so I am not likely to write this down to pass on formally to colleagues, although I may well share this 'knowledge' informally with them, perhaps by telling a story that showed how I recognised this extra need.

- *Dynamism*. Some knowledge may be subject to continuous change. For example, Moddens' price lists of fresh food such as vegetables could change frequently, so that any attempt to capture this detail manually will almost immediately be out of date and wrong in some detail.

- *Context-dependency*. Some knowledge may be extremely context dependent. For example, a recruitment plan for one section of the Moddens business in one country may not be applicable in another section of the business in another country, given what we know about national predispositions. Reusing the same campaign in a different country, ignoring the importance of context, is likely to prove ineffective and even produce the opposite effects to those expected.

- *Cost*. Some knowledge may cost more to codify than to learn by trial-and-error. For example, writing down detailed instructions for the Moddens' customer enquiry team about how to use a simple mechanical device like a stapler in their office environment is not likely to prove very useful. There is a lot of material 'written down' in an organisation which is rarely, if ever, referred to.

- *Politics*. Some knowledge may be politically too sensitive to codify. For example, very important knowledge when managing a project relates to who is a good teamplayer and who is likely to be obstructive and difficult. If I attempt to formally share this knowledge with others by putting personal opinions about people on a database (that 'Christine is a pain to work with', for instance), this might well be considered a libellous act as it has been formally codified.

A major difficulty of knowledge codification is related to the link between knowledge and power. Thus, if Christine feels that her knowledge is in short supply and yet central to the organisation, she may be reluctant to share this with others, since it confers personal advantages and so is secreted by the 'knower'. If she were to 'give it away', she would lose an important basis of power. This suggests that human resourcing tools and techniques are as important for effective KM as are IT tools and techniques. For example, incentive and reward schemes need to be devised to encourage knowledge-sharing and career development strategies need to be utilised, which recognise knowledge-sharing in appraisal and promotion decisions. In other words, human resourcing issues are key to the successful utilisation of knowledge in an organisation.

The tacit/explicit relationship

As we saw in the Moddens case study, the team members seemed consistently to share knowledge and ideas as they attempted to meet customers' needs over the telephone. Nonaka *et al.* (2002: 43) argue that in order to understand the appropriation and creation of knowledge we need to recognise that tacit and explicit knowledge are complementary, and that both types of knowledge are essential. They suggest that in order to become a true 'knowledge-creating company', an organisation must complete a spiral: tacit knowledge must become explicit via articulation through team-work and then re-internalised both in individuals and the organisation, to become part of the knowledge base. Once completed, the process starts over, spiralling at higher and higher levels to extend the application of knowledge throughout the organisation.

However, it can be argued that the distinction between tacit and explicit knowledge is oversimplistic, not least because each cannot be so clearly differentiated. Another problem is the difficulty in recording personal knowledge and locating it in a system accessible to everyone. One reason for this is that the 'transfer' of personal into explicit knowledge requires codification by someone else, which would need a shared implicit structure of understanding and a shared system of meaning (Trompenaars, 1994). So, even if personal knowledge is made available more widely in the organisation, it cannot necessarily be effectively used, because the potential users are not able to interpret or understand what has been codified by others with a different system of meaning. This is especially the case where the knowledge-sharing process involves individuals from different cultures (a key problem in multinational corporations), who may not share a common language, never mind a common system of meaning or understanding (Holden, 2002). Furthermore, to codify and store explicit knowledge in information systems, 'data warehouses' without recognising this can only, and inevitably, lead to organisational chaos, confusion and, inevitably, failure.

Tsoukas and Vladimirou (2001) do not engage at all with the tacit/explicit duality and do not complicate their definition of personal knowledge with problematic concepts such as 'justified true belief'. They prefer, instead, to focus on the *heuristic* nature of personal and organisational knowledge (that is, 'the knowledge that arises as individuals engage in their regular routines and improvise' (Orlikowski, 1996) 'in response to particular organisational situations encountered' (Collins, 1992)). So they focus on how an individual constantly and reflexively theorises during their knowledge development processes and on how organisational action might arise from this process. Their definition of personal knowledge reflects this: 'knowledge is an individual's capacity to draw distinctions, within a domain of action, based on an appreciation of context or theory, or both' (Tsoukas and Vladimirou, 2001: 1988).

Having considered the choices we have in conceptualising personal knowledge, our next exploration has to be 'how do we construe organisational knowledge?'

Organisational knowledge

An individual's knowledge has been regarded as an organisational asset (Wenger, 1998) because it is contextual, is the outcome of a highly reflexive process and has been interpreted to give meaning (Tsoukas and Vladimirou, 2001). However, we do need to take care that we do not view organisational knowledge as just a collection of the total personal knowledge of the individuals working in the organisation (Kay, 1993). The picture is far more complex than that, so producing a working definition of organisational knowledge is as complex an undertaking as trying to decide for ourselves how we might usefully construe the concept of personal knowledge. There are just as many variations of 'organisational knowledge' to choose from. For example, here is one from Davenport and Prusak:

> Knowledge is a flux mix of framed experiences, values and contextual information, and expert insight that provides a framework for evaluating and incorporating new experiences and information. It originates and is applied in the minds of knowers. In organisations, it often becomes embedded not only in documents or repositories but also organisational routines, processes, practices and norms.

> (Davenport and Prusak, 1998: 5)

Tsoukas and Vladimirou (2001) criticise Davenport and Prusak's definition for containing too many elements ('values', 'experiences' and 'contexts') without specifying their relationships and for neither stating in what form knowledge is embedded in organisations nor how individuals draw on it. However, they do commend this definition as demonstrating how knowledge is both an outcome (in this definition 'a framework') and a heuristic process. In this, they also suggest that such knowledge may be formally captured and, through its casting into propositional statements, can be turned into organisational knowledge. So this definition is useful in that there is an attempt to show a relationship between personal and organisational knowledge.

In developing *their* conception of organisational knowledge, Tsoukas and Vladimirou draw on writers such as Wittgenstein (1958), Penrose (1959), Polanyi (1975), Wenger (1998), Blackler (1995) and Collins (1992) and the following is a synthesis of their argument of how knowledge in organised contexts can be taken to be 'organisational'.

What is organisational knowledge?

Organisations can be said to be three things at once: concrete settings within which individual action takes place, sets of abstract rules in the form of propositional statements, and historical communities. In considering how we might construe organisational knowledge, we can usefully take as a starting point Wittgenstein's (1958) view that all knowledge is collective and link this to Penrose's (1959) definition that organisational knowledge is the set of collective understandings embedded in a firm, which enable it to put its resources to particular use. So knowledge becomes organisational when, as well as drawing distinctions in the course of their work by taking into account the contextuality of their actions, individuals draw and act on a corpus of generalisations in the form of generic rules produced by the organisation. Tsoukas and Vladimirou (2001) expand on this by taking a heuristic approach and their definition of organisational knowledge is worth quoting in full:

> Organisational knowledge is the capability members of an organisation have developed to draw distinctions in the process of carrying out their work, in particular concrete contexts, by enacting sets of generalisations whose application depends on historically evolved collective understandings and experiences. The more propositional statements and collective understandings become instrumentalised (in Polyani's sense of the term) and the more new experiences are reflectively processed (both individually and collectively) and then gradually driven into subsidiary awareness, the more organisational members dwell in all of them and the more able they become to concentrate on new experiences, on the operational plane.
>
> (Tsoukas and Vladimirou, 2001: 983)

To put it simply, then, organisational knowledge is a set of collective definitions that individuals in their working groups refer to in their decision-making processes.

We can see this in the day-to-day work of the Moddens' Gourmet Division customer enquiries section. There are a number of rules that exist in the section, such as how to answer customer enquiries and whom to contact when a price list might not be up to date. So the team are taking a generalised view and are developing a collective understanding (Penrose, 1959) by drawing collectively on these general rules and their knowledge of each other and other parties in order that they can respond to customers' queries in a standardised way. This collective understanding is also drawn on when each individual takes a call which is about their own specialist area. For example, when Andrea takes a call on her specialist area of wine and Jimi is asked about the price of a particular fish item, they individually draw on their past experiences of provision, as well as consulting the electronic database. When Byron, who has particular responsibility for meat products, is called on to stand in for Andrea, he can draw on the 'historically evolved collective understandings and experiences' of the other team members, because they, too, have had to deputise for each other.

Knowledge management and HR practice in organisations

In the business and management literature the management of knowledge is presented as a key strategic focus for managers today, where it is said that organisations are increasingly being viewed as knowledge systems which, if effectively managed, can provide an organisation with substantial competitive advantage (Davenport and Prusak, 1998). A number of authors have attempted to explain the nature of knowledge management (Bassi, 1997; Nahapiet and Ghoshal, 1998; Scarbrough et al., 1998; Petty and Guthrie, 2000), often combining both a systems and a processual perspective in their description. Their contribution can be synthesised (and at times criticised) as follows.

It has been strongly and persistently argued that knowledge management (KM) supports the strategic aims of attempting competitive advantage, particularly in a growing number of industries such as software and financial services (although few provide evidence for this link). Implicit in these definitions is Nonaka and Takeuchi's (1995) tacit/explicit knowledge relationship, where processes are said to be concerned with ensuring that once knowledge is acquired and used at one place and one time to solve a particular problem, this should be captured and shared so that the knowledge embedded in the solution can be reused at other places and times to enhance learning and performance in organisations. Davenport et al.'s (1998) definition seems to encompass the dominant view:

> Knowledge management is concerned with the exploitation and development of the knowledge assets of an organisation with a view to furthering the organisation's objectives. The knowledge to be managed includes both explicit, documented knowledge and subjective knowledge. Management entails all of those processes associated with the identification, sharing and creation of knowledge. This requires systems for the creation and maintenance of knowledge repositories, and to cultivate and facilitate the sharing of knowledge and organisational learning. Organisations that succeed in knowledge management are likely to view knowledge as an asset and to develop organisational norms and values which support the creation and sharing of knowledge.
>
> (Davenport et al., 1998: 17)

But there are other ways of defining knowledge management. For those interested in taking a strategic human resource development (HRD) perspective, one particularly helpful way of construing knowledge management is that of Tsoukas and Vladimirou (2001: 973) who, with an emphasis on reflective practice, argue that knowledge management could be taken to be about aiming to understand the practical mastery of employees and what those individuals are doing when they exercise that mastery. As they suggest, 'an unreflective practice involves us acting, doing things, effortlessly observing the rules of practice but finding it difficult to say what they are' (Tsoukas and Vladimirou, 2001: 990). The focus on reflection is interesting to develop.

It is not enough to unreflectively master a practice because, as we saw in the Moddens' customer enquiries team case study, if we need to teach new members effective practice or if we need to improve our own practice, then we need to be able to articulate and make explicit the rules and principles of our practice. So a definition of knowledge management that is quite different from others is that knowledge management is 'the dynamic process of turning an unreflective practice into a reflective one, by elucidating the rules guiding the activities of the practice by helping give a particular shape to collective understandings and by facilitating the emergence of heuristic knowledge' (Tsoukas and Vladimirou, 2001: 973).

Let us return to Jean Frear at Moddens' Gourmet Foods in her attempts to make sense of what could constitute 'knowledge management' at Moddens and what challenges there might be in organising knowledge in that organisational context.

Case Study 11.4

Making sense of knowledge management at Moddens' Gourmet Foods

Jean sat at her desk leafing through her back copies of her HR management magazine looking for articles on knowledge management. She wondered how she could usefully construe knowledge from an HR perspective. Juan Poort, the Group managing director, was fixated on recruiting and retaining people with the right sort of knowledge and skills. She would have to take account of this in any initiative by thinking of how to develop HR strategies and practices that could enable good utilisation of current employees' knowledge. She took up her pen and jotted down a few other questions she needed to think further about:

● How might 'organisational knowledge' be defined in the Moddens' Gourmet Foods context and how might the creation of such knowledge be encouraged?

● In what ways is organisational knowledge created in Moddens and what are the enablers and constraints of these processes?

● How could a culture of support for understanding the construction and use of knowledge be developed in order to keep pace with the profound changes that might impact on an organisation's position (such as the threatened takeover)?

● What activities could be useful for determining how appropriate HR knowledge related to organisational goals might be shared and disseminated?

● Might it be useful to do a business process re-engineering exercise where information flows were mapped in order to identify the what, where and when of knowledge-sharing in different contexts?

● What should be the role of IT, information systems (IS) and HR specialists as developers of systems for the gathering, sharing and creation of organisational knowledge?

> ### Activity 11.4 Defining organisational knowledge
>
> 1. How might organisational knowledge be defined in Moddens' Foods?
> 2. How would you define organisational knowledge in an organisation with which you are familiar?
> 3. In your view, what role might HR managers play in developing organisational knowledge?

As an HR director in Moddens, it is understandable that Jean wants to understand the relationship between any knowledge management activity required by company senior managers and the human resourcing task. There are a growing number of texts or journal articles on the human resourcing issues inherent in KM, with authors raising particular issues. These include difficulties in taking KM to be an unproblematic process of HRM (Scarbrough and Carter, 2000), losing knowledge through high turnover rates (Alvesson, 2000), the link between KM, HRM and employee commitment (Hislop *et al.*, 1997) and the difficulties in encouraging employees to share their knowledge (Robertson and O'Malley-Hammersley, 2000).

Scarbrough *et al.* (1998) argue that KM in an organisation builds on the interplay between tacit and explicit or articulated knowledge at the level of the individual, the group, the organisation and even the inter-organisational domain (Scarbrough *et al.*, 1998: 36). They suggest that the aim is to manage tacit knowledge by developing appropriate HR practices to locate experts with business-related tacit knowledge (which has an implication for recruitment and selection) and retain them within the organisation (via reward and appraisal systems). Then there should be an emphasis on explicating experts' knowledge and expertise into more codified forms (and therefore do not let people who have knowledge vital to core activities leave the organisation). Scarbrough *et al.*'s CIPD (2000) report identifies five specific ways in which HR can contribute to KM:

1. Best practice – which assumes that specific HRM models will help to deliver the behaviour required for KM to succeed. This does tend to imply that management need not concern itself with shaping HRM practices to meet the demands of KM programmers, but that by adopting best HR practice, commitment will be secured anyway.

2. Knowledge work – which focuses on the retention and motivation of knowledge workers, who are regarded as needing a distinctive culture and structure to motivate them.

3. Congruence – which emphasises the need for 'fit' between HRM and KM practices in the business strategy. This is based on the belief that organisations need to develop a 'systematic interaction between different functional areas' to enhance performance.

4. Human and social capital – this highlights the HRM implications of developing the human and social resources required for KM initiatives.

5. Learning – this focuses on the support needed from HRM for establishing and managing processes that develop learning at different levels from individual to organisational learning.

In a focus on knowledge workers ('people who use their heads more than their hands to create value' (Horibe, 1999: xi)), another CIPD study examined some of the people management issues specific to knowledge-intensive situations and professional knowledge workers. They advise that by managing the creation, development and sharing of knowledge both intra- and inter-organisationally, organisations can translate human capital into intellectual capital in the form of marketable products and services. They further suggest that knowledge workers have a number of distinct characteristics which mean application of their talents can be positively related to firm performance. It must therefore be appreciated that knowledge-intensive situations and workers must be managed successfully in order for the conversion process to be successful. Successful organisations are therefore adept at managing a number of dilemmas arising as a result of conflict between the needs and desires of knowledge workers and the needs and goals of the organisation.

Issues of learning, human and social capital will now be explored, linking them to the important HR activity of developing HR information systems in the increasingly popular way of developing cross-functional systems in many organisations. Point five on learning will be explored later.

Knowledge management and technology

In the early knowledge management literature KM was most frequently associated with the use of electronic means of communication, which requires two main types of activities. One is to document and appropriate individuals' knowledge and then disseminate it through such venues as a company-wide database. Another is the design of activities that facilitate human exchanges across the organisation using such information systems tools as groupware, e-mail and the internet. So, for example, where knowledge is important for product or service design, development or delivery and yet is widely dispersed, the solution presented was to use IT tools and techniques to transfer the knowledge from one person and place to another person and place. KM, therefore, was depicted as a linear process involving the use of technology for: knowledge 'capture' and codification; knowledge storage (a knowledge 'warehouse'); knowledge transfer (via an intranet, for example); knowledge access and retrieval ('data mining') (Newell *et al.*, 2002).

KM has been called a cult in pursuit of a new grail or a fad that shows how to capture, codify, use and exploit the knowledge and experience of employees by producing better tools and methods and by developing a willingness and ability to use those methods. This consideration of IS developments and practice in KM has been said to be to the detriment of attention to HR development and practice, which might in some way explain why HR practitioners have not engaged with the KM literature, nor identified how HR information systems (HRIS) influence KM. In this chapter we argue that a focus on the design and development of appropriate information systems is a necessary support to organising knowledge in organisations and that HRIS design and development is an essential part of this. We also argue that there is a need to consider the nature of KM with regard to the increasingly popular organisation-wide systems such as those developed to support Enterprise Resource Planning processes. Let us move on to consider both HRIS and ERP development in light of KM processes.

HR information systems

With the growing tendency to rationally define the organisation as a collection of knowledge assets, and the updating and management of information about those assets being seen to be of great importance, there is an increasing focus on the development of strategic computerised human resource information systems (Tansley *et al.*, 2001). There has been a marked improvement in the quantitative and qualitative provision of such systems (IS) since Richards-Carpenter (1991: 24) wrote about the lack of provision in that area. HR data is wide in its variety, and can include job history (transfers, promotions etc.), current and historical pay details, inventories of skills and competences, education and training records, performance assessment details, absence, lateness, accident, medical and disciplinary records, warnings and suspensions, holiday entitlements, pensions data and termination records.

An HRIS therefore provides an electronic database for the storage and retrieval of data, information and knowledge about human resources that is at least potentially available to anyone who may want to access it. Development of such systems, undertaken invariably in periods of major organisational as well as technological change, can be affected by social, technological, economic and political influences. There is an increasing tendency for several interested parties to be involved in this process. Inside the organisation these can include HR, information systems and business analyst specialists, line and senior management, and externally consultants and other guides to practice are likely to be involved.

Integrating HRIS with an Enterprise Resource Planning system

Increasingly, HRIS developments in larger organisations are undertaken as part of a major project to integrate all vital functional management information systems. The term given to this type of innovation is Enterprise Resource Planning (ERP). Knight defines innovation as 'the adoption of a change which is new to an organisation and to the relevant environment' (1967: 478) and he considers that innovation consists of special processes of organisational change. Given the tendency for larger organisations operating in a global environment to develop diverse systems and technologies in different parts of the organisation, ERP systems are designed with the objective of producing common business processes supported by an integrated IT infrastructure that will support business activity as a whole. The utilisation of ERP systems has increased rapidly and widely, based on their purported benefits, especially in terms of improved productivity and speed (Davenport *et al.*, 1998; Monk and Wagner, 2008). Where ERP systems are global, as Ferran and Kuossa (2008) argue, there are many issues and challenges to be faced.

Once a company decides to adopt an ERP system there are a number of stages to go through, as shown by Robertson *et al.* (2000), who outline a four-episode innovation model:

1. *agenda formation*, when the original idea, here to adopt ERP, is accepted and preparations made (e.g. formation of functional project teams) to facilitate adoption;

2. *design*, which involves understanding the ERP and organisational processes and fashioning a mutual fit;

3. *implementation*, which involves configuring the IT systems and changing organisational systems and processes;

4. *appropriation*, when the ERP system is fully embedded in the organisation so that it is accepted as routine.

These episodes should be seen as iterative, rather than linear.

So, once a company has decided to adopt an ERP system and has made its selection, it will typically set up one or more project teams to design and implement the system. This team must map existing organisational processes, identify the processes that are embedded in the ERP software, and define new organisational processes that fit both the software and the organisation. This design process necessitates the integration of knowledge. Let us return to the Moddens case study where an ERP project is about to begin.

Case Study 11.5

The work of an HR Enterprise Resource Planning team

At Moddens' Gourmet Foods, as part of a collection of organisational change programmes, an ERP programme was introduced to support business strategies and business activities and the realisation of functional objectives. The programme was designed to replace the current collection of information systems covering the organisation's core operational processes, such as HR, Finance and Production, in order to achieve optimum maximisation of the company's key resources via systems integration. This was considered to be one of the most important software implementation events in the history of Moddens.

The HR part of the ERP project was led by Jean Frear, because as HR director she felt she was the best person to be project leader and lead the setting up of the HR section of this important organisation-wide integrated system. Jean started the team recruitment process by engaging Caroline, an HR officer from the corporate HR planning section. She then proceeded to put out a general advertisement to all Moddens businesses to recruit staff for the project team, as well as (and vitally) using her own networks to find people with relevant knowledge and experience. Six additional members were recruited to the project team: four Moddens HR staff drawn from different areas of the company.

Caroline had previously been trained as a business analyst and over the last few years had gained excellent HR planning skills and competencies to add to her combination of IT and business expertise – exactly the combination that was required on the ERP HR project. She agreed to be on the project team, but only on a part-time basis while continuing to work in her previous role in HR planning. She had decided to have a baby some time in the future and thought that getting some ERP experience would make it easier to find a job once she returned from maternity leave, whether inside or outside Moddens. Likewise, she wanted to maintain her contacts in her corporate HR department so that she could return there should she want to. She thus agreed to work in the new project, but at the same time remaining firmly attached to her functional role.

Russell had been working as an HR manager on one of Moddens' Scottish sites. Over the course of his 20 years with Moddens, he had worked in many different parts of the HR function, so felt he would have a vast amount of knowledge to offer the team members who either had highly specialised knowledge or little knowledge and experience in the function. Russell had little IT knowledge (describing himself as 'computer illiterate') and it was because he wanted to add this to his skills portfolio that he said he wanted to join the team. His wife remained in the family home in Scotland while Russell obtained temporary accommodation at the Moddens company headquarters in Nottingham in order to be close to the project.

The HR ERP system was to include a payroll capability, so project manager Jean knew she would need someone with specialist knowledge in this area. She therefore gave a presentation about the project to the payroll management team, trying to encourage someone to join. Robin attended this presentation and, despite his recent promotion to payroll manager, agreed to join the project team. Like Russell, Robin saw this as an excellent opportunity to develop his IT systems skills, something he had wanted to do for some time. As he said, *'The main attraction for me to join the project was ERP software, the system itself, it clearly seems to be the way forward. It's had a lot of publicity.'* Once joining the project (supposedly full-time), like Caroline, Robin maintained his links with his functional area and regularly returned to do work there whenever he was needed, explaining, *'I've been supporting the payroll function . . . with the actual modifications that are needed to the current payroll software.'* So Robin joined the project team, and like Caroline when she said she could always return 'home', he said *'I could always fall back into the payroll manager's role.'*

Susan had been working in an HR functional role and so had general knowledge of the HR processes at Moddens. She was not happy in this role, however, and so applied to join the project team in order to get out of a line HR job that she did not like: *'It's more for myself really . . . it's what I can get out of it.'* However, once working on the project she continued to look for other opportunities in Moddens that would provide her with a more permanent role. This search intensified as the HR ERP project seemed to falter.

Rebecca was a placement student taking a business information systems degree who had been assigned to the project team. She had no ERP-specific knowledge but Jean had felt that this would provide her with valuable experience and that she could be useful in some of the more simple and mundane tasks that would need to be done. At the start of the project she was keen and eager, seeing it as a good opportunity to develop her skills. Over the course of the project she undertook more challenging tasks than administration, thus developing her knowledge at a more strategic rather than operational level. When she returned to university she was able to talk at great length about her experiences.

1. Agenda formation stage

As project leader for the HR ERP team, Jean was invited to attend briefings by senior managers of the strategy and plans for the ERP project across the company. On returning to the section, Jean called a meeting of the team, showed them a video of one of the management gurus explaining the benefits of ERP and the particular software they would be using. The team went away to make preparations for how they would implement the ERP strategy in HR, starting with the design and delivery of the process re-engineering workshops with the HR directors responsible for each designated HR process (called 'the process owners'). After the meeting the mood of the team was generally upbeat, although several found the language used to explain process re-engineering difficult to understand. One team member dismissed the video as *'all consultancy bollock-speak'*.

2. Design stage

Each team member had responsibility for a particular area of HR ERP implementation (e.g. employee resourcing, training and development, rewards) and they started to think about the design of the process re-engineering workshops. This proved a highly complicated endeavour because, while each member had worked in one area of the business, they were now required to design and run workshops where participants would be required to take a high-level view of current HR processes, then come up with plans to re-engineer them. One team member commented, *'It's like the blind leading the blind!'* However, Jean brought in consultants and, working in tandem, the team managed to design and run the workshops. Russell particularly was highly active in this. He enjoyed the workshops because it gave him an opportunity to show the senior manager participants how much he knew about their part of the HR function. It also gave him the chance to demonstrate his extensive HR experience and expertise to the other team members, all of lower status and more lowly paid than he was.

3. Implementation

Once the 'as-is' (current) processes were mapped, the team then had to work with senior managers responsible for particular HR processes in creating 'maps' of desired organisational HR processes ('to-be'). As they were doing this they also had to work with the IS specialists who were configuring the IT systems to suit requirements. It was at this stage that Russell was involved in a serious car crash and had a period in hospital so Susan had to run workshops instead of just assisting. Not surprisingly, the first workshop was not a great success. Fortunately, by now she had developed quite a network of senior managers so she was able to take advice from a number of these contacts and by the end of that period was running highly successful events.

Jean was aware of the difficulties of gauging how well the team was doing in their day-to-day 'deliverables', so she commissioned a team of researchers to interview the senior managers about their experiences of the process mapping activities and the findings were reported back to the HR ERP team and the senior managers in a joint workshop. This enabled a mid-stage review of the project to take place and activities were planned to answer some of the problems and complaints the senior managers had voiced about the way the project was progressing.

As the implementation stage began to draw to a close, Jean reflected on her own performance as leader. She had attempted to lead the team in developing their knowledge in their joint relations with each other and with their 'clients', the HR directors who were the 'owners' of the HR processes to be re-engineered. But this had been difficult because she had had to learn so much new knowledge herself, about the functionality of the software as well as the ERP methodology. She had thought she would be able to rely on Russell to support her in leading the team, but this had not happened because of Russell's unforeseen accident.

4. Appropriation

The HR element of the ERP system was fully implemented on time and to budget in the UK, so the team began to prepare to do the same in the company's other businesses in the rest of the world. A plan was drawn up by the team to do this and they began the same process again, this time in the international environment.

Activity 11.5   Before beginning an HR information systems project

In an organisation with which you are familiar:

1. How have computing and information technologies (C&IT) changed the work of the HR function over the last two years?

2. To what extent has the use of the C&IT changed communication processes between HR specialists and colleagues in other functions over the same period?

3. Think of a project you are familiar with in your recent organisational experience. What were the recruitment processes used and how did these link negatively or positively to the ultimate success or otherwise of the project?

4. In what ways did the recruitment process take into account project knowledge requirements?

In analysing this final episode of the case study, we could focus on how personal or organisational knowledge is created. However, in this section a different perspective of knowledge is taken, being viewed as neither individually tacit nor organisationally explicit but rather seen as knowledge that is continually constructed in social relations.

A relational perspective on knowledge

From the relational perspective, knowledge is viewed as being socially constructed in the shared social processes and negotiated understandings in which humans constantly engage (Berger and Luckman, 1966) and the joint activities of people's dialogues and actions together in particular institutional contexts and over time. Given the relational perspective being taken here, then, it is therefore not the *nature* of knowledge, but rather *how* people create knowledge of the local social and historical kind in their social interactions that is important (Burr, 1995). *Knowledge is therefore viewed here as being continuously created and re-created in people's joint activities of dialogue and action, as they share repertoires of meaning in particular contexts and over time.*

Let us return to our Moddens case study to understand some of these aspects.

Four innovation stages of an HR ERP project – a knowledge-based analysis

Stage 1: Agenda formation

As we saw in the Moddens HR ERP case study, various HR specialists joined the team to gain knowledge and skills that would enable them to develop in their careers. It is suggested here that the social capital of the project team leader was important in the recruitment process because of her need to find people with suitable skills and knowledge for the project. Nahapiet and Ghoshal (1998: 243) define social capital as 'the sum of actual and potential resources within, available through, and derived from the network of relationships possessed by an individual or social unit. Social capital thus comprises both the network and the assets that may be mobilized through the network'.

While the project team members had relevant and diverse knowledge and experience, their own goals and desires were also influential in their desire to join the project team. Jean herself was anxious to ensure that those getting involved did so because they were personally interested in the project. She was keenly aware that she was asking individuals for a high level of commitment, without offering any real job role security, so that when she made individuals an offer to join the team, she took great care to explain that this was a temporary project with no guarantees of success. Team members therefore only joined the project team if it suited their own personal agendas.

This orientation by organisational actors to undertake actions for their own as well as their organisation's benefit has been termed *strategic exchange* by Watson (1999). This term explains how human beings are strategically *shaping* their lives and Giddens' (1990) notion of *structuration* is drawn on with the argument that the structures and circumstances in which individuals find themselves partly shape what they think and do while, at the same time, individuals also shape those thoughts and circumstances (the extent to which they are able to do this varying with *power* associated with the position in which they find themselves). The notion of *shaping* is used throughout the theorising and the term *strategic* is used to highlight the ways in which human individuals on the one hand and work organisations on the other have to 'survive in a challenging and risk-filled world' which means that there always tends to be 'some pattern to the approach taken by any specified person or particular organisation to achieving that survival' (Watson, 1999: 26).

Stage 2: Design

At this stage of the project the team began to form as a group of specialists and, at the same time, make links with their 'clients' (the HR directors responsible for ensuring the HR process mapping was undertaken). As part of our relational analysis of the situation of HR specialists attempting to design the HR 'pillar' of the ERP programme, it will be useful a) to use a social rather than individualist theory of knowing and knowers, and b) to make some link to learning. The value of taking such a stance is demonstrated by Wenger (1998: 4), who argues that for us to 'know' something is a result of our gaining meaning by learning from our active engagement in social situations that he calls 'communities of practice'.

Communities of practice

In our analysis of the Moddens case study, we can usefully consider the HR ERP project team as a 'community of practice' (Wenger, 1998). Communities of practice can be defined as networks of people who work together in an organisation and who regularly share information and knowledge and learn in the process. Such people may be, but aren't necessarily, part of formal teams or units. They often collaborate on particular projects or products, or they hold the same or similar jobs. The notion of practice relates to the 'shared historical and social resources, frameworks and perspectives that can sustain mutual engagement in action' (Wenger, 1998: 5). Castells (1996) suggests that 'your knowledge is most valuable if it complements that of others in your immediate situation, thereby enabling all of you to collaborate in activities that will benefit each of you differently' (Castells, 1996 in Fuller, 2002).

So in HR information systems projects, such as the one we have seen in Moddens, a great deal of knowledge is produced and held collectively in often tightly knit communities of practice (such as a project team), so there is a shared experience that informs commonly held views about the type of information and systems that warrant attention and what to avoid. This bonding of such a community evolves from the interaction of these practitioners and gives meaning to shared information and knowledge.

According to Wenger (1998: 5), communities of practice are social configurations in which particular enterprises are considered to be worth pursuing and 'full participation' is recognisable as competence in that community. In the learning processes of these communities, members demonstrate their changing ability, individually and collectively, to experience life as meaningful while, at the same time, continuously (re)construct personal and group identities.

Human resourcing features of HR communities of practice

In the case study, we saw how Jean attempted to ensure a diversity of knowledge, skills and experience in this team of HR specialists. As many theories of team recruitment attempt to demonstrate, it is necessary to take into account the individual skills and characters of team members. Hackman (2002) advises that when you compose a team, you need to pay great attention to ensure that the team includes members who have the knowledge, the skills and the experience that are required for doing the work. But you also need to ensure that the team has a *diversity* of knowledge, skills, perspectives and experience. One aspect that was missing in the Moddens team was the inclusion of members with large-scale HRIS or ERP project development experience. For this Jean had to recruit consultants. This satisfied the need on the UK project but when the project 'goes global', if new members are not recruited with experience of different cultural environments, then we can anticipate further problems.

As Hackman (2002) argues, to derive real benefits from a team you need diversity of demography, or in terms of team members' knowledge base or skills repertoire. People often believe that harmonious relations are the main facilitator of team performance when this is not necessarily the case. This is further problematised when members select people who resemble themselves for the team. But to try to build a team that has the 'right mix' of personalities or behavioural styles is a fruitless exercise it is the diversity of knowledge, skills, perspective and experience that is so important.

The politics of team-work – team 'destroyers'

We saw evidence in the case study by some team members of negative views of the project – scathing comments about 'consultancy bollock-speak' on the video of the management guru and more commentary on the nature of management of the project where it was considered that 'the blind are leading the blind'. Sometimes in groups there are individuals who might be labelled with Hackman's (2002) term 'team destroyer'. It can be argued that team destroyers do exist. These are people who will undermine any team you put them in. Such people may be so unskilled in working collaboratively with other people, or so individualistic in their focus, that they should be invited to make what may be an excellent contribution to their organisation as solo performers. However, as Hackman (2002) argues, the reality is that, when teams encounter problems, or things aren't developing smoothly, team members frequently engage in a process of 'scapegoating'. They will pick on an individual to whom they assign personal responsibility for the difficulties. That person may then be labelled a 'team destroyer'. Scapegoating is not random. The individual selected tends to be different from the majority of the team, perhaps because of age, functional speciality, gender or ethnicity. Knowing this, we must guard against blaming individuals for problems that are team problems.

Whatever the original cause, this type of event can affect the successful knowledge development in a project. Three elements are worthy of consideration. First, is the team actually a clearly bounded group of people who accept a shared collective responsibility for the outcome? Second, has the person who created the team or the team leader established some basic norms of conduct and made these explicit, ensuring that all team members understand that certain behaviour is unacceptable? Third, is the reward system of the larger organisation such that collective team performance is recognised and rewarded, or is the team operating in a context in which only individual successes really 'pay off'? The risk of individual team members disrupting the team is much reduced if the answer to the first two questions, and first part of the third question, is 'yes'. Team success and a good group exert a powerful restraining influence on the behaviour of team members.

Given the potential for political difficulties arising within the team, the team leader needs to consider how they might assess how well a team is doing in terms of elements such as productivity and quality over time. We saw in Case Study 11.5 how Jean engaged a team of researchers to interview senior managers to gauge how well or otherwise the HR ERP team were progressing in their relationships and in developing processes for mapping HR activities. Thus a more qualitative approach was taken, rather than the typical response of considering available figures (usually financial) to plot trends and assess how well the team is doing. However, these figures do not necessarily demonstrate how well a team is working, in either the short or long term. In addition, a focus on the short term will yield very different results from a focus on the long term, and vice versa. A more qualitative approach allows opinion and interpretations of the 'client group' to be surfaced, and allows a determination of how well the team is doing at meeting the legitimate needs and expectations of these clients. As Hackman (2002) argues, looking at the numbers is not the only activity that should take place because they are generally not designed, intended or appropriate to assess team outcomes.

Hackman (2002) suggests a focus on the client, on the team itself and on the individuals in the team. Questions that might be asked are: 'Is the team meeting or exceeding the legitimate expectations of its clients?' 'What is happening to the team as a performing unit over time, i.e. is the team improving its performance, becoming better at assessing its environment and developing a strategy that is uniquely appropriate to it?' 'Is the team also drawing on all the talents, skills, knowledge, experience and perspectives of its members, promoting learning and personal and professional growth?' His three-item checklist for assessing how well a team is doing is: Are the clients happy? Is the team getting stronger as a performing unit over time? And, do the individual members of the team find in their work more learning and fulfilment than they do frustration?

As the project progressed, the team gained knowledge and competence in HRIS project work. Their learning and knowledge development were not just individually focused, however. Rather, members were active participants in a 'community of communities' (Spender, 1992). These communities included their own project group, other ERP functional groups (finance, production etc.), IT specialists, IT consultants and senior management. Participation in a community of practice such as the HR ERP project team is therefore both 'a kind of action and a form of belonging' (Wenger, 1998: 4).

Stage 3: Implementation

We saw in Jean's reflections at the end of stage three that she felt that she could have been a more effective project leader in the area of knowledge leadership.

It is rare to find anyone who devotes the time, expends the energy or has the self-knowledge required to develop strong leadership on the part of his or her peers to compensate for, supplement or complement his or her own weak side. It takes exceptional individuals to recognise that, despite their personal success and acclaim, part of their job is to develop other individuals to compensate for those areas where their own knowledge, skills, experience or style are less than satisfactory. Yet this is a critical requirement for a successful senior executive team. This said, it is not possible to identify all the pieces of the required skills 'jigsaw' ahead of time; nor can one simply administer personality tests and then assemble a team as you would the pieces of a jigsaw.

Stage 4: Appropriation

The fourth stage of the model suggests a rather rational approach – that the system is 'embedded' into the organisation, where members regard its use as routine. However, as we have seen by taking a relational approach to the other three stages, there are a myriad of elements that make up the social relations inherent in processes of knowledge construction.

We saw in the case how the project team engaged in a number of *situated* knowing (Amin and Roberts, 2008) and *situated learning* processes (Lave and Wenger, 1991) and how they were personally shaped when particular communities of practice were involved and particular managerial behaviours enacted. We also saw how, in gaining project skills in HRIS development work, team members moved from a position where they had little knowledge about necessary project processes, to a fuller understanding and engagement in those processes. This has been termed *legitimate peripheral participation* by Lave and Wenger (1991).

Legitimate peripheral participation

Legitimate peripheral participation refers to both the development of identity via the development of knowledge and skills in practice, and to the reproduction and transformation of communities of practice (Lave and Wenger, 1991: 55). Legitimate peripheral participation (LPP) considers the processes by which the shift from individual newcomer to community of practice 'old timer' occurs. It is an analytical viewpoint and a way of understanding learning. The emphasis is on connecting issues of socio-cultural transformation with the changing relations between newcomers and old timers in the context of a changing shared practice.

In their discussion on LPP, Lave and Wenger focus on the notion of the apprentice's learning journey towards attaining the level of skill and knowledge of the master (an 'old timer'). The apprentice is described as a 'newcomer' to the community of practice they are seeking to form. In our ERP tale we take as the community of practice the multidisciplinary world of the ERP development community consisting of a collection of functional specialists such as IT, IS and HR. In order for the HR ERP team to be successful, full legitimate peripheral participation for each member was a necessary, if unlikely, aim. However, as we saw in the case study, there were a number of difficulties that arose to influence this process, such as Russell's car accident and the feedback from the HR directors on the 'service' offered by the HR ERP team to the mapping teams.

Conclusions

To attempt to understand how knowledge might be understood in organisational life is quite a difficult undertaking, not least because of the lack of clarity in defining personal and organisational knowledge. It is also a challenging task for managers to understand how knowledge might be managed and the systems and processes necessary for this to be enabled. In this chapter a number of these challenging areas have been addressed and lessons drawn for HR practices.

Summary

In this chapter the following key points have been made:

- Knowledge in the organisational context can be construed in many different ways, but one useful way is that knowledge is a human resource that is socially constructed in the relational processes of human interaction and which is necessary for organisational survival and success.

- If managers use the notion of knowledge management in their practices, they need to take account of both the development of individual and organisational knowledge capabilities and of human resource information systems which facilitate understanding of the knowledge domains in an organisation.

- Learning in organisational life has to do with participating and becoming a member of a community, because social relations are important for the transmission of knowledge, the mastering of a situated curriculum (Gheradi *et al.*, 1998) and the relational development of both personal and organisational identity (Watson, 1994; Wenger, 1998) in the arena of social interaction (Gheradi and Nicolini, 2001).

- The social construction of knowledge in such occupational communities forms part of 'organisational learning'.

Discussion questions

1. What is 'knowledge' taken to be in your part of the organisation?
2. In what ways might it be argued that explicit knowledge is really just information?
3. In your experience, how are the knowledge economy, organisational knowledge and personal knowledge related?
4. To what extent do you think that 'knowledge management' is just another fad or fashion in the business and management field?
5. Give three examples of how knowledge might be managed in your part of the organisation. What implications do these practices have for managing knowledge across the organisation as a whole?
6. What constraints can we see in managing knowledge in a part of an organisation with which we are familiar?

7. To what extent could you be described as a knowledge worker?

8. Whose knowledge do you rely on for your own daily work? What constraints are there to your access to this knowledge of others?

9. How might taking a knowledge-based view of your current work tasks inform your future career development needs?

10. What do you see as the relationship between IT and the development of knowledge in your organisation?

Further reading

There are many texts on the various topics related to knowledge management and the most appropriate further reading for this chapter is indicated in the text, where readers can follow up citations that are most helpful to their particular interests. General texts that deal helpfully and broadly with such matters are those by Davenport and Prusak (1998), Newell *et al.* (2002), Nonaka and Takeuchi (1995), Little *et al.* (2002), Scarbrough and Carter (2000) and Wenger (1998). Knowledge management from the point of view of a particular sector (construction) can be found in Bartholomew (2008); from an information systems perspective in Mosco (2008), Ferran and Kuossa (2008) and Monk and Wagner (2008); from management consultancy in Sturdy *et al.* (2009); and with regard to communities of practice in Amin and Roberts (2008).

12

Managing processes of human resource development

Jan Myers and Susan Kirk

Learning outcomes

Having read this chapter and completed its associated activities, readers should be able to:

- Identify the changing nature of the contexts which may affect approaches to human resource development
- Articulate an understanding of human resource development as a strategic intervention
- Analyse approaches to employee development
- Critically evaluate potential and actual processes of human resource development
- Appreciate and describe the wider benefits of learning
- Critically analyse the contribution of human resource development and the changing role of HR practitioners in organisational changes and transition

Introduction

A key focus of this chapter is to consider the contribution of human resource development (HRD) in creating, enhancing or releasing the 'efforts, knowledge, capabilities and committed behaviours' (Chapter 1, p. 9) of individuals and groups and to consider the HR strategies and managerial interventions utilised within the context of organisations. It is increasingly being acknowledged that strategic management and development of skills and experience in organisations (often referred to as human capital or 'talent management') can actively contribute to organisational outcomes – employee and customer satisfaction, performance and quality levels and survival and sustainability. As such, it is important to place HRD firmly within the arena of wider strategic planning practices and to demonstrate how HRD contributes to and supports organisational aims and objectives. A number of activities, scenarios and case examples will be used throughout the chapter to develop discussion and provide opportunities for analysis and reflection.

HRD in context

Let us consider that in order for organisations to compete in an increasingly global market-based environment – whether to produce quality goods for niche markets, or to provide appropriate and accessible public services – that people, in this instance employees, are key players contributing to the core competences of the organisation (Hamel and Prahalad, 1994). We can begin to see, then, that harnessing the talents and capabilities of employees to the advantage of the organisation becomes a significant managerial activity; indeed the rise of so-called 'talent management' activities bears this out (Clarke and Winkler, 2006; Tansley *et al.*, 2006). However, while there are specifically articulated, good practice approaches and methods to educating, training and developing resourceful human beings (see Further reading, p. 412), there is clearly no one best way to managing the processes of HRD. Furthermore, as Livingstone and Roth (2001: 4) point out in relation to the Canadian experience of work-based learning, 'from a conventional management perspective, virtually the only relevant learning for employees is job training that can enhance the productivity and profitability of the company'.

This approach tends to ignore more informal learning in organisations as well as worker-investment in their own education and professional development. It can also lead, in some instances, to a more cost-orientation to training in organisations (as opposed to investment for future needs) and a short-term perspective on the immediate demands for skills, which may not be the same as those needed for future employability. This also raises the subtle differentiation between training (usually on-the-job) and development (often associated with personal and professional development, course/class-based learning and executive coaching). In Canadian studies, for example, it was found that employees who received the greatest amount of class-based training were university-educated employees, professionals and managers, and those employed in specific industries such as finance and insurance. Moreover, chances of receiving training were increased within larger companies (Statistics Canada, 2006: 53).

On a more general level, one of the major criticisms of British industry is that in comparison to some of its European neighbours, the UK has historically been seen as a poor investor in training and development (Redman and Wilkinson, 2001; Harrison, 2002) and, until recently, the national approach has been characterised by relatively little legal intervention and an emphasis on voluntarism. Often, this lack of investment is linked to levels of workforce productivity. In 2002, productivity levels (i.e. GDP per worker) were 16 per cent below those of Germany and 13 per cent below France, yet an estimated one-fifth of this difference is attributed to lower skills levels in the UK compared to Germany and France (Westwood, 2001; HM Treasury/DTI, 2004). In response to the need to meet skills gaps and increase productivity, what we are starting to see is a UK government keen to encourage a series of initiatives, and that recognises the importance of developing the skills both of people in the labour market and those working in private, public and voluntary sector organisations. In this way, we can see that developing an educated, capable and skilled workforce is also shaped by external forces exerted, in this instance, by government objectives, task force initiatives and country comparative benchmarking data. This together with, for example, trade union input into basic skills development and lifelong learning initiatives has contributed to the changing focus of training and development in both education leading to work and in the organisational work environment (Stubbs and Stubbs, 2008) – see the following Exhibit 12.1.

Exhibit 12.1

Union activities and learning

The Canadian Auto Workers Union

Since its breakaway from the US Auto Workers union, the Canadian Auto Workers Union (CAW) is the largest private-sector union in Canada. The first CAW Family Education Centre was set up in 1957 and over time there has been significant attention paid to education programmes for members. In 1988 a new facility was opened, set in a 47 acre site and, according to CAW, combines 'the best of a natural woodland setting and state-of-the art technology . . . it is an exceptional environment for reflection, discussion and recreation' (CAW, n.d., *History of the CAW Family Education Centre*).

The CAW education department offers one-day courses across Canada as well as paid education leave (PEL) courses at the Centre in Port Elgin, Ontario. For the latter all costs – travel, accommodation, course fees as well as lost time are covered by PEL funds. There are also two-week family education programmes in the summer for members and their families with recreational activities and childcare provided for teens and children. The courses generally focus on two purposes: promoting and developing union activism and skills on the one hand; and covering work-based issues and concerns on the other. A sample list is as follows:

- Aboriginal and Workers of Colour Leadership Training Program (running since 1992),
- Advanced Grievance Handling,
- Building a Respectful Workplace Environment (Anti Harassment),
- Confronting Homophobia – Understanding Sexuality,
- Women's Skilled Trades and Technology Awareness – geared to raising awareness soft skilled trades as a career option for women,
- Workplace Training: women's advocate.

Trades Union Congress (TUC), UK

The TUC is the largest umbrella union in the UK with 66 affiliated unions representing approximately 7 million members (TUC, 2008, *About the TUC*).

In 2006, what was TUC Education merged with Learning Services to become 'unionlearn'. The education programmes provided are geared to improving union activities and skills with specialist courses for union professionals and union representatives and they also provide basic skills development (reading, mathematics, English as a second language) as well as information and advice on career options.

Sources: Human Resources and Social Development Canada (2001) Corporate profiles: Canadian Auto Workers Union available from **www.hrsdc.gc.ca/en/lp/spila/wlb/ell/05canadian_auto_workers.shtml** Canadian Auto Workers Union website: www.**caw**.ca
Trade Union Congress website: www.**tuc**.org.uk
Unionlearn website: www.unionlearn.org.uk/

In many respects, this development reflects the view that by enhancing the skills base in the labour market, there will be an overall increase in human and social capital. Indeed the Department for Education and Skills recently published a summary of research carried out in the period 1999–06. This examines the wider benefits of learning, concluding that: 'The importance of learning is wide-ranging, extending well beyond qualifications and economic success' (Department of Education and Skills, 2006: 1). This report cites benefits from learning including enhanced mental and physical well-being, more positive attitudes and a reduction in crime (as a result of the introduction of two educational initiatives aimed at 16–18 year olds). This further reinforces the notion that the workplace is not the only arena in which people learn. As such, we can see that much of the UK government focus on learning opportunities is aligned with national, regional and local approaches to economic and social regeneration and fits with a broader international theme of building social capital and civil society.

The focus, for the UK, includes a top-down governmental push on education, training and lifelong learning. The notion of lifelong learning in this context is defined as both individuals and communities having equality of access to high quality learning opportunities throughout their lives. This approach to social and economic inclusion of individuals and communities brings together the contribution of schools and further and higher educational establishments and links into a planned modernisation of public sector organisations and an emphasis on cross-sector partnerships to provide opportunities for public, private and nonprofit sectors to work together. This emphasis on reciprocity of lifelong learning and individual, social and corporate responsibility is echoed in a 'Eurobarometer' – a specially commissioned survey of European citizens – which indicated that 8 out of 10 citizens surveyed viewed an integrated approach to lifelong learning as combining 'employability, personal development, active citizenship and social cohesion. This is especially so in Greece, Spain, Ireland and Sweden where around nine in ten support this approach' (CEDEFOP, 2003: 6).

In order to encourage a greater uptake of learning and development opportunities, we might see the need for (European and nation-state) government intervention: the willingness and ability to provide an infrastructure to support, both at an individual and organisational level, access to training, learning and development opportunities. The emphasis on development and skill acquisition is encouraged by the European Commission, which integrated its various educational and training initiatives under one umbrella in 2006 and launched the Lifelong Learning Programme. On a more local level, the recently published 'Statement of Priorities' from the UK Learning and Skills Council reports on the Council's key actions and priorities for 2008/9 to 2010/11. This outlines a wide-reaching action plan, 'creating a culture of demand for skills' through the so-called '14–19 reforms' aimed at raising attainment and participation in the education system through to an increased investment in the 'Train to Gain (TtG) service' and other initiatives such as the 'Personal and Community Development Learning (PCDL)' (Learning and Skills Council, 2007: 2). This requires the commitment and support of a range of key stakeholders, for example links to further and higher education, the collaboration with professional networks and institutions, and the input from trade unions and employee representative bodies.

Furthermore, there is also a growing emphasis on individual responsibility as well as encouragement and incentives to employers to provide and support continued employee development investment and opportunities. While the CEDEFOP survey (2003: 18) found that 44 per cent of all Europeans surveyed had taken up learning opportunities on their own initiative, half of these had been advised or required to do so by their employers. Moreover, many countries are also looking at the future face of labour markets given expected demographic changes. For example, in Canada it is expected that the majority of future employment opportunities will be as a result of retirements:

> 70 per cent of all job openings [3.8 million existing positions] during that period [2006–2015] will be associated with the need to replace retired workers, up from an average of about 51 per cent over the last ten years . . . [and most] expected to be in occupations usually requiring postsecondary (university, college or apprenticeship training) or in management.
>
> Lapointe *et al.* (2006: 2)

Impacts on HRD

As we can see from the discussion above, there are a number of external pressures and activities that impact on human resource management and development. Figure 12.1 summarises some of the key impacts on HRD policies and strategies: some of these impacts reflect the changing external environment (regulatory frameworks such as employment legislation); some link with internal management and HR activities (recruitment and selection); and others may be the result of specific strategic decision-making (outsourcing). HRD responses may include consideration of training and development to meet current needs and demands on the one hand, and on the other an anticipation of future skills and competences in the light of perceived changes and demands, which is touched on again later in this section.

Much of the language associated with increasing access to 'learning opportunities' through workplace activities is linked to increasing the (for-profit) organisation's competitive advantage. Language such as enhancing *sustainability*, increasing *efficiency* and *effectiveness*; of increasing *commitment* of employees; of creating *learning environments* where the unique skills of employees can be exploited for current needs and for the *long-term survival* of the company. Exploring training needs may often be used in conjunction with environmental scanning and assessment of external pressures and the internal strengths and weaknesses of the organisation to anticipate or respond to identified challenges and opportunities.

Figure 12.1 Impact on HRD strategies

Such responses may be rooted in the here-and-now of skills deficit analyses and meeting gaps – assuring that employee development is 'fit for purpose', that is, training geared to skills needed for specific tasks, or they may be more future orientated. This 'fit-for-future' agenda may be responding to anticipated skills needs and gaps and is also part of a wider reflection of changes in the labour market, for example attracting potential employees into areas where there are perceived likelihood of skills shortages (e.g. in the UK, teaching and nursing). However, the need to be accountable in terms of efficiency and effectiveness, to demonstrate sustainability and value is no less a priority for non-profit and public sector organisations, as the following case study shows.

Case Study 12.1

City School: HRD contribution to improving effectiveness and efficiency in an inner-city school

City School, catering for seven to eleven-year-olds, was facing closure because of the lack of students attending the school. It was seen to be no longer viable in the current economic environment. As a final attempt to revitalise the organisation, a new head was recruited. Within six years, the head had turned the school around.

The school was now in the position where it had to refuse entrance to some pupils because of the high number of parents wanting their children to attend the school. It had received national recognition for quality of leadership and teaching. It was able to attract additional funds to purchase high quality teaching equipment and IT resources for the pupils. It had become an employer of choice, with high numbers of candidates applying for any available teaching post or support role at the school. This had been achieved by:

- Changing the school name, adopting 'corporate' colours and upgrading premises.
- Open days and marketing events and increasing publicity about the school's achievements.
- Working in partnership with a teacher-training college to achieve 90 per cent of trainee time in class and therefore increasing numbers of classes while reducing class size.
- Appointing trained teachers for their expertise, then increasing their capacity to learn and share knowledge by assigning teaching away from their subject areas. For example, a staff member with a degree in theology actually teaches physical education (PE). This teacher is mentored by another member of staff who is qualified in PE and sports psychology, but teaches another curriculum subject. The PE teacher in turn mentors and supports the religious education teacher. This in turn fits with creating and managing an integrated curriculum and teaching programme for pupils by breaking down curriculum-defined categories. Staff are encouraged to think of themselves not as 'teachers' (of a particular subject) but as 'professionals' and 'educationalists', contributing to the organisation as a whole and the wider community in which the school is based.
- Pupils are encouraged to self-manage through use of support groups and participation in a School Council and there is an emphasis on collective responsibility for school policy (e.g. approaches to bullying) and life-skilling.
- All pupils and staff are expected to develop and maintain a personal development plan and record of achievement.
- Staff are encouraged to skills-share and provide learning opportunities for each other, for example lunchtime supervisory staff run a course for teaching staff on 'Coping with children with autism'.
- Systems and networks for collaboration and knowledge sharing with other schools and communities of practitioners are in place and regularly used.

There is little evidence of the use of generic strategy models (e.g. Porter's (1985) Five Forces or SWOT analyses), yet there is keen awareness of the environment and context in which the organisation operates, both at a local level and at a national and international sector level. There is considerable *social complexity* in the relationships between the staff and pupils, the culture and philosophies underpinning practice and the HRD contribution which enable the managers and staff in the school to 'conceive of and implement strategies that improve its efficiency and effectiveness' (Barney, 1991: 101).

Source: Myers (1996/7)

In the case study above, what we can see is an organisation that in the main employs individuals who arrive ready prepared and trained as teachers or specialist support staff. The managerial tasks include encouraging continuing learning and improving performance to benefit and satisfy a range of stakeholders, including staff, pupils, parents and government agencies. There is also an emphasis on continuous professional development that in turn links to career progression (generally moving out of the host organisation to another for promotion) and compliance with professional standards. Most of the learning in this example is work based and through internal and external networks. Yet, while we can pick out a number of initiatives that contribute to the success and sustainability of the school, this will not necessarily mean a successful outcome for another school or organisation wanting to imitate one or more of the initiatives. Blanket appropriation or copycat behaviour of successful methods and initiatives cannot necessarily be transferred wholesale from one organisation to another. Factors such as the historical development of the organisation, skills of employees and managers, and environmental and cultural issues need to be taken into consideration, to be appropriately contextualised, which again takes us away from the idea of direct transfer of 'best' practice to consider a range and diversity of 'good' and 'possible' practices (Myers and Sacks, 2001, 2003).

There is a further strand to developing resourceful human beings, which can be work based but also takes a focus on training *for* employment. The Organisation for Economic Cooperation and Development (OECD) reported that 'high and persistent unemployment has been a major blot on the economic and social record of most OECD countries since the early 1970s' (Martin, 1998: 5). This followed on from a strategy of improving education and training (OECD, 1996), particularly vocational education and training (VET) programmes linked to combating structural unemployment and quality-of-life issues.

Here emphasis has not only been on improving links between education and employers – for example, with successful use of apprenticeship schemes as evidenced in Austria, Germany, Switzerland and Denmark (Martin, 1998), but also in expanding and improving the quality of various VET initiatives along with recognised national standards and qualifications (OECD, 1998). The emphasis on this approach to individual learning is supported in the UK by initiatives such as Learn Direct, National Traineeships and Modern Apprenticeship schemes, together with adult work-based training. For those not yet in employment, there are pathways to work such as national vocational training qualifications tied to further education, Welfare to Work and New Deal initiatives, and less successful pilot schemes such as Individual Learning Accounts (withdrawn because of training provider misuse of the schemes – see Harrison, 2002; Marchington and Wilkinson, 2002b, for further discussion). All of these initiatives would fit in a framework of active measures identified for improvement by the OECD (see Martin, 1998: 6) which are aimed at achieving economic and social objectives in relation to job-related skills, responding to changes in labour markets and increasing access to employment.

Activity 12.1	Improving education and training: national initiatives

The OECD Jobs Strategy (1996) recommended improvements in education and training systems to tackle unemployment and skills shortages. We have seen some examples of government policy and public spending in responding to these challenges above. In addition, the OECD Economics Department (OECD, 1998: 20) highlights other initiatives, e.g.:

● Australia: government funding of off-the-job training for apprentices and trainees;

● Netherlands: training, apprenticeships, adult education and VET amalgamated into 46 regional centres;

● Norway: two-year programme of in-work training to all vocational school graduates;

● Denmark and Sweden: improving choice and reducing drop-out rates in upper secondary education;

● Finland: strengthening career guidance.

Furthermore, the OECD recently called for governments to do more to help workers adapt to the new global economy, arguing the need for improvements in labour regulations and social protection systems to help people adapt to changing job markets and the need to become more mobile to prevent them getting 'trapped in jobs with no future' (OECD, 2007: 1).

Identify and list government and work-based initiatives and support for training and education that impact on the labour markets in your country.

A strong influence on private sector employers' approaches to training and development has been through the promotion and encouragement of benchmarking and quality initiatives, such as Investors in People (IiP), which links training and development with business needs (for more in-depth discussion of IiP see Marchington and Wilkinson, 2002b). We can identify a similar move in the public sector. The UK public services as 'the main employers of highly educated and trained employees' (Marchington and Wilkinson, 2002b: 375) are increasingly using frameworks such as the European Quality Foundation Excellence Model, and adoption of tools such as the Balanced Scorecard (Kaplan and Norton, 1993). Both of these take a wider view of training and development as part of a whole systems approach linked to quality and transforming organisations to become 'world-class and successful' and so linked to processes of change, learning, knowledge management and innovation (Davenport and Prusak, 1998; Garvey and Williamson, 2002; Holden, 2002; Newell *et al.*, 2002).

However, Gibb and Megginson (2001) point to the development of these and other initiatives, such as the development of the Management Charter Initiative, as the emergence of old approaches in new forms. For example, new infrastructural organisations in the UK, such as the Learning and Skills Council – arising from closure of the Training and Enterprise Councils (see Activity 12.1 for comparison with the Netherlands' learning and training infrastructure), now with a strong workforce planning agenda; Sector Skills Councils – developing on from national training organisations.

This movement from 'old' to 'new' forms the heart of the UK government's drive to modernise public services, together with a partnership approach across sector boundaries of public, private and voluntary sectors (e.g. through public/private finance initiatives; cross-sector service provision; cross-sector mentoring schemes and an emphasis on employee volunteering as part of personal development initiatives). For example, the continued changes and developments in UK healthcare task the UK government and the NHS with investing in and providing 'high quality training and development' (Office of Public Service Reform, 2002: 21). However, research conducted over a two-year period into employee attitudes in two UK NHS acute Trusts found that 60 per cent of staff surveyed made neutral or negative comments in relation to the support that they received for professional development. Just under half of those questioned felt that the Trusts did not offer opportunities to learn new skills, with 80 per cent stating that resources are not made available for development opportunities (Fisher *et al.*, 2001). Some of these gaps have started to be addressed as this sector faces particular challenges with changing demographics (an ageing work population), labour shortages and meaningful career path development (Skills for Health, 2006). Even so, this suggests that the government is some considerable way from achieving its aims with regard to leadership and employee development and highlights an additional query on how strategic and creative public sector managers can be in determining organisational innovation and development given some of the constraints of public policy.

Some of the larger, national non-governmental organisations and development agencies may develop and run their own in-house training and development programmes, and there is growing recognition of the importance of training and career progression. Yet, an NCVO/VSNTO (2000: 1) report highlighted that 'two out of five voluntary organisations surveyed identified a gap between employees' current skills and those they need to do the job effectively'. Furthermore, while it was felt that management development was a priority for their organisation, approximately a third of respondents in this category lacked 'a strategy for delivering it', with constraints identified as lack of funding, pressures of work, level of priority, lack of leadership and inappropriate training provision (NCVO/VSNTO, 2000: 2). This situation becomes more complex when considering the training and development needs of volunteer workers associated with and working in non-profit and public sector organisations (Masterton and Pinnock, 2002).

It appears that while learning and development is seen to be a 'good thing', employers still need to be convinced of the economic necessity to invest in employee development. In his foreword in Holbeche (2002: xiv), David Hussey highlights how managers may feel that investment in developing human resources is an 'act of faith' due to the apparent difficulty in evaluating the effect on the bottom line. Indeed this difficulty in proving the value of training persists: a recent survey shows that 80 per cent of respondents report that their training activities are delivering greater value to the business than they are able to demonstrate (CIPD, 2006). This could be reflected in the seeming elasticity of training budgets experienced by HR practitioners and managers in some organisations and determined by the pressing needs of other departmental or organisation-wide priorities. In addition, the emphasis on 'must-do' training provision, such as that required by legislation around employment practices and health and safety, may also be a contributory factor. Similarly, this more instrumental approach, shown in the lack of take-up of more innovative learning and development processes, may be attributed to a lack of guidance and appropriate frameworks offered by governments and handbooks on management (Chaston *et al.*, 1999). Moreover, in a recent survey conflicting priorities and a lack of training for line managers themselves are attributed to the failure to provide effective learning and development support in two-fifths of organisations surveyed (CIPD, 2008e). It becomes necessary then to explore the changing emphasis on human resource development processes both from the internal needs and resources of the organisation and the contexts (social, political, environmental, local markets, national and global networks) in which organisations are operating. So, we might suggest that in conjunction with strategic shifts in levels of (UK) government intervention, there are, according to Desimore *et al.* (2002: 20), 'five challenges facing the field of HRD'. And, by implication, these are challenges facing HRD practitioners whether in specialist HR roles or acting as line managers with IIR responsibilities. In many ways, these challenges can be generalised across for-profit organisations and in some instances across sectors (public and non-profit) in different geographical locations. They include coping with and anticipating the needs brought about by changing workforce demographics; competing in a global economy, where one might also include the concept of the virtual marketplace offered by increasing technological capabilities; eliminating skills gaps; meeting the need for lifelong individual learning; and facilitating organisational learning.

We might therefore anticipate a continuing change in the role of HR practitioners in an effort to align employee development with business needs and where line managers are 'expected to develop into "business managers" with an awareness of the total organization' (Cunningham and Hyman, 1995: 6). Furthermore, where there is an emphasis on investing in *whole* workforce training and development (1995: 13), with associated concerns around equality of opportunity in accessing training and development, ethical considerations and managing diversity in human resource development is of key importance. What is in evidence from recent UK research, though, shows that the majority of organisations are identifying select groups of 'talented' individuals (rather than the whole workforce) and focusing their resources on these: thus issues of equal opportunities in terms of learning and development remain central (CIPD, 2006).

The changing nature of the role of HR practitioners can be seen in the job titles and job descriptions associated with the role: from personnel assistants, to learning tutors, to directors of organisational learning and development. We can see this demonstrated in the literature with reference to the move from the welfare role of HR professionals to the concepts of internal consultants and change agents, and HR practitioners and managers as coaches and facilitators of learning (CIPD, 2007c; Holbeche, 2002; Megginson *et al.*, 1999; Walton, 1999).

Activity 12.2   HRD over time

The changing organisation environment from local to global has an impact on the recruitment, training and development of staff, and retention of highly skilled individuals.

1. Consider the environment in which your organisation operates; is there a high or low degree of strategic uncertainty? (See p. 31 for an explanation of strategic uncertainty.)

2. Has the approach to employee development changed over time or in different circumstances (e.g. in response to government policy and action)?

3. Does it differ for different staff groups (whole organisational approaches or groups of 'talented' personnel?)

4. Are there any factors that are likely to change your organisation's approach within the next five years?

HRD as a strategic intervention

We can see examples of the changing role of HRD in organisations as they grow and develop over time and in relation to the complex challenges of changing sectors (e.g. privatisation of public services, the introduction and development of mobile technologies). We see these changes both reflected and shaped by the language associated with HRD as highlighted above and in the shift to a focus on the strategic intent of HRD activities.

The strategic focus on HRM and HRD is increasingly commented on (see, for example, Burgoyne, 1988; Garavan, 1991, 2007; Beaumont, 1994; Fredericks and Stewart, 1996; McCracken and Wallace, 2000; Simmonds and Pedersen, 2006) and follows from a distinction being drawn between three levels of thinking and action. The first, or highest, level is the strategic level (of managerial work), which deals with overall aims and objectives and formulation of plans and policies. This interconnects with the second, managerial level, which 'focuses on the processes by which the organisation obtains and allocates resources to achieve its strategic objectives' (Beaumont, 1994: 23). Finally, we have the operational level – the hands-on, day-to-day processes of managing and organising of work. Thus strategic HRD may be considered as a range of culturally sensitive interventions linked vertically to business goals and strategy, and horizontally to other HR and business activities, to actively encourage and support employee learning, commitment and involvement throughout the organisation.

In this sense, it could be seen that HRD may be following business goals and be part of the implementation strategy: where HR activities may be depicted as 'the servant of corporate strategy' (Chapter 1, p. 23) and where activities must 'match' or 'fit' (Fombrun et al., 1984; Beer and Spector, 1985) with the strategic direction of the company. If we think back to Moddens Foods (Case Study 1.2a, p. 17), the employers have a choice. They can choose to allow the skills and capabilities of some existing, highly skilled staff to 'lead' the strategy, i.e. they can produce high-quality foods aimed at niche markets, or they can choose to focus on producing high-volume, lower quality products which require only low-skilled labour. The strategic decision of which direction to take not only has implications for resourcing, together with ethical investment and sourcing issues, marketing and quality but also for skills requirements and delivery of employee development opportunities.

The decision-making process is made more complex at Moddens by the diversity of ideas and political alliances across the company. It illustrates some of the competing ideologies that may exist within organisations, which affect HRD processes. For example automate, mass-produce and so train for job or task-based needs for maximum efficiency and control compared to recognition of tacit knowledge and explicit skills, giving more autonomy with a tied emphasis on development and (product) innovation.

Case Study 12.2

Gourmet Delights: up-market or mass-market?

Gourmet Delights specialises in take-home delicacies for the professional life style, allowing hard working executives time to prepare quality food in minutes from a range of packaged fresh and frozen menus: ready made meals for 'discerning palate' with prices to match. The products have been extremely popular and the range and customer base has expanded rapidly since the company was formed in Julian Gilies' small, rural kitchen five years ago. Now employing 40 staff, the opportunity has arisen to develop into international markets but this has consequences for staffing, production and distribution as well as, some in the company would argue, goes against the quality label and lifestyle promises that the brand has come to represent. Following several heated discussions about the future direction of the company – to take the opportunity of foreign labour markets and mass-market production or to continue to develop quality niche production and marketing – Jean Brown, the recently-appointed learning and organisational development director, is anticipating lively discussion at the next board meeting when she presents her report on 'Knowledge Management for Competitive Advantage at Gourmet Delights'.

Having framed the basis of her report around the two options on the table, Jean has concentrated specifically on highlighting the HRD issues for each option together with some ethical and practical considerations that need to be made. While Jean favours the niche market route to growing the business, which she feels has been given an extra boost by some of the newer organic and GM-free products coming on-line and the consumer pressure for locally grown products, she is still very much aware of the case being put forward to increase the market base by lower-cost, mass-produced and more emphasis on frozen goods. She recognises that to give both arguments equal weight, she will need to present a robust business case to the board. Having had informal discussions with Sam Swift, regional sales manager, she is aware of his philosophical conviction regarding quality goods, but knows that at the end of the day, the bottom line is what counts and Sam will support his managing director, Julian Giles, if the niche marketing approach is seen to be lacking.

Jean is aware that the most persuasive argument for changing to mass production will come from Jorge Polo with regard to suggestions for improved production methods and skills required. While Jorge has given diligent attention to the technical and production implications of such a move and has been able to detail cost savings and potential growth markets, he has not considered the impact on the people in the company. There has been little in-depth discussion until now about the implications for training, for redeployment, for loss of key personnel and for possible redundancies of people who have been with the firm almost as long as some of the original members. Jean is resolved to give equally thorough consideration to both options to facilitate as well an informed debate as possible. After all, this will affect her job too.

| Activity 12.3 | Up-market or mass-market: implications for HRD strategy |

1. What links are there between organisational strategy and human resource development in this scenario for Gourmet Delights?

2. In presenting a critical evaluation of both options, what do you feel are the key implications for the company's HRD strategy that Jean needs to put forward in her report to the board?

3. Given this evaluation, which option might you recommend and why?

Some of the decision-making for Gourmet Delights may be linked to continued success of the company based on consideration of competitors in the industry sector or the wider market and stakeholder interests (e.g. growing consumer interest in organic and locally produced foods and quality products). However, Barney (1991) warns that sustainability of competitive advantage is achieved, not only 'through an analysis of its external market position, but through a careful analysis of the firm's skills and capabilities; characteristics which competitors find themselves unable to imitate'. For Gourmet Delights, this may be the knowledge held in the company of a sub-sector market and specialised product that could be developed in line with niche characteristics without losing highly trained and committed staff to outsourced producers with little connection to the product.

This internal focus, mirrored by Probst *et al.* (1998: 240), considers the internal labour market and emphasises an approach to employee development, which can both encompass the 'buying in' of appropriate skills when required and the development of in-house skills and knowledge. Here, we might also refer back to Case Study 1.1a: Meet the Aynshents (p. 7). As the need for more and diverse skills was growing, two coping strategies were identified – recruit into the tribe, 'capture one or two travellers' (although in this instance we are looking more at enforced labour rather than securing new and appropriate skills through open and negotiated exchange); and development of existing resources (retrain the eldest brother). Human capabilities become just one more of the recognised resources that a company has at its disposal or needs to acquire to utilise in ways that will achieve the best results for the company. At best, a resource-based view of the firm can give rise to consideration of work-based learning, which would place human resource development as a central tenet of strategic human resource management (Bratton and Gold, 2003).

Yet another perspective may be, rather than to view these two areas as distinct, to regard external and internal components as interrelated where one has an impact on the other in terms of strategic decision-making and sensemaking (Weick, 1995) in the organisation and that human resource development interventions can also be considered as part of this strategic consideration. In helping us to define whether human resource development activity is strategic, Garavan (1991) usefully suggests nine characteristics (see Figure 12.2). Commenting on the systemic nature of the nine characteristics, McCracken and Wallace (2000) suggest moving from a reactive role and status for strategic human resource development to a more proactive and promotional stance.

Here, HRD could be seen as moving from being part of an organisation's goals to actively shaping strategic direction, with an emphasis on outcomes as well as

Figure 12.2 Characteristics of SHRD

outputs and linked to a positive learning climate with specific policies, commitment and leadership. All this seems a far cry from HR practitioners having a nominal 'seat on the board'. It also brings to the fore environmental scanning linked to training, development and learning needs for the company and the role of the HRD practitioner and manager in managing processes of change and stakeholder perceptions.

To add to this, Ashton and Felstead (2001) identified several characteristics, pointing particularly to larger organisations where employment practices geared to employee investment and commitment also linked to the company being more committed to employee development. One might argue that while training and development investment is greater in larger companies with more money to spend and with specific HR functions and departments, smaller companies are traditionally seen to be poor investors in employee development. While this is the Canadian experience reported earlier, this view is not upheld by a recent CIPD survey of 101 organisations where small to medium enterprises employing fewer that 100 people were seen to spend more per capita on training than those with 500 plus employees (CIPD, 2008e). This suggests there might be room for a more strategic emphasis to be developed where HRD activities are dissipated throughout the organisation – favouring smaller, more dynamic organisations. Managers may need, therefore, to include in their strategic repertoire HRD considerations at every level of managerial operation. Size may matter, but large or small, centralised or networked, there needs to be a will and commitment to improve human resource development, which means appropriate resources and, as seen in Figure 12.2, leadership from the top and an emphasis on assessment of impact and outcomes.

However, if, as we are also told (e.g. Holbeche, 2002), many managers fail to invest in their own self-development (because of demanding workloads and a perception of training as being remedial rather than developmental), they may also find it difficult to assess what skills to train for in their workforce. Furthermore, in the absence of mandatory arrangements for training, many employers do not train. If they are short of particular skills, they poach or outsource, so reinforcing a short-term approach. This puts pressure on HR practitioners and managers to continue to work to define and provide an analysis for the contribution of HRD activities at all levels of an organisation as well as creating 'a culture in which learning is valued and supported, and where the enhanced skills of the individual are put to good use' (Holbeche, 2002: 211).

Activity 12.4   HRD: a centralised activity?

Thinking about your own organisation's structure, identify and critically evaluate the locations and roles of HRD.

1. To what extent are these activities centralised and/or decentralised in the organisation?

2. How does this relate to other HR or personnel (or other) activities? What are the advantages and disadvantages of these relationships?

3. Consider what alternative arrangements there might be and whether any benefits could be achieved by any changes.

Tensions between control and development

Taking the idea of short-term and long-term approaches to organisational strategy and HR, there could be seen to be a similar dichotomy reflected within work organisations resulting in a tension between control and development. This is often referred to as 'hard' and 'soft' approaches to human resource development (see, for example: Storey, 1992; Cunningham and Hyman, 1995; Legge, 1995; Guest, 1994). This can be further developed to consider low commitment and high commitment human resourcing strategies (see Chapter 1, p. 31), which brings to the fore the principles and ethical considerations underlying HRD approaches. Control, in this instance, is where training and development is tied into the aims and objectives of the company and bottom-line return on investment and with an emphasis on structure, instrumentalism and individual culpability. These tensions are represented graphically in Figure 12.3.

Where there is a high degree of *fit* between training and organisational immediate needs linked with a lack of investment in developing (high control/low development), then we are likely to observe a short-term approach based on training necessities and linked to individual job adherence and performance. Here, as mentioned earlier, we might see a defensive or protectionist approach to skills development, where additional skills may be bought in. Training may be viewed as a mechanism for controlling individual performance and maintaining current

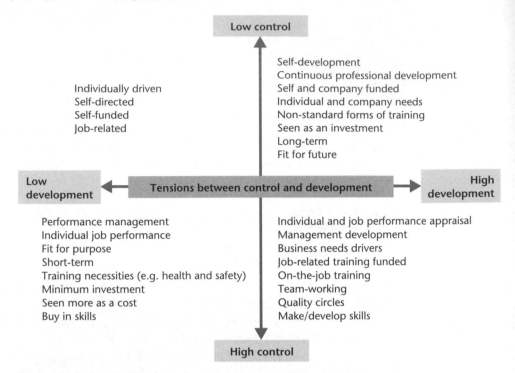

Figure 12.3 Tensions between control and development

systems and approaches, similar to Bennett and Leduchowicz's (1983) 'caretaker' approach to why and how organisations train (cited in Stewart *et al.*, 1999: 220–1).

Where we still can identify a high amount of control but where this is coupled with a high commitment to developing people, we can still see the relationship with performance management and overall company performance. However, we can also see a range of interventions, many job-related and located in the workplace (quality circles, team-working, on-the-job coaching) and to a certain extent these are learner-centred features of organisational approaches to training and development. Using Bennett and Leduchowicz's (1983) model again, this may be characterised by an 'evangelist' approach linked to maintenance and adaptation of what Boxall and Purcell (2002: 11) refer to as 'short-run responsiveness'.

A more innovative approach, which brings together learning and organisational change, according to Bennett and Leduchowicz (1983), is the 'innovator' approach where innovative training and development activities are encouraged. This may, in some instances, accord with the mix of high commitment to development and a low control level and links to Boxall and Purcell's (2002: 11) identification of 'long-run agility'. Here, we see training and development linked to organisational learning and a future orientation linked to the longer-term benefits of training and development activities, and this allows for increased stakeholder involvement and *multiple fits* (Boxall and Purcell, 2002: 54). We can consider this again later in relation to organisational approaches to employee development (see Figure 12.4 later).

In Figure 12.3, we identify a fourth focus by considering aspects of low control and low commitment to development, not identified by Bennett and Leduchowicz.

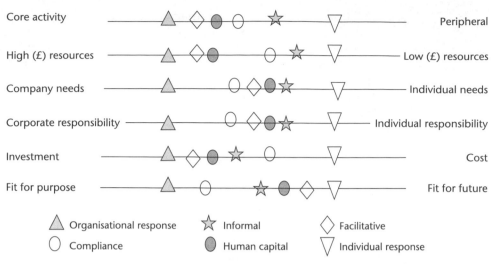

Figure 12.4 Organisational approaches to employee development

Here the combination highlights an individual commitment to training and development where there is little or no investment in training by the organisation.

Moving along and up and down each continuum may bring into focus different aspects of tensions between control and development. In considering the interplay of these tensions, it may also help us to expose some of the (in)congruence between a company's espoused values in relation to training and developing employees and its actual approaches and practice.

Activity 12.5	Investing in HRD

Think about your own organisation or an organisation with which you are familiar.

1. For what purposes does it invest in training and development of employees?
2. How are training needs identified?
3. Where does training take place and how is it undertaken?
4. Who has access to training and development opportunities and how is this decided on?
5. How would you evaluate your organisation in relation to the concepts of 'high control' focus or 'high development' focus?
6. Are there elements in the approaches you have identified in your organisation that you would like to change and how might this be achieved?
7. Looking back to both the Aynshents and the Moddens, can you identify any specific or nascent approaches in these case study examples?

Approaches to development processes

The trend to introduce more skills-specific forms of training and the growing recognition of individual learning contributing to organisational learning emphasise the

399

link between competitive advantage and training and development specifically around roles and tasks. Yet, this is criticised as being as 'short-sighted' and where a broader emphasis could be placed on 'identifying the skills and experiences, which the broad business direction suggests will be required in the future together with planning around developing talent at different levels in the organisation' (Holbeche, 2002: 285). This mirrors Watson's definition of human resources (see Chapter 1, p. 9) and Gardiner's (1999) suggestion that it is a manager's role to take a holistic view of the organisation and, again, emphasises the contextual and processual aspects of approaches to training and development in organisations.

While this brings back into view the role of HRD as a strategic intervention, if we turn our attention to the practical aspects of training and development, then we need to consider organisational approaches and commitment to employee development. In order for any real impact at a strategic level to occur, those organisational members involved in HR activities need to 'decide what combination of business and HR strategies offer the best way to make progress' and to see HR practitioners as business partners (Harrison, 2002: 65–7).

In many ways, this echoes a high commitment to HR practices and seeking good practice tools and techniques. Perhaps, then, the connections between employee development and management practices are more apparent when 'training is structured as set of continuous processes that are integrated with other systems and business strategies' (Blanchard and Thacker, 1998: 4) and where vertical links to business goals and horizontal links to other (HR) activities in the company can be more easily identified. This might also account for the sustained emphasis on systematic approaches to identifying training needs and planning for training activities consistently identified in training and development literature and 'how to' guides (see, for example, Jones, 1991; Bee and Bee, 1994). Additionally, this 'provides a framework for what trainers do and enables them to describe their professional practice in a coherent way' (Gibb and Megginson, 2001: 149). This, again, emphasises the need for a more integrative approach to employee development rather than seeing it as an occasional extra to other organisational activity. This is part of a debate, which partly culminates in the dialogue between the need for a more centralised HR role and function and the need to diversify and distribute HRM/D and particularly support for development activities within the organisation and promote the active involvement of line managers in these processes. However, in the UK to-date, it is suggested that only 12 per cent of employees feel that line managers take learning and development very seriously (CIPD, 2008e).

In addition to the role of line managers, part of this argument for additional support relates to the recognition of the complexities of how organisations work in practice (and that many small and medium-sized enterprises, especially in non-profit sectors, do not have any specialised HR function or associated practitioners and where responsibility for training and development issues lie with the governing committee, the chief officer or appropriate line manager). What is often forgotten is that we need different approaches for different contexts and in relation to the various stakeholders involved (Boxall and Purcell, 2002: 54). Here there might also be opportunities for alignment between employee and employer interests in the organisation and where there may well be conflicting interests at work.

We can see this developed further in Figure 12.4 when we begin to consider the different forces, pressures and attitudes surrounding approaches to employee development. Here we can see the identification of six interrelated approaches to employee development as a result of tensions such as whether the organisational approach to employee development is seen, for example, as a *core* activity or a *peripheral* activity (see Exhibit 12.2, below).

Exhibit 12.2

Organisational approaches to employee development

Organisational response

Key characteristics: high levels of employee development geared to current demands and skills needs; strategy-led HRD; seen as investment but safeguards and anti-poaching tactics observed; deficit focus; emphasis on function and control ('hard' approach).

Compliance

Key characteristics: formal activities, e.g. health & safety and must-do's training; bolt-on activity; HR driven from perceived external pressures, e.g. government intervention. Where based on company needs there is a specific top-down focus; deficit focused; emphasis on prescriptive training; incidental learning.

Informal

Key characteristics: informal exchanges and experiential learning through, for example, action learning; emphasis on development through on-the-job information exchange and training; job swaps; interpersonal skills; opportunist-type learning.

Human capital

Key characteristics: strong links to retention, reward and career development. 'Soft' approaches to increasing employee effectiveness and to compensate via increased employee satisfaction. It includes possibilities for personal development, mentoring, management development and time off for learning. More formalised, systematised and horizontally linked to other HR activities (e.g. planning, resourcing and performance appraisal).

Facilitative

Key characteristics: positive working environment linked to capturing learning; elements of learning organisations; more room for employee autonomy and experimentation. Interdependence between HR and line managers, geared to company and individual needs, continuous development focused on quality, effectiveness, outcomes and task flexibility and integrating work and learning.

Individual response

Key characteristics: little or no employee development support from the organisation; any significant training and development is instigated by the individual employee, is individually driven and therefore has, in the main, an individual focus. Training is ad hoc and individually negotiated with managers on a one-off basis. Self-funded and/or done in own time.

Similarly, these generalised approaches may be determined by the context in which the organisation works, the values and commitment to employees and the resources, such as time and money, available. Approaches may vary from one company to another, from one sector to another. There also may be differences within organisations relating to the power and status of certain groups of employees over others in their ability to attract investment in their own training and/or development within the company.

We can start to see the influences of some of these factors beginning to be mapped out in Figure 12.4. For each approach identified, we have applied a descriptor, which looks at *characteristics* associated with a particular approach, that is, the types of activities and perceptions of HRD that we *might* expect to see in typified organisations.

This represents a complex and dynamic picture of approaches to HRD, which is not adequately accounted for in some distinctions between 'hard' and 'soft' or 'traditional' and 'emerging' categorisations (Guest, 1994; Storey, 1994; Holbeche, 2002), but is, for example, captured in the growing literature on HRD (see Walton, 1999; McGoldrick *et al.*, 2002b). Indeed, the employment relationship is of a 'contested, contradictory and fragmented' nature (Marchington and Wilkinson, 2002b: 5) and this relationship will change over time and in relation to internal and external influences in and on the organisation.

In organisations where HRD is subordinate to strategy, 'unless training takes account and meets the expectations of the business, the business will institute sanctions on training systems (e.g. reduced budgets, staff and other resources), rather than provide it with more desirable inputs' (Blanchard and Thacker, 1998: 20). This might be a feature of a number of approaches to employee development, but we may associate it more with an organisation's pragmatic response geared to current demands and to formal training activities seen as necessary to carry out specific tasks and activities. This can be explored using Figure 12.4 where at one end of a spectrum we have an approach identified as *organisational response* and at the opposite end, *individual response*.

In responding from a basis of *organisational* needs, we may see a tendency towards high levels of employee development geared to here and now – to build capacity of individuals for the job in hand. By task-based training often on the job, this may focus development on skills and knowledge particular to that company. Cost effectiveness is key in terms of adequate return on investment in training opportunities and where there is an emphasis on addressing skills deficits ('fit for purpose'). While it builds the skills base of the organisation, it limits transfer of learning out of the firm (a defensive strategy). Investment in development opportunities may fluctuate within the organisation, like the ebb and flow of the tide. There may be high tides and a swell of investment, but as budgets tighten and managers look for cutbacks, investment may ebb away, for example in order to give higher returns to key stakeholders or for reinvestment in activities seen to more directly contribute to the bottom-line or core activities of the organisation.

At the opposite end of the spectrum, we have *individual response* characterised by little company involvement or support for employee development. Here we might see a tendency for individuals to determine their own training and development needs and seek solutions using their own resources to meet identified needs. This might accord with Holbeche's view that 'employees are making themselves increasingly employable, with or without the help of their organisations' (Holbeche, 2002: 47) in response to perceived needs for increased employability and employment mobility.

Of course, preferred organisational approaches can move along to different parts of each continuum at different times and according to different needs and circumstances. There may be other tensions that will affect HRD approaches, such as the adoption of generalist principles related to 'best fit' and 'best practice' or developing approaches consistent with the organisation's unique context (Boxall and Purcell, 2002).

Activity 12.6   Approaches to HRD

Use Figure 12.4 to think about your own organisation or an organisation you know.

1. Bearing in mind that employee development approaches in organisations will not necessarily conform to these 'ideal' types and that in fact within one organisation you may observe one or several approaches to employee development:

   a) How would you describe your organisation's approach to employee development?

   b) Does it link with or across any of the other identified approaches?

   c) Are there influences, which have not been identified, that apply to your organisation?

   d) Have approaches to employee development in your organisation changed over time?

2. Critically compare and contrast this model with other models and frameworks, for example you could choose two of the following:

   a) Ashridge Model in Woodall and Winstanley (1998);

   b) Fredericks and Stewart (1996): the strategy–HRD connection and strategic HRD;

   c) Guest (1987): soft and hard approaches;

   d) Lee (1997): developmental approach;

   e) Mabey *et al.* (1998): management development agendas;

   f) Megginson *et al.* (1999): approaches to development;

   g) Mumford in Stewart (1999): types of management development;

   h) Stewart (1999): dimensions of management development.

Managing learning opportunities

Although the systematic approach to learning and development through training needs assessment, skills gap analyses and planned approaches to training interventions are still a popular way of responding to the need to train and develop, there is growing interest in and recognition of experiential learning and professional assessment of prior learning (Critten, 1998). In this respect, understanding learning as a process – of activity, reflection, changes in behaviour, generating new learning and experiences – which is 'inherently social' (Clancey, 1995) gives rise to addressing issues of inclusion and participation, communication, and management or creation of learning opportunities (see Tansley's discussion on communities of practice, p. 346, and legitimate peripheral participation, p. 349).

Linking back to our earlier discussion between control and development or high commitment/low commitment, we need to consider organisational culture or climate for learning along with the dominant management ethos in the company. These are significant features in the literature on organisational learning and the learning organisation (e.g. Pedlar *et al.*, 1991; Senge, 1992) and knowledge management (Newell *et al.*, 2002) and are of continued interest. For example, a recent empirical study of large Australian firms (Dawe, 2003) identified three important elements contributing to the perceived success of training practices, including an organisational culture supporting learning, a capability to respond to change and where training was clearly linked to business strategy.

HR practitioners and managers have a key role to play in encouraging and maintaining an environment conducive to generating ideas and encouraging experimentation. Furthermore, in citing Ulrich *et al.* (1993), Gardiner (1999: 2) suggests that experimentation is key in terms of enhancing learning capability and writes:

> twenty-one per cent of the businesses in their [Ulrich *et al.*'s] study considered experimentation as a major source of learning. These companies experimented with process as well as product, testing new ideas not only in a number of manufacturing technologies, but also in other respects of the organisations, such as work teams, human resource systems and employee relations.

Learning in this context can therefore be linked with process and product innovation, knowledge management (Newell *et al.*, 2002) and change.

Activity 12.7   Managing information networks

Revisit Chapter 11 on knowledge management and consider the following scenario.

AB Links is a small non-profit organisation. Most mornings, two of its employees arrive around 8 a.m., have a coffee together and exchange news. While the team is small, the two work in very different areas and rarely have the chance for deep conversation. Gradually this has developed into a half hour of useful information exchange and problem-solving. The team leader generally arrives towards the end of the get-together and, on occasions, has joined in. Impressed by the opportunity for knowledge-sharing and learning, the team leader decided to build on this and instituted a team-wide morning meeting once a week, complete with timed opportunities for exchange of news and a regular agenda. The weekly meetings deteriorated soon after inception and the morning meetings between the two workers have dissolved.

Consider opportunities for informal networks and learning in your organisations.

1. What lessons can we learn from the above example?
2. How can opportunities for learning be facilitated?
3. What mechanisms could help to capture informal learning for the benefit of the organisation?

Change is something we cope with on a daily basis. Often it goes unnoticed but sometimes it can upset us even if only on a temporary and superficial basis upsetting our daily routines, our habited actions. How we cope with unexpected and anticipated changes may be partly due to our personality, partly to do with learned behaviour, partly to do with the importance we place on the outcomes and other stresses with which we have to cope at the same time. It can be therefore both a crisis and an opportunity for creativity and innovation where 'creativity and adaptation are born of tension, passion and conflict [which] propels us along the journey of development' (Pascale, 1991: 263).

Triggers, both internal and external, for learning in organisations could include one or more of the following:

● response to long- and short-term goals;
● skills supply and/or demand;
● acquisition of new technology;
● planned and emergent strategies;
● plans for growth or rationalisation, including mergers, restructuring etc.;
● rewards and performance management systems.

Any one of these or other events may result in a relatively minor shift in the way of working or may be experienced as fundamental and transformational in nature. Beckhard (1994: 6), for example, gives a useful outline of transformational change, which is seen as:

● a change in what *drives* the organisation;
● a fundamental change in the *relationships* between or among organisational parts;
● a major change in the *ways of doing* work;
● a basic *cultural* change in norms, values or reward systems.

The experience of change can be felt at an individual and/or a collective level. Think back to the response of the brother to suggestions of a change in his role in the Aynshents case study (p. 13). From one perspective, Brother Aynshent could be seen to be resisting the suggested changes from his sister. There was a lack of match or fit between sister's aims for the tribe and brother's personal vocation. From a different perspective, we can see he was planning (at least in his thoughts) a process of changing and developing his role in the tribe according to his desires and ambitions to gain, in his estimation, a more valued and meaningful contribution.

Current research into job satisfaction is showing that many people look for different jobs because the current work does not give them '*enough* stimulating change' (Boxall and Purcell, 2002: 159, authors' italics). This is compounded by the need to 'address the issues of balance, flexibility, learning [and] careers' especially, to repeat an earlier point, 'as employees are making themselves increasingly employable, with or without the help of their organisations' (Holbeche, 2002: 47).

A fundamental part of learning to adapt to change, and thus reduce resistance to change, is having the opportunity to participate. This would include having a degree of choice and control, to be able to take risks and to innovate and to reflect critically on personal experiences (see, for example, Blanchard and Thacker, 1998; Ulrich *et al.*, 1993 cited in Gardiner, 1999; Mullins and Cummings, 1991; Schein, 1997). This view is mirrored by Holbeche (2002: 3), who cites Ulrich (1997) arguing that 'the successful organisations will be those that can quickly turn strategy into action: to manage processes intelligently and efficiently; to maximise employee contribution and commitments; and to create the conditions for seamless change'. Bratton and Gold (2007: 307) are even more emphatic, suggesting that 'Learning is the only strategy to cope with change.' This is mirrored by the findings of a 2006 survey which found that 93 per cent of respondents stated that 'a consideration of the learning and development implications of change is critical to its success' (CIPD, 2007c). However, the degree to which employees are involved in decision-making concerning organisational change is questionable. The same survey reports one third of respondents as not participating in change planning processes.

With this in mind, reflect on the following example.

Case Study 12.3

Implementing change in City School: responding to an external trigger to improve quality of education and standards of achievement

Following an external evaluation report, City School called a staff meeting to look at recommended areas for action. The report suggested that to further improve the standards of achievement and quality of education, the governors, head teacher and staff should develop a curriculum framework to better support teachers' planning and ensure consistency, continuity and progression of learning for students.

Two members of staff were delegated to lead the discussion. The result was to conceptualise the curriculum in order to aid planning and set targets for learning outcomes in order to coordinate the subject areas to give the children a connected learning experience. One example: when studying history, a year group learning about battering rams will also explore pulley systems in technology classes, thereby connecting different subjects by transference of learning and aiding the planning process.

While the trigger for this change in ways of working had initially arrived from an external source, it was responded to and controlled by those responsible for delivery of the curriculum. By taking a team approach to the process and creating a critical incident from which to find a solution, staff did not react defensively to protect themselves from a change in structure and systems. Instead, through dialogue they aligned the problem to the culture and ways of working of the school to arrive at a solution for which all staff took ownership and responsibility to evaluate and monitor.

In this instance, the manager (head of school) provided a framework for working, delegated responsibility and provided support by personally covering classroom activities and not attending the meeting.

In using a processual and relational analysis, we need to consider how patterns of behaviours and critical events during processes of change in organisations may serve to ease transitions, impede progression or how issues may emerge which change the direction of the process. However, if 'UK managers see themselves as doers rather than "reflective practitioners"' then the opportunities for individual and organisational learning and change will be restricted (Marchington and Wilkinson, 2002b: 372, commenting on Keep and Rainbird's (2000) suggestions on inhibitors to workplace learning). For example, a non-profit agency running a large building with a number of voluntary groups as tenants needed to cut costs; we can see a useful example below of 'linear thinking' setting the 'basis for linear solutions' (Morgan, 1986: 248) with little consideration of consequences of actions.

Case Study 12.4

Cash problems at LDA

LDA is a medium-size non-profit organisation which, among its many services and areas of work, provides a community building with rental spaces for other small voluntary organisations and, with this, provides a reception and call-answering service. LDA is having problems meeting budget and needs to come up with ways of saving money. The problem and solution have been articulated in the format below and associated actions ensue:

Problem: funding has been cut . . . need to save money . . . need to cut back on services . . . conduct a skills audit . . . send out letters to staff to say may need to send out redundancy notices . . . close reception . . . reallocate people who have the required organisational skills . . . ask other organisations to contribute to costs (even though they already pay for this service with their rent) . . . Solution: save money and work to a decreased budget.

Very much a top-down approach, there was no consultation with staff or other stakeholders, resulting in immediate circulation of misinformation. Many of the reception staff thought they were losing their jobs because they had been told of possible redundancies while the skills audit was being undertaken. Other organisations already paying for the reception service thought they were seemingly being asked to pay twice (to continue to pay for reception costs in their rent and to contribute to the costs of 'redeploying' existing workers).

This change came at a time in the organisation's life cycle when a number of critical factors were coinciding and where, over a 12-month period, the organisation had employed five external consultants to look at the management and direction of the organisation.

Source: Myers (1996/7)

Take some time to reflect on the example above and the issues of trust, identified by Watson in Chapter 1.

Activity 12.8 Linking HRD activities and change

1. Think about your own personal and organisational experience of change and transition. In your opinion, what are the key factors that affect your ability to manage and cope with change?

2. Think about *planned* and *emergent* changes in your organisation – what have been the processes involved in initiating, shaping or responding to these events?

3. How have training and development activities supported change initiatives in your organisation?

Having had some time to think and reflect, let's look at continuing developments at Moddens; again, consider what you have learned about this particular company as its story has been told from different perspectives in the different chapters in this book.

Case Study 12.5

Gourmet Delights in transition

It's now been a year since the board took the decision to focus on the production of gourmet foods and there have been a number of significant changes in quick succession over a relatively short space of time. Not only has a decision been made to expand on the range of organic ingredients used in production, but also a new venture is coming on-line with the acquisition of a small specialist pastry- and pie-producing unit in Paris and several patisserie outlets in Paris and Brussels.

There has been a six-month exchange between the pastry and pie production unit manager from Paris and one of the junior production managers in the UK to look at harmonising production practices. One of a number of new developments emerging from this exchange has been the possibility of selling Belgian- and French-style patisseries via selected supermarkets and specialist delicatessens in the UK. After investigation, it has not been possible to import ready-made goods from the French unit and the decision has been taken to start production of a small range of patisseries in time for the Christmas market. This will start to happen in the East Counties Gourmet Division and will combine both fresh and frozen products.

In order to facilitate the transfer of some of the technical and specialist expertise required to produce the new goods and to provide instruction in using newly-acquired equipment, a team of French and Belgian chefs and food technicians together with a Belgian operations manager will be placed at East Counties for a period of three months. It is hoped that if this pilot works, then not only can production be replicated and expanded but also that a regular exchange of workers can be implemented between the three countries.

This way of expanding business through acquiring high-quality and reputable outlets in Europe and to a lesser extent North America is highly favoured by the Board and indications from Sam Swift and Julian Giles are that this strategy will be pursued more aggressively in future. In an effort to learn from managing this acquisition and the changes that are under way, Allan Baldwin – an external consultant and specialist in cross-cultural management and change issues – has been appointed to give an independent evaluation for future planning purposes.

While the expansion has proved successful in enlarging the profile and reputation of the organisation, it seems that the processes behind the transition have been less positive. In his visits to both the French production unit and to the East Counties Gourmet Division, Allan has been concerned about the low level of knowledge and understanding about the acquisition. Furthermore, following on from earlier rumours about opening low-cost factory units abroad, there is confusion and speculation in UK sites that all production of fancy pastries and gourmet 'instant' meals will be moved eventually to the French and Belgian units, leading to the closure of UK units. The employees in the French unit and French and Belgian outlets are concerned about having new 'British owners'.

Allan also learns that Gourmet Delight has seen a number of change initiatives around introduction of new technology and EPR systems and an influx of temporary staff to cope with seasonal variations in production. These changes together with announcements in ways of working – closing down potential markets, opening up new avenues for expansion through mergers and acquisitions – have left the majority of employees confused and in some instances critical of management and with decreasing motivation. Some staff have already left and some of the key employees from the Gourmet Division are being 'wooed' by rival companies. One of the employee focus groups was quite vocal in expressing its discontent with management's lack of consultation and there was little confidence in opportunities for international placements, which were compared to other potential development opportunities as being 'just for the managers or those in the "inner circle"'.

His discussions with the senior management members have pointed to a highly committed and skilled team, but there are tensions and resentments between certain managers over the way the developments have been handled and there is little evidence of cooperative working at this level. His interview with Jean Brown has also confirmed some of the complaints from employees.

Allan Baldwin is considering his final report to the board.

Activity 12.9 **HRD and change at Gourmet Delights**

1. What, in your opinion, are the key issues emerging from Allan Baldwin's evaluation?

2. Given the information you have, what do you consider the contribution could be for employee training and development in achieving a successful merger and managing change? What links with other HR activities might be needed?

3. From this, what role can you envisage for continued human resource development in the new organisation?

4. What key lessons do you feel can be learned from Moddens' experience for managing processes of change?

Changing role of HR practitioners and managers

Megginson *et al.* (1999) provide a useful historical analysis and summary of leading ideas associated with the changing role of the HR practitioner from 1964 through to 1998. We can associate with this change in role the concomitant concerns and debates about the nature and purpose of HRD, *per se* (McGoldrick *et al.*, 2002a; Walton, 1999). This includes direct links to corporate strategy, responsibility for and outcomes of learning, individual and team learning leading to organisational development, knowledge creation and management as well as internal consultancy (Woodall *et al.*, 2002).

The changes in HR roles swing from provider of training and associated services to facilitator of formal and informal learning networks and internal change consultant. This requires working with line managers and reflects the need for skills and knowledge of managing diversity, negotiation and team-based and cross-cultural learning. In addition although demand for ICT and blended learning is not as significant as was predicted, there will be increasing demand for these types of learning interventions in the future (Learning and Skills Council, 2006: 20). We can also trace the development of HRD practices against both the development of the modern work organisation and organisational life cycles and around the discourses of competition and collaboration, of inclusion and participation and of empowerment and control.

While there may be continued discussion on just how far HR practitioners' and line managers' roles have changed in practice, there is still evidence of a gap between normative theories and actual practice (Poell *et al.*, 2003) and resistance is still encountered (see, for example, Harris *et al.*, 2002; Poell *et al.*, 2003 for information on Dutch, Finnish and UK experiences). However, if HRD activities continue to become more strategic and with increased involvement of line managers in a wider range of operational HR activities, then we may see a continued movement away from analysis of training needs and direct training provision (Johnston, 2001) to one of supporting and developing a longer-range view of the organisation. HR practitioners and managers therefore need 'to look at the human dimension of the organisation in a broader and more corporate sense' (Chapter 1, p. 23).

Conclusion

In this chapter, we have examined different approaches to and processes associated with human resource development, recognising there is no one best way to manage the processes of HRD. Through an exploration of the social, economic and political contexts and external influences on practice, we have considered the growing emphasis on HRD's strategic contribution to organisational change and development, and the concepts of careers and roles in organisations and management development.

We have commented on the movement from training analysis and direct interventions to an approach which emphasizes the need for managing the processes of learning, taking account of a growing complexity and diversity of stakeholder needs. This has led to an increasing interest in continuous professional development and the concept of lifelong learning together with attention to knowledge creation and managing learning opportunities facilitated by internal and external networks and communities of practice. There is recognition, however, that there may be gaps between the academic and theoretical debates on learning and development in organisations and what can be seen in practice.

Even so, we have highlighted the implications for HR practitioners and managers in organisations, stressing the need for creation and development of environments conducive to encouraging workplace learning and innovation. Here, HRD is seen as an integral part of and contributor to an organisation's capacity and performance and, as such, is a significant managerial activity. In this way, we have argued for a more strategic approach to developing resourceful human beings in organisations for optimum benefit both to employees and to gain from the 'efforts, knowledge and committed behaviours' (Chapter 1, p. 9) that they can contribute.

Summary

Throughout this chapter, there has been a focus on different approaches to HRD and implications for HR practitioners. This has included the significance of context and external influences on practice; growing emphasis on organisational change and development; support for and facilitation of career and management development; creation of internal networks and the need for continuous learning and reflexive practice. In particular:

- The changing demands and stakeholder needs are pushing for current skills deficits to be matched as well as placing an emphasis on anticipating future needs.

- There is a move, particularly seen at senior practitioner level, from direct service provision through training analyses and training interventions to managing processes of learning, continuous professional development and knowledge management.

- HRD takes place at the nexus between external and internal organisational environments and links to strategic decision-making and specific employee and management development interventions.

- Learning and development therefore needs to be seen as an integral part of business processes rather than a bolt-on activity or an optional extra.

- HR practitioners still need to convince employers of the need to invest in learning opportunities and be proactive in promoting and accounting for the outcome of HRD activities if they are to be seen as key partners in the business.

- HRD is complex and dynamic and not always easily catered for in existing distinctions between 'hard' and 'soft' approaches; different approaches to HRD are needed in relation to the different and changing organisational contexts and stakeholder needs.

- Managers have a key role to play in encouraging and maintaining an environment conducive to generating ideas and encouraging experimentation that contributes to developing capacity for learning and for supporting organisational changes and transitions.

Discussion questions

1. To what extent does your organisation achieve vertical integration between HRD strategies and corporate goals? How would you suggest more synergy between the two can be achieved?

2. How will changing workforce demographics impact on the ways in which your organisation responds to the learning and development needs of current and future employees?

3. Consider how your organisation currently identifies the skills needs, i.e. on a deficit basis or looking more towards future needs. Project yourself into the future and explore the likely skills gaps. How do you envisage closing these gaps?

4. What do you consider to be the key drivers for change for HRD in the next five years?

5. In your opinion, is there an optimum balance required between the relationship of centralised HRD activities and line manager roles and responsibilities and, if so, how would you define this in terms of your own organisation?

6. Explore the criteria for making your workplace an effective learning environment.

Further reading

Readers who wish to develop a more in-depth appreciation of human resource development are encouraged to refer to Elliott and Turnbull (2005); Marchington and Wilkinson (2005); Dessler and Cole (2008); Van Woerkom and Poell (2009).

For a more pragmatic discussion of systematic approaches to training and development, useful resources include: Blanchard and Thacker (2003); Harrison (2005); Reid *et al.* (2004). For specific texts on employee and management development, including coaching and mentoring, see Devins and Gold (2000); Clutterbuck and Ragins (2001); Gibb and Megginson (2001); Megginson and Clutterbuck (2004); Hill and Stewart (2007); Megginson and Whitaker (2007). For a broad overview of learning and knowledge management, readers are encouraged to explore the work of: Brown and Duguid (2002); Garvey and Williamson (2002); Holden (2002); Newell *et al.* (2002); Wenger *et al.* (2002); Harrison and Kessels (2004); Harrison (2005); Easterby-Smith and Lyles (2006).

Associated reading on learning and change includes: Easterby-Smith *et al.* (2001); Dawson, 2003; Carnall (2007). For learning and sensemaking, see Weick (1995). Finally, for a research-based approach to HRD, see McGoldrick *et al.* (2002b); and for links to strategy and HRM, see Walton (1999); Redman and Wilkinson (2001); Boxall and Purcell (2003).

For web resources for specific information on education and learning development initiatives, see for example www.learndirect.co.uk/. Learndirect was set up by the University for Industry (www.ufi.com/home/default.asp) with a remit from government to provide post-16 learning opportunities. Over 800 online learning centres exist in England and Wales, providing access to a range of online learning opportunities. For networks for academics and practitioners, see for example International Alliance for Human Resources Research (www.yorku.ca/hrresall/); and the Chartered Institute of Personnel and Development (www.cipd.co.uk).

13

Developing managers and managerial capacities

Jim Stewart

Learning outcomes

Having read this chapter and completed its associated activities, readers should be able to:

- Articulate a range of perspectives on and definitions of management development
- Critically evaluate varying approaches to management development
- Describe the role and contribution of management development programmes and activities in wider human resourcing strategies
- Formulate and argue a position on the value of investment in management development
- Produce, justify and defend proposals for investment in management development

Introduction

This chapter will examine the concept and practice of management development (MD). This will include a consideration of the meaning of the terms 'management' and 'development' and the results of joining them together to construct the concept of 'management development'. The aim is to identify and examine some important arguments and debates surrounding management development, and to locate these in the wider context of human resourcing strategies.

As well as examining debates in the academic and professional literature, the chapter will also have a focus in application. This focus is concerned with questions to do with 'how'. Such questions can take three forms. First, how *is* management development done? Second, how *could* management development be done? Third, how *should* management development be done? Answering the last of these requires a prescription of what is 'right' or 'best'. The discussion of the notions of 'best practice' and 'contingent fit' in Chapter 1 would suggest that such prescriptions are at best problematic, assuming they are possible. That being the case, the chapter will be most concerned with the first two formulations of the 'how' questions. However, to support the focus in application and to help inform decisions on and in the practice of MD, the '*should*' question will be partly addressed through the use of the Aynshents and Moddens Foods case studies from Chapter 1.

An overview

The view adopted here is that management development is both complex and problematic. A recent example of this complexity and the problematic nature of MD is the (re)emergence of interest in the notion of 'leadership' and so in 'leadership development'. Many recent studies have focused on leader(ship) rather than management and on leader(ship) development rather than management development. There can be and is a debate about the extent to which these terms are synonyms: is a manager by definition a leader? and, are leaders only those in managerial roles and positions? What is clear is that there is much confusion around these questions. To illustrate this consider the following first sentence taken from a section in a chapter with the sub-title 'Leadership development':

How then does this affect how we see management development?

(Trehan and Shelton, 2007: 291)

It is clear that Trehan and Shelton are treating the terms as synonyms, at least in that part of their chapter, and they are not alone in that. Some though would argue significant differences between the concepts of management and leadership and so therefore between leadership development and management development (Stewart and Hill, 2007). This chapter does not directly address the questions posed on management and leadership but notes them as one example of uncertainty, confusion and complexity in the study and practice of management development.

Exhibit 13.1

Leadership development opportunities at the North East Wales NHS Trust

The North East Wales NHS Trust has an interesting approach to the notion of leadership. As well as focusing on managers they also focus on what they refer to as clinical leaders and leadership, and service leaders and leadership. So, managers are seen to occupy leadership positions and thus as needing to provide leadership. But non-managerial employees are also thought to be able to and actually do provide leadership to their colleagues. For example, a doctor, nurse or other health professional can provide leadership to colleagues by their example and being respected for their experience or ability. The same is true for those in service roles such as estates or administration. Employees also provide leadership because of their personal qualities and relationship with colleagues. Therefore leadership development opportunities in the Trust are not exclusively available to those in managerial positions.

Source: Tansley *et al.* (2007)

As we will see later in the chapter, further uncertainty, confusion and complexity arises in part from the complexity of 'managing' and 'development' and from the fact that the term 'management development' has no consistent or definitive meaning (Fee, 2001). An additional factor is that MD can and does pursue various

Table 13.1 **Management development agendas**

Type	Description
Functional performance	Focuses on knowledge, skills and attitudes of individual managers. Assumes unproblematic link between MD and performance.
Political reinforcement	Focuses on reinforcing and propagating skills and attitude valued by top managers. Assumes top managers are correct in their diagnosis and prescription.
Compensation	MD is seen as part of the reward system for managers. Assumes development is motivational and encourages commitment.
Psychic defence	MD provides a 'safety valve' for managerial anxieties. Assumes competitive careers and associated anxieties.

Source: Based on Mabey and Salaman (1995)

agendas (Lees, 1992). In other words, investment in MD can be undertaken to serve different and sometimes competing purposes (Hirsh and Carter, 2002). For example, Mabey and Salaman (1995) suggest four possible purposes, each with distinct characteristics and problems and derived from different assumptions. Their four purposes or 'agendas' are summarised in Table 13.1. This table questions what is arguably the conventional view, set out, for example, by both Woodall and Winstanley (1998) and Storey *et al.* (1997), that the purpose of MD is always and simply to improve organisational performance and success. This conventional view is also often associated with the argument that MD *should* be linked in some way with organisation strategy (see Hirsh and Carter, 2002, for example). Empirical research though suggests that this is not often the case (Seibert *et al.*, 1995).

A second problem with the conventional view on MD is that it assumes or implies formalised and structured systems in work organisations for the provision of MD (Mumford and Gold, 2004). Such systems, though, also assume medium-to-large-scale enterprises that can afford the levels of investment necessary for sophisticated approaches. There are two weaknesses with this perspective. First, the small firms sector is both a significant and growing feature of the EU economy (O'Dwyer and Ryan, 2002). Perspectives that assume formalised and structured MD systems will have little relevance or application in this important sector (O'Dwyer and Ryan, 2002). Second, an assumption of MD as a formal system excludes the role and contribution of what is variously referred to as 'accidental', 'informal' or 'situated' learning and development (see Fox, 1997; Mumford and Gold, 2004). It also fails to recognise and acknowledge the contribution of wider life experiences in management learning which, as Watson and Harris (1999) persuasively argue, are likely to be as significant as any systematic MD programme. The contrasting contexts of the Aynshents and Moddens illustrate both of these points.

This overview so far suggests that disagreement exists on the purpose of MD, and that conventional views on its practice tend to exclude both important contexts of application and a range of potentially significant learning and development opportunities. This rather confusing picture is complicated even further by examining the concepts of 'management' and 'development'.

The nature of managerial work

Perspectives on MD that emphasise formal and systematic approaches assume the possibility of clear and unambiguous specifications of managerial tasks and managerial behaviour. Such specifications are then assumed to enable identification and specification of the skills and capabilities which will constitute the required managerial resource in a given organisation. The latter are often referred to or described as competences which are often grouped together in competence frameworks (see, for example, Hamlin, 2005). However, this seemingly logical process is not quite as straightforward as is often argued, as the following activity should illustrate.

| Activity 13.1 | Managerial tasks in Aynshents and Moddens |

1. Re-read and recall your understanding of the Aynshents (Case Study 1.1a) and Moddens Foods (Case Study 1.2a) case studies in Chapter 1 (p. 7, p. 17).
2. Attempt to produce a broad specification of management tasks required in each enterprise.
3. Attempt to identify the key difference in managerial skills and capabilities required in each enterprise.

It is expected that this activity will prove difficult and not just because of the lack of contextual information. The argument here is that it is difficult to be clear and unambiguous in specifying tasks, behaviours, skills and capabilities. Managing is an ambiguous and uncertain activity (see, for example, Chia, 1997 and Thomas, 2003). Therefore MD must itself be ambiguous and uncertain since it is difficult, if not impossible, to devise a clear specification of what it is trying to achieve in terms of managerial skills and capabilities. A recent study conducted by Finch-Lees and Mabey (2007) both illustrates and extends this argument by applying a 'critical discursive' approach to analysing a MD programme. What becomes clear from this research is the contextual nature of both managing and management development. In simple terms, managing is a social process influenced by a myriad of variable, different and changing social conditions which are in a continuous state of flux over time and space. All of that also applies to MD with both managing and MD being not only influenced by, but constituted and constructed by, various and variable social processes and conditions. From a different perspective and with a different analysis, Iles and Preece (2006) make similar points on the uncertainty and ambiguity faced by managers and how these are surfaced in MD programmes. The point is also made by these authors that prescriptive MD programmes with predetermined content based on generic specifications are unlikely to address the realities faced by managers in their work.

Two more implications for MD arise from the two case studies. First, each makes clear that managing is a political process which in turn is influenced by personal values and interests (see also Finch-Lees and Mabey, 2007). As a result, and as argued in Chapter 1, strategy is more accurately understood as *emergent* rather than *planned* (though formal planning may play a part in the strategy-making process). A related argument on the need for a 'stakeholder' approach to MD itself is provided by an executive briefing from the CIPD (2002a). The conclusion seems to be that both the organisation strategy and any strategy for management development will be the outcome of a political process rather than the result of rational planning. However, such a situation does suggest that managers, including those with responsibility for MD, will be more effective if their behaviour reflects and applies political understanding and skills. This then suggests that development of such capability can be a useful and legitimate component of management development (see also Cunningham, 2008).

The second implication also concerns the connection between organisation strategy and management development. As indicated earlier, the conventional view is that there should be a direct connection. The CIPD report (CIPD, 2002a) suggests a mechanism for achieving this through what is referred to as a Business, Organisation and Management Review. There are, though, two problems with this approach. First, it assumes that MD is the 'servant' of organisation and business strategy. As Chapter 1 argued, this is not necessarily the case. Second, it also assumes that organisation strategy is settled and known. If, though, strategy is emergent over time, rather than a fixed plan, then it will be difficult to know exactly what it is that MD is supposed to 'serve'.

Exhibit 13.2

Strategic plans

Sir John Harvey Jones, speaking at a conference a number of years ago, recalled the strategic plans of ICI when he was chairman. He described very detailed papers collected into five volumes running to very many hundreds of pages. The questions he raised included who actually read all of those volumes. Since different parts of the strategic plan were written by different people in different divisions and departments it was not possible to be confident that even the authors had read all five volumes. A further question raised by Sir John was what influence, if any, these detailed strategic plans had on the day-to-day operations and business of the company if no one had read them.

The main point is that strategic plans may or may not exist but even when they do they cannot and do not control all decisions and actions taken by managers in organisations.

Source: Personal recollection

The nature of development

The concept of 'development' raises additional problems for thinking about what constitutes MD and how it could or should be practised. An analysis of the potential meanings to be attached to the concept has been provided by Monica Lee (Lee, 2003). Four different ways of understanding the term are suggested. Each varies in the assumptions and beliefs that are implicitly or explicitly applied to two factors. The first factor is the nature of the 'individual', which, according to varying perspectives, consists of either a unitary or co-regulated identity. The basic distinction here is the degree of involvement of others in creating and constructing 'individual identity'. In other words, the extent to which 'I' and 'I am'

Table 13.2 Approaches to management development

Approach	Characteristics
Maturation	Assumes a unitary identity and known end point. Development involves passing through known and predetermined stages.
Shaping	This approach combines a co-regulated identity and known end point. The basic difference to 'maturation' is that the end point is not determined by some inevitable process but is open to choice and decision. It is, though, known.
Voyage	Assumes unknown end point and unitary identity. Development represents a journey 'into the self'.
Emergent	Combines co-regulated identity and unknown end point. This approach, in simple terms, applies the idea of 'voyage' to the social system of which the individual is a part, and development therefore becomes a joint, interactive and interdependent process.

Source: based on Lee (2003)

exist independently of the perceptions, behaviour and actions of others and the social experience that 'I' share with others. The second factor concerns the 'end point' of development. This can be assumed to be either known or unknown. The two possibilities for the two factors gives four broad possible combinations: co-regulated identity and known end point; co-regulated identity and unknown end point; unitary identity and known end point; and unitary identity and unknown end point. Each of these combinations leads to a different understanding of the nature of development, summarised in Table 13.2.

Lee argues that these four varying conceptions of development can be and are applied to understandings of organisation, group or individual development. This will therefore include management development. While Lee herself argues for an holistic approach derived from all four conceptions, it is arguable that much or most MD in practice is informed by one understanding to the exclusion of the other three. It is also arguable that the influence of the one understanding is the outcome of implicit assumptions rather than the result of a deliberate choice. Those points aside, Lee's work supports the argument being advanced here that the concept of development is more complex and problematic than conventional treatments normally allow. Lee's work, though, can provide a useful framework for examining definitions of MD and the utility of varying methods.

Management development – purposes and meanings

The meaning to be attached to management development can often be associated with its assumed or declared purpose. A common distinction is the relative focus on *manager* as opposed to *management* development. The former implies a focus on *individual* learning and development and a purpose associated with improving individual capability and performance. The latter implies a concern with the development of a collective resource and a purpose associated with producing shared values and a common approach to managing. The focus here, then, is the organisation as an entity rather than the individual (see also Thomson *et al.*, 2001: 180). The need for each purpose is illustrated by the Aynshents case study in Chapter 1 through the proposed redeployment of the brother who was unsuccessful as a hunter, and through the need to sustain and promote trusting and supportive relationships between existing members and potential new entrants to the enterprise. However, there are often tensions between the two purposes and it is difficult to accommodate both in any single MD programme (Hirsh and Carter, 2002). Woodall and Winstanley (1998) label this tension as a need to achieve a balance between 'integration' and 'differentiation'.

As well as the two focuses on individual and organisation, the purpose of MD can also vary in terms of time-scale. A CIPD report (CIPD, 2002a) refers to this by arguing that the purpose of MD is a) to deliver the current business model and b) to contribute to developing future business models. The latter is associated in part with a rise in the past decade or so in the use of 'future studies' and its application to MD (Schultz, 2002, see Micic and Gold, 2008). The term 'business model' though can be taken to be synonymous with 'strategy' and so the difficulties identified earlier will apply to this prescription. There is, though, an alternative and potentially useful application of time-scale, and that is in relation to the current and future availability of managerial capability (Cappelli, 2008). In the case of the former, the concern is with current behaviours of managers, either as individuals or as a collective resource. In the case of the latter, the concern is usually with ensuring availability of skills and experience to meet future demands. This can focus on individuals to prepare them for future promotion opportunities, and/or on the organisation as an entity in the sense of ensuring a supply of managerial capability to fill senior positions as and when they become vacant. These can, of course, be related and directly connected since they both have a concern with attempts to manage internal labour markets through interventions in career progression. However, it can be useful to treat them separately since the nature of those attempts is likely to vary depending on whether the focus is the individual or the organisation. Of course, some recent works might question the possibility or advisability of 'managed careers' in the current and future employment context (see, for example, Arthur *et al.*, 1999). However, some current and established conceptions of MD continue to assume a purpose associated with managed career progression (Hirsh and Carter, 2002). In addition application of the notion of 'talent management', which is now popular in large if not all organisations, clearly assumes the possibility and desirability of managed careers (Tansley *et al.*, 2007).

The result of the analysis in this section so far suggests a framework for categorising varying conceptions and definitions of MD. The framework categorises definitions according to whether individual managers or the collective managerial cadre, referred to as 'organisation' in the framework, provide the *primary* FOCUS, and whether changing current behaviour or career progression provides the *primary* PURPOSE. The framework is given in Figure 13.1. The argument here is that any and every conception or definition of MD can be accommodated by one of the focus boxes in the framework. In addition, and as will be shown later in the chapter, the framework also has utility in categorising varying approaches to, and methods of, MD. This in part is because approaches and methods do have logical connections to conceptions and definitions.

		Focus	
		Individual	*Organisation*
Purpose	*Behaviour*	Quadrant 1	Quadrant 2
	Career progression	Quadrant 3	Quadrant 4

Figure 13.1 **Dimensions of management development**

The utility of the framework in relation to conceptions of MD can be examined by analysing definitions of MD. One broad and comprehensive example is that used by Thomson *et al.* (2001) in their major empirical study of MD practice in the UK. That definition suggests that MD is the 'different ways in which managers improve their capabilities' (Thomson *et al.*, 2001: 10). The elaboration which follows this rather all-embracing view suggests that 'managers' is used as a simple plural rather than to denote a collective, and so the *focus* is individual rather than organisation. The word 'capabilities' is developed in the elaboration in a way that suggests a *purpose* to do with current behaviour and performance. This definition therefore would seem to fit Quadrant 1 of the framework. In contrast, Reid and Barrington suggest that MD is concerned with 'preparation for future promotional moves, and the forward organisational planning that may be dovetailed with them' (1999: 26). This more specific example seems to have clear *purpose* associated with career progression. Thus, this definition seems to fit Quadrant 4 of the framework.

Discussion

The two definitions seem to illustrate and confirm the utility of the framework. Thus the argument that the framework will have practical value in aiding understanding and application of varying meanings and purpose of MD is supported. Such understanding will in turn have additional value in informing decisions and actions in professional practice.

There are, however, a number of problems with this argument. The first and perhaps most obvious is that the definitions have been deliberately selected. It will be instructive for readers to test this by applying the framework to alternative definitions (see Activity 13.2). Additional problems arise from the definitions themselves since they seem not to reflect some of the points made in earlier sections of the chapter. They do not, for example, directly or overtly acknowledge the complex and uncertain nature of managerial work and associated controversies (see Thomas, 2003). Each seems to assume, implicitly at least, that specifications of required 'capabilities', or the requirements of 'promotional moves', are unproblematic. The earlier analysis and works such as that of Thomas (2003) would suggest otherwise.

Activity 13.2   Clarifying and classifying definitions of MD

1. Through research, find three more definitions of MD. Journal articles as well as books will be useful.
2. Analyse the definitions using the framework in Figure 13.1.
3. Evaluate the utility of the framework using the results of 1) and 2).
4. Consider how the framework can be used to help MD practice.

The work of Lee (2003) on conceptions of development described earlier suggests additional problems. The two definitions both assume known end points in the form of 'capability' or 'promotion'. Each also seems to assume unitary identity. This limits the definitions to only one conception of development, that of 'maturation'. The remaining conceptions of development therefore do not seem to be accommodated in what can be argued to be mainstream and conventional definitions of MD. (In carrying out Activity 13.2 readers may also wish to analyse the additional definitions they access using Lee's categorisations of development.)

Perhaps more implicitly than explicitly, the two definitions also seem to reflect a 'unitary' conception of organisations (see Chapter 14). Such a conception assumes an unproblematic formulation of specifiable organisation goals and objectives. The Moddens case study in Chapter 1 clearly shows that this is not necessarily the case. So, too, do some alternative analyses of organisations (see Alvesson and Deetz, 1996; Morgan, 1997). In relation to MD, Burgoyne and Jackson (1997) provide an alternative perspective through their application of institutional theory to management learning. Burgoyne and Jackson term this perspective the 'arena thesis' which proposes greater validity and utility for pluralist rather than unitary conceptions of organisation, and a role for MD in providing a 'meeting point' where 'conflicting purposes and values can meet to be reinforced, reconciled or proliferated' (Burgoyne and Jackson, 1997: 68). The implication, therefore, for conventional definitions and treatments of MD is that if the assumed unproblematic nature and specification of organisation goals is questionable then so too are the conceptions of MD drawn from these assumptions. In defence of the originators of the definitions used here, it is fair and accurate to say that their analyses of MD go further to take account of the points made so far than their single-sentence definitions might suggest. There is, though, one final problem with the definitions where this is less true.

Processual perspectives and analyses of organising and managing both question and challenge the reification implicit in more conventional treatments. The language form of the preceding sentence makes the point. Conventional analyses treat organisations as independent, objective entities; in other words, an 'organisation' is a 'thing' or an 'it'. Such treatments suffer from what Chia (1996) refers to as 'misplaced concreteness' in their analyses. From a processual perspective, organisations do not have entitative status. Rather, organising is a process, with more or less patterning and regularity which produces and reproduces the shared experience that we label 'an' or 'the' organisation. 'Organisations' as entities are constructed by our shared experience and the language we use to make sense of that experience, and therefore 'they' do not have independent or objective existence (see Chia, 1996, 1997). The same arguments can be applied to management and managing and, as Lee's (2003) analysis of development shows, to individuals.

What are the implications of these arguments for our understanding of MD? They suggest that conventional definitions and conceptions do not, as they might claim and we might assume, provide accurate descriptions of an objective and given reality. It can be useful to conceive of organisations as objective entities, and to relate professional practice to such conceptions (see Stewart, 1999). However, it is also useful and instructive to think about organising, managing and professional practice from a processual perspective. It is perhaps particularly important to emphasise this point when leading and influential writers on MD continue to apply more traditional perspectives.

Exhibit 13.3

CapCo

CapCo is a UK multi-national with 25,000 employees and operates in 180 different countries worldwide. It has what it refers to as a capability-based MD programme focused on a framework of leadership capabilities. The language used in materials describing and promoting the MD programme internally suggest an objective view of individual characteristics being the basis of leadership and of the programme being able to develop these in participants to make them more effective leaders. According to research carried out into this programme, among the actual effects are identity construction and identity regulation. So, while overtly about individual learning, development and self-managed careers, the programme produces cohorts of CapCo managers meeting corporate requirements and a corporate specification of how leaders (managers) *should* behave.

Source: Finch-Lees and Mabey (2007)

Summary

The arguments in this section lead to a number of significant conclusions. First, influential analyses of MD practice continue to apply what might be termed conventional perspectives in organisation and management theory. Second, within that context, and partly because of it, variations in meaning attached to definitions of MD can be related to a small number of factors. Third, the framework in Figure 13.1 is capable of usefully categorising varying conceptions of MD arising from conventional analyses. Fourth, while what is termed here 'conventional analyses' remain influential and helpful, the processual perspective has utility in drawing attention to unstated and questionable assumptions informing conventional analyses (see also Finch-Lees and Mabey, 2007). This in turn both allows and encourages new insights into professional practice.

Case Study 13.1

Management development in ABC Consultants

While based in Northern Europe, ABC Consultants operates worldwide providing technical and professional consultancy services to charities and aid agencies involved in international economic development projects. At any one time, approximately 1500 employees work in the home office, with slightly more than 1700 consultants working in various parts of the world. Management development is a function managed by a centralised HR department. Perhaps because of the nature of the business operations, which are knowledge intensive and carried out by highly educated and qualified employees, HR staff adopt an internal consultancy role in support of line managers. Responsibility for learning and development, including MD, rests firmly with managers and individual employees. Senior managers create a supportive climate and other managers create personal development plans. The latter exist for each employee at all levels.

MD is supported by the central HR department and by a set of activities known as the Central Management Development Programme (CMDP). The primary purpose of the programme is, according to those who manage it, to support the creation of a supportive learning climate within ABC Consultants. It has a focus on self-awareness and reflection on personal identity, values, beliefs and attitudes, and the impact of these on the role of manager in the company. This is achieved by a combination of seminars and workshops, on-the-job exercises and practice and use of learning sets. One outcome of the CMDP is an individual learning and development plan for each participating manager. Another outcome is the formation of task groups, based on the learning sets, to address organisation performance issues.

Activity 13.3 — Linking the 'management' and the 'development' of MD

1. Analyse this case using the framework in Figure 13.1. In which quadrant would you place the CMDP? For what reasons?

2. What conceptualisation of development, using Lee's categories, informs the purpose and design of the CMDP?

3. Which features of the CMDP, if any, reflect a conventional view of MD? What organisational factors might help to account for this?

4. Conversely, which features of the CMDP, if any, reflect a processual view of MD? What organisational factors might help to account for this?

Management development – approaches and methods

The arguments so far suggest that approaches and methods to MD will be influenced by, and related to, the conception, or definition, being applied; for example, an understanding of MD associated with Quadrant 1 in Figure 13.1 is likely to lead to the use of methods different from those utilised if an understanding of MD associated with Quadrant 4 is applied. While managerial choice will play its part in selection of approaches and methods (Thomson *et al.*, 2001), additional contingency factors will also be influential in decisions on what approaches and methods to adopt. Jones and Woodcock (1985) argue that these factors are associated with what they term 'organisation readiness'. This concept suggests that particular approaches will be more appropriate than others, depending on particular organisational circumstances. A different way of framing this argument is to say that particular circumstances make it more likely that one approach rather than another will be adopted. The first formulation suggests a normative theory, i.e. one in which prescriptions are provided on how to practise MD to meet the requirements of varying circumstances; while the second formulation implies a descriptive theory, i.e. one which provides an account of why and how MD is practised in varying circumstances. The latter has received some support and analysis in recent empirical research (Thomson *et al.*, 2001; Storey *et al.*, 1997). What the significant contingency factors, or circumstances, might be is the subject of debate, but the following list is indicative (see also Harrison, 1997):

- level of top management support for MD;
- organisation/business priorities;
- intended or planned organisation and business strategies;
- economic sector;
- level of resources available/allocated to MD;
- clarity and specificity of managerial roles;
- size of organisation/numbers of managers.

These and other factors are unlikely to operate independently, since they have obvious connections and interrelationships. For example, resources allocated to MD will be influenced by the level of top management support which, in turn, will be influenced by their perception of the importance of MD to their intended business strategy. Taking potential relationships further, an intended business strategy of expansion will lead to increasing numbers of managers demanding or needing development.

A final point can be made on the indicative list. The factors do not operate independently in an additional and important sense. The factors are, as already argued, examples of 'organisational contingencies', also discussed in Chapter 1 and illustrated in Figure 1.1 (p. 28). Such contingencies, and their influence and consequences, are mediated by the interpretations and meanings assigned to them by decision-makers. It is not the case, therefore, that particular factors will or should determine particular approaches to MD. The meaning, and associated significance and influence, of each is not objectively given or predetermined. It will vary between different managers and over time.

Approaches to MD

The chapter so far has argued that approaches to MD will relate in part to variation in understanding of MD and to organisational contingencies, both mediated by individual and collective interpretation, and by conflicting and competing values and interests. Within that context, the available and possible approaches to MD are argued to be capable of categorisation. The typology suggested by Mabey and Salaman in Table 13.1 is one example. Two further typologies are of value and interest since, in more or less explicit ways, they can be related to the indicative organisational contingencies.

The first typology is that first suggested by Burgoyne in 1988 (Mumford and Gold, 2004). Which approach is adopted in Burgoyne's broad categories will depend, in part, on what Jones and Woodcock (1985) refer to as 'organisation readiness' which, in turn, will depend in part on the influence of organisational contingencies. Burgoyne uses the term 'organisation maturity' (Mumford and Gold, 2004) in a similar fashion to 'organisational readiness', and argues similar connections to organisational contingencies. The approaches are therefore a specific example, in relation to MD, of the 'best fit' arguments discussed in Chapter 1. The approaches are as follows:

1. no systematic management development;
2. isolated tactical management development;
3. integrated and coordinated structural and development tactics;
4. an MD strategy to implement corporate policy;
5. MD strategy input to corporate policy formulation;
6. strategic development of the management of corporate policy.

The basic premise of this typology is the link between MD and corporate or business strategy; what Burgoyne refers to as 'corporate policy'. This link has been used in more recent research, notably that by Thomson *et al.* (2001) with their notion of 'strong and weak' MD, and by Jansen *et al.* (2001) in their typology of approaches to MD. The latter in particular reflect similar arguments advanced by Burgoyne.

According to Burgoyne's original analysis, approach 1 is most likely to be evident in young and small organisations. Approaches 1 to 3 are probably the most commonly adopted, while approach 4 is likely to be associated with what is currently identified as 'HRM best practices' discussed in Chapter 1. Perhaps significantly, it also reflects the conventional view of HR being the servant of business strategy. This so-called 'best practice' approach is most likely to be found in large enterprises operating in well-established economic sectors. Examples of these include primary process industries, financial services, retailing, and public sector organisations such as those in local government and the health service. Given the first point, size seems to be a significant contingency factor influencing approaches to MD. So, too, does business strategy and, related to that, the degree of top management support. A final example from the list of influencing factors having an impact is economic sector.

As Mumford and Gold (2004) argue, one problem with Burgoyne's typology is that it assumes an understanding of MD as formalised and planned programmes. While Burgoyne recognises the occurrence and potential value of informal learning and development, which constitutes the whole of MD in the first approach in his typology, his descriptions of approaches 2 to 6 rely on planned and programmed activities. This analysis is confirmed by Burgoyne's definition of MD, which is 'the management of managerial careers in an organisational context' (Mumford and

Table 13.3 **Typologies of management development**

Type	Description
Type 1	Informal managerial – accidental process
Type 2	Integrated managerial – opportunistic processes
Type 3	Formal management development – planned processes

Source: Adapted from *Management Development: Strategies for Action*, 4th Edition, CIPD (Mumford, A. and Gold, J. 2004) with the permission of the publisher, the Chartered Institute of Personnel and Development, London (www.cipd.co.uk)

Gold, 2004). A potential weakness with this typology, therefore, is its failure to accommodate informal processes of learning and development. This will also be true of more recent but similar categorisations such as that offered by Jansen *et al.* (2001).

An alternative typology is that provided by Mumford himself (1993, 1997). This classification has two potential strengths. First, it accommodates dealing directly with informal processes of learning and development. Second, it is limited to three approaches. This makes the typology less conceptually complex and therefore easier to apply to inform practice. The three approaches are described in Table 13.3. They have some similarity with those suggested by Storey and his colleagues (Storey *et al.*, 1997), and also reflect the arguments put forward by, for example, Hirsh and Carter (2002), and by O'Dwyer and Ryan (2002) in support of what is termed 'blended learning'. In this context, the term refers to combinations of formal and informal processes within MD.

Each of the three types of MD in Table 13.3 has particular characteristics which, according to Mumford, will have implications and consequences for their effectiveness as an approach to MD. Type 1 has the strength and advantage of focusing on and occurring in 'real' work. According to the research conducted by Hirsh and Carter (2002), this focus on 'real' work is a growing trend in approaches to MD, even in the context of increases in investment in formal programmes (see Thomson *et al.*, 2001; Bristow, 2007). However, according to Mumford, learning in type 1 approach can be unconscious, undirected and insufficient. Type 3 overcomes these problems and disadvantages by being planned and therefore directed to serve desired purposes. But, and again according to Mumford, type 3 approaches have their own problems and disadvantages. First, the content of formal programmes may not be relevant to 'real' work. Second, participating managers may experience difficulties in transferring their learning to the work context. Both of these disadvantages are associated with the 'distance', both temporal and spatial, between formal learning and work. Mumford goes on to argue that type 2 approaches have the potential to maximise the advantages and minimise the disadvantages of each of the other two types. This argument relies in part on Mumford's contention that the either/or choice of formal or informal approaches is in fact a false dichotomy. This contention, in turn, seems to support the current arguments for 'blended approaches'. In any case, Mumford's work is valuable in emphasising the actual and potential learning inherent in the everyday experience of carrying out work tasks and activities.

One further factor arising out of Mumford's typology is of interest. Mumford suggests that a characteristic of both type 1 and type 2 approaches is that 'ownership' of MD processes and activities remains with managers themselves. Type 3 approaches, by contrast, imply ownership by professional practitioners. There is therefore in Mumford's typology a choice to be made in terms of the relative role and contributions of professional developers and other managers. Type 3 approaches provide professional practitioners with control and ownership. The other approaches do not. This issue of control and ownership is one of the main reasons for Mumford advocating type 2 approaches.

To return to Borgoyne's typology, and those with similar characteristics, there is one additional weakness which is not necessarily true of Mumford's typology. This is the separation of corporate strategy and human resourcing strategy. Perhaps more implicitly, such typologies also associate corporate strategy with the intentions and plans of senior managers. An alternative view of strategy as emergent and realised would suggest that Burgoyne's approach 6 more closely reflects the actuality of strategic processes and that therefore the other approaches are arguably false choices since they rest on false premises. This is not to say that the varying degree of formality and planning implicit in these typologies is without value. They do in practice generally have significant utility in making decisions concerning approaches to MD. For example, in circumstances where time and resources are devoted to producing detailed strategic plans for an organisation, it would be literally nonsensical not to undertake similar processes for MD, or not to contribute the views and ambitions of MD to the corporate planning process, or indeed not to take account of corporate strategic plans, where they exist, in formulating MD plans and programmes. However, more informed decisions in MD are likely when the actuality of organisation strategies as realised outcomes is recognised. Such recognition is likely to lead to greater focus on, and attention to, the informal processes of managerial action and behaviour, and this in turn will have implications for the content and design of formal MD programmes. For these reasons, Mumford's typology offers greater utility for understanding and making decisions about approaches to MD. In addition, his type 2 represents a commendable overall approach. It is fair to say also that Burgoyne's more recent work (e.g. Burgoyne and Jackson, 1997; Pedlar *et al.*, 1994) would support a similar conclusion.

Activity 13.4 — Approaches to MD

1. Identify some possible relationships and connections between organisation contingencies and the idea of 'organisation maturity'. Think about how a 'mature' and an 'immature' organisation might differ in relation to the contingencies.

2. Consider the likely implications for management development practice arising from changes in organisation contingencies.

3. Research and access some examples of management development practice from published cases in journals such as *People Management*.

4. Analyse the descriptions provided and categorise the approach adopted in each case according to the Burgoyne (1998) and Mumford and Gold (2004) frameworks.

5. Evaluate the utility of both frameworks and decide which is more effective, and for what reasons, in categorising varying approaches.

Methods

There are obvious connections between approaches to and methods of management development. A simple example would be that type 3 approaches in Mumford's typology are likely to be associated with formal programmes of management education and training, while type 2 approaches are likely to incorporate work and job-based methods such as action learning, coaching and mentoring (see Mumford and Gold, 2004; Stewart, 1996; Knights and Poppleton, 2008). There is, too, a vast array of methods available for use by professional developers (Fee, 2001) and by managers themselves (Pedler *et al.*, 1994). It is therefore necessary to be selective in the following discussion.

One commonly applied method of MD is to produce frameworks of management competence (Thomson *et al.*, 2001). As Thomson and his colleagues detail, there are a number of different meanings associated with, and methods of development attached to, this concept. It has, though, been applied within national policy through the work of the former Management Charter Initiative in creating occupational standards and National Vocational Qualifications (NVQs) for management (see Harrison, 1997). These occupational standards provide specifications of 'competences' that managers in various roles and hierarchical levels require to perform their jobs. The meaning of competence and the methodology applied to produce specifications of competence in NVQs have both been heavily criticised (see, for example, Bates, 1995; Stewart and Sambrook, 1995). Some empirical research, though, has claimed to demonstrate improvements in both individual and organisation performance through the use and application of management NVQs (Winterton and Winterton, 2002). It is the case that use of management NVQs provides opportunities for adoption of type 2 approaches since they require the generation and assessment of work-based evidence of competence. It is also true that NVQ-based specifications do not have to be used in competence-based methods of MD. Organisations can and do develop their own frameworks and specifications (Thomson *et al.*, 2001), and alternative generic specifications are also available (see, for example, Jones and Woodcock, 1985; Boyatzis, 1982).

Mumford (1997; Mumford and Gold, 2004) criticises management NVQs and the processes that led to their production. However, he does support the value of producing some framework or model of competence. He further argues, though, that such frameworks need an 'effectiveness' dimension as well as competence and, more importantly from our point of view, a focus on the vagaries and ambiguities of managerial work. Using these two criteria, Mumford also suggests a range of MD methods which, since they focus on combining learning and working and working and learning, enable application of type 2 approaches. The methods are categorised into three sets as follows:

- Changes in the job:
  - promotion;
  - job rotation;
  - secondments.
- Changes in job content:
  - additional responsibilities and tasks;

- specific projects;

- membership of committees or task groups;

- junior or shadow board.

● Within the job:

- coaching;

- counselling;

- monitoring and feedback;

- mentoring.

This list explicitly focuses on what might be termed informal methods of MD, which nevertheless are capable of, and perhaps would benefit from, some degree of planning and formalisation. The list does, however, exclude off-the-job and other methods that are normally associated with formalised and planned approaches. Alternative classifications are offered by Reid and Barrington (1994) and by Fee (2001). These classifications include the following methods:

● group-based methods, e.g. managerial grid;

● e-learning;

● outdoor development;

● in-house courses;

● planned experience outside the organisation;

● external courses, qualification or non-qualification based;

● role analysis;

● internal or external seminars;

● action learning;

● performance review;

● development centres;

● career management and development.

The latter three methods have links and connections with succession planning, discussed by Harrison (1997) as a method of MD. The two lists and individual methods in each are not mutually exclusive. Combinations of methods from both lists will enable and support application of Mumford's type 2 approach. Expressed another way, adoption of a type 2 approach is likely to lead to use of methods from both lists. It also needs to be recognised that the lists are not exhaustive (see Fee, 2001 for a comprehensive review of MD methods).

This discussion of methods illustrates an additional application of the framework in Figure 13.1. As well as being useful for categorising and comparing definitions and meanings, the framework can also be used to categorise methods. Figure 13.2 shows this by placing some methods in each of the quadrants. In closing this section, readers may find it useful to test this application of the framework by allocating the remaining methods from the two lists, and any others with which they are familiar, to one of the four quadrants.

		Focus	
		Individual	*Organisation*
Purpose	*Behaviour*	Coaching Competence Specifications	Promotion Managerial grid
	Career progression	Secondments Mentoring	Succession planning Career management

Figure 13.2 **Classification of management development methods**

Case Study 13.2

Management development in DEF

DEF is a large company with five divisions. There is a central corporate planning department reporting to the chief executive and each division also employs strategic analysts and planners responsible for producing divisional strategies and five-year plans. The company has clear statements of vision, mission, values and key strengths. Performance in all divisions and so at corporate level is currently impressive with annual growth in all indicators for the past five years. There is strong commitment to MD from the chief executive and sufficient resources allocated. There is an established Senior Management Programme for those appointed to senior roles in divisions. This includes a staged series of formal inputs on management theory and practice provided by a leading business school, although no element of the programme is accredited for qualifications. Simultaneously, participants work on a personal project to analyse and produce solutions to a strategic problem being experienced by their division. The projects are discussed by the group of participants following each get together for the formal inputs. Each individual though is personally responsible for their project and presents a report to the divisional management team at the end of the programme. The report has to include actionable recommendations. The individual project in this programme contrasts with the MD programme for the next lower level, which covers a population of around 300 managers and has a strong focus on group work, activity and projects across divisions. Both programmes have been running for a number of years. While evaluations have shown strong indicators of success the HR department feels that both need refreshing with some new approaches and methods.

> **Activity 13.5** **Approaches and methods in DEF**
>
> 1. How would you categorise the approach to MD for senior managers in DEF and why?
> 2. What different approaches could/should be adopted in refreshing the programme and why?
> 3. What do you think are the relative advantages and disadvantages of the individual focus in the programme for senior managers and the group focus in the middle manager programme? What are your reasons for these?
> 4. What methods would you recommend be incorporated in each programme and why?

Management development and HR strategy

This section is concerned with examining the relationship between MD and human resource strategy. The main focus therefore is with matters of *horizontal integration*. The section will draw on the arguments and conceptual frameworks presented in Chapter 1.

A useful starting point is always 'first principles'. Chapter 1 suggests two main alternative HR strategies, labelled high and low commitment. Variation across organisational hierarchies within a single human resourcing strategy is also possible. This might be expected to be common, with arrangements for managers being quite different from those for other employees. Certainly in terms of MD, conceptually at least, it is reasonable to expect approaches and methods to both assume and to be intended to encourage the principles of high commitment. This follows in part because managers as employees commonly exercise a high degree of discretion in their jobs and therefore create higher levels of uncertainty (see Chapter 1). That being the case, MD is more likely to exhibit the features of employee development detailed in the right-hand column of Table 1.2 (p. 27).

The other components of HR strategy listed in Table 1.3, though, suggest a complicating factor. This is simply that while it may be possible to have different development strategies for different categories of employees, and perhaps for other components such as rewards, mixing both low commitment and high commitment strategies in relation to some components will be more difficult; organisational culture and the role of the HR department, for example. Such variation, if achievable, will also create the problem of incongruence and 'mixed messages' across the organisation. In addition, it will work against the 'horizontal integration' argued to be necessary in HR strategy.

It is, of course, possible to adopt a single low commitment strategy which encompasses managers as well as other employees. The notion of commitment is linked to that of control; low commitment is associated with high levels of direct control and high commitment with indirect control, the notion of control being organisational processes to control employee behaviour (Watson, 1999). It is arguable that competence-based methods of MD, for example, are congruent with high levels of direct control and therefore with a low commitment strategy. This follows from the precise specification of desired behaviour associated with competency frameworks. Where performance management and rewards are also linked to the competency framework, 'horizontal integration' and congruence across organisation hierarchies can be achieved.

Activity 13.6   **HR and MD: a matter of congruence?**

Refer back to the Moddens case study in Chapter 1, and Case Studies 1.2c and 1.2d in particular (p. 24, p. 30).

1. How might difficulties in adopting a mix of high and low commitment HR strategies account for problems experienced in Moddens?

2. Based on responses to question 1, to what extent is HR strategy the servant of corporate strategy or integral to it?

Future developments in MD

New understanding of careers and how they are enacted (Arthur *et al.*, 1999), and in particular those of managers (Watson and Harris, 1999), suggests that our understanding of management development is also in need of reappraisal. This in turn means that approaches and methods associated with conventional definitions of MD are also likely to be continually questioned. One aspect of managing in particular which has until recently not featured significantly in approaches to, and methods of, MD is that of managerial values and ethics. Interest in this is currently higher than in the recent past because of increased attention to corporate governance and responsibility arising out of well-publicised cases of corporate wrong doing. While not directly related to these cases, the subject of ethics in MD practice is also receiving increased attention (Hatcher, 2007; Stewart, 2007).

According to research conducted by the CIPD (2002a) an additional challenge for MD in the future will be achieving integration of MD with organisation goals. That research indicated that over 80 per cent of senior managers rate such integration as their biggest challenge because senior managers perceive, and again according to that research, businesses as being more constrained by talent than by finance or the lack of commodities. As mentioned earlier in the chapter, the CIPD report proposes a prescriptive model for achieving vertical integration in MD practice. This model, though, is firmly within established and conventional understandings of MD and appears to be little different from the well-known training cycle (see Chapter 11). The notion of integration is also highlighted by additional research by Storey *et al.* (1997) and Hirsh and Carter (2002). In these cases, though, the focus is on 'horizontal' integration within MD practice itself. According to Hirsh and Carter, different methods of MD for managers of different levels can be integrated through 'blended' approaches to management development. In essence, though, this seems little different to a dual HR strategy based on both high commitment for senior managers and low commitment for other managers. However, it does seem that, based on this range of research, achieving both horizontal and vertical integration will be a continuing challenge for MD practice.

The research by Hirsh and Carter (2002) also suggests that MD practice will continue to experience a number of tensions in meeting the challenge of integration. These include the tension of organisation versus individual desires and agendas; that of learning theory versus development processes, with the 'bite size' chunks of e-learning, for example, conflicting with the holistic nature of learning suggested by theory; and tension over whom to target with investment in MD; e.g. talented managers or poor performers. There are, of course, no answers to these tensions but it seems clear that practitioners will need to work to resolve them in their own contexts.

These challenges have been confirmed and expanded in a collection of research produced by Hill and Stewart (2007). One challenge not yet mentioned though is the notion of global leadership and how to develop individual and collections of managers to meet the needs of global operations, and indeed global issues facing all organisations. There is much debate about what the notion means and so what exactly constitutes global leadership and, as a related question, whether it refers solely to leaders of multinational and global corporations or whether a different form of leadership, and so a different kind of leader, is needed for and in all organisations in a globalised and fast changing world (see Mendenhall, 2006). While the word used in this work is 'leadership' and 'leadership development', as we saw earlier these words are often used as synonyms for management and management development. We can say therefore that addressing the challenge will be on the future as well as current agenda of management development research and practice.

A final observation on future development may help to deal with at least some of these challenges and tensions. This is simply that perhaps in future the managerial resource will be understood as the capabilities, skills and efforts of managers as identified in Chapter 1, rather than managers as a collection of individuals. Such a view has clear potential for reducing the organisation–individual tension and some contribution to make to that of targeting MD investment whether for local or global operations.

Activity 13.7 Using MD to create a Modden(s) future

Return to the Moddens case study in Chapter 1 and consider the following questions.

1. What differences are we likely to see in approaches to MD in the two new divisions?
2. What factors will influence decisions on these approaches?
3. How are the tensions suggested by Hirsh and Carter likely to manifest themselves in the Gourmet Division?
4. What advice would you give Jean Frear to help her deal with and resolve the tensions?

Conclusion

This chapter has argued that MD can and does have a range of meanings and definitions. It has been further argued that definitions of MD will influence approaches and methods adopted in practice.

Additional influencing factors on practice will include 'organisations' contingencies' such as size, economic sector and top management support. Managerial values and choice, though, will also play a part in the end and MD practice will emerge from the interplay of the factors identified in Figure 1.1 (p. 28). Practice can also be associated with either a low or high commitment HR strategy, although in theory the latter is more likely for managers and therefore MD whatever the case for other employees. The chapter has, though, argued practical problems with adopting such a dual strategy. While the influence of contingency factors would suggest a 'best fit' rather than 'best practice' view of management development as being more appropriate, the ideas of Mumford and Gold and their type 2 approach do incorporate elements of relevance and value to most if not all contexts.

Summary

In this chapter, the following key points have been made:

- Both 'management' and 'development' are complex and problematic concepts.
- This complexity in part explains the variation in meanings attached to the term 'management development'.
- MD can focus on managers as a collective resource or as individuals and can have purposes related to developing capabilities and skills or to developing consistency in corporate culture.
- Alternative approaches to, and methods of, MD can support either a low or high commitment HR strategy.
- Attempts to adopt different HR strategies in relation to different categories of employees may encounter or engender practical difficulties, especially in relation to horizontal integration.
- Recent research suggests that MD practice will continue to experience a number of challenges and tensions.
- Research also suggests that perhaps the biggest challenge still facing MD practice is achieving vertical and horizontal integration.

Discussion questions

1. What is the relationship between different understandings of 'management' and assumptions about the purpose of management development?
2. How, if at all, can management development be designed to accommodate both individual and corporate aspirations?
3. What range of choices is available to professional practitioners in deciding approaches to management development? What factors might limit total freedom in making that decision?
4. Which factors influence the selection of management development methods? Which of the factors can be controlled or influenced by professional practitioners?

5. How can and should the outcomes of management development be evaluated?

6. How is management development practice likely to change in the future? And why?

Further reading

As with other chapters, the sources referenced in the text provide a rich variety of research and writing on MD. The text by Thomson *et al.* (2001) provides major empirical evidence as well as detailed and thoughtful analysis. While much briefer and narrower in scope, the work of Hirsh and Carter (2002) is a useful guide and pointer to current issues. Fee (2001) provides a clear practitioner-focused overview of MD methods. New perspectives on managing and the implications for management learning and development are important. The texts by Thomas (2003) and by Watson and Harris (1999) respectively deal with these issues in an exemplary manner. The works of Mumford and Gold (2004) and of Woodall and Winstanley (1998) are both 'must reads'. Finally, the most comprehensive coverage of recent research on MD is provided by the collection edited by Hill and Stewart (2007).

Part IV

Managing employment and other human resourcing relationships

Introduction to Part IV

In the fourth and final part of this book we explore a number of relationships that managers may have with organisations outside the immediate workplace. One aspect of strategic human resourcing is whether or not management is willing to mediate the employment relationship through trade unions. Aspects of managing the employment with and without employee voice articulated via trade unions are explored in Chapters 14 and 15. Finally, in Chapter 16 potential relationships with management consultants are explored.

The central argument of Chapter 14 is that there is a complex interrelationship between conflict and cooperation in the employment relationship and that this can best be understood by using a processual and pluralist approach rather than a systems and unitarist one. Conflict is neither the opposite of, nor the absence of, cooperation, but the two coexist and, indeed, interact with each other. Conflict may be covert or overt but the processual view leads us to suggest the continuous need for people to manage their differences. These can be between a variety of individuals and groups in the organisation, not simply between unions and management. Conflict may exist at the level of interests and at the level of behaviour and this understanding helps us distinguish between manifest conflict and latent conflict. These issues are explored through the device of a dialogue between two reflective practitioners of HRM and a case study of organisational conflict.

One arrangement employers use to manage conflict is to institutionalise it through collective bargaining with trade unions. However, union recognition is only one of a number of possible strategic directions that employers can and do follow. Others considered here are union de-recognition in the context where employers may wish to end or marginalise previously established relationships with unions, substitution strategies where employers seek to create an employment relationship in which employees do not seek to represent their views through unions or use them as a vehicle for improvement of terms and conditions of employment, or a 'black hole' strategy where unions are rejected and avoided by whatever means possible. The context for these possible strategic directions is examined in the light of the decline in union membership since the 1979 peak, the weakening and decentralisation of collective bargaining, and the reduction of the overt manifestation of conflict through strikes. It is suggested that employers might wish to reconsider their strategies in the light of statutory support for union recognition, but employers and trade unions are also likely to take account of the overall industrial relations context discussed above. Readers are invited to explore these possible strategic directions through a case study.

The ambiguous use of 'partnership' to describe employer–employee and/or employer–trade union relations is discussed and it is suggested that any attempt to mask conflict is unlikely to be successful. Approaches to partnership are linked to the unitarist/pluralist dichotomy introduced at the beginning of the chapter and, through an activity, readers are invited to consider their approaches to and understanding of these issues. The term 'partnering' is suggested as an alternative way of understanding these relationships, one that is more in tune with the processual approach adopted throughout this book.

In Chapter 15 issues related to employee participation, involvement and communications are considered. The differences in meaning between industrial democracy, employee participation and employee involvement are clearly established, as is the point that managers, employees and trade unions often seek different objectives from participation and involvement schemes. These differences are related to the Hyman and Mason (1995) differentiation of the two terms, and to a model of a participation continuum which permits an understanding of which participants are seeking what type of scheme and why. In particular, throughout the chapter the distinction between direct and indirect schemes, and job-related and business-related levels of decision-making, is drawn. Movements in the popularity of different schemes are discussed in terms of the cycles and waves models.

In the context of these general distinctions, a number of particular schemes of participation and involvement are examined, including representative participation, downward communication, upward problem-solving, task participation and financial involvement. The prospects for a change in approach in the way British managers, trade unionists and employees regard employee participation and involvement are considered in the light of developments in policy and practice in the European Union.

Finally, the notion of horizontal fit between different forms of employee participation and involvement and the relationship of these to overall human resourcing strategy is considered. In particular, the potential mismatch from a fads and fashions approach is highlighted, as are the tensions in operating schemes derived from the employee participation approach alongside the employee involvement one.

A different kind of external relationship that has become increasingly common is that with management consultants and specifically consultants specialising in strategic human resourcing issues. Often these consultants offer packaged solutions rather than bespoke ones and therefore the nature of managing consultancy and consultancy relationships is of particular importance. In Chapter 16 Diannah Lowry and Pam Stevens stress that the management of these relationships is inherently political and also involves other symbolic and structural dimensions. It is therefore necessary to appreciate the tensions, contradictions and challenges inherent in this. In the context of discussion about strategic human resourcing it is vital to recognise not only human resource strategy-makers, but also the constituents who feel that they are likely to be affected by the processes and outcomes of consultancy interventions that will be involved in these processes.

An essential defining feature of managing consulting and the consultancy relationship is that it involves the strategic exchange of knowledge. Issues about the nature of knowledge that consultants have are examined from both a strategic and a structural perspective and a way of integrating these two perspectives is proposed. The authors review a number of models designed to assist our understanding of the consultancy relationship and favour Kitay and Wright's (2003) model which distinguishes two categories of expertise, esoteric and structured, and relates these to the nature of the boundaries between the client and consultant. They then draw on the Alvesson and Johansson (2002) typology, which explores the inter-related issues of the 'professionalism' of consultancy, the nature of exchange between client and consultant, and issues of power, politics and negotiation. In the final section of the chapter the authors link us back to the concerns of Chapter 4 and ethical issues in managing consulting and the consultancy relationship. Issues explored include the nature of the consulting relationship and those surrounding the impact of consultancy interventions on other constituents both within and outside the organisation.

Strategic choice in patterns of employment relationships

Tony Watson, John Leopold and Derek Watling

Learning outcomes

Having read this chapter and completed its associated activities, readers should be able to:

- Recognise that alongside the cooperative activities which managers have to bring about in work organisations there will always and inevitably be conflicts and differences of interest

- Understand that conflicts in work organisations take a variety of forms – and that some aspects of conflict are more visible than others

- Appreciate that conflict is as much a phenomenon which has to be managed as is cooperation and that formalised arrangements, such as bargaining arrangements with trade unions, are one possible facet of this

- See some pattern in the changes that are occurring in employer–union relationships and note the strategic human resourcing options which relate to these

- Appreciate differing views of the notion of partnership as an employee relations strategy and the importance of the interrelationship of partnership principles, practices and processes

Introduction

Let us picture two young people sitting in the waiting room outside the office of the chief executive of a business which they each hope to join. They are both applicants for the new post of Human Resource Manager. Let us call them Unity Fairweather and Polly Politick. Both candidates have management studies qualifications and have worked for several years in human resourcing jobs. They are discussing how they would handle the question they had been told would be put to them by the interviewers, 'How would you contribute to taking the business forward as the HR manager?'

Some of the key underlying issues that are addressed in the present chapter are raised in the following dialogue which one can imagine taking place between these two *reflective practitioners* (Schön, 1983) of human resource management.

Unity Fairweather The main thing I'll stress is the need to get everybody to 'sign on' to the business's key objectives. I know this isn't a simple matter but I believe that if we clearly communicate to all employees what needs to be done to ensure a prosperous future for everybody then we really can move forward. Do you think that'll go down well, Polly?

Polly Politick Yes, I rather expect it will. It's the sort of thing the top managers who will be interviewing us like to hear.

UF Great. So you'll be saying something similar, then, I take it.

PP Well, I have a bit of a dilemma there. It would probably put me in a good light with the interview panel. But I am not sure that it's a realistic way of thinking.

UF But surely it is very realistic. Don't you think that a key part of the top manager's job, supported and guided by HR experts, is to persuade people in an organisation that they are all in the same boat and need to pull together so that everybody gets what they want in the long run?

PP Oh indeed. I agree that this is what you have to *try* to do. But I think that you are simply heading for disappointment, disillusion and failure if you convince yourself that you will ever achieve anything like this. You can only go so far. Managers must work at persuading people to 'pull together'. This is vital because without cooperation between people there is no organisation, let alone a successful organisation. But what you have to come to terms with is that this 'pulling together' can only come about if you recognise that you are dealing with people who are bringing a whole lot of different needs, wants or interests to the workplace. To get them to cooperate you have got to work all the time to get people with different interests to compromise. Conflicts are always there and . . .

UF Yes, I agree: conflict, conflict, conflict. But one of the reasons I want to change my job is because I am sick of all the conflict that I've put up with in my previous companies. It's sick. Don't you agree that we HR experts have got to find ways of getting rid of these artificial conflicts?

PP No, I don't, Unity. And I think I can put my finger on where we differ. You talk about these conflicts being artificial. I think that they are anything but artificial, you see. They are real and inevitable. At the most basic level, for example, the employer is trying to get the most out of employees that they can at the best cost they can achieve while the employees, not unreasonably, want to get the most out of the job they can for the best return they can get.

UF Polly, this really is depressing. If it really is like that, then there's no point in having 'people experts' like you and me trying to make things better.

PP Oh but there is, Unity. I shall talk in my interview about trying to make things better, as you put it, but I shall make my pitch in terms of 'managing conflict' – not getting rid of it. I'm happy to use rhetoric like 'we are all in the same boat' but I'm not stupid enough to believe my own propaganda. When

I try persuading the union people that we are all really on the same side, I am – in reality – trying to achieve a *management win*. I'm not daft enough to think that there really is no difference of interests between employers and employees. Our job is to get some cooperative work done, within the realistic recognition that underlying differences between people and between groups are regularly going to come back up to the surface and will continually need to be dealt with.

UF I see what you are getting at. I probably talk about the same things as you but in a different language. I like to talk ab_____ in place a strong and healthy culture which has clear and agreed _____ use to guide them in the right direction for the future _____ their personal goals. I also talk about sett_____ and employee development schemes whi_____ personal aspirations to be matched.

PP I go along with this – up to a point, Un_____ things that you talk about play a part in w_____ conflict. Perhaps you mean the same thing_____ 'matching business needs and personal aspi_____, though, is that you are never in any conclus_____ g to 'match' these different aims and wants. You ge_____ much as you can, to get things done. But things never settle. Ma_____ it is not a matter of designing systems which sort everything out. It is a process whereby you are all the time negotiating and renegotiating compromises and achieving working agreements.

Polly Politick operates with a view of management and work organisations which academics often characterise as processual – an approach which they contrast with a *systems* one (Watson, 2006). She sees management as a process in which managers are 'all the time negotiating and renegotiating compromises and achieving working agreements', rather than 'a matter of designing systems which sort everything out'. She is clearly implying that Unity Fairweather thinks about management in this latter non-processual way. But Polly Politick not only analyses organisational activities in processual terms. She also operates within what Fox (1966, 1974) calls a *pluralist* perspective – always taking into account the fact that there is a plurality of interests, goals, wants and priorities among the variety of people involved in any given organisation. (And note that pluralism does not necessarily imply an equality of power among the plurality of interest groups; Fox, 1979.) Unity Fairweather, in contrast, sees organisations and employment relations from what Fox calls a *unitary perspective*. This assumes the predominance of common interests and shared priorities across the organisation. Conflict is not an inevitable part of social life. It is pathological – a sickness to be cured as Unity sees it. This perspective is one that the writers of the present chapter, along with Polly Politick, feel to be unrealistic. And it takes managers towards the danger that Polly refers to – that of believing their own propaganda. The wise manager, we could say, may well try to persuade people that they are all 'on the same side', to encourage them to act cooperatively. The foolish manager is the one who assumes that this is actually the way the world is or that something close to complete harmony is, in fact, achievable.

Activity 14.1   **Polly Politick's processual and pluralist way of thinking**

Briefly look back to Chapter 1 and remind yourself about the 'processual' way of thinking about human resource strategy-making. Then come back to what Polly Politick is arguing and make a note of:

1. things she says about employment relationships which have some of these 'processual' characteristics;
2. things she says which indicate that she is working within a 'pluralist perspective'.

Whether we are focusing on human resource strategy-making or on employment relations, the main advantage of looking at organisations as ongoing processes rather than as fixed systems is that it keeps us aware that nothing ever settles into a steady state in organisational life. Organisations are not big machines which, once designed and 'put in place', will smoothly and harmoniously harness human energies to meet a set of clear 'organisational objectives'. Many managers aspire to making their organisation into this kind of smoothly functioning, perfectly designed set of goal-fulfilling systems and sub-systems. But this is not realistic. Organisations are made up of the activities of human beings – and every single one of these people (and every grouping of people) has their own interests, priorities or agenda. Also, organisations have to deal with numerous interests and pressures outside their boundaries. This means that there is continual adjustment, negotiation, balancing and rebalancing to be achieved to ensure that sufficient productive cooperation comes about for the organisation to continue in existence.

The handling of conflict is central to these processes. But what do we mean by conflict? To answer this question we have to establish, first, that it is not simply the opposite of cooperation or an absence of cooperation. Conflict and cooperation are intimately related and typically coexist. Once this point has been made we can go on to look at the two-sided nature of conflict itself – its darker or less visible side and its more visible or overt side. Having noted the very varied ways in which conflicts manifest themselves in organisations, we will then concentrate on the management–union relationship as an area in which strategic human resourcing options exist with regard to managing cooperation–conflict issues. Finally, we consider notions of 'partnership' and their relationship to our understanding of the interplay between conflict and cooperation.

The interplay of conflict and cooperation

It is vital for those involved in strategic human resource management to give full recognition to the existence of differences of interest, value and orientation in organisations. And this, in turn, entails applying the insights of the 'pluralist perspective' to employment relations. In practical terms, it draws to our attention the continual need for people to *manage their differences* so that they might cooperate sufficiently well to make it possible for them to stand any chance of achieving any of the different purposes which they may have. Conflict, we might say, is a facet of cooperation and cooperation is a facet of conflict. To explain this apparent paradox, we can take the simple example of a football match. There is conflict – each side wants to win by getting more goals than the other. Yet for this conflict to occur, there has to be cooperation. This is not just about following the same set of rules. It involves such matters as turning up on time at the same venue. Here we could say that cooperation was a means to conflict being expressed (the teams cooperate to enable one of them to defeat the other). But we could equally well say that the conflict was a means towards cooperation (the teams engage in a conflict in order to achieve the cooperative outcome of an entertaining football match). There can be no conflict without cooperation.

Note that even in what might at first look like the classical case of out-and-out conflict – a world war – there has to be cooperation over rules about prisoners of war or about which weapons are acceptable and which are not. Each side presumably recognises that without some degree of cooperation, there would be no victory worth having. And this is precisely the case in the employment context. In even the most bitter dispute between a capitalist employer and unionised employees, for example, there has to be cooperation in the handling of that dispute. This is vital to avoid a situation where the employing organisation collapses completely with the effect that there is neither work for the employees nor profits for the employer.

This coexistence and, indeed, interplay of conflict and cooperation in the work situation is something we all experience every day. As a departmental manager, for example, one might come into conflict with the staff in the department over the amount or quality of work they are producing. It is in the manager's interest to get as much 'output' as possible within a wage bill which is kept as low as is reasonably possible. And it is in the interests of the staff to avoid coming under too much pressure of workload while obtaining the best wage they can get. There is clearly an underlying conflict of interest here. Cooperative activities of consultation and negotiation between managers and staff would be one way of dealing with this – one way of 'managing' this basic conflict of interest. This would be a fairly normal way of proceeding. But the interplay of conflict and cooperation might go beyond this – as we see in the Dogger Bank loans department case.

Case Study 14.1a

Conflict and cooperation in the Dogger Bank loans department

Bill Borrack was the manager of the department of The Dogger Bank which processed loan applications. Constant complaints were made in the bank about how long it was taking his staff to deal with applications and Bill was told that he had to do something about this. At the same time, the accountants were telling him that his salary costs were unreasonably high. Bill felt that to keep his job – and his annual performance-related bonus – he would have to push his staff harder. But at the same time as he was coming to recognise this, Sandy Gate, the staff's elected union representative, was developing a claim to management for a salary improvement. This was said to be about bringing pay up to what was seen as a level equivalent to that paid by competing local financial services providers. And there was also a claim for reduced hours. This was based on observations about increasing stress levels in the department.

After a number of fairly heated arguments between Bill and Sandy, and following a refusal of the staff to do overtime at weekends, a crisis arose. The department developed a serious backlog of loan applications and Bill's annual appraisal review was approaching. The staff were increasingly uncooperative, both with managers and with other departments in the bank. Arguments and outbursts of ill-temper became more and more frequent. A higher number of resignations than usual started to come Bill's way.

Bill had no idea how to proceed. He decided to telephone a member of the human resources department to seek advice about what do.

Pause here in your reading and ask yourself what you might say to Bill if you were that HR person.

As it happened, the HR person concerned saw it as part of their job to keep informed about what was going on throughout the bank building and was aware of the frustration of the staff in the loans department. The suggestion was therefore made that Bill invite Sandy to help him form a 'working party' to examine how the work across the department was organised. This was an informal group whose brief excluded issues of pay or working hours. These would be dealt with in formal negotiations organised by the HR department and the trade union.

The working party spoke to every member of the department about how they did their jobs and ended up recommending a team-based reorganisation of the department along lines which the staff themselves felt would be more efficient and, at the same time, more satisfying.

Following the reorganisation, the tensions in the department reduced. There were fewer arguments and complaints became a rarity. The goodwill that was created enabled Sandy to strike a very good bargain with the bank over pay – one that involved dropping the claim for reduced working hours. Everything, Bill found himself boasting, was now sweetness and light.

What we see here is an increase or an improvement in the cooperative work done in the bank's loan department. But it has arisen out of a pattern of conflict which was growing in the department. The case illustrates that we cannot straightforwardly see conflict as a 'bad thing' (as 'dysfunctional' in the social science jargon). It produced better outcomes for both the employer and the employees. The conflicts – given skilled conflict management work both by managers and employee representatives – led to generally beneficial changes.

Activity 14.2   Constructive aspects of conflict

Can you think of any situation (real or imagined) where conflicts, tensions or rivalries between individuals or groups have led to improved outcomes for all parties concerned?

The 'sweetness and light' that Bill Borrack was so pleased about is something that we might expect to warm the heart of Unity Fairweather. In her terms, common objectives had come to be shared by everyone and new 'systems of working' had been put in place which ensured that those objectives continued to be fulfilled. Polly Politick, however, might see things a little differently. In her 'processual view' of management, nothing is ever finally settled you will remember. However effectively people at work might be persuaded to cooperate and might negotiate solutions to problems, underlying differences remain and conflict is always prone to return to the surface once again. Managing conflict, in Polly's terms, is an ongoing process. Differences between parties to the employment relationship are never resolved. They are simply more or less well handled at any given time. Let us return to the Dogger Bank loans department to see what occurred 12 months on.

Case Study 14.1b

Conflict and cooperation in the Dogger Bank loans department – 12 months on

Twelve months after Bill Borrack had concluded that his problems were over and that all was 'sweetness and light' in the Dogger Bank loans department, the staff put in a claim for a large salary rise. They argued that the department was so successful because they were working at a much higher skill level than previously and that this should be reflected in considerably enhanced pay levels. The bank's management argued in response that it could not afford such a rise because of the heavy competition for loans business which Dogger was experiencing. The trade union would not accept this and threatened strike action. The management at this stage, as part of a broader 'cost reduction programme', made two of the staff in the department redundant. Bitterness increased. The quality of work fell. A backlog of work built up. Bill did not know what to do. He telephoned the HR department. . . .

Conflict and cooperation, as two facets of human existence and behaviour, are constantly in a dynamic tension. And part of this dynamic tension is understood as involving deeper or 'underlying' differences of interest 'rising to the surface'. To make sense of processes of conflict and cooperation in organisations, then, we need a framework which distinguishes between aspects of conflict which can be said to exist at two levels.

Two levels of conflict and its variety of expressions

We often associate conflict with aggressive or argumentative *behaviour*. In terms of formal employment relations we think of strikes and other forms of so-called 'industrial action'. We would all readily label the bickering and arguing which occurred at the worst times in the bank loans department as 'conflict', as we would their threat to go on strike in support of their pay claim. However, social scientists typically see these behaviours as just one facet of conflict – it is the overt or *manifest* face of conflict. Behind the visible face – the fight or argument we see

Table 14.1 Two levels at which conflict exists in employment relations

Conflict at the level of interests	Conflict at the level of behaviour
Exists where there is a difference between employer/managers and employees over desired outcomes – a difference which is not necessarily stated or immediately obvious	Exists where parties desiring different outcomes either (a) directly and overtly clash over those differences and engage in open dispute, perhaps applying formal sanctions (such as one party stopping pay or locking people out or the other party going on strike) or (b) express their differences indirectly through such gestures as withdrawal of cooperation, generalised belligerence, destructive behaviour

going on – there is always some issue, some *difference* that exists between the protagonists. And this difference of interest does not necessarily lead to overt conflicts. It may stay buried or *latent* (where the two parties with different interests have not yet found an occasion to overtly fall out as a result of their different concerns). Or it might be handled or managed in a relatively peaceful way. To help us here we can make a distinction between conflict at the level of interests and conflict at the level of behaviour (Table 14.1).

Polly Politick expressed very clearly one of the most significant ways in which there is a conflict of interest at the heart of the employment relationship which is typical in the industrial capitalist type of economic and cultural order. She argued that

> at the most basic level, the employer is trying to get the most out of employees that they can at the best cost they can achieve while the employees, not unreasonably, want to get the most out of the job they can for the best return they can get.

Polly recognises that the economic system is set up this way: that there is the basic economic conflict of interest which exists between any buyer and seller (be they buyers or sellers of fish, bread or labour). In recognition that these conflicts are an inherent part of the way industrial capitalist society and economy is structured, Edwards (1986) provides us with the useful notion of *structured antagonism*. This conflict does not necessarily take a destructive form (although Marxist analysis suggests that, in the long run, it is bound to lead to the collapse of the economic order of which it is a part). We saw how, for example, the way the conflict was managed in Dogger Bank led to benefits for everyone concerned – for a certain period of time at least. But the banking case study also illustrates the other side of conflict represented in Table 14.1. The basic or underlying economic conflict of interest was expressed behaviourally in both the ways indicated on the right-hand side of the table. The 'industrial relations' dispute over pay and hours, the arguments between the manager and the union representative and the threat of 'industrial action' are all overt and direct manifestations of the conflict 'at the level of interest'. And the bickering, the uncooperative behaviour and the increased level of resignations from the department all illustrate how less obviously interest-based behaviours can be understood as related to such deeper differences.

If we think about the growing dissatisfaction which was developing in the loans department of the Dogger Bank as the staff came to believe that their higher

449

performance warranted a higher level of pay, we can see the logic of their threatening to withdraw their labour. But further thought might suggest that the strike threat was only one way in which this grievance might have been expressed. If the staff had not been relatively well organised as union members – and had Sandy Gate not been there to articulate their dissatisfactions – we might well have seen alternative expressions of the underlying conflict 'coming to the surface'. It could have meant a return to the awkwardness and bickering of the year before. It might have meant an increased rate of leaving the bank or increased absenteeism. It could have led to staff being less polite to customers or even to them sabotaging aspects of the loan operation. Yet again it might have seen staff slowing their work down by meticulously observing every detail of the official rules and procedures ('working to rule'). It could even have led to them refusing to comply fully with the Dogger Bank uniform requirements (a type of protest observed among airline cabin crew by Hochschild, 1983).

It has always been a key insight of industrial sociologists that underlying differences of interest or orientation between employers (or their managerial agents) and employees can be expressed in a range of interchangeable ways – including and going beyond those we have mentioned (Edwards and Scullion, 1982; Edwards and Whitson, 1989; Hyman, 1989; Turnbull and Sapsford, 1992; Watson, 2008). For the moment, however, we should note that several of these types of behaviour often appear together, the one reinforcing the other. At other times, however, they may shift from one form to another – high absenteeism disappearing, for example, as a group of workers move towards taking more concerted union-organised action to express dissatisfaction. And this example gives us some insight into the reasons why employers have often chosen to set up institutionalised conflict management procedures in the form of bargaining and consultative arrangements with trade unions. But such a strategic direction is not the only one open to employers, as we shall now see.

Traditional strategic human resourcing options in management–union relations

One of the major ways in which employing organisations can manage conflicts and handle many of the potential differences that can arise between employer and employee has been through institutionalised arrangements of collective bargaining and consultation with trade unions. A key human resourcing strategic decision for the managers of any employing organisation is whether or not they are going to recognise, or continue to recognise, a trade union (or several unions) as a legitimate vehicle for the expression of employee interests. While ultimately this decision is for the management of each organisation to decide in the light of all the contingent factors influencing human resourcing strategy decisions identified in Chapter 1, the decision is likely to be framed by two critical factors in the macro environment. On the one hand, managers will be aware of the decline of union membership and representation in the two decades since the peak of union density in 1979, and of the consequent decline in the proportion of employees having their pay and conditions determined through collective bargaining. On the other, they need to operate in the context of statutory support given to union recognition through the Employment Relations Act 1999. We shall examine each of these contexts in turn.

Patterns of change in union membership, collective bargaining and strike activity

The position of union membership in the UK is set out in Table 14.2.

The overall picture is that union membership has fallen dramatically since the peak in 1979, both in absolute terms and as a percentage of the working population. In fact, the period 1980–97 is the longest period of continuous annual membership decline since records began in 1892. Around 2000 there was a slight increase in the number of people in trade unions, but even so, as a proportion of employees in employment, union density continued to fall. Now, fewer than 3 out of every 10 employees is a union member compared with more than half only 25 years ago.

A number of competing explanations have been put forward to account for these dramatic changes – the impact of the business cycle (Disney, 1990), the changing composition of employment, with the loss of jobs in traditionally heavily unionised sectors of the economy and the growth of new jobs in traditionally less well-organised sectors (Millward and Stevens, 1986; Booth, 1989), changes in the legislation governing unions and their relations with employers (Freeman and Pelletier, 1990), the ways in which employers responded to the changed context by either pursuing high commitment policies or operating in an aggressive anti-union manner (Blyton and Turnbull, 2004; Kersley et al., 2006), and ways in which unions sought to respond to continuing decline and the relative success or failure of approaches such as recruitment campaigns among hitherto weakly organised areas, mergers to remain viable organisations, and developing an organising model to extend union recruitment in unorganised areas (Bassett, 1986; Heery et al., 2000; Mason and Bain, 1991; Willman, 1996).

Two important points need to be made about this analysis. First, the decline should not be attributed to any single cause, but rather to the interplay and interaction of them all (Disney et al., 1998; Metcalf, 1991; Waddington, 2003). Second, in changed economic and political circumstances it may be possible for unions

Table 14.2 **Changing levels of union membership**

Year	Unions	Number	Working population (%)	Employees in employment (%)
1979	453	13,289	50	57
1987	330	10,475	37	49
1992	268	9,048	36	32
1995	247	8,031	32	29
1997	234	7,801	31	28
2000	237	7,897	29	27
2001	226	7,781	27	29
2002	216	7,750	27	29
2005	201	7,559	26	29
2006	191	7,603	n/a	n/a

Sources: Annual Report of Certification Officer, Employment Gazette and Labour Force Trends (various)

to exert greater influence on their position and therefore employers may need to assess the circumstances and context in which they respond to employee and union demands differently from those which might have prevailed in the 1980s and early 1990s. After all, 44 of the UK's largest firms continue to recognise and operate with trade unions. Moreover, the overall decline in trade union membership masks some continuing pockets of strength, notably in the public sector, in banking and among professional employees. Of course, the corollary of this is that there are areas of trade union weakness such as in small firms, in newer private establishments, in private services and among young workers.

Many in the trade union movement hoped that the change of government in 1997 would lead to a change of their fortunes as well. However, the statutory union recognition procedures introduced in the Employment Relations Act 1999 were not as strong as some advocates had hoped. From 6 June 2000, the legislation provided that:

> Recognition should be granted where the union can demonstrate 50 per cent plus one membership among the proposed bargaining unit, or, where in a ballot 40 per cent of employees eligible to vote, vote for recognition. Recognition will cover pay, hours and holidays. The procedures will not apply to firms with 20 or fewer employees.

In the first 7 years of operation, of 566 initial applications to the Central Arbitration Committee, only 162 resulted in union recognition (CAC Annual Report, 2007). Beyond the statutory procedure, more recognition agreements were reached voluntarily and the incidence of voluntary recognition had increased sharply in the period under which the legislation was under discussion. Thus it appears as if the changed political climate about the value of trade union recognition has had an impact on the outcome. But smaller workplaces remain a problem area for unions to win members and gain voluntary recognition. In 2005, among workplaces employing fewer than 50 people, union density was 18.7 per cent compared with 38.5 per cent in larger workplaces (Grainger, 2006). Workplaces with under 20 employees continue to be excluded from the scope of statutory recognition.

We also need to consider union membership from the employee's point of view. Kochan (1980) has provided a useful model through which we may consider the line of thinking that most employees may go through in considering whether to join a trade union or not. This is presented in Figure 14.1. This model has

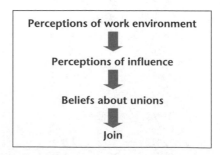

Figure 14.1 Why individuals join unions
Source: Kochan (1980)

recently been tested empirically using UK data and its main hypotheses supported (Charlwood, 2002).

The first stage in the employee's consideration is how they perceive the work environment. If it is a well-paid job, in excellent working conditions, with supportive managers and prospects of career advancement, then it may be the case that individual employees may not feel any need to seek to change this state of affairs. On the other hand, if pay is absolutely or relatively poor, if physical working conditions are poor, if managers are authoritarian and oppressive and future prospects are limited, then the employee may see a need to do something about the situation. However, it is not automatic that this will lead to joining a union and seeking a collective solution to collective problems. In some circumstances the employer may be known to be aggressively anti-union, or the situation may seem so desperate that a more immediate solution is sought. This is likely to be the individual one of seeking employment elsewhere rather than collectively seeking to improve the present employment. However, in some cases it may be perceived that unions might be able to negotiate changes, and certainly combined with union attempts at recruitment may lead to workers joining and seeking recognition. But even at this stage some employees may not support the principle of collective action and seek alternative solutions. At all of these stages in the process, employers may seek to intervene by unilaterally altering pay and conditions of employment, by changing management style or by making senior management views about unions known. Similarly, unions may seek to influence this process by emphasising the areas where they believe they can positively influence outcomes. We will return to these considerations when reviewing strategic options later in this chapter, but first we return to other changes to the environment which need to be borne in mind.

Related to the decline in trade union membership has been a decline in the coverage of collective bargaining and the decentralisation of the locus of bargaining where it continues to exist. Evidence from the surveys showed that the overall proportion of employees covered by collective bargaining fell from 71 per cent in 1984 to 41 per cent in 1998, and 35 per cent in 2005 (Cully *et al.*, 1999; Grainger, 2006). This decline occurred in every sector of the economy, even in the highly unionised public sector, as more groups of workers came under the remit of pay review bodies and the structure of employment was decentralised. National pay determination remains important in the public sector, but in most other parts of the economy where collective bargaining continues it has been decentralised from the multi-employer industry level to single-employer bargaining at either company or plant level. Jackson *et al.* (1993) relate these changes to a desire by employers to relate bargaining strategy to business strategy, and to link bargaining over market relations to bargaining over managerial relations. Even where recognition remained, the scope of collective bargaining has been diminished, especially on non-pay issues (Cully *et al.*, 1999; Kerlsley *et al.*, 2006; Millward *et al.*, 1992). The corollary of all this is that for the majority of employees, and even more so those in the private sector, their pay and conditions are determined unilaterally by management.

A final change in the macro environment of employee relations which managers may wish to take account of has been the decline in an overt manifestation of conflict, namely strikes. In Table 14.3 we present figures on the UK's strike record since the end of the Second World War.

Table 14.3 **The UK strike record after the Second World War**

Period	Number of strikes	Workers involved (000s)	Working days lost (000s)
1950–59	2119	663	3252
1960–69	2446	1357	3554
1970–79	2601	1615	12870
1980–89	1129	1040	7213
1990–99	273	202	660
2000–07	154	413	713

Source: Employment Gazette, Labour Market Trends and Economic and *Labour Market Review* (various)

From this information it can be seen that the number of strikes has declined since the peak decade of the 1970s and especially in the 1990s, though with a slight upward trend again in the mid-2000s. The numbers of workers involved and the number of working days lost have also declined but not as markedly as the number of strikes because these figures are influenced by large strikes which can affect the figures upwards and downwards. Thus the number of working days lost increased sharply in 1996, and again in 2002 and 2007, with large strikes in the transport and public administration sectors. Significantly, these were mainly in the public sector and it is here, where national pay determination has remained, that large national strikes have also remained a feature (Kessler and Bayliss, 1995). To put this another way, the greatest proportion of days lost is attributable to large stoppages, but very few stoppages are large. However, we should not conclude that the decline in strike activity should be equated with or indicative of a decline in industrial conflict, nor of the demise of trade union power (Blyton and Turnbull, 2004). As most commentators agree, both union and management negotiators have absorbed changes in the law regarding the conduct of strikes, especially those on balloting, into their practice (Kessler and Bayliss, 1995). Unions win the vast majority of pre-strike ballots (85 per cent in 2006; 98 per cent in 2007), but in most cases strikes do not occur because further negotiations to reach a final settlement occur (Labour Research Department, 1993). Thus Blyton and Turnbull (1998: 301) conclude that strikes may be viewed as a sign of union weakness, not of strength, because a strong union is able to achieve a negotiated settlement through the *threat* of strike action backed by membership support in a ballot rather than actually conducting a strike.

One final point about the decline of strikes in the UK needs to be made. It has not been a uniquely British phenomenon and, notwithstanding the acknowledged difficulties of comparing like with like, the incidence of strikes fell considerably in almost all industrial countries. Indeed it was only in the 1990s rather than the 1980s that the UK's position in any international league table changed to show relatively less incidence. Thus it is not possible to attribute the decrease of strikes in the UK solely, or even primarily, to changes in legislation under previous Conservative governments. Edwards (1995), for example, examines the interplay of five explanations for the decline in strike rates – economic conditions, the changing structure of employment, legal restrictions, improved means of dispute resolution and 'better industrial relations'. Like our examination of the reasons for union decline, it is safer to conclude that all of these factors played a part and not to attribute mono-causal explanations to any one of them. Rather it is better to follow the conclusions of Blyton and Turnbull (1998: 303) that 'over the long run, strikes have tended to occur in waves' and that their analogy of the spiral captures the interplay of continuity and change in the wavelike movements.

Faced with demands from a trade union for recognition, managers have conventionally adopted one of three broad strategies.

1. They could agree to the principle of recognition and seek to negotiate a recognition agreement with the trade union or trade unions which would establish the procedural parameters of the relationship.

2. They could seek to avoid employee demands for recognition by managing the employment relationship in such a way that employees feel no desire or need to seek union representation. They believe that the way the organisation is managed takes account of employee views and offers satisfactory rewards and working conditions that compare well in any comparison that may be made with similar organisations whether unionised or not.

3. They could seek to avoid recognition at all costs and may operate in what has become known as the 'black hole' of neither high commitment work practices nor traditional pluralist industrial relations.

Let us examine each of these possibilities – or strategic options – in turn.

A union-recognition strategic option

Recognition of one or more trade unions for collective bargaining implies that the employer is willing to reach joint agreements over certain areas of decision-making about the employment relationship and that consequently these will no longer be areas of unilateral management decision-making. Some might see this as a loss of management prerogative, others that joint decision-making is more likely to be acceptable to employees and therefore more likely to be adhered to and operated in practice than decisions solely made by managers. We have already discussed various ways in which employees can resist management decisions that are perceived as being contrary to their interests. Although employers may be faced with demands for union recognition, the process of reaching agreement with the union(s) is likely to lead to a clarification and codification of a number of key issues. One would be the establishment of the bargaining unit – the group of employees to be covered. Management may be willing to bargain over the pay and conditions of production workers, but not for supervisors or support staff. The union may only have organised production workers and therefore only seek recognition for that group, or it may seek a wider recognition covering all employees up to managerial grades.

Negotiations over recognition are also likely to confront a key issue that is seen by many managers to be at the heart of policy on union recognition. That is whether there will be more than one union or just a single union covering all the employees in the agreed bargaining unit. In Britain unions emerged as *trade* unions representing employees in particular trades and therefore their multiplicity in any workplace was the norm. In the 1960s and 1970s in particular it was alleged that the multi-union nature of unionised workplaces caused particular difficulties for British managers, especially over demarcation disputes, that were not faced by managers in West Germany where a smaller number of industry-based unions had been created after the Second World War. In subsequent years inward-investing companies which were prepared to recognise unions preferred to do so on a single-union basis or not at all. This was not an option for already unionised workplaces, but the 1990s saw moves towards the establishment of single-table bargaining where all the recognised unions in an organisation negotiated common pay and conditions agreements together rather than a series of separate agreements (Gall, 1994).

The final area of decision-making in a recognition agreement is over which issues are to be part of the substantive agreements, that is, which areas of decision-making are to be subject to joint decision-making. These are likely to include basic pay and conditions of employment such as hours of work and holidays, but when unions are strong they seek to extend the scope of collective bargaining into other areas such as pensions or training, whereas management might seek to restrict the areas covered when they feel that bargaining power is in their favour. Finally, a recognition agreement would also contain provisions for the resolution of disputes through conciliation or arbitration. Clauses would probably exclude the use of strikes or lockouts until these procedures had been exhausted, thus providing one of the key benefits to management of formal recognition – the avoidance of informal or wild cat strikes while disputes are considered through the formal procedures.

There is evidence of both de-recognition and marginalisation of unions in the 1980s and 1990s. Gall and McKay (1994) estimate that 200,000 employees were affected by explicit de-recognition strategies, but there is evidence of specific industries being greatly influenced by such an approach, for example provincial newspapers (Smith and Morton, 1993) and docks (Turnbull and Weston, 1993). However, with the change in political climate after 1997 Gall and McKay (1999) showed that the number of cases of recognition outnumbered those of de-recognition. Some employers have sought to marginalise unions by reducing the numbers of shop stewards, reducing union organising facilities, and increasing direct communication to individual employees and reducing the scope of collective bargaining. In both de-recognition and marginalisation, managers have to determine whether they are going to pursue a union substitution or a union avoidance policy and we consider different possible approaches to this in the next section.

A substitution strategic option

Beaumont (1987) distinguishes between union substitution and union avoidance as approaches to staying or becoming non-union. In considering union substitution approaches it might be useful to consider what unions have to offer employees and relate this to the chain of thought that employees might go through in deciding to join or not, which was discussed above. The implication is that if management can intervene to influence any of these decisions then the outcome may be that employees do not perceive any need to join a union as they do not believe that it would be able to improve the terms and conditions of employment or the nature of the employment relationship.

Essentially trade unions have three broad claims to make in order to attract employees into membership – that they can:

1. improve pay and conditions of employment through the strength of collective bargaining;

2. provide individual employees with insurance and protection against arbitrary management decisions;

3. provide membership services such as cheaper insurance and holidays.

The vulnerabilities of unions are therefore that employers are leading payers and providers of good working conditions in an industry or geographical area so that employees do not think that these can be improved on substantially through collective bargaining. Employers could seek to provide alternative channels of 'employee voice' through such devices as open-door systems, employee-based works councils and individual-based employee participation mechanisms (see Chapter 15), so that again employees do not feel that union channels of representation would significantly improve their situation at work. Finally, many alternative providers of membership services exist through other membership and commercial organisations so that this is not likely to be the prime route into union membership for non-members (Whitston and Waddington, 1994; Waddington, 2003). The essence of Beaumont's argument is therefore that employers can seek to introduce policies and practices that substitute for those which might follow from union membership and recognition. Employers can actively pursue such policies and in Chapter 1 we characterised such an approach as being a high commitment–indirect control one. Beaumont (1987) refers to 'household name' non-union companies such as IBM, Marks and Spencer and Hewlett Packard and they are presented as being distinctive from the traditional, sweatshop, non-union employer which we consider next. However, subsequent to Beaumont's analysis even the employment relations practices of his 'household name' companies have come under fire as they have reduced employment levels and evidence has emerged that their purchasing power forces poor employment practices onto their small suppliers (Blyton and Turnbull, 2004).

A 'black hole' strategic option

To the above categories of employer–employee relationships may be added the 'black hole' approach of operating with neither a high commitment–indirect control approach, nor industrial relations. The location of such an approach can be seen in Guest's (1995) fourfold classification of options for managing the employment relationship, as displayed in Figure 14.2.

Beardwell (1997) has researched the characteristics of companies operating in this sphere.

	HRM priority High	HRM priority Low
IR priority High	*New realism* High emphasis on HRM and ER	*Traditional collectivism* Priority to IR without HRM
IR priority Low	*Individualised HRM* High priority to HRM No IR	*The black hole* No HRM No IR

Figure 14.2 **Options for managing the employment relationship identified by Guest**

While there is no direct union recognition and consequent collective bargaining, there is evidence of a wide variety of pay determination mechanisms being used. The largest single category in his study was non-bargained collective pay, rather than an emphasis on individualised pay which being non-union might at first sight imply. Moreover, there were companies in his study that derived their pay structures, either wholly or in part, from collective bargaining mechanisms in the industry to which the firm belonged. The main conclusion was that pay settlement mechanisms were often unsystematic and this in turn reflected the absence of a clear overall strategy towards the management of the employment relationship. It is therefore no surprise to learn that not only did these firms lack unions, they also lacked personnel specialists, had patchy information flows and weak information channels. Or as Brown (1994) put it, 'we are not witnessing the emergence of a brave new world of non-union HRM but a tired old world of unrepresented labour'.

Case Study 14.2

Union recognition in Kleensweep

Kleensweep is a UK-based company which distributes hardware goods and garden supplies to a chain of retail shops throughout the country. Up until now the company has operated what might best be called a 'dual human resourcing' strategy. The 50 staff at head office in the Midlands are relatively well paid compared to other companies in the distribution industry. Other terms and conditions are perceived as being good, including a non-contributory pension scheme, share options and open access to senior managers. Most of these staff have been with the company a long time and willingly work long hours, especially at times of peak seasonal demand. These employees are not unionised and the company has had no requests for union recognition for this group of staff.

The 100 distribution drivers based at 10 depots throughout the UK, on the other hand, are paid around the average for the industry, have quite high levels of turnover and work long overtime hours to supplement their low basic pay. The company has successfully resisted two attempts by the main trade union that represents this grade of worker, Unite, to gain recognition for this group of employees.

Kleensweep has recently acquired a further distribution company in order to complete its national network of depots. This is likely to lead to redundancies in three areas where there is an overlap of depots, but potential expansion of employment in the South West of England and Scotland where the company had only a limited presence. The newly acquired company has a recognition agreement with Unite, for drivers, although not for its head office staff. Although an annual wage agreement is negotiated, depot managers believe that less than half the 60 drivers are members of the union.

Future policy

The board of directors has asked for an assessment of what the company's future policy on union recognition should be. They are particularly concerned about complying with legislation on union recognition but have an underlying preference to remain non-union as the parent company always has been. The board has asked for a report setting out three alternative strategies.

1. *Strategy A* – to adopt a hostile anti-union approach throughout the entire merged company and to de-recognise Unite in the newly acquired company.

2. *Strategy B* – to seek to develop and extend the high commitment approach adopted for head office staff, which has not led to any interest in union membership or demands for union recognition, to the rest of the company.

3. *Strategy C* – to consider extending union recognition in the company given the inheritance of this among drivers in the newly acquired company.

In reviewing the options here you should consider bargaining units, level and scope.

Activity 14.3   Strategic options on union recognition at Kleensweep

What do you see as the advantages and disadvantages of attempting to follow each of these possible strategic directions?

'Partnership' as an alternative strategic option for conducting the employment relationship?

During the late 1990s and early years of the new millennium a 'partnership approach' to the employment relationship became increasingly popular and was adopted by some employers who were faced with a claim for recognition by one or more unions or who felt a need to reassess and change their approach and relationship with their employees and their representative bodies (with reference to the latter see Gall, 2001; Haynes and Allen, 2001).

This chapter has emphasised that managing the employment relationship involves both conflict and cooperation. Many studies view the adoption of a partnership approach to employee relations as being more reflective of a cooperative, joint problem-solving atmosphere in employer–employee relations, where employers, employees and trade unions work together to achieve common goals, such as fairness and competitiveness, perhaps with some reassurances by employers over employment security. This is very different to an employment relationship dominated by adversarialism and conflict purported to be prominent in the UK during the 1970s, 1980s and early 1990s.

Various commentators have advanced different and contentious reasons why some employers, employees and their representative bodies believed it timely to embrace a more conciliatory partnership approach in the workplace. These reasons embrace the following:

● The need for employers to come to terms with increasing employee rights and a changing legal context impacting a variety of workplace matters. This changing legal environment has, in a variety of instances, required employers to engage in a dialogue with employees; for example, over the regulation of working time (Tailby and Winchester, 2005). It has also been suggested that further catalysts encouraging employers and employees to give consideration to a partnership approach have been the introduction of the statutory union recognition procedure in 2002 (Tailby and Winchester, 2005) and, more recently, the 2004 Information and Consultation of Employee Regulations (Guest *et al.*, 2008).

- An embryonic 'socio-political' nexus in the workplace focused on issues such as work–life balance, employee-initiated flexibility at work, and a greater concern with employer and employee conduct and behaviour (Martinez Lucio and Stuart, 2002).

- A belief on the part of management that employees and/or their representatives' involvement can help to facilitate organisational change emanating from competitive or financial crisis or as a result of mergers and acquisitions (Oxenbridge and Brown, 2002 and 2005).

- A belief by some trade union officials and representatives that a partnership approach might provide an opportunity for trade union renewal (Ackers and Payne, 1998).

In the UK this idea of partnership at work gained support from, and has been promoted by, a variety of people, institutions and organisations, for example the notion of partnership formed part of the Labour Party manifesto prior to its general election success in 1997. Tony Blair, Prime Minister at the time, explicitly stated in the foreword to the 1998 'Fairness at Work' white paper that a main element of the Employment Relations Act 1999 was to promote a partnership approach in the workplace (DTI, 1998). Government support for partnership at work was further demonstrated by the establishment of a 'Partnership Fund' which between 1999 and its closure in 2004 distributed over £12.5 million which funded 249 workplace partnership projects and a further 20 strategic projects (dberr.gov.uk accessed 4 June 2008; Terry and Smith, 2003). Support for the notion of partnership at work has also been displayed by the Trades Union Congress (TUC) as evidenced in its policy document *Partners for Progress: Winning at Work* (TUC, 2001b) and by the establishment, in 2001, of its 'Partnership Institute' which provides advisory and consultancy services to unions and employers (see www.partnership-institute.co.uk). The Involvement and Participation Association (IPA) has been an enduring supporter of partnership at work and, like the TUC, provides advisory and consultancy services to employees, unions and employers (see www.ipa-involve.com). A more guarded acceptance of partnership has been voiced by the Confederation of British Industry (CBI). It has been concerned that partnership approaches should not be seen to advance the influence of trade unions. Similarly, the Chartered Institute of Personnel and Development (CIPD) has supported the concept as long as the focus is on employer–employee relations rather than employer–trade union relations.

However, and notwithstanding the above overt and/or tentative support for the notion of partnership, Guest and Peccei during 2001, in what is arguably a seminal article, suggested that partnership is 'an idea with which anyone can agree, without having a clear idea of what they are agreeing about' (2001: 207), while Upchurch *et al.* suggested that partnership was a contentious subject (2003: 1). These concerns emanate from, and are reflective of the debates as to the meaning of the notion of partnership, the frames of reference informing the notion (see the first part of this chapter), the degree to which outcomes benefit employers or employees and their representative bodies (Kelly, 1996, 1999, 2005; Martinez Lucio and Stuart, 2002, 2005; Whitson, 2001; Wray, 2001), and the ability of a partnership approach to be sustainable in the long term (Brown, 2000; Bacon, 2001; Sisson and Marginson, 2003; Guest *et al.*, 2008).

In the following section of the chapter we briefly consider some of the issues arising from these concerns and debates.

Whilst the precise definition of partnership has been the subject of debate there have been a variety of published definitions of partnership emanating from bodies such as the IPA, ACAS, the EC, the TUC, various trade unions, the CBI and the CIPD. For example, in 1997 the IPA articulated a series of 'principles' and 'practices' associated with a partnership approach, they include:

● commitment to business success;
● employment security;
● employee voice;
● sharing the success of the organisation with all employees;
● training and development; and
● flexible job design and direct participation (IPA, 1997).

A notion of partnership based on the continental European model has been put forward by the British Trades Union Congress. This offers a legitimate role by both governments and employers to trade unions as representatives of employees and their involvement in various institutional fora at the economy and workplace levels. The TUC's formally adopted 'Six Principles of Partnership' include the following:

● a joint commitment to the success of the enterprise;
● unions and employers recognising each other's legitimate interests and resolving differences in an atmosphere of trust;
● a commitment to employment security;
● a focus on the quality of working life;
● transparency and sharing information;
● mutual gains for unions and employers, delivering concrete improvements to business performance, terms and conditions, and employee involvement. (TUC, 2001b)

While these two lists of 'partnership principles' do contain common elements, it is interesting to note that the TUC's definition of partnership explicitly identifies a place for union involvement, while the IPA's list refers to 'employee voice' and 'direct participation', implying that trade unions are not the sole preserve of independent employee representation, and we have already noted the reluctance of such bodies as the CBI and the CIPD to include reference to trade union involvement in their discussions of partnership, preferring to talk about direct employee engagement.

It is such ambiguities regarding the key ingredients of partnership arrangements that contributed to Guest and Peccei's conclusion that:

There is, in fact, no agreed definition or conceptualisation of partnership in either the academic or policy literature. Different writers tend to adopt different definitions and to emphasise potentially different elements and dimensions of partnership. Moreover, existing conceptualisations fail to provide a clear picture of the actual practices that characterise partnership systems, and of the specific principles that might underpin them.

(Guest and Peccei, 2001: 208)

According to Guest and Peccei (2001), a greater understanding of the varying interpretations of partnership may be gained by considering the different 'frames of reference' being adopted by the different protagonists of partnership. Just like the differing views held by Unity Fairweather and Polly Politick, mentioned earlier in this chapter, interpretations of partnership will be influenced by individuals' perspective on the employment relationship.

Guest and Peccei argue that a pluralist perspective on partnership accepts that a difference of interests may exist between coalitions of employees and employers. Such a perspective embraces a central role for directly elected employee representatives, usually in the form of trade union representation, to help secure an independent employee voice in the workplace. As examples of a pluralist approach to partnership, on a European-wide level, Guest and Peccei (2001: 209) make reference to the legislation on the Social Chapter and on European Works Councils.

A unitarist perspective on partnership, according to Guest and Peccei (2001: 209), can be seen to encompass two different 'strands' both of which seek to 'integrate employer and employee interests, while at the same time maximising employee involvement and commitment to the organisation'. The first strand, they identify, rests on employer policies and procedures that encompass financial incentives and shared ownership as the focus for cementing employer and employee interests. The emphasis, in this form of partnership, is on different forms of profit-sharing and share ownership which encourage employees to take a financial stake in their organisation. The second strand centres on various forms of direct employee participation and involvement in everyday workplace activities. The presupposition, here, is that employees' best interests are met when they can have some input into decisions which affect their day-to-day work activities, so long as these activities are restricted to work issues rather than wider organisational matters. Such an approach, it is suggested, may be supplemented by 'communication programmes' geared to improve employee commitment to company goals and values. Guest and Peccei (2001: 210) suggest that this approach can indicate a low level of trust and can, therefore, be criticised as being a 'rather one-sided form of partnership'.

Within the unitarist perspective on partnership Guest and Peccei also highlight a much more complex view of partnership emanating from the American literature which centres on maximising employee attachment, commitment and involvement to their company and therefore to its goals and values and to its success in attaining these. Key to this approach is the consistent use of a range of what have been referred to as 'progressive, high-performance, or high-involvement human resource practices in the areas of selection, training, job-design, communications, appraisals, rewards and so on, all designed to maximise individual–organisational linkages and to generate high levels of satisfaction, commitment and loyalty among the workforce' (Guest and Peccei, 2001: 210).

Guest and Peccei go beyond the dual model of pluralist and unitarist perspectives to suggest a third perspective on partnership which they term a 'hybrid' perspective. This 'hybrid' approach embraces elements of both pluralism and unitarism. It reflects the importance of employees being represented in the workplace while also accepting the importance of direct forms of employee involvement and participation. It also recognises the importance of the parties to the employment relationship working together to their mutual advantage. They suggest that this hybrid version is best exhibited by the 'mutual gains' model described by such writers as Kochan and Osterman (1994), 'where employees, both individually and through representatives, work with management to provide shared benefits such as job security and increased flexibility and productivity' (Guest and Peccei, 2001: 210). They further suggest that for this type of employer–employee partnership to flourish there is a need for a formal joint governance system, and that implicit in the model is a belief that formalised representative systems are a prerequisite both to sustain central aspects and processes of partnership and, maybe, to prevent exploitation by management.

Activity 14.4	'Partnership' as a strategic option for conducting the employment relationship

Guest and Peccei (2001) contend that approaches to 'partnership' may be influenced by individuals' perspectives (or frames of reference) on the employment relationship.

1. Consider an organisation for which you have worked or one with which you are familiar. Think about the employee relations context; compare your view of the employee relations context of your chosen organisation with Guest and Peccei's three approaches – pluralist, unitarist and hybrid, and then . . .

2. Assume your chosen organisation is considering changing its employee relationship to one that is more akin to a partnership. Which of the three approaches discussed by Guest and Peccei do you believe would most influence your organisation's approach to partnership?

3. What evidence would you use to support your conclusion?

Guest and Peccei (2001: 211) then argued that it was this 'hybrid' model that seemed to be the foundation of much of the UK policy debate on partnership at work. Certainly, the language used in Labour government publications embraced the tenor of the 'hybrid' approach with an emphasis on shared success and building trust, and this language also concurred with the IPA's position that employee representation need not necessarily be via trade union channels. Trade union statements on the later point, unsurprisingly, disagreed.

While the above analysis is helpful in explaining some of the variations in the positions adopted by protagonists of partnership it is, in many ways (as we have seen earlier in this chapter), reflective of traditional debates in the field of employee relations and HRM. Guest and Peccei acknowledge that the above analysis may simply refocus old debates. However, they, together with others at the time, argued that partnership could be seen as offering 'something distinctive', particularly by building on the notion of 'trust' (Fox, 1974) and the notion of 'mutuality', the idea that while two independent parties may have differing interests they could, at the same time, have shared interests and goals. While Guest and Peccei and other writers recognised that different parties may have varying views as to the exact nature of partnership, there also seemed to be some consensus which contended that the 'key notion underlying partnership was some idea of working effectively together to achieve shared or complementary goals' (Guest and Peccei, 2001: 212). Guest and Peccei, in their research, therefore, focused on identifying the types of institutional arrangements, policies and practices, and the interrelationship between them, which might have engendered this position of 'shared working' to the mutual benefit of both parties.

They gathered data from both employer and employee representatives of a sample of organisations, which they identified from the IPA's database, and which were representative of organisations which could be categorised as being at various stages of partnership relations. Their focus was to try to determine to what extent organisations claiming to operate on a partnership basis were actually demonstrating 'partnership practices' which could also be identified as leading to 'beneficial outcomes' for both parties. 'Beneficial outcomes', in this instance, for the employer might include higher employee commitment, a greater willingness to contribute, less absence, less labour turnover, less industrial conflict and superior performance. For the employees the benefits might include opportunities to exercise greater autonomy and direct participation, a more positive psychological contract, and an opportunity to share in the financial gains through employee share ownership. They also highlighted that there may also be beneficial gains for employee representatives, such as greater influence over employment issues and better representative organisational structures (Guest and Peccei, 2001: 215).

However, they highlighted that their results were 'far from straightforward' and that there were potential dangers in employers being selective about the practices that they choose to adopt to support a partnership approach. Their evidence concluded that partnerships seem to be more successful with the implementation of a 'bundle of partnership practices'. The most positive outcomes for all parties seem to emerge where organisations employed 'a high trust' form of partnership which encompassed a combination of direct and representative forms of participation, job design, a quality focus, and the use of employee share ownership. Using only some of these, most notably representative participation in isolation, would not produce similar benefits; indeed, if used on its own the evidence suggested that it had a negative impact on sales and profit (Guest and Peccei, 2001: 231–2).

Given that a distinguishing feature of partnership, according to Guest and Peccei, was a combination of 'trust and mutuality', it is interesting to note that they highlighted that for their sample of organisations, ones in which trust and mutuality might be expected to be highly visible, that the level of direct participation in work decisions and representative participation in wider organisational policy decisions was generally low, and that a greater emphasis seemed to be placed on employee contribution than on the promotion of employee welfare, rights and independent representation. Such managerial predispositions might have given rise to the conclusion that some employers displayed low trust in their employees and their representatives and that mutuality might have been somewhat balanced in favour of some managements, with the outcome that employers might have appeared to be gaining more from the operation of partnership practices.

Accepting potential problems with the direction of causality and the contentious nature of the items chosen for measurement purposes, Guest *et al.* more recently, using data from the Workplace Employment Relations Survey 2004 (Kersley *et al.*, 2006), confirmed their previous findings that 'partnership practices' seemed to display that 'the balance of advantage and power lay with management and as a result greater priority was given to performance management than to any sharing of control' (Guest *et al.*, 2008: 135). Thus, Guest and his colleagues were able to conclude that, 'there is little evidence from WERS 2004 of the kind of mutuality that we might expect to find in partnership at work' (Guest *et al.*, 2008: 135).

It is perhaps the potential existence of such an unbalanced position that enables some commentators to argue that entering into partnership arrangements can be detrimental to trade union, and hence employee, well-being. On some occasions, for instance when faced with managerial initiatives to erode terms and conditions of employment or when management do not seem to be taking employees' grievances seriously, the interests of employees are so different from management's that employees and their unions need the capacity to resist management. Kelly (1996, 1999) suggests that it is employee and union militancy that mobilises workers and unions to take action. He argues that conciliatory partnerships with employers by employees and their representatives diminish the latter's willingness and ability to challenge management when the need arises. He and other writers have highlighted evidence that indicates that partnership arrangements can also result in concession-bargaining, a limiting of the bargaining agenda, and the adoption of new (often non-union) consultative committees that erode or replace collective bargaining (Kelly, 1996; Bacon and Story, 2000; Watling and Snook, 2003). More recently Kelly contrasted the employment, wages and conditions, profit margins and union density outcomes in partnership and non-partnership organisations. He found scant support for the 'mutual gains' thesis. There seemed to be little evidence that workers were paid more highly or secured more favourable terms and conditions in partnership firms and their security of employment appeared worse than in the non-partnership organisations, at least in those sectors having to endure cutbacks and savings (Kelly, 2005: 202).

The potential for a partnership arrangement to be balanced in favour of management is bolstered by the long-term trade union membership decline and diminishing coverage of collective bargaining recorded earlier in this chapter (Kersley *et al.*, 2006). It is this trajectory of long-term union decline, however, which proved to be the catalyst for other early partnership commentators to be optimistic about the potential outcomes of partnership arrangements. Writers in this camp emphasised the fact that support for partnership by various bodies and organisations, including the government, and the pervasive influence of the European dimension might have afforded the potential to create a new type of engagement that might provide an accommodating employee relations landscape, in which trade unions could have the potential to regain the initiative and work to re-establish their institutional presence in the UK. According to some early commentators, 'social partnership appeared to be taking root' (Ackers and Payne, 1998; Brown, 2000).

It can be discerned from the above that early contributions to the partnership debate might be designated as either 'advocates' or 'critics' of partnership as an alternative strategic option for conducting the employment relationship. However, during more recent times according to Tailby and Winchester 'a wide range of intermediary positions has now been inserted in the debate' (2005: 438).

Reflecting the 'contentious reasons' for partnership expressed at the commencement of this section (p. 459) writers have considered partnership at work from a variety of different perspectives, using different research methodologies in different sectors, product and labour markets, including the investigation of non-union partnership arrangements (Upchurch *et al.*, 2006).

Notwithstanding the difficulties of evaluating this burgeoning literature Tailby and Winchester (2005) conclude that some patterns do emerge from the findings of these various studies. For example, a number of the early partnership agreements seemed to emanate out of organisational crisis where organisational survival was paramount or where organisations had given previous consideration to union de-recognition (Heery, 2002). Company financial difficulties, the need for organisational change, the desire to harmonise terms and conditions of employment and organisational competitiveness difficulties all seemed to be precursors to the arrival of partnership agreements in the organisations studied by Oxenbridge and Brown (2005). For them, mutuality of interest as an outcome of partnership seemed to be less important than securing union assistance in supporting a managerial response to these various organisational crises. As we have already seen this lack of mutuality was also a concern for Guest and Peccei (2001). Even Ackers' (Ackers and Payne, 1998) early optimism for union revival as a possible outcome of partnership seems to have diminished in his more recent work on employee involvement and partnership when he and his colleagues conclude that managers appeared to be shifting away from the, '1980s dualism of parallel union EI channels, either by drawing the unions into closer partnerships or by marginalising it, even in strongly unionised companies' (Ackers *et al.*, 2005: 41).

Given the above it would seem reasonable to conclude that, 'partnership presents high risks, rather than clear opportunities for trade unions' (Tailby and Winchester, 2005: 439). Even where partnership arrangements exist in non-union environments there is evidence to suggest that the reality of the 'partnership strategy both confirms and consolidates existing power discrepancies and presents only a façade of economic democracy . . .' (Upchurch *et al.*, 2006: 408).

While there are organisational and sectoral partnership arrangements still being concluded, for example the agreement arrived at during June 2007 in the papermaking industry between the Confederation of Paper Industries and Amicus and the TGWU (who have since merged to form Unite) and the GMB (see www.eurofound.europa.eu, 2007), the phenomenon does not seem to be extensive (Bacon, 2001). Indeed, Guest *et al.* (2008) cautiously conclude that Workplace Employment Relations Survey (WERS) 2004 panel data indicates 'no growth in partnership practices' (Guest *et al.*, 2008: 148–9).

Exhibit 14.1

Industry level partnership agreement

The papermaking industry in the UK employs over 10,000 people spread across 60 different geographical locations. Global competition is intense and the industry has suffered soaring energy prices. The papermaking sector is one of the few exceptions in the UK private sector to have maintained national level industry-wide collective bargaining arrangements. (The other sectors are printing, electrical contracting and engineering construction.)

A dispute over pay during 2004 was the catalyst which encouraged the employers and the trade unions to give consideration to improve ways of working together. In June of 2005 the bargaining parties namely the Confederation of Paper Industries (CPI) and the three recognised trade unions – AMICUS and the Transport and General Workers' Union (T&G), who have since merged to form Unite – plus the GMB general trade union decided to review and revise their existing national agreement which they believed was dated and did not take into account new employment legislation, 'green' and social issues, the globalisation of the sector and the competitive pressures this created for the industry. They gained support for this endeavour from the Department for Trade and Industry (now the Department for Business, Enterprise and Regulatory Reform (BERR)) and assistance from the Advisory and Conciliation and Arbitration Service (ACAS).

During a two-year period of consultation and negotiation involving a joint union–employer group with an independent chairperson – Professor Frank Burchill – the parties worked together to construct a modern agreement which would benefit both employers and employees and which would bolster the industry's requirement to enhance competitiveness. There was also a desire to ensure that the new agreement would ensure that the working practices and conditions would meet current and future needs. A draft agreement was reached in November 2006 and following further talks the agreement was overwhelmingly endorsed by union members in a ballot in June 2007.

The agreement is entitled the 'Papermaking Partnership' and according to its preamble it

> is intended to set standards across the industry and the Partners are committed to supporting successful companies in setting higher standards in the workplace.

The Partnership agreement covers production and engineering workers represented by the union partners. The accord has three main supporting themes, or as the agreement entitles them 'the three pillars of partnership'. The agreement summarises these three pillars using the following headings.

Working Together

The parties will, 'work together in a spirit of cooperation, based on mutual trust and respect, to maintain harmonious, productive and fulfilling workplaces, resolving problems and differences at the earliest possible stage through regular and open dialogue'. This element also embraces provisions on trade union recognition, union representatives, dispute resolution, information and consultation, dignity at work and privacy.

Grow Together

Through partnership the parties seek 'to maintain a successful papermaking industry as part of the UK manufacturing economy and strive for continuous improvement to the performance and profitability of companies and to the living standards and quality of life of employees'. This element also embraces provisions on pay, efficiency and productivity, working hours and work-life balance.

Stay Together

Working in partnership the signatories will overcome, 'short-term obstacles to achieve security of employment through successful companies employing a well-trained, fully-utilised, and flexible workforce'. This element also embraces provisions on learning and skills, temporary staffing, lay-off and short time working, health and safety, sickness and cancer screening.

A standing national Partnership Committee will oversee the application and the operation of the agreement. It will assess the effects of external changes upon the agreement, share information and promote the interests of the sector to the government at both national and European levels.

At the time the draft agreement was reached the Assistant General Secretary of AMICUS, Tony Burke, commented:

The new agreement is an important step in securing modern working terms across the industry, such as work-life balance, actively promotes learning and skills, provides a safer workplace, promotes dignity at work and gives employees an opportunity to be informed and consulted and actively involved in improving the performance of their workplace.

At the same time Martin Oldman, the Director General of the Confederation of Paper Industries said:

The new agreement takes us away from the old adversarial approach to a better common platform to jointly tackle the issues that hamper productivity and profitability in the workplace.

Whilst Professor Birchill suggested that:

The agreement provides an essential framework for all the parties to work as partners in talking the challenges together so that both mutual and different interests can be accommodated in securing a healthy future for the papermaking industry.

Sources: The Papermaking Partnership agreement can be found at www.amicustheunion.org/pdf/ CPI%20Partnership%20Agreement%20May%2007.pdf (accessed July 2008); Unite the Union news archive is at www.amicustheunion.org/Default.aspx?page=7302 (accessed July 2008) and www.amicustheunion. org/Default.aspx?page=5038 (accessed July 2008); Eironline www.eurofound.europa.eu/eiro/2007/08/ articles/uk0708019i.htm (accessed July 2008).

Given the above research and debate it might be concluded that 'the jury is still out' as to whether partnership is a viable and potentially enduring strategic option for conducting the employment relationship. If it is to be viable and enduring it seems that there are a number of potential barriers that will need to be resolved.

First, if it is accepted that the notions of 'mutuality' and 'trust' lie at the heart of partnership arrangements (Dietz, 2004; Guest and Peccei, 2001; Guest *et al.*, 2008), the question of how balanced the mutual exchange must be for trust to develop will need to be resolved. This will depend, in part, on management's attitudes towards their workers and their representatives. Arguably the achievement of a balance will require a genuine long-term strategic commitment on the part of management to work in a 'truly collaborative' way, characterised in Chapter 1 of this book as adopting a high commitment HR strategy. If employees perceive management's approach to be opportunistic or an attempt to marginalise them or their representatives, disillusionment will occur and the cooperative relationship will not endure.

Second, given that the evidence seems to suggest that the most 'successful' partnerships exist where both direct and indirect forms of representation are employed (Guest and Peccei, 2001; Guest *et al.*, 2008) views have been expressed that there is a need for greater legislative support for employee representation, be it trade union representation or otherwise (Upchurch *et al.*, 2003). Such legal support is particularly needed if the representational body is not a trade union. Many studies argue that the lack of statutory support for non-union bodies constitutes part of the reason why such representational arrangements fail (Gollan, 1999; Kidger, 1992; Terry, 1999; Watling and Snook, 2003; Upchurch *et al.*, 2006). Currently, such institutional support from the UK government is conspicuous by its absence (see DBERR, 2007).

Third, there is arguably a need for greater economic stability and a reduction in the short-term perspective of most employers. This, together with sustained high levels of employment, would engender an economic context more conducive for management to commit to greater employee job security. The absence of such economic stability makes the achievement of a 'mutual gains' culture less likely (Upchurch *et al.*, 2003). From the perspective of mid-2008 with the current 'credit crunch', the prospects of economic recession and increasing incidents of industrial action, particularly in the public sector (see Office for National Statistics, 2008), current and nascent partnership arrangements might find themselves facing challenging times.

The final issue potentially to be resolved is the acceptance of a partnership arrangement by the general workforce of an organisation. The majority of research so far has concentrated on employer and trade union representatives' views of partnership. There is a need, in the future, for even more research to ascertain the views of ordinary workers on partnership arrangements. If the workforce perceives partnerships simply to result in work intensification without commensurate improvements in terms and conditions they will reject the partnership paradigm (Danford *et al.*, 2004; Tailby *et al.*, 2004).

It is not unreasonable to suggest that many of these issues have still to be worked through by employers and employees, and that some of them are beyond the immediate control of management and the workforce, consequently they are not easily determined. Conflict and cooperation will be a pervasive aspect of the employment relationship even for those organisations moving towards partnership relations. Perhaps for these organisations the notion of partnership is better characterised as a 'continuum', reaching from those establishments in the early stages of adopting partnership practices to those establishments demonstrating high commitment HR strategies. Maybe 'partnering' as a term should be adopted as denoting a process shaped by specific and, at times, contradictory forces embracing economic and organisational factors, trade union factors and the political and regulatory contexts (Stuart and Martinez Lucio, 2005; Tailby and Winchester, 2005), which employers and employees may engage with and be more or less successful at managing, rather than 'partnership' which seems to denote an end state and an end in itself rather than a means to an end.

Activity 14.5   'Partnership' or 'partnering'?

Re-read Chapter 1 of this book.

1. To what extent do you believe that the term 'partnering' might be more appropriate than 'partnership' to describe the possible approach to the employment relationship outlined in the last section of this chapter?

2. Give reasons for and against such a view.

Conclusion

Strategic human resourcing is an ongoing process which itself involves cooperative work by managers who may well have different and conflicting priorities and values. This was demonstrated in the Moddens case study back in Chapter 1. But the strategy-making process then has to deal with the challenge of coming to terms with the multiplicity of potentially conflicting groups and individuals that make the broader organisation. Ways have to be found of managing differences and conflicts so that cooperative work can be done to sufficient a level to enable the organisation to continue healthily into the future. In this chapter we have demonstrated the necessity of analysing the events which occur in any specific organisation within a *processual* and *pluralist* framework. This is one which is sensitive both to the depth of the underlying conflicts which exist in workplaces and to the variety of ways in which these conflicts can be expressed or 'brought to the surface'.

We have also identified management–union institutionalised arrangements as one of the strategic options that may be followed to handle conflicts and differences. And this option is set alongside others. More recently a possible further approach of 'partnership' has been identified but this is seen as a problematic concept because of its variety of meanings and interpretations. Potentially these may seek to deny that the employment relationship involves both conflict and cooperation. The processual approach adopted in this book, however, emphasises the dual nature of the employment relationship involving both cooperation and conflict, not in a polarised, alternative way but intertwined and interrelated. Partnering is suggested as a way of bridging the gap.

Summary

In this chapter the following key points have been made:

- People tend to think about employment relations and organisational conflicts in one of two major ways. The first, associated here with Unity Fairweather, sees organisations as big systems which can be managed to achieve consensus and fully shared goals and priorities across the organisation. This is a systems-based and unitary perspective. The second is a processual and pluralist perspective, argued for here by Polly Politick. This sees managing organisations, and human resourcing issues specifically, as a process of continually adjusting, adapting and changing to cope with the constant interplay of pressures towards cooperation and pressures towards conflict.

- Conflict and cooperation are not opposites. They always exist alongside each other and, indeed, feed off each other.

- Conflicts exist at two levels: at the level of interests and at the level of behaviour (and activity).

- At the level of behaviour, underlying conflicts can be expressed in a wide variety of ways – these ranging from uncooperative behaviour or absenteeism to destructive behaviour or withdrawal of labour.

- Different expressions or manifestations of underlying conflicts are sometimes alternatives to each other (going on strike might replace working to rule, for example) or may reinforce each other (a strike threat might be reinforced by workplace belligerence).

- Trade union membership has declined markedly since 1979, but for an interplay of reasons rather than a single prime cause.

- The proportion of employees whose pay is determined through collective bargaining has also declined and the locus of bargaining has shifted from the industry to the single employer level.

- Various measures indicate that strike activity has also declined, but this is a feature of many Western capitalist economies and thus cannot be attributed to a UK-unique feature such as the Conservative government's legislation of the 1980s.

- The decline of strike activity is not to be equated with a decline in conflict in the employment relationship.

- Management–union arrangements represent one human resourcing strategic option relevant to conflict management. An alternative to it is a substitution approach (where management provide the benefits which union membership can give through other means – typically involving indirect control/high commitment practices). Another alternative is to allow a 'black hole' to persist – a relatively 'loose' strategy where there is neither a union–management relationship nor an attempt to build high commitment relationships directly with employees as individuals.

- 'Partnership' as a model of the employment relationship is shown to have a variety of meanings and to be problematic.

Discussion questions

1. Which perspective is the more 'realistic' about life in work organisations and management – that held by Unity Fairweather or Polly Politick? Consider this in the light of what you have personally seen in organisational contexts (including what you might have seen in your school, college or university).

2. Account for the decline in union membership in the UK after 1979.

3. Explore ways in which there might be an individual manifestation of conflict at work.

4. What are the prospects for union renewal and revival in the next five years?

5. What does the notion of 'partnership' mean to you? Is there any evidence of any of the meanings of partnership being practised in a workplace with which you are familiar?

Further reading

For a fuller discussion of conflict readers are advised to consult Watson (2008). Edwards (1986) provides both a critique of the Marxist analysis of conflict and an exposition based on a materialist analysis of the employment relationship.

An excellent coverage of issues such as union membership, recognition, collective bargaining and conflict is to be found in Blyton and Turnbull (2004). You could also usefully consult Edwards (2003).

15

Employee participation, involvement and communications

John Leopold

Learning outcomes

Having read this chapter and completed its associated activities, readers should be able to:

- Differentiate between industrial democracy, employee participation and employee involvement
- Explore different objectives held by managers, employees and trade unions in terms of employee involvement
- Consider these in terms of a participation continuum
- Review movements in employee participation in terms of waves or cycles
- Critically examine examples of representative participation
- Review and evaluate a number of forms of employee involvement
- Assess the potential impact of European Union policy and practice
- Show, through a case study, ways in which potentially conflicting objectives of participation and involvement schemes might be related to an organisation's overall human resourcing strategy

Industrial democracy, employee participation and employee involvement

Hyman and Mason (1995) offer a clear differentiation between three approaches to the employment relationship, related to the radical, pluralist or unitarist frame of reference. Industrial democracy flows from the radical frame of reference and involves a profound reordering of work relations which would allow workers to secure access to control over the means of production. This approach focuses on democratic control of the organisation, and while current at various points earlier in the twentieth century, is a concept which has disintegrated as a set of ideas and practice (Hyman and Mason, 1995: 8). The term 'industrial democracy' is not to be confused with the approach adopted by British unions in the 1970s in advocating worker representation at board level through statutory rights (Bullock Report, 1977). This approach is an example of Hyman and Mason's pluralist-based employee participation in that through the state, procedures are advocated or

473

introduced to regulate potential conflict between employers and labour. It is state supported, union initiated, usually based on indirect participation of union (rather than employee) representatives in joint union–management decision-making such as collective bargaining or as part of works councils.

Activity 15.1 Initial analysis of employee involvement and employee participation

Use Table 15.1 to relate to your experience of employee participation and involvement.

1. Which approach is currently dominant in an organisation known to you?
2. Offer specific examples to support your analysis.
3. What do you think are the aims of each type of scheme you have identified?

By contrast, employee involvement is seen as management initiated, attempting to secure the direct involvement of individual employees in various schemes designed to secure employee commitment, motivation and loyalty so as to contribute to the achievement of organisational goals and objectives. Unitarist in essence, this approach usually bypasses or ignores trade union presence, and while becoming the dominant approach in the latter decades of the twentieth century and into the twenty-first, it can in some organisations be found sitting alongside forms of the employee participation approach (Hyman and Mason, 1995; Kersley *et al.*, 2006).

The key points of contrast between employee involvement and employee participation are presented in Table 15.1. We will draw upon these points of distinction as we examine in detail some of the possible institutional forms of employee

Table 15.1 Employee involvement and participation compared

Employee involvement	Employee participation
Management inspired and controlled	Government or workforce inspired; some control delegated to workforce
Geared to stimulating individual employee contributions under strong market conditions	Aims to harness collective employee inputs through market regulation
Directed to responsibilities of individual employees	Collective representation
Management structures flatter, but hierarchies undisturbed	Management hierarchy chain broken
Employees often passive recipients	Employee representatives actively involved
Tends to be task based	Decision-making at higher organisational levels
Assumes common interests between employer and employees	Plurality of interests recognised and machinery for their resolution provided
Aims to concentrate strategic influence among management	Aims to distribute strategic influence beyond management

Source: *Managing Employee Involvement and Participation*, Sage (Hyman, J. and Mason, B. 1995). Reproduced by permission of SAGE Publications, London, Los Angeles, New Delhi and Singapore and produced by permission of Professor Jeff Hyman

participation and involvement. The essential point to establish is that the two approaches are distinct in their origin, advocacy and intended outcomes, and therefore we should avoid using the terms interdependently. Another term that is sometimes used is employee empowerment, but as Lashley (1999) admits there is considerable overlap between empowerment and involvement, participation and commitment. Indeed, many authors use them interchangeably. For Lashley, however, the forms that empowerment might take are the same as those that other authors argue constitute employee involvement and participation. Or as Hales (2000: 503) put it, 'empowerment is, in many respects, the "emperor's new clothes" (Argyris, 1998), the latest in a long line of cognate ideas which shares many of their contradictions'.

We can see this and the distinctions between them by considering the potential range of forms of employee participation and involvement in terms of a participation continuum as in Table 15.2. By use of this continuum we can differentiate clearly those institutional forms of participation and involvement that are management inspired or controlled, such as financial involvement or communication schemes, and those that are more likely to be worker and/or trade union inspired and controlled, such as collective bargaining or the election of worker directors.

Within the continuum there is an area where management and union aspirations overlap so that there are possibilities of areas of joint consultation and decision-making. On the other hand, managers are unlikely to advocate or actively support worker self-management, while unions are unlikely to be comfortable with a management which insists that the organisation has no form of involvement or participation, or only forms that are totally management controlled.

Two other points of distinction will be explored throughout this chapter. First, the distinction between direct involvement/participation of individual employees and of employees being represented indirectly by elected representatives. The other is the distinction between participation/involvement on task or job-related issues, and business-related levels of decision-making. First, it is necessary to trace the origins and trajectories of the various approaches.

Table 15.2 Employee participation and involvement continuum

Management inspired and controlled schemes							Worker/union inspired and controlled schemes	
Right to manage	Financial involvement	Downward communication	Upward problem-solving	Task participation	Consultation	Joint decision-making	Worker representation on final decision-taking bodies	Self-management
Job roles	Profit-sharing	Briefing groups	Quality circles	Job enrichment	Joint consultative committee	Collective bargaining through a joint negotiating committee	Worker directors	Worker cooperatives
	ESOPs	Company reports	Attitude surveys	Team-working	Domestic and European works councils			
			Suggestion schemes			Partnership forums		
						Co-determination		
	Direct					Indirect		Direct

The distinctions we have established between employee involvement and employee participation relate directly to the distinction established in Chapter 1 between a high commitment and a low commitment approach to strategic human resource strategy-making.

Employee involvement, with its emphasis on winning employee cooperation, commitment and contribution, links directly to the high commitment approach and to managing change through employee commitment. The more adversarial union-based employee participation approach relates more to a low commitment route. Of course, as emphasised in Chapter 1, these are ideal types and many organisations try to operate with elements drawn from each. Ultimately managers have to seek to control labour, while at the same time finding ways of unleashing creativity and cooperation. The tensions and dilemmas of this contradiction will unfold in our examination of employee participation and involvement.

Waves or cycles?

Study of the movements in the incidence of various possible forms of employee participation and involvement has centred round the debate on whether fluctuations in the incidence of various forms is best characterised by the metaphor of cycles or of waves. Ramsey (1977, 1983, 1990) was the main advocate of the theory that the incidence of employee participation moves in cycles, in particular that management are forced to introduce concessions of employee participation in periods when a strong organised labour movement presents a challenge to management control, so that management can regain control by appearing to share it and incorporate the threat from trade unions. The converse of this argument is that when the pressure ebbs, so too does the practice of participation. The 'cycles approach' stands in contrast to the evolutionary view which suggests that factors such as more educated employees, an erosion of differential attitudes and managers being more willing to treat their staff as 'resourceful humans' mean that, from the 1970s, employee participation, and joint consultation in particular, is here to stay (Marchington, 1994). Ackers *et al.* (1996), while also refuting the evolutionary view, took issue with the cyclical explanation arguing that employers introduce employee involvement for a variety of reasons, not just to counter strong trade unions. This has been particularly so from the 1980s onwards in response to tighter labour and product markets. Consequently, they argue that while the 'cycles of control' thesis may have had explanatory value up until the 1970s, it no longer does, and these authors prefer the 'waves' metaphor to explain more recent change. Marchington (2005) suggests that cycles may best account for movements in participation at the macro level, whereas explanations of changes in direct involvement require a micro focus on contingencies within the individual firm, especially managerial relations.

The waves metaphor allows for varying degrees of intensity in the incidence of particular forms of participation or involvement, for the movement to be differently paced and timed in different organisations, and for the various forms to have separate rhythms. Marchington (1992) argues that the wave metaphor allows for management simultaneously supporting various forms of participation, even if the objectives of these initiatives are contradictory. The mix of institutional forms being practised in any organisation is related to managerial choice and organisational context, not just to broader movements in the relationship between employers and trade unions (Marchington *et al.*, 1993).

This in turn reminds us of a central point of this book, namely the creation and development of strategic human resourcing and the need to consider the broad goals being pursued and how the specific tools of employee participation and involvement might contribute to them. This cannot be done by considering management alone but requires consideration of potential differences within management, as well as the interplay of tensions and commonalities between employees and unions.

We have already identified that in the 1970s indirect representation schemes such as joint consultation and moves towards worker directors were dominant (Hyman and Mason, 1995: 29–30). These debates were union led, but through the 1980s the focus shifted to management-led initiatives. Marchington (1995: 187) quotes a manager in a food factory who summarises the dynamics of the change in emphasis and position along the participation and involvement continuum: 'It's pushing negotiations down to consultation, and consultation down to communication.' Or as Millward *et al.* (2000: 136) put it: by 1998 'there had been a major shift from collective, representative, indirect and union-based voice to direct, non-union channels'.

Having established these concepts to use in trying to understand and explain employee participation and employee involvement, we now need to examine the operation of a number of specific examples of institutional forms of these practices. We will pay particular regard to the extent of their use, the main purposes behind their use, and finally to problems and issues concerned with their use. We will first address examples of employee participation and then examples of employee involvement.

Representative participation

Joint consultative committees (JCCs) are the most commonly found form of representative participation where management and employees' representatives, usually but not always trade union-based, meet on a regular basis to discuss issues of mutual concern, but where the final decision on any matter under consideration will be taken by management. JCCs have waxed and waned in terms of popularity, which can be interpreted in terms of cycles (Ramsey, 1977). In the 1960s it was argued that they would fade away as workers would prefer to have issues pursued through strong shop steward organisations (Clegg, 1985). But JCCs went through a resurgence in the 1970s, before declining to being present in just under 30 per cent of workplaces by the end of the 1990s (Millward *et al.*, 2000) and further declining to a presence in only 14 per cent of workplaces in 2004 (Kersley *et al.*, 2006). Formal JCCs are more likely in unionised than in non-union companies (29 per cent, cf 8 per cent), in larger companies (73 per cent if more than 500 employees, cf 4 per cent with less than 25 employees) and in the public sector (28 per cent cf 11 per cent). This appears to confirm the duality of representative participation identified by Hyman and Mason (1995: 127), of formal approaches in large manufacturing companies and the public sector, but informal and loose structures in smaller organisations and the service sector.

Exhibit 15.1

Consultation arrangements in a non-unionised organisation

Sense is a charity that works for people with deaf-blind and associated disabilities, providing residential care and other service. It employs 1,500 staff nationwide, split into 5 main regions. The organisation identified that there was no means of communication or mechanism for two-way dialogue with its disparate workforce and that as a result opportunities were being missed to improve the service.

In 2001, Sense asked the Involvement and Participation Association (IPA) to assist with a project to establish a staff consultation forum in one region, Sense East, with a view to rolling this out to the other regions. A constitutional framework for the new consultation forum emerged from workshops, facilitated by the IPA, which looked closely at the nature and role of consultation for groups of senior regional managers, managers and employees, in relation to themselves and the wider organisation.

The constitution sets out the principal aim of the forum as: 'to contribute to the continuous improvement of services and the working environment in Sense East'. This aim is reinforced by commitments to:

- Share information and seek the views of staff through consultation with elected representatives.
- Work to enable employees' views and interests to be expressed more effectively.
- Promote open and timely communications with all staff.

The role of the forum was also discussed in the workshops and agreed to cover:

- Reports on organisational performance and discussion of strategic plans.
- New or significant changes to personnel policies, including health and safety, training and development, and equal opportunities.
- Proposals for, and the implementation of, organisational change.
- All matters where consultation and/or agreement with representatives of the workforce is required by law.

The next stage involved the IPA managing the nomination and balloting process to select the first team of employee representatives for the forum. In total 15 representatives were elected, each representing a constituency based on location or function. In addition, the regional director and HR manager joined the forum as non-elected members.

The IPA trained the newly elected representatives to ensure they were aware of their new role and its responsibilities, and to equip them with the appropriate skills to undertake their duties effectively. This included communication skills and exercises in effective consultation.

Though it is early days, the Regional Direction of Sense East summed up the benefits the new forum was already revealing: 'Implementing the forum has made a positive contribution to two-way communications and has demonstrated real business advantages. It has been a significant factor in Sense East in being recognised for Investors In People.'

Source: Health and Safety Commission and Health and Safety Executive Collective Declaration on Worker Involvement, 2004, reproduced under the terms of the Click-Use Licence

Table 15.3 Models of consultation

	Non-union	Competitive	Adjunct	Marginalistic
Purpose	Prevent unions	Reduce union influence	Problem-solving, cooperative	Symbolic, keep representatives busy
Subject matter	'Hard' and 'soft' information	'Hard' high-level information	'Hard' high-level information	'Soft' information and trivia
Representation	Employees	Shop stewards and other employees	Shop stewards	Union and non-union representatives
	Line or personnel manager	Line manager	Line manager	Personnel manager
Process	Educative	Educative	Mutual influence	Fire-fighting
	Grievance procedure	Advance information	Advance information	
	Chaired by management	Chaired by management	Pre-meetings for reps Rotating chair	
Levels/layers	Establishment level and no links	Establishment level and below	Multi-tiered and clear links	Establishment level, no links

Source: Marchington (1988)

Beyond the debate on the rise and fall of JCCs in practice is the question of the significance of those committees where they continue to exist. Marchington (1988) offers four models of joint consultative committees which might exist and these are presented in Table 15.3.

These alternatives are presented as ideal types, but they serve to stress that joint consultation is not monolithic and that it can vary between organisations as well as within the same organisation over time (Marchington, 1992, 1994). However, the 1998 Workplace Employment Relations Survey (WERS) provided some clear evidence that joint consultative committees were not being used as a substitute for trade union representation when they reported that 'union representation and indirect employee participation go hand-in-hand rather than being substitutes for one another' (Cully *et al.*, 1999: 100). In other words, the adjunct model was to the fore.

In the participation continuum, consultation sits at the boundary between the clearly management led and initiated employee involvement schemes and the more trade union-based collective bargaining and strong worker representation schemes. Part of being on the boundary may lie in the ambiguity of what the participants believe is occurring in joint consultative committees. For management the ability to make the final decision may be to the fore and they may believe that the purpose of the committee is to secure legitimacy for management decisions, to develop cooperative rather than conflictual industrial relations, or even to marginalise trade unions. Union representatives, on the other hand, may blur the distinction between consultation and bargaining and see the consultative committee as a way of gaining leverage over a wider range of issues. Indeed, these ambiguous boundaries may be formalised by some bodies, being titled joint negotiating and consultative committees. Partnership, as discussed in Chapter 14, can then be seen as a way of trying to manage this ambiguity.

> ## Activity 15.2 | Joint consultative committees
>
> 1. Does the experience of organisations with which you are familiar fit into any of these ideal types?
> 2. If not, why not?
> 3. Has there been any attempt to change the focus of these JCCs in recent years? If so, in what ways?

Employee representation on health and safety

Employee participation in health and safety issues is, in the UK at least, an example of participation rights being enshrined in statute, namely the Safety Representatives and Safety Committees Regulations 1997. In force from October 1978, they decisively moved health and safety from being an issue almost wholly within management prerogative, to one with substantial rights for employees. Initially these statutory rights were only conferred on representatives of recognised trade unions, but subsequently the rights were extended to all employees working on offshore installations in 1989, and to all employees in non-unionised situations under the Health and Safety (Consultation with Employees) Regulations 1996. However, representatives of employee safety have fewer statutory powers than their equivalents in unionised workplaces established under the SRSCs Regulations (James and Walters, 2002). But the duty to consult on health and safety can also be achieved through direct communication with employees and the 2004 WERS discovered an increased use of this approach, especially in new and growing workplaces (Kersley *et al.*, 2006).

There remains strong evidence of a well-established link between trade union support for health and safety representation and its effectiveness (Walters, 2000: 418). However, the decline in union recognition and representation through the 1980s and 1990s meant that the proportion of workplaces with SRSC-appointed safety representatives declined (James and Walters, 2002).

The current mixed system of indirect representation through trade union-based representatives, indirect representation via RESs in non-union workplaces, and direct consultation with employees in non-union firms results in weaknesses in representation in non-unionised workplaces and at the same time a decline in the coverage of the more effective union-based system (James and Walters, 2002).

> ## Exhibit 15.2
>
> ### Involvement and participation in workplace health and safety
>
> *Extracts from the Health and Safety Commission and Health and Safety Executive Collective Declaration on Worker Involvement (2004)*
>
> #### 4. A statement on methods of worker involvement
>
> By involvement we specifically mean relationships between workers and employers based on collaboration and trust and nurtured as part of the management of health and safety. The most common and widespread arrangements are those developed through trade union safety representatives

and safety committees. Evidence outlined in section 5 makes clear that trade union safety representatives, through their empowered role for purpose of consultation, often lead to higher levels of compliance and better health and safety performance than in non trade union systems. . . .

However as we noted above many workers, particularly those working in small and medium sized organisations, may not belong to trade unions and do not have access to trade union safety representatives. So we need to encourage workers to want to get involved and we encourage various methods of involvement appropriate to different circumstances. Examples we support for getting involved include ownership by workers of action pans and risk assessments; arrangement for feedback between workers and employers; works councils with dedicated health and safety meetings and honest, open and supportive safety cultures. We will encourage employers to ensure workers take part in health and safety and listen and respond to their opinions, views and advice. . . .

5. A statement of evidence

We believe the statement of principle is based on evidence. We also believe, as described in section 4, that there are different methods for how workers can be actively involved and consulted on health and safety which may be more appropriate in some of the organisations in existence today. Organisations should assess the goals they need to achieve to ensure good occupational health and safety and deploy the appropriate methods and techniques for worker involvement and consultation to achieve them.

There is an imbalance in the available evidence showing the impact of these ranges of methods and this can be summarised diagrammatically [in Figure 15.1].

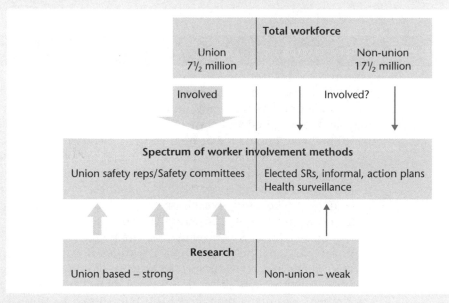

Figure 15.1 Impact of ranges of methods

Source: Health and Safety Commission and Health and Safety Executive Collective Declaration on Worker Involvement, 2004, reproduced under the terms of the Click-Use Licence

Within this large amount of research into the trade union impact there is evidence of the positive impact trade unions have on health and safety performance, particularly where health and safety hazards are overt, showing they 'react by reducing injury rates'.[1] There is further evidence that trade union safety representatives, through their empowered role in consultation 'shows the strongest relationship with safety compliance'.[2]

On the other end of the scale there is less evidence of successful methods of involvement and consultation in small businesses where trade unions are not recognised or are without safety representatives for any other reason. Historically research has not penetrated in these areas and our understanding of what works is limited here. Of course this is the business environment for most businesses and about half the workforce.'

1 Trade unions and Industrial Injury in Great Britain, Adam Seth Litwin, LSE, Centre for Economic Performance, 2000
2 Safety Behaviour in the Construction Sector, HAS/HSE Northern Ireland by Nick McDonald and Victor Hrymak

Activity 15.3   Employee representation on health and safety at work

1. What is the basis, if any, of employee representation on health and safety in a company known to you?
2. Is this effective?
3. In what ways might it be improved?

European comparators

A central theme of this chapter has been the marked shift along the participation continuum from worker/trade union inspired and controlled schemes towards management inspired and controlled schemes over the period from the 1970s to the 2000s. The dominance of involvement mechanisms in the 1980s and 1990s has been assisted by enabling legislation (such as that for financial involvement); government exhortation (on flexibility and efficiency); through the example of inward-investing industry, particularly Japanese and American; and because of some managers' focus on competitive advantage through efficiency and quality.

However, throughout this period the spectre of Europe has haunted both the former Conservative government and many British managers. The practice of employee participation in much of continental Europe, with worker directors, works councils and consultation, often with statutory backing, and attempts to generalise this throughout the European Union via directives has horrified both government and many managers in Britain (Burchill, 1997: 197; Department of Employment, 1989; Hyman and Mason, 1995: 30). Based on the employee participation approach, such measures and practice rub against the grain of experience and policy in Britain. Above all, the former Conservative government and most

British employers were opposed to the idea of legislation to require companies to adopt such practices. Rather, the Conservative government implemented legislation that deregulated the labour market, while at the same time weakening the position of trade unions. The government took a voluntarist approach to participation in an attempt to demonstrate to Europe that the statutory alternatives were neither required nor helpful in pursuing competitive advantage. At the same time the British Conservative government blocked progress on measures under consideration in the European Union that might have enhanced worker and trade union rights. These included the draft Fifth Directive on employee directors, the Vredeling proposals on information and consultation in multinational companies, and the European Company Statute with its implication for employee participation. This policy culminated in the opt-out of the Social Chapter at the Maastricht agreement in 1991 (Hall, 1992).

In 1997, however, the newly elected Labour government reversed these policies and signed the Social Chapter of the 1997 Amsterdam Treaty on European Union. Specifically, this led to the European Works Council Directive being implemented in Britain through The Transnational Information and Consultation of Employees Regulations 1999. The directive provides for a pan-European-wide information and consultation system to be set up in all organisations with at least 1000 employees in the states covered by the directive (the EU member states plus Iceland, Liechtenstein and Norway); and 150 employees in at least 2 of these countries. Affected companies had until 22 September 1996 to agree a customised system under article 13 before the Special Negotiating Body procedure laid down in the directive took effect.

Many British companies such as BT, ICI and United Biscuits had established voluntary agreements at an early stage (Cressey, 1998). By negotiating voluntary agreements companies were able to influence the tone, approach and constitution of the European Works Council. Management could seek to use it as a vehicle to project management plans, demonstrate management expertise and seek to elicit trade union and employee commitment for the espoused strategy. Moreover, through early agreement management could seek to influence whether worker representation would be employee- or trade union-based, and whether any trade union representation would include full-time officials or be confined to lay representatives working in the company (Cressey, 1998; IDS, 1997a). Wills (1999) believes that management have attempted to use EWCs as a vehicle to promote their own agenda and vision, and to help build a European corporate culture. By contrast, the European Trade Union Confederation seeks to reform EWCs in a way that would emphasise a more power-centred process and less of an information and consultation one, especially if meetings were required to reach agreement on issues discussed. After a decade of legislation, only around one third of eligible companies have established a EWC, and following the failure to reach a new agreement on the future of EWCs after a prolonged period of consultation between the social partners, the European Commission launched its own proposals for reform in 2008. However, given the difficulties in reaching agreement it may be some time before employers, unions and national governments have to respond to any new legislation.

Other European legislation in this area includes the Transfer of Undertakings (Protection of Employment) Regulations 1981, or TUPE, which provides for trade unions to be consulted when there is a transfer of a business to which these regulations apply. These are based on the EU Acquired Rights Directive 1977, which has been updated by Directive 2001/23/EC in March 2001.

The Trade Union and Labour Relations (Consolidation) Act 1992 requires employers to consult with trade unions when 20 or more redundancies are proposed. This is based on the EU Collective Redundancies Directive 1975.

The initial legislation gave rights to consultation and information to trade unions as the single channel of employee representation. However, following a European Court of Justice ruling in 1994 the British government was required to make provision for 'the designation of employee representatives for the purposes of information and consultation' where recognised trade unions did not exist. A similar amendment had to be made to legislation on consultation over health and safety at work (Sargeant, 2001). Thus a dual channel of employee representation, both union and non-union, was established through the influence of European legislation and this dual channel was subsequently repeated in the implementation of both the Working Time and Parental Leave Directives through provision for 'workforce agreements' as well as collective bargaining.

The principle of dual representation was continued with the Directive for Informing and Consulting Employees, March 2002, which aims to promote greater social dialogue in undertakings, to encourage greater anticipation of developments which may lead to changes in employment, and more action to prevent negative effects of change, and to ensure that the information and consultation of employees occurs in a timely manner. Specifically the directive requires employers to *inform* employee representatives on the organisation's activities and economic situation. It further requires employers to go beyond pure information to *consult* with employee representatives on the 'situation, structure and probable development of employment' as well as any future plans, particularly where jobs are at risk. *Consultation* will also be required on decisions likely to lead to substantial changes in work organisation or contractual relations, including redundancies and transfers as at present, and in these areas consultation should be 'with a view to reaching an agreement'. This directive was implemented in the UK progressively for different sized organisations between 2005 and 2008 depending on organisational size, but does not apply at all in organisations employing fewer than 50. Initial findings from research commissioned by the CIPD on the operation of these arrangements for informing and consulting employees is that their success depended on the attitude and commitment of management. If management wanted the bodies to be successful, then this might be possible. But if management believed beforehand that they were likely to be ineffective, and if employee representatives became disillusioned because they were not consulted about major issues in the way they had anticipated and then resigned, the subsequent failure of the body served to reinforce management's prior belief that they would be a waste of time (Hall *et al.*, 2008).

European practice

As many of the continuing examples of employee participation have their origins in European Union legislation, it may be fruitful to review the practice of employee participation in European countries other than the UK, and to this end we will look at both domestic and European works councils.

One key issue in understanding domestic works councils is that of the channel of employee representation. We have seen above that the traditional union single channel in Britain has been widened through recent legislation. In countries such as Germany and the Netherlands works councils are employee-only bodies with no formal roles for trade unions, but in practice in Germany 80 per cent of all works councillors are union members (Keller, 2004). On the other hand, in Denmark and Luxembourg they are joint employer/employee bodies and in France the Comité d'enterprise is chaired by the employer. Works councils are usually enshrined in legislation and have rights to information and consultation. In certain cases there are also rights to co-determination as in the German or Dutch situation over issues such as training and working hours arrangements. But even in Germany there is a growing trend for the emergence of participation-free zones as there are fewer works councils in the SME sector. The unions successfully campaigned to revise the Works Constitution Act in 2001 to make it easier to establish works councils in smaller firms.

Employee involvement

The change from employee participation to employee involvement highlights a number of points of contrast as presented in Table 15.1.

As Hyman and Mason (1995) argue (see Table 15.1 on p. 474), there are different supporting mechanisms, trajectories and objectives underpinning employee participation and employee involvement. The objectives of management-initiated employee involvement includes educating employees about the realities of the business; gaining employee commitment to corporate goals; developing employee contributions to increased efficiency; improving productivity and customer service. The term empowerment is sometimes used interchangeably with involvement. Wilkinson (1988: 40) argues that empowerment should be applied properly to information-sharing, upward problem-solving, task autonomy, attitude-shaping, and self-management. What all these schemes have in common is that they are based on the unitarist frame of reference and 'take place within the context of a strict management agenda'. Marchington and Wilkinson (1996) identify four categories of employee involvement:

1. downward communication;
2. upward problem-solving;
3. task participation;
4. financial involvement.

Each of these will be considered in turn.

Downward communication

The principle objective of such schemes is for managers to inform and educate employees directly so that they accept management plans. A variety of techniques are available which vary in their degree of formality/informality, their regularity and in whether they rely on oral or written communication, and whether they are face-to-face or indirect. They include formal written communication such as employee reports, house journals or company newspapers, videos and increasingly e-mail; informal and non-routinised communications between managers and their staff; formal team briefings based on a cascade system; and larger meetings of groups of employees, representing of all the employees in the organisation (IDS, 1997b).

Townley (1994b), drawing on a number of surveys conducted in the 1980s and early 1990s, reveals that while management use a number of different methods of communication, oral rather than written methods of communication are preferred. Larger companies preferred use of the management-chain meetings with all employees, and newsletters, whereas small and medium-sized companies were more likely to use face-to-face communication and staff meetings. The 2004 Workplace Employment Relations Survey (Kersley *et al.*, 2006) revealed that 71 per cent of companies surveyed used team briefing, with an even higher proportion in the public sector and in larger workplaces. These figures demonstrate a steady increase in the use of this method compared with both the 1990 and 1998 surveys.

Reports on the operation of direct communication in practice, and team briefing in particular, indicate that there are a number of problems in practice which may well inhibit the achievement of senior management objectives (Townley, 1994b). Prime among these is the lack of commitment of middle managers to implement the briefing system in practice, combined with a lack of appropriate skills to enable them to do this. Thus a device designed to demonstrate management dominance and control may in practice highlight weaknesses such as management incompetence or lack of commitment.

Team briefing also faces problems of maintaining regularity. It is often set aside to meet pressures of output or customer service, to maintain flows of relevant and detailed information, or to deal with changing staff working patterns. Managers also face the problem of overcoming deep-seated employee cynicism and suspicion (Townley, 1994b). Attempts to resolve some of these problems include the use of 'communicators' to reach part-time staff at Sainsbury's, and company intranets at ICL to update staff regularly (IDS, 1997b).

Managers themselves may perceive the increased dissemination of information to subordinates as threatening and undermining (Marchington *et al.*, 1992). Finally, introduction of new downward communication schemes in a unionised organisation may be seen by the union as a threat and challenge to established means of communication through the union and its representatives. Attempts to go over the head of the union and communicate directly with employees can be met by attempts by the union to resist and undermine the new system. A more common union response is to improve their own communication network to their members, as a counter to any views management are communicating through the briefing system.

Upward problem-solving

The principal objective of participation schemes that come under this subheading is to permit management to draw on employees' knowledge of their jobs. This can be either at an individual level through attitude surveys or suggestion schemes, or at a group level through quality circles or total quality management. Marchington and Wilkinson (1996: 262) argue that though these managers wish 'to increase the stock of ideas in the organisation, to encourage cooperative relations at work, and to legitimate change'. Increasingly such schemes are part of an overall continuous improvement approach.

Survey evidence reveals that two-way communication systems are used in a minority of companies. Although attitude surveys have a long history (Townley, 1994b: 604), the latest WERS found that only 42 per cent of organisations used them (Kersley *et al.*, 2006). The use of suggestion schemes has remained around 30 per cent of organisations over WERS from 1990 to 2004, although larger organisations are more likely to use such schemes. One final point from this survey evidence is that unionised workplaces were more likely to utilise the full range of communication methods than non-union ones.

At first sight this low usage of attitude surveys and suggestion schemes seems puzzling. There are a number of high profile accounts of companies saving large sums of money from suggestions made and of employees receiving financial rewards for their suggestions. A UK Association of Suggestion Schemes survey found savings to companies of almost £40 million, including as much as £2.75 million at British Airways, and payments to employees of nearly £2 million (IDS, 1997b). The IPM (1988) believe that in addition to the financial returns, there are also benefits in that the climate of employee relations can improve, as can two-way communications because employees feel that management is prepared to ask for their views. Finally, some organisations believe that knowledge of a successful suggestion scheme enhances their position both with customers and potential employees.

These schemes may not be so universal because in practice such formality may not be necessary in smaller organisations. But Marchington (1992: 185) has pointed out three drawbacks which may make organisations wary of adopting them. First, while some employees may feel good about the pay-out from the scheme, others may be resentful of the amount or of the amount relative to the size of savings made. Second, supervisors may feel that their position is threatened or undermined by senior management going directly to employees rather than through the line. Finally, and this relates to other upward problem-solving approaches such as quality circles and TQM, why should some staff be specifically rewarded for good suggestions, when the alternative approach requires a constant search for continuous improvement by all staff?

Exhibit 15.3

Suggestion scheme at Lloyds TSB

Lloyds TSB, employer of 80,000 employees across 2000 branches, has rejuvenated its staff suggestion scheme, receiving nearly 30,000 suggestions in 2002 alone. Comments were encouraged through a reward system, including a £5 high street voucher for the first suggestion, and supplemental rewards for new suggestions, with the possibility of a limited number of £10,000 prizes for the best suggestions.

The system uses the firm's intranet to process the suggestions, which are then analysed by a team of 200 'core' evaluators, supported by a further 200 'specialists'. Each idea is graded according to certain criteria including practicality, money saving potential and imagination.

Besides the obvious primary benefits, the iLine database (which stores all suggestions) can be used to track employees' attitude to aspects of the company and, as each suggestion must be thoroughly researched before its submission, offers good support for why changes ought to be enacted in the future.

Source: *Suggestion Schemes*, IDS Study 752, June 2003

Quality circles and total quality management

Quality circles and total quality management (TQM) may be considered together. Tuckman (1994, 1995) has pointed out that British companies' interest in quality management practices began in the late 1970s with some experimentation with quality circles, but by the mid-1980s, as these showed signs of failure, the focus shifted to TQM. Hill (1991: 15) accounts for the failure of quality circles in Britain primarily because they were implemented as a grafted-on technique and often without management training, whereas TQM was expected to have a greater potential for success precisely because it is total rather than partial.

Wilkinson *et al.* (1992) offer a framework to compare quality circles with TQM (Table 15.4).

From this we can examine areas where the operation of quality circles may run into difficulties. Quality circles in practice are groups of volunteers, usually between four and eight in number, who meet regularly to identify, analyse and solve job-related problems, generally under the guidance of a supervisor. They present their solutions for management to decide whether to implement them or not. Researchers (Collard and Dale, 1989; Hill, 1991) have identified two distinct, although related, management objectives for quality circles to enhance organisational performance and to improve employee relations. WIRS3 (Millward *et al.*, 1992) found that only 5 per cent of manufacturing organisations operated quality circles, whereas the 1990 ACAS survey found them in 27 per cent of its sample (ACAS, 1990). The general view is that they grew rapidly in the mid-1980s, but then declined rapidly (Geary, 1994: 640; Gennard and Judge, 1997: 131). Using a wider concept of problem-solving groups, the 2004 WERS found these to exist in only 21 per cent

Table 15.4 The differences between quality circles and TQM

Factor	Quality circles	TQM
Choice	Voluntary	Compulsory
Structure	Bolt-on	Integrated quality system
Direction	Bottom-up	Top-down
Score	Within departments/units	Company-wide
Aims	Employee relations improvements	Quality improvements

Source: Wilkinson *et al.* (1992)

of workplaces, up from 16 per cent in 1998 (Kersley *et al.*, 2006). Even where they exist in an organisation the number of employees actually participating is often less than 10 per cent of those eligible to join (Black and Ackers, 1988; Hill, 1991). Moreover, there is a clearly identified susceptibility of quality circles to fall into disuse over time; Bradley and Hill (1987: 73) found that only 20 per cent of circles were still in operation three years after the inception of the programme.

A number of reasons have been put forward to account for this lack of success of quality circles. One major area concerns the position of management. Quality circles can threaten the position of middle managers and supervisors, partly because they are tackling problems which they might have been expected to identify and solve, partly because they change the relationship between the managers and the workforce in ways in which they perceive in being 'soft', and because quality circles add to their workloads for comparatively small returns (Bradley and Hill, 1987: 75–6). Yet senior managers find a need to engage in some form of upward problem-solving and so periodically reinvent quality circles under a different name. Rees (1999) cites a bank changing from Quality Service Action Teams to Quality Improvement Teams.

The evidence on the impact of quality circles on employees is mixed. Evidence from the US suggests that involvement in them can have a positive impact on attitudes and performance (Griffin, 1988). This is supported by research in the UK (Webb, 1989: 23), but this and other research (Bradley and Hill, 1983: 303; Marchington and Parker, 1990: 199) suggests that any such improvement may not be sustained over time and that there can be differences between members and non-members of circles which can have an overall disadvantageous impact.

Quality circles can be perceived by unions as being a threat to their position in that established working practices and agreements may be undermined by decisions of quality circles without reference to established procedures, or that employees will come to identify more closely with the employer to the detriment of the relationship with the union. In reviewing the evidence of the influence unions can have over the success or failure of quality circles, Marchington (1992: 90) concludes:

> In situations where circles are an integral part of union-based EI schemes, unions may have little to fear from their introduction. Conversely, where quality circles are implemented in an attempt to reform industrial relations in a climate of mistrust, the end-result is likely to depend more on the relative balance of power in the workplace.

Tuckman's (1994) analysis of the situation following the fizzling out of quality circles was that management turned to TQM because it appeared to offer a solution based on the notion of a *total* management system. Drawing on the contrasts in Table 15.4, TQM was to become everyone's concern and responsibility, not just the small minority who volunteered to participate; it would be company-wide rather than confined to departments which opted in; and be led by senior management. The aim of the approach shifted from improving employee relations to improving quality in order for the organisation to remain competitive. In the later 1980s these concepts spread from manufacturing to the service sector in the guise of customer care (Tuckman, 1995). In approaching this, however, TQM necessitated a workforce willingly cooperating in continuous improvement rather than merely complying with existing approaches and methods. Or as Geary (1994: 643) put it:

TQM places considerable emphasis on enlarging employees' responsibilities, reorganising work and increasing employees' involvement in problem-solving activities. The search for continuous improvement is the responsibility of all employees, management and manager alike, and all functions. TQM requires quality to be 'built in' to the product and not 'inspected in' by a separate quality department. Where employees are not in direct contact with the organisation's customers they are encouraged to see their colleagues at successive stages of the production process as internal customers. Thus, a central part of TQM is the internalisation of the rigours of the marketplace within the enterprise.

Marchington (1992: 93–5) distinguishes a 'hard' and 'soft' approach to TQM in practice. On the one hand are those advocates, following the 'excellence school of management', who call for open management styles, delegated responsibility and increased autonomy to staff. This 'soft' approach is contrasted with the 'hard' operations management view which stresses measurement and arguably leads to less discretion for employees. The third, 'mixed' approach borrows from both the other approaches but in a unitarist fashion. Putting TQM into practice means balancing the production-orientated and employee relations-orientated elements which, as Marchington clearly identifies, means managing 'the tensions between, on the one hand, following clearly laid-down instructions while, on the other, encouraging employee influence over the management process' (1992: 94).

Work by Wilkinson *et al.* (1998) allows us to assess how these tensions have been played out in the 1990s, as the authors put it, between the promise of TQM and its principles of continuous improvement, or TQM as a slightly longer-lived management fad. The evidence appears to be mixed. Wilkinson *et al.* review a number of studies from the UK and the USA as well as presenting their own survey and case study results. They conclude that TQM has become more widespread in both countries, is usually implemented in response to perceived competition, and represents an attempt to win and sustain competitive advantage. But 'while there is evidence of successful implementation with a significant impact on organisational performance, the results are disappointing for the proponents of TQM in a large number of cases' (Wilkinson *et al.*, 1998: 86). Problems in implementing TQM included severe resource limitations, costs constraints, an emphasis on short-term goals, the impact of the reduction on staff morale and difficulties in the measurement of quality and lack of commitment in the organisation, including top management (Wilkinson *et al.*, 1998: 181). There was, however, little evidence of union resistance to quality management despite the suspicions unions may have about the implicit unitarism of TQM. McCabe's (1999: 688) study of TQM in a vehicle components firm in the Midlands leads to the conclusion that 'TQM does not automatically marginalise or incorporate trade unions', but while these dangers exist, its implementation throws up new opportunities for resistance and possible gains for labour.

However, the unitarism can give rise to contradictions. For example, TQM is based on high trust, building employee commitment to the need for service quality and continuous improvement, but in their food retailing case 'mystery shoppers' were used to check that predicted norms of customer care behaviour were being implemented. This low-trust compliance approach could backfire when set alongside the commitment approach. The fundamental unresolved tension is between 'the call for empowerment and individual innovation on the one hand and the requirement for conformance to tight behavioural specifications on the other' (Wilkinson *et al.*, 1998: 179).

Wilkinson *et al.* examine the views expressed by some (Hammer and Champy, 1993) that TQM is not capable of effecting the transformational change which is believed necessary to regain competitive advantage because it is too much based on incremental change. Thus TQM is seen as a fad whose time has gone and is being replaced by business process re-engineering and stretch management. Wilkinson *et al.* dispute this view and suggest that 'while the high tide of the TQM movement may have receded, this does not mean that its impact has been negligible or insignificant; it has left its mark on British management' (1998: 188). But they do concede that TQM is often reinterpreted by managers who are reluctant to give up power and are driven by short-term considerations. Thus they suggest that what exists in the UK is Partial Quality Management. Such a view is confirmed by Glover (2000) who believes that TQM in the UK has been implemented in an ad hoc manner and that this is because of management intransigence and the short-term focus of British shareholders seeking immediate returns rather than long-term improvements.

Task participation

Task participation is a form of direct employee involvement in which employees are encouraged or expected to extend the range and type of tasks undertaken at work (Marchington and Wilkinson, 1996: 262). Here we consider three examples of task participation: job redesign, job enrichment and team-working. Marchington (1992) identifies three separate, but potentially overlapping, reasons why employers may introduce task participation – as a counter to work alienation; as an attempt to increase employee commitment; and as a contribution to competitive advantage. These three reasons may be linked to Buchanan's (1994) contention that historically there has been a periodisation of approaches to work design – scientific management (1900–50), quality of working life (1950–80); and high performance work systems (1980–).

Task participation as a counter to work alienation was in effect a reversal of scientific management and emphasised job redesign and job enrichment. While these approaches were meant to satisfy employee needs for more interesting and satisfying work, they also addressed management needs to reduce absenteeism and labour turnover and increase productivity. There is, however, a tension between satisfying employer and employee needs simultaneously (Kelly, 1982). Recent work in this area has highlighted management responses to a highly competitive and unpredictable operating environment which has turned attention to ways of improving flexibility and performance through work and organisational design (Buchanan, 1994: 106). Hence a greater emphasis on commitment and competitive advantage and less emphasis on the needs of workers.

The restructuring of jobs

Other methods designed to increase employee commitment in the workplace include job redesign and job enrichment programmes. This work restructuring can range from horizontal job redesign to vertical job enrichment. The former involves only changes in what Goss (1994) called the *content* of the work, i.e. changes the number or variety of operations an individual performs at the same skill level (Marchington, 1992). It is task, rather than decision, based participation and can result in job rotation programmes which do little to alleviate the stress and monotony of boring, repetitive jobs.

Job enrichment schemes, on the other hand, may either offer employees increased task responsibility or, more radically, are intended to alter the *form* of participation and provide workers with increased discretion over decision-making. Derived from Herzberg's Two-Factor Theory of Motivation developed in the 1950s, this type of participation is also reflected in so-called 'empowerment' initiatives such as the 'Whatever it Takes' programme in Marriott Hotels which sought to empower staff to satisfy customer needs (Lashley, 1997: 49–50).

Herzberg's work has been criticised in terms of the research methods employed but also methodologically on the grounds of psychological universalism (Hackman *et al.*, 1985). In other words, every employee may not share the need, for example, for increased responsibility in the workplace. In short, even though employers may find the notion of obtaining functional flexibility through multi-skilling beguiling, to some workers (and indeed managers) these types of programmes may be an increased source of stress and demotivation (Marchington, 1992: 113–14).

Team-working

The concern about flexibility is reflected in the use of team-working as the 1990s manifestation of job redesign. In its ultimate form it has been labelled high performance work design (Buchanan, 1994) and involves a group of multi-capable workers who switch between tasks, organise and allocate work, and are responsible for all aspects of production, including quality. Buchanan (1994: 100) sees this approach as being quite different from the QWL (quality of working life) approaches of later decades in that 'management motives are therefore strategic rather than operational, concerned with competition and customer satisfaction rather than with employment costs'.

As Geary (1994: 441) notes, team-working is a term used in a variety of different ways, a unitarist rousing cry for all employees to work together, not least as forms of team-working range from groups of individuals simply sharing skills and knowledge to more or less self-managing work units. He suggests that this latter, more sophisticated form is largely confined to a small number of well-publicised companies, many of which were originally established on greenfield sites, and indeed often incoming Japanese companies (1994: 642). Marchington (2000: 66) suggests that greater care is need in defining team-work so that it can be properly evaluated. To assist this he suggests analysing team-working in terms of its *scope*, the technical requirements of work, and its *degree*, the extent of employee influence and control over these requirements.

Team-working can face similar problems to those with experienced job restructuring programmes. It can be stressful (Berggren, 1989; Black and Ackers, 1990) for workers and managers alike. In addition, it can be viewed by the workforce as an attempt to increase control over the labour process and intensify work (Parker and Slaughter, 1988). Marchington (2000: 73) argues that senior management support and commitment is essential and if this is not forthcoming it is not likely to be reciprocated by employees. Rees (1999: 471) concludes from his study of team-working in a hotel and a bank that team-working represents 'a constrained and limited form of involvement, which allows for greater detailed control for employees at the point of production or service delivery at the same time as providing management with increasing general control'.

Financial involvement

A number of different schemes aimed at linking part of an individual employee's rewards to the success of the unit and/or of the organisation as a whole exist. These include profit-sharing and/or share incentive plans, employees save as you earn schemes employee and ESOPs (employee share ownership plans). These schemes have been encouraged by successive UK governments since 1978, and although there have been many changes in the detail, the essence of state support is through tax relief which benefits both the individual employee and the organisation offering the scheme. Pendleton (2005: 79) argues that these 'statutory frameworks and fiscal concessions are key determinants of the incidence of financial participation'.

Management have a number of objectives behind their introduction and while these may be overlapping, they can also be competing and contradictory. Baddon *et al.* (1989) discovered, from a survey of 1000 companies and detailed case study work in five organisations, four main management objectives behind the introduction of profit-sharing and ESOPs:

- encouraging the cooperation and involvement of all employees in improving the performance of the business;
- giving employees a sense of identification with the company;
- rewarding employees for past performance;
- generating a sense of business awareness among employees.

A fifth possible rationale for management introduction of profit-sharing is a union deterrence motive. While found historically (Bristow, 1974; Ramsey, 1977), it was not prevalent in the Baddon *et al.* (1989) or other recent surveys. The Baddon *et al.* survey did show that financial involvement schemes were almost invariably introduced without negotiation or consultation with trade union where recognised, but also that the union attitude towards them was one of 'bored hostility'. This was because they were not a threat to mainstream pay determination through collective bargaining but were seen as a bonus or an add-on. Perhaps one of the reasons that union opposition to financial involvement schemes is so muted is that, despite government facilitation and encouragement, the take-up has not been extensive. The Inland Revenue (2003) estimates that since the inception of all-employee schemes, and up to the end of March 2001, some 2.75 million people have received shares under profit-sharing schemes, and 2 million have received share options. It is recognised that there is a considerable overlap of participants in both types of scheme. All companies in the FTSE 100 had one scheme or another and 75 per cent of those in the FTSE 250. More recently (2000), the Enterprise Management Incentives scheme was introduced to provide incentives to help smaller, higher-risk companies recruit and retain high calibre staff. This scheme is attractive to unlisted companies, but for, on average, only five employees per company, and it is found in les than 1 per cent of work-places (Kersley *et al.*, 2006).

A number of points can be made about these figures. First, after 25 years of tax relief, the numbers covered by such schemes represent only around 10 per cent of the employed labour force, but those working for large plcs are much more likely to be involved than those in other parts of the economy. The smaller number of employees involved in SAYE schemes suggests that the requirement of the employee to contribute some of their own money and to commit to a medium-term savings plan is a barrier to employees expressing their commitment to their employing organisation through purchasing shares in it. Indeed, the Baddon *et al.* (1989) study suggested that rather than share schemes being a vehicle for elicit-ing employee commitment, it was only already committed and loyal employees, whose personal finances permitted, who took up share schemes. Moreover, this was more likely to be white-collar workers and managers than blue-collar work-ers. In other words, those employees with whom management would most like to build a commitment relationship are the very ones who are least likely to take up financial involvement.

A claim made by advocates of employee share ownership was that this would end 'them and us' and help build employee commitment and loyalty. However, between 1984 and 1996, the practice of most companies was to offer share option schemes to senior executives only. This may have been driven by the need to recruit and retain such staff, and/or to establish a vehicle to encourage and reward short-term performance. Criticism of such narrowly constructed schemes led to revisions to their tax status in 1996. After this the number of staff involved increased from an average of 80,000 per year to 280,000, but the average share value per employee decreased from c. £20,000 to £5000 (Inland Revenue, 2003).

A final tax beneficial scheme, ESOPs, was introduced in 1988. These schemes permit the participation of employees in the ownership of companies; but use in Britain has largely been confined to the privatised bus industry (Pendleton, 2001). Here the majority of such ESOPs were what Pendleton calls 'representative' in that the employees played a major part in the design and implementation of the new firm. There was thus a potential for this form of financial involvement to move more decisively along the participation continuum. However, although 21 per cent of those surveyed believed that they had more say in decisions, further analysis revealed only a relatively limited impact on employee attitudes and commitment. But the ESOPs were short lived, averaging less than four years, and the subsequent takeover of these companies by larger companies has meant that employee owners have, like many non-employee owners, preferred capital gains to long-term ownership of the firm that they worked for (Trewhitt, 2000).

Impact of financial involvement

A number of studies have been conducted which have tried to assess the impact that the various forms of financial involvement have had. An early attempt, admittedly from two strong advocates of such schemes, was from Bell and Hanson (1984) who argued that financial involvement schemes are warmly welcomed by employees and that it is seen as 'good for the company and its employees'. While their research might suggest that such schemes do have an impact on employee commitment and loyalty, a number of other more detailed research studies cast doubt on this. Work by Baddon *et al.* (1989) reveals that profit-sharing and employee share ownership is seen by employees in very instrumental ways. They conclude that:

> The benefits of most schemes are generally too small to have much prospect of making the kind of impact management would wish. The benefits tend not to be seen by employees as an essential element of pay which would generate commitment but are more typically regarded as 'just another kind of bonus'.
>
> (Baddon *et al.*, 1989: 274)

The emphasis on an instrumental approach is confirmed by other research. Poole and Jenkins (1990) conclude that the impact of profit-sharing on company performance is likely to be minor as both profits and share price are affected by a number of factors such as exchange rate movements or cost of materials, which are beyond the day-to-day influence of employees. However, once a financial participation scheme is in place, failure to maintain the benefits may actually have an adverse impact on employee commitment and on employee perceptions of the competence of top management.

A long-standing trade union objection to share ownership is that of 'double jeopardy', i.e. that employees should not have their jobs and their capital both tied up in the same company, because redundancies would lead to a loss of income and of savings simultaneously. From the employees' perspective, two further potential drawbacks about financial participation exist. First, none of these schemes, with the exception perhaps of ESOPs, offer employees any increased participation in decision-making. At best they may elicit an orientation towards an appreciation of the marketplace and an understanding of business priorities as seen by top management, but they do not permit employees to exercise a voice in decision-making even in their role as share owners. Nor, with many of the schemes, is there a direct link between the schemes and the effort expected of the employee on a day-to-day basis, nor is the pay-out regular enough to act as a motivator. Other payment and motivation systems would be necessary to provide such links. Moreover, the existence of share ownership schemes which focus on the parent plc may not sit comfortably with other involvement schemes which focus on the subsidiary company or on the work team.

Finally, we can obtain a European perspective on financial participation by considering the findings of the European Union sponsored research on PEPPER (Promotion of Participation by Employed Persons in Profits and Enterprise Results). Poutmsa *et al.* (1999) review the main findings of the second PEPPER report. Drawing on the societal approach (Lane, 1989), they anticipate that workers and employers in different countries will have different attitudes towards financial involvement. The 1996 PEPPER report bears this out, with a range from strong government support for financial participation schemes only in France and the UK, to a lack of official government support in countries such as Denmark and Greece (Poutsma *et al.*, 1999: 177–82). Despite the initial similarity between France and the UK, Poutsma and his colleagues differentiate between the UK logic of contract, the French logic of opposition and the German logic of cooperation.

They characterise the British schemes discussed above as occurring in a situation where the government creates permissive legislation that offers tax incentives within which employers and employees can operate voluntarily. The relative weakness of trade unions has enabled employers to introduce such schemes on a contract basis with very little comment, although where share ownership was linked to privatisation there was greater union opposition. In the French situation, on the other hand, governments have also offered a permissive legal framework in which employers can introduce profit-sharing but only after a company-level agreement. These have largely been introduced through company-level agreements with unions involved in only 13 per cent of cases. French unions remain ambivalent about profit-sharing and have been involved in some negotiated agreements while at the same time opposing them at national level. In Germany, there are no state incentives for profit-sharing, but such schemes are regulated between management and works councils at company level, while at national level unions remain sceptical.

A final tentative conclusion that Poutsma and his colleagues postulate is the thought that the countries with the weakest financial participation schemes, the Rhineland countries, are characterised by cooperation and they query whether financial participation is irrelevant to this. On the other hand, in more antagonistic systems where financial participation is more prevalent, they wonder whether this could be a means for employers to obtain commitment and collaboration from their employees in the absence of other cooperative participation schemes (Poutmsa *et al.*, 1999: 191–2).

Activity 15.4   Financial participation

1. Does the organisation you work for, or any you may have worked for, operate any form of financial participation?

2. If so, which of the five reasons for such schemes mentioned above seems to best explain the motives of senior managers?

3. What do you think the impact of the schemes has been on employees?

4. Drawing on your reading and knowledge of financial participation in a number of countries, do you think there is substance in the conclusions reached by Poutsma and his colleagues (1999) about the differences between the Rhineland countries and those like the UK and France characterised by more antagonistic industrial relations?

Conclusion

In this chapter we have stressed the differences between employee participation and employee involvement and demonstrated the prevalence of employee involvement forms in the 1980s and 1990s. We have related this to a concern by management to elicit employee commitment and identification as part of an overall strategy to gain and retain competitive advantage. At the same time we have shown that although employee involvement approaches may be dominant over employee participation ones, neither are a majority practice. In many cases employee involvement initiatives are more likely to be found in foreign-owned companies in large organisations and in the public sector. By no measure are the practices widespread and dominant.

We now turn to consider the extent to which the various forms of employee involvement and participation which we have identified and considered fit together, either with each other or with the overall human resourcing strategy of the organisations. Wilkinson *et al.* (1998: 50) argue that empowerment needs to be situated in the whole work environment within which it operates and not be an isolated initiative. Here we need to consider the extent to which various forms of EI are merely management fads and fashions which come and go. Indeed Hales (2000: 507) gives us an example where managers recognised the danger of this and 'eschewed the term "empowerment" in order to avoid its faddist "flavour of the month" associations, but espoused the associated rhetoric in asserting the importance of employees as the key element in "delivering the magic"'.

We have already suggested that some approaches might be contradictory. For example, a share ownership scheme which focuses on the parent company might not sit comfortably with a team-working initiative which focuses on the immediate work group. Similarly, a communications approach which emphasises line management's position and authority might not be compatible with a task participation approach which seeks to eliminate immediate supervision and emphasise autonomous work groups. At a higher level there is a tension between the recent emphasis on an employee involvement approach with earlier approaches based on employee participation. This is often common in public sector organisations where union-based joint consultative committees operate alongside team briefing and other communication schemes based on direct involvement between management and employees that have been introduced more recently in response to 'Best Value' or other such initiatives. McCabe and Wilkinson's (1991) account of TQM at Medbank offers an example of a unitarist-based employee involvement initiative failing, partly because of poor implementation, but more significantly due to its unitarist vision not being shared by all staff, nor even by all managers. Moreover, concurrent restructuring and consequent redundancies emphasised the contradiction between a unitarist TQM vision based on customer service, and recessionary and competitive pressures forcing large-scale redundancies. Here the strategy behind the TQM initiative was overtaken and overwhelmed by that of restructuring and redundancies.

Marchington *et al.* (1993) provide a useful device which allows us to make sense of the dynamics of schemes and their interrelationship which we have explored in detail earlier (Figure 15.2).

In this the dynamics of EI are graphically represented as a series of waves thus capturing the ebbs and flows of a particular technique over time and in comparison with each other, in this case a large private sector firm. This diagram can be replicated for any organisation.

Activity 15.5	Waves exercise

Draw the equivalent diagram for an organisation with which you are familiar. Consider the trajectories of each form and why they declined or continue to (co)exist.

It is also suggested that the confused and confusing pattern which emerges can be further complicated by interdepartmental rivalries over the ownership and

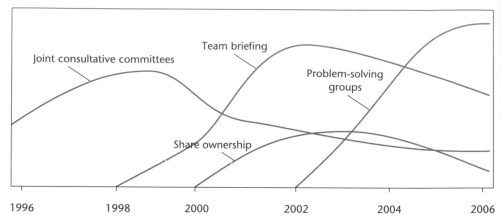

Figure 15.2 Movements of employee involvement and participation schemes within an organisation over time

Source: Adapted from Marchington *et al.* (1993)

objectives of particular initiatives. Figure 15.2 suggests that there is no guarantee of success for EI initiatives. Indeed Marchington (2000: 76) argues that 'if integrated effectively, the combination of different EI techniques was beneficial, but any contradictions between them were soon noticed and exposed by employees'. We have stressed that one of the distinguishing features of EI is that it is management led. Yet the practices we have examined here suggest that it can fail or move into decline because of the action of managers. The messages can be contradictory and competing, the penetration of the initiatives can be weak, and first-line managers, on whom much depends, can feel threatened or bypassed by initiatives and may not actually implement them. Moreover, there is evidence that the training of managers to implement schemes is often inadequate and that, when faced with the dilemma of spending time and money on developing initiatives and the rigours of meeting production or service demands, the latter take priority.

We have stressed that employee involvement is based on a unitarist view of the organisation; that there is an identity of interest between employee and employer. Yet many of the initiatives we have examined are designed to create the very commitment and identity which is presumed to exist. Marchington (1995: 290), on the basis of a review of survey evidence, concludes that employees are attracted to the general concept of involvement and participation but somewhat cynically points out that this is unremarkable since the alternative is an autocratic and non-communicative management style. But often, as we have shown above, their support is based on instrumentalism, a share bonus or time off monotonous work, rather than signs of commitment and loyalty. Many schemes, such as team briefing and quality circles, only involve a minority of employees for a minority of their working time and therefore their potential to transform the total employment relationship must be limited. That is why approaches such as TQM, which are intended to form an employment relationship rather than be built on one, might be expected to be more successful (Hill, 1991). Even here the evidence from Wilkinson *et al.* (1998) suggests that it is only Partial Quality Management which is practised in Britain at the end of the 1990s.

The final point of contrast between participation and involvement is to consider the role and position of trade unionism. Participation is seen as being union led whereas not only is involvement management led, it is often designed to undermine or bypass union organisation (Kelly, 1988; Smith and Morton, 1993). The biggest threat to unions is that management may attempt to weaken collective bargaining, where unions effectively have a right of veto, to channel more issues through joint consultation and to increase direct communication to employees so as to reinforce the management message. On the other hand, union responses to some specific involvement initiatives have tended to be more in the 'bored hostility' camp than outright opposition.

While there is some evidence of non-union firms using a combination of EI techniques to maintain a non-union presence, the survey evidence indicates that non-union firms as a whole are less likely than their union counterparts to operate them (Sisson, 1993). In many cases EI and collective bargaining run in parallel (Storey, 1992). A more recent trade union approach (Monks, 1998) is to take the rhetoric of employee involvement and to turn it into a trade union demand for greater involvement in the management operation of the workplace. Combined with the window of opportunity offered by the European Works Council Directive, this may allow unions in the workplaces where they are still strong to put the employee participation approach back on the agenda. But for many employers operating in the 'black hole' of neither traditional industrial relations nor HRM, employee involvement is alien. Here we might let Marchington have the final say by repeating his words (1995: 302):

> It could be argued that the haphazard, uneven and piecemeal way in which EI has been introduced into most employing organisations so far may not provide a fair indication of what it can achieve under a regime of 'soft' HRM.

Activity 15.6 Employee involvement and participation at Moddens Foods

We will now return to the developing case of Moddens Foods. We have seen in Chapter 1 that the two branches of the company adopted different routes to their healthy continued existence; routes we have called high commitment and low commitment. We will now examine how these differing approaches relate to employee involvement and employee participation.

You are an HR consultant who has been called into Moddens Foods. Your task is to advise the senior management of both the Gourmet Division and the Volume Division on the potential and possibilities of introducing forms of employee participation and employee involvement into each division.

You are expected to draw on the range of forms of employee participation and employee involvement discussed in this chapter. However, you must come up with an appropriate mix or 'bundle' of measures which takes account of:

a) The likely philosophy towards management and the personal preferences of the senior managers involved, given the information in Chapter 1.

b) The circumstances of each division and how the proposals might achieve the notion of 'fit', both vertical and horizontal.

You might like to refer back to Table 1.3 (p. 31) in considering this.

Summary

In this chapter the following key points have been made:

- Industrial democracy, employee participation and employee involvement have been differentiated.

- An employee participation and involvement continuum can be used to distinguish between those initiatives that are wholly management led as opposed to those that are worker/union controlled.

- Explanations of changing form and content of employee involvement and participation in organisations in terms of the cycle and wave metaphors have been offered.

- From the 1970s to the present day, the dominant approaches in organisations have largely been management inspired and controlled.

- Managers have sought to use employee involvement techniques in an attempt to gain employee commitment to organisational goals.

- Legislation from the European Union, together with a more pro-European stance of the Labour government, may see a movement towards employee participation.

- Four models of joint consultative committee have been identified and explained.

- Four main approaches of involvement – downward communication, upward problem-solving, task participation and financial involvement have been outlined and analysed.

- A framework to understand the movement of particular forms of employee participation and involvement within an organisation over time, the relationship between different forms, and between these and HR strategy has been utilised.

Discussion questions

1. How would you differentiate between industrial democracy, employee participation and employee involvement?

2. In your view, which metaphor best describes movements in the incidence of forms of employee participation and involvement, waves or cycles?

3. Examine ways in which European Union policy and practice has influenced the policies of UK governments and/or the practices of UK companies.

4. Take one form of employee involvement and examine the arguments for and against using it from an employer, employee and trade union point of view.

5. Take one form of employee involvement and analyse what barriers there are to management achieving its intended objectives.

Further reading

Employee participation, involvement and communications issues appear as topics in most HRM and industrial relations textbooks. Appropriate references for specific topics have appeared in the text and are listed in the bibliography where readers can follow up citations that are most helpful to their particular interests. There have been no recent overview texts, but one text that addresses all the issues covered in this chapter is Hyman and Mason (1995). Readers should also consult Harley *et al.* (eds) (2005). This book of essays examines a number of features of employee involvement and participation in the context of Ramsey's work on cycles.

16

Managing consulting and consultancy relationships

Diannah Lowry and Pam Stevens

Learning outcomes

Having read this chapter and completed its associated activities, readers should be able to:

- Understand the tensions, contradictions and challenges inherent in managing consulting and consultancy relationships
- Identify a number of different dimensions and frameworks associated with processes of managing consulting and consultancy relationships
- Appreciate that organisational actors have a range of options concerning the type of consultancy relationship they engage in
- Understand that processes associated with managing consulting and the consultancy relationship potentially impact on a wide group of constituencies, not just the 'target' organisation
- Understand some of the ethical issues associated with managing consulting and the consultancy relationship

Introduction

The structure of the strategic human resourcing function has evolved dramatically over the past few years, evidenced by the emergence of shared services centres and business partner models, leading many HR specialists to develop consultancy-style relationships with line managers as well as 'external' clients (Wright, 2007; Cooke, 2006; Francis and Keegan, 2006). This is coupled by the increasing trend of organisations turning to management consultancies for guidance on a range of other strategic human resourcing 'problems' and interventions. Indeed, it is likely that few of us have escaped the effects of some type of intervention that has been led by a management consultant or consultancy group. Consultants are typically associated with some type of organisational change effort associated with restructuring, reward systems, cultural programmes, the 'learning organisation', total quality management and other programmes that are considered by some to be more 'faddish' in nature. They are portrayed in the consultancy literature generally as having a 'contract for services' relationship with the organisation.

In this chapter we do not focus on the nature of the content of consultancy programmes, instead the focus will be on the dynamics and processes underlying managing consultancy and the consultancy relationship. Specifically, we will explore the nature of managing consultancy and consultancy relationships in a way which is consistent with the notion that HR strategies emerge from political processes of debate, negotiation and argument among strategic decision-makers, and from the way that managers interpret the circumstances affecting the organisation. If we refer back to Figure 1.1 (p. 28) we can see that such debate and negotiation is informed by, and contributes to, the values and interests (both personal and group interests) of the strategy-makers.

We take the view that the traditional internal/external boundaries of the consultancy relationship are becoming blurred, as in many organisations a 'contract for services' arrangement exists between various parties *within* the organisation. As noted above, within HR we have seen the emergence of a shared services model, the growth of call or contact centres and the development of business partner models which all bear the hallmarks of a consultancy arrangement exemplified by such things as service level agreements (Cooke, 2006; Francis and Keegan, 2006). The subcontracting or outsourcing of the HR function has externalised what was previously an internal relationship and has led to HR specialists having a consultancy-style relationship with line managers, creating tensions as well as a need to work together cooperatively.

Against this backdrop, the processes associated with managing consultancy and the consultancy relationship are seen as a further 'layering' of debate, negotiation and argument. What characterises the consultancy relationship then, is a set of complex political processes, since each strategy-maker engaged in the consultancy relationship is acting from a different set of personal and group values and interests (see, for example, Czarniawska and Mazza, 2003). Alongside this political dimension of the consultancy relationship, there are also other symbolic and structural dimensions, due to the different values and interests not *just* from strategy-makers, but also from those constituents who perceive that they are likely to be affected in varying ways by the *outcomes* of the processes associated with managing any consultancy intervention.

An implicit assumption throughout this chapter is that the process of managing consulting and the consultancy relationship is one of strategic exchange. The chapter will open with a critical exploration of the nature of this exchange; more specifically, we will examine what is being exchanged and why such exchange occurs. This also involves some discussion of the tensions, contradictions and challenges that are inherent in managing consulting and consultancy relationships. Following on from this we will explore some different models and frameworks associated with management consultants. This will involve an examination of what it is that consultants 'do', and the various devised means of classifying such activity. The chapter then concludes with a discussion of ethical issues associated with managing consulting and the consultancy relationship.

The nature of exchange in the consultancy relationship

Managing consulting and the consultancy relationship involves the notion of exchange, specifically exchange in terms of *knowledge*. Our typical conception of management is that they are expected to have certain skills and competences as well as an appropriate knowledge base from which they 'construct' their managerial activity. This begs the question, then, as to *why* consultants are used, and why such an exchange of knowledge is considered necessary. One simple explanation for the use of consultants may be that managers operating under demands and pressures within tight deadlines see consultancy as a solution. In other words, the immediacy of an intervention may form the justification for turning to outside the organisation. Managers may have the ability and knowledge to generate options and solutions but there is no time, little opportunity and higher priorities. This observation may be accurate in one sense, but it raises several points that require some careful consideration. First, what is the nature of the body of knowledge that consultants profess to have access to? Typically, consultants set about persuading clients that they possess 'a plethora of distinctive bodies of knowledge' rather than a 'distinctive domain of knowledge' (Clark, 1995). In other words, the knowledge-base is fluid, and draws from a broad range of models and frameworks such as organisational development models, learning theory, Gestalt theory, role theory, as well as consultancy-generated frameworks such as the Boston Consulting Group matrix.

It is important to note that consultancy roles are typically (rightly or otherwise) described in ways that reinforce the professional status and autonomy of the consultant, and attribute an acknowledged body of 'professional' knowledge (Boussebaa, 2008). But if we accept that consultants have access to a fairly 'fluid base' of knowledge as discussed above, can consultants' knowledge be considered 'professional' knowledge, and can consultants be considered professionals? Strictly speaking, in order to be labelled as a profession, an occupation will have a defined body of scientific knowledge, acquired through long formal education, autonomy, ethical rules, a distinct occupational culture and client orientation, and the occupation would be socially 'sanctioned' (authorised) in some manner (Abbott, 1988, cited in Alvesson and Johansson, 2002: 230). The extent to which consultancy can be considered a 'profession' from this type of definition is somewhat questionable. As noted above, consultants have no distinct 'domain of knowledge'; the body of knowledge from which consultants draw is largely non-codified, and their expertise is somewhat ambiguous. Consultants come from a wide range of educational backgrounds, and anyone can start a consulting firm. Moreover, there is no evidence of a distinct occupational culture or socialisation process, and while some firms have ethical codes, these are a fairly recent phenomena and their application and interpretation are, in some cases, arguably ambiguous.

Such factors beg the question, *why* do managers seek the knowledge and 'expertise' of consultants? From where does the knowledge and apparent expertise of consultants originate, and why is it considered to have such force of legitimacy? In order to address such questions, let us examine two noted perspectives of the process of consultancy, strategic and structural perspectives.

Strategic perspectives of consultancy

Earlier in this chapter we emphasised the importance of strategic exchange and processes of negotiation as a crucial feature of the consultant–client relationship. A case can thus be made that consultants have become influential in part due to their powers of persuasion and other related symbolic factors. Clark (1995: 18), for example, argues that it is the intangibility of consultants' knowledge that gives them leeway to 'construct a reality which persuades clients that they have purchased a high quality service . . . each assignment provides an opportunity for a consultant to create or sustain his or her reputation'. Clark (1995) thus argues that consultancy is usefully perceived in terms of a dramaturgical metaphor; in other words, consultancy is a 'performance', an exercise in persuasive communication. Clients are made receptive in the same way that an audience is captive, as consultants adopt a posture of 'conviction and certainty' (Clark, 1995: 117). The client becomes vulnerable and unsettled in the presence of such conviction, with the consultant often playing on any detected uncertainties by convincing the client they 'know' the client's problems. Indeed, consultants could be extremely convincing from this perspective, since their own intangible expertise is very similar to the ultimately ambiguous nature of much management activity. It is through this strategic process of 'impression management' (Clark, 1995: 110) that consultants create their legitimacy and influence. Such strategies involve 'true power/knowledge interactions' (Fincham, 1999: 339):

> Not only does their knowledge empower consultants in relation to clients, but knowledge categories themselves are formed by practitioners. As well as defining their own indispensability, consultants construct client dependency and the problems clients experience so that they are responsive to predefined solutions. The emphasis on strategies of persuasion therefore does much to account for the unexpected power of the consultancy discourse and how consultancy activity is socially accomplished'

> (Fincham, 1999: 339)

While this type of observation is indeed interesting, it does assume that the client plays a fairly passive role in the consultancy–client relationship. Let us now turn to an approach that imparts a more active role to the client.

Structural perspectives of consultancy

As with the strategic perspective briefly outlined above, the structural perspective is also concerned with power. In this case, however, power is not necessarily in the hands of the consultants, rather this perspective presents consultants as a sort of 'by-product' of corporate power. One version of this perspective proposes that consultants are merely a response to corporate demand by large 'capital extensive' organisations that have developed out of global capitalism (Ackroyd and Lawrenson, 1996). The growth dynamics underlying such large organisations means that there is much room for consultants, who are seen largely as a means to introduce efficiency (Taylorist) 'solutions' that assist the process of capital growth, rather than as a source of innovative knowledge.

Jackall (1988) proposes a less radical and slightly different view of the structural perspective. He argues that managers need a constant influx and supply of ideas since they need to appear to be abreast of the latest thinking and ideas, in order to secure career advantage and influence in the organisation's hierarchy and political arena. Far from being dependent on consultants, clients *use* consultants in an active, discriminative and instrumental fashion as a source of ideas that in turn keeps managers ahead of the game. Moreover, consultancy ideas play an important role in legitimising the power of management and their role as important decision-makers in the hierarchy:

> (consultancy ideas) define the executive as the group with the capacity to, and responsibility for, redesigning the organisation. They locate and define the role of the senior management as the authority that has the responsibility and capacity and knowledge to define the structure and design the processes of the organisation.
>
> (Salaman, 2002: 253)

Activity 16.1   Hiring consultants

1. Identify a consultancy intervention that has taken place in your own organisation and reflect on the circumstances surrounding the acquisition of the services of the consultant(s). (If you have no knowledge of the surrounding circumstances you will need to interview someone who does.)

2. Identify any strategic or structural factors associated with the decision to hire the consultant(s). Does one perspective appear to 'fit' better than the other?

Integration of the strategic and structural perspectives

The strategic and structural perspectives are not necessarily at odds, and can be usefully integrated to provide a more encompassing view of managing consulting and the consulting relationship (Fincham, 1999). Both perspectives emphasise the importance of power, despite their respective emphasis on the different sources of such power. Taken together, the two perspectives capture the essential complexity of processes associated with consultancy. In the process of exchange of knowledge, consultancy involves a range of different types of relationships which involve, to varying degrees, the notions of dependency, interdependency, underpinned by dynamics associated with power and manipulation, stemming from either the consultant *or* client camp. Having now explored some of the underlying dynamics and nature of the exchange in the consultancy relationship, let us now examine some of the models and frameworks associated with what consultants actually 'do'.

Models of managing consulting and the consultancy relationship

Early frameworks of management consulting tended to be classificatory schema, which adopted a variety of metaphors to explain the consultancy relationship. Typically, early models of management consulting tended to focus on the role of the consultant as 'helper' – a consultant was brought in to help a client who felt they lacked the skills or knowledge in some aspect or another of managing. Schein (1969) is perhaps the strongest proponent of this view of consulting – his typology has been influential in the prescriptive literature and is typical of the early classifications. His initial proposition was that there were three types of models of consultancy, briefly summarised below:

1. 'Purchase of expertise' model – the client identifies a problem and then purchases the required service.

2. 'Doctor–patient' model – in this case the client is not sure of the cause of a problem. The consultant is brought in to diagnose what is wrong, and then recommends a solution.

3. 'Process consultation' – this involves the client and consultant jointly involved in the process of diagnosis and problem solution. This model emphasises 'empowering' the client towards greater self-sufficiency.

More recently, Schein (2002) has emphasised the increased relevance and importance of this last model of 'process consultation'. He appears to reject the idea that the role of consultants is to provide advice, arguing that 'giving advice in the arena of human problems is generally one of the quickest paths to failure as a consultant' (Schein, 2002: 21). Schein thus sees that consulting is about managing the interpersonal process between client and consultant rather than providing content expertise. Essentially Schein stems from a social psychology perspective, adopting a prescriptive view of consulting which emphasises the psycho-dynamics underlying the consultancy relationship. A fundamental psycho-dynamic, according to Schein, involves the degree of felt dependence of the client towards the consultant. The role of the consultant then is to reaffirm the 'status' and self-esteem of the client in order to ensure mutual trust. To Schein this notion of mutuality is pivotal – in order to build mutual trust, mutual expectations must be explored in the early stages of the consulting relationship, and ultimately the consulting relationship is seen by Schein as one that involves 'mutual helping':

> (The consulting process) can be viewed as one of mutual helping. The helper can create trust by really accepting at every level what the client reveals which requires the helper to change his own conceptions of what may be going on. In a sense the helper is dependent on the client for accurate information and feelings, and the helper must be willing to be helped in order for the client to build up the trust necessary to reveal deeper layers. The relationship gradually becomes equilibrated as both parties give and receive help.
>
> (Schein, 2002: 27)

Schein's view of the consulting relationship is not entirely at odds with the idea that managing consulting and the consultancy relationship is inherently characterised by negotiation, debate and choice. The processes of establishing mutual expectations and 'mutual helping' referred to in the quote above implicitly acknowledges processes associated with debate and negotiation, and associated transmutations of values and interests between consultant and client. However, while Schein does acknowledge issues related to power and the need for negotiation in the consulting relationship, his view is confined to consulting on an individual basis, and his discussion of power is thus based on a limited conception of interpersonal power and interpersonal negotiation. Another criticism lies in the assumption that it is the consultant who initiates the client into 'mutuality' and ensures this process of mutual helping, an assumption which implies an inherent power asymmetry in the relationship, regardless of the stated aim of mutual helping. Finally, Schein's conception fails to consider the symbolic aspect of much consulting work, a point which the following story illustrates.

Exhibit 16.1

The symbolic aspects of consultancy

A management consultant was presenting his report to a group of senior executives. He could tell by the first break for coffee that his presentation was not being well received. This was evidenced by the lack of eye contact, the general shuffling of papers by the executives and the way in which they avoided talking to him over coffee. He was puzzled by this reaction but nonetheless carried on with his presentation after the break, continuing to watch for signs of discomfort and resistance.

At lunchtime, he approached one of the people he knew and asked her why the group were unreceptive to his ideas. The executives, she told him, were used to informal presentations using flip charts and with plenty of interaction. His formal use of sophisticated slides and complex models was alienating the group. They felt uninvolved and would take no ownership of the consultant's ideas unless there was an opportunity to translate these ideas into the language and culture of their own organisation.

The consultant abandoned the rest of his presentation that afternoon. Instead, he invited the main group to split up into smaller groups and discuss his proposals. This then generated lively debate, many flip charts were produced and mounted all over the room, with the kernel of his original ideas now being translated into more familiar organisational language which the executives could make sense of, and accept.

Kitay and Wright (2003) have developed a different model of consulting roles, which attempts to 'map' more fully the various dimensions of consultant activity and the nature of the exchange in the consultancy relationship. Kitay and Wright interviewed 90 consultants and managers in client firms across a broad spectrum of large and small consultancies as well as different 'functional specialisms' (strategy, IT and HR consulting). The resultant typology relies on Watson's (1995) observation that work is structured along the primary axes of administrative and occupational principles as an organising framework. Administrative principles refer to the organisational context of work, while occupational principles refer to 'distinctive' features of the work being performed. The dimensions Kitay and Wright develop from these axes in the context of consultancy are first, differences in expertise, and second, the nature of the boundaries between client and consultant (in terms of being clear or blurred).

With regard to the dimension of expertise, Kitay and Wright distinguish two categories of expertise. The first is termed 'esoteric knowledge', defined as 'specialised knowledge inaccessible to the uninitiated, with a wide ambit to define problems and recommend creative solutions for clients' (Kitay and Wright, 2003: 23). This type of consulting is typically associated with strategy consulting, and is of particular interest for our purposes here, with HR strategy consulting. The second category of expertise is 'technical', usually based on codified packages.

From this view, consultancy activity consists of providing access to a body of knowledge of a more routine nature, for example systems related to recruitment, attitude surveys, reward surveys or implementation of reward.

Kitay and Wright then go on to develop two ideal types within the dimension of 'organisational boundaries'. They argue:

> a crucial difference between consulting roles revolves around the extent to which the consultant is clearly external to the client organisation, with the transaction based primarily on market principles, or has developed a range of social ties with the client, such that the boundary between the client and consulting organisation is to some extent blurred.
>
> (Kitay and Wright, 2003: 24)

They propose then that consultants can be regarded as 'insiders' or 'outsiders'. The former develops long-term relationships with clients, while the latter operates with a relationship based mainly on market criteria.

Kitay and Wright's (2003) typology of consulting roles based on the dimensions and ideal types discussed above is presented in Table 16.1.

From Table 16.1, we can see that what Kitay and Wright (2003) term 'advisers' are consultants with an esoteric knowledge base and whose relationship is mainly a market transaction. This fits with the typical role of the detached external 'expert' called in to solve a problem that may involve much complexity and uncertainty. In this case the consultant is contracted to gather information, and write a report, leaving the client to follow through and implement the recommendations. A 'partner' role also rests on the generation of esoteric knowledge and advice; however, it goes beyond a simple market relationship. In this case, social ties are constructed, and the boundaries between client and consultant become fuzzy or blurred. Perhaps the outsourcing or subcontracting of HR most closely resembles this new partner relationship.

Consultants operating from the position of a more technical knowledge base may also have different levels of interacting with the client. 'Providers' have a low level of interacting with a client, usually limited to a simple market-based relationship. 'Implementers', on the other hand, also provide a technical service but take on some of the characteristics of 'insiders'; in other words, there is more two-way interaction between client and consultant, with the relationship being more consolidated and moving beyond one of simple market transaction. The movement from a simple market-based transaction to an 'insider' relationship can be illustrated by the following account which also highlights some of the difficulties of this transition.

Table 16.1 Kitay and Wright's (2003) typology of consulting roles

| | | Type of knowledge | |
		Esoteric	Technical
Organisational boundaries	Outsider	Adviser	Provider
	Insider	Partner	Implementer

Source: Expertise and Organizational boundaries: the varying roles of Australian management consultants, *Asia Pacific Business Review*, 9(3), pp. 21–40 (Kitay, J. and Wright, C. 2003), reprinted by permission of the publisher (Taylor & Francis Ltd, http://www.informaworld.com)

Exhibit 16.2

The blurring of organisational boundaries

Angie works for a large IT consultancy which specialises in the installation of Human Resource information systems. She is based on the client's site and spends anything up to two years testing the software, training the staff how to use the software and helping them to transfer the data from the existing manual or computer files. During this period of time, although still an employee of her IT company, she spends all of her working time with her clients, in effect acting as a project manager.

Thus, while her initial role, according to the Kitay and Wright typology, classifies her as an outsider with esoteric knowledge (adviser), as time goes by she inevitably forms relationships and friendships with the employees of the host company. This has the effect of blurring the boundaries between client and consultant (partner) as Angie is increasingly assimilated into the group norms and values of her working colleagues. She says that this can be an uncomfortable situation, as the following incident illustrates.

On one particular occasion, an employee of the host company and someone she was training made a serious error which resulted in the loss of substantial amounts of information requiring a manual re-inputting of data at considerable cost. Angie was asked to be a witness and provide 'expert' analysis of the error during the ensuing disciplinary investigation of this employee. She declined to do so. She felt that her position as 'consultant' to the company was compromised as they were treating her as if she was one of their own employees. Her role as consultant over a period of some months had become that of implementer, providing technical knowledge but now with considerable two-way interaction in the client–consultant relationship.

Eventually, Angie was able to persuade the managers in the host company that it would be inappropriate and potentially unethical for her to be involved in a disciplinary investigation and she was able to negotiate her way out of it.

It is important to note that the ideal types developed in Kitay and Wright's (2003) model are not static 'types'. Kitay and Wright propose that at different times, a consultant will take on different roles, in their words 'depending upon the outcome of negotiations with the client and the changing nature of projects' (2003: 26). Again, we find ourselves back to the fundamental notion that managing consulting and the consultancy relationship are based on processes of negotiation, debate and choice.

The processes of negotiation, debate and choice between client and consultant involve a number of factors that go beyond the 'rational' planning of a consultancy intervention and resultant change. Throughout this text it is emphasised that if we want to understand how long-term changes to whole organisations occur, we must examine the managerial politics, and the values and interests of those actors who are responsible for such change. Bringing in an 'outsider' to influence the strategy-making process adds a further layer of complexity to this subjective aspect of strategy-making. In addition to the 'rational' task of formulating a required intervention, the consultant will be subjected to the political dynamics surrounding the processes of negotiation and choice. Against this backdrop, the consultant will also be engaged in his or her own construction of meaning within the organisation, as well as engaged in the processes of 'impression management' discussed earlier in this chapter.

Let us now return to the Moddens Foods case study (introduced in Chapter 1), where it has become apparent that the different actors in the firm hold different views on the firm's strategic direction.

Case Study 16.1

A consultant is hired at Moddens Foods

It is now a few months since Sam Modden, company chairman, supported by the marketing director Hal Selz, had serious misgivings and arguments with the managing director, Juan Poort, and Frank Angle, the operations director. The basis for this disagreement was a difference of opinion as to whether Moddens Foods should follow a strategy of producing 'cheap chicken nuggets' or whether it should maintain the family reputation as 'a purveyor of fine quality game and sausages to the discriminating classes'.

In spite of his position as company chairman, Sam has been unable to resolve this conflict among the directors of the company and they are no closer to achieving a satisfactory solution. Jean Frear, the HR director, is concerned that the schism will have a detrimental effect on the workings of the company. She has noted that the managers reporting to each director are beginning to form factions and the ripple of unrest is spreading around the company.

Jean has had separate meetings with both Sam and Juan in which she has proposed a 'middle ground' to try to resolve the conflict. In the meetings she suggested to them that she contract a business consultant to carry out an independent review of the company's strategy. The response of both Sam and Juan was initially negative, albeit for different reasons. Sam couldn't see how an 'outsider' would be able appreciate the history and 'culture' of Moddens Foods. Jean assured Sam that she would give the consultant a full briefing of the origins and aims of the company, and fully explain 'how things were done' at Moddens. Sam was satisfied with this and agreed to her proposal.

Juan's concerns were somewhat different. He didn't like the idea of what he called 'some geeky graduate consultant' with no real experience coming into Moddens with 'new-fangled ideas'. His real concern, which he didn't voice to Jean, was simply that some young, ethically sensitive and environmentally aware consultant would indeed come up with a plan that did not fit in with his own plan of routinising production methods and using cheap labour. Jean convinced Juan that she would carefully source the consultant from a reputable firm, and would consider only a seasoned and experienced consultant. Juan felt reassured by this, and even felt a little confident that any experienced consultant worth their weight would recognise the financial benefits his desired changes would bring. To help this process along, he decided to tell his ally Frank Angle about the possibility of the consultant, and together they could plan a little chat to the consultant on his or her arrival at Moddens.

Jean was pleased that her idea to contract a consultant was accepted. She felt that the arrival of a consultant would send the message to everyone at Moddens Foods that the conflict surrounding the strategic direction was being taken seriously and that 'best practice' would be applied. Jean also felt that an external consultant's ideas would be less likely to meet with resistance since they were essentially 'neutral'. Jean also had a different set of motivations for hiring the consultant – if the consultant's ideas proved a success she would ensure that such praise be redirected towards her; after all, it was her idea to contract the consultant in the first place. On the other hand, she thought that if the ideas or interventions proved unpopular or even failed, the consultant could take the blame.

Jean went to three of the leading consulting firms before being satisfied that she had found the 'right' person. She checked academic qualifications of individual consultants in the firms, checked whether they had previous experience in similar firms, and also followed up with previous clients as to their satisfaction with the service. Eventually she chose Max Athlone from the Peterson Group of consultants, and she gave him a full and detailed picture of Moddens Foods. This included a detailed history of the firm, emphasising its traditional commitment to high-quality output. Max listened intently and patiently to Jean before asking a series of questions. He had several years of consultancy experience – he realised the complexity of the situation at Moddens Foods, and considered that it required a fairly creative approach. Based on what Jean had told him, he realised that Moddens Foods could be a long-term client, and he suspected that his services could be required in carrying out any recommendations, rather than simply presenting a report.

Activity 16.2 The Moddens Foods' consultant – Max Athlone

1. Using Kitay and Wright's typology, identify which 'type' of consultant Max Athlone most closely resembles.

2. In what way are the interests, values and ideas of the strategy-makers likely to impact on the task facing Max Athlone?

In Chapter 1 we noted the two main factions at Moddens, and also noted that the HR director was doing her best to remain neutral. From the developments outlined in the case above we can see that Jean's interests and values have (however unwittingly) infiltrated her intention to remain neutral. Her briefing to Max Athlone focused strongly on the desire of Moddens to continue to produce a quality product, a view no doubt that Sam Modden would also express to the consultant on his arrival. Juan Poort's values and interests are also evident – he has clear plans to lobby Max Athlone, and intends to conscript other members of his faction to do the same. Another issue that surfaces in the case study is that there are some official and unofficial side-functions associated with Max's role. For example, aside from the official function of sorting out the strategic direction of Moddens

Foods, Jean clearly sees other more subtle and unofficial 'uses' for Max, mainly that he will legitimise the process of strategic redirection, and that his actions may even potentially positively affect her career. Managing consulting and the consultancy relationship involves an understanding of the 'official and unofficial side-functions' associated with the consultancy role. Kieser (2002), for example, proposes that management contract consultants for carrying out a number of additional functions, most of which are not explicitly included in their contracts:

- *Legitimisation.* Bringing in a consultant sends signals throughout the organisation that 'best practices' are being applied.

- *Stimulation of acceptance.* Consultants bring expert power into the change process. They also are likely to be persuasive, with powerful presentation and rhetorical techniques that will overcome organisational members' resistance to change.

- *Providing weapons for politics.* As their project becomes accepted, consultants can be instrumental in increasing the power of some management groups while undermining the projects of rival groups. Also, consultants may take the roles of scapegoats. For example, they may propose to downsize by making 3000 workers redundant, thereby opening up negotiations which give management and employee representatives the opportunity to agree to the laying off of fewer workers.

- *Fostering careers of sponsors.* Consultants typically portray the managers that hired them in a favourable manner and allow them to claim much of the praise for themselves if an assignment is declared successful.

- *Interpretation.* Consultants often take on the role of a sounding board, since managers have a need for 'impartial' discussion partners so they can reflect on their actions and generate ideas.

So far we have touched on a number of different issues associated with managing consultancy and the consulting relationship. We have examined issues related to the 'professionalism' of consultancy, discussed the nature of the exchange between client and consultant, and briefly explored issues related to power, politics and negotiation. A model that incorporates many of these issues has been neatly articulated by Alvesson and Johansson (2002). Table 16.2 provides a summary of their typology. Like Kitay and Wright (2003), they argue that consultants are not locked into any one type of role, rather consultants continually negotiate their approach, not just from assignment to assignment but also within a specific assignment. Alvesson and Johansson's model is interesting since they consider and incorporate the additional dimensions of 'elements of professionalism', have attempted to map the nature of political activity, and have also considered the type of client in relation to the consultant.

From Table 16.2 we can see that Alvesson and Johansson (2002) label one type of consultant the 'esoteric expert'. The emphasis here is on the consultant who possesses considerable academic education and organisational experience, with an emphasis on rationality, predictability and careful judgement. This type of consultant is objective and neutral in the types of 'best practice' that they advocate. The esoteric expert addresses problems that are seen as 'non-political', and if his or her integrity is threatened, ethical standards prevail. The corresponding client is likely to be a lay person, a purchaser of intangible services. The 'strength' of the client in this case determines the extent and breadth of the assignment.

Table 16.2 Varieties in types of consultants and clients in management consultancy work

Type of management consultant	Claim of professionalism	Significant elements of anti-professionalism	Politics	Corresponding type of client
Esoteric experts	Strong: firmly founded in knowledge, technocratic	Hiding technical core with socio-political skills, questionable knowledge base	Technocratic politics, expert rule	Lay person, purchaser of service
Brokers of meaning	Relatively weak: creative application of a body of partly established vocabularies	Downplaying of expert role	Manipulation, management of meaning	Conversation partner, co-maker of meaning
Traders in trouble	Ambiguous: context-sensitive process or problem-solving expertise	Subordination to interests of power, axeman	Direct support for and legitimisation of top management	Ruler, director or troubleshooter
Agents of anxiety and sellers of security	Weak: developer and exploiter of new standards, novel/repackaged ideas and vocabularies	Messianic and revolutionary ideas, breaking with tradition, including science and established, tested 'truths', fashion orientation	Disciplinary power, normalisation	Victim of uncertainty, cultural dupe

Source: Alvesson and Johansson (2002: 234)

Despite the neutrality of this role, the reality is perhaps somewhat different, since different values, interests and perceptions in most complex organisational settings mean that claims to neutral expertise are quite difficult to maintain (Alvesson and Johansson, 2002).

'Brokers of meaning' are consultants who specialise in the production and delivery of linguistic artefacts. This role comes close to the process consulting role proposed by Schein (1969), for the role of consultant is not to provide expert advice, rather they construct language tools and metaphors for understanding issues in order to clarify them. This type of consultant falls relatively lower on professionalism, with the emphasis on social processes rather than specified solutions. Power and politics are also somewhat downplayed in this metaphor, although there is the possibility that language may be used for manipulation.

In contrast to the neutrality in the two previous categories, 'traders in trouble' are associated with power and political issues. This category highlights the various interest of different actors and the conflict-ridden nature of problems that consultants are contracted to deal with. From this perspective, consultants are typically used when a senior executive identifies less than desired performance in some area. There may be some blaming and loss of status, but more serious issues may be involved, such as promotion, demotion, loss of resources or even employment. The client here is strong, and plays a powerfully directive role with the corresponding weaker consultant. This is the consultant who is viewed as the 'whore in pinstripes' (Jackall, 1988: 140), one who is completely subordinated to the authority of the client. This category involves the standard notion of professionalism, since clients use consultants they can trust to serve their interests. The consultant in this category may be used as a scapegoat but the 'trader in trouble' is required to accept that they are paid well for doing so.

The final consultancy type in Alvesson and Johansson's (2002) model is consultants as 'agents of anxiety and sellers of security'. This label highlights the role of consultants in the creation of fads, fashions and 'new solutions'. Managers operate in the context of stress and uncertainty in an ever-changing economic, technical and social environment. New skills and qualities are necessary to adapt and change within this context. Consultants serve to fuel anxiety by creating new schemes and fads, constantly being replaced by even newer packages. With each new management fashion, existing skills are seen as obsolete, and tremendous efforts to bridge the gap between current skills and abilities and more up-to-date ones are encouraged. Consultants, as the instigators of such management fashions, then serve to trigger and reinforce the anxiety that creates receptivity for the employment of consultancy services to remove such anxiety. Here the power lies with the consultant. However, the metaphor works against traditional conceptions of professionalism. The consultant merely claims to 'know better' than the client, and the knowledge employed has little to with science or validated practice (Alvesson and Johansson, 2002).

Activity 16.3	Identifying a successful consultancy intervention

1. Reflect on the types of management consultancy outlined in Table 16.2 with reference to the same (or a different) consultancy intervention which you considered in Activity 16.1. Identify which label, if any, most closely applies to your chosen intervention and the reasons why this label applies.

2. Consider whether the particular management consultancy type you have identified was in fact, appropriate for that particular consultancy intervention. In other words, to what extent were the outcomes of the intervention 'successful' relative to the original objectives and to the parties concerned?

3. Reflect on the lessons learned from the above analysis which could be taken forward to help with the planning of any future consultancy intervention.

Having now reviewed various models of managing consulting and the consultancy relationship, let us turn our attention to the matter of ethical issues and consultancy.

Ethical issues in managing consulting and the consultancy relationship

The increasing popularity of the use of consultants has arguably led to an increase in client expectations of consultants' services, which in turn has led to increased competition *between* consultants. It is perhaps not surprising that in the United States, consultants and consulting firms are finding themselves to be the target of litigation, typically due to 'overstated contract offers'. Such action is also potentially likely in the UK and Europe. The issue of ethics and consultancy has come to the fore with events such as the Enron scandal, however, it is not just accounting consultancy firms who have ethical 'responsibilities'. The decisions made by consultants who advise on strategic human resourcing issues may also have far-reaching effects not just for shareholders, but for other actors both inside and outside the organisation. Consultants advise on reward systems, job design, recruitment and selection, and strategies such as downsizing, all of which have potential ethical implications (refer to Chapter 4).

In Chapter 4 we examined ethical issues associated with strategic human resourcing; in particular, we focused on the ethical 'choices' available to those responsible for strategic human resourcing. In this section a similar approach will be taken; however, the discussion has a slightly more prescriptive flavour. The same continuum of ethical stances highlighted in Figure 4.1 (p. 108) can be applied in the context of managing consulting and the consultancy relationship. Importantly, *either party* (client or consultant) involved in the consulting relationship may adopt a variety of ethical stances ranging from 'quietism' to 'ethical assertiveness' in relation to any unethical aspects of a consultancy intervention.

If we refer back to the strategic and structural perspectives of consultancy discussed earlier in this chapter, we can see ethical issues in both perspectives. In the strategic perspective, the notion of 'impression management' is 'ethically loaded' since it implies that consultants *induce* a state of ongoing dependency in the client. Echoing Schein's conception of consultation as activity that involves 'mutual helping', Ozley and Armenakis (2000) argue that the level of dependency is a crucial issue in 'ethical consulting'. They view the level of dependency as being the first in a series of steps which should be encountered in order for ethical consulting to eventuate. Figure 16.1 neatly outlines their model. From it, you can see that the consultancy relationship is the first 'block', and that each block in the model provides the foundation for the next block. It must be noted that this is a heavily prescriptive model, and is subject to the same critique as given to Schein's model of consulting discussed earlier in this chapter. For example, the model assumes the initial power dominance of the consultant, who then initiates and assumes responsibility for ensuring mutuality. Despite the logical problems underpinning this approach, the authors feel the model has its merits, particularly in

Figure 16.1 A model of ethical consulting
Source: Ozley and Armenakis (2000)

acknowledging that the consultancy relationship is dynamic and likely to go through various stages over time. The model also broadly fits with the notion that the consultancy relationship is a negotiated relationship.

Based on their research, Ozley and Armenakis (2000) have suggested that the consultancy relationship moves through three stages of development. The first of these is 'dependency', since managers have (assumedly) called in a consultant to solve a problem, and as a result the organisation is dependent in varying degrees on the consultant for advice, suggestions, solutions and so on. If for any reason either party is perceived as unhelpful, then this can lead to a 'counter-dependent' relationship. Here we might find comments from the client such as 'What are those people doing here?' or 'They're getting loads of money to say/do what we've been trying to do for years', or even worse 'What a racket!' (Ozley and Armenakis, 2000). Ozley and Armenakis suggest that counter-dependency is difficult to avoid. The extent to which the consultant engages in ethical practices will expedite moving through this stage, which results from a variety of causes such as unrealistic expectations, impatient clients and resource allocation problems. Negotiation and debate are essential in this stage of the relationship. The ultimate and desired stage according to Ozley and Armenakis is the 'interdependent' client/consultant relationship. In this type of relationship the consultant only does for the client 'what they cannot and/or will not' do for themselves and the consultant and client mutually agree on what those issues are. Again, this stage implicitly suggests the ongoing processes of negotiation, debate and choice, in order to avoid falling back into the counter-dependent stage. From this stage of relationship development, the other 'blocks' in the model progress through stages of implementation until the relationship is terminated. Again, this process of disengagement of the consultant is a negotiated process.

We have just examined ethical issues in the context of the strategic perspective of consulting, focusing on the consultancy relationship. In the structural perspective, ethical issues may also arise. Senior decision-makers in organisations may bring in consultants to maximise expansiveness and efficiency at all costs, potentially exploiting the human resources of the firm. Additionally, ethical issues may also arise if managers engage consultants purely to keep ahead of the game and to advance their own status and power.

Activity 16.4   Ethics and managing consultants

Identify a consultancy intervention that has taken place in your own organisation, perhaps the same one you identified in Activity 16.1. Identify any ethical issues associated with the way the consultancy was managed and in the consultancy relationship. Also, identify any ethical impacts of the intervention.

Summary

In this chapter the following key points have been made:

● HR strategies emerge from political processes of debate, negotiation and argument among strategic decision-makers, and from the way that managers interpret the circumstances affecting the organisation. Against this backdrop, the processes associated with managing consultancy and the consultancy relationship are seen as a further 'layering' of debate, negotiation and argument.

- What characterises the consultancy relationship is a set of complex political processes, since each strategy-maker engaged in the consultancy relationship is acting from a different set of personal and group values and interests.

- Symbolic and structural dimensions also characterise the consultancy relationship, owing to the different values and interests not just from strategy-makers, but also from those constituents who perceive that they are likely to be affected in varying ways by the outcomes of the processes associated with managing any consultancy intervention.

- An essential defining feature of managing consulting and the consultancy relationship is that it involves the strategic exchange of knowledge. In particular, there is recognition of the involvement of all managers in dealing with human resourcing matters and an emerging change in direction for HR specialists in the processes of knowledge exchange.

- Strategic and structural perspectives of consultancy help us understand why consultancy is desired by strategic decision-makers.

- Managing consulting and the consultancy relationship involves the acknowledgement of both 'official' and 'unofficial' aspects of consultancy.

- Consultancy roles are varied according to factors such as the type of knowledge base that is required, the degree of dependency of the client, the nature of the market transaction, and whether the consultancy relationship is short- or long-term.

- There are a number of ethical issues associated with managing consulting and the consultancy relationship, and such ethical issues can arise from activities of either the client or the consultant (or both). Such ethical issues include the nature of the consulting relationship (such as the degree of induced dependence), managers using consultants solely for their own means, as well as more substantive issues surrounding the impact of consultancy interventions on other constituents both inside and outside the organisation.

Discussion questions

1. To what extent do you agree that engaging an external consultant conveys a message throughout an organisation that 'best practices' are being applied?

2. Is HR changing to a consultative model or business partner model in your organisation? In terms of the tensions, contradictions and challenges inherent in the consultancy relationship, what implications does this changing model of HR have for:

   a) HR specialists?

   b) line managers?

   c) the relationship between HR specialists and line managers?

3. What are the arguments for and against the introduction of a 'code of conduct' and/or a 'licence to operate' for anyone who claims to be a consultant?

4. How far, if at all, is it possible to anticipate the unofficial side-functions associated with consultancy? Consider this in relation to a consultancy intervention with which you are familiar.

5. Consider the fact that the literature on consultancy is characterised by attempts to attribute *labels* to different kinds of consultancy or to establish *typologies*. What are the main problems with this approach?

Further reading

Readers wishing to further explore some of the more critical approaches associated with managing consulting and the consultancy relationship should consult Clark and Fincham (2002). More prescriptive accounts of managing consulting and the consultancy relationship can be found in Wickam (1999) and Sadler (1998). For some interesting reading on issues related to ethics and consultancy, readers are directed to von Weltzien Hoivik and Føllesdal (1995). This chapter has not touched on the origins or history of modern consulting; however, interested readers are directed to McKenna (1995) and Kipping (1996, 2002).

Bibliography

Abraham, S.E., Karns, L.A., Shaw, K. and Mena, A.M. (2001) 'Managerial competencies and the managerial appraisal process', *Journal of Management Development*, 20 (10), pp. 842–52.

ACAS (Advisory, Conciliation and Arbitration Service) (1990) Consultation and communication Occasional Paper 49, London: ACAS.

ACAS (Advisory, Conciliation and Arbitration Service) (1991, 2007) *Annual Reports 1991, 2007*, ACAS.

ACAS (Advisory, Conciliation and Arbitration Service) (2006) *Advisory Booklet – Managing Attendance and Employee Turnover*, London: ACAS.

Ackers, P. (2001) 'Employment ethics', in *Contemporary Human Resource Management*, Redman, T. and Wilkinson, A. (eds), London: Pearson.

Ackers, P. and Payne, J. (1998) 'British trade unions and social partnership: rhetoric, reality and strategy', *The International Journal of Human Resource Management*, 9 (3), pp. 529–50.

Ackers, P., Marchington, M., Wilkinson, A. and Dundon, T. (2005) 'Partnership and voice, with or without trade unions: changing UK management approaches to organisational participation', in *Partnership and Modernisation in Employment Relations*, Stuart, M. and Martinez Lucio, M. (eds), London: Routledge, pp. 23–45.

Ackers, P., Smith, C. and Smith, P. (1996) *The New Workplace and Trade Unionism; Critical Perspectives on Work and Organisation*, London: Routledge.

Ackroyd, S. and Lawrenson, D. (1996) 'Knowledge work and organisational transformation: analysing contemporary change in the social use of expertise', in *New Relationships in the Organised Professions*, Fincham, R. (ed.), Aldershot: Avebury.

Adams, J.S. (1963) 'Toward an understanding of inequity', *Journal of Abnormal and Social Psychology*, 67 (4), pp. 422–36.

Adams, J.S. (1965) 'Inequality in social exchange', in *Advances in Experimental Social Psychology*, Vol. 2, Berkowitz, L. (ed.), New York: Academic Press.

Adler, N.J. (1997) *International Dimensions of Organisational Behaviour*, 3rd edition, Cincinnati: South-Western College Publishing.

Algera, J.A. and Greuter, M.A. (1993) *Functie-analyse. Nieuw Handboek A&O-psychologie*, Aflevering 11.

Allen, M.R. and Wright, P. (2007) 'Strategic management and HRM', in *The Oxford Handbook of Human Resource Management*, Boxall, P., Purcell, J. and Wright, P. (eds), Oxford: Oxford University Press.

Alvesson, M. (2000) 'Social identify in knowledge intensive companies', *Journal of Management Studies*, 37 (8), pp. 1101–23.

Alvesson, M. and Deetz, S. (1996) 'Critical theory and postmodernism approaches to organisation studies', in *Handbook of Organisation Studies*, Clegg, S.R., Hardy, C. and Nord, W.R. (eds), London: Sage.

Alvesson, M. and Johansson, A. (2002) 'Professionalism and politics in management consultancy work', in *Critical Consulting*, Clark, T. and Fincham, R. (eds), Oxford: Blackwell.

Amin, A. and Roberts, J. (eds) (2008) *Communities of Practice: Community, Economic Creativity, and Organization*, Oxford: Oxford University Press.

Anderson, N. (2001) 'Towards a theory of socialization impact: selection as pre-selection socialization', *International Journal of Selection and Assessment*, 9 (1–2), pp. 84–91.

Anderson, N. and Herriot, P. (1997) *International Handbook of Selection and Assessment*, Chichester: John Wiley and Sons.

Anderson, N. and Ostroff, C. (1997) 'Selection as socialisation', in *International Handbook of Selection and Assessment*, Anderson, N. and Herriot, P. (eds), Chichester: John Wiley and Sons, pp. 543–66.

Anderson, N. and Witvliet, C. (2008) 'Fairness reactions to personnel selection methods', *International Journal of Selection and Assessment*, 16 (1), pp. 1–10.

Anderson, N., Silvester, J., Cunningham-Snell, N. and Haddleton, E. (1999) 'Relationships between candidate self-monitoring, perceived personality, and selection interview outcomes', *Human Relations*, 52 (9), pp. 1115–31.

Andrews, K. (1971) *The Concept of Corporate Strategy*, Homewood, IL: Dow Jones Irwin.

Ansoff, H.I. (1965) *Corporate Strategy*, New York: McGraw Hill.

Anxo, D. and O'Reilly, J. (2000) 'Working-time regimes and transitions in comparative perspective', in *Working Time Challenges*, O'Reilly, J., Cebrian, I. and Lallement, M. (eds), Cheltenham: Edward Elgar.

Argyris, C. (1998) 'Empowerment: the emperor's new clothes', *Harvard Business Review*, May/June, pp. 98–105.

Arkin, A. (1996) 'Open business is good for business', *People Management*, 2 (1), pp. 24–7.

Armstrong, M. (1995) *Personnel Management Practice*, 5th edition, London: Kogan Page.

Armstrong, M. (2002) *Employee Reward*, 3rd edition, London: Chartered Institute of Personnel and Development.

Armstrong, M. and Baron, A. (2005) *Managing Performance: Performance Management in Action*, London: Chartered Institute of Personnel and Development.

Armstrong, M. and Brown, D. (2001) *New Dimensions in Pay*, London: CIPD.

Armstrong, M. and Murlis, H. (1998) *Reward Management: A Handbook of Remuneration Strategy and Practice*, 4th edition, London: Kogan Page.

Armstrong, M. and Murlis, H. (2007) *Reward Management: A Handbook of Remuneration Strategy and Practice*, 5th edition, London: Kogan Page.

Arnold, J., Cooper, C.L. and Robertson, I.T. (1997) *Work Psychology: Understanding Human Behaviour in the Workplace*, London: Pitman Publishing.

Arrowsmith, J. and McGoldrick, A. (1995) 'A flexible future for older workers?', *Personnel Review*, 26 (4), pp. 258–73.

Arthur, M.B., Inkson, K. and Pringle, J.K. (1999) *The New Career: Individual Action and Economic Change*, London: Sage.

Ashton, C. and Morton, L. (2005) 'Managing talent for competitive advantage', *Strategic HR Review*, 4 (5), pp. 28–31.

Ashton, D. and Felstead, A. (2001) 'From training to life-long learning: the birth of knowledge society?', in *Human Resource Management: A Critical Text*, Story, J. (ed.), London: Thomson.

Assen van, M., Berg van den, G. and Wobben, J.J. (2008) *Excelleren = Optimaliseren en Innoveren*, Assen: van Gorcum.

Atkinson, A., Burgess, S., Croxson, B., Gregg, P., Propper, C., Slater, H. and Wilson, D. (2004) 'Evaluating the impact of performance-related pay for teachers in England', CMPO working paper No 04/113, University of Bristol: Centre for Market and Public Organisation.

Atkinson, J. (1984) 'Manpower strategies for flexible organisations', *Personnel Management*, August, pp. 28–31.

Atkinson, J. (1987) 'Flexibility or fragmentation? The UK labour market in the eighties', *Labour and Society*, 12 (1), pp. 87–102.

Atkinson, J. (1996) *Temporary Work and the Labour Market, Report 311*, Brighton: Institute of Employment Studies.

Atkinson, J. and Meager, N. (1986) *Flexibility in Firms: A Study of Changing Working Patterns and Practices*, Brighton: Institute of Manpower Studies.

Audit Commission (1993) *Citizen's Charter Indicators; Charting a Course*, London: Audit Commission.

Autor, D. (2000) *Why do Temporary Help Firms provide Free General Skills Training?* Working paper 7637. Cambridge MA: National Bureau of Economic Research.

Bach, S. (ed.) (2005) *Managing Human Resources – Personnel Management in Transition'*, 4th edition, Oxford: Blackwell.

Bach, S. and Sisson, K. (eds) (2000) Personnel Management in Britain – A Comprehensive Guide to Theory and Practice, Oxford: Blackwell.

Bacon, N. (2001) 'Employee relations', in *Contemporary Human Resource Management: Text and Cases*, Redman, T. and Wilkinson, A. (eds), London: Financial Times/ Prentice Hall.

Bacon, N. and Story, J. (2000) 'New employee relations strategies in Britain: towards individualism or partnership?', *British Journal of Industrial Relations*, 38 (3), pp. 407–27.

Baddon, L., Hunter, L., Hyman, J., Leopold, J. and Ramsay, H. (1989) *People's Capitalism? A Critical Analysis of Profit Sharing and Employee Share Ownership*, London: Routledge.

Baier, K. (2002) 'Egoism', in *A Companion to Ethics*, Singer, P. (ed.), Oxford: Blackwell.

Bailyn, L. (2002) 'Time in organizations: constraints on, and possibilities for, gender equity in the workplace', in *Advancing Women's Careers*, Burke, R.J. and Nelson, D.L. (eds), Oxford: Blackwell.

Baker, E. and Jennings, K. (2000) 'Limitations in "realistic recruiting" and subsequent socialization efforts: the case of Riddick Bowe and the United States Marine Corps.', *Public Personnel Management*, 29 (3), pp. 367–78.

Ball, R. and Monaghan, C. (1996) 'Performance review: the British experience', *Local Government Studies*, 22 (1), Spring.

Ball, S. (2001) 'The European employment strategy: the will but not the way?', *Industrial Law Journal*, 30 (4), pp. 353–74.

Bamberger, P. and Meshoulam, I. (2000) *Human Resource Strategy: Formulation, Implementation, and Impact*, Thousand Oaks, CA: Sage.

B&Q, (2008) http://www.jobs.diy.com/jobs/about/diversity.html. (accessed 20 May 2008).

Barber, A.E. (1998) *Recruiting Employees: Individual and Organizational Perspectives*, Thousand Oaks, CA: Sage.

Barnes, L. and Ashtiany, S. (2003) 'The diversity approach to achieving equality: potential and pitfalls', *Industrial Law Journal*, 32 (4), pp. 274–96.

Barnes, N. (1997) 'Invisible workers: a study of academic employees on fixed term contracts in Higher Education', MBA dissertation, University of Sussex.

Barnett, A. (1996) 'Gas regulator cools cuts', *The Observer*, 11 August, Business Section, p. 3.

Barnett, D. (2002) *Managing Dismissal: Practical Guidance on the Art of Dismissing Fairly*, London: Tolley.

Barney, J.B. (1991) 'Firm resources and sustained competitive advantage', *Journal of Management*, 17 (1), pp. 99–120.

Barney, J.B. (1992) 'Integrating organizational behaviour and strategy formulation research: a resource based analysis', in *Advances in Strategic Management*, Shrivastava, P., Huff, A. and Dutton, J. (eds), Greenwich, CT: JAI Press, Vol. 8, pp. 39–61.

Baron, R. (1989) 'Impression management by applicants during employment interviews: the "too much of a good thing" effect', in Eder, R.W. and Ferris, G.R. (eds), *The Employment Interview: Theory, Research and Practice*, Newbury Park, CA: Sage Publications, pp. 204–15.

Barrick, M., Mount, M. and Judge, T. (2001) 'Personality and performance at the beginning of the new millennium: what do we know and where do we go next?', *International Journal of Selection and Assessment*, 9, pp. 9–30.

Barrow, S. and Mosley, R. (2005) *The Employer Brand: Bringing the Best of Brand Management to People at Work*, Chichester: John Wiley and Sons.

Barsoux, J.L. and Lawrence, P. (1990) *Management in France*, London: Cassell.

Bartholomew, D. (2008) *Building on Knowledge: Developing Expertise, Creativity and Intellectual Capital in the Construction Professions*, Oxford: Wiley Blackwell.

Bartlett, C.A. and Ghoshal, S. (1989) *Managing Across Borders: The Transnational Solution*, Boston: Harvard Business School Press.

Bassett, P. (1986) *Strike Free*, London: Macmillan.

Bassi, L.J. (1997) 'Harnessing the power of intellectual capital', *Training and Development*, 51 (12 December) (1–2), pp. 9–29.

Bates, I. (1995) (ed.) 'Special Issue on competence and the NVQ framework', *British Journal of Education and Work*, 8 (2).

Bauman, Z. (1993) *Postmodern Ethics*, London: Blackwell.

BBC (2003) The Money Programme: 'The Great British Job Take-Away', 22 October.

BBC (2006) Supermarkets covet Polish spend. http://news.bbc.co.uk/1/hi/business/5332024.stm. (accessed 22 May 2008).

Beach, L.R. (1990) *Image theory: Decision Making in Personal and Organisational Contexts*, Chichester: John Wiley and Sons.

Beard, D. (2003) 'Structural and Cultural Change – Reasons to Leave or not to Leave: A Research Attempt to Unravel the Mystery of Leaving', MBA dissertation, Nottingham Trent University.

Beardwell, I. (1997) 'Into the "black hole"? An examination of the personnel management of non-unionism', *New Zealand Journal of Industrial Relations*, 22 (1), pp. 37–49.

Beatson, M. (1995) *Labour Market Flexibility*, Employment Department, Research Series No. 48.

Beaumont, P.B. (1987) *The Decline of Trade Union Organisation*, London: Croom Helm.

Beaumont, P.B. (1993) *Human Resource Management*, London: Sage.

Beaumont, P.B. (1994) 'US Human Resource Management Literature: a review', in *Human Resource Strategies*, Beaumont, P.B. (ed.), London: Sage, pp. 20–37.

Beavis, S. and Barrie, C. (1996) 'Problems lurk in the gas pipeline', *The Guardian*, 2 August, p. 10.

Becker, B. and Gerhart, B. (1996) 'The impact of human resource management on organizational performance: progress and prospects', *Academy of Management Journal*, 39 (4), pp. 779–801.

Beckhard, R. (1994) 'A model for the executive management of transformational change', in *Human Resource Strategies*, Beckhard, R. (ed.), London: Sage, pp. 95–106.

Bee, F. and Bee, R. (1994) *Training Needs Analysis and Evaluation*, London: CIPD.

Beer, M. and Spector, R. (1985) *Human Resource Management: A General Manager's Perspective*, New York: Free Press.

Begley, A. and Thomas, M. (1998) 'Coping strategies as predictors of employee distress and turnover after an organisational consolidation: a longitudinal analysis', *Journal of Occupational and Organisational Psychology*, December, 71 (4).

Bell, W. and Hanson, C. (1984) *Profit Sharing and Employee Shareholding Attitude Survey*, London: Industrial Participation Association.

Bennett, R. and Leduchowicz (1983) 'What makes for an effective trainer?', *Journal of European Industrial Training*, 7 (2), pp. 1–31.

Bercusson, B. (1995) 'The conceptualisation of European law', *Industrial Law Journal*, 24 (1), pp. 3–18.

Bercusson, B. (1999) 'Democratic legitimacy and European labour law', *Industrial Law Journal*, 28 (1), pp. 153–70.

Berger, P.L. and Luckmann, T. (1966) *The Social Construction of Reality*, Harmondsworth: Penguin.

Berggren, C. (1989) 'New production concepts in final assembly in the Swedish experience', in *The Transformation of Work?* Wood, S. (ed.), London: Unwin Hyman.

Bevan, S. and Thompson, M. (1992) *Pay and Performance – the Employer Experience*, The Institute of Employment Studies, Report 258.

Beynon, H. (1984) *Working for Ford*, 2nd edition, Harmondsworth: Penguin.

Bhatt, G.D. (2001) 'Knowledge management in organisations: examining the interaction between technologies, techniques, and people', *Journal of Knowledge Management*, 5 (1), pp. 68–75.

Bibby, A. (2002) 'Home start', *People Management*, 8 (1), pp. 36–7.

Bierhoff, H.W., Cohen, R.L. and Greenberg, J. (1986) *Justice in Social Relations*, New York: Plenum.

Biernacki, R. (1995) *The Fabrication of Labour: Germany and Britain 1640–1914*, Berkeley: University of California Press.

Biesebroeck, J. van (2007) 'The cost of flexibility', *Assembly Automation* 27 (1), pp. 55–64.

Billig, M. (1995) *Banal Nationalism*, London: Sage.

Black, J. and Ackers, P. (1988) 'The Japanisation of British industry: a case study of quality circles in the carpet industry', *Employee Relations*, 10 (6), pp. 9–16.

Black, J. and Ackers, P. (1990) 'Voting for employee involvement at General Motors', paper presented to the *8th Labour Process Conference*, University of Aston, March.

Black, J.S., Gregersen, H.B., Mendenhall, M. and Stroh, L. (1999) *Globalizing People through International Assignments*, Boston, MA: Addison-Wesley.

Blackler, F. (1995) 'Knowledge, knowledge work and organisations: an overview and interpretation', *Organisation Studies*, 16 (6), pp. 1021–46.

Blanchard, N.P. and Thacker, J.W. (1998) *Effective Training: Systems, Strategies and Practices*, Englewood Mills, NJ: Prentice Hall.

Blanchard, N.P. and Thacker, J.W. (2003) *Effective Training: Systems, Strategies and Practices*, 2nd edition, Englewood Mills, NJ: Prentice Hall.

Blinkhorn, S. and Johnston, C. (1990) 'The insignificance of personality testing', *Nature*, 348, pp. 671–2.

Blyton, P. and Morris, J. (1991) *A Flexible Future*, Berlin: de Gruyter.

Blyton, P. and Turnbull, P. (1992) *Reassessing Human Resource Management*, London: Sage.

Blyton, P. and Turnbull, P. (1998) *The Dynamics of Employment Relations*, 2nd edition, London: Macmillan.

Blyton, P. and Turnbull, P. (2004) *The Dynamics of Employee Relations*, 3rd edition, London: Palgrave Macmillan.

Boisot, M. (1998) *Knowledge Assets Securing Competitive Advantage in the Information Economy*, New York: Oxford University Press.

Bolton, S. and Houlihan, M. (2007) *Searching for the Human in Human Resource Management: Theory, Practice and Workplace Contexts*, Basingstoke: Palgrave Macmillan.

Booth, A. (1989) 'The bargaining structure of British establishments', *British Journal of Industrial Relations*, 27 (2), pp. 225–34.

Boring, E.G. (1923) 'Intelligence as the tests test it', *New Republic*, 35, pp. 35–7.

Borman, W., Penner, L., Allen, T. and Motowidlo, S. (2001) 'Personality predictors of citizenship behaviour', *International Journal of Selection and Assessment*, 9 (1–2), pp. 52–69.

Bosch, G. (2006) 'Working time and the standard employment relationship', in *Decent Working Time: New Trends, New Issues*, Boulin J., Lallement, M., Messenger, J. and Michon, F. (ed.), Geneva: ILO, pp. 41–64.

Boulin, J., Lallement, M., Messenger, J. and Michon F. (2006) *Decent Working Time: New Trends, New Issues*, Geneva: ILO.

Boussebaa, M. (2008) 'Are consultants simply bluffing?' Book review of *Sociologie du conseil en management*, by Michel Villete, *Organization*, 15, pp. 298–300.

Bowen, D.E., Ledford, G.E. and Latham, B.R. (1991) 'Hiring for the organisation, not the job', *Academy of Management Executive*, 5 (4), pp. 35–50.

Bowey, A., Thorpe, R., Mitchell, F., Nicholls, G., Gosnold, D., Savery, L. and Hellier, P. (1982) 'Effects of incentive payment systems, United Kingdom 1977–1980', *Department of Employment Research Paper, No. 36*, London: DE.

Bowles, L.M. and Coates, G. (1993) 'Image and substance: the management of performance as rhetoric or reality', *Personnel Review*, 22 (2), pp. 3–21.

Boxall, P. (1996) 'The strategic HRM debate and the resource-based view of the firm', *Human Resource Management Journal*, 6 (3), pp. 59–75.

Boxall, P. and Purcell, J. (2002) *Strategy and Human Resource Management*, London: Palgrave.

Boxall, P. and Purcell, J. (2003) *Strategy and Human Resource Management*, Basingstoke: Palgrave Macmillan.

Boxall, P. and Purcell, J. (2008) *Strategy and Human Resource Management*, 2nd edition, Basingstoke: Palgrave Macmillan.

Boxall, P., Purcell, J. and Wright, P. (2007) (eds) *The Oxford Handbook of Human Resource Management*, Oxford: Oxford University Press.

Boyatzis, R. (1982) *The Competent Manager*, Chichester: John Wiley and Sons.

Boyer, R. (1987) 'Labour flexibilities: many forms, uncertain effects', *Labour and Society*, 12 (1), pp. 107–29.

Boyer, R. and Hollingsworth, R. (1997) 'How and why do social systems of production change?', in *Contemporary Capitalism: The Embeddedness of Institutions*, Hollingsworth, J.R. and Boyer, R. (eds), Cambridge: Cambridge University Press, pp. 189–96.

Bradley, H., Erickson, M., Stephenson, C. and Williams, S. (2000) *Myths at Work*, Cambridge: Polity.

Bradley, K. and Hill, S. (1983) 'After Japan: the quality circle transplant and productive efficiency', *British Journal of Industrial Relations*, 21 (5), pp. 291–311.

Bradley, K. and Hill, S. (1987) 'Quality circles and managerial interests', *Industrial Relations*, 26, pp. 68–82.

Braid, M. (2008) 'Revolt over forced retirement', *Sunday Times*, March 30th, p. 6.7 (Recruiter Forum Supplement).

Bratton, J. and Gold, J. (2003) *Human Resource Management: Theory and Practice*, Basingstoke: Palgrave.

Bratton, J. and Gold, J. (2007) *Human Resource Management. Theory and Practice*, 4th edition, Houndsmill: Palgrave Macmillan.

Brewerton, P.A. (1997) '360° feedback: the enthusiasts and the suspicious', unpublished MSc. (HRD) dissertation, The Nottingham Trent University.

Brewster, C. and Hegeswich, A. (1994) *Policy and Practice in European Human Resource Management*, The Price Waterhouse Cranfield Survey, London: Routledge.

Brewster, C., Hegeswich, A., Lockhart, T. and Mayne, L. (1992) *Issues in People Managment No. 6: Flexible Working Patterns in Europe*, London: IPM.

Brewster, C., Mayne, L., Tregaskis, O., Parsons, D. and Atterbury, S. (1996) *Working Time and Contract Flexibility in the EU*, Report for the European Commission, Cranfield University School of Management.

Brewster, C., Sparrow, P. and Vernon, G. (2007) *International Human Resource Management*, London: CIPD.

Bridges, W. (1994) *Jobshift: How to Prosper in a World without Jobs*, Cambridge: Nicholas Brealey.

Bristow, E. (1974) 'Profit-sharing, socialism and labour unrest', in *Essays in Anti-Labour History*, Brown, K.D. (ed.), London: Macmillan.

Bristow, N. (2007) 'Clinical leadership in the NHS: evaluating change through action learning', in *Management Development: Perspectives from Research and Practice*, Hill, R. and Stewart, J. (eds), London: Routledge.

Brockner, J. (1992) 'Managing the effects of lay-offs on survivors', *California Management Review*, 34 (2), pp. 9–28, cited by Redman, T. and Wilkinson, A. (2006) *Contemporary Human Resource Management: Text and Cases'*, Harlow: Financial Times/Prentice Hall, p. 359.

Brown, D. (2000) *Guide to Bonus and Incentive Plans*, London: Tower Perrins/CIPD.

Brown, D. and Armstrong, M. (1999) *Paying for Contribution*, London: Kogan Page.

Brown, J.S. and Duguid, P. (1991) 'Organisational Learning and communities of practice: towards a unified view of working, learning and innovation', *Organisational Science*, 2 (1), pp. 40–57.

Brown, J.S. and Duguid, P. (2002) *The Social Life of Information*, Boston: Harvard Business School Press.

Brown, W. (1981) *The Establishment Survey of Warwick 1977/98*, Warwick: Industrial Relations Research Unit.

Brown, W. (1994) *The Establishment Survey of Warwick 1977/8*, Industrial Relations Research Unit (IRRU).

Brown, W. (2000) 'Putting partnership into practice in Britain', *British Journal of Industrial Relations*, 38 (2), pp. 299–316.

Bryson, C. (1996) 'The use of fixed term contracts in HE: not such a flexible solution for all parties', paper presented at the *International Labour Process Conference*, 27–29 March, Aston.

Bryson, C. (1997) 'Do fixed term contracts mean a better or a worse deal for women?', paper presented at the *International Labour Process Conference*, 25–27 March, Edinburgh.

Bryson, C. and Barnes, N. (1997) 'Professional workers and fixed term contracts: a contradiction in terms', paper presented at the *ERU Conference*, Cardiff, September.

Bryson, C. and Barnes, N. (2000) 'The casualisation of HE in the UK', in *Academic Work and Life*, Tight, M. (ed.), Amsterdam: JAI.

Buchanan, D. (1994) 'Principles and practice in work design', in *Personnel Management*, Sisson, K. (ed.), Oxford: Blackwell.

Buglear, J. (1986) 'Appraisal: what it is and why we should fight it', *Evaluation Newsletter*, Society for Research into Higher Education (SRHE), 10 (2), Winter.

Bullock Report (1977) *Report of the Committee of Inquiry in Industrial Democracy*, Chairman Lord Bullock, Cmnd, London: HMSO.

Burchell, B., Lapido, D. and Wilkinson, F. (2002) *Job Insecurity and Work Intensification*, London: Routledge.

Burchill, F. (1997) *Labour Relations*, Basingstoke: Macmillan.

Burgess, S., Prentice, G. and Propper, C. (2007) 'Performance pay in the public sector: a review of the issues and evidence,' *Report for the Office of Manpower Economics*, Bristol University: The Centre for Market and Public Organisation, November.

Burgoyne, J. (1988) 'Management development for the individual and the organisa-tion', *Personnel Management*, June, pp. 40–4.

Burgoyne, J. and Jackson, B. (1997) 'The Arena thesis: management development as a pluralistic meeting point', in *Management Learning*, Burgoyne, J. and Reynolds, M. (eds), London: Sage.

Burns, T. and Stalker, G.S. (1994) *The Management of Innovation*, 2nd edition, Oxford: Oxford University Press.

Burr, V. (1995) *An Introduction to Social Constructionism*, London: Sage.

Business Europe, Etuc/Ces, Ueapme and Ceep (2007) *Key Challenges Facing European Labour Markets: A Joint Analysis of European Social Partners*, Brussels.

Butterfield, K., Trevino, L. and Weaver, G. (2000) 'Moral awareness in business organ-isations: influences of issue-related and social context factors', *Human Relations*, 53 (7), pp. 981–1018.

CAC (Central Arbitration Committee) (annual), Annual Reports.

CALM (Computer Assisted Learning for Managers) (n.d) *Setting Objectives*, Brighton: Maxim Training Systems Ltd.

Campbell, J. and Knapp, D. (eds) (2001) *Exploring the Limits in Personnel Selection and Classification*, Mahwah, NJ: Lawrence Erlbaum Associates, p. 637.

Canadian Auto Workers Union (n.d.) *History of the CAW Family Education Centre*, avail-able from URL: http://www.caw.ca/educationcentre/history/index.asp (accessed 2 September 2008).

Cannell, M. (2005) *Performance Management Survey Report.* London: CIPD.

Cannell, M. and Wood, S. (1992) *Incentive Pay: Impact and Evolution*, London: IPM.

Capelli, P. (1995) 'Rethinking employment', *British Journal of Industrial Relations*, 33 (4), December, pp. 563–602.

Cappelli, P. (2008) 'Talent management for the twenty-first century', *Harvard Business Review*, 86 (3), pp. 74–81.

Carlson, K., Connerley, M. and Mecham III, R.L. (2002) 'Recruitment evaluation: the case for assessing the quality of applicants attracted', *Personnel Psychology*, 55 (2), pp. 461–90.

Carnall, C.A. (1999) *Managing Change in Organisations*, London: Financial Times/ Prentice Hall.

Carnall, C.A. (2007) *Managing Change in Organisations*, 5th edition, London: Financial Times/Prentice Hall.

Caroli, E. (2007) 'Internal versus external labour flexibility: the role of knowledge codification', *National Institute Economic Review*, 201, pp. 107–18.

Carvalho, A. and Cabral-Cardoso, C. (2008) 'Flexibility through HRM in management consulting firms', *Personnel Review*, 37 (3): 332–49.

Casey, B. (1988) 'The extent and nature of temporary employment in Britain', *Cambridge Journal of Economics*, 12 (4), pp. 487–509.

Casey, B. (1995) *Redundancy in Britain*, DoE&E, Research series No. 62, London.

Casey, B., Metcalf, H. and Millward, N. (1997) *Employers' Use of Flexible Labour*, London: Policy Studies Institute.

Cass, B. (1995) 'Overturning the male breadwinner model in the Australian social protection system', in *Social Policy and the Challenges of Social Change*, Saunders, P. and Shaver, S. (eds), University of New South Wales: Social Policy Research Centre, Reports and Proceedings no. 122, pp. 47–66.

Castells, M. (1996) *The Rise of the Network Society*, Oxford: Blackwell.

Castells, M. (1998) *End of Millennium*, Oxford: Blackwell.

Cattell, R.B. (1965) *The Scientific Analysis of Personality*, Harmondsworth: Penguin.

CBI (Confederation of British Industry) and William M. Mercer (2000) *Employment Trends Survey 2000: Measuring flexibility in the labour market*, London: CBI.

CEDEFOP (2003) *Lifelong Learning: Citizens' Views*, Luxembourg: Office for Official Publications of the European Communities.

Challis, D.J. (1981) 'The measurement of outcome in social care of the elderly', *Journal of Social Policy*, 10 (2), pp. 179–208.

Charlwood, A. (2002) 'Why do non-union employees want to unionize? Evidence from Britain', *British Journal of Industrial Relations*, 40 (3), pp. 463–91.

Chaston, I., Badger, B. and Sadler-Smith, E. (1999) *Organisational Learning and Knowledge Acquisition in Small, Entrepreneurial, UK Manufacturing Firms*, GOLDE, Plymouth Business School, University of Plymouth, available at: http://www.developingmanagement.com (accessed 2001).

Chia, R. (1996) *Organisational Analysis as Deconstructive Practice*, Berlin: de Gruyter.

Chia, R. (1997) 'Process philosophy and management learning: cultivating foresight in management', in *Management Learning*, Burgoyne, J. and Reynolds, M. (eds), London: Sage.

Child, J. (1972) 'Organisational structure, environment and performance', *Sociology*, 6 (1), pp. 2–22.

Child, J. (1997) 'Strategic choice in the analysis of action, structure, organizations and environment: retrospect and prospect', *Organization Studies*, 18 (1), pp. 43–76.

Chryssides, G. and Kaler, J. (1996) *Essentials of Business Ethics*, Maidenhead: McGraw Hill.

Chubb, L. (2008) 'Organisations are failing to learn from their mistakes, says HSE' *People Management On-Line*, 30 April, http://www.peoplemanagement.co.uk/pm/articles/2008/04/corporate-memory-loss-to-blame-for-workplace-accidents.htm (accessed 19 May 2008).

CIPD (Chartered Institute of Personnel and Development) (2001) *Competency Frameworks in UK Organisations*, London: CIPD.

CIPD (Chartered Institute of Personnel and Development) (2002a) *Developing Managers for Business Performance: What Your Board Needs to Know Today*, London: CIPD.

CIPD (Chartered Institute of Personnel and Development) (2002b) *Redundancy – Survey Report 2002*, London: CIPD.

CIPD (Chartered Institute of Personnel and Development) (2003a) *Redundancy, Quick Facts*, http://www.cipd.co.uk/subjects/emplaw/redundancy/redundancy.htm?IsSrchRes=1

CIPD (Chartered Institute of Personnel and Development) (2003b) *Recruitment and Retention 2003*, Survey Report, London: CIPD.

CIPD (Chartered Institute of Personnel and Development) (2004) *Labour Turnover Survey, 2003*, London: CIPD.

CIPD (Chartered Institute of Personnel and Development) (2005a) *Performance Management Survey Report*, London: CIPD.

CIPD (Chartered Institute of Personnel and Development) (2005b) *The Change Agenda: Managing Diversity, Linking Theory and Practice to Business Performance*. London: CIPD.

CIPD (Chartered Institute of Personnel and Development)/Lovells (2005) *Employment Law – Burden or Benefit?* Survey Report, London: CIPD.

CIPD (Chartered Institute of Personnel and Development) (2006) *Learning and Development Annual Survey and Report*. London: CIPD.

CIPD (Chartered Institute of Personnel and Development) (2007a) *Annual Survey Report Recruitment, Retention and Turnover 2007*, London: CIPD.

CIPD (Chartered Institute of Personnel and Development) (2007b) *Reward Management Survey Report 2007*, London: CIPD.

CIPD (Chartered Institute of Personnel and Development) (2007c) *Learning and Development Annual Survey and Report*, London: CIPD.

CIPD (Chartered Institute of Personnel and Development) (2008a) *Reward Management Survey Report 2008*, London: CIPD.

CIPD (Chartered Institute of Personnel and Development) (2008b) *Team Reward Fact Sheet*, London: CIPD.

CIPD (Chartered Institute of Personnel and Development) (2008c) *Performance Management Survey Report 2008*, London: CIPD.

CIPD (Chartered Institute of Personnel and Development) (2008d) *Redundancy, Factsheet*, http://www.cipd.co.uk/subjects/emplaw/redundancy/redundancy.htm

CIPD (Chartered Institute of Personnel and Development) (2008e) *Learning and Development Annual Survey and Report*, London: CIPD.

Clancey, W.J. (1995) 'A tutorial on situated learning', in *Proceedings of the International Conference on Computers and Education*, Taiwan AACE, pp. 49–70.

Clark, H., Chandler, J. and Barry, J. (1994) *Organization Identities: Texts and Readings in Organizational Behaviour*, London: Chapman and Hall.

Clark, T. (1995) *Managing Consultants: Consultancy as the Management of Impressions*, Buckingham: Open University Press.

Clark, T. and Fincham, R. (2002) (eds) *Critical Consulting: New Perspectives on the Management Advice Industry*, Oxford: Blackwell Publishers Ltd.

Clarke, R. and Winkler, V. (2006) *Change Agenda. Reflections on Talent Management.* London: CIPD.

Clawson, D. (1980) *Bureaucracy and the Labour Process*, New York: Monthly Review Press.

Clegg, H. (1985) 'Trade unions as an opposition which can never become a government', in *Trade Unions*, 2nd edition, McCarthy, W.E.J. (ed.), Harmondsworth: Pelican.

Clegg, S., Kornberger, M. and Rhodes, C. (2007) 'Business Ethics as Practice', *British Journal of Management*, 18 (2), pp. 107–22.

Clutterbuck, D. and Megginson, D. (1998) *Mentoring in Action*, London: Kogan Page.

Clutterbuck, D. and Ragins, B.R. (2001) *Mentoring and Diversity: An International Perspective*, Oxford: Butterworth-Heinemann.

Cockburn, C. (1991) *In the Way of Women: Men's Resistance to Sex Equality in Organisations*, London: Macmillan.

Cohen, D. (2003) *Our Modern Times. The New Nature of Capitalism in the Information Age*, Cambridge: MIT Press.

Cole, R.E. and Scott, W.R. (2000) *The Quality Movement and Organization Theory*, London: Sage.

Collard, R. and Dale, B. (1989) 'Quality circles', in *Personnel Management in Britain*, Sisson, K. (ed.), Oxford: Blackwell.

Collins, H. (2000) 'Justifications and techniques of legal regulation of the employment relation', in *Legal Regulation of the Employment Relation*, Collins, H., Davies, P. and Rideout, R. (eds), London: Kluwer Law International.

Collins, H. (2001) 'Regulating the employment relation for competitiveness', *Industrial Law Journal*, 30 (1), pp. 17–48.

Collins, H. (2003) *Employment Law*, Oxford: Oxford University Press.

Collins, H., Davies, P. and Rideout, R. (eds) (2000) *Legal Regulation of the Employment Relation*, London: Kluwer Law International.

Collins, M. (1992) *Artificial Experts: Social Knowledge and Intelligent Machines*, Cambridge, MA: MIT Press.

Commission on Vulnerable Employment (CoVE) (2008) 'Hard Work, Hidden Lives', TUC Report by the Commission on Vulnerable Employment, Trade Union Commission (TUC). http://www.vulnerableworkers.org.uk/2008/05/ (accessed 10 July 2008).

Conner, K. (1991) 'A historical comparison of resource-based theory and five schools of thought within industrial organization economics: do we have a new theory of the firm?' *Journal of Management* 17 (1), pp. 121–54.

Cook, M. (1993) *Personnel Selection and Productivity*, Chichester: John Wiley and Sons.

Cooke, F.L. (2006) 'Modelling an HR Shared Services Centre: Experience of an MNC in the United Kingdom' *Human Resource Management*, 45 (2), pp. 211–27.

Cooper, C. (2003) 'Minority support', *People Management*, 9 (24), pp. 24–7.

Cornwell, R. (2008) 'Starbucks Chokes on its Latte', *The Independent*, 01 August, p. 56.

Costa, P.T. Jr. and McCrae, R.R. (1992) 'Four ways five factors are basic', *Personality and Individual Differences*, 13, pp. 653–65.

Cox, T. (1993) *Cultural Diversity in Organizations: Theory, Research and Practice*, San Francisco: Berrett-Koehler Publishers.

Cox, T. and Blake, S. (1991) 'Managing cultural diversity: implications for organizational competitiveness', *Academy of Management Executive*, 5 (3), pp. 45–56.

Crane, A. and Matten, D. (2007) *Business Ethics*, 2nd edition, Oxford: Oxford University Press.

Crane, A., McWilliams, A. Matten, D., Mood, J. and Siegal, D. (2008) *The Oxford Handbook of Corporate Social Responsibility*, Oxford: Oxford University Press.

Cressey, P. (1998) 'European works councils in practice', *Human Resource Management Journal*, 8 (1), pp. 67–79.

Critten, P. (1998) 'From personal to professional development: creating space for growth', in *Managing Human Resources*, Critten, P. (ed.), London: Arnold, pp. 920–1110.

Croner (2007) Employment Law: Questions and Answers, Issue No 132, 19 October, Croner Publications.

Cully, M., O'Reilly, A., Millward, N., Forth, J., Woodland, S., Dix, G. and Bryson, A. (1998) *The 1998 Workplace Employee Relations Survey*, London: DTI.

Cully, M., Woodland, S., O'Reilly, A. and Dix, G. (1999) *Britain at Work as Depicted by the 1998 Workplace Employee Relations Survey*, London: Routledge.

Cunningham, I. (2008) *Developing Senior Managers*, CIPD Factsheet, www.cipd.co.uk/subjects/lrnanddev/mmtdevelop//devsnrman/htm (accessed 18 August 08).

Cunningham, I. and Hyman, J. (1995) 'Transforming the HRM vision into reality: the role of line managers and supervisors in implementing change', *Employee Relations*, 17 (8), pp. 5–20.

Cunningham, I. and Hyman, J. (1999) 'Devolving human resource responsibilities to the line. Beginning or the end or a new beginning for personnel?', *Personnel Review*, 28 (1), pp. 9–27.

Custodial Care Training Organisation (n.d.) *Custodial Healthcare Standards*, http://www.themsc.org/standards/custodial.html

Czarniawska, B. and Mazza, C. (2003) 'Consulting as a liminal space', *Human Relations*, 56 (3), pp. 267–90.

Daily Routine Arrangements: Experiment in the Netherlands (2002), published by the Ministry of Social Affairs and Employment, The Hague.

Dale, M. (2006) *The Essential Guide to Recruitment: How to Conduct Great Interviews and Select the Best Employees'*, London: Kogan Page.

Danford, A., Richardson, M., Stewart, P., Tailby, S. and Upchurch, M. (2004) 'High performance work systems and workplace partnership', *New Technology, Work and Employment*, 19 (1), pp. 14–29.

Daniels, K. and Macdonald, L. (2005) *Equality, Diversity and Discrimination: A Student Text*, London: CIPD.

Davenport, T.H. (1997) *Information Ecology*, Oxford: Oxford University Press.

Davenport, T.H. and Prusak, L. (1998) *Working Knowledge: How Organisations Manage What They Know*, Boston: Harvard Business School Press.

Davenport, T.H., De Long, D.W. and Bets, M.C. (1998) 'Successful knowledge management projects', *Sloan Management Review*, 39 (2), pp. 43–57.

Davidge, E. (2007) 'The changing reward scene in local government', *The Reward Quarter*, Winter 2007/08, Manchester: E-Reward.

Dawe, S. (2003) *Determinants of Successful Training Practices in Large Australian Firms*, London: National Centre for Vocational Education Research.

Dawson, P. (2003) *Understanding Organisational Change: The Contemporary Experience of People at Work*, London: Sage.

DBERR (2007) *Workplace representatives. A Review of their Facilities and Facility Time: Government Response to Public Consultation*, London: DBERR.

De Cieri, H. and McGaughey, S. (1998) 'Relocation', in *The IEBM Handbook of Human Resource Management*, Poole, M. and Warner, M. (eds), London: International Thomson Business Press.

De Vita, E. (2007) 'John Lewis: Partners on Board', *Management Today*, August.

Deakin, S. and Wilkinson, F. (1996) *Labour Standards Essential to Economic and Social Progress*, London: Institute of Employment Rights.

Deery, S. and Mahoney, A. (1994) 'Temporal flexibility: management strategies and employee preferences in the retail industry', *Journal of Industrial Relations*, 36, pp. 332–52.

Delery, J. and Doty, D. (1996) 'Modes of theorizing in strategic human resource management: tests of universalistic, contingency and configurational performance predictions', *Academy of Management Journal*, 39 (4), pp. 802–35.

Delsen, L. (1998) 'Why do men work part-time?', in *Part-time Prospects: An International Comparison of Part-time Work in Europe, North America and the Pacific Rim*, J. O'Reilly and C. Fagan (eds), London and New York: Routledge, pp. 57–76.

Delsen, L. (2001) *Exit Poldermodel? Sociaal-economische ontwikkelingen in Nederland*, Assen: Van Gorcum.

Dench, S., Hurtsfield, J., Hill, D. and Akroyd, K. (2006) 'Employers' use of migrant labour', *Home Office On Line Report*, www.homeoffice.gov.uk

Department of Education and Skills (2006) *The Wider Benefits of Learning: A Synthesis of Findings from the Centre for Research on the Wider Benefits of Learning 1999–2006*, Brief No: RCB05-06.

Department of Employment (1989) People and companies; employee Involvement in Britain, London: HMSO.

Department of Health (1989) *Working for Patients; Working Paper No. 7: NHS Consultants Appointments, Contracts and Distinction Awards*, London: HMSO.

Desimore, R.L., Werner, J.M. and Harris, D.M. (2002), *Human Resource Development*, 3rd edition, Orlando FL: Harcourt College Publishers.

Dessler, G. and Cole, N.D. (2008) *Human Resources Management in Canada*, Canadian 10th edition, Toronto: Pearson/Prentice Hall.

Devins, D. and Gold, J. (2000) 'Cracking the tough nuts: mentoring and coaching the managers of small firms', *Career Development International*, 5 (4/5), pp. 250–55.

Dex, S. and McCulloch, A. (1997) *Flexible Employment; The Future of Britain's Jobs*, Basingstoke: Macmillan.

Dey, I. (2008) 'RBS poised for record bank loss', *The Sunday Times*, 03 August, Business Section, p. 1.

Dickens, L. (1994) 'The business case for women's equality: is the carrot better than the stick?', *Employee Relations*, 16 (8), pp. 5–18.

Dickens, L. (2000) 'Still wasting resources? Equality employment', in *Personnel Management – A Comprehensive Guide to Theory and Practice*, 3rd edition, Bach, S. and Sisson, K. (eds), Oxford: Blackwell, pp. 137–69.

Dickens, L. (2005) 'Walking the talk? Equality and Diversity in Employment', in *Managing Human Resources*, (previously Personnel Management), 4th edition, S. Bach (ed.). Oxford: Blackwell Publishers.

Dickens, L. (2008) 'Legal Regulation, institutions and industrial relations', Warwick Papers in Industrial Relations, Number 89.

Dickens, L., Jones, M., Weekes, B. and Hart, M. (1995) *Dismissed: a Study of Unfair Dismissals and the Industrial Tribunal System*, Oxford: Blackwell.

Dierdorff, E. and Wilson, M. (2003) 'A meta-analysis of job analysis reliability', *Journal of Applied Psychology*, 88 (4), pp. 635–46.

Dietz, G. (2004) 'Partnership and the development of trust in British workplaces', *Human Resource Management Journal*, 14 (1), pp. 5–24.

Dipboye, R.L. (1997) 'Structured selection interviews: Why do they work? Why are they underutilized?', in *International Handbook of Selection and Assessment*, Anderson, N. and Herriot, P. (eds), Chichester: John Wiley and Sons, pp. 543–66.

Dipboye, R.L. and de Pontbriand, P. (1981) 'Correlates of employee reactions to performance appraisal and appraisal systems', *Journal of Applied Psychology*, 66, pp. 248–51.

Disney, R. (1990) 'Explanations of the decline in trade union density in Britain', *British Journal of Industrial Relations*, 28 (2) April, pp. 165–76.

Disney, R., Gosling, A., Machin, S. and McCrae, J. (1998) 'The dynamics of union membership in Britain', *Employment Relations Research Series, Research Report 3*, Department of Trade and Industry.

Dobson, P. (1989) 'Reference reports', in *Assessment and Selection in Organisations*, Herriot, P. (ed.), Chichester: John Wiley and Sons.

Doherty, N. and Horstead, J. (1995) 'Helping survivors to stay on board', *People Management*, 12 January, pp. 26–31, cited by Redman, T. and Wilkinson, A. (2006) *Contemporary Human Resource Management: Text and Cases*, Harlow: Financial Times/Prentice Hall, p. 359.

Donkin, R. (2003) 'How to learn a lesson from the leavers', *The Financial Times*, 11 September, p. 23.

Donovan, Lord (1968) *Report of the Royal Commission on Trades Unions and Employers' Associations*, London: HMSO.

Doorne-Huiskes van, A., Dulk den, L. and Peper, B. (2005) 'Organizational change, gender and integration of work and private life', in *Flexible Working and Organizational Change*, Peper, B., Doorne-Huiskes van, A. and Dulk den, L. (eds), Cheltenham: Edward Elgar.

Dougherty, R.L., Turban, D.B. and Callender, J.C. (1994) 'Confirming first impressions in the employment interview', *Journal of Applied Psychology*, 71 (1), pp. 9–15.

Dowling, B. and Richardson, R. (1997) 'Evaluating performance related pay for managers in the National Health Service', *The International Journal of Human Resource Management*, 8 (3), pp. 348–67.

Dowling, P.J., Festing, M. and Engle, A. (2008) *International Human Resource Management: Managing People in a Multinational Context*, London: Thomson Learning.

Dreaper, J. (2008) 'How do foreign staff view the NHS', BBC News. http://news.bbc.co.uk/1/hi/health/7307575.stm (accessed 28 March 2008).

Drucker (1993) *Post-Capitalist Society*, Oxford: Butterworth-Heinemann.

DTI (Department of Trade and Industry) (1998) *Fairness at Work*, CM 3968. London: HMSO.

Dulk, den L. (2001) 'Work-family arrangements in organisations: a cross-national study in the Netherlands, Italy, the United Kingdom and Sweden', PhD, University of Utrecht.

Dyson, R. (1991) 'Changing labour utilisation in NHS Trusts: the reprofiling paper', University of Keele.

Eagly, A. and Carli, L. (2007) 'Women and the labyrinth of leadership', *Harvard Business Review*, 85 (9), pp. 63–71.

Easterby-Smith, M. and Lyles, M.A. (2006) *Handbook of Organizational Learning and Knowledge Management*, Oxford: Blackwell.

Easterby-Smith, M., Burogoyne, J. and Araujo, L. (eds) (2001) *Organisational Learning and the Learning Organisation*, London: Sage.

Echteldt van, P. (2007) *Time Greedy Employment Relationships*, PhD. University of Groningen.

Economic and Labour Market Review (2008) http://www.statistics.gov.uk/elmr/10_08

Edwards, C.C. (1995) '360 degree feedback', *Management Services*, June: p. 24.

Edwards, P. (2007) 'Justice in the workplace: why it is important and why a new public policy initiative is needed', *Provocation Series*, 2 (3), Warwick Business School: Industrial Relations Research Unit.

Edwards, P., Ram, M. and Black, J. (2003) *The Impact of Employment Legislation on Small Firms: A Case Study Analysis*. DTI Employment Research Series No. 20.

Edwards, P.K. (1986) *Conflict at Work: A Materialist Analysis of Workplace Relations*, Oxford: Blackwell.

Edwards, P.K. (1995) 'Strikes and industrial conflict', in Edwards, P.K. (ed.), *Industrial Relations: Theory and Practice*, Oxford: Blackwell.

Edwards, P.K. (2003) *Industrial Relations: Theory and Practice in Britain*, 2nd edition, Oxford: Blackwell.

Edwards, P.K. and Scullion, H. (1982) *The Social Organisation of Industrial Conflict*, Oxford: Blackwell.

Edwards, P.K. and Whitson, C. (1989) 'Industrial discipline, the control of attendance and the subordination of labour', *Work, Employment and Society*, 3, pp. 1–28.

Edwards, R. (1979) *Contested Terrain: The Transformation of the Workplace in the Twentieth Century*, London: Heinemann.

Eglin, R. (2002) 'Diversity boosts the bottom line', *Sunday Times*, November 17th, p. 6 (Features Supplement).

Elliot, C. and Turnbull, S. (2005) *Critical Thinking in Human Resource Development*, Oxford: Routledge.

Elliott, L. (1998) 'Globalisation in need of repairs', *The Guardian Weekly*, 8 February.

Elliott, L. (2008) 'Doha: not dead, just resting', in *The Guardian*, 30 July, p. 23.

Elmuti, D. (1993) 'Managing diversity in the workplace: an immense challenge for both managers and workers', *Industrial Management*, 35 (4), pp. 19–22.

Emmott, M. (2008) 'The case for a Workplace Commission', *Impact*, 23, London: CIPD.

Emmott, M. and Harris, L. (2004) *Shared HR Schemes for Small Firms. A Report for the DTI on the Shared HR Pilot Schemes for Small Firms*. London: CIPD.

Equal Opportunities Commission (2002) 'The Labour market', http://www.equalityhumanrights.com

Equal Opportunities Commission (2006) 'Sex and power: who runs Britain?', London: Equal Opportunities Commission.

E-reward (2004) 'What is happening on contingent pay today, Part 1', Research Report No. 18., Manchester.

Esping-Andersen, G. (1990) *The Three Worlds of Welfare Capitalism*, Cambridge: Polity Press.

Esping-Andersen, G. (1999) *Social Foundation of Post-industrial Economics*, New York: Oxford University Press.

European Commission (1999) 'Equal opportunities for Women and Men in the European Union 1998', Brussels.

European Commission (2000) *Employment in Europe 2000*, Luxembourg: Office for official publications of the European Committees.

European Commission (2004) 'Proposition de directive du parlement europeen et du conseil', SEC 1154, 22 September.

European Commission (2007) 'Report from the Commission to the Council, the European Parliament, the European Economic and Social Committee and the Committee of the Regions – on equality between men and women 2007', Commission of the European Communities.

European Commission (2008) *Equality between Men and Women*, http://ec.europa.eu/employment_social/publications/2008/keaj08001_en.pdf (accessed 28 August 2008).

European Foundation for the Improvement of Living and Working Conditions (EFILWC) (2003) *A New Organization of Time and Working Life*, Luxembourg: Office for Official Publications of the European Commission.

Eysenck, H.J. (1953) *The Structure of Human Personality*, London: Methuen.

Fagan, C. and O'Reilly, J. (1998) *Part-time Prospects*, London: Routledge.

Farnham, D. (2000) *Employee Relations in Context*, London, CIPD.

Farnham, D. and Giles, L. (1996) 'People management and employment relations', in *Managing the New Public Services*, Farnham, D. and Horton, S. (eds), Basingstoke: Macmillan.

Farnham, D. and Horton, S. (2000) *Human Resource Flexibilities in the Public Sector: International Perspectives*, Basingstoke: Macmillan.

Fee, K. (2001) *A Guide to Management Development Techniques*, London: Kogan Page.

Felstead, A. and Jewson, N. (1999) *Global Trends in Flexible Employment*, London: Macmillan.

Ferran, C. and Kuossa, R.S. (eds) (2008) *Enterprise Resource Planning for Global Economies: Managerial Issues and Challenges*, Hershey, Pennsylvania: Medical Information Science Reference.

Filipczak, B. (1997) 'Managing a mixed workforce', *Training*, 34 (10), pp. 96–101.

Financial Times (2008a) 'Gloom surrounds equities', 27 June, p. 37.

Financial Times (2008b) 'FT Global 500', 28 June, Financial Times Magazine.

Fincham, R. (1999) 'The consultant-client relationship: critical perspectives on the management of organizational change', *Journal of Management Studies*, 36 (3), pp. 335–51.

Finch-Lees, T. and Mabey, C. (2007) 'Management development: a critical discursive perspective', in *Management Development: Perspectives from Research and Practice*, Hill, R. and Stewart, J. (eds), London: Routledge.

Finlay, W. and Coverdill, J. (2002) *Headhunters: Matchmaking in the Labor Market*. Ithica, New York: IRL.

Fisher, C. (2000) 'Human resource managers and quietism', *Business and Professional Ethics Journal*, 19 (3&4), pp. 55–72.

Fisher, C. and Lovell, A. (2009) *Business Ethics and Values 3rd edition*, London: Prentice-Hall.

Fisher, C., Harris, L., Kirk, S., Leopold, J. and Leverment, Y. (2001) 'Job satisfaction and the modernisation project: the dynamics of expectations and satisfaction in NHS hospitals', paper presented at the *Annual Conference of the European Group of Public Administration*, Vaasa, Finland.

Fisher, C., Harris, L., Kirk, S., Leopold, J. and Leverment, Y. (2003) 'Job satisfaction and the modernisation project: a longitudinal study of two NHS acute Trusts', in *Health*

Care Policy, Finance and Performance, Tavakoli, M. and Davies, H. (eds), London: Ashgate, pp. 252–69.

Fisher, C.M. (1995) 'The differences between appraisal schemes: rhetoric and the design of schemes', *Personnel Review*, 24 (1), pp. 51–66.

Flanagan, J.A. (1954) 'The critical incident technique', *Psychological Bulletin*, 51, pp. 327–58.

Fleetwood, S. (2007) 'Why work-life balance now?', *International Journal of Human Resource Management*, 18 (3), pp. 387–400.

Fletcher, C. (1989) 'Impression management in the selection interview', in *Impression Management in the Organization*, Giacalone, R.A. and Rosenfeld, P. (eds), Hillsdale, NJ: Lawrence Erlbaum Associates, pp. 269–81.

Fletcher, C. (2001) 'Performance appraisal and management: the developing research agenda', *Journal of Occupational and Organisational Psychology*, 74, pp. 473–7.

Flexicurity Pathways (2007) Report by the European expert group on flexicurity, Brussels.

Floodgate, J.F. and Nixon, A.E. (1994) 'Personal development plans: the challenge of implementation – a case study', *Journal of European Industrial Training*, 18 (11), pp. 43–7.

Fogarty, T. (2000) 'Socialization and organizational outcomes in large public accounting firms', *Journal of Managerial Issues*, 12, pp. 13–34.

Folger, R. and Cropanzano, R. (2000) *Organisational Justice and Human Resource Management*, Thousand Oaks, CA: Sage.

Fombrun, C.J., Tichy, N. and Devanna, M.A. (1984) *Strategic Human Resource Management*, New York: John Wiley and Sons.

Foote, D. and Robinson, I. (1999) 'The role of the human resources manager: strategist or conscience of the organisation?', *Business Ethics: A European Review*, 8 (2), pp. 88–98.

Ford, V. (1996) 'Partnership is the secret of success', *People Management*, 2 (3), pp. 34–6.

Forster, N. (1994) 'The forgotten employees? The experiences of expatriate staff returning to the UK', *The International Journal of Human Resource Management*, 5 (2), pp. 405–25.

Foss, N.J. (1996) 'More critical comments on knowledge based theories of the firm', *Organization Studies*, 7 (5), pp. 519–23.

Foster, C. (2003) *Understanding and Implementing Managing Diversity in Organisations: a study in the retail sector*, PhD thesis, Nottingham Trent University.

Foster, C. and Harris, L. (2005) 'Easy to say, difficult to do: diversity management in retail', *Human Resource Management Journal*, 15 (3), pp. 4–17.

Foucault, M. (1980) *Power Knowledge*, Brighton: Harvester.

Fowler, A. (1999) *Managing Redundancy*, London: IPD.

Fox, A. (1966) *Industrial Sociology and Industrial Relations*, London: HMSO.

Fox, A. (1974) *Beyond Contract: Work, Power and Trust Relations*, London: Faber and Faber.

Fox, A. (1979) 'A note on industrial relations pluralism', *Sociology*, 13 (1).

Fox, S. (1997) 'From management education and development to the study of management learning', in *Management Learning*, Burgoyne, J. and Reynolds, M. (eds), London: Sage.

Fox, S., Bizman, A. and Garti, A. (2005) 'Is distributional appraisal more effective than the traditional performance appraisal method?', *European Journal of Psychological Assessment*, 21 (3), pp. 165–72.

Francis, H. and Keegan, A. (2006) 'The changing face of HRM: in search of balance', *Human Resource Management Journal*, 16 (3), pp. 231–49.

Fredericks, J. and Stewart, J. (1996) 'The strategy–HRD connection', in *Human Resource Development*, Stewart, J. and McGoldrick, J. (eds), London: Pitman.

Fredman, S. (1997) 'Labour law in flux: The changing composition of the workforce', *Industrial Law Journal*, 26 (4), pp. 337–52.

Fredman, S. (2001) 'Equality: a new generation?', *Industrial Law Journal*, 30 (2), pp. 145–68.

Freeman, R. and Pelletier, J. (1990) 'The impact of industrial relations legislation on British union density', *British Journal of Industrial Relations*, 28 (2), pp. 141–64.

Frenkel, S.J. (2006) 'Towards a theory of dominant interests, globalization, and work', in *Social Theory at Work*, Korczynski, M., Hodson, R. and Edwards, P. (eds), New York: Oxford University Press.

Fuller, G. (2008) 'Smashing the glass ceiling', *Employers' Law*, April, pp. 12–13.

Fuller, S. (2002) *Knowledge Management Foundations*, Oxford: Butterworth-Heinemann.

Galin, A. (1991) 'Flexible work patterns – why, how, when and where?', *Bulletin of Comparative Labour Relations*, 22, pp. 3–18.

Gall, G. (1994) 'The rise of single table bargaining in Britain', *Employee Relations*, 16 (4), pp. 62–71.

Gall, G. (2001) 'From adverserialism to partnership? Trade unionism and industrial relations in the banking sector in the UK', *Employee Relations*, 23 (4), pp. 353–75.

Gall, G. and McKay, S. (1994) 'Trade union derecognition in Britain, 1988–1994', *British Journal of Industrial Relations*, 32 (3), pp. 433–48.

Gall, G. and McKay, S. (1999) 'Developments in recognition and union derecognition in Britain 1994–1998', *British Journal of Industrial Relations*, 37 (4), pp. 601–14.

Garavan, T.N. (1991) 'Strategic human resource development', *Journal of European Industrial Training*, 15 (1), pp. 17–30.

Garavan, T.N. (2007) 'A strategic perspective on human resource development', *Advances in Developing Human Resources*, 9 (1), pp. 11–30.

Gardiner, P. (1999) 'Creativity, experimentation and innovation in small businesses', Management First, available at: http://www.managementfirst.com/articles (accessed 18 September 2002).

Garvey, B. and Williamson, B. (2002) *Beyond Knowledge Management*, London: Financial Times/Prentice Hall.

Geary, J. (1992) 'Employment flexibility and human resource management: the case of three American electronics plants', *Work, Employment and Society*, 6 (2), pp. 251–70.

Geary, J. (1994) 'Task participation: employees' participation enabled or constrained', in *Personnel Management*, Sisson, K. (ed.), Oxford: Blackwell.

Gennard, J. and Judge, G. (1997) *Employee Relations*, London: IPD.

Gennard, J. and Judge, G. (2005) *Employee Relations*, 4th edition, London: CIPD.

Gheradi, S. and Nicolini, D. (2001) 'Learning through knowledge management', in *Handbook of Organizational Learning and Knowledge*, Dierkes, M., Berthoin Antal, A., Child, J. and Nonaka, I. (eds), Oxford: Oxford University Press, pp. 35–60.

Gheradi, S., Nicolini, D. and Odella, F. (1998) 'Toward a social understanding of how people learn in organisations: the notion of the situated curriculum', *Management Learning*, 29, pp. 273–98.

Gibb, F. (2007) 'Should judges face appraisals?' *Times Online*, 27 September, http://business.timesonline.co.uk/tol/business/law/columnists/article2544364 (Accessed 1 April 2008).

Gibb, S. (2002) *Learning and Development*, London: Palgrave Macmillan.

Gibb, S. and Megginson, D. (2001) 'Employee development', in *Contemporary Human Resource Management*, Gibb, S. and Megginson, D. (eds), London: Financial Times/Prentice Hall, pp. 128–63.

Gibbons, M. (2007) *Better Dispute Resolution: A Review of Employment Dispute Resolution in Great Britain, Department of Trade and Industry Report*, London: DTI.

Giddens, A. (1990) *The Consequences of Modernity*, Cambridge and Oxford: Polity and Blackwell.

Giddens, A. (2006) *Europe in the Global Age*, London: Polity Press.

Giles, A., Lapointe, P., Murray, G. and Belanger, J. (1999) 'Industrial relations in the new workplace', *Relations Industrielles*, 54 (1), pp. 15–25.

Gill, P. (1996) 'Managing workforce diversity – a response to skills shortages?', *Health Manpower Management*, 22 (6), pp. 34–7.

Gilligan, C. (1982) *In a Different Voice*, Cambridge, MA: Harvard University Press.

Gilmore, D.C., Stevens, C.K., Harrell-Cook, G. and Ferris, G.R. (1999) 'Impression management tactics', in *The Employment Interview Handbook*, Eder, R.W. and Harris, M.M. (eds), London: Sage, pp. 321–36.

Glaze, T. (1989) 'Cadbury's dictionary of competence', *Personnel Management*, July.

Glover, L. (2000) 'Neither poison nor panacea: shopfloor responses to TQM', *Employee Relations*, 22 (2), pp. 121–45.

Golden, L. (2005) 'The flexibility gap: employee access to flexibility in work schedules', in *Flexibility in Workplaces*, Zeytinoglu, I.U. (ed.), Geneva: ILO.

Gollan, P. (1999) 'Having a voice – non-union forms of employee representation in the United Kingdom and Australia', paper presented to the 49th BUIRA Conference.

Gonzales-Rendon, M., Alcaide-Castro, M. and Florez-Saborido, I. (2005) 'Is it difficult for temporary workers to get a permanent job? Empirical evidence from Spain', in *Flexibility in Workplaces*, Zeytinoglu, I.U. (ed.) Geneva: ILO.

Goodman, J., Earnshaw, J., Marchington, M. and Harrison, R. (1998) 'Unfair dismissal cases, disciplinary procedures, recruitment methods and management style. Case study evidence from three industrial sectors', *Employee Relations*, 20 (6), pp. 536–50.

Goodpaster, K. (1995) 'Commentary on "MacIntyre and the Manager"', *Organisation*, 2 (2), pp. 212–16.

Goss, D. (1994) *Principles of Human Resource Management*, London: Paul Chapman, pp. 164–72.

Govindarajan, V. and Gupta, A. (1998a) 'Setting a course for the new global landscape', in *Mastering Global Business*, The Financial Times, part 1 of 10.

Govindarajan, V. and Gupta, A. (1998b) 'Success is all in the mindset', in *Mastering Global Business*, The Financial Times, part 5 of 10.

Gower (n.d.) *Appraisal Skills*, a training video package.

Grace, D. and Cohen, S. (2000) *Business Ethics: Australian Problems and Cases*, Melbourne: Oxford University Press.

Grainger, H. (2006) 'Trade union membership 2005', *Employment Market Analysis and Research*, DTI, March 2006.

Grant, R.M. and Zack, M.H. (1999) 'The resource-based theory of competitive advantage: implications for strategy formulation', in *Knowledge and Strategy*, Zack, M.H. (ed.), Woburn, MA: Butterworth-Heinemann, pp. 3–23.

Gratton, L., Hope-Hailey, V., Stiles, P. and Truss, C. (1999) *Strategic Human Management*, Oxford: Oxford University Press.

Greenberg, J. (1987) 'A taxonomy of organisational justice theories', *Academy of Management Review*, 12, pp. 9–22.

Griffin, R. (1988) 'Consequences of quality circles in an industrial setting', *Academy of Management Journal*, 31, pp. 338–58.

Grimshaw, D. (1999) 'Changes in skills-mix and pay determination among the nursing workforce in the UK', *Work, Employment and Society*, 13 (2), pp. 293–326.

Grimshaw, D. and Rubery, J. (2007) 'Economics and HRM', in *The Oxford Handbook of Human Resource Management*, Boxall, P., Purcell, J. and Wright, P. (eds), Oxford: Oxford University Press.

Grint, K. (2000) *The Arts of Leadership*, Oxford: Oxford University Press.

Grubb, D. and Wells, W. (1993) 'Employment regulation and patterns of work in EC countries', *OECD Economic Studies*, 21, pp. 7–56.

Gudex, C. (1986) *QALYs and their use by the Health Service*, discussion paper No. 20, Centre for Health Economics, University of York.

Guest, D. (ed.) (1994) *Human Resource Strategies*, London: Sage.

Guest, D. (1995) 'Human resource management, trade unions and industrial relations', in *Human Resource Management: A Critical Text*, Storey, J. (ed.), London: Routledge.

Guest, D. (1997) 'Human resource management and performance: a review and a research agenda', *International Journal of Human Resource Management*, 8 (3), pp. 263–76.

Guest, D. (2002) 'Perspectives on the Study of Work-life Balance', Social Science Information, 41 (2), pp. 255–79.

Guest, D.E. (1987) 'Human resource management and industrial relations', *Journal of Management Studies*, 24 (5).

Guest, D.E. (2007) 'HRM and performance: can partnership address the ethical issues?', in *Human Resource Management: Ethics and Employment*, Pinnington, A., Macklin, R. and Campbell, T. (eds), Oxford: Oxford University Press.

Guest, D.E., Brown, W., Peccei, R. and Huxley, K. (2008) 'Does partnership at work increase trust? An analysis based on the 2004 Workplace Employment Relations Survey', *Industrial Relations Journal*, 39 (2), pp. 124–52.

Guest, D.E. and Conway, N. (1997) *Employee Motivation and the Psychological Contract*, Report No. 21, London: Institute of Personnel and Development.

Guest, D.E. and Peccei, R. (2001) 'Partnership at work: mutuality and the balance of advantage', *British Journal of Industrial Relations*, 39 (2), pp. 207–36.

Guion, R.M. (1997) 'Criterion measures and the criterion dilemma', in *International Handbook of Selection and Assessment*, Anderson, N. and Herriot, P. (eds), Chichester: John Wiley and Sons, pp. 543–66.

Hackman, J.R. (2002) *Leading Teams: Setting the Stage for Great Performances*. Boston, MA: Harvard Business School Press.

Hackman, J.R. and Oldham, G.R. (1976) 'Motivation through the design of work: a test of a theory', *Organisational Behaviour and Human Performance*, 16 (2), pp. 250–79.

Hackman, J.R., Oldham, G.R., Janson, R. and Purdy, K. (1985) 'A new strategy for job enrichment', *California Management Review*, 17 (4), pp. 57–71.

Hagström, P. (2000) 'New wine in old bottles: information technology evolution in first strategy and structure', in *The Flexible Firm. Capability Management in Network Organization*, Birkinshaw, J. and Hagström, P., Oxford: Oxford University Press.

Hakim, C. (1990) 'Core and periphery in employers' workforce strategies: evidence from the 1987 ELUS survey', *Work, Employment and Society*, 4 (2), pp. 157–88.

Hales, C. (2000) 'Management and empowerment programmes', *Work, Employment and Society*, 14 (3), pp. 501–19.

Hall, C. (2003) 'Nurse shortage in NHS is "near to crisis point"', *The Daily Telegraph*, April 29th.

Hall, E.J. and Hall, M.R. (1990) *Understanding Cultural Differences*, Yarmouth, ME: Intercultural Press.

Hall, L. and Torrington, D. (1998) *The Human Resource Function: The Dynamics of Change and Development*, London: Financial Times Management.

Hall, M. (1992) 'Behind the European works councils directives: the European Commission's legislative strategy', *British Journal of Industrial Relations*, 30 (4), pp. 547–61.

Hall, M., Purcell, J. and Terry, M. (2008) Implementing Information and Consultation: Early Experience under the ICE Regulations-interim update report. London: CIPD.

Hamel, G. and Prahalad, C.K. (1994) *Competing for the Future*, Boston, MA: Harvard University Press.

Hamlin, R. (2005) 'Towards universalistic models of managerial leader effectiveness: a comparative study of recent British and American derived models of leadership', *Human Resource Development International*, 8 (1), pp. 5–25.

Hammer, M. and Champy, J. (1993) *Re-engineering the Corporation: A Manifesto for Business Revolution*, New York: Harper Business.

Hammermesh, D. (1987) 'The demand for workers and hours and the effects of job security policies: theories and evidence', in *Employment, Unemployment and Labour Utilisation*, Harr, R. (ed.), Boston: Unwin.

Harley, B., Hyman, J. and Thompson, P. (eds) (2005) *Participation and Democracy at Work*, Basingstoke: Palgrave Macmillan.

Harris, H. (2001) 'Researching discrimination in selection for international management assignments: The role of repertory grid technique', *Women in Management Review*, 6 (3), pp. 118–26.

Harris, L. (1999) 'Employment law and human resourcing: challenges and constraints', in *Strategic Human Resourcing: Principles, Perspectives and Practices*, Leopold, J., Harris, L. and Watson, T. (eds), London: Financial Times/Pitman Publishing.

Harris, L. (2000) 'Procedural justice and perceptions of fairness in selection practice', *International Journal of Selection and Assessment*, 8 (3), pp. 148–57.

Harris, L. (2001a) 'Rewarding employee performance – line managers' values, beliefs and perspectives', *International Journal of Human Resource Management*, 12 (7), pp. 1182–92.

Harris, L. (2001b) 'Employee rights – better employment relationships or the growth of the organisational rule book?', *16th Annual Employment Research Conference*, Cardiff Business School, 'Politics, Public Policy and the Employment Relationship', 10–11 September.

Harris, L. (2002a) 'Achieving the balance in approaches to human resourcing between the "employee rights" agenda and care for the individual', *Business and Professional Ethics Journal*, 21 (2), pp. 45–60.

Harris, L. (2002b) 'Small firm responses to employment regulation', *Journal of Small Business and Enterprise Development*, 9 (3), pp. 296–306.

Harris, L. (2003) 'Home-based teleworking and the employment relationship', *Personnel Review*, 32 (4), pp. 422–37.

Harris, L. (2008) 'The changing face of the HR function in UK local government and its role as "employee champion"', *Employee Relations*, 30 (1), pp. 34–47.

Harris, L. and Bott, D. (1996) 'Limitation or liberation? The human resource specialist and the law', *Journal of Professional HRM*, Issue No. 4.

Harris, L. and Foster, C. (2005) *Small, Flexible and Family Friendly – Work Practices in Service Sector Businesses*, Employment Relations Research Series No. 47, London: DTI.

Harris, L., Doughty, D. and Kirk, S. (2002) 'The devolution of HR responsibilities – perspectives from the UK's public sector', *Journal of European Industrial Training*, 26 (5), pp. 218–29.

Harris, L., Foster, C. and Whysall, P. (2007) 'Maximising women's potential in the UK's retail sector', *Employee Relations*, 29 (5), pp. 492–505.

Harris, L., Tuckman, A., Snook, J., Tailby, S., Hutchinson, S. and Winters, J. (2008) Small Firms and Workplace Disputes Resolution, Research Paper Ref: 01/08, ACAS.

Harrison, R. (1997) *Employee Development*, London: Institute of Personnel and Development.

Harrison, R. (2002) *Learning and Development*, 3rd edition, London: CIPD.

Harrison, R. (2005) *Learning and Development*, 4th edition, London: CIPD.

Harrison, R. and Kessels, J. (2004) *Human Resource Development in a Knowledge Economy: an Organisational View*, Basingstoke: Palgrave Macmillan.

Harvey-Jones, J.E. and Taffler, R. (2000) 'Biodata in professional entry-level selection: statistical scoring of common format applications', *Journal of Occupational and Organizational Psychology*, 73 (1), pp. 103–18.

Harzing, A-W. and Ruysseveldt van, J. (2004) (eds) *International Human Resource Management*, 2nd edition, London: Sage.

Hatcher, T. (2007) 'The fallacy of ethics and HRD: how ethics limits the creation of a "deep" profession', in *Critical Human Resource Development*, Rigg, C., Stewart, J. and Trehan, K. (eds), Harlow: Financial Times/Prentice Hall.

Hayfield, A. (2003) 'Meet the "out" laws', *People Management*, 9 (24), p. 21.

Haynes, P. and Allen, M. (2001) 'Partnership as union strategy: a preliminary evaluation', *Employee Relations*, 23 (2), pp. 164–87.

Heap, D. (2004) 'Redundances in the UK: An update of previous analyses of redundances in the UK in relation to age, sex, occupation, industry and region', *Labour Market Trends*, 112 (5), pp. 195–201.

Heenan, D.A. and Perlmutter, H.V. (1979) *Multinational Organisation Development*, Reading, MA: Addison-Wesley.

Heery, E. (1998) 'A return to contract? Performance-related pay in a public service', *Work, Employment and Society*, 21 (1), pp. 73–95.

Heery, E. (2000) 'The new pay: risk and representation at work', in *Ethical Issues in Contemporary Human Resource Management*, Winstanley, D. and Woodall, J. (eds), London: Macmillan.

Heery, E. (2002) 'Partnership versus organising: alternative futures for British trade unionism', *Industrial Relations Journal*, 33 (1), pp. 20–35.

Heery, E. and Noon, M. (2001) *Dictionary of Human Resource Management*, Oxford: Oxford University Press.

Heery, E. and Salmon, J. (1999) *The Insecure Workforce*, Andover: Routledge.

Heery, E., Simms, M., Delbridge, R., Salmon, J. and Simpson, D. (2000) 'The TUC's organising academy: an assessment', *Industrial Relations Journal*, 31 (5), pp. 400–15.

Heider, F. (1958) *The Psychology of Interpersonal Relations*, New York: John Wiley and Sons.

Heinsman, H., de Hoogh, A., Koopman, P. and van Muijen, J. (2007) 'Competencies through the eyes of psychologists: a closer look at assessing competencies', *International Journal of Selection and Assessment*, 15 (4), pp. 412–28.

Hendry, C. (1994) *Human Resource Strategies for International Growth*, London: Routledge.

Hendry, C. and Pettigrew, A. (1992) 'Patterns of strategic change in the development of human resource management', *British Journal of Management* 3 (3), pp. 137–56.

Hendry, C., Bradley, P. and Perkins, S. (1997) 'Missed a motivator?', *People Management*, 3 (10), pp. 21–5.

Hendry, C., Woodward, S., Bradley, P. and Perkins, S. (2000) 'Performance and rewards: clearing out the stables', *Human Resource Management Journal*, 10 (3), pp. 46–64.

Hepple, B. (1995) 'The future of labour law', *Industrial Law Journal*, 24 (4), pp. 303–22.

Hepple, B. and Morris, G. (2002) 'The Employment Act 2002 and the crisis of individual rights', *Industrial Law Journal*, 31 (3), pp. 245–69.

Hermelin, E. and Robertson, I. (2001) 'A critique and standardization of metaanalytic validity coefficients in personnel selection', *Journal of Occupational and Organizational Psychology*, 74 (3), pp. 253–77.

Herriot, P. (1984) *Down from the Ivory Tower*, Chichester: John Wiley and Sons.

Herriot, P. (1989) 'Attribution theory and interview decisions', in *The Employment Interview*, Eder, R.W. and Ferris, G.R. (eds), London: Sage.

Herriot, P. and Anderson, N. (1997) 'Selecting for change: how will personnel and selection psychology survive', in *International Handbook of Selection and Assessment*, Anderson, N. and Herriot, P. (eds), Chichester: John Wiley and Sons, pp. 1–38.

Herriot, P. and Pemberton, C. (1995a) *New Deals: The Revolution in Managerial Careers*, Chichester: John Wiley and Sons.

Herriot, P. and Pemberton, C. (1995b) 'Psychological contracts – a new deal for middle managers', *People Management*, 1 (12), pp. 32–4.

Herzberg, F. (1966) *Work and the Nature of Man*, Cleveland, OH: World Publishing Company.

Hibbett, A and Meager, N. (2003) 'Key Indicators of women's positions in Britain', *Labour Market Trends*, 111 (10), pp. 503–12.

Hickson, D.J., Hinnings, C.R., Lee, C.A., Schneck, R.E. and Pennings, J.M. (1971) 'A strategic contingencies theory of interorganisational power', *Administrative Science Quarterly*, 16 (2), pp. 216–29.

Hill, A. (2007) 'The changing face of British cities by 2010', *The Observer*, 23rd December.

Hill, R. and Stewart, J. (eds) (2007) *Management Development: Perspectives from Research and Practice*, London: Routledge.

Hill, S. (1991) 'Why quality circles failed but total quality might succeed', *British Journal of Industrial Relations*, 29 (4), pp. 541–69.

Hilpern, K. (2003) 'The rich rewards of racial equality', *The Independent*, 30 October.

Hirsh, W. and Carter, A. (2002) *New Directions in Management Development*, Brighton: Institute for Employment Studies.

Hislop, D., Newell, S., Swan, J. and Scarbrough, H. (1997) 'Innovation and networks: linking diffusion and implementation', *International Journal of Innovation Management*, 1, pp. 427–48.

Hitt, M., Bierman, L., Shimizu, K. and Kochar, R. (2001) 'Direct and moderating effect of human capital on the strategy and performance in professional service firms: a resource-based perspective', *Academy of Management Journal*, 44, pp. 13–28.

HM Treasury/DTI (Department of Trade and Industry) (2004) *Productivity in the UK 5: benchmarking UK productivity performance*, Norwich: HMSO, available from http://www.hm-treasury.gov.uk/consultations_and_legislation/productivity_indicators/consult_productivity_indicators_index.cfm.

Hochschild, A.R. (1983) *The Managed Heart: The Commercialisation of Human Feeling*, Berkeley, CA: University of California Press.

Hoecklin, L. (1995) *Managing Cultural Differences: Strategies for Competitive Advantage*, Wokingham: Addison-Wesley.

Hoeft, S. and Schuler, H. (2001) 'The conceptual basis of assessment center ratings', *International Journal of Selection and Assessment*, 9 (1–2), pp. 114–23.

Hofer-Alfeis, J. (2008) 'Knowledge management solutions for the leaving expert issue', *Journal of Knowledge Management*, 12(4): 44–54.

Hofstede, G. (1984) *The Game of Budget Control*, London: Tavistock.

Hofstede, G. (1991) *Cultures and Organisations: Software of the Mind*, London: McGraw Hill.

Hogarth, R. (1980) *Judgement and Choice*, New York: John Wiley and Sons.

Hogarth, T. and Barth, M. (1991) 'Costs and benefits of hiring older workers: a case study of B&Q', *International Journal of Manpower*, 12 (8), pp. 5–17.

Hogg, C. (1998) 'In my opinion', *Croner Reference Book for Employers Magazine*, Issue 8, March, London: Croner, p. 5.

Holbeche, L. (2002) *Aligning Human Resources and Business Strategy*, Oxford: Butterworth-Heinemann/Roffey Park Institute.

Holden, N.J. (2002) *Cross-cultural Management*, London: Financial Times/Prentice Hall.

Honey, P. (1980) *Solving People-Problems*, London: McGraw-Hill.

Hope-Hailey, V., Gratton, L., McGovern, P., Stiles, P. and Truss, C. (1997) 'A chameleon function? HRM in the '90s', *Human Resource Management Journal*, 7 (3), pp. 5–18.

Horibe, F. (1999) *Managing Knowledge Workers: New Skills and Attitudes to Unlock the Intellectual Capital in Your Organization*, Chichester: John Wiley and Sons.

Hotopp, U. (2002) Teleworking in the UK, *Labour Market Trends*, 110 (6), pp. 311–18.

HR Focus (2008) 'What is diversity? Not many places know the answer', *HR Focus*, 85 (5), p. 8.

Human Resources and Social Development Canada (2001) *Corporate Profiles: Canadian Auto Workers Union* available from URL: http://www.hrsdc.gc.ca/en/lp/spila/wlb/ell/05canadian_auto_workers.shtml (accessed 2 September 2008).

Human Synergistics/Center for Applied Research (n.d.) *Individual Diagnostics*, available at http://enteract.com/-car/diag2.html (accessed 29 January 1998).

Hunter, J.E. and Schmidt, F.L. (1990) *Methods of Meta-analysis: Correcting Error and Bias in Research Findings*, Newbury Park, CA: Sage.

Hunter, L., McGregor, A., MacInnes, J. and Sproull, A. (1993) 'The "flexible firm": strategy and segmentation', *British Journal of Industrial Relations*, 31 (3), pp. 383–407.

Huselid, M. (1995) 'The impact of human resource management practices on turnover, productivity and corporate financial performance', *Academy of Management Journal*, 38 (3), pp. 635–72.

Hutchinson, S. and Purcell, J. (2003) 'Bringing policies to life: the vital role of front line managers in people management', *Executive Briefing*, London: CIPD.

Hutchinson, S. and Purcell, J. (2007) 'Learning and the line: the role of the line manager in training, learning and development', in *The Change Agenda*, London: CIPD.

Hyman, R. (1989) *Strikes*, 4th edition, London: Macmillan.

Hyman, R. (1991) 'Plus, ça change', in *Farewell to Flexibility*, Pollert, A. (ed.), Oxford: Blackwell.

Hyman, J. and Mason, B. (1995) *Managing Employee Involvement and Participation*, London: Sage.

Ibbetson, A. and Newell, S. (1998) 'Don't blame the provider', *International Journal of Training and Development*, 1 (4), pp. 239–58.

Ichniowski, C., Shaw, K. and Prennushi, G. (1997) 'The effects of HRM practices on productivity', *American Economic Review*, 86, pp. 291–313.

IDS (Incomes Data Services) (1997a) *European Works Councils*, IDS Study 637, London: IDS.

IDS (Incomes Data Services) (1997b) *Suggestion Schemes*, IDS Study 638, November, London: IDS.

IDS (Incomes Data Services) (2001) *Competency Frameworks*, IDS Study 706, London: IDS.

IDS (Incomes Data Services) StudyPlus (2001) Autumn.

IDS (Incomes Data Services) (2003) *Performance Management*, IDS Study 748, London: IDS.

IDS (Incomes Data Services) (2003) *Suggestion Schemes*, IDS Study 752, London: IDS.

IDS (Incomes Data Services) (2007a) *Bonus Schemes*, IDS Study 843, London: IDS.

IDS (Incomes Data Services) (2007b) *Performance Management*, IDS Study 839, London: IDS.

IDS (Incomes Data Services) (2007c) *Employee Benefits*, IDS Study 856, London: IDS.

IDS (Incomes Data Services) (2008) *HR*, IDS Study 871, London: IDS.

IDS (Incomes Data Services) (2008) *Work-Life Balance*, IDS Study 873, London: IDS.

Iles, P. and Preece, D. (2006) 'Developing leaders or developing leadership? The Academy of Chief Executives' programme in North East England', *Leadership*, 2 (3), pp. 317–40.

Illes, P. and Robertson, I. (1997) 'The impact of personnel selection procedures on candidates', in *International Handbook of Selection and Assessment*, Anderson, N. and Herriot, P. (eds), Chichester: John Wiley and Sons, pp. 543–66.

Industrial Relations Services (1997) 'The changing nature of the employment contract', *IRS Employment Trends*, July.

Inland Revenue (2003) 'Employee Share Schemes' www.inlandrevenue.gov.uk/stats/emp_share_schemes (accessed 22 October 2003).

International Labour Office (2002) *An Inclusive Society for an Aging Population: The Employment and Social Protection Challenge*, Geneva: ILO.

IPA (Involvement and Participation Association) (1997) *Towards Industrial Partnership*, London: IPA.

IPD (Institute of Personnel and Development) (1997) *A Vision for the Development of Equal Opportunities: Managing Diversity*, an IPD position paper, London: IPD.

IPD (Institute of Personnel and Development) (1998) *IPD 1998 Performance Pay Survey*, Executive Summary, London: IPD.

IPM (Institute of Personnel Management) (1988) 'Suggestion schemes', *Personnel Management Factsheet 11*, November.

IPM (Institute of Personnel Management) (1992) *Performance Management in the UK. An Analysis of the Issues*, London: IPM.

Jackall, R. (1988) *Moral Mazes: The World of Corporate Managers*, Oxford: Oxford University Press.

Jackson, M.P., Leopold, J.W. and Tuck, K. (1993) *Decentralisation of Collective Bargaining: An Analysis of Recent Experience in the UK*, Basingstoke: Macmillan.

Jacques, D. (1992) 'Self-appraisal; problems and insights, conference presentation', at *Appraisal: Implications for Academic Staff Development in Higher Education*, organised by the Standing Conference on Educational Development and Derbyshire College of Higher Education.

Jacques, E. (1961) *Equitable Payment*, London: Heinemann.

James, P. and Walters, D. (2002) 'Worker representation in health and safety: options for regulatory reform', *Industrial Relations Journal*, 33 (2), pp. 141–56.

Jansen, P., van der Velde, M. and Mul, W. (2001) 'A typology of management development', *Journal of Management Development*, 20 (2), 106–20.

Janz, T., Hellervik, L. and Gilmore, D.C. (1986) *Behaviour Description Interviewing: New, Accurate, Cost-effective*, Boston, MA: Allyn and Bacon.

Jarzabkowsky, P. (2005) *Strategy as Practice*, London: Sage.

Jefferson, M. (1997) *Principles of Employment Law*, 3rd edition, London: Cavendish Publishing Ltd.

Jensen, M. and Meckling, W. (1976) 'Theory of the firm: managerial behaviour, agency costs and ownership structure', *Journal of Financial Economics* 3, pp. 305–60.

Jewson, N. and Mason, D. (1986) 'The theory and practice of equal opportunities policies: liberal and radical approaches', *Sociological Review*, 34 (2), pp. 307–34.

Johns, T. (1995) 'Don't be afraid of the moral maze', *People Management*, 1 (20), pp. 32–5.

Johnson, G., Langley, A., Melin, L. and Whittington, R. (2007) *Strategy as Practice: Research Directions and Resources*, Cambridge: Cambridge University Press.

Johnson, G., Melin, L. and Whittington, R. (2003) 'Micro strategy and strategizing: towards an activity-based view', *Journal of Management Studies*, 40 (1), pp. 3–22.

Johnson, L. and Johnstone, S. (2000) 'The legislative framework', in *The Dynamics of Managing Diversity: a critical approach*, Kitron, G. and Greene, A.M. (eds), Oxford: Butterworth Heinemann.

Johnson-Hillery, J., Kang, J. and Tuan, W. (1997) 'The difference between elderly consumers' satisfaction levels and retail sales personnel's perceptions', *International Journal of Retail & Distribution Management*, 25 (4), pp. 126–37.

Johnston, R. (2001) 'Supporting learning in the third millennium', in *Human Resource Development*, Johnston, R. (ed.), London: Kogan Page, pp. 475–94.

Johnston, W. and Packer, A. (1987) *Workforce 2000: Work and Workers for the 21st century*, Indianapolis: Hudson Institute.

Jones, A. (1991) *Handbook of Training*, London: Gower.

Jones, J.E. and Woodcock, M. (1985) *Manual of Management Development*, Aldershot: Gower.

Jones, N. and Fcar, N. (1994) 'Continuing professional development: perspectives from human resource professionals', *Personnel Review*, 23 (8), pp. 48–61.

Judge, T.A. and Ferris, G.A. (1992) 'The elusive criterion of fit in human resources staffing decisions', *Human Resource Planning*, 15, pp. 47–67.

Kahn-Freund, O. (1972) *Labour and the Law*, London: Stevens and Sons.

Kaler, J. (1999) 'What's the good of ethical theory?', *Business Ethics: A European Review*, 8 (4), pp. 206–13.

Kandola, R. and Fullerton, J. (1994) 'Diversity: more than just an empty slogan', *Personnel Management*, 26 (11), pp. 46–50.

Kandola, R. and Fullerton, J. (1998) *Diversity in Action: Managing the Mosaic*, 2nd edition, London: CIPD.

Kandolin, I. and Kauppinen, K. (1996) 'New working time models in comparison: 6 + 6 hour day shift and compressed work week', *Finnish Work Research Bulletin*, 4, pp. 31–5.

Kane, J.S. (2000) 'Accuracy and its determinants un distributional assessment', *Human Performance*, 13, pp. 47–85.

Kaplan, R.S. and Norton, D.P. (1992) 'The balanced scorecard – measures that drive performance', *Harvard Business Review*, Jan–Feb, pp. 71–9.

Kaplan, R.S. and Norton, D.P. (1993) 'Putting the balanced scorecard to work', *Harvard Business Review*, Sept–Oct, pp. 134–42.

Karstcn, L. and Leopold, J. (2003) 'The need for Hora management', *Personnel Review*, 32 (4), pp. 405–21.

Karuppan, C.M. (2004) 'Strategies to foster labour flexibility', *International Journal of Productivity and Performance Management*, 53 (6), pp. 532–47.

Kauffman, J.R., Jex, S.M., Love, K.G. and Libkuman, T.M. (1993) 'The construct validity of assessment centre performance dimensions', *International Journal of Selection and Assessment*, 1, pp. 213–23.

Kay, E., Meyer, H.H. and French, J.R.P. (1965) 'Effects of threat in a performance appraisals interview', *Journal of Applied Psychology*, 49, pp. 311–17.

Kay, J. (1993) *The Foundations of Corporate Success*, Oxford: Oxford University Press.

Keenan, T. (1995) 'Graduate recruitment in Britain: a survey of selection methods used by organisations', *Journal of Organisational Behaviour*, 16, pp. 303–17.

Keenan, T. (1997) 'Selection for potential', in *International Handbook of Selection and Assessment*, Anderson, N. and Herriot, P. (eds), Chichester: John Wiley and Sons, pp. 507–28.

Keenoy, T. (1990) 'IIRM. A case of the wolf in sheep's clothing', *Personnel Review*, 19 (2), pp. 3–9.

Keep, E. and Rainbird, H. (2000) 'Towards the learning organisation', in Bach, S. and Sisson, K. (eds) *Personnel Management*, Oxford: Blackwell.

Keller, B. (2004) 'Employment relations in Germany', in *International and Comparative Employment Relations*, 4th edition, Bamber, G., Lansbury, R. and Wailes, N. (eds), London: Sage.

Kelliher, C. and Desombre, T. (2005) 'Breaking down boundaries: functional flexibility and occupational identity in health care in *Flexibility in Workplaces*, Zeytinoglu, I.U. (ed.), Geneva: ILO.

Kelly, A. and Monks, K. (1998) 'View from the bridge and life on deck: contrasts and contradictions in performance-related pay', in *Experiencing Human Resource Management*, Mabey, C., Skinner, D. and Clark, T. (eds), London: Sage, pp. 113–28.

Kelly, G.A. (1955) *The Psychology of Personal Constructs*, New York: Norton.

Kelly, J. (1982) Scientific Management, Job Redesign and Work Performance, London: Academic Press.

Kelly, J. (1988) *Trade Unions and Socialist Politics*, London: Verso.

Kelly, J. (1996) 'Union militancy and social partnership', in *The New Workplace and Trade Unionism*, Ackers, P., Smith, C. and Smith, P. (eds), London: Routledge, pp. 77–109.

Kelly, J. (1999) *Rethinking Industrial Relations: Mobilisation, Collectivism and Long Waves*, London: Routledge.

Kelly, J. (2005) 'Social Partnerships in Britain', in *Partnership and Modernisation in Employment Relations*, Stuart, M. and Martinez Lucio, M. (eds), London: Routledge, pp. 188–209.

Kerr, S. (1991) 'On the folly of rewarding A while hoping for B', in *Motivation and Work Behaviour*, Steers, R.M. and Porter, L.W. (eds), New York: McGraw-Hill, pp. 485–97.

Kersley, B., Carmen, A., Forth, J., Bryson, A., Bewley, A., Dix, G. and Oxenbridge, S. (2006), *Inside the Workplace – Findings from the 2004 Workplace Employment Relations Survey*, London: Routledge.

Kessler, I. (1994) 'Performance pay', in *Personnel Management, a Comprehensive Guide to Theory and Practice in Britain*, Sisson, K. (ed.), Oxford: Blackwell, pp. 465–93.

Kessler, I. (1995) 'Reward systems', in *Human Resource Management, A Critical Text*, Storey, J. (ed.), London: Routledge, pp. 254–79.

Kessler, I. (2000) 'Remuneration systems', in *Personnel Management, a Comprehensive Guide to Theory and Practice in Britain*, Bach, S. and Sisson, K. (eds), Oxford: Blackwell, pp. 264–86.

Kessler, I. (2005) 'Remuneration Systems', in *Managing Human Resources: Personnel Management, a Comprehensive Guide to Theory and Practice in Britain*, 4th edition, S. Bach (ed.), Oxford: Blackwell.

Kessler, I. (2007*)* 'Reward choices: strategy and equity', in *Human Resource Management – A Critical Text*, 3rd edition, J. Storey (ed.), London: Thomson.

Kessler, I. and Bayliss, F. (1995) *Contemporary British Industrial Relations*, 2nd edition, London: Macmillan.

Kessler, K. and Purcell, J. (1992) 'Performance related pay: objectives and application', *Human Resource Management Journal*, 2 (3), pp. 16–33.

Kidger, P. (1992) 'Employee participation in Occupational Health and Safety: Should union appointed or elected representatives be the model for the UK?', *Human Resource Management Journal*, 2 (4), pp. 21–35.

Kieser, A. (2002) 'On communication barriers between management science, consultancies and business organizations', in *Critical Consulting*, Clark, T. and Fincham, R. (eds), Oxford: Blackwell.

King, S. (1994) 'Opportunity 2000: three years on', *Management Development Review*, 7 (5), pp. 23–5.

Kipping, M. (1996) 'The US influence on the evolution of management consultancies in Britain, France, and Germany since 1945', *Business and Economic History*, 25 (1), pp. 112–23.

Kipping, M. (2002) 'Trapped in their wave: the evolution of management consultancies', in *Critical Consulting*, Clark, T. and Fincham, R. (eds), Oxford: Blackwell.

Kirk, G.S. (1976) *The Nature of the Greek Myths*, Harmondsworth: Penguin.

Kirkpatrick, D.L. (1967) 'Evaluation of training', in *Training and Development Handbook*, Craig, R.L. and Bitten, L.R. (eds), New York: McGraw-Hill.

Kirton, G. and Greene, A. (2005) *The Dynamics of Managing Diversity: A Critical Approach*, 2nd edition, Oxford: Elsevier Butterworth-Heinemann.

Kitay, J. and Wright, C. (2003) 'Expertise and organizational boundaries: the varying roles of Australian management consultants', *Asia Pacific Business Review*, 9 (3), pp. 21–40.

Klein, N. (2000) *No Logo: Taking Aim at the Brand Bullies*, London: Harper Collins.

Knight, K.E. (1967) 'A descriptive model of the intra-firm innovation process', *Journal of Business Strategy*, 40 (4).

Knights, A. and Poppleton, A. (2008) *Developing Coaching Capabilities in Organisations*, London: CIPD.

Knights, D. and Raffo, C. (1990) 'Milk round professionalism in personnel recruitment: myth or reality', *Personnel Review*, 19, pp. 28–37.

Kochan, T. (1980) *Collective Bargaining and Industrial Relations*, Homewood, IL: Irwin.

Kochan, T. and Barocci, T.A. (1985) *Human Resource Management and Industrial Relations*, Boston: Little Brown.

Kochan, T. and Osterman, P. (1994) *Mutual Gains Bargaining*, Boston, MA: Harvard Business School Press.

Kolb, D., Rubin, M.I. and McIntyre, J.M. (1974) *Organizational Psychology: an Experimental Approach*, 2nd edition, Englewood Cliffs, NJ: Prentice Hall.

Krause, D., Kersting, M., Heggestad, D. and Thornton, G. (2006) 'Incremental validity of selection center ratings over cognitive ability tests', *International Journal of Selection and Assessment*, 14 (4), pp. 360–80.

Kremer, M. (2005) *How Welfare States Care*, PhD. University of Utrecht.

Kurtzberg, T., Naquin, C. and Belkin, L.Y. (2005) 'Electronic performance appraisals: the effects of e-mail communication on peer ratings in actual and simulated environments', *Organisational Behaviour and Human Decision Processes*, 98: 216–26.

Labour Force Survey (2002) http://www.statistics.gov.uk/StatBase/Source.asp?vlnk=358

Labour Research Department (1993) *Labour Research*, 82/2, February.

Lane, C. (1989) *Management and Labour in Europe*, Aldershot: Gower.

Lane, D.A. (1988) 'Redundancy counselling for those still in employment', *Journal of Managerial Psychology*, 3, pp. 17–22.

Lapointe, M., Dunn, K., Tremblay-Côté, N., Bergeron, L.-P. and Ignaczak, L. (2006) *Looking Ahead: a 10-year outlook for the Canadian Labour Market (2006–2015)*, Quebec: Human Resources and Social Development Canada.

Lashley, C. (1997) *Empowering Service Excellence: Beyond the Quick Fix*, London: Cassell.

Lashley, C. (1999) 'Employee empowerment in services: a framework for analysis', *Personnel Review*, 28 (3), pp. 169–91.

Latham, G.P., Saari, L.M., Pursell, E.D. and Campion, M. (1980) 'The situational interview', *Journal of Applied Psychology*, 65 (4), pp. 422–7.

Laurent, A. (1983) 'The cultural diversity of western conception of management', *International Studies of Management and Organisation*, 13 (1–2), pp. 75–96.

Lave, J. and Wenger, E. (1991) *Situated Learning: Legitimate Peripheral Participation*, Cambridge: Cambridge University Press.

Lawler, E. (1973) *Motivation in Work Organisations*, California: Brook Cole.

Lawler, E. (2000) *Rewarding Excellence: Pay Strategies for the New Economy*, San Francisco: Jossey-Bass.

Lawler, E. and Porter, L. (1968) *Management Attitudes and Behaviour*, Homewood, IL: Irwin-Dorsey.

Lazar, A., Kravetz, S. and Zinger, A. (2004). 'Moderating effects of rater personality on the relation between candidate self-monitoring and selection interview ratings', *International Journal of Selection and Assessment*, 21 (4), pp. 321–6.

Learning and Skills Council (2006) *The Provider for the Future: Draft E-Learning* Vision, April, Coventry: LSC.

Learning and Skills Council (2007) *Better Skills, Better Jobs, Better Lives: Priorities and Key Actions for 2008/9 to 2010/11*, Coventry: LSC.

Lee, M. (1997) 'The development approach: a critical reconsideration', in *Management Learning*, Burgoyne, J. and Reynolds, M. (eds), London: Sage.

Lee, M. (ed.) (2003) *HRD in a Complex World*, London: Routledge.

Lees, S. (1992) 'Ten faces of management development', *Management Education and Development*, 23 (2), pp. 89–105.

Legge, K. (1988) 'Personnel management in recession and recovery: a comparative analysis of what the surveys say', *Personnel Review*, 17 (2), (monograph issue).

Legge, K. (1995) *Human Resource Management: Rhetorics and Realities*, London: Macmillan.

Legge, K. (1998a) 'The morality of HRM', in *Strategic Human Resource Management*, Mabey, C., Salaman, G. and Storey, J. (eds), London: Sage.

Legge, K. (1998b) 'Is HRM ethical? Can HRM be ethical?', in *Ethics and Organisations*, Parker, M. (ed.), London: Sage.

Legge, K. (2001) 'Silver bullet or spent round? Assessing the meaning of the "high commitment management"/performance relationship', in *Human Resource Management: A Critical Text*, 2nd edition, Storey, J. (ed.), London: Thomson Learning.

Legge, K. (2005) *Human Resource Management, Rhetorics and Realities*, 2nd edition, Basingstoke: Macmillan.

Lehman Brothers (1994) *Jobs Study*, Paris: OECD.

Leighton, P. and Syrett, M. (1989) *New Work Patterns: Putting Policy into Practice*, London: Pitman.

Lengnick-Hall, C. and Lengnick-Hall, M. (1988) 'Strategic human resources management: a review of the literature and a proposed typology', *American Management Review*, 13 (3), pp. 45–70.

Leopold, J. (ed.) (2002) *Human Resources in Organisations*, London: Financial Times/ Prentice Hall.

Leopold, J. and Hallier, J.P. (1998) 'Approaches to the employment relationship on greenfield sites: an international comparison', paper presented at the Sixth Conference on International Human Resource Management, Paderborn, June.

Leung, L. and Li, W. (1990) 'Psychological mechanisms of process-control effects', *Journal of Applied Psychology*, 75, pp. 613–20.

Lewis, J. (1995) 'The contractor factor', *Computing Weekly*, 3 January.

Lewis, P. (1991) 'Performance-related pay: pretexts and pitfalls', *Employee Relations*, 13 (1), pp. 12–16.

Lewis, P. (1993) *The Successful Management of Redundancy*, Oxford: Blackwell.

Lewis, P., Thornhill, A. and Saunders, M. (2003) *Employee Relations: Understanding the Employment Relationship*, Harlow: Prentice Hall.

Lewis, S. (1997) 'An international perspective on work–family issues', in *Integrating Work and Family: Challenges for a Changing World*, Parasurama, S. and Greenhaus, J. (eds), Westport: Praeger, pp. 91–103.

Li, Y., Vanhaverbeke, W. and Schoenmakers, W. (2008) 'Exploration and exploitation in innovation: reframing the interpretation, *Creativity and Innovation Management*, 17 (2), pp. 107–26.

Lievens, F. (1998) 'Factors which improve the construct validity of assessment centres: a review', *International Journal of Selection and Assessment*, 6 (3), pp. 141–52.

Liff, S. (1989) 'Assessing equal opportunities policies', *Personnel Review*, 18 (1), pp. 27–34.

Liff, S. (1999) 'Diversity and equal opportunities: room for a constructive compromise?', *Human Resource Management Journal*, 9 (1), pp. 65–75.

Liff, S. and Dickens, L. (2000) 'Ethics and equality: reconciling false dilemmas', in *Ethical Issues in Contemporary Human Resource Management*, Winstanley, D. and Woodall, J. (eds), London: Macmillan.

Linehan, M. and Hanappi-Egger, E. (2006) 'Diversity and diversity management: a comparative advantage?', in *Managing Human Resources in Europe*, Larsen, H. and Mayrhofer, W. (eds), Abingdon: Routledge, pp. 217–33.

Lister, R. (2003) *Citizenship: Feminist Perspectives*, London: Palgrave.

Little, S., Quintas, P. and Ray, T. (eds) (2002) *Managing Knowledge: An Essential Reader*, London: Sage.

Livingstone, D.W. and Roth, R. (2001) *Workers' Knowledge: An Untapped Resource in the Labour Movement*, WALL Working Paper No 31, Toronto: Centre for the Study of Education and Work, Ontario Institute for Studies in Education of the University of Toronto.

Locke, E. and Latham, G. (1984) *Goal Setting: A Motivational Technique that Works*, Englewood Cliffs, NJ: Prentice Hall.

Locke, E. and Latham, G. (1990) *A Theory of Goal Setting and Task Performance*, New York: Prentice Hall.

Locke, E., Shaw, K., Saari, L. and Latham, G. (1981) 'Goal setting and task performance 1969–1980', *Psychological Bulletin*, 90, pp. 125–52.

Lowry, D. (2006) 'Human resource managers as ethical decision-makers: mapping the terrain', *Asia Pacific Journal of Human Resources*, 44 (2), pp. 171–83.

Lowson, C. and Boyce, R. (1990) 'The development of the performance management programme', *Management Services*, September, pp. 6–9.

Mabey, C. and Salaman, G. (1995) *Strategic Human Resource Management*, Oxford: Basil Blackwell.

Mabey, C., Salaman, G. and Storey, J. (1998) (eds) *Strategic Human Resource Management*, London: Sage.

Macan, T.H., Avedon, M.J., Paese, M. and Smith, D.E. (1994) 'The effects of applicants' reactions to cognitive ability tests and an assessment centre', *Personnel Psychology*, 47, pp. 715–38.

Macduffie, J.E. (1995) 'Human resource bundles and manufacturing performance: organisational logic and flexible production systems in the world auto industry', *Industrial and Labor Relations Review*, 48 (2), pp. 197–221.

MacIntyre, A. (1985) *After Virtue: A Study in Moral Theory*, 2nd edition, London: Duckworth.

Mackay, L. and Torrington, D. (1986) *The Changing Nature of Personnel Management*, London: Institute of Personnel Management.

Mackinnon, C. (1987) *Feminism Unmodified*, Cambridge, MA: Harvard University Press.

Macklin, R. (2006) 'The moral autonomy of human resource managers', *Asia Pacific Journal of Human Resources*, 44 (2), pp. 211–21.

Maddock, S. and Parkin, D. (1993) 'Gender cultures: women's choices and strategies at work', *Women in Management Review*, 8 (2), pp. 3–9.

Mahoney, J. (1998) 'Cultivating moral courage in business', *Business Ethics: A European Review*, 7 (4), pp. 187–92.

Mainiero, L.A. and Sullivan, S.E. (2006) *The Opt-Out Revolt: Why People are Leaving Companies to Create Kaleidoscope Careers*, Palo Alto, CA: Davies-Black Publishing.

Makinson, J. (2000) *Incentives for Change*, London: HMSO.

Malhotra, N., Budhwar, P. and Prowse, P. (2007) 'Linking rewards to commitment: an empirical investigation of four UK call centres', *International Journal of Human Resource Management*, 18 (12), pp. 2095–127.

Marchington, M. (1988) 'The four faces of employee consultation', *Personnel Management*, May.

Marchington, M. (1992) *Managing the Team*, Oxford: Blackwell.

Marchington, M. (1994) 'The dynamics of joint consultation', in *Personnel Management*, Sisson, K. (ed.), Oxford: Blackwell.

Marchington, M. (1995) 'Employee relations', in *Strategic Prospects for HRM*, Tyson, S. (ed.), London: IPD.

Marchington, M. (2000) 'Teamworking and employee involvement: terminology, evaluation and context', *Teamworking*, Proctor, S. and Mueller, F. (eds), Basingstoke: Macmillan Business.

Marchington, M. (2005) 'Employee involvement: patterns and explanations', in *Participation and Democracy at Work*, Harley, B., Hyman, J. and Thompson, P. (eds), Basingstoke: Palgrave Macmillan.

Marchington, M. and Grugulis, I. (2000) ' "Best practice" human resource management: perfect opportunity or dangerous illusion?', *International Journal of Human Resource Management*, 11 (4), pp. 905–25.

Marchington, M. and Parker, P. (1990) *Changing Patterns of Employee Relations*, Hemel Hempstead: Harvester Wheatsheaf.

Marchington, M. and Wilkinson, A. (1996) *Core Personnel and Development*, London: IPD.

Marchington, M. and Wilkinson, A. (2002a) *Core Personnel and Development*, London: CIPD.

Marchington, M. and Wilkinson, A. (2002b) *People Management and Development*, London: CIPD.

Marchington, M. and Wilkinson, A. (2005) *Human Resource Management at Work: People Management and Development*, London: CIPD.

Marchington, M. and Wilkinson, A. (2008) *Human Resource Management at Work*, 4th edition, London: Chartered Institute of Personnel and Development.

Marchington, M., Goodman, J., Wilkinson, A. and Ackers, P. (1992) *New Developments in Employee Involvement*, London: Employment Department, Research Series No. 2.

Marchington, M., Wilkinson, A., Ackers, P. and Goodman, J. (1993) 'The influence of managerial relations on waves of employee involvement', *British Journal of Industrial Relations*, 31 (4), pp. 553–76.

Marginson, P. (1989) 'Employment flexibility in large companies: change and continuity', *Industrial Relations Journal*, 29 (2), pp. 101–18.

Marinker, M. (ed.) (1990) *Medical Audit and General Practice*, London: British Medical Journal.

Markwick, N. and Fill, C. (1997) 'Towards a framework for managing corporate identity', *European Journal of Marketing*, 31 (5/6), pp. 396–409.

Marsden, D. (2004) 'Unions and procedural justice: an alternative to the common rule', in *Unions in the 21st Century: An International Perspective*, A. Verma and T.A. Kochan (eds), London: Palgrave Macmillan.

Marshall, A. (1890) *Principles of Economics*, London: Macmillan, p. 1972.

Martin, J.P. (1998) 'What works among economy active Labour market policies: evidence from OECD's countries' experiences', *Labour Market and Social Policy Occasional Paper No. 35*, Paris: OECD.

Martinez Lucio, M. and Stuart, M. (2002) 'Assessing the principles of partnership. Workplace trade union representatives' attitudes and experiences', *Employee Relations*, 24 (3), pp. 305–20.

Martinez Lucio, M., and Stuart, M. (2005) *Partnership and Modernisation in Employee Relations*, London: Routledge.

Mason, R. and Bain, P. (1991) 'Trade union recruitment strategies: facing the 1990s', *Industrial Relations Journal*, 22 (1), pp. 36–45.

Masterton, A. and Pinnock, N. (2002) *UK Voluntary Sector Training Courses Review*, London: Directory of Social Change.

Matlay, H. (1999) 'Employee relations in small firms – a micro-business perspective', *Employee Relations*, 21 (3), pp. 285–95.

Mavin, S. and Girling, G. (2000) 'What is managing diversity and why does it matter?', *Human Resource Development International*, 3 (4), pp. 419–33.

Maxwell, G., Blair, S. and McDougall, M. (2001) 'Edging towards managing diversity in practice', *Employee Relations*, 23 (5), pp. 468–82.

Mayerhofer, W. (1997) 'Warning: flexibility can damage your organisational health', *Employee Relations*, 19 (9), pp. 519–34.

Mayne, L., Tregaskis, O. and Brewster, C. (1996) 'A comparative analysis of the link between flexibility and HRM strategy', *Employee Relations*, 18, pp. 5–24.

McCabe, D. (1999) 'Total Quality Management: anti-union Trojan horse or management albatross', *Work, Employment and Society*, 13 (4), pp. 665–91.

McCabe, D. and Wilkinson, A. (1991) 'The rise and fall of TQM: the vision, meaning and operation of change', *Industrial Relations Journal*, 29 (1), pp. 18–29.

McCartney, C. (2007) *Diversity and Equality Survey Results*, Horsham: Roffey Park Institute.

McCormick, E.J., Jeanneret, P.R. and Mecham, R.C. (1972) 'A study of job characteristics and job dimensions as based on the Position Analysis questionnaire', *Journal of Applied Psychology*, 56, pp. 347–68.

McCracken, M. and Wallace, M. (2000) 'Towards a redefinition of strategic HRM', *Journal of European Industrial Training*, 24 (5), pp. 281–90.

McEvoy, G.M. (1990) 'Public sector managers' reactions to appraisals by subordinates', *Public Personnel Management*, 19 (2), Summer, pp. 201–12.

McFarlin, D.B. and Sweeney, P.D. (1992) 'Distributive and procedural justice as predictors of satisfaction with personal and organisational outcomes', *Academy of Management Journal*, 35 (3), pp. 626–37.

McFarlin, D.B. and Sweeney, P.D. (2001) 'Cross-cultural applications of organizational justice', in *Justice in the Workplace Volume 2: from Theory to Practice*, Cropanzano, R. (ed.), Mahwah, NJ: Lawrence Erlbaum Associates Inc.

McGoldrick, J., Stewart, J. and Watson, S. (2002a) 'Researching HRD: philosophy, process and practice', in *Understanding Human Resource Development: a research based approach*, McGoldrick, J., Stewart, J. and Watson, S. (eds), London: Routledge, pp. 1–17.

McGoldrick, J., Stewart, J. and Watson, S. (eds) (2002b) *Understanding Human Resource Development: a research-based approach*, London: Routledge.

McGovern, P., Gratton, L., Hope-Hailey, V., Stiles, P. and Truss, C. (1997) 'Human resource management on the line?', *Human Resource Management Journal*, 7 (4), pp. 12–29.

McGovern, P., Hope-Hailey, V. and Stiles, P. (1998) 'Human resource management on the line?', *Human Resource Management Journal*, 7 (4), pp. 13–29.

McGregor, A. and Sproull, A. (1991) *Employers' Labour Use Strategies: Analysis of an Employer Survey*, Employment Dept. Research Paper No. 83.

McKenna, C. (1995) 'The origins of modern management consulting', *Business and Economic History*, 24 (1), pp. 51–8.

Meager, N. (1985) *Temporary Work in Britain: Its Growth and Changing Rationales, IMS Report No. 106*, Brighton: Institute of Manpower Studies.

Meehl, P.E. (1986) 'Causes and effects of my disturbing little book', *Journal of Personality Assessment*, 50, pp. 370–5.

Meekings, A. (1995) 'Unlocking the potential of performance measurement: a practical implementation guide', *Public Money and Management*, Oct–Dec.

Megginson, D. (2000) 'Current issues in mentoring', *Career Development International*, 5 (4/5), pp. 256–60.

Megginson, D. and Clutterbuck, D. (2004) *Techniques for Coaching and Mentoring*, Oxford: Butterworth-Heinemann.

Megginson, D. and Whitaker, V. (2007) *Continuing Professional Development*, 2nd edition, London: CIPD.

Megginson, D., Banfield, P. and Joy-Matthews, J. (1999) *Human Resource Development*, 2nd edition, London: Kogan Page.

Mendenhall, M.E. (2006) 'The elusive, yet critical challenge of developing global leaders', *European Management Journal*, 24 (6), pp. 422–9.

Mento, A.J., Steel, R.P. and Karren, R.J. (1987) 'A meta-analytical study of task performance: 1966–1984', *Organisational Behaviour and Human Decision Processes*, 39, pp. 52–83.

Metcalf, D. (1991) 'British unions: dissolution or resurgence?', *Oxford Review of Economic Policy*, 7 (1), pp. 18–32.

Miles, R.E. and Snow, C.C. (1978) *Organization Strategy, Structure and Process*, New York: McGraw-Hill.

Milkovich, K.T. and Newman, J.M. (1987) *Compensation*, Illinois: Business Publications.

Miller, B. (1989) *Management Skills for the Technical Professional: Workbook*, Milton Keynes: Career Track International.

Millward, N. and Stevens, M. (1986) *British Workplace Industrial Relations: 1980–1984*, The DE/ESRC/PSI/ACAS Survey, London: Gower.

Millward, N., Bryson, A. and Forth, J. (2000) All change at work, British employment relations 1980–1998, *Workplace Industrial Relations Survey Series*, London: Routledge.

Millward, N., Stevens, M., Smart, D. and Hawes, W.R. (1992) *British Workplace Industrial Relations in Transition*, Aldershot: Dartmouth Publishers.

Micic, P. and Gold, J. (2008) *Future management: Towards a model of future learning for managers*, 9th International Conference on Human Resource Development Research and Practice across Europe: Developing Leaders and Managers, IESEG School of Management, Catholic University of Lille, 21st–23rd May.

Mintzberg, H. (1994) *The Rise and Fall of Strategic Planning*, Hemel Hempstead: Prentice Hall.

Mohrman Jnr, A., Resnick-West, S.M. and Lawler III, E.E. (1989) *Designing Performance Appraisal Schemes: Aligning Appraisals and Organisational Realities*, San Francisco: Jossey-Bass.

Moir, J. (2008) 'Has the froth finally blown off the coffee?', *The Daily Mail*, 01 August, p. 28.

Molleman, E. and Slomp, J. (2003) 'The impact of team and work characteristics on team functioning', *Proceedings of the Group Technology/Cellular Manufacturing World Symposium*, Columbus, OH, July 28–30.

Monbiot, G. (2003). *The Age of Consent: A Manifesto for a New World Order*, London: Flamingo.

Monbiot, G. (2003) 'The Flight to India', *The Guardian*, 21 October, p. 25.

Monk, E. and Wagner, B. (2008) *Concepts in Enterprise Resource Planning*, 3rd edition, Florence, KY: Delmar.

Monks, J. (1998) 'Trade unions, enterprise and the future', in *Human Resource Management The New Agenda*, Sparrow, P. and Marchington, M. (eds), London: Financial Times/Pitman.

More, E. (2002) 'How to set up a CSR programme', *People Management*, 8 (20), pp. 50–1.

More, T. (1978 [1516]) *Utopia*, Harmondsworth: Penguin.

Morgan, G. (1986) *Images of Organisation*, London: Sage.

Morgan, G. (1997) *Images of Organisation*, London: Sage.

Morgeson, F., Campion, M., Dipboye, R. and Hollenbeck, J. (2007) 'Reconsidering the use of personality tests in personnel selection contexts', *Personnel Psychology*, 60 (3), pp. 683–729.

Morley, M. (2007) 'Person-organization fit', *Journal of Managerial Psychology*, 22 (2), pp. 109–17.

Morris, M.W. and Peng, K.P. (1994) 'Culture and cause: American and Chinese attributions for social and physical events', *Journal of Personality and Social Psychology*, 67, pp. 949–71.

Mosco, V. (2008) *Knowledge Workers in the Information Society*, Lanham, MD: Lexington Books.

Mucha, R. (2004) 'The art and science of talent management', *Organizational Development Journal*, 22 (4), pp. 96–101.

Mullins, J.W. and Cummings, L.L. (1991) 'Situational strength – a framework for understanding the role of individuals in initiating proactive strategic change', *Journal of Organisational Change Management*, 12 (6), pp. 462–79.

Mumford, A. (1993) *Management Development: Strategies for Action*, 2nd edition, London: Institute of Personnel Management.

Mumford, A. (1997) *Management Development: Strategies for Action*, 3rd edition, London: IPD.

Mumford, A. and Gold, J. (2004) *Management Development: Strategies for Action*, 4th edition, London: CIPD.

Myers, J. (1996/7) 'Dynamics of organization change and development: crisis or creativity?', unpublished MSc dissertation, Nottingham Business School, Nottingham Trent University, Nottingham, UK.

Myers, J. and Sacks, R. (2001) 'Harnessing the talents of a "loose and baggy monster"', *Journal of European Industrial Training*, 25 (9), pp. 454–64.

Myers, J. and Sacks, R. (2003) 'Tools, techniques and tightropes: the art of walking and talking private sector management in non-profit organisations', *Financial Accountability and Management*, 19 (3), pp. 283–301.

Nahapiet, J. and Ghoshal, S. (1998) 'Social capital, intellectual capital and the organisational advantage', *Academy of Management Review*, 23 (2), pp. 242–66.

Nalbantian, H.R., Guzzo, R.A., Kieffer, D. and Doherty, J. (2003) *Play to Your Strengths: Managing Your Internal Labour Markets for Lasting Competitive Advantage*, New York: McGraw-Hill.

NCVO/VSNTO (2000) *Leading Managers: A Guide to Management Development in the Voluntary Sector*, London: NCVO/VSNTO.

Neathey, F. and Hurstfield, J. (1995) *Flexibility in Practice: Women's Employment and Pay in Retail and Finance*, EOC Research Discussion series, London: IRS.

Nelson, R.R. and Winter, S.G. (1982) *An Evolutionary Theory of Economic Change*, Cambridge: Belknap Press.

Newell, S., Robertson, M., Scarbrough, H. and Swan, J.A. (2002) *Managing Knowledge Work*, London: Palgrave.

Nonaka, I. (1994) 'A dynamic theory of organizational knowledge creation', *Organization Science*, 5 (1), pp. 14–37.

Nonaka, I. and Takeuchi, H. (1995) *The Knowledge-Creating Company*, Oxford: Oxford University Press USA.

Nonaka, I., Toyama, R. and Konno, N. (2002) 'SECI, Ba and leadership: a unified model of dynamic knowledge creation', in *Managing Knowledge: An Essential Reader*, Little, S., Quintas, P. and Ray, T. (eds), London: Sage, pp. 41–67.

O'Dwyer, M. and Ryan, E. (2002) 'Management development – a model for retail business', *Journal of European Industrial Training*, 26 (9), pp. 420–9.

OECD (Organisation for Economic Co-operation and Development) (1996) *The OECD Jobs Strategy*, Paris: OECD.

OECD (Organisation for Economic Co-operation and Development) (1998) 'The OECD Jobs Strategy: program report on implementation of country-specific recommendations', Economic Department Working Papers No. 196, Paris: OECD, available at http://www.oecd.org/dataoecd/49/29/20686301/HTM#1988 (accessed June 2003).

OECD (Organisation for Economic Co-operation and Development) (2001) 'Eurostat Labour Force Surveys 1999', *Labour Market Trends*, September 2001, p. 453.

OECD (Organisation for Economic Co-operation and Development) (2004) 'Employment Protection Regulation and Labour Market Performance', in *OECD Employment Outlook*, Paris: OECD.

OECD (Organisation for Economic Co-operation and Development) (2007) *Employment Outlook*, Paris: OECD.

Oeij, P.R.A. *et al.* (2002) De Toekomst van Flexibilisering van Arbeid en Arbeidsrelaties, TNO Hoofddorp.

Office for National Statistics (2008) 'Labour Disputes in 2007', *Economic and Labour Market Review*, 2 (6), pp. 18–29.

Office of Public Service Reform (2002) *Reforming our Public Services: Principles into Practice*, London: OPSR.

Olmsted, B. and Smith, S. (1989) *Creating a Flexible Workplace*, New York: Amacom.

Ones, D., Dilchert, S., Viswesvaran, S. and Judge, T. (2007) 'In support of personality assessment in organizational settings', *Personnel Psychology*, 60 (4), pp. 995–1028.

Ones, D. and Viswesvaran, C. (2001) 'Integrity test and other criterion-focused occupational personality scales (COPS) used in personnel selection', *International Journal of Selection and Assessment*, 9 (1–2), pp. 31–9.

O'Reilly, C.A., Chatman, J. and Caldwell, D. (1991) 'People and organisational culture: a profile comparison approach to assessing person–organisation fit', *Academy of Management Journal*, 34, pp. 487–516.

O'Reilly, J. (1992) 'Banking on flexibility: a comparison of the use of flexible employment strategies in the retail banking sector in Britain and France', *International Journal of Human Resource Management*, 3 (1), pp. 35–58.

O'Reilly, J. and Fagan, C. (1998) *Part-time Prospects*, London: Routledge.

O'Reilly, J., Cebrian, I. and Lallement, M. (2000) *Working Time Changes*, Cheltenham: Edward Elgar.

Orlikowski, W. (1996) 'Improvising organisational transformation over time: a situated change perspective', *Information Systems Research*, 7 (1), pp. 63–92.

Ostroff, C. and Rothausen, T.J. (1996) 'Selection and job matching', in *Handbook of Human Resources*, Lewin, D., Mitchell, D. and Zaidi, M. (eds), Greenwich, CT: JAI Press.

Overell, S. (1998a) 'All things not being equal', *People Management*, 4 (23), pp. 32–6.

Overell, S. (1998b) 'Missionary statements', *People Management*, 16 April, pp. 32–7.

Oxenbridge, S. and Brown, W. (2002) 'The two faces of partnership? An assessment of partnership and co-operative employer/trade union relationships', *Employee Relations*, 24 (3), pp. 262–76.

Oxenbridge, S. and Brown, W. (2005) 'Developing Partnership Relations', in *Partnership and Modernisation in Employment Relations*, Stuart, M. and Martinez Lucio, M. (eds), London: Routledge, pp. 83–100.

Oxford Polytechnic Educational Methods Unit. (n.d.) *Academic Staff Development and Appraisal*, Oxford: Oxford Polytechnic.

Ozley, L. and Armenakis, A. (2000) ' "Ethical consulting" does not have to be an oxymoron', *Organizational Dynamics*, 28 (4), pp. 38–51.

Palmer, D.K., Campion, M.A. and Green, P.C. (1999) 'Interviewing training: interviewer and interviewee perspectives', in *The Employment Interview: Theory, Research, and Practice*, 2nd edition, Eder, R.W. and Harris, M.M. (eds), Newbury Park, CA: Sage.

Parekh, B. (1998) 'Integrating minorities', in *Philosophy, Politics and Society*, 2nd series, Blackstone, T., Parekh, B. and Sanders, P. (eds), Oxford: Blackwell.

Parker, M. (1998a) 'Business ethics and social theory: postmodernising the ethical', *British Journal of Management*, 9, pp. 27–36.

Parker, M. (ed.) (1998b) *Ethics and Organizations*, London: Sage.

Parker, M. and Slaughter, J. (1988) *Choosing Sites: Union and the Team Concept*, Boston: South End Press.

Parry, E. (2008) *Managing an Ageing Workforce: The Role of Total Reward, Research Insight*, London: CIPD.

Pascale, R. (1991) *Managing on the Edge*, London: Penguin.

Patterson, M., West, M., Lawthom, R. and Nickell, S. (1997) *Impact of People Management Practices on Business Performance*, London: IPD.

Pedlar, M., Burgoyne, J. and Boydell, T. (1991) *The Learning Company: a Strategy for Sustainable Development*, Maidenhead: McGraw-Hill.

Pedlar, M., Burgoyne, J. and Boydell, T. (1994) *A Manager's Guide to Self-Development*, 3rd edition, London: McGraw-Hill.

Pegg, M. (1999) *The Art of Mentoring*, Gloucestershire: Management Books 2000.

Pendleton, A. (2001) *Employee Ownership, Participation and Governance: A Study of ESOPs in the UK*, London: Routledge.

Pendleton, A. (2005) 'Employee share ownership, employment relationships and corporate governance', in *Participation and Democracy at Work*, Harley, B., Hyman, J. and Thompson, P. (eds), Basingstoke: Palgrave Macmillan.

Peng, M.W. (2001) 'The resource based view and international business', *Journal of Management*, 27, pp. 803–29.

Penrose, E. (1959) *The Theory of the Growth of the Firm*, Oxford: Blackwell.

Peper, B., Doorne-Huiskes van, A. and Dulk den, L. (eds) (2005) *Flexible Working and Organisational Change*, Cheltenham: Edward Elgar.

Perkins, S.J. and White, G. (2008) *Employee Reward*, London: CIPD.

Perlow, L. (1998) 'Boundary control: the social ordering of work and family time in a hightech corporation', *Administrative Science Quarterly*, 43, pp. 328–57.

Perrow, C. (1986) *Complex Organisations*, London: Tavistock.

Pettigrew, A. and Whipp, R. (1991) *Managing Change for Competitive Success*, Oxford: Blackwell.

Petty, R. and Guthrie, J. (2000) 'Intellectual capital literature review', *Journal of Intellectual Capital*, 1 (2), pp. 155–76.

Pfeffer, J. (1981) *Power in Organisations*, Marshfield, MA: Financial Times/Pitman.

Pfeffer, J. (1994) *Competitive Advantage through People*, Boston: Harvard Business School Press.

Pfeffer, J. (1998) 'Six dangerous myths about pay', *Harvard Business Review*, May and June, pp. 109–19.

Philpott, J. (2008) 'A barometer of HR trends and prospects 2008', London: CIPD.

Pickard, J. (1995) 'Prepare to make a moral judgement', *People Management*, 1 (10), pp. 22–5.

Pillinger, J. (2006) *Challenging Times: Innovative Ways of Organising Working Time: The Role of Trade Unions*, Brussels: ETUC Publications.

Piore, M. and Sabel, C. (1984) *The Second Industrial Divide*, New York: Basic Books.

Poell, R.F., Pluijmen, R. and Van der Krogt, F. (2003) 'Strategies of HRD professionals in organising learning programmes: a qualitative study among 20 Dutch HRD professionals', *Journal of Industrial Training*, 27 (2/3/4), pp. 125–36.

Polanyi, M. (1966) *Personal Knowledge: towards a post-critical philosophy*, New York: Harper Torchbooks.

Polanyi, M. (1975) 'Personal knowledge', in *Meaning*, Polanyi, M. and Prosch, H., Chicago, IL: University of Chicago Press, pp. 22–45.

Pollert, A. (1991) *Farewell to Flexibility*, Oxford: Blackwell.

Pollitt, C. (1985) 'Measuring performance: a new system for the NHS', *Policy and Politics*, 13, pp. 1–15.

Poole, M. and Jenkins, G. (1990) *The Impact of Economic Democracy: Profit Sharing and Employee Shareholding Schemes*, London: Routledge.

Porter, M. (1980) *Competitive Strategies: Technologies for Analyzing Industries and Firms*, New York: Free Press.

Porter, M. (1985) *Competitive Advantage: Creating and Sustaining Superior Performance*, New York: Free Press.

Posthuma, R., Morgeson, F. and Campion, M. (2002) 'Beyond employment interview validity: a comprehensive narrative review of recent research and trends over time', *Personnel Psychology*, 55 (1), pp. 1–81.

Poutsma, E., de Nijs, W. and Doorewaard, H. (1999) 'Promotion of employee ownership and profit sharing in Europe', *Economic and Industrial Democracy*, 20, pp. 171–96.

Presser, H.B. (2003) *Working in a 24/7 Economy: Challenges for American Families*, New York: Russell Sage Foundation.

Presser, H.B., Gornick, J.C. and Parashar, S. (2008) 'Gender and nonstandard work hours in 12 European countries', *Monthly Labour Review*, February, pp. 83–103.

Pritchard, C., Hull, R., Chumer, M. and Willmott, H. (2000) *Managing Knowledge*, Basingstoke: Macmillan.

Probst, G., Buchel, B. and Raub, S. (1998) 'Knowledge as a strategic resource', in *Knowing in Firms: Understanding, Managing and Measuring Knowledge*, Von Krogh, G., Roos, J. and Kleine, D. (eds), London: Sage.

Proctor, S. (2003) *Managing Flexibility*, Andover: Routledge.

Proctor, S., Rowlinson, M., McCardle, L., Hassard, J. and Forrester, P. (1994) 'Flexibility, politics and strategy: in defence of the model of the flexible firm', *Work, Employment and Society*, 8 (2), pp. 221–42.

Prowse (1990) 'Assessing the flexible firm', *Personnel Review*, 19 (3), pp. 13–17.

Pucik V. (1998) 'Creating leaders that are world-class', in *Mastering Global Business*, The Financial Times, part 5 of 10.

Pugh, D.S. and Hickson, C.D. (1976) *Organisation Structure: Extensions and Replications*, Farnborough: Saxon House.

Pukas, A. (2008) 'Storm in a coffee cup', *The Express*, 02 August, p. 44.

Punnett, B.J. (1998) 'Culture, cross-national', *The IEBM Handbook of Human Resource Management*, Poole, M. and Warner, M. (eds), London: International Thompson Business Press, pp. 9–26.

Purcell, J. (1995) 'Corporate strategy and its link with human resource strategy', in *Human Resource Management: A Critical Text*, Storey, J. (ed.), London: Routledge, pp. 63–86.

Purcell, J. and Hutchinson, S. (2007) 'Front-line managers as agents in the HRM performance causal chain: theory, analysis and evidence', *Human Resource Management Journal*, 17 (1), pp. 3–20.

Purcell, J. and Kinnie, N. (2007) 'HRM and Business Performance', in *The Oxford Handbook of Human Resource Management*, Boxall, P., Purcell, J. and Wright, P. (eds), Oxford: Oxford University Press.

Purcell, J., Kinnie, N., Hutchinson, S., Rayton, B. and Swart, J. (2003) *Understanding the People and Performance Link: Unblocking the Black Box*, London, CIPD.

Purcell, K. (2000) 'Gendered employment insecurity?', in *The Insecure Workforce*, Heery, E. and Salmon, J. (eds), Andover: Routledge, pp. 112–39.

Purcell, K. and Purcell, J. (1999) 'Insourcing, outsourcing and the growth of contingent labour as evidence of flexible employment strategies', in *Non-standard Work and Industrial Relations*, Blanpain, R. (ed.), The Hague: Kluwer Law International.

Purcell, K., Hogarth, T. and Simm, C. (1999) *The Costs and Benefits of Non-standard Working Arrangements and Contracted Relations*, York: Joseph Rowntree Foundation.

Quinn, J. (2008) 'Never mind the sex . . . stick to merit', *Personnel Today*, 8 July, p. 9, www.personncltoday.com.

Quinn, J.B. (1980) *Strategies for Change: Logical Incrementalism*, Homewood, IL: Irwin.

Quinn, J.B. (1992) *Intelligent Enterprise: a Knowledge and Service Based Paradigm for Industry*, New York: Free Press.

Quintas, P. (2002) 'Managing knowledge in a new century', in *Managing Knowledge: an Essential Reader*, Little, S., Quintas, P. and Ray, T., London, Sage: 1–14.

Race for Opportunity (2002) available from http://www.raceforopportunity.org.uk (accessed 10 June 2002).

Rajan, A. and Harris, S. (2003) 'The business impact of diversity', *Personnel Today*, 2 September, pp. 18–21.

Ramsey, H. (1977) 'Cycles of control: worker participation in sociological and historical perspectives', *Sociology*, 11 (3), September, pp. 481–506.

Ramsey, H. (1983) 'Evolution or cycle? Worker participation in the 1970s and 1980s', in *Organisational Democracy and Political Processes*, Crouch, C. and Heller, F. (eds), International Yearbook of Industrial Democracy, London: Wiley.

Ramsey, H. (1990) *The Joint Consultation Debate: Soft Soap and Hard Cases*, discussion paper no. 17: Glasgow: Centre for Research in Industrial Democracy and Participation.

Rawls, J. (1971) *A Theory of Justice*, Cambridge, MA: Harvard University Press.

Reber A.S. (1985) *Dictionary of Psychology*, Harmondsworth: Penguin.

Redman, T. and Snape, E. (1992) 'Upward and onward: can staff appraise their managers?', *Personnel Review*, 27 (7), pp. 32–46.

Redman, T. and Wilkinson, A. (2001) *Contemporary Human Resource Management*, Harlow: Financial Times/Prentice Hall.

Redman, T. and Wilkinson, A. (eds) (2006) *Contemporary Human Resource Management: Text and Cases*, Harlow: Financial Times/Prentice Hall, Chapter 14, 'Downsizing': pp. 356–81.

Reed, M. (1996) 'Expert power and control in late modernity: an empirical review and theoretical synthesis', *Organisation Studies*, 17 (4), pp. 573–97.

Rees, C. (1999) 'Teamworking and service quality: the limits of employee involvement', *Personnel Review*, 28 (5/6), pp. 455–73.

Reid, M. and Barrington, H. (1994) *Training Interventions*, 4th edition, London: IPD.

Reid, M.A. and Barrington, H. (1999), *Training Interventions*, 6th edition, London: CIPD.

Reid, M.A., Barrington, H. and Brown, M. (2004) *Human Resource Development: Beyond Training Interventions*, 7th edition, London: CIPD.

Reilly, P. (2001) *Flexibility at Work*, Burlington: Gower.

Reilly, P. (2003) 'New approaches in reward: their relevance to the public sector', *Public Money and Management*, October, pp. 245–52.

Reilly, P. and Tamkin, P. (2007) *The Changing HR Function: Transforming HR?* CIPD Research Report, London: CIPD.

Renton, D. (2008) 'Deliver us from employment tribunal hell?' Employment law, industrial relations and the Employment Bill, Working Paper Series Ref UHBS2008:3, University of Hertfordshire: Centre for Research in Employment Studies.

Renwick, D. (2003) 'HR Managers – Guardians of employee well being?', *Personnel Review*, 32 (3), pp. 341–59.

Rest, J. (1986) *Moral Development: Advances in Research and Theory*, New York: Praeger.

Rest, J., Narvaez, D., Thoma, S. and Bebeau, M. (2000) 'A neo-Kohlbergian approach to morality research', *Journal of Moral Education*, 29 (4), pp. 381–95.

Richards-Carpenter, C. (1991) 'Celebration of an era', *Personnel Management*, February, p. 24.

Richardson, R. (1999) *Performance-related Pay in Schools: An Assessment of the Green Papers*, London: National Union of Teachers.

Rifkin, J. (1995) *The End of Work*, New York: Putnam.

Robertson, I.T., Illes, P., Gratton, L. and Sharpley, D.S. (1991) 'The impact of personnel selection and assessment methods on candidates', *Human Relations*, 44, pp. 963–82.

Robertson, M. and O'Malley-Hamersley, J. (2000) 'Knowledge management practices within a knowledge-intensive firm: the significance of the people management dimension', *Journal of European Industrial Training*, 24 (2), pp. 241–52.

Robertson, M., Swan, J. and Sorensen, C. (2000) 'Facilitating knowledge creation within GroupWare: A case study of a knowledge intensive firm', *Proceedings of the 33rd Hawaiian International Conference on System Sciences*.

Robinson, G. and Dechant, K. (1997) 'Building a business case for diversity', *Academy of Management Executive*, 11 (3), pp. 21–31.

Robinson, P. (2000) 'Insecurity and the flexible workforce: measuring the ill-defined', in *The Insecure Workforce*, Heery, E. and Salmon, J. (eds), London: Routledge, pp. 25–38.

Rodger, A. (1970) *The Seven-Point Plan*, London: National Foundation for Educational Research.

Rogers, C.R. (1970) *On Becoming a Person*, Boston, MA: Houghton Mifflin.

Rollinson, D. and Dundon, T. (2007) *Understanding Employment Relations*, London: McGraw-Hill Education.

Rosenfeld, P. (1997) *Impression Management in Organizations*, London: Routledge.

Rothwell, S. (1986) 'Comparative labour costs: getting the right mix', *Manpower Policy and Practice*, 1 (3), pp. 217–35.

Rousseau, D. (2004) 'Psychological contracts in the workplace: understanding the ties that motivate', *The Academy of Management Executive*, 18 (1), pp. 120–35.

Rousseau, D.M. (1995) *Psychological Contracts in Organizations: Understanding Written and Unwritten Agreements*, Thousand Oaks, CA: Sage Publications.

Rousseau, D.M. (1996) *Psychological Contracts in Organisations: Understanding Written and Unwritten Agreements*, Thousand Oaks, CA: Sage.

Rubery, J. (1995) 'Performance-related pay and the prospects for gender-related equity', *Journal of Management Studies*, 32 (5), pp. 637–55.

Rubery, J. and Wilkinson, F. (1994) *Labour Markets and Flexibility*, Oxford: Oxford University Press.

Sabel, C.F. and Zeitlin, J. (eds) (1997) *Worlds of Possibilities: Flexibility and Mass Production in Western Industrialization*, Cambridge: Cambridge University Press.

Sadler, P. (ed.) (1998) *Management Consultancy*, London: Kogan Page.

Salaman, G. (2002) 'Understanding advice: towards a sociology of management consultancy', in *Critical Consulting*, Clark, T. and Fincham, R. (eds), Oxford: Blackwell.

Sargeant, M. (2001) 'Employee consultation', *Employee Relations*, 23 (5), pp. 483–97.

Saville and Holdsworth Ltd (1995) *Work Profiling System* (WPS, updated version), London: Saville and Holdsworth.

Saville and Holdsworth Ltd (1997) *UK Survey of Views of Performance Appraisal*, Thames Ditton: Saville and Holdsworth.

Sayer, A. (2007a) 'Understanding why anything matters: needy beings, flourishing, and suffering', in *Critical Realism and the Social Sciences: Heterodox Elaborations*, Frauley, J. and Pearce, F. (eds), Toronto: University of Toronto Press.

Sayer, A. (2007b) 'Moral economy and employment', in *Searching for the Human in Human Resource Management: Theory, Practice and Workplace Contexts*, Bolton, S. and Houlihan, M. (eds), Basingstoke: Palgrave Macmillan.

Scarbrough, H. and Carter, C. (2000) *Investigating Knowledge Management*, London: CIPD.

Scarbrough, H., Swan, J.A. and Preston, J. (1998) *Knowledge Management and the Learning Organisation*, London: Institute of Personnel and Development.

Schein, E. (1969) *Process Consultation: Its Role in Organizational Development*, Reading, MA: Addison-Wesley.

Schein, E. (2002) 'Consulting: what should it mean?', in *Critical Consulting*, Clark, T. and Fincham, R. (eds), Oxford: Blackwell.

Schein, E.H. (1997) 'The concept of "client" from a process consultation perspective: a guide for change agents', *Journal of Organisational Change Management*, 10 (3), pp. 202–16.

Schneider, B. (1987) 'The people make the difference', *Personnel Psychology*, 40 (3), pp. 437–54.

Schneider, S.C. and Barsoux, J.L. (1997) *Managing Across Cultures*, Hemel Hempstead: Prentice Hall.

Schön, D.A. (1983) *The Reflective Practitioner: How Professionals Think in Action*, New York: Basic Books.

Schuler, R. (1998) 'Human resource management', in *The IEBM Handbook of Human Resource Management*, Poole, M. and Warner, M. (eds), London: International Thomson Business Press.

Schuler, R.S. and Jackson, S.E. (1987) 'Linking competitive strategies with human resource management practices', *Academy of Management Executive*, 1 (3), pp. 209–13.

Schuler, R., Dowling, P. and De Cieri, H. (1993) 'An integrative framework of strategic international human resource management', *Journal of Management*, 19 (2), pp. 419–59.

Schuler, R.S., Jackson, S.E. and Storey, J. (2001) 'HRM and its link with strategic management', in *Human Resource Management: A Critical Text*, 2nd edition, Storey, J. (ed.), London: Thomson Learning.

Schutz, A. (1967) *The Phenomenology of the Social World*, Evanston, IL: Northwestern University Press.

SCP/CBS (Sociaal cultureel Planbureau/Centraal Bureau voor de Statistiek) (2006) *Emancipation Monitor*, The Hague.

Searle, R. (2004) *Selection and Recruitment: A Critical Text*, Basingstoke: Palgrave Macmillan.

Sector Skills for Health (2006) *Delivering a Flexible Workforce to Support Better Health and Health Services – The Case for Change*, Sector Skills for Health, Stage 3, Bristol: Skills for Health, available from www.skillsforhealth.org.uk/js/uploaded/Sector%20Skills%20Agreement/Research%20and%20publications%20/Caseforchange-Final.pdf

Seibert, K., Hall, D. and Kram, K. (1995) 'Strengthening the weak link in strategic executive development: integrating individual development and global business strategy', *Human Resource Management*, 34 (4), pp. 549–67.

Sels, L. and van Hootegem, G. (2001) *Measuring the Degree of Organisational Transformation: A Methodological Benchmark of Organisation Surveys*, Leuven: Katholieke Universiteit Leven.

Senge, P. (1992) *The Fifth Discipline*, London: Century.

Sennet, R. (2000) 'Street and office: two sources of identity', in *On the Edge*, Hutton, W. and Giddens, A. (eds), London: Jonathan Cape.

Shackleton, V. and Newell, S. (1994) 'European management selection methods: a comparison of five countries', *International Journal of Selection and Assessment*, 2 (2), pp. 91–102.

Shackleton, V. and Newell, S. (1997) 'International selection and assessment', in *International Handbook of Selection and Assessment*, Anderson, N. and Herriot, P. (eds), Chichester: John Wiley and Sons, pp. 81–96.

Sheppard, B., Lewiicki, R. and Minton, J. (1992) *Organisational Justice*, New York: Lexington.

Sheppard, B.H., Blumenfield-Jones, K., Minton, W.J. and Hyder, E. (1994) 'Informal conflict intervention: advice and dissent', *Employee Responsibilities and Rights Journal*, 7, pp. 53–72.

Shorthose, J. (2004) 'Like summer and good sex? The limitation of the work-life balance campaign', *Capital & Class*, 82 (1), pp. 1–9.

Siler, C. (1996) 'Embarrassed Ford acts to assuage minorities', *Advertising Age*, 67 (9), p. 42.

Silverman, D. (1970) *The Theory of Organisations*, London: Heinemann.

Silverman, M., Kerrin, M. and Carter, A. (2005) *360 Degree Feedback: Beyond the Spin*, Institute for Employment Studies (IES) Report No. 418, IES: London.

Silvester, J., Anderson-Gough, F., Anderson, N. and Mohamed, A. (2002) 'Locus of control, attributions and impression management in the selection interview', *Journal of Occupational and Organizational Psychology*, 75 (1), pp. 59–77.

Simmonds, D. and Pedersen, C. (2006) 'HRD: the shapes and things to come', *Journal of Workplace Learning*, 18 (2), pp. 122–35.

Simon, H.A. (1977) *The New Science of Management Decision*, Hemel Hempstead: Prentice Hall.

Simpson, R. (2000) 'Presenteeism and the impact of long hours on managers', in *Ethical Issues in Contemporary Human Resource Management*, Winstanley, D. and Woodall, J. (eds), London: Macmillan.

Singer, M. and Singer, A. (1991) 'Justice in preferential hiring', *Journal of Business Ethics*, 10 (10), pp. 797–803.

Sisson, K. (1993) 'In search of HRM', *British Journal of Industrial Relations*, 31 (2), pp. 201–10.

Sisson, K. (1999) 'The new European social model: the end of the search for an orthodoxy or another false dawn?', *Employee Relations*, 21 (5), pp. 445–62.

Sisson, K. and Marginson, P. (2003) 'Management: systems, structure and strategy', in *Industrial Relations*, Edwards, P. (ed.), Oxford: Blackwell, pp. 157–88.

Skills for Health (2006) *Delivering a Flexible Workforce to Support Better Health and Health Services – the Case for Change (Sector Skills Agreement Stage 3)*. Bristol: Skills for Health available at http://www.skillsforhealth.org.uk/js/uploaded/Sector%20Skills%20Agreement/Research%20and%20publication%20/Caseforchange-Final.pdf

Skyrme, D.J. and Amdon, D.M. (1998) 'New measures of success', *The Journal of Business Strategy*, 19 (1), pp. 20–24.

Sly, F. and Stillwell, D. (1997) 'Temporary workers in Great Britain', *Labour Market Trends*, September: 347–54.

Smith, A. (1776) *An Inquiry into the Nature and Causes of the Wealth of Nations*, 6th edition, London: Methuen, 1950.

Smith, G. and Cantley, C. (1985) *Evaluating Health Care: A Study in Organisational Evaluation*, Milton Keynes: Open University Press.

Smith, I. (1983) *The Management of Remuneration – Paying for Effectiveness*, London: IPD and Gower.

Smith, I. (1993) 'Reward management: a retrospective assessment', *Employee Relations*, 15 (3), pp. 45–59.

Smith, M. (1994) 'A theory of the validity of predictors in selection', *Journal of Occupational and Organisational Psychology*, 67, pp. 13–31.

Smith, P. (1995) 'Performance indicators and outcome in the public sector', *Public Money and Management*, Oct–Dec.

Smith, P. and Morton, G. (1993) 'Union exclusion and the decollectivisation of industrial relations in contemporary Britain', *British Journal of Industrial Relations*, 31 (2), pp. 97–114.

Smith, M., Masi, A., Berg, A. and Smucker, J. (1995) 'External flexibility in Sweden and Canada: a three industry comparison', *Work, Employment and Society*, 9 (4), pp. 689–718.

Snyder, M. (1974) 'Self-monitoring of expressive behaviour', *Journal of Personality and Social Psychology*, 30, pp. 526–37.

Sparrow, P. (1998) 'New organisational forms, processes, jobs and psychological contracts: resolving the HRM issues', in *Human Resource Management – The New Agenda*, Sparrow, P. and Marchington, M. (eds), London: Financial Times/Pitman.

Sparrow, P. (2000) 'International reward management', in *Reward Management – a Critical Text*, White, G. and Druker, J. (eds), Routledge Studies in Employment Relations, London: Routledge, pp. 196–214.

Sparrow, P. and Marchington, M. (1997) *Human Resource Management – The New Agenda*, London: Financial Times/Pitman.

Spender, J.C. (1992) *Knowledge Management: Putting your Technology Strategy on Track*, New York: Institute of Industrial Engineers.

Spidla, V. (2007) Green Paper: 'Modernising labour law to meet the challenges of the 21st Century', Brussels: Commission of the European Communities http://ec.europa.eu/employment_social/labour_law/docs/2006/green_paper_en.pdf (Accessed 28 August 2008).

Stark, A. (1994) 'What's the matter with business ethics?', *Harvard Business Review*, May–June, pp. 38–48.

Statistics Canada. (2006) *The Canadian Labour Market at a Glance*. Catalogue no. 71–222–XWE, Ottawa: Statistics Canada.

Steel, R. (2002) 'Turnover theory at the empirical interface: problems of fit and function', *Academy of Management Review*, 27 (3).

Stewart, J. (1996) *Managing Change Through Training And Development*, 2nd edition, London: Kogan Page.

Stewart, J. (1998) 'Intervention and assessment: the ethics of HRD', *Human Resource Development International*, 1 (1), pp. 9–12.

Stewart, J. (1999) *Employee Development Practice*, London: Financial Times/Pitman Publishing.

Stewart, J. (2007) 'The ethics of HRD', *Critical Human Resource Development*, in Rigg, C., Stewart, J. and Trehan, K. (eds), Harlow: Financial Times/Prentice Hall.

Stewart, J. and Hill, R. (2007) 'Researching and practicing management development', in *Management Development: Perspectives from Research and Practice*, Hill, R. and Stewart, J. (eds), London: Routledge.

Stewart, J. and Knowles, V. (2000) 'Graduate recruitment and selection practices in small businesses', *Career Development International*, 5 (1), pp. 21–38.

Stewart, J., Manhire, E. and Hall, R. (1999) 'Employee training and development', in *Strategic Human Resourcing: Principles, Perspectives and Practices*, Leopold, J., Harris, L., and Watson, T. (eds), London: Financial Times/Pitman, pp. 217–38.

Stewart, J. and McGoldrick, J. (eds) (1996) *Human Resource Development: Perspectives, Strategies and Practice*, London: Pitman.

Stewart, J. and Sambrook, S. (1995) 'The role of functional analysis in NVQs: a critical appraisal', in Bates, I. (ed.), 'Special Issue On Competence and the NVQ Framework', *British Journal of Education and Work*, 8 (2), pp. 93–106.

Stewart, J. and Tansley, C. (2002) *Training in the Knowledge Based Economy*, London: CIPD.

Stewart, T. (1997) *Intellectual Capital: The New Wealth of Organisations*, London: Nicholas Brearley.

Stiglitz, J.E. (2003) *The Roaring Nineties: A New History of the World's Most Prosperous Decade*. New York: W.W. Norton.

Stiles, P. (1999) 'Performance management in fast-changing environments', in *Strategic Human Management*, Gratton, L., Hope-Hailey, V., Stiles, P. and Truss, C. (eds), Oxford: Oxford University Press, pp. 59–78.

Stiles, P., Gratton, L., Truss, C., Hope-Hailey, V. and McGovern, P. (1997) 'Performance management and the psychological contract', *Human Resource Management Journal*, 7 (1), pp. 57–66.

Stokes, G.S., Hogan, J.B. and Snell, A.F. (1993) 'Comparability of incumbent and applicant samples for the development of biodata keys: the influence of social desirability', *Personnel Psychology*, 46, pp. 739–62.

Stopford, J., Markides, C., Roberts, A. and Vagneur, K. (1994) *Building Global Excellence*, monograph, The BOC Group.

Storey, J. (1992) *Developments in the Management of Human Resources*, Oxford: Blackwell Publishers Ltd.

Storey, J. (1994) 'Human resource management in the public sector', in *Human Resource Strategies*, Storey, J. (ed.), London: Sage, pp. 47–58.

Storey, J. (2007) *Human Resource Management – A Critical Text*, 3rd edition. London: Thomson.

Storey, J., Edwards, P. and Sisson, K. (1997) *Managers in the Making*: Careers, Development and Control in Corporate Britain and Japan, London: Sage.

Storey, J., Quintas, P., Taylor, P. and Fowle, W. (2002) 'Flexible employment contracts and their implications for product and process innovation', *International Journal of Human Resource Management*, 13, pp. 1–18.

Strebler, M. (2004) *Tackling poor performance*, Institute for Employment Studies (IES) Report No. 406, IES: London.

Strebler, M. and Bevan, S. (2001) *Performance Review: Balancing Objectives and Content*, Report 370, Institute of Employment Studies, Brighton.

Strebler, M., Robinson, D. and Bevan, S. (2001) *Performance Review: Balancing Objectives and Content*, Report No. 370, Institute for Employment Studies, Brighton.

Streeck, W. (1988) comment on Ronald Dore, 'Rigidities in the labour market', *Government and Opposition*, 23 (4), pp. 413–23.

Stuart, M. and Martinez Lucio, M. (eds) (2005) *Partnership and Modernisation in Employment Relations*, London: Routledge, pp. 23–45.

Stubbs, D. and Stubbs, C. (2008) *The EU Lifelong Learning Programme: A Handbook for Trade Unions* (V.2 ed.), Brussels: The European Trade Union Institute for Research, Education and Health & Safety.

Sturdy, A., Clark, T., Fincham, R. and Handley, K. (2009) *Management Consultancy: Boundaries and Knowledge in Action*, Oxford: Oxford University Press.

Sturgeon, T.J. (2002) 'Modular production networks. A new American model of industrial organization', *Industrial and Corporate Change*, 11, pp. 451–96.

Suff, P. (2001) 'The new reward agenda', *IRS Management Review 22*, London: Industrial Relations Series.

Supiot, A. (1999) *Audela de l'emploi: Transformations du travail et devenir du droit du travail en Europe*, Paris: Flammarion.

Supiot, A. (2001) Beyond Employment: Changes in Work and the Future of Labour Law in Europe, Oxford: Oxford University Press.

Susskind, R. (2003) 'In the modern world, should the judges themselves be judged?', *The Times*, 22 July, features: Law, 6.

Taguchi, S. (2002) *Hiring the Best and the Brightest*, New York: Amacom.

Tailby, S. and Winchester, D. (2005) 'Management and Trade Unions: Partnership at Work', in *Managing Human Resources: Personnel in Transition*, 4th edition, S. Bach (ed.), Blackwell: Oxford, pp. 424–51.

Tailby, S., Richardson, M., Stewart, P., Danford, A. and Upchurch, M. (2004) 'Partnership at work and worker participation: An NHS case study', *Industrial Relations Journal*, 35 (5), pp. 403–18.

Tam, M. (1997) *Part-time Employment: A Bridge or a Trap?* Aldershot: Avebury.

Tam, Y.M., Korczynski, M. and Frenkel, S.J. (2002) 'Organisational and occupational commitment: knowledge workers in large corporations', *Journal of Management Studies*, 39 (6), pp. 775–801.

Tansley, C., Harris, L., Stewart, J. and Turner, P. (2006) *Talent Management: Understanding the Change Dimension*, London: CIPD.

Tansley, C., Newell, S. and Williams, H. (2001) 'Effecting HRM transformation through the implementation of an information system – an e-greenfield site?', *Personnel Review* (special greenfield sites issue), 30 (3), pp. 351–70.

Tansley, C., Turner, P.A., Foster, C., Harris, L.M., Stewart, J., Sempik, A. and Williams, H. (2007) *Talent: Strategy, Management, Measurement*, London: CIPD.

Taylor, F.W. (1911, 1998) *The Principles of Scientific Management*, Atlanta: Engineering and Management Press.

Taylor, R. (2002) *Diversity in Britain's Labour Market*, Economic and Social Research Council.

Taylor, S. (2000) 'Debates in reward management', in *Strategic Reward Systems*, Thorpe, R. and Homan, G. (eds), Harlow: Financial Times/Prentice Hall.

Taylor, S. (2002) *The Employee Retention Handbook*, London: CIPD.

Taylor, S. and Emir, A. (2006) *Employment Law-An Introduction*, Oxford: Oxford University Press.

Teece, D.J. and Pisano, G. (1994) 'The dynamic capabilities of firms: an introduction', *Industrial and Corporate Change*, 3 (3), pp. 537–56.

Teece, D.J., Pisano, G. and Shuen, A. (1997) 'Dynamic capabilities and strategic management', *Strategic Management Journal*, 18 (7), pp. 509–33.

Temporary Agency Work: National Reports: The Netherlands (2002) European Foundation for the Improvement of Living and Working Conditions.

Terry, M. (1999) 'Systems of collective employee representation in non-union firms in the UK', *Industrial Relations Journal*, 30 (1), pp. 16–30.

Terry, M. and Smith, J. (2003) 'Evaluation of the Partnership at Work Fund', *Employment Relations Research Series No. 17*. DTI.

Thibaut, J. and Walker, L. (1975) *Procedural Justice: A Psychological Analysis*, Hillsdale: Erlbaum.

Thomas, A.B. (2003) *Controversies in Management: Issues, Debates, Answers*, 2nd edition, London: Routledge.

Thomas, D. and Ely, R. (1996) 'Making differences matter: a new paradigm for managing diversity', *Harvard Business Review*, 74 (5), pp. 79–90.

Thomas, K. (1973) *Religion and the Decline of Magic: Studies in Popular Beliefs in the Sixteenth and Seventeenth Centuries*, Harmondsworth: Penguin Books.

Thomas, R. (1991) *Beyond Race and Gender*, New York: Amacom.

Thompson, M. (2002) 'Salary progression schemes', in *Reward Management – a Critical Text*, Routledge Studies in Employment Relations, White, G. and Druker, J. (eds), London: Routledge, pp. 126–51.

Thompson, P. (2002) *Total Reward*, Executive Briefing, London: CIPD.

Thompson, P. and Milsome, S. (2001) *Reward Determination in the UK*, London: CIPD.

Thomson, A. *et al.* (2001) *Changing Patterns of Management Development*, Oxford: Blackwell Business.

Thorpe, R. and Homan, G. (2000) *Strategic Reward Systems*, Harlow: Financial Times/ Prentice Hall.

Tietze, S. and Musson, G. (2005) 'Recasting the homework relationship: A case of mutual adjustment?', Organization Studies, 26 (9), pp. 1331–52.

Tietze, S., Musson, G. and Scurry, T. (2006) 'Improving services. Balancing lives? A multiple stakeholder perspective on the work-life balance discourse', in *Work-Life Integration. International Perspectives on the Balancing of Multiple Roles*, Blyton, P. (ed.), London: Palgrave, pp. 180–95.

Toffler, A. (1980) *The Third Wave*, New York: William Morrow.

Torrington, D. (1989) 'Human resource management and the personnel function', in *Human Resource Management: A Critical Text*, Storey, J. (ed.), London: Routledge, pp. 87–109.

Torrington, D. (1994) *International Human Resource Management: Think Globally, Act Locally*, Hemel Hempstead: Prentice Hall International.

Torrington, D. and Hall, L. (1987) *Personnel Management – a new approach*, Hemel Hempstead: Prentice Hall.

Torrington, D. and Hall, L. (1998) *Human Resource Management*, London: Prentice Hall Europe.

Townley, B. (1991) 'The politics of appraisal: lessons of the introduction of appraisal in UK universities', *Human Resource Management Journal*, 1 (2), pp. 27–42.

Townley, B. (1993) 'Foucault, power/knowledge and its relevance for human resource management', *Academy of Management Review*, 18 (3), pp. 518–45.

Townley, B. (1994a) *Reframing Human Resource Management*, London: Sage.

Townley, B. (1994b) 'Communicating with employees', in *Personnel Management*, Sisson, K. (ed.), Oxford: Blackwell.

Trehan, K. and Shelton, R. (2007) 'Leadership development: a critical examination', in *Management Development: Perspectives from Research and Practice*, Hill, R. and Stewart, J. (eds), London: Routledge.

Trevino, L. (1992) 'Moral reasoning and business ethics: implications for future research, education, and management', *Journal of Business Ethics*, 11 (5, 6), pp. 445–59.

Trevino, L. and Nelson, K. (1999) *Managing Business Ethics: Straight Talk about How to Do It Right*, 2nd edition, New York: John Wiley.

Trewhitt, L. (2000) 'Employee buyouts and employee involvement: a case study investigation of employee attitudes', *Industrial Relations Journal*, 31 (5), pp. 437–53.

Trompenaars, F. (1994) *Riding the Waves of Culture: Understanding Diversity in Global Business*, London: Harper Collins.

Tsoukas, H. and Vladimirou, E. (2001) 'What is organizational knowledge?', *Journal of Management Studies*, 38 (7).

TSSA (Transport Salaried Staffs' Association) (2007) *Network Rail Management Grades 2007 Pay Award*, TSSA.

Tsutsui, W.M. (1998) *Manufacturing Ideology: Scientific Management in Twentieth-Century Japan*, Princeton: Princeton University Press.

TUC (Trades Union Congress) (2001a) 'Focus on union recognition', *TUConline*, www.tuc.org.uk.

TUC (Trades Union Congress) (2001b) *Partners for Progress: Winning at Work*, London: TUC. Partnership Institute.

Tuckman, A. (1994) 'The yellow brick road: total quality management and the restructuring of organisational culture', *Organisation Studies*, 15 (5), pp. 727–51.

Tuckman, A. (1995) 'Ideology, quality and TQM', in *Making Quality Critical: Studies in Organisational Change*, Wilkinson, A. and Willmott, H. (eds), London: Routledge.

Tung, R.L. (1998) 'Human resource management, international', in *The IEBM Handbook of Human Resource Management*, Poole, M. and Warner, M. (eds), London: International Thomson Business Press.

Turnbull, P. and Sapsford, D. (1992) 'A sea of discontent: the tides of organized and "unorganized" conflict on the docks', *Sociology*, 26 (2), pp. 291–309.

Turnbull, P. and Wass, V. (1997) 'Job insecurity and labour market lemons: the (mis)management of redundancy in steel-making, coal mining and port transport', *Journal of Management Studies*, 34 (1), pp. 27–52.

Turnbull, P. and Weston, S. (1993) 'Co-operation or control? Capital restructuring and labour relations on the docks', *British Journal of Industrial Relations*, 31 (1), pp. 115–34.

Tyson, S. (1997) *The Practice of Human Resource Strategy*, London: Pitman.

Tyson, S. and York, A. (2003) *Essentials of HRM*, London: Butterworth-Heinemann.

UKCC (United Kingdom Central Council for Nursing, Midwives and Health Visitors) (1996) 'PREP: you and your guide to profiling', *Register*, No. 17, Summer.

Ulrich, D. (1997) *Human Resource Champions: The Next Agenda for Adding Value and Delivering Results*, Boston: Harvard Business School.

UNDP (United Nations Development Programme) (2001) *Human Development Report, 2000*, Oxford: Oxford University Press.

Upchurch, M., Danfold, A., Stewart, P., Tailby, S. and Richardson, M. (2003) 'Partnership at work, the third way, and democracy', paper presented to the *Policy and Politics Conference*, July, Bristol.

Upchurch, M., Richardson, M., Tailby, S., Danford, A. and Stewart, P. (2006) 'Employee representation and partnership in the non-union sector: a paradox of intention?', *Human Resource Management Journal*, 16 (4), pp. 393–410.

Valdiserri, T. (2002) '"Pink" market needs respect', *Precision Marketing*, 14 (23), p. 9.

Van Woerkom, M. and Poell, R. (eds) (2009) *Workplace Learning: Concepts, Measurement and Application*, Oxford: Routledge.

Vance, C.M., McClaine, S.R., Boje, D.M. and Stage, H.D. (1992) 'An examination of transferability of traditional performance appraisal principles across cultural boundaries', *Management International Review*, 32 (4), pp. 313–26.

Varma, A., Soo Min Toh, S-M. and Pichler, S. (2006) 'Ingratiation in job applications: impact on selection decisions', *Journal of Managerial Psychology*, 21 (3), pp. 200–12.

Vass, P. (1996) 'Regulated industries', in *Public Services Yearbook 1996–7*, Jackson, P. and Lavender, M. (eds), London: Pitman Publishing.

Visser J. (2000) *The First Part-time Economy in the World. Does it work?* http://www.uva-aias.net/files/working_papers/WP1.pdf (accessed 4 September 2008).

Visser, J. and Hemerijck, A. (1997) *A Dutch Miracle*, Amsterdam: University Press.

Volberda, H.W. (1998) *Building the Flexible Firm*, Oxford: Oxford University Press.

Vorster, G. (2008) 'Age discrimination set to become most common form of discrimination', *Personnel Today*, 7th January.

Vroom, V. (1964) *Work and Motivation*, New York: John Wiley and Sons.

Waddington, J. (2003) 'Trade union organisation', *Industrial Relations Theory and Practice*, 2nd edition, Edwards, P. (ed.), Oxford: Blackwell.

Walby, S. (1989) 'Flexibility and the changing sexual division of labour', in *The Transformation of Work? Skill, Flexibility and the Labour Process*, Wood, S. (ed.), London: Union Hyman.

Walsh, D. (2008) 'Starbucks to close 61 Australian outlets', *The Times*, 30 July, p. 40.

Walsh, D.A. (1992) 'Recruitment for new superstores: A-B-Zee', in *Case Studies in Personnel*, Winstanley, D. and Woodall, J. (eds), London: IPM.

Walsh, J. (2007) 'Equality and diversity in British workplaces: the 2004 Workplace Employment Relations Survey', *Industrial Relations Journal*, 38 (4), pp. 303–19.

Walters, D. (2000) 'Employee representation on health and safety and European Works Councils', *Industrial Relations Journal*, 31 (5), pp. 416–36.

Walters, M. (1995) *The Performance Management Handbook*, London: IPD.

Walton, J. (1999) *Strategic Human Resource Development*, London: Financial Times/Prentice Hall.

Walton, R.E. (1985) 'From control to commitment in the workplace', *Harvard Business Review*, March–April, pp. 77–94.

Wang, l. and Hinrichs, K. (2005) 'Realistic expatriate assignment preview: a potential solution to expatriate premature return', *International Journal of Organizational Analysis*, 13 (3), pp. 269–82.

Wanous, J.P. (1980) *Organisational Entry: Recruitment, Selection and Socialisation of Newcomers*, Reading, MA: Addison-Wesley.

Ward, P. (1995) 'A 360° turn for the better', *People Management*, 1 (3), pp. 20–2.

Watling, D.F. and Snook, J. (2003) 'Works council and trade unions: complementary or competitive? The case of SAGCo', *Industrial Relations Journal*, 34 (3), pp. 260–70.

Watson, T.J. (1977) *The Personnel Managers*, London: Routledge and Kegan Paul.

Watson, T.J. (1986) *Management, Organisation and Employment Strategy – New Directions in Theory and Practice*, London: Routledge and Kegan Paul.

Watson, T.J. (1994) *In Search of Management: Culture, Chaos and Control in Managerial Work*, London: Routledge.

Watson, T.J. (1995) *Sociology, Work and Industry*, London: Routledge.

Watson, T.J. (1999) 'Human resource strategies: choice, chance and circumstances', in *Strategic Human Resourcing: Principles, Perspectives and Practices*, Leopold, J., Harris, L. and Watson, T. (eds), London: Financial Times/Pitman Publishing.

Watson, T.J. (2001) *In Search of Management, revised edition*, London: Thomson Learning.

Watson, T.J. (2002) *Organising and Managing Work: Organisational, Managerial and Strategic Behaviour in Theory and Practice*, Harlow: Financial Times/Prentice-Hall.

Watson, T.J. (2003) 'Ethical choice in managerial work: the scope for moral choices in an ethically irrational world', *Human Relations*, 56 (2), pp. 167–85.

Watson, T.J. (2004) 'Human resource management and critical social science analysis', *Journal of Management Studies*, 41 (3), pp. 447–67.

Watson, T.J. (2006) *Organising and Managing Work: Organisational, Managerial and Strategic Behaviour in Theory and Practice*, 2nd edition, Harlow: Financial Times/Prentice Hall.

Watson, T.J. (2008) *Sociology, Work and Industry*, 5th edition, London: Routledge.

Watson, T.J. and Harris, P. (1999) *The Emergent Manager*, London: Sage.

Watson, T.J. and Watson, D.H. (1999) 'Human resourcing in practice: managing employment issues in the university', *Journal of Management Studies*, 36 (4), pp. 483–504.

Wayne, S.J. and Ferris, G.R. (1990) 'Influence tactics, affect and exchange quality in supervisor–subordinate interactions: a laboratory experiment and field study', *Journal of Applied Psychology*, 74 (3), pp. 487–99.

Webb, S. (1989) *Blueprint for Success: A Report on Involving Employees in Britain*, London: Industrial Society.

Weber, J. (1992) 'Scenarios in business ethics research: review, critical assessment and recommendations', *Business Ethics Quarterly*, 2 (2), pp. 137–60.

Weber, M. (1978) *Economy and Society*, Berkeley, CA: University of California Press.

Webster, J. (2001) *Reconciling Adaptability and Equal Opportunities in European Workplaces*, London: Research and Consultancy in Work and Employment.

Wedderburn, Lord (1986) *The Worker and the Law*, 3rd edition, Harmondsworth: Penguin Books Ltd.

Weick, K.E. (1979) *The Social Psychology of Organizing*, Reading, MA: Addison-Wesley.

Weick, K. (1995) *Sensemaking in Organizations*, London: Sage.

Weir, G. (2003) 'Job Separations', *Labour Market Trends*, March, London: Office for National Statistics.

Welch, J. (1997) 'New Model Army', *People Management*, 4 December, pp. 22–7.

Weltzien Hoivik von, H. and Føllesdal, A. (eds) (1995) *Ethics and Consultancy: European Perspectives*, Dordrecht: Kluwer.

Wenger, E. (1998) *Communities of Practice*, Cambridge: Cambridge University Press.

Wenger, E., McDermott, R. and Snyder, W. (2002) *Cultivating Communities of Practice: A Guide to Managing Knowledge*, Boston: Harvard Business School Press.

Wentling, R. and Palma-Rivas, N. (1998) 'Current status and future trends of diversity initiatives in the workplace: diversity experts' perspective', *Human Resource Development Quarterly*, 9 (3), pp. 235–53.

West, M.A. and Allen, N. (1997) 'Selection for teamwork', in *International Handbook of Selection and Assessment*, Anderson, N.R. and Herriot, P. (eds), London: Wiley, pp. 493–506.

Westwood, A (2001) *Not Very Qualified*, London: The Work Foundation.

Whipp, R. (1992) 'HRM, competition and strategy', in *Reassessing Human Resource Management*, Blyton, P. and Turnbull, P. (eds), London: Sage.

White, G. and Druker, J. (2000) *Reward Management – a Critical Text*, Routledge Studies in Employment Relations, London: Routledge.

Whitehead, M. (1999) 'A time for buy-in', *People Management*, 2 (11), pp. 54–6.

Whitener, E., Brodt, S., Korsgaard., M. and Werner, J. (1998) 'Managers as initiators of trust: an exchange relationship for understanding managerial trustworthy behaviour', *Academy of Management Review*, 23 (3), pp. 513–30.

Whitson, C. (2001) 'The chimera of social partnership', paper presented to the *Assessing Partnership* conference at Pinset Curtis Biddle, Leeds.

Whitston, C. and Waddington, J. (1994) 'Why join a union?', *New Statesman and Society*, 18 November, pp. 36–8.

Whittaker, S. and Marchington, M. (2003) 'Devolving HR responsibility to the line. Threat, opportunity or partnership?', *Employee Relations*, 25 (3), pp. 245–61.

Wickens, P. (1987) *The Road to Nissan*, London: Macmillan.

Wickham, P. (1999) *Management Consulting*, London: Pitman.

Wilcox, T. (2006) 'Human resource development as an element of corporate social responsibility', *Asia Pacific Journal of Human Resources*, 44 (2), pp. 184–96.

Wilcox, T. and Lowry, D. (2000) 'Casual workers and the human centered organisation', *Business and Professional Ethics Journal*, 19 (3&4), pp. 29–54.

Wilkinson, A. (1988) 'Empowerment: theory and practice', *Personnel Review*, 27 (1), pp. 40–56.

Wilkinson, A., Marchington, M., Goodman, J. and Ackers, P. (1992) 'Total quality management and employee involvement', *Human Resource Management Journal*, 2 (4), pp. 1–20.

Wilkinson, A., Redman, T., Snape, E. and Marchington, M. (1998) *Managing with Total Quality Management*, London: Macmillan.

Williams, N. (2008) 'Many firms failing to tackle ageist policies', *Personnel Today*, 1st April, p. 47.

Willman, P. (1996) 'Merger propensity and merger outcomes among British unions 1986–1995', *Industrial Relations Journal*, 27 (4), pp. 331–8.

Wills, J. (1999) 'European works councils in British firms', *Human Resource Management Journal*, 9 (4), pp. 19–38.

Wilson, E. and Iles, P. (1999) 'Managing diversity – an employment and service delivery challenge', *International Journal of Public Sector Management*, 12 (1), pp. 27–48.

Wilson, F. and Nutley, S. (2003) 'A critical look at staff appraisal: the case of women in Scottish universities', *Gender, Work and Organisation*, 10 (3), pp. 301–19.

Wilson, J.P. (ed.) (2001) *Human Resource Development*, London: Kogan Page.

Wilson, T. (1991) 'The proletarianisation of academic labour', *Industrial Relations Journal*, 22 (4), pp. 250–62.

Winstanley, D. and Stuart-Smith, K. (1996) 'Policing performance: the ethics of performance management', *Personnel Review*, 25 (6), pp. 68–84.

Winstanley, D. and Woodall, J. (2000) *Ethical Issues in Contemporary Human Resource Management*, London: Macmillan Business.

Winterton, J. and Winterton, R. (2002) 'Evaluating the impact of management development on performance', in McGoldrick, J. *et al.* (eds), *Understanding HRD: A Research Based Approach*, London: Routledge.

Wittgenstein, L. (1958) *Philosophical Investigations*, Oxford: Blackwell.

Wolf, M. (2008) 'A year of living dangerously for the world', *The Financial Times*, 16 July, p. 9.

Womack, J.P., Jones, D.T. and Roos, D. (1991) *The Machine that Changed the World: The Story of Lean Production*, New York: Harper.

Women and Work Commission (2006) *'Shaping a Fairer Future'*, Equality Challenge Unit, www.equalities.gov.uk/women_work/women_work_commission.htm

Women and Work Commission (2007) *Towards a Fairer Future*, Executive summary, Crown Copyright, www.equalities.gov.uk/women_work_commission.htm

Women's National Commission (2002) *Women in Public Life Today: A guide*. London.

Wood, S. (1995) 'The four pillars of HRM: are they connected?', *Human Resource Management Journal*, 5 (5), pp. 53–8.

Wood, S. and de Menezes, L.M. (2008) 'Comparing perspectives on high involvement management and organizational performance across the British economy', *The International Journal of Human Resource Management*, 19 (4), pp. 639–82.

Woodall, J., Alker, A., MacNeil, C. and Shaw, S. (2002) 'Convergence and divergence in HRD: research and practice across Europe', in *Understanding Human Resource Development: A Research Based Approach*, McGoldrick, J., Stewart, J. and Watson, S. (eds), London: Routledge, pp. 339–54.

Woodall, J. and Winstanley, D. (1998) *Management Development: Strategy and Practice*, Oxford: Blackwell.

Woodward, J. (1994), *Industrial Organisation*, 2nd edition, Oxford: Oxford University Press.

Worley, C. and Lawler, E. (2006) 'Designing organizations that are built to change', *MIT Sloan Management Review*, 48 (1), pp. 18–23.

Wray, D. (2001) 'Working a partnership: a case study', paper presented to the *Assessing Partnership* conference at Pinset Curtis Biddle, Leeds.

Wright, C. (2007) 'A consultant to the business: professionalising the human resource function?', paper presented at the *5th Critical Management Studies Conference*, Manchester, 11–13 July.

Wright, G. (1984) *Behavioural Decision Theory: An Introduction*, Harmondsworth: Penguin.

Zeitlin, J. (2003) 'Productive alternatives, flexibility, governance and strategic choice in industrial history', in *Business History around the World*, Amatori, F. and Jones, G. (eds), Cambridge: Cambridge University Press.

Zeytinoglu, I.U. (ed.) (2005) *Flexibility in Workplaces*, Geneva: ILO.

Zhou, J. and George, J. (2001) 'When job dissatisfaction leads to creativity: encouraging the expressive voice', *Academy of Management Journal*, pp. 682–96.

Zingheim, P.K. and Schuster, J.R. (2000) *Pay People Right: Breakthrough Reward Strategies to Create Great Companies*, San Francisco: Jossey-Bass.

Index